CONTENTS

KU-066-622

FEATURE BOXES

FOREWORD BY BRUCE DICKINSON

So why are you reading this book? Whether it came from Santa, or was a birthday present, or your sister threw it at your head, its arrival is quite timely, in light of heavy metal's recent renaissance.

Music journalists are notoriously fickle, they don't always tell the truth (No! Really?), so when one attempts to write a volume as comprehensive as this, applause is in order. To write a book of this nature requires passion, determination and years of patient research.

I'm sure that there will be some opinions in this book with which some might disagree. Indeed, spot the rock stars peeking at their entries in bookstores and snorting in disbelief, or emerging smug and triumphant – it's all part of the media circus!

I was involved with heavy metal before it was even called heavy metal. Back in the day, the roots of what is now known as "metal" lay in "blues rock", "heavy rock", "progressive rock" and even the curious beast that briefly emerged as "jazz rock". It was then, and is now, a heady mix of great songs, blood-curdling guitar riffs, pomp, pretence and idiocy, chemically supercharged by an excess of creativity, testosterone or ego – take your pick.

Metal's founding fathers (heavy metal also had a mutha!) still command respect from legions of new fans. In the world of pop culture, where throwing things away is considered a virtue, this must rate as most unusual.

Metal has been constantly portrayed as violent, evil, the work of the Anti-Christ, etc., yet in reality, it is curiously traditional (if the critics only knew the boring truth!)

When I was fifteen I hurled myself into a bass bin in a sugar-and-caffeine-crazed frenzy seeing my first rock concert. I remember the adrenaline pumping, the sheer joy of being able to fling myself around and not to give a fuck about what I looked like or what anyone

else thought. I signed up at the crossroads and rock became my music; it belonged to me and no one could take that away. Indeed, the more it was lambasted or ridiculed, the more angry and determined I became. It seems I am not alone, and thirty years later, I can look out on a Maiden crowd and see my adolescent self reflected in its faces.

Because of the ever-changing nuances of metal, and its constant invention (or rediscovery) of various niches within its own cabal, this book makes a valuable contribution to the understanding and history of the genre. If you never want to be a chartered accountant … read on.

Bruce Dickinson

If you were to ask the venerable Lemmy what kind of music Motörhead play he would fix you with a beady eye and tell you in no uncertain terms that it's all just rock'n'roll, which goes to show how perceptions of genres can differ.

There are so many sub genres in heavy music that there ought to be some description of heavy metal itself, referring to the specific period when the broadening of sound occurred.

The roots of rock and metal can be traced back to the blues of the 60s. But it was an upswing in the popularity of distorted guitar sounds, along with the audacity of the players, which led to greater volume, power and aggression in the music. Some point to the Kinks' UK #1 "You Really Got Me" (1964) as an early example of the metal riff in action (it's no coincidence that the tune became identified as one of Van Halen's favourite cover versions); others point to the fuzzy, acid-fuelled bombast of Blue Cheer; Led Zeppelin are often considered the fountainhead; while sometimes Black Sabbath are cited because they were just so much scarier sounding than everyone else; and then there's Steppenwolf's famous use of the phrase "heavy metal thunder" in their 1969 hit "Born To Be Wild". Despite the song's chugging riff and biker theme it would be a while before the name stuck to the nascent genre.

Heavy metal solidified as a popular concept around the mid-70s, came into its own and then gradually began splintering in the 80s – so pure metal (a contentious term if ever there was one) in many ways relates to this era. What confuses things is that bands such as early Sabbath are tagged 'metal', even though they were really playing a kind of heavy blues, complete with the occasional harmonica break.

From the late 60s and into the 70s this bluesy, riff-based music gradually became more intense and theatrical; as musicians upped the extremity and drama quotient, so critics and journalists cast around for adequate tags. The blues influence began to take a back seat and the music became increasingly heavy – the dour grind of later Sabbath and the wildly overdriven riffing of Montrose, for instance. Not being harnessed to a specific sound and style allowed greater experimentation and energy to be introduced; by the late 70s the first bands appeared who promoted the idea that they were metal and nothing else, not just the largely interchangeable hard or heavy rock.

And yet metal's identity was inextricably linked with hard and heavy rock. Just think of the archetypal fan's biker-look, complete with badges and patches, and epitomised by Saxon's headbanging classic "Denim And Leather". The style encompassed a whole host of bands and sounds – from Judas Priest to Uriah Heep and beyond – the common factor among them being they were very loud and they rocked.

And as the metal tag gelled, the band images hardened – Venom, for instance, were about to burst through as the most extreme looking band. The aim was to sound as dramatic and heavy as possible, while the lyrics were increasingly about the dark side of life, taking the original Sabbath horror factor even further.

The advent of the New Wave Of British Heavy Metal (itself a term coined by the music press) in the late 70s can be looked upon as a kind of watershed. Suddenly things became even more extreme, which eventually resulted in a series of sub-genres. There was thrash, death, and black metal; plain old hard rock, glam and hair metal; while grunge and nu-metal were not far behind. There was a type of metal to suit almost every taste.

The influence of other musical styles, such as goth, punk and hardcore, in turn led to such a profusion of heavy and obscure sounds – each with an obscure tag – that it is hard to pin down certain bands. As a result of all this, today even heavy metal is sometimes referred to as old-school metal and gets put into the classic rock box alongside hard and heavy rock.

So where does this leave a book on a subject that is so diverse? Clearly it's impossible to write about every single band, and inevitably some will quibble over the inclusion of certain artists over others; why, some may ask, is grunge included when the plaid-clad mopers from Seattle apparently killed off real metal in the early 90s? Why include effete hair metallers and pop-oriented lightweights instead of umpteen Scandinavian black metal outfits? The idea behind this book is to detail the stages and history of metal in all its flavours and guises; thus you will find Bon Jovi cuddling up to industrial deathsters The Berzerker; Nirvana duking it out with grind-core veterans Napalm Death; and Thin Lizzy sharing the bill with abrasive art-metallers Tool; there is even a nod or two to the most recent garage-flavoured sounds. In addition, the book offers descriptions of the wide variety of heavy genres as well as a giddy mosh pit of related subjects, such as concept albums, metal soundtracks, guitar heroes and more.

Ultimately, though, with such a head-spinning confusion of bands, genres and possibilities it's very tempting simply to do as Lemmy does and just think of it all as rock'n'roll. After all, he should know – he was there when it all started.

A note on the Structure and Icons

The individual entries in the guide are arranged alphabetically by band or artist and their albums are reviewed at the end of their biographies. For an index of all bands and artists discussed at any length, turn to page 407. Within the entries, you'll notice groups and individuals in **this font**, which means they have their own individual entry which can be referred to for more detail.

The selective discographies at the end of each entry are listed in order of their original recording dates.

Author's Acknowledgments

So many people have been helpful in this endeavour, providing historical information, statistics, back catalogue, photo assistance, opinions, ideas, and plain old inspiration. Thank you one and all for dealing with my endless questions about line-ups, discographies, and who did what, when and how.

Donna Doling, Andy Turner, Lisa @ Peaceville Records, Dave Pattenden, Bruce Dickinson, Malcolm Dome, Dave Ling, James Sherry, Mark Osterloh, Nick Ryan, Valerie Potter, Daniel Lane, Sarah Lees, Dan Tobin, Darren Edwards, Doug Wright, Michelle Kerr, Alison Edwards, Kirsten Lane, Roland Hyams, Nik Moore, Jamie Fisher, Owen Packard, Liz Fairweather, Kas Mercer, Hayley Connelly, Dorothy Howe, Sarah Watson, William Luff, Becky Deayton, Amy Bowles, Nita Patel, Ben Myers, Catherine Yates, Vanessa Cotton, Andreas @ Metal Blade Records, Karl Demata, Catherine Roe, Nicky Hobbs, Gillan Porter, Neil Smith, Anthea Thomas, Duff Battye, Anna Maslowicz, Louise Mayne, Anton Brookes, Anthony Gibbons, Louise Molloy, Lisa Freeman, Joolz Bosson, Zac Crossfire, Gary Levermore, Lisa Weaving, Polly Birkbeck, Phoebe Sinclair, Lee Dorrian, Will Palmer, Matt Vickerstaff, Sepi Berelian, Mussadiq Ahmed, Leigh Marklew, Mike Gitter, Paula Hogan.

And, of course, the splendid people at Rough Guides: Michelle Bhatia, Peter Buckley, Andrew Lockett, Mark Ellingham.

Sincere apologies to anyone I might have accidentally overlooked. So many people chipped in, it's tricky keeping track. I'd also like to say a big thank you to all those individuals who have been so helpful over the years in my day-to-day music writing – you know who you are.

This book is dedicated to Lisa, Mum and Dad, and Amelie and Eloise (you cats rule!).

Essi Berelian (2005)

A PERFECT CIRCLE

Formed Los Angeles, US, 1999

A Perfect Circle was a side project born out of frustration that went on to enjoy a very convincing life of its own.

In the late 90s nihilistic rockers **Tool** were in legal dispute with their record label after the recording of their *Ænima* album, leaving the various band members with time on their hands to explore other musical avenues. During the creation of the album, Tool guitar tech **Billy Howerdel** played a few demos he had been working on to Tool mainman **Maynard James Keenan** (vocals). Howerdel's skills and vision had been shaped by working with a number of notable bands in the past, such as **Nine Inch Nails** and **Smashing Pumpkins**, and Keenan could see the possibilities inherent in Howerdel's writing. Other musicians were drafted in – **Paz Lenchantin** (bass), **Troy Van Leeuwen** (guitar; ex-Failure) and **Josh Freese** (drums; ex-pretty much everyone!). A Perfect Circle were formed, their debut performance taking place at LA's Viper Room.

In the studio Howerdel's writing complemented Keenan's lyrical sensibilities and *Mer De Noms* (2000) – meaning "sea of names" – was an instant hit, riding mainly upon the back of Keenan's reputation. Comparisons with Tool were inevitable – especially once Circle's choppy and intense first single "Judith" was aired – but in reality the album's sound was far more expansive in both mood and texture. Lenchantin was also an accomplished violinist and her talent for string arranging brought a bruising emotional depth to the album; the spooky strains of "Renholdër", in particular, benefit from sinuous, haunting violins over spare and intricate percussion. The mood was mellower than on Tool's grimy, sordidly metallic workouts, with an emphasis on slow-burning power and invention, rather than shock-tactic eruptions of fury.

With plenty of time on their hands the band were able to take the Circle out of the studio to tour and transform the critical acclaim into actual butts-on-seats popularity.

The project, however, was put on hold as Tool cranked back into life with the release of *Lateralus* in 2001. It would be 2003 before another Circle set was ready to go, but after such a daring and brilliant debut there was no doubt that *Thirteenth Step* – a reference to the typical twelve-step rehab programme – would duplicate, if not exceed, expectations. Musically, A Perfect Circle had achieved an amazing balance between tension and beauty, between lyrical weight and sonic prowess.

In the time it had taken to record the album, Lenchantin had left to join **Billy Corgan** (ex-Smashing Pumpkins) in Zwan, and her place was taken by **Jeordie White** (aka Twiggy Ramirez, ex-**Marilyn Manson**); after recording part of the album Van Leeuwen left to join **Queens Of The Stone Age**. Additional guitars had been provided by Nine Inch Nails' **Danny Lohner** in the studio, with **James Iha** (ex-Smashing Pumpkins) finally stepping in for touring duties.

The release of the second album ensured that A Perfect Circle were seen not just as a mere offshoot of an already established band, but were appreciated as a genuine supergroup capable of selling millions of records.

Mers de Nom
2000; Virgin

Satin and steel: an expression of beauty and power in a sublime package. This album displays a sense of finesse lacking in Tool's more muscular outings.

Thirteenth Step
2003; Virgin

An assured follow-up proving that Keenan can pull it off outside his day job, provided he has a stellar cast along for the ride.

ACCEPT

Formed Solingen, Germany, 1977

Without doubt **Accept** are up there with the Scorpions as one of the definitive German heavy metal bands of the 80s. They might not have been as commercially successful as Klaus Meine and co, but when it came to twin screaming axes, coordinated headbanging antics and impossibly shrill vocals, Accept were masters through and through, earning the immortal accolade of "Teutonic top-string torturers" from *Kerrang!*.

Accept's roots can be traced back to the early 70s when **Udo Dirkschneider** (vocals) put together his first band, but it wasn't until the mid-70s that the unit was a viable proposition, with a line-up featuring guitarist **Wolf Hoffmann** and bassist **Peter Baltes**. Despite having some key players in place, the late 70s and early 80s found the band still trying to shape their identity. As a result *Accept* (1979), *I'm A Rebel* (1979) and *Breaker* (1980) were rather hit-and-miss affairs with the infamous Udo shriek not quite fully formed.

An early support slot with Judas Priest, however, would change all that. Some of the Brummie's chrome-plated style must have rubbed off on the Germans because, with a line-up that now included guitarist **Hermann Frank** and drummer **Stefan Kaufmann**, 1983's *Restless And Wild* was a storming

coming of age. Hoffmann and Frank were now precision riff dealers and Udo at last sounded like the inhuman siren that would define Accept's identity – listening to his feral, snarling delivery was akin to having your ears shredded by sandpaper. In addition, their songwriting had improved immeasurably. Sure, their desire to sing in English resulted in some gloriously bizarre lyrics – "Flash Rockin' Man" anyone? – but there was no denying the sheer power of proto-thrash opener "Fast As A Shark", which began with a jokey German folk intro before Udo's mental scream kicked off a guitar-fest of primal fury.

From beginning to end *Restless And Wild* remains a classic, a trick which the band pulled off for a second time with *Balls To The Wall* (1983), the record that would launch their bid to break the US. With its controversial title track, its baffling homage to "London Leatherboys" and a homo-erotic sleeve, Accept were virtually guaranteed to stir up a hornet's nest of conjecture. Most importantly, the record rocked in the most obscenely over-the-top manner imaginable, leading to support slots with Ozzy Osbourne, Mötley Crüe and Kiss, not to mention an appearance at the *Donington Monsters of Rock* festival in 1984.

Their thirst for commercial success eventually led them to choose Scorpions producer **Dieter Dierks** for *Metal Heart* (1985), bringing a more melodic polish, which obscured what had made Accept lovably abrasive in the first place. The new album was more musically accomplished but occasionally lacking in the aggression stakes; one thing that

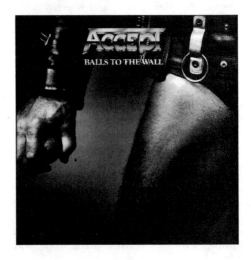

didn't change, though, was the band's slightly off-kilter lyrics – the *pièce de résistance* was Udo proclaiming that he was "Screaming For A Love-Bite".

Despite the change of direction nothing could stop the tour machine and a trip to Japan resulted in live mini-album *Kaizoku-Ban* being released shortly before *Russian Roulette* (1986). Back to the old headbanging approach, Accept were seemingly unstoppable: the twin guitar assault was as intense as ever while Udo's vicious vocal volleys were complemented with some fabulously operatic gang choruses. Meanwhile, the stage shows included the bizarre sight of Udo in combat fatigues goose-stepping wildly alongside his guitar-wielding comrades.

With such a winning combination of songwriting and performance panache, Accept should have gone on to top the metal league well into the 90s, but long-standing tensions began to take their toll and the remainder of their story is rife with missed opportunities.

The rot set in when Udo, none too impressed with his bandmates' desire to make things more lightweight, disappeared to form **U.D.O.** and continue his career in the same vein as *Restless And Wild* and *Balls To The Wall* – oddly enough his first album, *Animal House*, was basically a bunch of Accept songs deemed unsuitable by his former outfit. The remainder of Accept, however, were in trouble; how could they replace a singer who had come to be identified as the definitive voice of the band? They ended up going for American **David Reece** and recorded the disastrous *Eat The Heat* (1989). Reece was no Udo and the fans steered well clear of the record and the gigs. The situation was dire and only *Staying A Life* (1990), a live album from the vaults featuring Udo, kept the band's name afloat until, amazingly, Udo returned for 1993's *Objection Overruled*. Sadly, despite solid performances, the early 90s were not the ideal times for relaunching a career in heavy metal, with grunge saturating the airwaves. Accept trundled on with *Death Row* (1994) and *Predator* (1996), toying with their sound to meet the climate, but they were clearly struggling to make any kind of a significant commercial impact, in spite of the loyalty of old fans and some relatively successful touring. A live DVD package, *Metal Blast From The Past*, featuring concert footage

from the 80s and 90s as well as demo rarities and unreleased tracks, has prevented the band from slipping out of view. Udo, meanwhile, seems unstoppable and continues to keep the metal flame burning.

Restless And Wild
1983; Portrait

A screaming Germanic classic. Huge riffs, taut drumming and powerful vocals – you can just picture the synchronized headbanging on stage.

Balls To The Wall
1983; Portrait

Wildly over-the-top lyrics and crunching guitars make this another must-have. Ridiculous and unstoppable.

Russian Roulette
1986; Portrait

Songs about war, death and destruction – very, very heavy metal. And they're all dressed up in military uniform. What more do you want?

AC/DC

Formed Sydney, Australia, 1973

"They had a brilliant idea to put me on stage in a phone box ... I was supposed to spring out as Superman but when I got in the door jammed and I was stuck in there for fifteen minutes!" Angus Young

What can one say about **AC/DC**? Their electrifying moniker is synonymous with heavy rock of the highest order. To any lover of raucous riffing these Aussies are gods. In lead guitarist **Angus Young** they have a genuine iconic guitar hero, an instantly recognizable figure with his archetypal schoolboy uniform and bright red Gibson guitar. And then, of course, there are the songs. AC/DC are responsible for some of rock's finest moments – their album *Back In Black* is one of the biggest-selling records of all time. According to Elektra Records, total US sales for all their albums clocked in at over 63 million units in 2001, and over 140 million units worldwide, making them one of the world's major recording acts, exceeded only by artists such as Pink Floyd, Led Zeppelin and the Beatles.

AC/DC, one of the longest-running, most theatrical hard-rock bands of the last three decades were formed by **Malcolm**

Young (guitar) when his previous outfit, uncannily named the Velvet Underground, hit the rocks. Malcolm enlisted younger brother **Angus** (lead guitar) and it was their sister who suggested Angus wear his school uniform on stage, a gimmick that would still be employed more than twenty years into the band's career.

The two Young brothers made their debut at the Chequers club in Sydney with **Dave Evans** on vocals, **Larry Van Knedt** on bass and **Colin Burgess** on drums. Another early incarnation saw **Rob Bailey** and **Peter Clark** form the rhythm section and it was this line-up that recorded a rather glam version of "Can I Sit Next To You Girl", which became their first single in July 1974. A move to Melbourne brought yet another change, as **Mark Evans** (bass) and **Phil Rudd** (drums) were brought in. One night, when Dave Evans refused to go on stage, the band's chauffeur, **Bon Scott**, was asked to take over. In Scott they had the perfect combination of rasping, sleazy vocals, a knack for smutty lyrics and a magnetic frontman able to hold his own against Angus's bad-schoolboy image.

Having signed to Albert Productions, the next couple of years brought the release of *High Voltage* (1974) and *TNT* (1975). The pop-glam that had influenced their first single had been stripped away and in its place a love of blues-based rock'n'roll gave them a raucous and raw studio sound. All you had to do was listen to their pumped-up cover version of Chuck Berry's "School Days" to know exactly where they were coming from. Neither album was officially released outside Australia, but upon signing to Atlantic and moving base to the UK a selection of cuts from both sets was released under the moniker *High Voltage* (1976).

Once the band began touring beyond the shores of Australia, notoriety and a cult following ensued. The stage show was a furious mixture of hard-rocking, bad-boy boogie conducted with salacious glee by the twin focus of Bon and Angus, the former often bare-chested and menacing, the latter indulging in manic duck-walking solos. Their first UK headlining tour was dubbed *Lock Up Your Daughters*, the summer of 1976 brought an appearance at the Reading Festival and the winter saw the release of *Dirty Deeds Done Dirt Cheap* (1976) – yet another collection of tracks from the Australian albums and not to be confused with the Antipodean version bearing the same name. For years to come the different versions of this and the previous albums would provide plenty of fun for fans trying to track down all the songs.

By now the band were alternating their touring and recording schedules at a hectic pace. Unable to take the pressure, Evans was replaced by **Cliff Williams**. Up to this point the band's ideas were often stretched to the point of tedium – witness the Status Quo-like monstrosity that is "Ain't No Fun Waiting Round To Be A Millionaire" – but with *Let There Be Rock* (1977) the band at last began to produce material destined to be classic. From the bawdy, bouncing boogie of kick-off stunner "Go Down", via the opening fumbled bars of "Overdose" – one of their finest, least-acknowledged compositions – to the ballsy brilliance of "Whole Lotta Rosie", it was clear that they were well into their creative stride. The sound was as raw as before but with a crackling full-on live intensity so far lacking. The album hit the UK charts – some feat considering much of the rock world was gripped by punk at the time – and the mighty follow-up, *Powerage* (1978), featuring hit single "Rock 'N' Roll Damnation", proved the addictive power of simple heartfelt rock'n'roll. The inclusion of the magnificent "Down Payment Blues", featuring some of Scott's best lyrics, was worth the price tag alone. And just to keep the collectors happy the album was released at different times across the world with different tracklistings and different mixes; "Cold Hearted Man", for example, was a gem appearing only on the European version.

As a live attraction, their appeal was simply staggering; widely acknowledged as one of the all-time great live rock albums, *If You Want Blood – You've Got It* (1978) peaked at #13 in the UK charts. The opening electrical hum of towering amplifiers erupting into "Riff Raff" remains one of the greatest moments of any live album recording in rock, and "Whole Lotta Rosie" is often considered the definitive version, the crowd chanting for Angus leading into the famous stop-start riff.

But it wasn't until producer Mutt Lange was brought in for *Highway To Hell* (1979) that they became true international stars. The bad-boy image coupled with their risqué lyrics made them obvious targets for moral extremists and also ensured that the US finally took notice; the album became their first million-seller and climbed to #17 in the US. The album was gutsy but polished to hard-rocking perfection, ideal for any radio station willing to air the nudge-nudge innuendo of Scott's lyrics and Angus's fretboard freakery. This first highly successful collaboration with Lange also proved to be the last with Scott. Following a heavy drinking binge in Camden Town, on February 20, 1980, Scott was found dead, having choked on his own vomit. The coroner stated that he had "drunk himself to death".

Scott had been one of the main attractions and it seemed inconceivable that any replacement could hope to emulate his charisma or vulgar turn of lyrical phrase. Incredibly AC/DC found **Brian Johnson** (former lead singer with UK band Geordie) and were recording a new album within two months. With Lange guiding the production, *Back In Black* (1980) was a storming return to form, with the band giving the collective finger to their detractors on the closing anthem, "Rock And Roll Ain't Noise Pollution". The album went on to sell more than ten million copies over the next decade in the US alone.

It was business as usual on *For Those About To Rock (We Salute You)*, released in 1981, although it was clear to some that the band could do better – "Night Of The Long Knives" and "Breaking The Rules" sounded lazy compared to the epic title track and revved-up rockers such as "Let's Get It Up" and "Put The Finger On You". Nevertheless, the headlining slot at the UK Monsters Of Rock Festival in 1981 added to their list of effortless conquests; they would headline again in 1984 and 1991. After *Flick Of The Switch* (1983) Rudd left due to exhaustion and **Simon Wright** took his place. But it wasn't just Rudd who was tired: the songwriting for the album was disappointing, with the exception, perhaps, of "Bedlam In Belgium" and the heavy riffing of "Nervous Shakedown". In addition, the self-produced album was possibly the heaviest thing the band had put their name to so far.

Despite signs that they were running out of ideas, the fact that they had entered rock's superleague meant that the insipid *Fly On The Wall* (1985) sold millions worldwide; in particular the heavily reverbed production on Johnson's vocals rendered his usual harsh scream virtually unintelligible.

Angus Young stubs his toe on the monitor.

The following year brought *Who Made Who* (1986), essentially a compilation album with a handful of tracks recorded especially for the Stephen King movie *Maximum Overdrive*. Following a lengthy silence the band returned with the relatively dull *Blow Up Your Video* (1988) – a workmanlike outing, its one distinguishing feature being the hit single "Heetseeker". The set was eclipsed only by the monumental tedium of *The Razor's Edge* (1990) – by now with veteran **Chris Slade** taking over from Wright. Although they managed to knock out hit singles with relative ease, they were clearly becoming self-parodies; it was as though they were their own covers band, recycling their finest moments into faded carbon copies of the originals. 1992's *Live* album failed to capture the sweaty intensity of *If You Want Blood – You've Got It*, though the longer special collector's edition did provide more bangs for your buck.

The last few years have seen the band sticking to an increasingly relaxed schedule, with bouts of touring carefully planned to support each unchanging release. A collaboration with producer Rick Rubin on the track "Big Gun", used on the soundtrack of the Arnold Schwarzenegger movie *Last Action Hero*, was a return to form of sorts and *Ballbreaker* (1995) was a vast improvement on the stale material from the mid-80s. Producer Rick Rubin had always professed to being a major AC/DC fan and his crisp and clear recordings brought back some of the organic rocking edge the band had lost in the studio. *No Bull*, a live document from Madrid in July 1996, captured the sheer scale of the *Ballbreaker* concert experience.

Christmas 1997 brought the band's first foray into box-set territory with *Bonfire*. Put together as a tribute to Scott it included some classic concert recordings, rarities and more. It also served as a useful stopgap while the band started work on a new studio album. In the meantime, in 1999 the band also received a Diamond Award for over ten million sales of *Back In Black* in the US, while a wholesale repackaging programme began reissuing all the albums yet again.

When the new album, *Stiff Upper Lip* (2000), finally emerged, a full five years after their last studio effort, it was hailed by some as a return to form and nabbed the band the honour of being immortalized on the Hollywood Rock Walk. Whether it could ever hope to capture the imagination in the same fashion as albums from their 70s and early 80s heyday was debatable, but it certainly recaptured the raw blues flavour lacking in some of their more recent works. And if the album was sonically more successful, the live shows were nothing short of spectacular; the towering bronze statue of Angus glowering from the stage took its place next to the giant bell (for "Hells Bells") and cannons (for "For Those About To Rock We Salute You") in the line-up of classic AC/DC stage props. The whole gloriously over-the-top extravaganza, the biggest tour the band had ever organized, including their first dates in Japan since 1982, was captured for posterity on the *Stiff Upper Lip Live* (2001) DVD. Somehow Johnson also found time during 2001 to play a few dates with his old band Geordie.

The band have always been media-shy and even now only break cover to play the odd massive gig or pick up the occasional accolade.

If You Want Blood – You've Got It
1978; Atlantic

The last word in live hard rock albums. If the amplifier hum and opening notes of "Riff Raff" don't hook, then you must be dead. This album takes the studio tracks and transforms them into timeless classics. Definitive and indispensable.

Highway To Hell
1979; Atlantic

One of their finest studio albums. Mutt Lange's production is crisp and powerful, fully harnessing their filthy Gibson guitar sound. "Touch Too Much" and "Shot Down In Flames" are two of the best tracks on an album groaning under the weight of potential hit singles.

Back In Black
1980; Atlantic

Brian Johnson's voice bears a passing similarity to Bon Scott's but altogether it's the quality of the writing that makes this a remarkable album. They were at their peak here and it shows.

Bonfire
1997; EMI

One for the collectors out there. A stonking box set including the famed Atlantic Studios radio session from 1977 on CD for the first time; a double-CD album of the soundtrack to the concert movie *Let There Be Rock*; and a CD called *Volts* featuring a whole host of Bon Scott demo rarities and live cuts. Cool, and an excellent investment.

AEROSMITH

Formed New Hampshire, US, 1970

In common with many other long-running hard rock bands, **Aerosmith** owe their longevity to a combination of star quality – most notably in vocalist **Steven Tyler** and guitarist **Joe Perry** – and an acute sense of their own place in the sprawling landscape of modern American music. They have suffered personal clashes and nearly bitten the dust as a result. However, they always bounce back with a renewed commitment to being one of the best damn rock bands on the planet – and if that means employing the odd outside composer or undergoing a change in image and production values to survive, then so be it. The results might sometimes be uneven, but they're always quintessentially Aerosmith.

Aerosmith's genesis stems from Tyler meeting Perry at a holiday resort in Sunapee, New Hampshire, where the latter, a member of the **Jam Band**, would frequent a club called the Barn. With another Jam Band veteran, **Tom Hamilton** (bass), they formed a trio, but it wasn't until **Brad Whitford** (guitar) and **Joey Kramer** (drums) joined and they established themselves as a Boston band that it all fell into place. The early 'Smith sound was a tight blend of rough Rolling Stones swagger – with Tyler possessing more than a passing resemblance to Mick Jagger – and sleazy R'n'B attitude; it was gritty, dirty and unashamedly bluesy, making it perfect for smoky bar rooms and clubs.

By 1972 they had signed to Columbia for a healthy $125,000 and set about creating *Aerosmith* (1973). The album contained a rollicking cover of the R'n'B classic "Walkin' The Dog", the sublime strut of "Mama Kin" – a song that Guns N' Roses would go on to immortalize on their classic debut *Live?!*@ *Like A Suicide* – and the heart-rending ballad "Dream On", a tune that marked Aerosmith's talent for bringing a tear to the eye of even the most hardened rocker. The latter was released as a single but only met with moderate success; however, on re-release in 1976 it would go on to peak at #6 in the US and become their first million-selling record.

In the interim, major touring commitments – playing with the likes of Mott The Hoople and The Kinks – and their second album, *Get Your Wings* (1974), helped along by producer **Bob Ezrin**, would consolidate their early promise. Their breakthrough set came in the unfaultable form of *Toys In The Attic* (1975), which was every rock fan's vision of perfection, especially hit singles "Sweet Emotion", "Walk This Way" – with its silver-tongued proto-rap – and the manic title track. And who could resist the emotional wringer of closing ballad "You See Me Crying"?

Superbly honed studio material coupled with a frenetic live show made Aerosmith one of the hottest bands to tour America in the mid-70s, and with commercial success came chemical excess of legendary proportions.

Tyler and Perry were well on the way to earning their reputation as the Toxic Twins; to live was to party and no one liked to party harder than Aerosmith. Their hedonistic lifestyle inspired them to record *Rocks* (1976), one of the definitive albums of the era, and one that would influence the next generation of sleazy rockers in the 80s. Kicking off with the crazed rocking rodeo of "Back In The Saddle", the track was a classic; "Rats In The Cellar" echoed the rampaging insanity of "Toys In The Attic", "Combination" was a loose-limbed, ballsy stomper, while "Nobody's Fault" was nightmare-inspired and one of the heaviest things they had recorded to date. The album closed with Tyler coming over all sentimental in "Home Tonight".

All of which was a major contrast to *Draw The Line* (1977), often cited as the point at which things went awry, despite the fact that the band had actually been allowed to rest after nearly five solid years of work. It lacked the cohesion and, let's face it, the decent songwriting of its predecessors, but the momentum already created propelled Aerosmith onto even bigger stages, in front of even more people. In 1978 they headlined the California Jam II festival before a crowd that was measured in hundreds of thousands, alongside artists such as Heart and Ted Nugent; they took part in the Texxas World Music Festival aka Texxas Jam, in Dallas. In the same year they recorded a cover of "Come Together" with producer George Martin for inclusion in the *Sgt Pepper's Lonely Hearts Club Band* movie, in which they played the **Future Villain Band**.

"Come Together" went to #23 in the US charts and ensured that *Live! Bootleg* (1978) kept their profile high as they ploughed on with yet more touring commitments and preparation for *Night In The Ruts* (1979) – the best thing about the latter being the cunning spoonerism of the title.

But Aerosmith were faltering: Perry and Tyler were almost constantly at loggerheads, a situation not helped by the band's appetite for the rock'n'roll lifestyle. In late 1979 Perry quit the band to form the **Joe Perry Project**. **Jimmy Crespo** took up the impossible task of replacing him. Just a month or two down the line Whitford also left to form the imaginatively named **Whitford/St Holmes Band** with ex-Ted Nugent guitarist Derek St Holmes; he was replaced by **Rick Dufay**. This left one of the biggest bands in the US without their original killer guitar duo. It could have spelt disaster, and many thought the 'Smith were flogging a dead horse, but *Rock In A Hard Place* (1982) wasn't the dog's breakfast many fans thought it was going to be. True, it wasn't brilliant but under the circumstances it was an acceptable effort.

And this was the situation until Valentine's Day 1984 when Perry and Whitford ended up backstage after a 'Smith gig in Boston and, like the plot of some cheesy Hollywood movie, everybody got on so well that within a couple of months the pair had rejoined. The band decided to set off on the Back In The Saddle tour (well, what else would they call it?) and had their eye on writing the next album.

1985's *Done With Mirrors* (the band had somewhat cleaned up) emerged on Geffen and was produced by Ted Templeman, the man who had worked miracles with the early Van Halen. While everyone was falling over themselves to grab the first slice of Aerosmith to emerge in three years and *Classics Live!* (1985) was keeping the band hot in the charts, it took the help of another group to truly relaunch their career in an era where MTV ruled supreme. In autumn 1986 **Run-D.M.C.** covered "Walk This Way" with the help of Tyler and Perry; the single was a smash and introduced the band to a whole new generation of rock fans. The following year Aerosmith performed the single with Run-D.M.C. at the MTV Awards, ensuring success for the comeback album *Permanent Vacation* (1987). And just to make sure, they drafted in a bunch of outside talent – notably **Desmond Child** and **Jim Vallance** – to hone and polish the material until almost every single track had chart potential: "Angel", "Dude (Looks Like A Lady)" and "Rag Doll" all guaranteed heavy MTV exposure. Notably, on the US leg of their tour, the band asked that support act Guns N' Roses confine all boozing and partying to their own dressing rooms in order not to interfere or tempt the members of Aerosmith into falling off the wagon – now that they had gained the initiative, the last thing they needed was for the ol' Bolivian marching powder to get them under its spell again.

The new healthier regime and slick formula of *Permanent Vacation* led naturally to *Pump* (1989), with writers Vallance and Child bringing their commercial sensibilities to the songs, and the album being lovingly orchestrated by producer **Bruce Fairbairn**. Smutty, innuendo-strewn single "Love In An Elevator" was a hit and, the band, having largely been a US phenomenon for much of their career, actually made it to the UK and Europe for their first tour in twelve years. At the London gig they were joined onstage during the encores by **Whitesnake** vocalist **David Coverdale**.

Steven Tyler makes fun of his audience.

RICHARD E AARON/REDFERNS

As Aerosmith cruised into the new decade they were on an all-time high, and 1990's hectic schedule of vast outdoor gigs and a seemingly never-ending stream of accolades underlined how far the five skinny white boys who had started out jamming blues covers had come: they were inducted into Hollywood's Rock Walk on Sunset Boulevard; *Rolling Stone* voted them Best Heavy Metal Band and at Boston's prestigious Music Awards they walked away with a fistful of gongs for both their musicianship and *Pump*. In the UK they played at the Monsters Of Rock festival and were joined on stage by **Jimmy Page** for "Train Kept A Rollin'" and "Walk This Way", while single "Janie's Got A Gun" (from *Pump*) won in the Best Metal/Hard Rock Video and Viewer's Choice categories at the MTV awards. Then, the following year they did it all over again with awards and plaudits raining in from all directions, including a Grammy.

It was the perfect time to unleash the huge *Pandora's Box* (1991) box set, which was packed with rare goodies from the vaults. This was followed by *Get A Grip* (1993), another chart-topping Bruce Fairbairn-masterminded album. Yes, it was the old formula yet again, but no one gave a damn. Cue yet more awards and platinum-rated sales. What could they do? Where else could they go? Even the advent of grunge hadn't dented their stadium status too badly. *The Big Ones* (1994) compilation was next and then a massive breathing space of three years which was followed by *Nine Lives* (1997). Despite a healthy clutch of singles from the latter, the song that eclipsed pretty much everything else and gave them their first US #1 (#4 in the UK) was "I Don't Want To Miss A Thing" from the *Armageddon* soundtrack. It was a shameless weepie that used their talent for creating gentler numbers and cranked the sentiment levels way into slush territory; mums and grannies the world over were suddenly fans. And it wasn't even a genuine 'Smith song, having been penned by Diane Warren, who had written hit tunes for several other artists. It took *A Little South Of Sanity*, essentially a greatest hits live set, and *Just Push Play* (2001) to even things out a little, but the latter fell short of most fans' expectations.

Three years on and *Honkin' On Bobo* (2004), a set of smokin' blues covers, was released. Aerosmith had opted to go back to their roots – they were financially secure and an established part of the mainstream so could pretty much do whatever they liked. Joe Perry did just that by releasing his fourth solo effort, *Joe Perry* (2005).

⦿ Toys In The Attic
1975; Columbia

Worth the price just to hear the original version of "Walk This Way" and the superb "Sweet Emotion". The fact that the rest of the album's excellent is a bonus.

⦿ Rocks
1976; Columbia

Taken with its predecessor you have two albums that define an era of American music. Great songwriting and terrific performances make this a classic.

⦿ Permanent Vacation
1987; Geffen

A return to form after a period out in the cold. The original line-up back together with a little outside songwriting help and without the aid of chemical stimulation.

⦿ Pump
1989; Geffen

The MTV revolution starts here because this one is packed with hits – "Love In An Elevator", "Janie's Got A Gun", "The Other Side". They're all here and more great stuff besides.

AKERCOCKE

Formed London, UK, 1996

When bands such as Black Sabbath and Led Zeppelin dabbled in the occult it was all largely seen as theatre, a little bit of salacious window-dressing to their burgeoning legendary status. Throw a few Alistair Crowley quotes about, liberally season with mentions of Hammer horror flicks and you bring an instant and gratifying frisson of danger to the music, guaranteed to rub moral guardians up the wrong way and sell a few more records. **Akercocke** – named after Satan's capuchin monkey messenger in Robert Nye's *Faust* – however, are the real deal: genuine devil-worshipping metallers of the highest order; quintessentially English, fearlessly uncompromising, oddly eccentric and ruthlessly efficient, they bring both style and grace to a genre that most hear simply as a blur of guttural noise.

The band's roots can be traced back to an early 90s band called **Salem Orchid** where **David Gray** (drums) first met **Jason Mendonca** (guitar/vocals). The aim had been to create a truly satanic thrash band but the concept had faltered due to the usual wranglings about musical direction and the bruising of attendant egos.

A few years down the line and practising Satanists Mendonca and Gray realized they still enjoyed making an unholy racket. So they recruited **Peter Theobalds** (bass) and **Paul Scanlan** (guitar) to the cause of "blasting for Satan", as they called it: the brutal fusion of philosophical and musical paths in total harmony. It might have sounded faintly absurd to the uninitiated, but there was nothing ridiculous about the searing precision and utter conviction of their delivery. Furious blastbeat drumming, face-shredding guitar, a unique deathly vocal style babbling arcane lyrics and a desire to confound even extreme metal purists with their intricate arrangements were key to their vision.

Influenced by bands such as Emperor, Possessed, Deicide, Suffocation and Necromantia, they quickly made a name for themselves through a series of gigs around London, most notably their first outing in 1998, at a pub called the Red Eye, where they stood out from the normal heavy metal cognoscenti by electing to wear suits. By adopting a well-tailored and gentlemanly twist to their image, the intent was to present a visual manifestation of their disciplined approach to black metal; devil knows what the punters must have thought when, seemingly a bunch of accountants – albeit long-haired ones – took to the stage.

Their first album, *Rape Of The Bastard Nazarene* (1999) – a collection of songs based around the Faust mythos – was a poorly produced, self-financed affair sold at gigs. But the utterly evil and incredibly inventive nature of the songwriting brought them to the attention of extreme metal mag *Terrorizer*, who awarded them *Album Of The Month*. That year they supported the likes of Morbid Angel and Hecate Enthroned. The following year, an intense bout of touring climaxed with a benefit gig for Chuck Schuldiner, frontman of Florida thrashers Death, who had recently undergone surgery.

Akercocke were now well and truly on the underground metal map, resulting in a deal with Peaceville Records and the release of

Goat Of Mendes (2001), an album that incorporated infernal carnality and sado-masochistic eroticism into the equation. The band were quick to follow in the footsteps of pioneering UK black metallers Cradle Of Filth with their merchandising, one of Akercocke's more popular T-shirts featuring the horned one himself pleasuring the odd nun or two.

Album number three was a major breakthrough for the band following a signing to extreme label Earache. Titled *Choronzon* (2003) – named, naturally enough, after one of the demonic guardians of the abyss as seen in an episode of the cult *Hammer House Of Horror* television series – the album was a quantum leap forward in terms of production. The standard hallmarks of speed and attitude were all present as was an undiluted sense of total, cacophonous apocalypse; electronic nuances and samples along with excerpts from horror movies provided a terrifying sense of sonic evil. It was hell captured on tape. The album was instantly hailed as one of the best records of the year by the metal press. The following year Akercocke were featured in a BBC Radio 1 documentary about extreme music and duly asked to join the bill at the Donington Download festival. Paul Scanlan left the band in late 2004 as the band were working on their new album.

⊙ Choronzon
2003; Earache

From opener "Praise The Name Of Satan" to closer "Goddess Flesh" this is one hell of a ride. Diversity is the name of the game; black metal melds seamlessly with a profusion of musical styles and quiet chilling interludes to create an atmosphere of total menace. Recommended only for those with a taste for the extreme.

ALCATRAZZ

Formed Los Angeles, California, US, 1983;
disbanded 1987

The rather short period in the limelight enjoyed by **Alcatrazz** would hardly be worth mentioning were it not for the fact that throughout the band's career the line-up included some of the best, most talented guitarists ever to burn up a fretboard.

When vocalist **Graham Bonnet** found himself without a band – he had fronted **Rainbow** and **The Michael Schenker Group** – the logical thing to do was to create his own vehicle of excessive six-string fire power. With **Jimmy Waldo** (keyboards) and **Garry Shea** (bass), both formerly of melodic rockers **New England**, they set about looking for a drummer and axe wizard. Auditions were held and **Clive Burr** (Iron Maiden) and **Aynsley Dunbar** (Journey) were among those who pounded the skins, though the job finally went to **Jan Uvena**, who had worked with a wide variety of bands including **Alice Cooper**. Finding a scorching guitarist as good as Michael Schenker or Rainbow fella Ritchie Blackmore posed its own problems. What they needed was a combination of genuine musicianship and flashy finger-flinging, power and poise. One relatively unknown, classically influenced guitarist by the name of **Yngwie J. Malmsteen**, who had been impressing L.A. rock club punters in a band named **Steeler**, fronted by Ron Keel, was chosen to join the group. Malmsteen, as luck would have it, was a huge Blackmore fan, making him the ideal choice.

The first excellently titled album from this prodigiously skilled unit was *No Parole From Rock'N'Roll* (1984). Malmsteen widdled and soloed for all he was worth and Bonnet belted out his granite-tinged vocals. Among the best tunes to be found on the debut were the single "Island In The Sun" and "Hiroshima Mon Amour", a tune about the dropping of the first atomic bomb. Curiously enough the band soon became a hit in Japan where the record rapidly went gold and where they recorded the incendiary *Live Sentence* (1984); this included their version of the Rainbow hit "Since You've Been Gone".

Inevitably, however, a line-up this crammed with sizeable egos was doomed to failure. The chief problem was Malmsteen's rampant soloing – something that has always been a major feature of his style. He had to go.

The new kid on the block was **Stevie Vai**. The hideously brilliant guitarist had spent a good while as chief plank spanker with Frank Zappa. Vai's style, while technically superb, was more conducive to producing tightly rocking tunes. *Disturbing The Peace* (1985) was his first outing with Alcatrazz and the cohesion in the songs was apparent from the outset. Highlights included the frenetically riffy "Stripper" and humorously scorching "God Blessed Video". Yet more touring, including a return to Japan, ensued but management problems meant that the new album's potential wasn't fully exploited.

Joining forces with Ronnie James Dio's management team seemed like the best way forward but it was a little too late for the mercurial Vai whose stock was on the rise. His next move would secure his place in metal history. He was offered the chance to join **David Lee Roth** who was looking for a guitar genius of his own with which to whip Van Halen, whom he had left to start a solo career. Vai went off to record the magnificent *Eat 'Em And Smile* with Roth, leaving Alcatrazz to find yet another replacement.

Next up for the guitarist's job was **Danny Johnson**, whose more bluesy style brought yet another facet to the ever adaptable unit. *Dangerous Games* (1986) was a largely overlooked slice of hard rocking mayhem. Another major US tour ensued but by now they were battling the immutable law of diminishing returns; they could play as hard as they liked but that wouldn't change the fact that they had produced three different sounding albums and had lost what little momentum they had started off with.

Come the beginning of 1987 and they folded, abandoning what hopes they had of world domination through the power of the guitar solo. Their legacy was a clutch of fascinating albums that will reward those eager enough to hear the dynamically dextrous playing of some of rock's greatest showmen.

⊙ No Parole From Rock'N'Roll
1984; Rocshire

A great title to get things rolling. Malmsteen's stamp is all over this album as he unleashes torrent after torrent of berserk fret work. When he calms down a bit, from time to time, the songs really shine.

Live Sentence
1984; Rocshire

You just can't help feeling that Malmsteen is absolutely loving the attention when you hear the crowd. A worthy little addition to the Alcatrazz catalogue if only because it sounds a touch more spontaneous than their debut.

Disturbing The Peace
1985; Capitol

This album sounds far more together than their first, largely thanks to Vai's willingness to be a team player rather than swamping everything with blustering solos. When he gets into his stride the sound is awesome.

Dangerous Games
1986; Capitol

Polished and professional, this is a fine example of 80s melodic metal; plenty of guitar riffing combined with some smooth keyboard parping and shamelessly hooky vocals.

ALICE IN CHAINS

Formed Seattle, US, 1987; disbanded 2002

Despite the platinum-selling albums, heavily rotated MTV videos and the major influence on a huge number of 90s metal bands, the story of **Alice In Chains** is also characterized by drug-induced frustration and ultimately tragedy, a waste of potential that could have seen the band trump all-comers for many years to come.

In **Jerry Cantrell** they had an immensely talented guitarist able to grind out massive riffs in the grand classic rock style, but temper the histrionic excesses through his masterful control of mood. In **Layne Staley** they had a singer who, rather than embrace the full-on glaring glory of rock stardom, chose to dwell in the shadows, his vocal style both soaring and mordant. All of which made them perfect representatives of the burgeoning grunge scene alongside contemporaries such as Soundgarden and Pearl Jam – except that the roots of the band lay, somewhat ironically given grunge's supposed rock dinosaur-culling qualities, in a distinctly glam outfit, **Diamond Lie**. But when Staley kicked off the AIC trajectory the dark chemistry was obvious to most who heard them. Completing the line-up were **Mike Starr** (bass) and **Sean Kinney** (drums).

Grunge hadn't even been thought of when the band signed to Columbia in 1989. The world had yet to learn of Nirvana's might, or indeed appreciate the music-changing power of the gathering wave of alternative rock that would wash away the legacy of the 80s. They released the *We Die Young* EP in 1990, and found themselves supporting bands such as Poison. *Facelift* followed soon after, a powerful slab of early-90s metal, all twisted riffs and desperate vocal shadows, the material dwelling on depravity and depression – giving the first inklings that AIC would soon be embroiled in a deadly chemical romance.

The following year, however, found the band quickly rising in prominence. They made a cameo appearance as a bar band in Cameron Crowe's Seattle-based romantic comedy *Singles* and contributed "Would?" to the soundtrack, the tune apparently inspired by the death of Andrew Wood, vocalist of Seattle band Mother Love Bone; the song gave a teasing indication of where the band would be heading on their second watershed album. In the meantime, the single "Man In The Box" began a gruelling six months grind into the top 20 – helping *Facelift* to chart finally – aided by a heavily rotated MTV video, high profile support slots with Megadeth, and the Clash Of The Titans tour featuring Slayer, Megadeth, Anthrax and Van Halen. They rounded out the year with their *Sap* EP.

When *Dirt* (1992) arrived, produced by Dave Jerden, the critical and fan reaction was astonishing, with the album reaching #6 in the US. While *Facelift* had hinted at the finely wrought misery AIC were capable of creating, *Dirt* was the sound of souls in torment, a bleak but mesmerizing descent into self-destruction. Staley might have kept the drug use relatively veiled previously but songs such as "Junkhead" and "God Smack" were verging on the confessional. The album was a harrowing display of revulsion and resignation – in other words a masterpiece. An album this black fitted in perfectly with what was now perceived as a new musical movement: grunge. "Would?", "Them Bones", "Angry Chair" and "Down In A Hole" all charted. Even Staley injuring his foot while the band toured with Ozzy Osbourne couldn't prevent their sudden rise in stature and he was able to continue, playing in a wheelchair. The album would be Starr's last with the band; his replacement was **Mike Inez**. By the end of the year *Dirt* had gone platinum twice over in the US.

There seemed no stopping them and early 1994 saw their icy *Jar Of Flies* become the first ever EP to top the *Billboard* chart. Despite the critical kudos and demand for their music, the band refrained from touring – they pulled out of a support slot with Metallica in the summer, one day before they were due to hit the road. Rumours began to spread that heroin was to blame – it had fuelled their genius and was unravelling their lives at the same time. At one point it looked like AIC had split: Staley had turned up with **John Baker Saunders, Pearl Jam**'s **Mike McCready** and Screaming Trees' **Barrett Martin** in a band first dubbed the **Gacy Bunch** and then **Mad Season**; they proceeded to record *Above* (1995).

Desperate to give the band another go, AIC reconvened to begin recording their next album and Staley was invited to rejoin. Preceded by the single "Grind", *Alice In Chains* debuted at US #1 towards the end of 1995, another assured helping of gloom and despondency. The trend for acoustic albums resulted in *MTV Unplugged* (1996), Staley's soul-baring lyrics going down well as minimal Cantrell compositions. But problems were just around the corner.

As a unit AIC were becoming increasingly unviable and unreliable due to Staley's inability to control his habit, and 1998 eventually saw the release of Cantrell's solo *Boggy Depot*, material he had started working on the year before. Meanwhile, Columbia began amassing material for an AIC blow-out; in mid-1999 *Nothing Safe – The Best Of The Box* pre-empted the box-set madness of *Music Bank*. The fact that there was newly recorded material present provided a faint glimmer of hope, soon extinguished by a protracted period of inactivity – the label occasionally chucked out a live album or compilation, while Cantrell continued working on his own songs. This culminated in the release of his *Degradation Trip* (2002). However, just a couple of months prior to the album's launch, fans of the band suffered the ultimate blow: Staley was found dead of a drugs overdose in April 2002.

⊙ Dirt
1992; Columbia

An apt title for a thoroughly depressing but classic record. They might not have started off as a grunge band but they came to define the morbid angst of the genre with these tales of drug-fuelled dejection and misery.

⊙ Music Bank
1999; Columbia

A massive collection of AIC brilliance, though this much Alice in one go is not recommended. *Nothing Safe* is a more digestible compilation of the band's finest moments.

ALIEN ANT FARM

Formed Riverside, California, US, 1995

Let's face it, there aren't many metal bands out there who can claim to have come to prominence through an off-kilter cover of a Michael Jackson tune. That's precisely what **Alien Ant Farm** achieved when they issued "Smooth Criminal" as a single in 2001 and almost instantly found themselves catapulted towards the top of the nu-metal heap, over the heads of their peers.

Things had started off at a more modest pace, however, when **Dryden Mitchell** (vocals), **Terence Corso** (guitar), **Tye Zamora** (bass) and **Mike Cosgrove** (drums) first got together, jamming on a diet of covers: the traditional apprenticeship of any aspiring rock group. Moonlighting from their various other bands, it became apparent that, as a group, they were destined for greater things. Their name was apparently conjured up by Corso during a daydream about aliens cultivating human civilization on earth.

Mitchell's father was a guitarist, and got the youngster interested in six-string finger flinging. Later, Mitchell decided to hone his vocal skills; he often namechecks the likes of Edie Brickell and Tracy Chapman as sources of inspiration. The other band members came from backgrounds of varying musicality: Corso's budding brilliance was encouraged by his mother and he gained formal training in band workshops; Zamora started out on the guitar, but was soon seduced by bands like Primus, who promoted the joys of the four-string rumble; and Cosgrove was a self-taught skin pounder. The resulting amalgam of metal, funk, pop and hard rock was topped off with a deliberately oddball stage presence, featuring Zamora's weird adventures in gurning and Mitchell's geeky dancing. This – along with their notorious EPs *$100 Tape* and *Love Songs* – gradually won them a loyal fan base in the punk and metal scene of southern California. Their tightness as a unit made them stand out from the crowd and their association with fellow scenesters Papa Roach raised their profile. The two outfits would promote each other whenever the opportunity arose.

The band's first independently released album, the ironically titled *Greatest Hits* (1999), landed them a gong at the LA Music Awards for Best Independent Rock Album and proved to be just a taster of the plaudits they would eventually earn. Even better was *Anthology* (2001), released on Papa Roach's New Noize imprint, giving them the benefit of major label distribution via Dreamworks. Nestling within the polished nu-metal grooves was hit single "Movies" and their blistering, heavied-up take on Jacko's "Smooth Criminal". The former featured lyrics penned by Mitchell, exploring relationships and their demise. As well as displaying impressively tight musicianship, this track showed a little more poetic bite than average chart fodder, yet it was the aggressive jokey pop-metal of "Smooth Criminal" that really kick-started the Ant Farm phenomenon. As big fans of Jackson's output, great care was taken to create a classic cover version and so, complete with all the requisite yells and whoops, the single

made a home in the pop charts and sent the band stratospheric.

Success was halted somewhat abruptly in May 2002, however, when the band's tour bus collided with a truck in Spain. The bus driver was killed and the band came away with a variety of serious injuries – not least Mitchell, who broke his neck. Recovery was slow. Remarkably, despite the critical nature of his injuries, Mitchell bounced back almost completely – the nerve damage he had suffered meant almost constant pain in his upper body, but to all intents and purposes he was a fully functioning frontman again. In order to cope with the situation the band indulged their puerile sense of humour to make light of the fact that they had almost been derailed permanently; in several interviews Mitchell revealed that, though none of their new songs dealt directly with the bus crash, he had written one called "Spain In The Neck" that might surface as a B-side. They also toyed with the idea of including on their forthcoming album a mobile phone voice message that had captured the crash – Corso had been leaving a voice message for his girlfriend and had fallen asleep without hanging up. They decided not to: to their minds, it would have interfered with the mood of the record.

Despite such a major trauma, *Truant* (2003) was recorded and released in less time than many metal bands take to get their equipment into the studio. At the production helm were brothers **Robert** and **Dean DeLeo** (ex-**Stone Temple Pilots**). The resulting sound, broadened with acoustic and Latin textures, gave greater variety to AAF's hallmark tight riffing.

Unfortunately the positive aspects of their comeback were overshadowed by the sudden departure of Corso – due to "irreconcilable differences" – to be replaced, at least on a temporary basis, by **Victor Camacho**, an old friend of the band, allowing tour dates to be honoured without a break.

Dryden Mitchell offers to clean the photographer's lens.

Anthology
2001; Dreamworks

Polished and commercial, this is chart-friendly nu-metal at its most professional. Worth checking out, if only for "Movies" and "Smooth Criminal".

Truant
2003; Dreamworks

Gradually moving away from the nu-metal style of their debut, this follow-up broadens their sound and should, therefore, improve their longevity.

THE ALMIGHTY

Formed Glasgow, Scotland, 1988

"Me and Stumpy were in the pub one night and I said I had an idea for a band called The Almighty… A year later we were in Abbey Road recording our first album." Ricky Warwick

It seems only right that a tough city such as Glasgow produced a band like **The Almighty**. Formed at the tail end of the 80s, when the size of the hair was more important than the power of the music, they were one of the hardest and toughest-sounding bands to emerge from the UK.

Mad, bad, tattooed and positively bristling with an attitude akin to Motörhead after a rough night on the meths, they evolved from the aptly named **Rough Charm** in 1988. At their heart was chief songwriter, guitarist and vocalist **Ricky Warwick** along with drummer **Stumpy Monroe**; **Floyd London** (bass) and **Tantrum** (guitar) completed the line-up. Warwick had been a member of New Model Army's touring unit trekking across the States and had decided to launch his own career upon returning to the UK. The idea for his new band was somewhat removed from the visceral protest polemics of NMA. Instead he envisioned a brutally raw and pulverizing heavy rock outfit, a diesel'n'Jack-fuelled nightmare on wheels. The image of the band as a bunch of brawling desperadoes was topped off with a logo that bore a striking resemblance to the Hells Angels' motif; in fact, so uncomfortably similar were the designs that the band had to change theirs for fear of angering the rather possessive owners of the original.

The band's early performances were somewhat under-rehearsed and shambolic, but such was their self-belief and the quality of the songs that within a year of forming they had signed to Polydor and were in Abbey Road studios recording their debut. Taking a leaf out of The Cult's sweat-stained bible of leather-clad excess, *Blood, Fire & Love* (1989) was a shape-throwing titan of a debut, studded with gloriously overblown titles such as "Wild And Wonderful", "Resurrection Mutha" and the frankly ridiculous "Full Force Lovin' Machine". It was bold, brilliant and unrepentantly grand, a chest-beating display of testosterone and musical muscle.

The *Power* EP followed and "Wild And Wonderful" made a modest top-fifty entry in the UK charts, but the band's forte lay in live bluster, and *Blood, Fire & Live* (1990) became their first album to chart. The real gold, however, lay in their top-thirty follow-up effort *Soul Destruction* (1991), produced by Duran Duran guitarist **Andy Taylor**. Preceded by the anthemic delights of top-forty single "Free'n'Easy" it marked the most successful period the band were to enjoy. "Devil's Toy" and "Little Lost Sometimes" also made appearances in the charts despite being accompanied by some of the worst video promos ever recorded.

After these early, seemingly effortless triumphs, the band were actually on the verge of cracking up thanks to Tantrum, who was living up to his name and indulging far too much in the booze-soaked rock'n'roll lifestyle. He was eventually sacked and replaced by ex-**Alice Cooper** guitarist **Pete Friesen**, with whom the band had struck up a friendship while touring across the UK and Europe. Fortunately they got their act together and gave a powerful opening slot performance at Donington supporting Iron Maiden in 1992. It rained hard during their performance, but the Almighty were buoyed by the rapturous support of the fans keen to show their appreciation for such a genuine and unpretentious band.

Although 1993's grunge-flavoured *Powertrippin'* had some critics calling foul because of its apparent bandwagon jumping, a change in tone was arguably the best way forward at this point, given the ubiquitous nature of the Seattle sound. The fans agreed and sent it to #5 in the UK.

Even though the Almighty appeared to be real contenders for international success, problems with Polydor led to a signing with Chrysalis. Wasting little time, *Crank* (1994) appeared. Far from toning things down in an effort to gain commercial ground, if anything they seemed to have become even heavier, while Warwick had apparently become angrier: "Jonestown Mind", "United States Of Apathy", "Sorry For Nothing" and "Welcome To Defiance" spoke volumes about the guitarist's state of mind. It was another top-twenty album, but things were about to go horribly wrong with *Just Add Life* (1996).

The band had spent a year trying to get the label on their side, but a buy-out by EMI resulted in most of those with an interest in the band being shown the door. They had no one willing to push them and the album, by their recent standards, stiffed. The Raw Power label briefly took control but, frustrated by the whole process, the band called it a day. Warwick went off to form the uncommercially named **(sic)**, which was basically the Almighty in another guise. Unfortunately, this fact was obvious to the majority of the punters who came to see them and they kept asking when his former outfit would once again hit the stage.

It wasn't long before the Almighty's old line-up was resurrected, with guitarist **Nick Parsons** in place of Friesen, for a storming eponymous set in 2000. Four years in the wilderness had not mellowed Warwick's characteristic fire and the new album, released on Sanctuary, boasted such subtle tunes as "I'm In Love (With Revenge)" and "USAK-47".

The comeback, however, failed to ignite quite the same level of ardour as they had enjoyed the first time round; nu-metal had seen to that. Nevertheless *Psycho-Narco* (2001) waded back into the fray, knuckles bleeding and veins bulging, to be followed by *Wild And Wonderful* (2002), a compilation album.

Since then Warwick has launched an acoustic career, releasing *Tattoos And Alibis* (2003). Featuring **Joe Elliott (Def Leppard)** and **Thin Lizzy** guitarist **Scott Gorham**, and also co-produced by Elliott, the new songs led Warwick to support Def Leppard as a one-man band.

⊙ Blood, Fire & Love
1989; Polydor

This has it all: big guitars, big choruses and an even bigger heavy rock attitude. A monster was born and no mistake.

⊙ Blood, Fire & Live
1990; Polydor

Record labels like to milk bands for all their worth; this album was rushed out to make the most of the band's sudden rise in popularity. Good thing it's a pretty decent effort.

⊙ Soul Destruction
1991; Polydor

Makes their debut sound like they were just getting warmed up. Contains some great singles, including "Free'n'Easy", and the album's highlight track "Bandaged Knees". A classic? Quite possibly.

⊙ Powertrippin'
1993; Polydor

By now no one could call their blood-and-thunder success a fluke. Warwick outdoes himself with the bile and bullets on offer here; "Jesus Loves You ... But I Don't" says it all.

⊙ The Almighty
2000; Sanctuary

A great comeback. Parsons fits in well and contributes to the overall feel of the album, which goes back to the heart of what they were all about in the first place.

AMEN

Formed Los Angeles, US, 1994

"I apologize for being sick!" Casey Chaos leaning out over a seething mosh pit in the Garage, August 2000

For **Amen** frontman **Casey Chaos** it's not about gold records and it's not about the money. The motivating force behind the creation of this rabidly unstable punk metal band was being real, delivering killer records and performing live psychomania blowouts with utter put-you-in-accident-and-emergency conviction. That the band hasn't become huge comes down to Chaos's unbending, uncompromising stance and – that hoary old chestnut – record company politics.

Chaos's vision for the ultimate band came at an early age. A rootless and directionless youth, self-abuse and hard drugs were an antidote to the emotional and mental confusion of his childhood, as was skateboarding, which allowed him to earn a modest living. According to Chaos, a fellow skater played him a Black Flag tape one day and he enjoyed a life-changing epiphany. Music became his life, so the logical thing to do was to move from conservative Florida to liberal Los Angeles where a punk-rock freak could find like-minded people.

Chaos was overflowing with ideas, riffs and tunes that he would play and record at home. The first product of his enthusiastic amateurism, under the Amen moniker, was *Slave* (1995), a release limited to only 2000 copies on indie Drag-U-La Records. Amen had been born out of torment, and Chaos aimed his vitriol at the fakery he perceived about him – life in LA presented plenty of targets. Sonic tantrums such as "Safety In Suicide" and "Celebrate Annihilation" rammed home his nihilistic agenda.

Such caustic outpourings were all very well but he needed a band and a record deal to wreak real revenge on the world. First to enter the picture was **Paul Fig** (guitar), along with **Shannon Larkin** (drums); the line-up was completed by **Sonny Mayo** (guitar) and **John 'Tumor' Fahnestock** (bass). A deal was struck with the I Am label, an imprint of Roadrunner Records and, with nu-metal godhead **Ross Robinson** at the helm, an eponymous set was released in 1999. According to Chaos the genesis of the album was tortuous and as the songs were his vision he insisted on playing pretty much everything except the drums. But the result was an astonishingly visceral collection of tunes. Anything and everything came under fire: television, politics, greed, America. "Coma America", "No Cure For The Pure", "When A Man Dies A Woman", "TV Womb", "Everything Is Untrue" all raged with unhinged abandon. The message was nothing new, of course, but with the punk attack given a murderously metallic spin, the album suddenly propelled them into the limelight. And then there were the legendary gigs where Chaos came on like a hurricane, a cross between Iggy Pop and human disaster area G.G. Allin, swapping the injuries and broken bones of skateboarding for the blood sport of performing live.

However, the band were not interested in writing cuddly made-for-radio hits and the fickle record industry soon lost interest, especially as the band did not fit in with the all-encompassing wave of nu-metal. Dropped by Roadrunner but picked up by Virgin, their second album, *We Have Come For Your Parents* (2001) – produced by Robinson – repeated the same trick, albeit with a more musically focused set of tunes. As a consolidation effort it was right on the money, though it was becoming clear that, while the band were making major headway in the UK and around Europe, they were relatively unknown in the US. This was a situation that would be made worse in the aftermath of an Australian tour. On their return, they found that the new regime at the label wasn't particularly sympathetic to the Amen cause.

Gradually the money began to dry up and Chaos lost his band, though he eventually put

together another line-up featuring **Rich Jones** (guitar), **Scott Sorry** (bass), **Matt Montgomery** (guitar) and **Luke Johnson** (drums). In 2002 Chaos hit his nadir – without a deal Amen were going nowhere. However, a chance meeting at the Big Day Out festival in Australia with **System Of A Down** guitarist **Daron Malakian** proved to be the turning point. They struck up a friendship – fuelled by their common interests in punk and black metal – and Chaos eventually let Malakian hear some of the demos he had been working on. Extremely excited and enthusiastic about what he had heard, Malakian thought Amen should be the first signing to his new label, EatUrMusic.

In true do-or-die style Chaos maxed out his credit cards to put the new recording sessions together and called in favours from anyone who had access to studios and equipment. Again he played everything bar the drums, with input coming from Malakian in the form of arrangement suggestions and moral support, as well as co-production. *Death Before Musick* (2004) chronicled the frustration and anger Chaos had felt over the preceding eighteen months; it was yet another furious slab of metal-inflected punk, bleeding over with such cathartic anthems as "The Abolishment Of Luxury", "Oblivion Stereo" (featuring a scary vocal approximation of the Dead Kennedys' Jello Biafra), "Please Kill Me" and "Money Infection".

Provided they can avoid being dropped again, Amen have the potential to become one of the most dangerous bands on the face of the planet.

Amen
1999; Roadrunner

A violent, screaming punk'n'metal wake up call. Robinson might have made his name producing nu-metal bands, but the kind of anger channelled here is way more unpredictable and exciting.

We Have Come For Your Parents
2001; Virgin

More tightly constructed but with the same deadly intent. Chaos sheds blood on both the stage and in the studio, making this one pissed-off mutha of a rock album.

Death Before Musick
2004; EatUrMusic/Columbia

The songs are short sharp shocks and instantly gratifying. The catalogue of over seventy original tunes was whittled down to fifteen of the most savage and direct. A welcome and disturbing return to form.

AMPLIFIER

Formed Manchester, UK, 1999

A band needs real ability to take a classic heavy rock sound and fashion it into an experience that is both reverential to the rock tradition and utterly, compellingly modern. The **Amplifier** story began when **Matt Brobin** (drums) met **Sel Balamir** (vocals/guitar) while they were both university students with vague ideas about making it in the music business. **Neil Mahoney** (bass) became part of the plan when the other two met him working at a local musical equipment shop. A mere three-piece, their band name would soon become synonymous with a sprawling metallic soundscape so vast and titanic it could crush the breath from your lungs.

Their desire to dabble in chemical recreation opened their minds to the possibilities inherent in prog and space rock. Present within the early Amplifier sound were elements of Hawkwind's spacy drone, Pink Floyd's bizarre psychedelia, and good old-fashioned fuzzy garage metal, greasy riffs and well-oiled rhythms. Many jam sessions and minor gigs later they were picked up by Music For Nations in 2002 who duly put them in the studio to record their debut. The record was completed in 2003 but, typically, the marketing department of the label wanted a solid buzz about the band before releasing it. A swathe of club gigs, both headlining and supporting, garnered a resoundingly positive response from both press and the fans; one early coup for the band was being picked from over 200 acts to support The Deftones in Manchester in May 2003.

Finally, *Amplifier* (2004) was unveiled, to almost unanimously positive reviews. Here was a band that lived up to its name. It wasn't just that they were loud – that went without saying – everything about their sound was shamelessly proggy and bruisingly huge, and drew upon both classic metal and more modern purveyors such as Soundgarden. Here were volcanic drums, bass lines of sinuously steel-warping power, mountain-levelling guitar riffs, all falling together to create music of grandiose proportions. "Motorhead" was a hymn to the classic speedfreak aesthetic; "Panzer" was the soundtrack to a corporate world apocalypse; "UFOs" was a histrionic sci-fi epic, a majestic, sweeping rush of seismic proportions.

The summer found the band preparing for a clutch of festival dates, at which they were one of the must-see bands.

Amplifier
2004; Music For Nations

A stunning debut. Everything about these songs screams epic; a modern metallic masterpiece and no mistake.

ANATHEMA

Formed Liverpool, UK, 1990

Anathema are one of the UK's best-kept secrets. It could be the relative lack of rock star posing or it could be the reticence of the mainstream to embrace a band that originally started off as a death metal outfit. Whatever the reason for the lack of immense success in their home country, Anathema are one of the few metal bands of the early 90s to convincingly metamorphose beyond their influences into a band of genuine power and prowess, fusing their love of crunching metal with a peculiarly maudlin English proggy quirkiness.

Like so many of their contemporaries, Anathema were hugely affected by the thrash explosion of the 80s. Brutality was the name of the game and if you could throw in some religion-baiting then so much the better. Hence, when they first strapped on their guitars, the name **Pagan Angel** winged its way into their excited and furtive imaginations. The line-up consisted of **Darren White** (vocals), **Danny Cavanagh** (guitar), plus his brothers **Vincent** (guitar) and **Jamie** (bass), and drummer **John Douglas**; Jamie would soon be replaced by **Duncan Patterson**.

Drawing on the legacy of doomsters and deathsters such as Candlemass and Morbid Angel, the band played basic grinding thrash, veering from snail-pace to all-out blitz, complete with tortured demon vocals. The rough demos they recorded – "An Iliad Of Woes" and "All Faith Is Lost" – attracted the attention of cult Swiss metal label Witchunt, who released their bouncily titled "They Die". This became something of a cause célèbre in the metal underground, in turn attracting interest from the Peaceville label.

They were soon in the studio and an appearance on a compilation with "Lovelorn Rhapsody" led to their *Crestfallen* EP and debut effort *Serenades* (1992). It was rough-sounding stuff for sure, with the band already showing dangerous genre-bending tendencies, but got the vital thumbs up from the UK metal press. European festival appearances beckoned as did the odd dalliance with MTV on *Headbangers Ball,* alongside labelmates My Dying Bride and At The Gates.

The real transformation began with the *Pentecost III* EP and long-awaited follow-up album, *The Silent Enigma* (1995). Now without White, who had gone on to form **The Blood Divine**, the band decided not to waste time searching for a replacement frontman; **Vincent Cavanagh** took over lead vocals. Icily doom-laden throughout and with the ghost of Celtic Frost lurking somewhere in the background, the new album showcased

adventurous arrangements, more orchestral touches than their debut and greater versatility in the vocal department; dripping with misery, the minutiae of life were processed through the Cavanagh lyric mill. Even "Nocturnal Emission", a tune about wet dreams(!), sounded like the death throes of a condemned man.

It was almost as though Anathema wanted to be the metal world's Pink Floyd. Indeed, this was the thrust of the critical reception for *Eternity* (1996), with its drifting three-part title track and, wait for it, cover version of an old Roy Harper/David Gilmour song, "Hope". There were instrumental passages and atmospherics; the ghost of death metal had faded into oblivion and a finely wrought, genre-crossing soundtrack quality was creeping in. Soon after, however, drummer problems left them without someone permanent behind the kit. So, for Peaceville's tenth anniversary compilation, they decided to record some tunes that didn't need driving rhythm, namely Pink Floyd's "One Of The Few" and "Goodbye Cruel World", and Bad Religion's "Better Off Dead".

The challenging nature of the music developed even further with *Alternative 4* (1998), featuring drummer **Shaun Steels**. Now even the gothic feel of their image was for the chop; previous album art had reflected the gravity of the band's music and lyrical sentiments, and always had a strange flavour of the crypt to it, but the new songs came wrapped in a stark white cover depicting an astronaut with angels wings. Needless to say, the prog odyssey continued in the music as well, given a suitably modern polish by veteran producer **Kit Woolven**. On the personnel front, this was the last album to feature Patterson; he was replaced by **Dave Pybus**, while drummer John Douglas returned to the fold.

The next album, *Judgement*, followed a year later on Music For Nations, eliciting yet more comparisons to Floyd, but the driven riffing and plaintive vocals were about to undergo yet another transformation. Bands such as Radiohead, often dubbed the "new prog", had long since infiltrated the mainstream and it was in this direction that *A Fine Day To Exit* (2001) was reaching – featuring the talents of ex-**Cradle Of Filth** keyboardist **Les Smith**. Its suicidal cover theme was a visual expression of the troubled lyrics and harrowing rock contained within; from the opening chords of "Pressure", through the helter-skelter momentum of "Panic", to the closing refrain of "Temporary Peace" it was a *tour de force* of inspired writing and execution – that was roundly ignored by the mainstream.

Somewhat chastened by the indifferent reaction, *A Natural Disaster* (2003) – featuring Cavanagh's brother Jamie back on bass, Douglas's sister **Lee** providing vocals on the title track and Les Smith's new baby on gurgling infant duties for "Childhood Dreams" – reined in the previous album's overwhelming sense of fragility and bolstered the guitar muscle to create the band's most harmoniously balanced record to date. It was lush in all the right places without compromising on the heaviness; it was emotional without bleeding over into histrionics, making it yet another underground hit for this most underrated and enigmatic of UK bands.

The Silent Enigma
1995; Peaceville

Gathering storm clouds on the sleeve and a photo of the Horsehead nebula within, and with music to match. Doomed and despairing, this is inventive yet bleak, marking out a transitional period for the band.

Eternity
1996; Peaceville

Death and doom carried off in the style of Pink Floyd's *Wish You Were Here*, with multi-sectioned epics and a much broader approach to the writing. Acoustic textures, piano arrangements and a firm grasp of dynamics make this a fine and engrossing experience.

Judgement
1999; Music For Nations

"As ye sow, so shall ye weep", proclaims the legend on the sleeve. The slow-burning-to-driven breakdown of the title track alone is extraordinary, not to mention the swathes of suicidal darkness permeating the remainder of the tunes.

A Natural Disaster
2003; Music For Nations

The transformation is complete. This is a set of powerfully arranged modern rock with prog nuances, heavy in both content and execution. Simply amazing.

ANDREW WK

Born Los Angeles, California, US, May 9, 1979

From time to time an artist seems to appear with an almost fully formed public persona. Meet **Andrew WK**. Seemingly from nowhere he exploded onto the rock scene in a shower of sweat and a manic blur of headbanging. With the "W" representing eternal mental strength and resilience, and the "K" representing the mystical power of the universe – or it could just be that his family name is Wilkes-Krier – it was obvious that there was a little bit more to this prodigiously talented musician than simply the ability to pen a catchy tune or two.

Andrew was tinkling the ivories from around the age of four, encouraged by his parents. His family moved to Michigan and in his teens the young lad began playing in various punk and metal bands around the Detroit area, developing his playing skills to embrace drums as well as keyboard and guitar. He kicked off his solo recording career by moving to New York and circulating demos, and by the age of twenty he had earned a reputation for some extremely hard-rocking solo shows along the Eastern seaboard.

Girls Own Juice, an EP culled from early recordings was released on an indie label and was soon followed by *Party Til You Puke*, another EP; no prizes for guessing that he was promoting a party-hard manifesto but, bizarrely, as a route to spiritual enlightenment – the focus being purity of purpose and hedonistic happiness as the ultimate goal.

By the time Andrew was 22 he had a band in place, a record deal and an album in the bag. The title, *I Get Wet* (2001), suggested, according to the man himself, that in committing yourself one hundred percent to any course of action you're going to get wet – it could be "blood, sweat, urine, semen or girls' lubricant". This attitude gave the album a somewhat manic and uplifting quality; it sounded like Kiss playing thrash with lyrics cobbled together from a self-help book.

Everything was recorded, seemingly, on eleven; the drums didn't just provide a spine to the tunes, they propelled them at breakneck speed while the guitars never dipped below the red zone. With ballsy baroque melodies, perfect harmonies and killer choruses, these were tunes guaranteed to work their way into your memory with the irritating insistence of deranged nursery rhymes.

On top of the happy metal formula came an extremely energetic live show featuring mucho headbanging and frantic jumping around, while Andrew – wearing his standard uniform of sweat-drenched, filthy T-shirt and jeans – exhorted the crowds to go nuts. This was the perfect occasion to pick up the

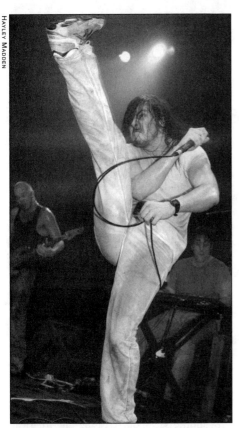

HAYLEY MADDEN

Andrew lets rip!

mashingly annoying gang choruses and yet more jackhammer rhythms.

With such an extreme and unsubtle formula to his rock it's hard to know quite where Andrew WK is going to take things next. Wherever it may be you can bet that it'll be very, very loud indeed.

⊙ I Get Wet
2001; Mercury

The maddest party soundtrack you could hope to find. This doesn't just encourage a good time it commands it, by its crunching guitars and some irritatingly catchy tunes. It's basic, good-time rock from a bloke who believes in the liberating power of never changing your underwear.

⊙ The Wolf
2003; Mercury

No marked shifts in style and content, just more hell-for-leather pounding, bright and beefy keyboards and impossibly happy riffing locked together in a rubber room for a jolly old punch-up.

ANGEL WITCH

Formed London, UK, 1979

his basic but inventive trio were one of the leading lights of the New Wave Of British Heavy Metal back in the late 70s. Alongside Iron Maiden, Saxon and Def Leppard, they brought a fresh burst of energy to the UK's metal scene in the wake of the drubbing dished out by punk; they were brash, unpretentious and played with real passion. Sadly, their rather erratic career, like that of Diamond Head's ill-fated stab at fame, can be put down to a number of factors, not least the evil machinations of the record industry. However, when **Angel Witch** did manage to get records out, the songs would be cited as formative influences by bands such as Megadeth and Metallica.

The band's story begins back in the mid-70s with an outfit called, imaginatively, Lucifer, featuring one **Kevin Heybourne** (guitar/vocals). Another band with the same name threatened to wipe the floor with them in court if they didn't come up with something else. Casting around for inspiration they latched onto the title of one of their own songs and Angel Witch were born. They didn't enjoy a stable line-up until **David Hogg** (drums) and **Kevin "Skids" Riddles** (bass) joined **Heybourne** to create a

odd black eye or broken rib. At his UK debut performance at the Garage club in London, he became the chief casualty and had to be rushed to hospital after colliding with a stage diver.

Needless to say, a stupendous amount of touring ensued in the wake of *I Get Wet*, so it wasn't until 2003 that *The Wolf* came howling and headbanging into the shops. The single "We Want Fun" had already been selected for inclusion on the soundtrack to the incredibly successful and stupid *Jackass* movie – the song had been accompanied by a heavily MTV-rotated video featuring him and the *Jackass* loonies acting, well, like loonies really. The new album was yet more of the same.

In typically shy and retiring style he described it as, "pure, unadulterated triumph, unmitigated glory, absolute, complete euphoria, melodic ecstasy, and true human victory!" Again it sounded like an epic pogo party crammed onto CD, complete with brain-poundingly exuberant keyboards, ear-band that made up for in sound what they lacked in visuals – while their contemporaries were aware of stagecraft and image, Angel Witch simply looked odd. Riddles commanded attention through his impressive seventeen-stone frame, in contrast with Heybourne's lean and wiry build.

Nevertheless, they earned themselves a major and dedicated following through some tireless gigging and by being offered a place on the Metal Crusade tour. Instigated by **Neal Kaye** of the Heavy Metal Soundhouse, they played alongside Iron Maiden, Praying Mantis and Saxon. But while their contemporaries were being snapped up by labels, Angel Witch were about to suffer the taste of bitter rejection from EMI. One of the band's earliest appearances on record was the legendary *Metal For Muthas* compilation issued by the label, of which "Baphomet" was one of the outstanding cuts – a crunching cod-satanic number featuring some fine soloing and a dizzying array of time changes. EMI also put out their "Sweet Danger" single, but no sooner had the song made a modest #75 dent on the charts and subsequently disappeared, the label cut them loose.

With time ticking by and the band losing ground they managed to secure a deal with Bronze and set about working on their debut. "Angel Witch", the single, preceded their eponymous debut; however, the set completely failed to set the world on fire. Fans loved it but critics laid into the weak production. The guitars were a weedy carbon copy of their live intensity and the drums were woefully limp. The songs, however, were great, combining bags of invention and melody with a raw sense of aggression. The title song featured a daft but enjoyable chant-along chorus to complement the speedy riffing and "Atlantis" chugged along at a pleasing gallop. Meanwhile "Angel Of Death" featured precisely the kind of pounding and sinister riff that Metallica would use to make a fortune.

With the subsequent touring finished, Hogg called it a day; he was replaced by **Dave DuFort** (brother of Girlschool's drummer, Denise). This line-up only managed one EP, prophetically called *Loser*, in 1981. The title track was a great song, spitting with the kind of energy lacking on the debut album. Shortly afterwards they disbanded; despite some triumphant live dates, the odds seemingly stacked against them.

The following year Heybourne attempted to resuscitate the band as a four-piece, but achieved little of note other than *82 Revisited – Live At The East Anglia Rock Festival –* and that wasn't issued until 1997. The band folded once more. But, as the 80s thrash boom began to gain momentum and the leading lights of the movement cited Angel Witch as an inspiration, the tenacious Heybourne couldn't resist trying to get things going once more.

Unfortunately the results of the re-formation – *Screamin' 'N' Bleedin'* (1985) and *Frontal Assault* (1986) – were less than impressive. For some reason they decided a more melodic sound might be the way to go. It was a mistake compounded by poor mastering and production, all topped off with some of the worst album art ever plastered on a sleeve.

In 1989 Angel Witch toured with US band Lääz Rockit, resulting in *Live* (1990) on Metal Blade, a competent but unremarkable gig document, again besmirched by a truly cack-handed album sleeve. It was during this period that Heybourne decided that the band needed to be relocated to the US, a decision which his UK bandmates wouldn't go along with. Ever the enthusiastic optimist, Heybourne set about creating an American line-up, striking up a writing partnership with Lääz Rockit bassist **Jon Torres**. Just as it seemed the band might actually make some headway, Heybourne was deported for not having a work permit, leaving the new line-up to crumble. Amazingly Heybourne and Torres managed to maintain a working relationship by swapping tapes and by Torres occasionally flying over to the UK to write.

The real testament to the enduring popularity of this ill-starred band, however – apart from the odd live date now and then – must be the release of several latter-day compilations: a cracking reissue of their debut album expanded to include a clutch of single cuts, *Sinister History* (1999), a collection of demos called *Resurrection* (2000), and *2000: Live At The LA2* (2001).

⊙ Angel Witch
1981; Bronze

Ignore the weird production and revel in the headbanging brilliance of the riffs. Throw in some crazy time changes and clever arrangements and you have a flawed classic. The chant-along of the title track chorus is just one of the album's more endearingly daft moments.

ANTHRAX

Formed New York, US, 1981

Emerging from the thrash explosion of the 1980s, **Anthrax** are one of the few bands that have managed to endure and adapt to the wild and various fashion changes in the rock scene of the last fifteen years.

The band's early line-up consisted of key songwriter **Scott "Not" Ian** (guitars), the diminutive **Danny Spitz** (guitars), **Dan Lilker** (bass), **Neil Turbin** (vox) and **Charlie Benante** (drums). Brought together by a mutual love of skateboarding, comics, and the New York hardcore punk scene, their early material bears all the hallmarks of their clashing influences – heavy metal given a vicious shot of hardcore speed and attitude.

After a bout of hectic small-town touring in 1982, the band met thrash guru **Johnny Z** who signed them to his Megaforce label; "Soldiers Of Metal" was released upon a rock audience hungry for the adrenaline rush that thrash metal could provide. Under his guidance, the band took support slots with macho metalmen Manowar, and the fledgling Metallica.

Their first full album release, *Fistful Of Metal* (1984), was of little note apart from the savage speed of the guitar work, unless you count the appalling title and highly dubious cover art. During this development period Anthrax coexisted with Ian, Lilker and Benante's side-project, the **Stormtroopers Of Death** (SOD). Taking a distinctly hardcore stance, the result was just one album, *Speak English Or Die* (1984). Lilker left to form **Nuclear Assault** soon afterwards and roadie **Frank Bello** stepped in as a permanent replacement. The stability was short-lived, however, as Turbin was fired, to be replaced first by **Matt Fallon** and then ex-Bible Black member, **Joey Belladonna**.

Belladonna's power and operatic style gave their subsequent work a depth and polish they had previously lacked. The five-track mini-LP *Armed And Dangerous* (1985), their first release with the revamped line-up, featured a muscular reworking of the Sex Pistols' classic "God Save The Queen" which was to become a live favourite. Having attracted the attention of some

major labels with their steadily growing popularity, they recorded their next album for Island Records. *Spreading The Disease* (1986) successfully catapulted them into the mainstream and effectively set the tone for the next five years. There were songs about all the usual heavy-metal favourites such as nuclear war ("Aftershock") and mythical monsters ("Medusa"), but a fun quotient was maintained by the hit single "Madhouse" and the spaghetti western-inspired "Lone Justice".

The band's image at this time also contributed to their popularity; they single-handedly made gaudy surfing shorts, baseball caps and skateboarding the latest rock fashion trends. Although subsequent years would see them trying hard to shake off the cartoon goofball image, at the time, they were too busy giving bands like Metallica a run for their money as they supported them in late 1986.

With the release of *Among The Living* (1987) their style had finally crystallized. Under the guidance of legendary producer **Eddie Kramer**, they produced stand-out material in the shape of hit single "Indians" (#44 in the UK) and the epic "ADI/Horror Of It All". And the fun factor was still present in full force: both the title track and "Skeleton In The Closet" were based on Stephen King stories, while the band endeared themselves to British heavy metal fans with "I Am The Law" based on 2000 AD's legendary lawman, Judge Dredd (#32 in the UK). With the album going gold in America and a UK chart position of #18, the band enjoyed two sell-out shows at the Hammersmith Odeon, preceded by an appearance at the Donington Monsters of Rock festival. Oddly enough their biggest hit of this period came with the B-side to "I Am The Law". Released as a single in its own right, "I'm The Man" – a spoof rap crossover – reached #20 in the UK. The apparently throwaway nature of the rap connection would prove to be significant some way down the line.

The following year brought a consolidation of the band's commercial success with a gold album in *State Of Euphoria* (1988) – the lyrical content of the set stemming, largely, from a preoccupation with popular films and culture. The single "Make Me Laugh" reached #26 in the UK, but the fact that a cover version of Trust's "Anti-social" was one of the stand-out cuts on the album showed in reality how patchy their latest LP was.

Dodgy quality control aside, the band seemed to have an unstoppable momentum – not even a fire at their Yonkers rehearsal studio, which destroyed $100,000 worth of equipment, could slow them down. *Persistence Of Time* (1990) punched effortlessly into the UK charts and peaked at #13, though again, the most memorable cut on the album was a cover – the melodic and superswift version of Joe Jackson's "Got The Time". A distinctly odd choice of single, given their ensuing experiment with rap, it nevertheless gave Anthrax a #16 chart place, and showed up the quality of the songwriting on the rest of the album.

It was at this point that their enduring fascination with rap music reached fruition. In an experiment that would have made more traditional rock acts go pale at the thought, they teamed up with Public Enemy's **Chuck D** on "Bring The Noise" and released *Attack Of The Killer B's* (1991), a mixture of rap, re-recorded old SOD material and B-sides.

By now it was gradually becoming apparent that the band were no longer functioning as a group despite their commercial success. In the grunge climate of the early 1990s, rock music underwent a radical ground shift and heavy metal dipped in popularity. Coupled with this general trend, Belladonna's

feather-headed approach to the music began to grate with the other members. He was eventually jettisoned and replaced by the less polished but tougher sounding **John Bush**.

By the time *Sound Of White Noise* (1993) emerged on Warners, the band had done their utmost to adopt a more contemporary flavour to their trademark guitar barrage. But it was still hard to ditch the frivolous cartoon image that had dogged them for so many years, and although the album entered the *Billboard* chart at #7 it did not attain the same heights scaled by their previous efforts.

The dissatisfaction with Belladonna had resulted in change but things were still not running smoothly; the problem this time was Dan Spitz. The band's unease with Spitz had been growing for a number of years and while his playing was assuredly professional, his lead style and less-than-enthusiastic stage attitude were holding the band back. His minimal songwriting input and self-exclusion from band activities led to his departure in 1995.

After an unremarkable concert effort, *Live: The Island Years* (1994), the band put out *Stomp 442* (1995) – again on Warner – with guitar duties split between Benante, Ian, **Dimebag Darrell** (**Pantera**) and friend **Paul Crook** (who had played guitar in

ANDY BUCHANAN

Anthrax peering into the abyss?

Belladonna's old band), proving to be one of their strongest albums to date. It stiffed, but more because of the US heavy metal scene's plunge, amid grunge fallout, than through any fault of their own.

When *Stomp 442* failed to set the world alight, the band retreated to rethink their approach as a four-piece. The time away resulted in one of their most accomplished releases in *Volume 8: The Threat Is Real* (1998). Though still recognizably Anthrax, the songwriting took the sound they had experimented with over the preceding five years and guided it to its logical conclusion. The heaviness of the new material compared more than favourably with fresh-faced nu-metal bands hungry for success, but the band seemed powerless to halt what seemed to be a tortuously slow slide into obscurity.

Return Of The Killer A's (1999), a self-explanatory compilation album sought to remind the dwindling numbers of fans just how potent Anthrax's hook-laden thrash could be; the highlight was a duet between Bush and Belladonna on a cover of the Temptations' "Ball Of Confusion". The idea behind the track was to hype up an impending tour featuring both singers and a set split between old and new material. It seemed like a great way to hook in fans of both eras but the idea hit the rocks when Belladonna pulled out, allegedly over financial wrangles.

And then the truly bizarre happened. A new horror gripped the US following the September 11 attacks on New York: biological terrorism, namely anthrax. Suddenly the band's name was synonymous with real death and destruction. In the face of this blow the band characteristically chose to fight on with more touring and recording. *We've Come For You All* (2003) was a gloriously melodic album with new member **Rob Caggiano** on lead guitar; in a couple of neat additions, the album also included guitar contributions from **Dimebag**, and guest vocals by **Roger Daltrey** (**The Who**). Cult comic book artist **Alex Ross** provided the sleeve art in a subtle nod to one of the band's formative influences.

Having survived numerous setbacks and ructions Anthrax seemed truly indestructible at this point. Not even the surprise departure of long-standing bass monster Frank Bello (to join a re-formed **Helmet**) stopped the band from touring – veteran player **Joey Vera** (**Armored Saint**, **Fates Warning**) stepping in to fill the gap. *Music of Mass Destruction: Live*

From Chicago (2004) – on both DVD and CD – and *The Greater Of Two Evils* (2004), a set featuring reworked and re-recorded classics, were duly issued to great acclaim before the band stunned the metal world by announcing in March 2005 the re-formation of the classic mid-80s line-up, including Belladonna, Spitz, and Bello. Where this will lead only time can tell.

Spreading The Disease
1985; Island

A brash and enthusiastic second outing bursting with energy and speedy riffing; the dumb, manic blur of "Gung Ho" is stunning. Elsewhere the preoccupation with war, fantasy, and heavy metal makes for an entertaining blitz through one of the finest albums of this genre.

Among The Living
1987; Island

Another colourful trawl through popular culture with songs inspired by Judge Dredd, and Stephen King horror stories. There are stabs at more serious subjects such as world peace ("One World") and the plight of Native Americans ("Indians").

Sound Of White Noise
1993; Elektra/Warners

Having ditched Belladonna, they produced an album brimming with an intensity and fury rarely paralleled. Trying to leave the dumb excesses of their cartoon image behind they sound wired and fierce.

Stomp 442
1995; Elektra/Warners

Possibly their heaviest, most angry album to date. The absence of Spitz' tuneless lead solos gives the songs greater cohesion while the guest guitarists add an extra dimension and colour to the brutal sonic attack.

We've Come For You All
2003; Nuclear Blast

Yet more bloodshot brilliance. Taut and muscular guitar lines weave dextrously around crushing drums and percussion. "Cadillac Rock Box", "Taking The Music Back" and the majestic salute to the old school of metal "Strap It On" are three of the outstanding cuts studding this *tour de force*.

ARCH ENEMY

Formed Sweden, 1995

One of the finest, most inventive extreme metal bands to emerge from Sweden during the last few years started out as not much more than a side project for

AOR: Adult Oriented Rock

Primarily a term used during the 80s to denote pretty much any kind of ear-friendly rock, it is sometimes used interchangeably with tags such as "melodic rock" and "soft rock". All of which should make it clear what we're driving at here: rock'n'roll which is accessible and tuneful, the kind of thing that used to thrive on commercial radio stations, particularly in the US. To its detractors this was precisely the problem; to them it was rock music with pretty much all the rebellion sucked out of it.

This criticism could be levelled at the bands at the lighter end of the spectrum, such as **REO Speedwagon** and **Toto**, but groups such as **Journey**, **Foreigner** and **Boston** were among those worshipped by rock fans in the 70s and 80s, not least because they were also known for rocking out in classic style – albeit in a very tasteful and well-produced fashion.

evil guitar genius **Michael Amott**. Amott had left UK gore metal pioneers **Carcass** after falling out of love with the direction they were taking and decided to form stoner band **Spiritual Beggars**. However, he obviously missed the stench of death, for it wasn't long before he had roped in his brother **Chris** (ex-**Armageddon**) on guitar, along with drummer **Daniel Erlandsson** (also of Armageddon) and vocalist **Johan Liiva**, for new band Arch Enemy's *Black Earth* (1996), released on indie label Wrong Again. It was a brutal, technical thrash-fest which took the fire and energy of the genre into hitherto unexplored quarters. In fact, the flavour of classic metal was one of the prominent aspects of their early sound, a characteristic that would come to the fore on subsequent releases.

The quality of the first album was such that Century Media pounced on the band for their next outing, 1998's *Stigmata*, which was put together with a different rhythm section (**Peter Wildoer** and **Martin Bengtsson**). Again, the critics and fans loved it, lamenting the fact that things only seemed to happen when Spiritual Beggars were off the road. By the next album, 1999's *Burning Bridges*, the rhythm section had stabilized to **Erlandsson** and **Sharlee D'Angelo** (ex-**Mercyful Fate**, ex-**Witchery**), making the set yet another underground success; the band were enjoying a burgeoning reputation in Europe, across the Asian subcontinent and into Japan where Amott was hailed as something of a guitar god. This ravenous fan base prompted the release of *Burning Japan Live* (1999), but Amott was convinced that Arch Enemy had even greater potential. He decided that a more musical approach was needed and that Liiva's powerful bark had had its day.

Step in **Angela Gossow**, an attractive extreme metal fan from Germany. It was a

very smart move by Amott; in one fell swoop Arch Enemy had not only recruited a charismatic and vocally agile new member, they had also gained a new focal point, one the magazines couldn't resist splashing all over their glossy pages. *Wages Of Sin* (2001) confirmed that Gossow was a remarkable talent, her demonic rasp confidently duelling with the increasingly intricate old-school-influenced guitar lines provided by the Amott brothers. In fact, musically the band had pushed even further into melodic territory adding Iron Maiden-esque flourishes to the speedy riffing. It was exactly the kind of outing that would bridge the gap between fans of old and newer forms of extreme metal – even the usually cynical UK audiences was beginning to take notice.

By the time of *Anthems Of Rebellion* (2003) – packed with songs questioning the nature of both political and religious authority – they had established themselves as one of the premier melodic extreme metal bands in the world.

Burning Bridges
1999; Century Media

A roaring, malevolent and melodic collection of tunes. The songwriting is as assured as the bone-crunching power of the music. Not bad going for what was essentially a side-project.

Wages Of Sin
2002; Century Media

Sounding more like a creature from the pit than human being, Angela Gossow's first album is an incredibly catchy collection of old-school power metal riffing and deathly extremes.

Anthems Of Rebellion
2003; Century Media

A stonkingly solid follow-up, the decision to go with Gossow's infernal throat mayhem pays dividends. Their tendency to throw in the odd Iron Maiden tweak provides a cool melodic counterpoint to the relentless thrashing.

ASIA

Formed London, UK, 1981

A cynical exercise in commercial melodic rock, or a worthy addition to the softer end of the rock spectrum? Whatever the perspective there's no getting around the origins of this archetypal supergroup: US record label Geffen was looking around for a suitable AOR commodity; **Asia** stepped in to fill the gap at a time when FM radio was absolutely lapping up material from bands such as Bad Company, Foreigner, Journey and Boston.

When it comes to supergroups it's hard to imagine a line-up quite this super. Asia consisted of well-travelled musos **Steve Howe** (guitar, ex-Yes), **Geoff Downes** (keyboards, ex-Yes, and, believe it or not, Buggles!), **John Wetton** (vocals/bass, ex-King Crimson) and **Carl Palmer** (drums, ex-Emerson, Lake & Palmer). Their old school prog credentials were impeccable, instantly bringing to mind the kind of ludicrous instrumental excesses for which the 70s were infamous. However, what they rapidly became renowned for was the ultra-smooth AOR of their eponymous debut in 1982 – complete with a characteristically brilliant **Roger Dean** sleeve – which was light on frenetic guitar and overflowing with Downes' lush keyboards and Wetton's passionate vocals. The album did relatively well in the UK but America went positively nuts for them, the debut topping the chart and "Heat Of The Moment" going top-five.

A new arena-filling phenomenon had arrived but, unfortunately, standards were about to start sliding. Although *Alpha* (1983) kept them rolling with almost the same degree of success, as singles "Don't Cry" and "The Smile Has Left Your Eyes" made decent dents on the charts, tensions were rising between Howe and Wetton, the strain of which would snowball beyond endurance. When Wetton was ousted to be replaced by **Greg Lake** (ex-ELP) it made little difference to their live profile, but was the first in a series of line-up shifts as various management and record label personnel kept trying to tinker with the band's chemistry. This in turn began to have a detrimental effect on their recorded work. It soon became apparent

that Lake wasn't a suitable singer, so what did the powers that be do? Tempted Wetton back, of course. But that meant Howe had to go; his replacement was ex-Korkus guitarist **Mandy Meyer**.

A not-so-supergroup now, their third album, *Astra* (1985), completely failed to get the juices of the label moneymen flowing; the best thing about it was another very fine Roger Dean sleeve. As the album flopped, so the band folded and the various members went off to lick their wounds and dabble in their own projects.

The possibility of rekindling the flame remained and in the early 90s Asia was resurrected by Wetton, Palmer and Downes with **Pat Thrall** on guitar. *Then & Now* (1990) featured some new songs among the old hits but the line-up faltered again, until another concerted effort by Downes got things going for another album. *Aqua* (1992) lacked Wetton but did feature help from Howe, Palmer, **John Payne** (bass) and **Al Pitrelli** (guitar, ex-**Alice Cooper** and Danger Danger) plus session drummer **Michael Sturgis**. Live dates followed but as far as relaunches of careers go they couldn't have picked a worse time, as grunge began to take over the world. *Aria* (1994) followed and so did the interminable line-up shifts and management hassles, leading to *Arena* (1996) – really the Downes and Payne show.

An inevitable trip to the vaults led to *Archiva 1* and *2* (1996) but it would be nearly another five years before an actual studio effort from the band, *Aura*. By now Asia basically revolved around the axis of Payne and Downes. The *America: Live In The USA* (2002) album and DVD plus a US acoustic tour kept the Asia brand ticking over where it mattered most while *Silent Nation* (2004) was in preparation.

Asia
1982; Geffen

For many fans this is the best. Big keyboards, big melodies, and big vocals make this a pomp rock classic.

Alpha
1983; Geffen

It might not hit all the highs of the debut but there is some great AOR to be found here, again with giant keyboards and a suitably shiny production job making the most of the arrangements.

BAD COMPANY

Formed London, UK, 1973

Blues-based rockers **Free** had already enjoyed considerable success when personality clashes and the drug habit of their lead guitarist **Paul Kossoff** precipitated a split. While bassist **Andy Fraser** went on to develop a career as a songwriter, Kossoff's brief attempt to become a solo star ended abruptly when he died as a result of substance abuse. **Simon Kirke** (drums) and **Paul Rodgers** (vocals) decided to put together another band – named after the 1972 Robert Benton-directed Civil War western – this time with **Mick Ralphs** (guitar, ex-Mott The Hoople) and **Boz Burrell** (bass, ex-King Crimson).

Initially **Bad Company** were seen by detractors as just a variation of Free – mainly down to the familiarity of Rodgers' warm and lucid vocals – but the band soon quietened critical voices by charting a successful direction for themselves. How could they fail with such a line-up of eclectic, but complementary, well-seasoned musos? Despite The Hoople and Crimson's reputation for the weird and wonderful, however, Bad Company offered straight down the line melodic rock. The classic *Bad Company* (1974) was bookended by the singles "Can't Get Enough" and "Movin' On", all three of which zipped straight into the charts on a fistful of smooth hooks and well-judged performances. The album, in particular, narrowly missed topping the charts in the UK but was a number one hit in the US, the prime

market for their brand of tough but tuneful heavy rock.

One of the chief reasons for their quick ascent was doubtless the input from **Led Zeppelin** manager **Peter Grant**. Grant's reputation was formidable and his guidance invaluable; while the Company were on Island Records in the UK (the previous home of Free) they were the first band signed to Zeppelin's own Swan Song label in the US – they even got to use Led Zep's mobile studio for their first album.

With such heavyweight support behind them, Rodgers and co found themselves filling stadiums with consummate ease, and it's fair to say that the Bad Company sound heavily influenced the American melodic rock scene of the 70s and 80s. *Straight Shooter* (1975) and *Run With The Pack* (1976) were both hits in rapid succession, though the extremely mediocre *Burnin' Sky* (1977) was an indication that there was only so much mileage in the formula. Of these three records, *Straight Shooter*, with its instantly recognizable rolling dice cover art, is often cited as being the tidiest and most solidly rocking, with plenty of lyrics about lurve. Witness hit singles "Good Lovin' Gone Bad" and "Feel Like Makin' Love" – delivered in Rodgers' husky hard rock howl, with Ralphs laying down some glorious guitar lines.

There was a distinct feeling, however, by the mid-70s that things were going a touch stale. Although *Desolation Angels* (1979) sold well, the songs were rather bland. With the exception of "Rock'n'Roll Fantasy" which was a hit in the US, the album would be their last major selling record before things started going awry.

Although by now signed to Swan Song in the UK as well as in the US, no amount of pushing could disguise the fact that *Rough Diamonds* (1982) was, well, pretty rough. There had been speculation that Bad Company were on their last legs for a while and the band split before they mired their reputation with any more dull records. Of the main players it was Rodgers who made the most of the 80s by heading off to form **The Firm** with Led Zep guitarist **Jimmy Page**.

This, however, wasn't the last to be heard from Bad Company. Given the little success that most members enjoyed outside the band, the mid-80s saw an inevitable reunion – minus Rodgers. Compilation album *10 From 6* (1986) was released, followed by *Fame And Fortune* in the same year, with **Brian Howe** (ex-**Ted Nugent**) replacing Rodgers. Bad Company were back, albeit a pale shadow of the hard rock supergroup that had packed out vast venues a decade earlier; the album was at best a lightweight AOR effort aimed squarely at the US market. *Dangerous Age* (1988) merely reinforced the problem, though for many Bad Company diehards the songs stacked up much better than on the predecessor.

The fact that the band spent a good portion of 1990 touring with the super-melodic Damn Yankees should give an indication of what Bad Company had become. Some might argue they weren't even the same band given that new album *Holy Water*

(1990) featured only Kirke from the original line-up. Fortunately Ralphs was back after a sabbatical for *Here Comes Trouble* (1992), though they changed vocalist again, adding **Steve Walsh** (ex-Kansas).

Much of the 90s was thus spent trading on former glories – *What You Hear Is What You Get* (1993, a live best-of album), was followed by *Company Of Strangers* (1995) and *Stories Told And Untold* (1996, a combination of new and old songs). *The Original Bad Company Anthology* (1999), however, was to mark a new era and a reunion tour of the US, with all the original members back together again. The momentum that was generated prompted the release of *Bad Company In Concert – Merchants Of Cool* (2002).

⊙ Bad Company
1974; Island

Straight in with a bullet. Lots of great songs moving away from the bluesy template of Free but retaining the hard rock vibe, injected with loads of melody.

⊙ The Original Bad Company Anthology
1999; Elektra

Not only does it draw heavily from the first two studio albums but there are plenty of rarities and out-takes to keep the fans happy, along with some new numbers.

BAD NEWS

First sighting UK, 1983

Some might suggest that it doesn't take a bunch of comedians to make heavy metal funny, but if you were going to take the mick then *The Comic Strip Presents* British TV series would be a damn good place to start.

The Comic Strip were the team behind some of the first comedy productions commissioned for the then new Channel 4, and *The Comic Strip Presents: Bad News Tour* was part of the first series, broadcast in 1983. So, technically, the programme predated that other classic metal piss-take, *This Is Spinal Tap* (1984), though they were both presumably in production around the same time.

While Spinal Tap were a US band with a history and a catalogue of work to their name, **Bad News** couldn't actually play an instrument between them. But fuelled by

their dreams – dreams well beyond their abilities – they set off on a UK tour pursued by a documentary crew. The band comprised chief metalhead **Vim Fuego** (guitar/vocals, known as **Alan Metcalfe** to his mum and dad) aka **Ade Edmondson**, the obnoxious **Colin Grigson** (bass, a banker by day and by nature) aka **Rik Mayall**, and the stupendously thick **Den Dennis** (guitar) aka **Nigel Planer** – in other words three quarters of the *Young Ones*. Completing the incompetent line-up was insane druggie **Spyder Webb** (drums) aka **Peter Richardson**.

The episode was so successful that the foursome teamed up again in 1986 to play Donington, headlined by Ozzy Osbourne, where they were higher on the bill than Motörhead. The now mythical performance became the highlight of the sequel episode, *More Bad News*. The band popped up a few more times, including a charity gig at the then Hammersmith Odeon in November 1986 – apparently there was a bit of a guitar duel between the band, **Brian May** and **Jimmy Page** – and an appearance at Reading in 1987 when Brian May turned up again.

Brian May produced the band's eponymous 1987 debut; it featured their mangling of "Bohemian Rhapsody". The seasonal "Cashing In On Christmas" followed, with *Bootleg* appearing in 1988, after which the band was laid to rest. *The Cash In Compilation* (1993) pulled together some of the best bits of the earlier releases but it wasn't until 2004

that EMI saw fit to reissue the debut album, along with a bunch of bonus tracks.

 Bad News
1987; EMI; reissued 2004

The two episodes of *Bad News* on video are pretty hard to track down, but these ridiculous songs interspersed with dialogue are a fine way to experience this uniquely Brit-flavoured metal spoof.

THE BERZERKER

Formed Melbourne, Australia, 1995

Could this bunch of Aussies be the heaviest band on the planet? Quite possibly. Meaner and nastier than Carcass, Cannibal Corpse or any other wussy death metal mob, they make Slipknot sound like Boyzone. Following Samuel Johnson's famous quote, "He who makes a beast of himself gets rid of the pain of being a man", **The Berzerker**'s goal is to descend to the most primal level of brutality in music; they achieve this with blistering precision through a liberal injection of nuclear strength beats and samples. A typical Berzerker song sounds like Slayer immolating Ministry deep within the bowels of a concrete mixer. Definitely not suitable listening for granny – or indeed most of the human race.

What's more, it's all delivered in a totally faceless manner, that's to say, all the members of the band sport standard issue black garb, wear hideous sci-fi alien-demon prosthetic

Bad News, portrayed by (from left to right) Planer, Richardson, Mayall and Edmondson.

masks and go by such informative handles as **The Guitarist**, **The Bassist** and **The Drummer**. Naturally, stage front we have **The Singer**, or **The Berzerker** himself, orchestrating a mighty aural meltdown. Many would point out that Slipknot had the dehumanizing mask thing down pat, but The Berzerker will always insist, with a shrug of resignation, that he eradicated his identity far earlier.

The history of The Berzerker's reign of sonic terrorism can be traced back to the mid-90s when Mr Berserker was a relatively normal drummer. Unfortunately, he injured his back in a car accident which rendered him unable to play. As a result, he began exploring new musical avenues, including techno DJing. Before long he had garnered something of a reputation for aggressive industro-gabba noise, and a number of EPs were issued on various labels, including Speedcore and Industrial Strength. In 1998 he provided remixes of various **Morbid Angel** tunes – including "Day Of Suffering", "Abominations" and "The Ancient Ones" – for the Earache label.

Suddenly The Berzerker had become a going concern with a proper album deal. The first rancid fruit was 2000's eponymous debut, a record calculated to make grown metal fans weep in terror; just one listen to the distorted blastcore drumming, pushing the bpm meter well beyond the red, alongside the jagged bonesaw guitars, was all it took. And then there were the lyrics; titles such as "Cannibal Rights", "Massacre" and the suspiciously Carcass-like "Chronological Order Of Putrefaction" made the bile rise with unerring ease. Of course, a fully functioning band was required for touring. So the search began for individuals capable of tolerating extreme discomfort while pummelling audiences' hearing beyond salvation.

A second album, *Dissimulate* (2002), honed the ferocity of the techno-metal tornado even further, the manic intensity of the beats alone capable of total head removal. And again, the song titles had a familiar ring of toxic misanthropy – "Death Reveals", "Pure Hatred", and "The Principles And Practices Of Embalming".

With a growing reputation for extremity, the band were naturals for some of the heaviest touring bills doing the rounds; possibly the most successful was their 2003 US tour alongside Nile, Napalm Death, Dark Tranquillity and Strapping Young Lad.

Is it possible for The Berzerker to become even more extreme? Time will tell – but when it comes to pushing the envelope of death metal this band will stop at nothing.

⊙ **The Berzerker**
2000; Earache

This delivers a demented level of lethal blastbeats per minute. Possibly the most evil-sounding debut ever.

⊙ **Dissimulate**
2002; Earache

Well, things have gotten a lot heavier ... if that were possible. Barked vocals gabble through a tirade of hate, guitars slash wantonly, jackhammer rhythms threaten to destroy anything in their path. Dare you try this at home?

BIOHAZARD

Formed New York, US, 1988

Defiant, bruising and brutal, it's only fitting that this pulverizing outfit from New York should incorporate the street-level elements of hip-hop and hardcore in their shellshock metal formula. Not so much a band as a four-man wrecking crew, **Biohazard** have suffered the usual knocks and setbacks that often plague bands. Yet, every time they encounter bad luck or record label stupidity they just bounce back, madder and meaner than ever.

A living product of the mean streets of Brooklyn, Biohazard were created when **Evan Seinfeld** (bass/vocals), **Billy Graziadei** (guitar/vocals), **Bobby Hambel** (guitar) and **Danny Schuler** (drums) wanted a vehicle in which to comment on the strife of urban living – the gang wars, the drugs, the squalor and daily injustices. Emerging from a blue-collar background they told it how they saw it – without any rock star pretensions. With a punishing tour schedule they set about building a solid fan base by putting in the hours and applying some good old-fashioned sweat and passion.

Their hard work led them to the small Maze label who put out their eponymous debut in 1990. Just a single glance down the track listing betrayed the band's hardcore credentials and do-or-die attitude: "Scarred For Life", "Retribution", "Wrong Side Of The Tracks", "Survival Of The Fittest" and "Justified Violence". So assured was their

DARREN EDWARDS

Evan Seinfeld in unfortunate on-stage guitar-strap-chafes nipple incident.

bellicose ranting – they didn't so much carry a tune as nail it to the floor – that a deal with Roadrunner Records was secured soon afterwards.

There was plenty more bile to be spewed; *Urban Discipline* (1992) was their watershed release, sales of which were helped by the video for "Punishment", which found favour on MTV's Headbanger's Ball. This pounding album secured them support slots on a wide variety of tours – alongside the likes of House Of Pain, Sick Of It All and Kyuss – taking their message of survival against the odds to a wider audience. Another coup was working with Onyx on a version of the rappers' "Slam" hit single. This in turn led to a collaboration on the title song for the soundtrack to *Judgment Night*. It was a fitting way to gain ground, especially at a time when the typical metal paradigm had been thoroughly mangled by team-ups between bands such as Anthrax and Public Enemy.

State Of The World Address (1994), released on Warners, was a suitably fist-banging consolidation of their work ethic and growing global following. While the previous albums had been slow-burners, amassing sales and kudos gradually, the new record actually made a decent dent on the US charts, peaking at #48.

Despite their ever-expanding horizons this turned out to be the last album to feature Hambel. They recorded their follow-up, *Mata Leão* (1996) – meaning "to kill the lion" – as a trio, but it was something of a mediocre effort. Internal tensions and drink and drug problems had all reached critical point when they headed back to Roadrunner for the follow-up live album *No Holds Barred* (1997), which at least showcased the band on slaying form in Europe, with new guitarist **Rob Echeverria** (ex-Helmet).

It seemed as though they just couldn't find a stable label platform from which to lob their Molotov cocktails of street-level enlightenment; *New World Disorder* (1999) emerged on Mercury. Never the happiest bunch, the lyrics to the new songs seemed to suggest deep-seated problems, especially the searching tone of "End Of My Rope". Once again, their new home proved to be another dead end. They left Mercury during the wrangling that took place when the label, along with several others, was merged with Universal. Not only that, but once again they found themselves without a lead guitarist.

Now without a deal, backs against the proverbial wall, they hit the road, taking their show to Japan and Europe, while a compilation, *Tales From The B-Side*, condensed a few rarities and remixes for the fans. The result of their bullish tenacity was a split deal with SPV and Sanctuary and a brand spanking new set of thuggish anthems in *Uncivilization* (2001), a critically lauded album powered by a new sense of conviction and focus. It featured the fresh six-string talents of **Leo Curley** and a bunch of guest slots filled by **Roger Miret** (Agnostic Front), **Jamie Jasta** (Hatebreed), **Phil Anselmo (Pantera)**, **Corey Taylor (Slipknot)**, **Igor Cavalera**, **Derrick Green** and **Andreas Kisser** (all of **Sepultura**), **Pete Steele (Type O Negative)** and **Sen Dog** (Cypress Hill).

The album was recorded at Rat Piss Studios, the band's own space, which had recently been refurbished with state-of-the-art equipment. The security that came with being signed again allowed them to hone their production skills and, therefore, direct their own recording work – they could now do things at their own pace without the interfering presence of record label executives.

As well as setting up a permanent studio they indulged in a few side projects: Graziadei dabbled with trip-hop; Schuler helped out New York band **Among Thieves**; and Seinfeld landed a role in hard-hitting prison drama *Oz*.

The revitalization seemed complete; *Kill Or Be Killed* (2003) snarled into view with yet another new lead guitarist, **Carmine Vincent**, in the line-up. Utilizing the same studio set-up meant little time was wasted on trivialities and more energy was spent on creating another vein-bulging, eye-popping bunch of protest anthems.

Urban Discipline
1992; Roadrunner

The unreconstructed macho promise of their eponymous debut finds full realization with a proper record deal. Stoked and furious they rail hard against the injustices of modern life.

State Of The World Address
1994; Warners

Still angry, still fuming, the songs are tighter and more focused. It's worth enduring the pummelling just to hear "What Makes Us Tick".

No Holds Barred
1997; Roadrunner

Recorded in Hamburg during a full-scale European assault, this live album captures a band righteously pissed off with record company politics.

Uncivilization
2001; SPV

Spot the guest star. The other albums have featured the odd helping hand here and there but this one really is bulging with interesting names. And the songs are good, blending just the right level of brutality with chant-along choruses.

BLACK CROWES

Formed Atlanta, US, 1988

S ultry, smoky and packing a kick like a mule on moonshine, the brand of hard rock peddled by these good ol' boys was as refreshing as an ice-cold one, yet steeped in the traditions of the south. For them, time seemed to have stopped round about 1974, when the music was unsullied by commercial considerations, when a band was judged by how long and how convincingly they could jam before the industrial strength hooch knocked 'em cold.

Chief songwriting brothers **Chris** (vocals) and **Rich Robinson** (guitar) assembled the **Black Crowes** during a decade that valued flash over substance and pop hooks over integrity. Starting around 1984 with an outfit named **Mr Crowe's Garden**, they started gravitating towards the grass roots rock that would catapult them into the limelight just as grunge was on the ascent. Towards the end of the 80s they added **Jeff Cease** (guitar), **Johnny Colt** (bass) and **Steve Gorman** (drums), to the line-up. With Rich's soulful and bluesy guitar lines providing a sublime complement to Chris's rich and husky drawl, they came over as a heady cross between the Faces, the Allman Brothers and Lynyrd Skynyrd.

The quality of their material attracted the attention of producer and A&R man **George Drakoulias**, who signed them to Def American for *Shake Your Money Maker* (1990). The album would eventually reach the US Top 5 after extensive touring and a string of excellent singles, the most notable being a sassy cover of Otis Redding's classic "Hard To Handle". The album swung with a loose and easy vibe, driven by memorable riffs and Chris's world-weary rasp; piano and organ embellishments were added by **Chuck Leavell** (ex-**Allman Brothers**), bringing that all-important bar-room roll to the Robinsons' gloriously ragged, pot-fuelled rock.

Their desire to keep things pure extended beyond the confines of the studio, however, and they carved something of a reputation for being difficult when on tour, supporting ZZ Top in 1991. Tour sponsorship was provided by Budweiser and the Crowes just couldn't resist putting an elegantly scuffed boot into the corporate face of the music industry when they took the stage. The result? They were kicked off the tour. This strong-willed, some might say guileless stance, would be a feature of the Crowes over the coming years.

However, none of this prevented the eventual platinum status of the debut album or the various accolades being heaped upon the band by magazines such as *Rolling Stone*. All the hard work put into touring the UK and playing Donington paid off handsomely with the magnificent second album, *The Southern Harmony And Musical Companion* (1992), which extended beyond the naive charm of the debut to create a harder, but no less accessible, sound; highlights included "Hotel Illness", "Remedy" and "Thorn In My Pride". The record reflected the natural growth of the band, which now featured **Marc Ford** (guitar, replacing Cease) and **Ed Hawrysch** tinkling the ivories.

Arguably, this was their peak – the album topped the charts in the US and only Iron Maiden's *Fear Of The Dark* stopped it from doing the same in the UK.

The same, however, couldn't be said of *Amorica* (1994). The band were on a high after playing the Glastonbury and Phoenix festivals, but nothing could mask the rather pedestrian feel of the new material. The sleeve – with its close up of an immodestly tiny pair of stars'n'stripes bikini briefs – might have hinted at some cheeky hard-rock fun to be found within, but maybe it was too much to ask of a band that had been virtually wedded to the road since their debut album. Certainly the volatile nature of the relationships within the band – especially between the two Robinsons – couldn't have helped and the odd rumour about a split began to surface.

Three Snakes And One Charm (1996) was better, with great tunes such as the Zeppelin-esque "How Much For Your Wings", the loping slide riffed "Under A Mountain" and melancholy gospel-tinged "Girl From A Pawnshop". Not that they had totally abandoned their penchant for jamming. The

BLACK METAL

Critics might suggest that black metal is just a wall of noise influenced of the pointy-tailed one and channelled through the inadequate musical abilities of sulky teenagers. But to others the genre is characterized by unflinching musical invention and a dedication to the underground.

But there is so much more to take into account than just the music. There is the philosophical aspect – as an antidote to Christianity – drawing in the occult musings of the likes of Alistair Crowley and Anton LaVey, as well as ancient pagan traditions.

Leaving the infernal chin-stroking to one side, however, what is black metal exactly and when did it first erupt? The answer is to be found in the state of metal during the very late 70s and early 80s with bands such as **Venom** in the UK and **Bathory** in Sweden. Demonic imagery and the occult were already part and parcel of the rock arsenal – **Black Sabbath**, among others, had seen to that – but in the hands of Venom it took on a far more theatrical and evil twist. *Welcome To Hell*, *Black Metal* and *At War With Satan* were landmark releases at the start of the 80s and though not particularly well produced, the raw and evil vibes contained had a major influence on the thrash explosion just around the corner. In the press, photos of **Cronos**, **Mantas** and **Abaddon** clad in leather and studs, wielding axes and swords, surrounded by skulls and bleached bones, made just as much of an impression as the music. As for Bathory – which basically consisted of one man, the enigmatic **Quorthon** – the self-titled debut was an unholy racket and helped mark the path for black metal's future development, while subsequent albums would incorporate more Nordic and gothic elements.

Throughout the 80s a legion of thrashers were using satanic imagery. **Slayer** and **Celtic Frost** were among the key players, propelling the music into the 90s, when, arguably, the Scandinavian scene – featuring Christian-hating bands such as **Darkthrone**, **Emperor** and **Mayhem** – came to epitomize black metal. And not just for the music, which by now featured even more extreme guitar and vocal brutality. Church burnings, murder, suicide and all manner of unsavoury events provided the notoriety. In addition, the overt fascist leanings of some of the bands brought yet another disturbing dimension.

Modern black metal is often characterized by an epic, near classical sound – though some bands across Europe and Russia incorporate indigenous folk flavours of their own – and includes bands such as **Dimmu Borgir**, **Satyricon**, **Borknagar** and the UK's biggest extreme export, **Cradle Of Filth**. The latter's more literate, lyrical approach and symphonic sound have given them the artistic and commercial edge over more basic practitioners.

subsequent touring found the band tapping into the joys and excesses of protracted instrumental noodling, on a stage decked out with exotic rugs and candles.

Having recovered some of their original fire, *By Your Side* (1998) finally emerged on Columbia, featuring another revised line-up. The infamous pressure-cooker dynamic within the band, again instigated by the friction between the two brothers, led to Ford leaving and Colt being replaced by **Sven Pipien**. As such, the album was penned without a second guitarist with Rich soloing in the studio for the first time. The result was bittersweet and satisfyingly accomplished. Songs explored relationships (the sizzling single "Kicking My Heart Around"), drugs (the sinister "HorseHead") and plain ol' hard rock hedonism (the reckless "Go Faster").

The return to form was topped by the release of *Live At The Greek* (1999), which featured none other than guitar legend **Jimmy Page** ripping through a set of **Led Zeppelin** songs – try "Custard Pie", "Sick Again" and "In My Time Of Dying" on for size! The stunning collaboration was hatched after Page had asked for the Crowes to provide some musical support for a charity gig at the Café du Paris in London in June 1999. The idea rapidly snowballed and a handful of concerts were announced across the US which sold-out in minutes. The two shows at Los Angeles' Greek Theatre formed the basis of the album with Page, Rich Robinson and the Crowes' new touring guitarist **Audley Freed** playing their fingers off.

This coup was rounded off with the release of *The Greatest Hits* 1990-1999: *A Tribute To A Work In Progress...* which marked a move from Columbia to V2, for *Lions* (2001). The new album was heavier than their previous efforts but still shot through with their familiar funky Stones and southern rock vibe. However, it was to be the last studio outing for the band; things were put on hold with *Live* (2002), allowing Chris Robinson the time to indulge in a solo album, *New Earth Mud* (2002). Now married to *Almost Famous* film actress Kate Hudson and with nothing left to prove, it was a relaxed and very laid-back solo debut.

Whether this means the end of the Crowes or just a long break from their deliberately anachronistic brand of rock remains to be seen.

⊙ Shake Your Money Maker
1990; Def American

A basic debut with pronounced southern rock influences and an extremely Faces-style vibe.

⊙ The Southern Harmony And Musical Companion 1992; Def American

Considered by many to be their finest collection. Strong performances, great lyrics and a more mature and accomplished feel.

⊙ By Your Side
1998; Columbia

After the detour provided by the mid-90s and all the infighting, the band return with a fistful of terrific songs, which try to get back to the heart of what it means to be in a great rock band.

⊙ Live At The Greek
1999; SPV

If you want to hear where the Crowes derive some of their inspiration just listen to them shred through these timeless Zeppelin rockers. And it's made all the more incredible by the presence of one Jimmy Page.

BLACK SABBATH

Formed Birmingham, UK, 1969

"I was never a Black Sabbath fan. I always liked Ozzy better without them."
Lemmy on Black Sabbath

What can you say about **Black Sabbath**? A legendary band without whom the history of heavy metal would have been drastically different and so much poorer. Alongside their contemporaries Deep Purple and Led Zeppelin, this ragtag four-piece laid down some of the heaviest, doomiest riffs ever recorded, influencing an uncountable number of upcoming artists and providing several of metal's splinter genres with inspiration. Where would doom metal be without Sabbath's cast-iron grooveprint? Would today's black metallers be quite as scary if it hadn't been for Sabbath's much-hyped occult leanings? And to whom would today's champions of classic metal turn to whip the minions of nu-metal into submission?

The classic Sabbath line-up has been heaped with praise for many reasons, though when the band first started critics were only too willing to give these hairy oiks a sound drubbing. In singer **Ozzy Osbourne** they had a real working-class hero with a fabulous banshee wail, who could captivate an audience by his sheer stage presence; guitarist **Tony Iommi** was a veritable riff machine, forging some of metal's finest moments; bassist **Geezer Butler**'s solid and sinuous style provided the all-important bowel-rumbling bottom end; and drummer **Bill Ward**'s rocking thunder anchored all the components in concrete. Truly, the whole exceeded the sum of the parts. Influenced by the heavy blues and jazz scene of which they were a part during the 1960s, Sabbath transcended their roots to produce a sound that was genuinely scary and copied by a whole generation of rockers desperate to follow in their mighty, though somewhat coke- and alcohol-addled, footsteps.

Back in their native Birmingham the band went under a variety of names as they scrabbled for the break that would make their career. **Polka Tulk** became **Earth**, which eventually turned into Black Sabbath, the name borrowed from an old Boris Karloff horror flick. The new horror slant, helped along by Butler's modest enthusiasm for the occult, gave the band a hook upon which to hang their tough bluesy bombast. They first tried their hand at a cover of American band **Crow**'s "Evil Woman (Don't Play Your Games With Me)" on the Fontana label, which completely failed to make an impression on the charts. Switching to Vertigo, their first album, produced by Roger Bain and done in two days for £600, was

another matter. *Black Sabbath* (1970) stayed in the UK album chart for five months and peaked at #8. The album was a classic – right from the driving rain and tolling bell of the doomy opening title track, it was packed with gargantuan riffing.

What would really propel Sabbath into the public eye, however, arrived in the summer of 1970: "Paranoid" was a galloping little ditty knocked off in a spare few minutes in the studio. The single went Top 5 in the UK and prompted a last-minute album title change for their next opus. *Paranoid* (1970), like its predecessor, consisted of songs that had formed part of the band's live set. Opening anti-war anthem "War Pigs" went on to become one of the band's stage faves, alongside the lumbering "Iron Man" and the ludicrously dubbed "Fairies Wear Boots". The entire set was seamlessly brilliant. There was even time for a slice of cosmic mellowness in the sublime, dark shades of "Planet Caravan". The album went to the top slot in the UK and in America narrowly missed the Top ten.

The 70s marked the beginning of Sabbath's rocketing to fame across the globe, and all kinds of pressures which accompany such fame. There was drug and alcohol excess, copious numbers of groupies, management wrangles and all manner of attendant madness. Roger Bain was again at the production helm for *Master Of Reality* (1971), another brace of classics. High points include the magnificent herbal high of "Sweet Leaf" and the brisk

Ozzy demonstrates the art of making giant bunny rabbit finger shadows.

rumble of "Children Of The Grave". The album went Top 5 in the UK and Top 10 in the US. *Vol. 4* (1972) was another hit album on both sides of the Atlantic, this time self-produced, with tunes such as "Snowblind" indicating exactly where the band's heads were at; in fact a cursory glance at the credits for the album will reveal a thank you to the "great COKE-Cola Company of Los Angeles", where the songs were recorded. With full-blown chemical blizzards raging in their heads the band decided that different management would be a wise move – a decision that would have major repercussions down the line. With *Sabbath bloody Sabbath* (1973) – another superb album, though one labouring under more involved production – just released and climbing the charts, the decision to move was about to backfire: in January 1974, as Ozzy walked on stage during a US tour he was handed a writ from their old manager which effectively put the band on ice for nearly a year.

This enforced break was a double-edged sword – it allowed the band to rest, but it also meant Ozzy was free to focus upon the self-destructive habits nurtured while on the road. The singer was also unhappy with the increasingly tortuous recording sessions they had been indulging in. The drug, drink and mental problems would eventually come to a head, but not before *Sabotage* (1975) – funnily enough featuring a cracking little tune called "The Writ" – stormed up the charts. While its predecessor had a layered and polished feel to it, true to Ozzy's wish to get back to basics, the new album was a more aggressive and punchy affair. The brutal charge of "Symptom Of The Universe" harked back to the band's primitive roots, but with Ozzy singing the lyrics to "Am I Going Insane (Radio)", the album had a distinctly portentous and sinister feel. It was the beginning of the end for the classic line-up.

Technical Ecstasy (1976) was a relatively patchy effort, paling next to the band's previous highpoints. Ozzy was becoming increasingly unstable – he also couldn't stand the more experimental aspects of the new album – and in 1977, he left the band, unable to get along with the others any longer. Unbelievable as it may sound, the band drafted in **Savoy Brown** singer **Dave Walker** as vocal cover. Ozzy was coaxed back for *Never Say Die* (1978) but the results were just as ropy as before. Sporting a title intended to

defy the burgeoning punk movement, fans had expected something with greater fire and passion. To make matters worse, during the tour Iommi was the spotlight attraction on stage, with Ozzy relegated to the level of side-kick. They were also roundly upstaged by their support act, young US whippersnappers Van Halen. The situation couldn't last and Ozzy never made it to the next album; in 1979 he was replaced by ex-**Rainbow** warbler **Ronnie James Dio**.

Ozzy, of course, went on to enjoy a phenomenally successful solo career. Sabbath were in the awkward position of having to break in a new singer. Ozzy's speciality had been proficient, gut-level rabble rousing, whereas Dio brought with him an acute musical ability as well as a love of heroic romance. These qualities were at the heart of *Heaven And Hell* (1980), a quite stunning return to form. Even those who couldn't stand Dio's purple lyrical fare had to admit he was a far more accomplished singer than his predecessor. The album peaked at #9 in the UK. Following this, the frankly rubbish *Live At Last* – put together from the tapes of a mid-70s show – was issued without the approval of the band; the album nevertheless went top five. Such ignominious stunts aside, the way was clear for *Mob Rules* (1981), another Dio-led stomper with a killer title track and bags of theatrical attitude. Unfortunately, Bill Ward who was suffering from ill health induced by years of bad behaviour on the road, wasn't on the album; he was replaced by **Vinnie Appice**.

The relative upturn in fortune soon went sour, however, as ego friction threatened to scupper the band again. Infamously, these came to a head during the mixing of *Live Evil* (1983), with Dio and Iommi at loggerheads over the volume of Dio's vocals. In the end Dio left with Appice to form **Dio** and events took such a bizarre twist as to make the months of wrangling appear to be small beer in comparison.

Again without a singer, the band needed focus – Iommi and Butler came up with **Deep Purple** singer **Ian Gillan**. *Born Again* (1983), the one album to result from this line-up, was certainly heavy enough but there was no disguising the lack of chemistry. Things got stranger still: at Reading in 1983 they unveiled a life-size Stonehenge set – in case you were wondering, this is where Spinal Tap got the idea – that was so big they could only get parts of it on stage. Then there was the dwarf in the red leotard who was supposed to imitate the demonic baby on the album cover. And the band even took to encoring with "Smoke On The Water", which must have seemed quite surreal to the audience.

Ward returned to the fray but the reunion was somewhat muted – he still wasn't well enough to play live, so the job went to ELO's **Bev Bevan**. Things got worse when Gillan left to rejoin Deep Purple in 1984.

With Gillan gone, much of the 80s and early 90s saw Black Sabbath turned into the Tony Iommi show while a seemingly endless succession of musos and singers trundled in and trundled off again. *Seventh Star* (1986), *The Eternal Idol* (1987), *Headless Cross* (1989) and *Tyr* (1990) represented the band at their nadir. And then there was the questionable decision to play South Africa's Sun City in 1987. The only faint glimmer of their glory days came in 1985 when the original line-up got together to play *Live Aid* at the JFK stadium in Philadelphia – but even that was a damp squib of a reunion.

With Dio back on board in the early 90s the band pulled the old *Mob Rules* line-up back together again for *Dehumanizer* (1992). But it was not the smash they had been hoping for. Ozzy then invited Sabbath to play at the final two dates of his farewell tour in California in November 1992, but Dio wanted no part of it. So Sabbath were fronted by **Judas Priest** screamer **Rob Halford** on the first night, with Ozzy taking over on the second. Although there were subsequent announcements that Sabbath would reform, nothing happened for a while; *Cross Purposes* (1994) and *Forbidden* (1995) plugged the gap until three-quarters of Sabbath – Ward was apparently deemed too ill to join in the fun – got together for Ozzfest *1997*.

Ozzy was back in the fold but it wasn't a true reunion until all four of the original members were back on stage together; the event occurred in December 1997 at Birmingham's National Exhibition Centre. It was a truly historic occasion. The recording of the second night was issued as *Reunion* (1998), along with two new studio tracks, "Selling My Soul" and "Psycho Man". The Sabbath touring unit made several more appearances across Europe; this included a show at the first UK Ozzfest, in 1998, though Ward suffered a

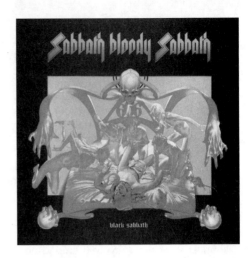

heart attack during rehearsals and had to be replaced by Appice again.

Following the gigs there was a massive amount of speculation as to whether the band would record a new album together. We live in hope.

Black Sabbath

1970; Castle

You can imagine how scary this must have sounded at the time. Four hairy blokes with a penchant for the occult dishing out head-cracking heavy blues. Awesome.

Paranoid
1970; Castle

A classic and no mistake. Doomy and dark with Iommi cranking out some marvellously inventive riffing. Worth it just for the title song.

Master Of Reality
1971; Castle

Total magic right from the coughing kick-off into the grinding "Sweet Leaf". Brooding and bloody, Ozzy bares his soul throughout, with "Solitude" one of the major highlights.

Sabotage
1975; Castle

More brutal and basic than their previous effort, while "Symptom Of The Universe" is a classic. And check out Bill Ward's red tights and Ozzy's snazzy silk kimono and stack-sole combo.

Heaven And Hell
1980; Vertigo

Dio's golden gob leads the band through a belting selection of terrific songs; "Neon Knights" is a cracking opener and the title track is a masterpiece. Very different to Ozzy-era Sabbath, this is nevertheless a quality album.

BLACKFOOT

Formed Florida, US, 1972

W hen it comes to stormingly heavy southern rock in a classic style, **Blackfoot** were one the best bands to ever strut a stage. With the likes of the far more laidback Lynyrd Skynyrd out of action after their tragic plane crash, Blackfoot became one of the most popular live draws of the late 70s and early 80s, their hell-raising style owing as much to AC/DC as to any traditional southern influences.

The history of the band stretches way back to Florida of the late 60s when Blackfoot mainman **Rick 'Rattlesnake' Medlocke** (guitar/vocals) was trying to get himself started in the music business. The grandson of bluegrass veteran Shorty Medlocke, the young Rickey was steeped in the sounds of the south and itching to express himself. His early attempts weren't particularly successful and he ended up playing drums in **Lynyrd Skynyrd** until he decided to form Blackfoot with old friends **Jackson 'Thunderfoot' Spires** (drums/vocals), **Charlie Hargrett** (lead guitar) and **Lenny Stadler** (bass), who was eventually replaced by **Greg T. Walker** (bass/keyboards/vocals).

The band debuted with *No Reservations* (1975) followed closely by *Flyin' High* (1976), but they didn't receive much coverage, probably in part due to the records coming out on different labels (Island and Epic respectively), the first appearing only in the UK and the latter only in the US. By 1979 they were on Atco and the magnificent *Strikes* was the first of a series of ballsy and soulful albums rich in tradition and positively smokin' with raucous riffing, topped off with Medlocke's resonant blues howl. The album spawned the crowd-pleasing US hit single "Highway Song". *Tomcattin'* (1980) and *Marauder* (1981) cemented the band's reputation as dealers of prime hard rock – enough to get them on the bill at Donington in 1981– but the real breakthrough came with the live album *Highway Song* (1982), which went to #14 in the UK charts. Recorded while on tour in the UK, the raw and unrelenting vibe neatly encapsulated just how much harder and faster the band played in front of a rabid crowd.

Unfortunately this would prove to be the band at their peak. **Ken Hensley** (keyboards, ex-**Uriah Heep**) joined for the slicker *Siogo* (1983) which found the band going for a more melodic metal sound in an effort to crack the charts. When that failed, *Vertical Smiles* (1984) was wheeled out, to the horror of old-time fans – Blackfoot's transformation into a generic radio rock band was almost complete. The most interesting aspect of this album was the controversial sleeve featuring Polaroids of women's legs – it looks tame now but along with the risqué title it caused a fuss at the time. Something had to give under the mounting pressure and the band split while on tour.

When *Rick Medlocke And Blackfoot* (1987) was released, none of Medlocke's old cohorts was in sight, and the fact that the songs were still of the radio-friendly variety made one suspect that he was just working through his contract with the label; the photo on the sleeve looked more like a very serious-looking David Lee Roth than a veteran heavy rocker. *Medicine Man* (1990) and *After The Reign* (1994) were Medlocke's last attempts to keep the flame burning, while 1994's *Rattlesnake Rock 'n' Roll: The Best Of Blackfoot* reinforced just how exciting the early days had been compared to what the band had become. By the time a *King Biscuit Flower Hour* live concert recording had been released in 1998 Medlocke had rejoined his old pals Lynyrd Skynyrd.

⊙ **Rattlesnake Rock'N'Roll: The Best Of Blackfoot** 1994; Rhino

Strikes is probably the best studio effort but, for a good delve into what Blackfoot were all about, this compilation covers a lot of ground. From start to finish this is butt-kickin' rock'n'roll of the highest order.

BLUE CHEER

Formed San Francisco, US, 1967

I s this where it all started? For people who enjoy arguing about such things, nailing down exactly when heavy metal appeared leads to all sorts of chin-stroking musings. On any list of likely suspects, this lot – named after a particularly potent strain of acid tab – must rank near the top.

The legend goes that the band (as a six-piece) clocked Jimi Hendrix doing his wild thing at Monterey and were sold on the idea of pushing everything to the max – the distortion, the volume, everything. So the slimmed-down line-up of **Leigh Stephens** (guitar), **Dick Peterson** (bass/vocals) and **Paul Whaley** (drums) headed into the studio to record their debut. With studios being relatively primitive affairs back in the late 60s there wasn't much scope for refinement or flexibility, and the studio technician wanted them set up as though they were going to play live. It only took a few power chords to blow up the control board. Blowing things up would prove to be something of a regular occurrence; and there was nothing remotely subtle about the loose garage blues which they would play at ear-shattering volume, complete with distorted guitar, bass and frenetic thrash'n'jazz drumming. The control board repaired, *Vincebus Eruptum* – surely one of the best album titles ever – was completed in a just three days of manic sessions.

The six tracks would go down in history as some of the most primal and influential heavy music ever committed to tape. They landed a hit single with their brain-mashing cover of Eddie Cochrane's "Summertime Blues", which brought with it almost instant notoriety. Other highlights – or disasters, if the critics were to be believed – included the fuzzy blues breakdown of "Rock Me Baby", the shuddering but groovy fire of "Out Of Focus" and immense closer "Second Time Round". The latter blasted in on a drum track that sounded like the studio ceiling was caving in, before the riff and howling vocals entered to jump up and down on your spine. It also enjoyed the dubious distinction of containing (possibly) the first ever rock drum solo captured on tape. It was a sound that would go on to form the blueprint for so many bands; where would grunge, stoner and garage rock be without *Vincebus Eruptum*'s success through excess aesthetic?

When it came to recording a follow-up, again legend has it that they were so loud they blew the studio monitors and ended up having to play outside. Naturally enough the album was called *Outsideinside* (1968). If anything, it was a refinement over the free-form chaos of the debut, if it was possible to describe anything they did as refined.

Certainly the recording sounded more balanced despite the extreme volume at which everything was belted out, and this time the odd smattering of keyboards added a little more variety to the saturated sonics. Otherwise, they did exactly what came naturally, which was to reduce everything to matchwood – witness the closing violence of "Just A Little Bit" and the swooping bassy boom of "Gypsy Ball". Hoping perhaps to score another hit they pounded through a rousing rendition of the Stones' "(I Can't Get No) Satisfaction" and plodded (in a good way) through a cover of Booker T. Jones's "The Hunter".

At this point the Blue Cheer story gets mired in all sorts of personnel changes and lost potential. Four more albums followed, but by 1974 it was all over. Since then there have been various re-formations – not least in the 80s which resulted in an album on metal label Megaforce – but nothing really comes close to the furious racket captured on the first two albums. So, is this where it started? Quite possibly. But who cares? What matters is that these albums rock – big time.

⊙ Vincebus Eruptum
1968; Track

Six tracks of bonkers riffing, mad drumming and blues howling. A classic, unhinged debut that has gone down in history as a major paradigm shift.

⊙ Outsideinside
1968; Track

Album number two in the same year. A much better recording, with stronger songs and even bigger balls – an essential album for lovers of heavy vibes, man.

BLUE ÖYSTER CULT

Formed New York, US, 1971

A loud and menacing riposte to the swirling psychedelia of the 60s, **Blue Öyster Cult** were intended to be the US equivalent of Black Sabbath, though just a cursory journey through their early-70s albums ought largely to dispel the idea. Sure, they had the occult leanings and a wanton way with a face-melting riff or two but, whereas Osbourne, Iommi et al revelled in doom and gloom horror, BÖC were all together more sprightly and inventive, blessed with a

Blue Öyster Cult: "Now look lads, this is how you play it."

RICHARD E AARON/REDFERNS

tongue-in-cheek wit that leavened their sinister lyrics with a knowing pinch of irony.

For a group that would come to represent some of the best in 70s heavy metal the band's genesis was something of a muddle. The nucleus was formed when **Donald 'Buck Dharma' Roeser** (guitar/vocals) met **Albert Bouchard** (drums/vocals) at university in the 60s. The two jammed with an assortment of musicians and under various names – **Soft White Under Belly** and **Stalk-Forrest Group**, most prominently – under the guidance of manager/mentor **Sandy Pearlman**. Pearlman was a prominent journalist writing for *Crawdaddy* magazine and, along with his writer friend Richard Meltzer, they envisaged a band that could take American rock'n'roll to the next level. Blue Öyster Cult would be that band. The line-up was completed by **Eric Bloom** (lead vocals/ "stun" guitar), **Joe Bouchard** (bass/ vocals), **Allen Lanier** (keyboards/guitar); the latter would eventually add the all-important metal-signifying umlaut to the band name.

When their eponymous album, produced by Pearlman and **Murray Krugman**, appeared in 1972 on Columbia, the first glimmerings of the classic BÖC sound were in place, even though the production lacked the sonic punch that would propel future studio efforts. Clearly there was still something of the late-60s Stalk-Forrest Group flavour to the tunes but with Pearlman and Meltzer doing their best on the press front and "Cities On Flame With Rock And Roll" getting New York radio airplay, it was just a matter of time before the US would be drawn into the peculiar metal world of BÖC. Already there was an inkling of the wit and humour present in the band's writing – "I'm On The Lamb But I Ain't No Sheep" and "She's As Beautiful As A Foot" were just two of their early and most intriguing song titles.

Key to their future status as weirdo sci-fi occultists was the adoption of the "Kronos" hook and cross logo – a symbol representing the Roman god Saturn – placed prominently on the monochrome album sleeve designed by **Bill Gawlik**. It added to the gathering sinister mystique of the band – even if it eventually took a support slot with **Alice Cooper** for them to really learn the art of stagecraft. The ominous logo was perfect for everything from tattoos, through T-shirts, to graffiti.

Tyranny And Mutation (1973) featured an even more striking Gawlik sleeve, upping the band's occult ante, and finally found them ditching the last vestiges of the 60s for something altogether more strident and crunchy. At last they were coming close to the ideal of a US Black Sabbath, though they were also incorporating harmonies and technical virtuosity into their powerhouse sound. With one side of the album red and the other black, the intention was to indicate the album's contrast of moods; the subtle, shimmering shades of tunes such as "Wings Wetted Down" and "Teen Archer" against the all-out bombast of "Hot Rails To Hell" and future stage fave "7 Screaming Diz-Busters". Pearlman and Meltzer were practising their lyrical alchemy throughout. And "Baby Ice Dog" even featured lyric contributions from future punk-poetess Patti Smith, at the time an item with Lanier, a writing partnership that would last well into the 80s.

Ending what came to be known as their "black and white" period was the consistent masterpiece *Secret Treaties* (1974). The arrangements were moody and lithe, the poetry of the lyrics was intelligent, arcane and dark; **Patti Smith** contributed to the opening "Career Of Evil", while Meltzer, enjoying the shock value, provided lyrics to "Harvester Of Eyes". The album gave them such concert standards as "Flaming Telepaths", "Dominance And Submission" and "Astronomy", helping their live reputation as a killer unit to grow. Live album *On Your Feet Or On Your Knees* (1975) showcased a band so at home on stage that even the shaky production couldn't mask their spitfire energy.

They just needed a little boost to project them into the super league, and that came in the shape of *Agents Of Fortune* (1976) and its massive US hit single "(Don't Fear) The Reaper", which helped raise their profile in the UK no end. While the single was uncharacteristically gentle and almost Byrds-like in sound, the album was far more experimental and diverse. BÖC were now music magazine cover stars and with the pressure on to provide a convincing follow-up, *Spectres* (1977) was an over-polished disappointment. Far more satisfying was the short but punchy *Some Enchanted Evening* (1978) which again proved that live was where the band excelled.

The desire to keep the momentum up resulted in the lightweight *Mirrors* (1979). This was after they ditched Pearlman and Krugman as producers and opted for **Tom Werman** who had worked with the likes of Ted Nugent and Cheap Trick. Pearlman had become manager of Black Sabbath during this period and, as a result, the producer of *Heaven And Hell,* **Martin Birch**, was given the job of helping create first *Cultosaurus Erectus* (1980) and then *Fire Of Unknown Origin* (1981). The former was relatively weak but sold well – it made #12 in the UK charts but did less spectacularly in the US – while the latter featured much stronger material with a surprise hit in "Burnin' For You", originally intended for a Buck Dharma solo LP. Both albums took the group's penchant for flights of sci-fi fantasy to new heights, with lyrical contributions from cult novelist **Michael Moorcock**.

The Sabbath and BÖC collision went further, in their team-up for the *Black And Blue* tour, making BÖC seem at last to be heading in the right direction – yet more problems were about to torpedo their career. Following a spate of peculiar behaviour and a less than auspicious appearance at Monsters Of Rock in 1981, Al Bouchard left the band to be replaced by **Rick Downey**. Minus a founding member and with Dharma working on his solo effort *Flat Out*, 1982 looked decidedly shaky, with only another gig document, *Extraterrestrial Live*, filling a yawning chasm in their schedule. It was a contractual obligation and a waste of time for the fans who had had their fill of live albums. *The Revolution By Night* (1983) couldn't be saved by a powerful Bruce Fairbairn production job, and the realization that the band was crumbling was beginning to dawn.

Three years passed before *Club Ninja* (1986) hammered the nails firmly into the coffin. Even when *Imaginos* (1988) appeared – a logic-teasing concept album, touted as a "random access myth" – no one could quite understand what it was they were listening to. The album was based upon a series of lyrical ideas put together by Pearlman back in the 60s and had originally been a solo album project, with Al Bouchard at the helm. The only way the label could be persuaded to release it was if it was issued as a bona fide BÖC record, hence parts were reworked and rerecorded with the original members in place. By some it was viewed as genius – apparently Metallica were big fans – to others it was a mess. It bombed and the band were dropped the following year, effectively sealing BÖC's fate as the group on tour forever, but with no deal. Only the soundtrack to the awful horror movie *Bad Channels* (1992) resulted in any new Cult material.

Finally, in 1998, a deal was landed with CMC. *Heaven Forbid* was their first proper album for a decade – with a sizeable lyrical injection from sci-fi writer **John Shirley** – though only Bloom, Lanier and Roeser remained from the original line-up. It was a return to form, but far too late to make an impression on a music scene reeling from alternative rock and the first formative wailings of nu-metal. A new deal with Sanctuary resulted in the enjoyable if unspectacular *Curse Of The Hidden Mirror* (2001) followed by yet another live package, *A Long Day's Night* (2002).

Despite the huge drop in popularity, BÖC continue to tour – a revolutionary, thundering and intelligent live unit – even as their old label continues to churn out repackaged albums and compilations, mining the band's commercial peak for all it's worth.

Blue Öyster Cult
1972; Columbia

A loose and slightly muffled production can't mask the addictive quality of songs such as "Transmaniacon MC", "Cities On Flame With Rock And Roll" and "Workshop Of The Telescopes". Brilliant riffy tunes, pure and simple.

Tyranny And Mutation
1973; Columbia

A vastly improved studio sound makes songs such as the chugging "Hot Rails To Hell" and the blinding "7 Screaming Diz-Busters" absolutely essential.

Secret Treaties
1974; Columbia

For many fans this is the BÖC at their best and it's not hard to understand why. "Career Of Evil", "Dominance And Submission", "Flaming Telepaths" and the sublime "Astronomy" (since covered by Metallica) make this one of their most consistent sets.

Agents Of Fortune
1976; Columbia

Nice and heavy, this is another classic of esoteric rock poetics and it contains one of the most enduring riffs in "(Don't Fear) The Reaper".

BODY COUNT

Formed South Central LA, US, 1989

Set aside rap metal and the pretensions of nu-metal and consider for a moment the real deal. The creation of this hybrid hip-hop metal band is worthy of note because the man behind it was bona fide rap star and self-proclaimed original gangster, **Ice-T**. While so many predominantly white rock bands had begun to appropriate black rap stylings in the alternative early 90s, there was a distinct lack of hip-hop stars moving into metal. This lot would break new ground, though they didn't capitalize fully on their early success, becoming something of a footnote in Ice-T's ever-diversifying media and music career.

The rapper had first met guitarist **Ernie-C** at Crenshaw High School, South Central,

Los Angeles and when their respective musical careers were under way, Ice-T would turn to him whenever a vicious guitar riff was required. **Body Count** officially came into existence in 1989; with a line-up that also included the hockey mask-wearing **D-Roc** (guitar), **Mooseman** (bass) and **Beatmaster V** (drums), they were blowing people away on the very first Lollapalooza tour before they'd even released an album.

The overwhelmingly positive feedback from their first appearance set the tone for their eponymous debut, which screeched into view in a hail of Uzi fire in 1992. *Body Count* was an amazing amalgamation of thundering metal and Ice-T's brazen, tongue-in-cheek lyrics honed from years of the hippest hip-hop; it was so full-on and hardcore in its portrayal of Ice-T's world of the street that some critics couldn't tell whether the thing was for real. As a crossover album it was unique in that it didn't feature any wannabe white-boy rappers making fools of themselves; but nothing could have prepared the band for the song that really broke them into the popular consciousness.

The profanity-strewn *pièce de résistance* was the deliberately abrasive "Cop Killer". With its inflammatory story about a black man taking revenge on behalf of Rodney King and encouraging the use of violence to get even with the police, it had the moral guardians and political authorities up in arms. In the end the record label (Warners) had to remove the track from the album after the band and company staff received death threats. While some of the other songs dealt with serious subjects such as racism in a sick but humorous way ("Momma's Gotta Die Tonight"), others were hammered home in classic gangster style with plenty of "Muthafuckas!" and "Bitches!" thrown in for good measure.

After this incendiary start the band had a lot to live up to; *Born Dead* (1994) delivered more of the same, albeit without a song of the same headline-grabbing proportions as "Cop Killer". By now the band had moved to Virgin and it would be the label for their final album, the far more consistent *Violent Demise (The Last Days)* (1997).

After this, little was heard of the band, though it seems unlikely that Ice-T will attempt to resurrect their fortunes, given the string of tragedies suffered by the various members. Beatmaster V succumbed to leukemia in 1996;

Mooseman was an innocent victim in a drive-by shooting in 2000; and D-Roc died in August 2004 after suffering from lymphoma.

Body Count
1992; Warners

Hugely offensive, wildly over-the-top, this is the world of gangster rap colliding violently with metal – gangster metal, if you will. Huge, heavy and uncompromising, there is a mad sense of humour lurking beneath the riffing and Ice-T's manic persona. Look hard and you might find a version with the controversial "Cop Killer" on it.

BON JOVI

Formed New Jersey, US, 1983

Just mention the name and visions of stadiums packed with adoring fans springs to mind, that and vast record sales. What **Bon Jovi** brought to rock in the 80s was slick showmanship, a sense of fun and an ultra-polished songwriting talent; when firing on all cylinders the band were a sight to behold, a smooth and loose-limbed entertainment machine. In the 90s and beyond they transformed themselves into a mature megaband, with a frontman who had transcended rock stardom to become a bona fide celebrity, developing an acting career alongside the singing.

It all started with **Jon Bon Jovi** (vocals, born **Bongiovi**) harbouring a desire to emulate his rock heroes. Influenced by artists as diverse as Bruce Springsteen and Thin Lizzy,

the young Bon Jovi was a member of several bands during his school years. But the first moves toward stardom were taken when he joined forces with school buddy **David Bryan** (keyboards, born **Rashbaum**) **Richie Sambora** (guitar) **Alec John Such** (bass), and **Tico Torres** (drums). It was a solid line-up, one which lasted for over twenty years. They recorded a demo at New York's Record Plant studio and a Jon Bon Jovi-penned tune called "Runaway" ended up on a radio station compilation album of unsigned acts. What marked Bon Jovi out as having a better-than-average chance of success was the hunger and burning ambition of their singer. Not only that but they looked great in an era when poodle-permed hair and terrific teeth almost guaranteed magazine coverage, even without a hit tune. In short, they had it all. All they needed was a couple of lucky breaks.

A deal was signed with Mercury and "Runaway" was rerecorded; it became their first US top-forty single in early 1984. Their eponymous first album followed and was lauded as a great debut by *Kerrang!* magazine, pushing the band into the limelight; their slot supporting Kiss across Europe further raised their profile. However, the follow-up album, 7800° *Fahrenheit,* although decent enough, lacked the killer cuts necessary to catapult them to stardom.

That breakthrough eluded them until *Slippery When Wet* (1986). The Springsteen-like preoccupation with the song as a story was fused to the shamelessly commercial don't-bore-us-get-to-the-chorus writing ethic and all of it was given a suitably huge production by **Bruce Fairbairn**. The magic ingredient was the drafting in of outside songwriters, most notably **Desmond Child,** whose slick tricks with hooks and lyrics were second to none. The result was commercial dynamite: a US #1 album that narrowly missed the Top 5 in the UK. Previous singles such as "In And Out Of Love" and "The Hardest Part Is The Night" had barely tickled the charts, but "You Give Love A Bad Name" and "Livin' On A Prayer" were in with a bullet. And our Jon got to play the mythical cowboy troubadour on "Wanted Dead Or Alive", charming everyone with his guitar-strumming antics; it was an image he would exploit to great effect over the coming years.

Whereas they had been placed somewhere mid-bill at Donington in 1985, dodging bottles and clumps of mud, the major hit single

Bon Jovi in all their 80s glory.

"Never Say Goodbye", just one of the many slushy lighters-in-the-air ballads produced over the years landed them the top slot in 1987; always the showman, Jon swung down on a rope for the opening song – too bad the spotlight operator wasn't fast enough to catch the action.

From this point the flow of accolades and huge sales seemed like a certainty. In an effort to repeat the magic, the same production and writing team were reassembled for *New Jersey* (1988) and the album topped the charts in both the UK and the US. The hits came thick and fast, not least the Desmond Child-assisted "Bad Medicine" and soft-focus ballad "I'll Be There For You" – the latter topping the US charts shortly after Jon got married to his childhood sweetheart in the spring of 1989. The only blot on an otherwise spotless horizon was the conviction of the band's manager **Doc McGhee** on drug smuggling charges in 1988 – 40,000lbs of grass to be precise – from six years earlier. Amazingly he got away with fines, a suspended prison sentence and community service, which involved setting up the Make A Difference anti-drink and drug foundation.

Predictably, the touring that accompanied *New Jersey* put the band through a punishing global schedule that included headlining appearances at the Moscow Music Peace Festival – alongside Ozzy Osbourne, Skid Row, Scorpions, Cinderella and Mötley Crüe – and at the Milton Keynes Bowl. The marathon trek over with, the band effectively took a break from each other. Bon Jovi headed off into the desert sun wielding his trusty six-string, to do his modern cowboy thing with the soundtrack to *Blaze Of Glory: Young Guns II* (1990) – he also landed a cameo part in the movie. The lead track became his first solo number one in the US and the album went Top 5 on both sides of the Atlantic, prompting speculation that the band were finished now that their mainman had scored so easily on his own.

While Bon Jovi cleaned up at various awards ceremonies, Sambora also issued a bluesier solo set, *Stranger In This Town* (1991), helped out by Torres and Bryan and a smokin' solo provided by **Eric Clapton** on "Mr Bluesman". While in many ways it was a more appealing set than the usual Bon Jovi fare – for one thing Richie has a fine singing voice – predictably it didn't bother the charts with quite the same longevity.

With the spectre of a group split haunting fans, the only thing that assured them of Bon Jovi's continuing existence was *Keep The Faith* (1992), this time produced by **Bob Rock** who had worked as engineer on their previous recordings. Everything about the new album was calculated to break through the grunge monopoly that had effectively killed off the kind of rock'n'roll with which they had made their fortune. Gone was the rock-star glitz, Jon had cut his hair, and the feel was of a band that had matured. The record was another chart-topper and several of the tunes were hits of varying proportions; however, it marked the least successful phase of their career.

Crossroad (1994) was a tidy best-of compilation, but the chart-topping success was not enough to convince Such to stay in the band. The *Best Of...* album kept interest in the band relatively high while they worked on their next effort, *These Days* (1995), their first studio recording for three years. In the same fashion as *Keep The Faith,* the new material seemed to be better appreciated in the UK and across Europe, where the dour effects of alternative rock hadn't permeated the airwaves to the same extent as in the US.

The knock they suffered in the US charts didn't prevent Bon Jovi from undertaking sellout stadium-sized tour dates, however. And when he wasn't fronting the band Jon made himself busy with his fledgling acting career. A part in *Moonlight And Valentino* led to a role in *The Leading Man* and, although he didn't swap the role of lead singer to lead on screen, he seemed to pop up from time to time in various small roles – the most high profile of which included the wartime submarine drama *U-571* and the TV series *Ally McBeal*.

In 1997 it was time to flex the old solo career again. *Destination Anywhere* proved to be something of a departure from the usual Jon Bon Jovi fare, helped by the use of several different producers including **Dave Stewart** and Desmond Child, and a large selection of musos, all bringing their own unique twist to the tales of lost love. The following year, Sambora issued *Undiscovered Soul*, again prompting positive reviews but registering little more than a blip compared to Jon and his cowboy hat.

By this point in their career the band had shifted a staggering eighty million albums around the world, achieving the status of rock giants. And when *Crush* (2000), their first studio effort in five years, cruised into view the world stadium tour covered eleven countries; they even played two sell-out shows at Wembley Stadium, the last rock performances there before it was torn down. The album was decked out with a pumping modern production which worked well on the tried-and-trusted blend of ballads, gentle rockers and full-on pop-metal gems – in particular, the single "It's My Life". Especially successful was the ripping party anthem "One Wild Night" which gave its name to the live album of the following year *One Wild Night: Live 1985-2001*. However, it was a pretty lacklustre effort for their first official concert album. Still, this mediocre album did nothing to defuse the enthusiasm of the fans for the subsequent tour, which was even more ambitious than the last.

The pattern continued with *Bounce* (2002), undaunted and undented by trends such as nu-metal; while Ozzfest kids may have had little interest in the band, their carefully orchestrated and managed mainstream success had ensured the group a loyal and stable fanbase who wanted big, bold feel-good ballads and sing-along rockers. In a smart move *This Left Feels Right: Greatest Hits With A Twist* (2003) recycled some of their best-known songs – ignoring tunes from *These Days* – by rerecording them with a slower, mellower feel. It was considered money for old rope by some and a highly desirable exercise by others.

Love 'em or loathe 'em, the way Bon Jovi are going they'll be filling stadiums in true Mick and Keef style for at least the next decade.

⦿ Bon Jovi
1984; Vertigo

It's all here right from the off. Big fat choruses and lots of 80s-style strutting and preening. Contains the early promise of greatness in "Runaway" and a deceptive little tune called "Shot Through The Heart", prefiguring the huge change that would take place in '86.

⦿ Slippery When Wet
1986; Vertigo

Suddenly it all makes sense. No duff tracks and a seamless flow from ballsy rockers to ballads and all points in between. Makes you want to raise your fist and yell in a big-haired, spandex-loving kind of way.

⦿ New Jersey
1988; Vertigo

Basically this is a sequel to their monster breakthrough album with a massive production and lots of irritatingly catchy tunes, especially the insanely energetic "Bad Medicine".

⦿ Keep The Faith
1992; Vertigo

Bon Jovi grow up and reinvent themselves for the miserable early 90s. The cheese factor is kept in check, though the trademark licks and tricks are still in place.

⦿ Crush
2000; Vertigo

A comeback of major proportions, bolstered by a tougher-sounding production and oodles of melodic, classy writing. Worth checking out for the brash "I Got The Girl" and good-time rocker "One Wild Night".

BOSTON

Formed Boston, US, 1975

For many fans of loud guitars the notion of a band usually involves like-minded individuals getting together to celebrate their love of sex, drugs and rock'n'roll – usually in that order. **Boston**, however, are one of the most successful exceptions to the rule. They have sold squillions of records over the last thirty or so years – recently they received a coveted Diamond award for vast sales – yet their formula basically involves raising the roof with anthems about the power of lurve. The main man behind these creations is the multitalented, multi-instrumentalist and all-round technical and scientific wizard, **Tom Scholz**. Unusually, the remarkable sales figures have been generated by one of the smallest back catalogues in modern rock history; in the time it takes Scholz to tune up, some bands can enjoy entire careers. But what Boston lack in quantity, they more than make up for in quality – making them one of the most influential bands of the 70s and 80s.

The Boston story started with Scholz working as a design scientist for Polaroid, having obtained a master's degree in mechanical engineering. Despite the secure day job, Scholz harboured a desire to rock; he put together a basement studio where he slowly and carefully toiled, trying his hardest to craft the sounds he imagined into note-perfect songs. The creation of some superb demo tracks eventually led to a deal with Epic Records. So good were the tunes that they formed the basis of the legendary eponymous debut album which landed in 1976, complete

with garish Technicolor guitar-shaped UFO artwork on the sleeve. There was some input from other musos, but essentially it was Scholz at the controls, guiding his personal vision to fruition. And what a vision it was. *Boston* (1976) was a testament to meticulous sonic engineering. The album was brimful of solid harmonies and driving guitar power, a fact readily apparent on its monster smash hit single "More Than A Feeling" (a top-5 hit in the US). The effect of this almost symphonic-sounding melodic marvel was extremely far-reaching – as has often been pointed out, Nirvana's "Smell's Like Teen Spirit" owes just as much to that famous riff as to any number of obscure punk bands.

The other chief ingredient, aside from Scholz's precision songwriting, was the soaring vocal contribution provided by **Brad Delp**, meshing beautifully with the sublime guitar harmonies to produce timeless nuggets of classic rock. The result was a debut that, while narrowly missing #1 in the US and the Top 10 in the UK, would go on to sell ridiculous amounts around the world, making it one of the most successful rock albums of all time.

Naturally, a full line-up was required to tour such a commercial behemoth; Scholz and Delp were joined by **Barry Goudreau** (guitar), **Fran Sheehan** (bass) and the marvellously afroed **Sib Hashian** (drums). Considering this was the hirsute mid-70s, never before had there been such a fine selection of moustaches and beards assembled – they were a sight to behold with Scholz the only member to abstain from ludicrous fuzzy-face furniture.

Two years on, *Don't Look Back* (1978) arrived and, despite the title, it took the basic sound of the debut and rearranged the pieces, to create yet another brace of ultra-melodic hard rock. It went to the top of the US charts and hit the Top 10 in the UK. Despite the amazing sales racked up by their sophomore effort it wasn't deemed as big a success; Scholz put it all down to a hasty genesis – he would much rather have taken more time to get the second one up to the flawless standard of the first.

Scholz's desire to take time to put out records resulted in a wave of legal action against him. The chief wrangle – setting aside actions launched by disgruntled band members – lay with Epic who wanted hit albums and plenty of them, while Scholz wasn't ready to play ball. Epic eventually lost their seven-year battle in 1990 and had to settle Scholz's counterclaim that he was owed huge amounts in unpaid royalties.

In the meantime, the various band members got fed up hanging around; Goudreau first went solo in 1980 and then formed **Orion The Hunter**, enjoying modest success on the back of his Boston career. As for the mothership, it wasn't until 1986 that she would fly again, this time on MCA records. The sleeve to *Third Stage* proclaimed that the material within was arranged by Scholz with a little help from his friends – the new look line-up featuring **Gary Pihl** (guitar, ex-**Sammy Hagar**) and **Jim Masdea** (drums). Masdea had actually helped Scholz out with the two earlier records and the first demos. Despite the #1 US hit single "Amanda", a rather soppy ballad, ideal for mid-80s FM radio, the new album sold less than the previous two outings – that said, we're still talking sales in the millions. The reality was that Scholz had alienated many of the fans by not getting albums out more quickly; some people had just forgotten how great Boston were in the 70s. Their influence, however, was prevalent in the vast number of AOR bands that had sprung up in the 80s.

After *Third Stage* Boston disappeared yet again. No one knew when Scholz would deem any new material ready for release, so in 1991 Delp and Goudreau formed **Return To Zero** with **Tim Archibald** (bass), **Brian Maes** (keyboards) and **Dave Stefanelli** (drums). An eponymous album enjoyed a little chart action in 1992 but nothing to rival the success of Boston.

By the time *Walk On* (1994) registered on radar, the line-up had been tweaked once more, with the addition of **Fran Cosmo** and

Tommy Funderburke on vocals. By now it really was a case of diminishing returns; after all, grunge had pretty much wiped out the market for precision-played melodic rock. A relatively short three years later, *Greatest Hits* arrived, featuring three whole new songs and the return of Brad Delp.

Again Boston fell silent on the recording front, though the thoroughly inventive Scholz continued to busy himself with his company, Scholz Research & Development, responsible for creating various amazing bits of electronic kit for musicians, and supporting various organizations – the ethically aware Scholz is involved in a variety of environmental, homeless and animal charities. It was his social awareness that informed the creation of *Corporate America* (2002) – the title track taking a stab at America's culture of greed – with a line-up now augmented by **Kimberley Dahme** (bass) and **Anthony Cosmo** (guitar).

Much touring of America's arenas followed; however, when Scholz will decide to release another new album is anybody's guess. Until then the first two albums will continue to pop back into the charts every now and then, bringing some of the most distinctive power chords in rock to new generations.

⊙ Boston
1976; Epic

Overshadowed by the mighty success of "More Than A Feeling" this album is actually studded with classics. The production is awesomely polished, the instrumentation lovingly layered and lush, the guitar playing sweet and fiery.

⊙ Don't Look Back
1978; Epic

More of the same. Big, bold hooks, tons of guitars made to sound like an orchestra of rock and beautiful harmonies.

⊙ Greatest Hits
1997; Epic

A collection of superb songs. If you need to carry around a selection of Boston tunes, then this is it.

BUDGIE

Formed Cardiff, Wales, 1967

One of the UK's best heavy rocking bands of the 70s and 80s, **Budgie** never hit the same stratospheric heights as contemporaries such as Deep Purple or Black Sabbath. But their idiosyncratic riffy style and love of weird and wonderful song titles influenced not only bands in the New Wave Of British Heavy Metal – Iron Maiden covered "I Can't See My Feelings" – but a few heavyweight US bands as well. Soundgarden owe more than a packet of birdseed to the crunchy power trio's fuzzed and furious attack; they covered "Homicidal Suicidal". Most famously of all, however, is Metallica's passion for the feathered ones' tricky, bass-heavy riffing; the Bay Area thrashers covered both "Breadfan" and the fantastically titled "Crash Course In Brain Surgery".

The band originally started off under the chucklesome name of **Six Ton Budgie**, bassist/vocalist **Burke Shelley**'s peculiar sense of humour already shaping the band's identity. There were plenty of pub and club gigs to be had around south Wales and, with a stable line-up including **Tony Bourge** (guitar) and **Ray Phillips** (drums), they set about becoming one of the heaviest rock bands doing the rounds in the early 70s. Bourge's primal riffing combined with Shelley's pumping bass lines and helium-pitched vocals to create something akin to a proggy Black Sabbath, or a skull-crackingly powerful version of Rush.

The constant gigging led to a tight portfolio of tunes; they came to the attention of producer **Rodger Bain**, who had been working with Brummie metallers Sabbath, and detected a similar tough and brutal edge in Budgie's efforts. A deal with MCA resulted in *Budgie* (1971), home of the original version of "Homicidal Suicidal" and featuring the first

Better Than The Movie: Metal Soundtracks

There is no shortage of great rock and metal soundtracks. The animated movie *Heavy Metal* (1981) features an intriguing snapshot of rock sounds from the late 70s and early 80s; *Singles* (1992) captures the grunge phenomenon early on; **Pink Floyd**'s *The Wall* (1982) is simply awesome; while possibly the greatest Sex Pistols documentary, *The Filth And The Fury* (1999), features some authentic punk, pop and rock vibes of the era. And then we have pretty much anything that **The Who** put their name to, such as *Tommy* (1975), *The Kids Are Alright* (1979) and *Quadrophenia* (1979) – if you look for them, the goods are there. But what about metal soundtracks that are vastly superior to the films? The following ten soundtracks are worth checking out even if you never see the movies in question…

The Return Of The Living Dead (1985; Restless Records)
The film is something of a cult favourite among B-movie aficionados and the soundtrack features an excellent clutch of early to mid-80s goth and punk gems from the likes of **The Damned**, **TSOL** and the superb **45 Grave** whose "Partytime (Zombie Version)" is worth the price of admission alone – it's like listening to Mötley Crüe gone goth. Truly a rave from the grave.

Who Made Who (1986; Atlantic)
Maximum Overdrive is a schlocky mess of a horror movie directed by Stephen King from one of his own short stories, but the soundtrack rocks from start to finish. This is basically an **AC/DC** compilation with a couple of instrumental guitar workouts thrown in for good measure. There were some other interesting compositions and remixes created for the film but they didn't make the soundtrack – for those you'll have to watch Emilio Estevez battling a bunch of possessed trucks.

Last Action Hero (1993; Sony)
The movie stiffed because it couldn't decide if it was an action thriller, a comedy or a fantasy. No such identity problems with the soundtrack though because it kicks off with AC/DC's "Big Gun" and brings along **Alice In Chains**, **Queensrÿche**, **Def Leppard**, **Anthrax** and **Megadeth** for the ride.

Spawn: The Album (1997; Sony)
This is either a stroke of genius or an act of sacrilege, depending upon your point of view. While the film was an unholy mess the soundtrack takes some of the meanest electronic and techno wizards and slings them into the pit with a few choice metal bands. The result is artists such as **Atari Teenage Riot** and **DJ Spooky** getting down and dirty with **Marilyn Manson** and **Metallica**. These songs could well rip your ears off.

Escape From L.A. (1996; Atlantic)
Snake Plissken rides again – in a John Carpenter movie that's not a patch on the original *Escape From New York*. The soundtrack, however, features one of the rare instances in which **White Zombie** turn up. They are without doubt one of the highlights while **Sugar Ray** remind everyone what they sounded like before they lightened up for the radio. Elsewhere **Tool**, **Ministry**, and **Gravity Kills** ensure that the atmospherics are nice and dark.

Strangeland (1998; TVT)
Written by and featuring **Twisted Sister's Dee Snider** this horror flick is quite terrible. The music, however, is an interesting collision of old and new. **Crisis** and **dayinthelife** tackle the two parts of Twisted Sister's "Horror Teria" that inspired the script, while the Sister themselves reunite for "Heroes Are Hard To Find". And then we have Megadeth, Anthrax, **Sevendust** and **Soulfly** among a bewildering array of bands, making this one hell of a menacing album.

End Of Days (1999; Interscope)
Another dodgy Arnie vehicle, this time ruined by a nonsensical apocalyptic plot. The soundtrack, however, features one of the few **Guns N' Roses** appearances of the late 90s with "Oh My God". It's far from vital G N'R but it does make the album unique. Elsewhere the likes of **Korn**, **Limp Bizkit** and **Powerman 5000** give this a punchy nu-metal flavour.

Dracula 2000 (2000; Sony)
The film was a turkey but the bands gathered on this little beauty make for a blisteringly punishing experience. **Slayer**, Powerman 5000, **Pantera**, **Monster Magnet** and **System Of A Down** all rub shoulders alongside a whole bunch of noisy bruisers all going for the jugular. Let the blood flow.

Queen Of The Damned (2002; Warner Bros)
Forget about the movie, the soundtrack is a must for nu-metal lovers and Korn fans in particular. Frontman **Jonathan Davis** helped write five of the songs with the vocals tackled by the likes of Marilyn Manson, **David Draiman** (Disturbed), **Wayne Static** (Static-X), **Jay Gordon** (Orgy), and **Chester Bennington** (Linkin Park). And then there are some already-out-there cuts from **Papa Roach** and **Deftones** among others.

of Shelley's inspired song titles – the classic "Nude Disintegrating Parachutist Woman". The sleeve also established a running theme – their "Budgie man" character.

Squawk (1972) followed soon after, establishing a prolific one album per year pattern that the band stuck to, with only a couple of exceptions. "Hot As A Docker's Armpit" was the stand-out crazy title this time; overall the playing and production was an improvement on their debut.

The band were already picking up a sizeable following thanks to DJs such as Kid Jensen plugging them constantly on Radio Luxembourg, but the real leap came with *Never Turn Your Back On A Friend* (1973). The record was a stormer. The chugging "Breadfan" led into a cracking cover version of "Baby Please Don't Go"; the barmy song titles were there too – "You're The Biggest Thing Since Powdered Milk" and "In The Grip Of A Tyrefitter's Hand" – proving that Shelley truly had a gift for off-the-wall metal monikers. Occasional acoustic passages decorated arrangements of great invention, all helped along by a self-handled production job; nowhere was this more apparent than in the mellow "Riding My Nightmare", leading into the ten-minutes-plus journey of "Parents". The album cover featured the Budgie man struggling with a giant-sized bird of prey in a classic Roger Dean painting.

Never Turn Your Back... proved to be the last album to feature Phillips; soon **Pete Boot** was behind the kit for *In For The Kill* (1974) which actually went top 30 in the UK. Curiously the album contained "Crash Course In Brain Surgery", which had been their first single back in 1971 but had somehow not been included on any album so far. Boot was eventually replaced for the next album, the consistent and tightly rocking *Bandolier* (1975), by **Steve Williams**.

With a sizeable and loyal UK following already won over, Budgie set their sights on the US and first toured there in 1976. This focus led to a slight change of tack musically, in an effort to win over a new audience. The inspired title for their next effort was *If I Were Brittania I'd Waive The Rules,* and with it came a more refined and less aggressive approach – especially during the title track which featured a classic heavy Budgie riff leading into bouncy funk verses. Suffice it to say, it disappointed fans who wanted more of the Budgie of old. They got this in the form

of *Best Of Budgie,* which condensed some of their best songs into one volume.

Impeckable (1978) made an effort to balance the less in-your-face style with a heavier vibe and, to a large extent, it succeeded. But it is still regarded as something of a disappointment. During this period the band were still staging gigging raids across the US and the album was recorded in Ontario so that they could keep to their live schedule without missing a beat. The constant slog of the road took its toll on Bourge who eventually bailed out; another guitarist, **Rob Kendrick**, stepped into the fold but didn't last long.

The man who would become their permanent guitarist was **"Big" John Thomas** and with him came another pronounced shift in direction. With punk on the rise, metal bands had upped the speed and aggression stakes in the New Wave Of British Heavy Metal, but Budgie proved without a doubt that they could more than compete with the younger whippersnappers. Thomas brought with him a distinct metallic edge and Budgie moved away from their slightly crustier sound of old to riffing with the best of them. Their 1980 *If Swallowed Do Not Induce Vomiting* EP contained four tracks of crunching metal with "Wildfire" and "Panzer Division Destroyed" being the ripsnorting highlights. The EP was just a taster of what was to follow with *Power Supply* (1980); kicking off an album with a song titled "Forearm Smash" explained exactly where they were coming from, their new, more commercial style allied to a terrific amount of energy. Thanks to the waves created by the NWOBHM, *Nightflight* (1981) and *Deliver Us From Evil* (1982) made modest dents on the album charts.

Though the band continued to gig and write material right up to 1988, no albums were released – except for another *Best Of Budgie* (with a different tracklisting) – and they eventually decided to take a break. Shelley formed the **Superclarkes** while the others stayed quiet until there was a resurgence in the band's popularity, helped along by Metallica covering their songs. In the mid-90s Budgie played in San Antonio, marking their return.

Since then sporadic gigging has been accompanied by a steady stream of anthologies, live CDs and rarities: *An Ecstasy Of Fumbling* is a damn-near definitive double album compilation; *We Came, We Saw...* presents BBC recordings of the band's Reading appearances in 1980 and 1982; *Heavier Than Air – Rarest Eggs* pulls together a tantalizing fistful of radio sessions; *Life In San Antonio* captures a US live set from 2002. Most recently a comprehensive re-issue campaign has begun remastering the old albums with bonus tracks, and to really get the feathers flying *The Last Stage* contains material the band were working on in the mid-80s but never released.

Budgie
1971; Repertoire

If you want to hear where the likes of Soundgarden got their inspiration then look no further. "Homicidal Suicidal" is the obvious highlight.

Never Turn Your Back On A Friend
1973; Repertoire

Another classic, this time providing Metallica with one of their best cover version selections, "Breadfan".

Bandolier
1975; Repertoire

Considered by some one of their finest albums and certainly one of the most consistently rocking; "Breaking All The House Rules" is an all-time cracking opener. Yet again Budgie provide material for others to cover; "I Can't See My Feelings" turned up as an Iron Maiden B-side.

Power Supply
1980; Repertoire

The reissued version of this album also includes the excellent *If Swallowed...* EP, which is also essential.

The Definitive Anthology: An Ecstasy Of Fumbling 1996; Repertoire

One of the best compilation albums currently available, this double-CD package contains killer track after killer track and throws in one or two rarities as well.

BUSH

Formed London, UK, 1992

"I don't know why you can get criticized for saying things as they are. I can call an orange a melon if I want – I often have – but sometimes I wanna call it an orange." Gavin Rossdale

Bush are one of those rare examples of a UK rock band that can whip up a storm in the US but meet relative indifference in their homeland. Maybe it has something to do with the fact that they landed a deal in the US before the UK; maybe it has something to do with them being first embraced by American rock lovers and thus perceived as sell-outs or, worse still, deliberate grunge copyists – a UK band adopting what was almost exclusively an alternative US rock identity. Whatever. When **Gavin Rossdale** (guitar/vocals), **Nigel Pulsford** (guitar), **Dave Parsons** (bass; ex-**Transvision Vamp**) and **Robin Goodridge** (drums) began rehearsing, thoughts of American domination were just a fantasy, albeit one that would be realized through a combination of good luck and bloody-minded hard work.

Nearly two years of gigging had led to little, when one of the band's demo tapes was passed via DJ Gary Crowley to Trauma Records in the States, specifically George Michael's ex-manager **Rob Kahane**. With Nirvana having abruptly ended, following Kurt Cobain's suicide, one could say that there was something of a gap in the US market for powerfully delivered grunge with a knowing pop sensibility. Call it cynical, or just good marketing, Bush, while far from being identical to Cobain and crew, did nonetheless fulfil much of the criteria. Kahane was savvy enough to allow Rossdale free reign in the creation of *Sixteen Stone* (1994) and the driving "Everything Zen" wreaked havoc on the US Modern Rock singles chart as it carved its way to #2. With Rossdale's fashionably tousled look and square jaw the band had a model frontman; he not only looked good, but sounded suitably husky and vulnerable, delivering his own emotionally charged, often abstract lyrics. Chuck in some hooky, menacing guitar and Bush were channelling the spirit of Seattle, only with an English accent. A successive series of singles eventually bled over from the rock charts to the mainstream top 40, ensuring that *Sixteen Stone* eventually went to number 4 in the US charts.

While they were doing the business Stateside, the band still couldn't get airplay in their home country. It would take a second album, *Razorblade Suitcase* (1996), for the UK to sit up and take notice. Stung by suggestions that the band weren't for real, they decided to let **Steve Albini** loose on their grungy sound. Albini's infamous non-production techniques – he is usually credited as simply having "recorded" a band – had worked brilliantly with artists such as the

Bizarre Cover Versions

It's hard to imagine a non-metal artist convincingly covering a metal tune; likewise who can imagine a heavy band playing anything other than the most intense music?

One of the few bands to get away with the latter is **Faith No More**, who built a reputation around being as off the wall as possible. True, they did cover Black Sabbath's "War Pigs", which isn't such a stretch, but with singer Mike Patton's amazing vocal dexterity they also tackled such songs as their hit cover of the Commodores' "Easy", the Bee Gees' "I Started A Joke" and Bacharach and David's "This Guy's In Love With You".

But what of other bands and artists? One of **Anthrax**'s best-loved live tunes is a fairly well honed version of **Joe Jackson**'s "Got The Time", given a turbo-charged thrash kick in the butt, but others don't fare quite so well. Girl band **All Saints** covered the **Red Hot Chili Peppers**' "Under The Bridge" despite the fact that the song is about heroin addiction; **Motörhead**'s **Lemmy** and **Wendy O Williams** of the **Plasmatics** infamously covered **Tammy Wynette**'s "Stand By Your Man"; power metallers **Gamma Ray** gave the **Petshop Boys**' "It's A Sin" a thorough going over; **Cradle Of Filth** gave Sir Cliff's "Devil Woman" a good seeing to, and **Mariah Carey** got all over-wrought on **Def Leppard**'s "Bringing On The Heartbreak". Meanwhile, in a slightly punkier vein, ska nuts **Less Than Jake** have tackled **Slayer**'s "Antichrist" and emo jockies **Coheed And Cambria**, apparently big fans of **Iron Maiden**, have covered "The Trooper". One of the unlikeliest combinations, however, must be **Avril Lavigne** covering **Metallica**'s "Fuel" at the third MTV Icons tribute show, neck and neck with **Tori Amos** covering Slayer's "Raining Blood" on her covers album *Strange Little Girls*. Then again that honour might well go to **Manowar** doing a version of "Nesum Dorma", or possibly avant-garde thrashers **Celtic Frost** covering **Dean Martin**'s "In The Chapel In The Moonlight".

Keeping the unlikely in mind – and sidestepping the obvious **Guns N' Roses** covers of **Dylan**'s "Knocking On Heaven's Door" and their wholesale destruction of **Paul McCartney**'s "Live And Let Die" – there is one band that has inspired perhaps more cover versions than any other: **Led Zeppelin**. The *Encomium* tribute album features a motley crew of odd acts from **Duran Duran** to **Hootie & The Blowfish** giving various Zeppelin tunes a good hiding. Their majestic "Stairway To Heaven", however, has been a seemingly endless source of inspiration with everyone from **Elkie Brooks** and **Dolly Parton** to **Rolf Harris** and the **Sisters Of Mercy** (responsible for many a weird cover version, especially live) climbing those mythical stairs into the clouds, and in the case of Rolf armed with a wobbleboard. And then, of course, there was the incomparable **Dread Zeppelin** who took on **Page** and **Plant**'s compositions reggae style on *Un-Led-Ed* (1990).

The market is awash with tribute albums allowing labels to cobble together just about anything to appeal to just about anyone. Hardcore noise merchants **Dillinger Escape Plan**, who also covered **Billy Idol**'s "Rebel Yell", took on Guns N' Roses' "My Michelle" on *Bring You To Your Knees: A Tribute To Guns N' Roses* (2004), an album packed with dodgy covers by a whole host of unlikely bands. Its awfulness is about equal to *Punk Goes Metal* (2000), but not nearly as terrible as *In A Metal Mood: No More Mr. Nice Guy* (1997) from the spotless **Pat Boone**, a record so bad it's almost genius. Boone's irreverent big band deconstruction of tunes such as "Smoke On The Water" (featuring **Ritchie Blackmore**) and "Holy Diver" (featuring **Ronnie James Dio**) angered his natural constituency of morally upright Christians and some humourless metal fans.

For more wholesale cover version mayhem look no further than bluegrass and country combo **Hayseed Dixie** who have created a nice little niche for themselves recording tribute albums to **AC/DC** and **Kiss**, plus one consisting of melodic rock covers. Not strictly speaking a covers band but well worth mentioning is the web-based parody outfit **Beatallica** whose name should give a major clue as to what they're about: mop top metal. Let's face it, anything is better than *St Anger*.

Pixies, PJ Harvey and, of course, Nirvana, and the idea was to bring a scathing and aggressive edge to Rossdale's angst. Thirteen raw and aching slabs of grating noise graced the set; it went to #1 in America and #4 in the UK, helped by their first top ten single, "Swallowed". Meanwhile, in the US, Rossdale's chiselled appearance landed him with the dubious honour of being nominated as one of the *Fifty Most Beautiful People In The World* by *People* magazine in 1997. Gwen Stefani of No Doubt probably agreed – she and Rossdale had first met when her band had supported Bush in 1996 and he would eventually propose to her on New Year's Day 2002.

Deconstructed (1997) followed shortly after *Razorblade Suitcase*, and basically featured a fistful of remixes, making it something of a curio rather than a must-have release for the fans. *The Science Of Things* (1999), their next album proper, was also a strange beast. The urge to incorporate something of a modern industrial sound resulted in a rather half-hearted combination of electronics and samples peppering the songs. It wasn't a particularly convincing effort, sounding rather more confused than ultramodern,

Gavin Rossdale's fretwork is head and shoulders above the rest.

and this was reflected in muted performances in the charts.

Far more effective was a return to the bone-breaking approach of their first album for *Golden State* (2001). Gone were the unnecessary studio embellishments; instead there was greater focus and power to Rossdale's typically anguished compositions. For the US tour, **Chris Traynor** (guitar; ex-**Helmet**) stepped in – Pulsford intended to continue with his new solo career and also wanted to stay at home with his newly expanded family. Traynor became a permanent fixture some months down the line.

 Sixteen Stone
1994; Trauma

Rossdale sounds impassioned and fiery on this debut of nail-hard and psychotically-driven grunge gems. A perfect recipe of angry introspection, obscure poetics and catchy caustic choruses.

 Razorblade Suitcase
1996; Trauma

Albini's abrasive techniques scratch all the superficial gloss from the songs allowing Rossdale's natural way with hooky choruses to do all the work. It sure ain't pretty.

Golden State
2001; Atlantic

A return to the basic riffy sound of their debut. Emotionally wound-up and pulsing with steely conviction, this is their most consistent set to date.

CANDLEMASS

Formed Stockholm, Sweden, 1985; disbanded 2004

At a time when every one was upping the speed levels of metal in an effort to be harder and nastier than anyone else, a hairy bunch of Black Sabbath and Trouble fans decided to hit the brakes and in the process help kick-start doom metal. **Candlemass** will forever be associated with the (mostly) excellent clutch of albums they released in the late 80s, each one an attempt to push the boundaries of metal beyond the accepted norms of the genre.

Originally starting out as **Nemesis**, the band decided on Candlemass to avoid confusion with another group named Nemesis. **Johan Lanquist** (vocals), **Mats Björkman** (guitar), **Leif Edling** (bass) and **Matz Ekstrom** (drums) were keen on emulating the strident, lumbering power of very early Black Sabbath rather than indulging the fashion for thrash. They began writing material in a small, unheated house at the top of a mountain. On a budget of next to nothing, they turned out *Epicus Doomicus Metallicus* (1986); this was an album of raw, glowering, primeval metal, epic in scope, with downbeat lyrics and a general atmosphere of suicidal sloth. But after the band delivered this startling debut, Lanquist decided to quit.

The new singer was **Messiah Marcolin**, an excellent frontman with mad hair and a penchant for wearing a monk's habit onstage. His immense vibrato could level

mountains. *Nightfall* (1987) – which added **Lars Johansson** (guitar) and **Jan Lindh** (drums) – was an international cult classic, packed with titanic future faves such as "Dark Are The Veils Of Death" and "At The Gallows End". At Marcolin's behest they recorded a version of Chopin's "Marche Funèbre", a tune that would be used as a suitably atmospheric and sombre intro to their shows, and used Thomas Cole's *The Voyage Of Life: Old Age* as a cover painting. Candlemass received plaudits from both fans and critics amazed to hear a band railing so convincingly against the prevailing trends in rock.

The level of success attained by *Nightfall*, however, put an increasing amount of pressure on the band. A support slot with Motörhead was in the offing and they needed new material. *Ancient Dreams* (1988) was rush released, and it showed: it was a decent enough doom record but failed to scale the heights of their blackly charming debut. *Tales Of Creation* (1989) was a more assured and far more worthy successor to *Nightfall*, with Edling delving into his old stock of songs and dusting down some classy material from early demo days. And instead of opting for another Cole painting, an etching from an old family Bible gave the sleeve the required level of morbidity. The band headed into the new decade with *Live* (1990), recorded in their home town, an album that captured a definitive Candlemass show, with next to no overdubs. This was a defining era for doom.

Sadly, cracks were already beginning to show and a huge amount of stress had resulted

a comeback album, but egos and musical differences proved to be insurmountable clichés, dead set on sending the band to the grave. Come early 2004, Candlemass once again split – presumably with "Marche Funèbre" echoing ethereally in the background.

⊙ **Epicus Doomicus Metallicus**
1986; Black Dragon

Such a perfect album title – Epic Doom Metal. The vocals are adequate but the real joy lies in the trudging pace and atmosphere of menace.

⊙ **Nightfall**
1987; Axis

A masterpiece. Marcolin's supernatural, operatic style gives the songs real towering stature. For mist-shrouded gloom and depression, this one is hard to beat.

CANNIBAL CORPSE

Formed Buffalo, New York, US, 1988

If heavy metal were a form of blood sport Cannibal Corpse would surely be the masters of the hunt. And you would pity their prey. In short, this band are an explosion in a sonic abattoir, a blood-spattered, entrail-festooned abomination, purveying some of the nastiest death metal to ever offend ears. Over the years they have courted more than their fair share of controversy with their song and album titles and graphically violent sleeve art, though the vocals have usually been so over the top as to make their manifestos of carnage, thankfully, unintelligible.

Way back in 1988 the Buffalo underground metal scene was positively buzzing with activity. **Chris Barnes** (vocals), **Jack Owen** (guitar), **Bob Rusay** (guitar), **Alex Webster** (bass), **Paul Mazurkiewicz** (drums) set out with the express desire to be as savagely offensive and extreme as possible, providing their "Skull Full Of Maggots" demo to record labels as a calling card. Incredibly they found takers for their Slayer-on-crack thrash and signed to Metal Blade for *Eaten Back To Life* (1990). While a death-dealing band like the UK's Carcass obviously had a streak of very black humour running through their bloody outpourings, Cannibal Corpse's approach was so damn misanthropically brutal that only those with very strong stomachs could take

in a major break from recording. Egos were running amok, especially Marcolin's, and internal wrangling was making their writing sessions a very ugly affair. The huge, doom-dancing monk had made himself the vocal and visual focus of the band and thought himself to be irreplaceable. A few bouts of weird behaviour later and they replaced him with **Tomas Vikström** for *Chapter IV* (1992). This really was the beginning of the end, even though the subsequent touring went relatively well. A tired Edling sensed that *Chapter IV* wasn't going to do the Candlemass reputation any good; he held back on the writing front and no one was happy with the end result.

By the following year Candlemass had split. Marcolin formed **Memento Mori**, Edling formed **Abstrakt Algebra**, and the others recorded as **Zoic**. Needless to say none of these acts enjoyed the same success as Candlemass, so, on the verge of financial ruin, Edling decided to resurrect the band. Unfortunately, he was the only original member and *Dactylis Glomerata* (1998) and *From The 13th Sun* (1999) failed to match the grinding majesty of early Candlemass releases, despite containing some decent songs.

Finally, in 2001, with remastered versions of their albums ready to go, the original line-up got talking again and decided that Candlemass should be given another shot; they fixed their sights on a clutch of festival dates across Europe while *Doomed For Life* (2003), a massive double CD packed with live material, was trundled out. Everything seemed to be progressing; new songs were demoed with a view to writing their extremity. Amazingly, a rabid cult following sprang up to consume the band's necrotic wares.

There was even more horror to be found on *Butchered At Birth* (1991) and *Tomb Of The Mutilated* (1992). The zombie birth depicted on the sleeve of the former was pretty tasteless, but the representation of cadaverous oral sex on the latter resulted in bans from retail chains – and so the art had to be toned down. With such catchy titles for tunes as "Meat Hook Sodomy", "Necropedophile", "Addicted To Vaginal Skin" and the ultra-offensive "Entrails Ripped From A Virgin's Cunt", the band were by now infamous.

The *Hammer Smashed Face* EP followed in 1993. Rusay was fired and **Rob Barrett** (ex-Malevolent Creation) took his place just in time for the band, incredibly, to make a cameo appearance alongside Jim Carrey in *Ace Ventura: Pet Detective*. It was possibly their only brush with the mainstream world; for *The Bleeding* (1994) they were roaming the crypts once more for fresh flesh. Such charming ditties included "Fucked With A Knife", "Stripped, Raped, And Strangled" and "Force Fed Broken Glass". Amazingly, some fans consider the latter to be one of the band's more accessible albums.

Preparing for their next round of aural violence the band became increasingly dissatisfied with Barnes's vocals; he was replaced by **George 'Corpsegrinder' Fisher** for the recording of *Vile* (1996). The following year Barrett decided he'd had his fill of rotting flesh and **Pat O'Brien** stepped in for *Gallery Of Suicide* (1998). Compared with previous albums, the set featured relatively inoffensive song titles, making it something of a letdown for the band's more hardcore hounds – although the music was still as harsh as ever. The band continued to churn out the gore with frightening regularity; *Bloodthirst* (1999), *Live Cannibalism* (2000) and the unsurprisingly titled *Gore Obsessed* (2002) followed. After the Corpse's most recent offering, *The Wretched Spawn* (2004), Owen left to pursue other projects and was replaced by **Jeremy Turner**.

 15 Year Killing Spree
2003; Metal Blade

You can take a stab at pretty much any Corpse album and be greeted with extreme death, but this four-disc eruption of blood and filth distils much of their output into a "best of".

CARCASS

Formed Liverpool, UK, 1986

There are bands who step into a ready-made genre and go on to become superstars, and there are those who play for the fun of it and influence thousands with their uncompromising approach along the way. So it was for **Carcass**, one of the most brutal and extreme metal bands ever to emerge from the UK; from sound to on-stage visuals, everything about Carcass was calculated to shock, though in a tongue-in-cheek fashion.

Carcass was created by **Bill Steer** (guitar) and childhood friend **Ken Owens** (drums). Heavily influenced by early thrash and death metal bands, Steer was playing guitar in one of the early incarnations of **Napalm Death**, while dabbling in a little side project or two; practice sessions would take place at Steer's parents' house in the attic, where the two would work on formulating their sound which, at the time, was influenced by hardcore punk. When **Jeff Walker** (bass/vocals; ex-**Electro Hippies**) joined, their direction shifted onto a sludgy path of hardcore, death metal and pure thrash. Walker had started as a hardcore punk and then grew into the metal scene. He brought to the band a voice that sounded like he was gargling battery acid, but a keen artistic sense. He had already designed the album sleeve for Napalm Death's seminal *Scum* album and set about creating a band logo and the artwork to go with Carcass's first album, *Reek Of Putrefaction* (1988), released on the extreme Earache label.

Reek... was a revelation in terms of both style and content. Although the production was abysmal, nothing could hide the fact that Carcass were an underground force to be reckoned with. Walker had found inspiration in his sister's nursing textbooks and the colour of the creative juices that flowed was blood-red, not to mention necrotic black and putrefaction green. The sleeve was a collage of carnal and medical atrocities, the lyrics were tongue-twistingly absurd and dwelt on every imaginable form of disease and medical butchery. Song titles included "Genital Grinder", "Manifestation On Verrucose Urethra", "Mucopurulence Excretor" and the unforgettable "Vomited Anal Tract". Musically the songs were short, sharp detonations of noise, doubtless as a result of the Napalm Death hardcore aesthetic, though the influence of bands such as Repulsion, Death, Slayer, Morbid Angel and Discharge was also evident.

It was obvious that the band's humour was pretty dark and seemed to revolve around the idea of humans as slabs of meat – a satirical stance perhaps, stemming from their vegan/vegetarian and anti-vivisection stance. Live shows would have their chosen horrific imagery flashed up on the backdrop.

As befits a band who stumbled upon new ground, Carcass were rapidly hailed as gore pioneers, streets ahead of mere grind and death practitioners. The late John Peel did much to spread the word – he loved the first album, voting it his favourite release of the year in high-brow broadsheet newspaper *The Observer* and gave it much airplay on his Radio 1 show. He even invited Carcass into the studio to record a couple of exclusive sessions for broadcast. Second album *Symphonies Of Sickness* (1989) proved that their formula was a potent one. A better studio sound and production brought power and depth to Owens' frenetic blastbeats and Steer's voracious riffing, and yet again Walker growled menacingly. "Excoriating Abdominal Emanation", "Exhume To Consume" and "Swarming Vulgar Mass Of Infected Virulency" were brutal, violent, and nightmarish, and who could forget live fave "Crepitating Bowel Erosion"? The album included yet another sleeve featuring festering flesh, a fact that had the tabloid papers up in arms and led the police to charge the band under obscenity laws, though the charges were eventually dropped.

By the time of *Necroticism: Descanting The Insalubrious* (1991), things had become serious enough for Steer to leave Napalm Death and concentrate on Carcass full-time. In addition, a second guitarist, **Michael Amott** (ex-**Carnage**), brought a further boost to their already rampant attack. And at this point a more melodic direction was developing, though without sacrificing the speed or the horrific content. Once again the medical dictionary was resulting in such catchy titles as "Corporal Jigsore Quandary" and "Lavaging Expectorate Of Lysergide Composition". By heading in a slightly more accessible musical direction the band were able to headline the Gods Of Grind tour with Entombed, Cathedral and Confessor in support.

The following year brought only their *Tools Of The Trade* EP as a prelude to *Heartwork* (1993), which featured a change in lyrical direction and more musical refinement. Believing that they had pushed the medical torture idea to its limits, songs were based more around life events than morbid mortuary splatter, and the sound pushed further into melodic death metal territory. It was a change that signalled a more mature style and opened the door to greater commercial possibilities. The band were persuaded to record an album for Columbia in the US, but not before **Carlos Regedas** replaced Amott, who went off to form **Spiritual Beggars**.

As is often the case, the move to a major label was fraught with problems. Here was a band that had started out as hardcore punks dabbling in metal, which led to their courting by a money-making business machine looking for the next big thing – at a time when Nirvana had blown a gaping hole through the traditional rock and metal scene. Creatively speaking, the band and the label never really saw eye to eye, a fact underlined by the story that an A&R man apparently suggested Walker should abandon his larynx-ripping guttural roar and take a few singing lessons. In the end *Swansong* (1996) was released via Earache and proved to be possibly the most stripped-down and direct set of songs they had created so far. It was rapidly followed by the *Wake Up And Smell The...*(1996) compilation.

By this point Steer was rapidly losing interest in the band – he went off to form retro rockers **Firebird** – so the remaining members mutated into **Blackstar**, who managed one album and then bit the dust. Another compilation album celebrating Carcass's influence on the death and grind metal scene was scheduled for 1999 but was delayed when Owens suffered a brain haemorrhage and ended up in a coma. The band agreed that the album would not be released until he had recovered sufficiently; in 2004 *Choice Cuts* was released with major input from Owens.

Reek Of Putrefaction
1988; Earache

Vicious, horrific, brutal thrash informed by hardcore. The tunes rarely exceed one or two minutes in length but that's quite long enough. The aural equivalent to wading through a vat of human offal.

Necroticism: Decanting The Insalubrious 1991; Earache

For many this is the perfect mix of gore and thrash. Musically and technically this is hard to beat.

Heartwork
1993; Earache

More melody, less blood but a crunching and muscular romp nonetheless. A blueprint for the future of melodic death metal.

THE CASANOVAS

Formed Melbourne, Australia, 1999

It's no coincidence that **The Casanovas** chose to cover AC/DC's classic "Riff Raff" on their "Shake It" single. The love of the Young brothers' heavy blues riffing is evident in much of the output mustered by this trio, who have been hailed alongside bands such as The Datsuns as antipodean saviours of heavy rock'n'roll. Unlike the feted and rolling Datsuns, however, The Casanovas' rise to notoriety has been rather slower, hampered by personnel confusion and a false start when trying to record their debut.

The love of monster riffs and axe-strangling solos should come as no surprise considering Australia's track record for producing great rock bands, and brothers **Patrick** (drums) and **Tommy Boyce** aka **Tommy Love** (guitar/vocals), plus **Jimmy Lewis** aka **Jimmy Heat** (bass) were throwing shapes from an early age. Tommy Boyce, in particular, rapidly earned a reputation as a perfectionist looking for that heavy rock sound and would scout for equipment that would deliver just the right vibe and tone.

Their first gig, so the story goes, came about by accident. Having rehearsed just a handful of times, the Boyce brothers were in the audience to see one of their favourite bands, the Powder Monkeys, when Lewis's other band, **Red Shift**, pulled out of their support slot. So, with borrowed equipment the lads took the stage and blasted through a short sharp set that went down in local rock history.

Unfortunately this sudden kick-start didn't lead to instant success. Yes, their classic heavy rock influences and their punky delivery, ensured that their gigs went down a storm. But when it came to issuing records things didn't go quite according to plan – if you could say they actually had one. First single "10 Outta 10"/"Too Cool" (released in 2000 on Full Toss Records) had classic stamped all over it with its rock'n'roll high school-themed lyrics, and the ...*Keep It Hot* EP (2002 on Rubber Records) added another tightly rocking ace in the hole with "Nasty". The only trouble was the time taken between one output and the other. Early recording sessions with power punk producer **Kim Salmon** fell short of expectations and slowed their progress towards an album. And to make matters worse, Lewis decided to quit, in order to keep his day job and play with one of his other bands. Eventually **Damian Campbell** stepped in as replacement.

On the strength of ...*Keep It Hot* they were signed to Alan McGee's new label, The Singles Society, which issued "Nasty"/"Too Cool", songs already out on the debut EP. Meanwhile, antipodean contemporaries such as The Datsuns and Jet were starting to make waves internationally. A tour of the UK was arranged as support to The Datsuns, a single, "Shake It", followed and then more touring ensued; they also contributed a version of Ted Nugent's "Just What The Doctor Ordered" to the *Valentine Killers* compilation.

Gradually inching towards a full-length debut the band hit another glitch when Patrick Boyce left during recording sessions. **Jordan 'Jaws' Stanley** (ex-**Onyas**), a speedy hard-hitter, came on board and the album was completed.

The Casanovas
2004; Rubber

This eponymous debut turned out to be more solid and majestic than the early flurry of singles and EPs had suggested. Pure retro-rock exhilaration.

MARTIN PHILBEY/REDFERNS

The Casanovas Fidel with their Castros.

CATHEDRAL

Formed Coventry, UK, 1989

Heavier than a concrete battleship, **Cathedral** are masters of doom metal – slow, ponderous, despairing, thundering and very often surprisingly groovy. It must come as something of a revelation to the uninitiated, then, that the man responsible for Cathedral's rise to the top of the modern doom heap is vocalist **Lee Dorrian**, ex-member of UK hardcore punk thrashers, **Napalm Death**.

The story goes that at a Carcass show, Dorrian, and roadie **Mark Griffiths,** got chatting about their favourite doom metal bands. Names such as Trouble, St Vitus, Black Sabbath and Candlemass were mentioned, and the idea formed that they should try to create their own monster heavy metal outfit, drawing from the music they found so inspirational. Griffiths knew guitarist **Garry Jennings** to be a big fan of the genre – even though he had been a member of comic thrashers **Acid Reign** – so after a few jam sessions the line-up finally settled on Griffiths playing bass (though he had originally started on guitar) with **Ben Mochrie** on drums. The final addition was second guitarist **Adam Lehan**, also ex-Acid Reign. The *In Memorium* EP was released in 1990 on Dorrian's nascent Rise Above label, and the lumbering doom beast that is Cathedral was born. The frontman's

rasping lung power can be heard on lyrics inspired by cult sci-fi and horror films, and the odd bit of social commentary, while his bandmates dirge and thunder away very, very slowly. Their early sound was akin to being trampled to death by a herd of somnambulant elephants. Also key to Cathedral was their excellent sleeve art; **Dave Patchett**, who provided unique, fantastical and eerily stylized artwork for almost all of their albums, rendered each one instantly recognizable.

For 1991's *Forest Of Equilibrium* on Earache, Mochrie was replaced by **Mike Smail**; the album was so slow and heavy that it had the doom underground positively rabid with excitement. The music had that all-important laboured edge, and Dorrian was proving to be something of a keen lyricist with an eye for a catchy title or two – standouts being "Ebony Tears" and "Reaching Happiness, Touching Pain". And what better place to display their new wares than on the Gods Of Grind tour alongside Carcass, Entombed and Confessor? The tour was a triumph, with audiences initially flummoxed, then enraptured by Dorrian's new direction.

Despite their rise in popularity, Cathedral just couldn't seem to hold on to drummers; eventually Smail was replaced by yet another ex-member of Acid Reign, **Mark Ramsey Wharton**, for the *Soul Sacrifice* EP in 1992, a record which gave an indication of the groovier aspect they would add to their

Sabbath-on-Mogadon grind. It was also the band's first outing for Columbia in the States, a relationship that would be fraught with difficulties.

By the following year Jennings found himself having to handle bass duties as well as guitar on *The Ethereal Mirror*, not that it made the slightest bit of difference to the thick monolithic slabs of 70s-inspired noise they were hewing – tunes such as "Ride" and "Midnight Mountain" would prove to be huge stage favourites. Critics were at last taking note and new markets were opening up, not least in Japan where they made major headway promoting the new album.

Problems, however, were just around the corner, many of them stemming from the group's relationship with Columbia. The band ended up being kicked off a series of dates supporting Mercyful Fate, after they disagreed with the label's tour choices. The tensions created resulted in Cathedral seemingly haemorrhaging members, even as they released one of their most challenging records, the *Statik Majik* EP, featuring the incredibly long and off-the-wall "The Voyage Of The Homeless Sapien". Although the band were promised creative control, Columbia tried to tamper with the tracks and released the EP in America with different sleeve art. In the midst of all this strife, Dorrian and Jennings – by now the only two stable members of a line-up that seemed to vary from month to month – were at least heartened to be complimented on their new sound as a four-piece by none other than Tony Iommi. The Black Sabbath guitarist reckoned they sounded far more powerful with one less guitar in their live mix.

Unsurprisingly, after the problems with Columbia they were dropped by the label, which came as something of a relief. They needed some new momentum, not to mention a bassist and drummer, and they recruited **Leo Smee** and **Brian Dixon**. At last they had a rock solid line-up and no major label trying to act the puppet master; Earache handled their releases on both sides of the Atlantic.

The Carnival Bizarre (1995) was the sound of a newly revitalized band keen to make up for the time lost simply battling for existence. The set was a fiery, loose-limbed canter, drawing on all manner of retro hard-rocking influences and, best of all, the cosmic fury of "Utopian Blaster" featured a guitar solo provided by **Tony Iommi**. Elsewhere tunes such as "Night Of The Seagulls" and "Hopkins (The Witchfinder General)" had Dorrian unearthing a couple of cult horror movies for inspiration. The latter tune was also the lead track to one of their most unusual EPs, which featured a hilarious cover of The Crazy World Of Arthur Brown's "Fire", the decidedly weird disco of "Purple Wonderland", complete with electronic beats and processed strings, and the sub-James Brown saxophone-driven funk doom of "The Devils Summit" – the latter is possibly the only place you will ever hear Dorrian yell the word "Superfly!". These departures illustrated Cathedral's drollness, sense of irony and desire to experiment – never let it be said that doom equals humourless.

Despite being less than ready to record *Supernatural Birth Machine* (1996) the result was surprisingly assured, although Earache's US office decided to try to make the band look more like a stoner outfit by changing their usual Dave Patchett art for a simple photo cover. The set featured even more diverse elements to their trademark doomy grunt. This was speedier, bouncier, more melodic and altogether a satisfying development.

Sadly, the headway they had forged was lost when yet more legal hassles with their label meant there were no releases for three years. However, when *Caravan Beyond Redemption* (1999) arrived, it proved to be yet another triumph of inventive songwriting, with their sense of humour making their groovy metal even more accessible – not that this meant they had compromised on the heaviness, for Jennings' blistering

riffing was as iron-clad and headbanging-friendly as ever.

By the time *Endtyme* (2001) was released, marking their final album for Earache, Dorrian reckoned a change was in order. So Cathedral went back to their roots with a more primitive and aggressive approach; if anything, the band were even heavier than before, with a raw and impassioned feel that carried over to *VIIth Coming* (2002) which emerged on Dream Catcher.

Forest Of Equilibrium
1991; Earache

The sound of a storm gathering. From the distant mists of time guitarist Jennings conjures up pile-driving riff after riff. It's a morbid and raw ride into the dark side of depression.

The Carnival Bizarre
1995; Earache

No longer content to deliver their metal at a crawl, Cathedral have added a touch of speed to their punishing groove. A diverse and amusing collection with Dorrian grunting and rasping through some of his best lyrics.

Endtyme
2001; Earache

Back to their roots, Dorrian and co don't want to play safe. Heavier than before, if that's at all possible, Cathedral outdo themselves with this aggressive approach.

CELTIC FROST

Formed Switzerland, 1984

"If people want to rock their fuckin' brains out, they should come and see us." Thomas G Warrior

Singular and uncompromising in their vision, **Celtic Frost** are one of the most important European bands to emerge from the thrash explosion of the 80s. For them, to simply rage and roar was not enough. With guitarist and vocalist **Thomas Gabriel Warrior** at the helm, each new album signals some kind of evolutionary leap forward; over the years this has included the use of samples, electronics, female vocals, spoken word interludes and a marked classical influence. Dubbed avant-garde by just about every critic and admired for their daring attitude by their loyal fan base, their arty approach to the darker side of metal has influenced countless death- and black-metal bands.

Warrior (aka **Fischer**) first fell in love with heavy metal after exposure to the late 70s and early 80s New Wave Of British Heavy Metal, and his first foray into creating music was to form **Hellhammer**. This was a primal metal outfit that landed a record deal and issued *Apocalyptic Raids* (1983). After this one album Warrior and **Martin Eric Ain** (bass) felt that the band had run its limited course, so they formed Celtic Frost, with the specific aim of being a cutting-edge metal outfit, unrestricted by genre – and indeed, as the band progressed, their art-rock and goth credentials would gradually come to the fore. Drummer **Stephen Priestly** helped out in the studio for *Morbid Tales* (1984) on Noise Records, an astonishingly assured thrash album, which catapulted the band into the limelight as Europe's answer to US bands such as Metallica and Megadeth. Warrior had developed a unique growling vocal style, punctuated by what would become known as his infamous death grunts, and alongside the innovatively arranged, grinding guitar onslaught were the first glimmerings of experimentation using violins and weird sound effects. Visually, they could have passed for cousins of Venom – they appeared clad in leather, spikes, studs and deathly make-up, a perfect foil for their occult and dark fantasy leanings.

With Priestly not wanting to be the band's full-time drummer, Warrior roped in **Reed St Mark** for the *Emperor's Return* EP in 1985. This was to be just the start of the band's line-up woes. For the recording of *To Mega Therion* (1985), **Dominic Steiner** had stepped in to replace Ain, who, after suddenly quitting, had reconsidered his rash move and decided to return. Personnel ructions aside, the album (the title of which means "the big beast") was a triumph of dark and mystical slabs of brutal thrash, neatly packaged with a Satanic sleeve – courtesy of cult artist **H.R. Giger**, famed visual creator of the beast in the *Alien* movies. Female vocals and classical instrumentation peppered the songs – to stunning effect in the epic and brooding "Dawn Of Meggido" – bringing an extra dimension of doom and menace to the band's idiosyncratic brand of metal. The *Tragic Serenades* EP followed and their place at the vanguard of Euro-thrash was assured.

Next came *Into The Pandemonium* (1987). Packaged in a sleeve featuring the suitably ominous Hieronymus Bosch painting *Garden Of Earthly Delights*, this album was their landmark release. If the previous albums had featured the odd wacky moment, this one stuck a great big one right up front by kicking off with a bizarre cover of Wall Of Voodoo's "Mexican Radio". It was an inspired move, priming the listener for a rampaging thrash album that went places they never imagined a metal album might go. "One In Their Pride" was a brave attempt at dance metal; "Tristesses De La Lune" set a female vocal reciting French poetry over a sparse classical arrangement; "Rex Irae (Requiem)" was a dirge-like death march complete with operatic female vocals. And just to flummox people further, they recorded a cover of the Dean Martin classic "In The Chapel, In The Moonlight", a version that became much sought-after. Apparently they originally intended to do Nancy Sinatra's "These Boots Are Made For Walking" but Megadeth had got there first, so they opted for something with a Slayer-esque title, as a joke.

Despite having recorded a terrific album the subsequent touring brought the band to their knees. Personality clashes with second guitarist **Ron Marks** didn't help, while the band experienced huge money hassles exacerbated by their label; legend has it that the road crew had to hold equipment hostage at the end of the tour in order to get paid.

Such pressures were beyond endurance and the band folded, only to reconvene once the touring debacle had died down. Only Warrior remained from the original line-up but he was joined by **Curt Victor Bryant** (bass), **Oliver Amberg** (guitar) and old friend Stephen Priestly (drums). Celtic Frost were back in business, but at this point Warrior inexplicably decided that the band should evolve into a glam-death outfit. Some of the impetus for the change can be put down to Amberg's input and producer **Tony Platt**'s commercial bent. But most fans couldn't believe that Warrior – who was now using his surname of Fischer – would be involved in the creation of the disaster that was *Cold Lake* (1988). The album and tour flopped and, as a measure of how bad it was, in the band's 1999 reissue programme *Cold Lake* was resolutely ignored.

So, for the next project, Amberg was out while Ain and Marks were back in again. *Vanity/Nemesis* (1990) was the true follow-up to *Into The Pandemonium*, featuring nods to their arty tastes with covers of **David Bowie**'s "Heroes" and **Roxy Music**'s "This Island Earth". Subsequently, however, they only managed the compilation album of rarities and rerecordings, *Parched With Thirst Am I And Dying* (1992), before pulling the plug. Yet more disastrous dealings with record labels had sapped them of their will to go on, and a mammoth double album entitled *Under Apollyon's Sun* was shelved even though some material was ready to go.

When Warrior eventually stepped back into making music he chose **Apollyon Sun** as the name of his new band. The *God Leaves (And Dies)* EP heralded a new sound steeped in industrial and electronic metal and an album, *Sub* (2000), pushed the formula further. It failed to garner the interest it should have (given Warrior's reputation) but at the time of writing Celtic Frost are apparently back in business – taking a very long time to issue their album, tentatively titled *Probe*.

Morbid Tales
1984; Noise

Very heavy, very raw, and ever so slightly off-the-wall thrash. A perfect answer to US thrash of the same vintage.

To Mega Therion
1985; Noise

Pushing the envelope further, Warrior and his noisy mates rip up a storm of consistently evil metal and courageous experimentation.

Into The Pandemonium
1987; Noise

Dark and morose, the classical arrangements and gothic tone were highly influential. This album still sounds as fresh as it did way back when. A classic.

CHEAP TRICK

Formed Illinois, US, 1973

A sublime fusion of solid metal crunch and smooth pop melodies, for a while during the late 70s and early 80s **Cheap Trick** were a band that managed terrific commercial success without selling out their roots. So powerful and influential was their blend of heavy tunefulness and oddball eccentricity that they inspired many of the bands – Nirvana, Smashing Pumpkins and Everclear among those name-checking them – that would be responsible for the wave of alternative rock that swept the world in the early 90s.

Back in the late 60s and early 70s **Rick Nielsen** (guitars – lots and lots of guitars) joined forces with **Tom Petersson** (bass), and with a couple of other musos they gigged and released an album for Epic Records under the name **Fuse** before becoming the **Sick Man Of Europe**. So far so dull. It took the addition of drummer **Bun E Carlos** and vocalist **Robin Zander** for the Cheap Trick formula to really take off, but when it did, the effect was deliciously mesmerizing. Taking their cue from bands such as the Beatles, ELO and The Move, Cheap Trick worked shameless pop hooks and harmonies into bright'n'bouncy nuggets of sugar-coated hard rock. In Zander and Petersson they had the debonair looks and in Nielsen and Carlos they had, well, the opposite really. Carlos just looked like an unlikely rock star while Nielsen, in particular, played up to the nerdy muso image. While guitar heroes such as Jimmy Page looked incredibly cool throwing shapes and pealing off solos Nielsen looked like he had dressed himself from jumble-sale castoffs; his monogrammed sweater, wacky baseball cap and bad-taste bow-tie combo rapidly became a trademark in just the same way that Angus Young's schoolboy outfit signalled the arrival of AC/DC. The thing was that Nielsen wasn't covering for any inadequacy – with his insatiable hunger for weird guitars and even weirder licks he was quite rightly revered as a genius.

The first example of their hard-as-nails yet sweet-as-candy heavy rock was their early 1977 eponymous debut. They had spent much of the mid-70s gigging fervently supporting the likes of Kiss and Queen and had developed into a super-tight unit with more than a few killer tunes in their armoury; during the Queen tour Nielsen wrote a kind of journal for a Japanese music paper, a clever move which gave the band a high profile before they had even released an album there. Launching with the glammy stomp of "ELO Kiddies", they were also capable of dishing out commercial tunes such as "Oh Candy" (which failed to chart!) and booty-shaking rockers such as "He's A Whore" – they had it all: humour, hooks and terrific tunes. In fact

Rick Nielson: who said less is more?

they had so many great songs, their second album followed in the latter half of 1977.

In Color was a far more crafted affair. While the debut sounded tough, the follow-up concentrated far more on delivering memorable tunes. The key commercial track was the cheerful "I Want You To Want Me". The album was a joy to listen to and the fun angle was emphasized by the inspired cover art: Zander and Petersson looking every inch the rock gods astride Harleys and very much "in color", while Carlos and Nielsen appeared on the flip teetering on push-bikes and very much "in black and white".

The two albums had sold respectably in their homeland but it was in Japan that they were already celebrities. Their touring during 1978 confirmed that stardom was just round the corner as venues such as the famous Budokan Arena were selling out in less than two hours. *Heaven Tonight* (1978) proved to be the studio album to break the band – well almost. Opening album track and single "Surrender" was a modest chart entry in the US but stylistically the album was a triumph. If the first had been too hard for its own good and the second maybe just a tad too polite, then the third was layered and lush, combining keyboards with the best elements of the previous two; it rocked hard and with depth, barbed hooks and ironic lyrics working their way into your brain in a wicked subversion of the rock star myth; rockers aren't supposed to have brains but even a cursory listen revealed a band able to revel in the absurdity of stardom and explode expectations from within. All of these things made *Heaven Tonight* a classic, though one which still only made a slight dent on the chart.

The band's first real commercial success came with *Cheap Trick At Budokan* (1979). The Japanese crowd sounded ecstatic and the band were captured delivering in the frenetic and spitfire style they had assiduously honed during the 70s; if it's possible to encapsulate stagecraft on an album this was a supreme example. And ironically the song that helped it along was a live version of "I Want You To Want Me", which this time went top 10 while the album went top 5 in the US and entered the top 30 in the UK.

Now on a roll, *Dream Police* (1979) was another hit album in the mould of its predecessor; plenty of big guitars and clever melodic arrangements boosting it up to #6 in the US. Always ones for a nifty joke sleeve, this time they were dressed as the titular law enforcers, Nielsen looking particularly daft.

Clearly they were at their peak, they were packing out arenas and selling millions of records, but events after *All Shook Up* (1980) would cause a lamentable slide in popularity. For a start, working with Beatles producer **George Martin** wasn't perhaps the smartest thing for a band influenced by the Fab Four to do, but the biggest headache came when Petersson bailed out to be replaced first by **Peter Comita** and then **Jon Brant**.

One On One (1982) marked the beginning of a woeful mid-80s period during which time the band actually ended up supporting acts such as Ratt and Mötley Crüe. The cheekily titled *Next Position Please* (1983) failed to do the trick (cheap or otherwise – it stayed in the chart for only eleven weeks) while *Standing On The Edge* (1985) sounded somewhat prophetic. By the time of *The Doctor* (1986) something had to give – and it turned out to be the band giving in to record label pressure. Petersson returned to the fold and outside writers were drafted in to write some big 80s-style ballads. The result was the rather sanitized *Lap Of Luxury* (1988) and the monster #1 hit single "The Flame". They

were back but at the price of their identity. Another top-five US hit with a cover version of "Don't Be Cruel", however, was the last time they would enjoy anything even remotely approaching their previous popularity levels.

An attempt to utilize their new style on *Busted* (1990) was muted by the law of diminishing returns. And no record label is happy with those kinds of figures. *The Greatest Hits* (1991) signalled the end of their relationship with Epic, leaving the band without a deal just as grunge was starting to wipe the floor with anyone not sporting a plaid shirt and a frown.

After Zander had managed a solo effort in 1993 the band issued *Woke Up With A Monster* (1994) for Warners – supposedly a return to their raucous recipe of old – but it was a failure that ironically seemed to propel the band into the embrace of the new generation of alternative bands who had grown up listening to Cheap Trick and who were now riding high. The next few years found the band opening for Smashing Pumpkins, the Stone Temple Pilots and playing Lollapalooza among the more traditional rock slots; in 1997 they even issued a one-off single, "Baby Talk", recorded with **Steve Albini** on the Sub Pop label. Meanwhile their new label Red Ant also issued *Cheap Shots*, a tribute album featuring bands such as Everclear and the Posies covering classic Cheap Trick songs. Finally, the band themselves returned with *Cheap Trick* (1997), a melodic but rough-edged collection of tunes. But just as it sounded like the band might have a modest success on their hands, the label declared itself bankrupt and the album was pulled off the shelves.

Teetering on the edge of bankruptcy themselves the band decided to tour behind the expanded reissue of *At Budokan: The Complete Concert* (the new album added the tracks that had already been issued in 1994 as *Budokan 2*) with a similarly titled live show. Taking advantage of the situation they took one night's set and issued it as *Music For Hangovers* (1999) on their own Cheap Trick Unlimited label. Another storming live set arrived a couple of years later in the shape of the double album, *Silver*.

Back in the studio the band proved that they still had plenty of life left in them with *Special One* (2003), an eclectic set showcasing their disparate influences perfectly.

Cheap Trick
1977; Columbia

Nielsen might look like a plonker but there's nothing foolish about the writing here: "Hot Love", "He's A Whore", "Speak Now Or Forever Hold Your Peace" are absolute hard rock gems.

Heaven Tonight
1978; Columbia

This set combines just the right amount of pop to hard rock. The title track and their cover of The Move's "California Man" are two instant classics and the rest aren't too shabby either.

Dream Police
1979; Columbia

"The House Is Rockin' (With Domestic Problems)" is an ironic masterpiece, while "Gonna Raise Hell" is nine minutes plus of superb classic rock.

At Budokan: The Complete Concert
1998; Columbia

Live albums were all the rage when this little beauty first arrived in 1979. It was stunning on vinyl all those years ago and this CD reissue adds in the songs originally cut due to lack of space. It's urgent stuff and positively crackling with energy.

CHIMAIRA

Formed Cleveland, Ohio, US, 1998

Named after the mythical Greek creature with the head of a lion, body of a goat and tail of a dragon, this terrifying beast of a band reflect their namesake by fusing the fury of thrash, the emotional power of metalcore and the cold precision of modern electronics. In fact, **Chimaira**, along with several other bands, such as Killswitch Engage, God Forbid and Shadows Fall, have been lumped into what has been dubbed the New Wave Of American Heavy Metal, the US counterpart of the British Wave that, twenty years ago, gave us bands such as Iron Maiden and Venom. The reason for the emergence of these new bands is simple: as nu-metal dies on its arse, the revitalizing spark will come from groups such as Chimaira who survive through their professionalism and down-to-earth blue-collar work ethic.

As is often the case, the death of one band leads to the birth of another; back in 1998 guitarist **Jason Hager** of now defunct **Ascension** was casting around for new and like-minded musicians. Singer **Mark Hunter** was the first to join and a line-up gradually came together with **Rob Arnold** (guitar), **Jim LaMarca** (bass), **Andols Herrick** (drums) and **Chris Spicuzza** (electronics). The addition of Spicuzza gave Chimaira an all-important edge over the competition – they were free to indulge their old-school thrash influences, yet introduce a cutting-edge, almost Fear Factory-esque flavour.

This Present Darkness (1999), released on indie East Coast Empire, was their boot in the door – shifting nearly ten thousand copies in the process – with "Painting The White To Grey" securing several weeks worth of vital airplay on local radio stations. The degree of self-belief and professionalism present in those budget-produced grooves caught the attention of Roadrunner Records. However, while the band looked to be making progress, founding member Hager had to leave due to personal problems. **Matt DeVries** stepped in for 2001's *Pass Out Of Existence*, an album which translated the raw ideas from their debut into a solidly produced slab of brutal bludgeon. Hunter's fearsome screech was ear-manglingly harsh enough to appeal to the nu-metal kids, as were the angst-flavoured lyrics, but there was a distinct refusal to indulge in any other nu-metal games. This was modern metal with a dash of hardcore, helped along with the scything power of electronic special effects – making it both spine-chillingly eerie and gloriously abrasive. Experimentation was also there in the shape of closing track "Jade", a full twelve minutes of cleansing noise.

Chimaira crank it up to #11.

CHRISTIAN METAL

If the devil has all the best tunes then it makes you wonder what's left for the bearded chap upstairs. This little conundrum aside, it's bands such as **Stryper** and the melodic sound of the mid-80s that pretty much sum up what most people think of as Christian metal. Taking their name from *Isaiah 53:5*, this US band became one of the biggest-selling Christian groups of the decade, their *To Hell With The Devil* (1986) album going platinum when they crossed over effectively to a secular metal audience. Unfortunately, most people remember them for their nifty line in yellow and black stripy spandex and a penchant for lobbing copies of the Good Book into crowds, rather than the music. Other bands of the era, such as **Barren Cross** and **Bloodgood**, had their fair share of fans, but nothing in quite the same league as Stryper.

As the metal scene has expanded and taken on myriad forms, so Christian metal has adapted. It is now possible to find bands truly extreme-sounding bands espousing a Christian perspective, taking styles as diverse as death metal, hardcore and pure unadulterated thrash. The quality of the music varies, as with all metal styles, but among the best are the likes of the highly successful nu-metallers **P.O.D.**, metalcore practitioners **Norma Jean** and **Zao**, the death-leaning **Extol** and **Living Sacrifice** (now disbanded) and the doom-laden **Paramaecium**. Perhaps the ultimate irony is Christian black metal, though the debate continues (in circles where people care about such things) as to whether it is correct to call music black metal if the satanic is replaced with the Godly.

By the time of *The Impossibility Of Reason* (2003) they had honed their approach with the clinical precision of a surgical strike. Another twelve-minutes-plus closer, "The Implements Of Destruction" had them flexing their progressive metalcore tendencies, but for the most part, it was an album that, when it didn't indulge in minor key introspective shadowplay, compared favourably to Slayer in its dynamics and pure thrashing power. In fact they found themselves being championed by none other than Slayer guitarist Kerry King, who wholeheartedly approved of their stripping away of pretension to let the speed and aggression do the talking.

Serious touring commitments eventually took their toll on Herrick. Burned out and in desperate need of time off, he left the band in early 2004. **Richard Evens** (ex-**Dog Faced Gods**) stepped in as the band headed into yet more intense gigging with the NWOAHM 2004 tour, alongside God Forbid, Killswitch Engage and Shadows Fall. Subsequently, they released their first DVD, *The Dehumanizing Process* (2004).

⊙ Pass Out Of Existence
2001; Roadrunner

This is one tormented clutch of tunes. Heavy, pounding and relentless metalcore.

⊙ The Impossibility Of Reason
2003; Roadrunner

More refined than its predecessor, this set relies less on shock tactics and more on gut-level brutality, with a good deal of old-school muscle.

CINDERELLA

Formed Philadelphia, US, 1983

You shall go to the ball. The legend goes that Jon Bon Jovi had quite a hand in getting this lot signed, for the self-styled rock'n'roll cowboy apparently discovered them and introduced them to Mercury Records. In reality Cinderella had been going for a while and had built up something of a local reputation for some seriously rocking live shows on the club circuit.

Whatever Mr Bon Jovi's involvement, there was no disguising the ambition and songwriting prowess of this fine example of 80s hair metal. The band was formed by **Tom Keifer** (vocals/guitar), **Jeff LaBar** (guitar), and with **Eric Brittingham** (bass) providing the nucleus. **Jody Cortez** was the initial drummer before **Fred Coury** stepped in eventually to create a stable line-up.

The impact that Cinderella made when they first appeared was quite remarkable. Slap-bang in the mid-80s you were no one on the metal scene if you didn't have enormous hair or dress like your girlfriend, and Cinderella were experts in the application of lip gloss and eye shadow as well as the delivery of power chords. The sleeve of their excellent debut album, *Night Songs* (1986), shows four cocksure poseurs pouting and preening for the camera, while the music within was straight-up glammy good-time pop metal – the record shot to

#3 in the US charts. There was nothing particularly original about the music. Rather it was the strength of the songwriting, with catchy songs such as the wonderfully sleazy "Push, Push", the big ballad hit single "Nobody's Fool" and cheeky stomp rocker "Shake Me" pushing all the right buttons to encourage air guitar action and ensure maximum airplay. The chief weapon in their arsenal was Keifer's wicked way with a guitar and his incredible shrieking vocals which were not a million miles in style from those of AC/DC's Brian Johnson. It was a formula that went down well with the crowds when they supported the likes of David Lee Roth and Bon Jovi – ol' Jon had also helped out with some backing vocals on their debut.

Such instant success meant the following album had a lot to live up to; *Long Cold Winter* (1988) was a valiant effort which didn't quite match its predecessor for chart action but actually contained songs of longer-lasting appeal. To be fair, the band avoided trying to ape the overt poppiness of their debut by giving the songs a bluesier spin. And by the time of *Heartbreak Station* (1990) the love of old Stones records was really shining through. Unfortunately, the effect was to alienate the fans who remembered the spandex and make-up.

Cinderella had found themselves in the unenviable position of still trying to make a major breakthrough at a time when the dour wind of change was making it impossible – Seattle was gradually beginning to kill off the old guard. The only thing that kept fans going over the next few years was a Japanese mini-LP, *Live Train To Heartbreak Station* (1991). It wasn't until 1994 that the knowingly titled *Still Climbing* arrived, and by that point grunge was in full swing. So even though the record boasted some strong songs and a heavier feel no one was really interested.

For a while the band went on hold and Mercury issued the *Once Upon A…* (1997) compilation, a reasonable enough collection of their finest moments. To make matters worse Keifer began to suffer from vocal chord problems, which effectively prevented the band from playing gigs, though *Live At The Key Club* (1999), a totally unpolished, warts-and-all concert recording was a decent addition to their catalogue.

Since then the Cinderella name has been kept alive by the occasional tour across the US – they are booked for the Rock Never Stops tour in summer 2005 and will be supported by Quiet Riot and Ratt. They also have a new compilation and DVD – *Rocked, Wired & Blessed*. Keifer is apparently working on a solo album and Coury is producing other bands, while LaBar and Brittingham tour with Naked Beggars.

⊙ Night Songs
1986; Vertigo

A glorious hair metal effort. The songs simply scream good time rock'n'roll with huge pompous choruses and instantly memorable melodies. Keifer's voice sounds amazing.

⊙ Live At The Key Club
1999; Cleopatra

As good as being there really. The liner notes claim that this album hasn't been doctored or overdubbed, providing the fans with a fine and raw gig experience.

CLUTCH

Formed Germantown, Maryland, US, 1991

To call **Clutch** a stoner band would be to do them a disservice. True, they do have that lumbering and greasy feel to their sound but there is so much more going on, from funk to punk, to full-on metal. At the centre of the chunky slabs of discordant guitar, however, lies the band's ace in the hole, their very own poet laureate, vocalist **Neil Fallon**. Completely defying the usual rock clichés with lyrics that range from the beautifully wrought to the fabulously weird and surreal, he delivers his wino wisdom and flights of narcotic fantasy in anything ranging from an elephantine roar to a peculiarly languid style of rap.

Clutch's singular and idiosyncratic adventures in rock began when Fallon was joined by **Tim Sult** (guitar), **Dan Maines** (bass), and **Jean-Paul Gaster** (drums) for their highly collectible 1991 "Pitchfork" single on indie Inner Journey Records. The four tracks within caught the attention of Earache who released the *Passive Restraints* EP in 1992, which in turn landed them a deal with Eastwest. From nothing to a major label deal in just two years.

Their first helping of wigged-out heavy rock didn't pander to any corporate ideals, however. *Transnational Speedway League: Anthems,*

Anecdotes, And Undeniable Truths (1993) was as eclectic as its title suggested. Working away from their band's initial hardcore punk-oriented sound towards a sort of ragged Pantera-esque power groove, the set was tempered by Mogadon-fuelled doom passages, with some fine and funky percussion thrown in too. Fallon's vocals were odd too, ranging from a tortured bellow to a growling croon, and his gift for humorous off-the-wall lyrics was already taking shape.

With much touring completed *Clutch* (1995) followed. By now the stoner vibe was beginning to shine through – it was like listening to ZZ Top circa *Tres Hombres* covering tunes from *Paranoid*. It was poundingly heavy but also loose and twangy, with Fallon's Twilight Zone lyrics eloquently taking on the politics of heavy guitars ("Rock'N'Roll Outlaw"), pirate adventures on the high seas ("Big News I") and a strange little tale about a fisherman landing the coffin of an infamous presidential assassin ("I Have The Body Of John Wilkes Booth"). And we haven't even touched on the robots, UFOs and super-strength weed.

In 1997 Earache rereleased the *Passive Restraints* EP in expanded form as the *Impetus* mini-LP and the "Pitchfork" single also got another airing in 1999. Sandwiched between these two releases came Clutch's masterful *The Elephant Riders* (1998), the title song featuring the curious central image of soldiers during the American Civil War riding into battle astride elephants. With a more basic and under-produced feel, *Jam Room* (1999) was a self-financed album which took a couple of years to get a proper worldwide release.

Pure Rock Fury (2001) returned to the bigger studio sound and another set of seer-like musings from Fallon. Carried by a huge drum sound and superbly dirty riffing, the back-to-back rumble of "Open Up The Border" (basically a surreal shopping list and history of world trade) and "Careful With That Mic…" (a brilliantly off-kilter rap poem) were obvious highlights. In keeping with the psychedelic thrashing, the record thrived thanks to the help of fellow Maryland rockers **Sixty Watt Shaman**, Mountain's **Leslie West** and Spirit Caravan's **Scott "Wino" Weinrich** (also famed for fronting doomy stoners Obsessed).

What followed was a period of protracted touring with *Live At The Googolplex* (2002), a so-so concert recording, and *Slow Hole To China: Rare And Unreleased* (2003) keeping Clutch going while they retired to their drummer Gaster's abode for a spot of riff-forging. The result was *Blast Tyrant* (2004) which returned to the spirit of *Jam Room* for inspiration and rejoiced under the marvellously ornate full title of *Blast Tyrant's Atlas Of The Invisible World Including Illustrations Of Strange Beasts And Phantasms*.

A law entirely unto themselves, Clutch occupy that unique hinterland where cult status mingles with the heroically offbeat, to produce work of great imagination and flair. They are intelligent and utterly compelling – not bad going for four hairy mountain blokes with a liking for Kentucky Fried Chicken.

⊙ Clutch
1995; Eastwest

With their style gradually settling down, this is the first taste of Clutch moving away from the hardcore blasts and investigating the possibilities of 70s sonics.

⊙ The Elephant Riders
1998; Eastwest

Considered one of their best albums by those in the know. Fallon's penchant for trippy lyrics with allusions to literature, history and the occult will have your head reeling.

⊙ Jam Room
1999; Spitfire

Back to basics with a rawer, downhome feel. Despite the lo-fi production this rocks like the bastard offspring of ancient ZZ Top and Blue Cheer.

COAL CHAMBER

Formed Los Angeles, US, 1994; disbanded 2003

When nu-metal gradually came to prominence in the mid-90s, **Coal Chamber**, alongside their geographical contemporaries Deftones and Korn, were chief among the purveyors of the new style.

It was the time-honoured fashion of replying to classified ads that had **Dez Fafara** (vocalist) joining forces with **Miguel "Meegs" Rascon** (guitarist). **Mike Cox** (drums) and bassist **Rayna Foss** (soon to become **Foss-Rose**) then completed the line-up. In the pioneering spirit of nu-metal the band began bolting together a mutant metal monster, consisting of heavily downtuned guitars, splashes of hip-hop, a touch of punk'n'goth, and plenty of roaring schizophrenic vocals; it was an angry, bass heavy attack with just a nod to the fuzzed-out doom of old Black Sabbath. Band members looked as outlandish as the music sounded – there were plenty of facial piercings and a decidedly freakish style; the ensemble went down a storm at LA clubs such as the *Roxy* and the *Whisky A-Go-Go*. This was weird metal for spooky kids. The underground buzz about the band began to pique various labels' interest, but it was the championing of their demo tape by Fear Factory guitarist **Dino Cazares** that gave them their first big break. Cazares tipped off producer **Ross Robinson**; the tune "Loco" stood out as being particularly indicative of the future direction of metal, and was enough to land them a deal with Roadrunner.

But for a while it seemed Coal Chamber might never get off the ground. Fafara had quit the band to concentrate on his relationship with his wife – the stresses of working with a band had been less than conducive to a happy home life. But in the end the lure of the music and the lifestyle drew him back to his old bandmates and, subsequently, the band's eponymous 1997 debut was injected with extra emotional juice. They had already been cultivating a major following through heavy touring, and 1996's Ozzfest was invaluable in getting the Chamber out to alienated kids across the US. The album served to consolidate their position as pulverizing sonic contenders with its solid, if somewhat unvarying groove. Fafara was adept at both guttural shrieking and whispered menace,

with stand-out cuts including "Loco", "Big Truck" and live fave "Sway".

Over the ensuing bouts of touring **Nadja Peulen** helped out on bass as Foss-Rose took maternity leave. Meanwhile the band's relationship with Ozzfest ensured that they enjoyed massive exposure, but their follow-up album, *Chamber Music* (1999), was something of a disappointment. In an attempt to incorporate yet more gothy, industrial and electronic influences the band lost sight of the songs, and while the material was more varied and inventive, the focus was lost. Also the decision to cover Peter Gabriel's "Shock The Monkey" with help from **Ozzy Osbourne** on vocals was just plain wrong. Inconsistencies aside, *Chamber Music* proved to be more chart-friendly than their first effort, making #21 and #22 in the UK and US respectively.

By the time of *Dark Days* (2002) Peulen had become their permanent bassist, and the desire to push themselves beyond the bounds of the nu was still strong. "I don't wanna put any tags on it", said Fafara of the new album, "I've been told by everybody that's heard it so far that it's 'new' music, which is what we were striving for. We never want to do anything that's in the box. It's much more driving, more raw … I think fans of Coal Chamber and fans of heavy genres are gonna love it!"

Such positive words, however, couldn't hide the fact that the album wasn't nearly as popular as the band expected, due, in part, to the shift in metal and the band's inability to

NIGEL CRANE/REDFERNS

Coal Chamber: "Look into my eyes. On the count of three you will wake up and you won't remember any of our records."

Concept Albums

These two words strike fear into the heart. Just mention the notion to any self-respecting rock fan and immediately the worst excesses of 70s prog loom out of the mists, conjuring images of hobbits, elves, magical swords, dragons and a time when bands such as **Pink Floyd**, **Yes**, **Jethro Tull** and **Genesis** peddled albums with overarching themes. You might think that metallers would steer well clear of the concept album. Not so, for the annals of metaldom are littered with 'em.

Cult books and comics have always been a favourite source of ideas – just pop down the local library, pick a popular classic, rip it apart and cobble it back together in a Frankenstein's monster patchwork of metal. **Steel Prophet**'s *Dark Hallucinations* (1999), for example, was a retelling of Ray Bradbury's dystopian sci-fi tale *Fahrenheit 451*; and legendary brainy rockers **Rush** adapted Ayn Rand's *Anthem* – though whether it can be considered a classic is another matter. It did, however, inspire them to create an all-time 70s masterpiece in the shape of *2112*, with side one devoted to describing an artless totalitarian future.

At some point Tolkein must figure in this fantastical landscape, cue Blind Guardian's *Nightfall In Middle Earth* (1998) which takes JRR's most impenetrable book, *The Silmarillion*, and gives it the concept album treatment. And while we're on the subject of elves, **Kiss** dabbled in the idea of fantasy led rock'n'roll on 1981's *(Music From) The Elder*. About a young hero out to slay an elf, it was effectively the soundtrack to a mythical story cooked up by Gene Simmons, with a view to possible sequel releases and a movie, and must rank as one of the worst albums – concept or otherwise – ever recorded.

The long-running **Iced Earth** have also dabbled on and off with concepts – *The Dark Saga* (1996) displays a neat popular touch as Todd MacFarlane's hit *Spawn* comic gets suitably metallized.

Much better with the fantasy is arch sword-and-sorcery fan **Ronnie James Dio** who, after a fallow period, brought himself in from the cold with 2000's *Magica*. And while we're on the subject of fantasy it's worth mentioning **Blue Öyster Cult**'s complicated and weird *Imaginos* (1988) – dubbed a "random access myth" – wherein strange extra-dimensional beings interfere with human history. In a league of their own when it comes to sci-fi concept albums are **Fear Factory**. Most of their work explores the way in which man and technology interface, but in *Obsolete* (1998) they go one step further by providing the *Terminator*-esque story of Edgecrusher's battle against the machines, with directions for a screenplay.

Horror is, of course, a heavy metal staple and **King Diamond**'s *Abigail* (1987) and **Cradle Of Filth**'s *Cruelty And The Beast* (1998) must rank among the best collisions of gore and metal. The former recounts an occult-friendly story of infanticide and ghostly reincarnation, which was so successful almost every King Diamond album thereafter featured some sort of narrative framework. And the latter finds the Brit black metallers getting their fangs stuck into the claret-spouting legend of Countess Bathory and her penchant for bathing in virgins' blood. The Filth also borrowed heavily from horror writer Clive Barker's *Nightbreed* for their *Midian* album.

Horror of a different, more satirical variety is conjured up by **Marilyn Manson** in *Antichrist Superstar* (1996), where the loose story of "Wormboy" allows Manson to lay into America's soft white conservative underbelly. Indeed, the idea of an outsider as a central character is key to some of metal's more memorable conceptual excursions. Incredibly, two of shock rockers **WASP**'s more mature albums – *Crimson Idol* (1992) and *The Neon God: Part I The Rise* (2004) – have developed the idea, the former in particular following the trials of a rock star in torment. This is an idea also explored by **Savatage** on *Streets: A Rock Opera* (1991). **Alice Cooper** has also experimented with themes – to greatest effect with *Welcome To My Nightmare* (1975). Later came *From The Inside* (1978), the musical result of Cooper's spell in a mental asylum trying to dry out.

The *pièce de résistance* in metal's collection of outsider myths, however, must be **Queensrÿche**'s classic *Operation: Mindcrime* (1988) which tells the story of junkie Nikki and how his naive idealism is harnessed by the evil Dr X for his own political ends. It's a powerful, emotional and intelligent example of what can be achieved in a metallic framework. And any fan of cerebral metal can't afford to ignore **Dream Theater**'s *Metropolis Part 2: Scenes From A Memory* (1999), a complex emotional story of love, tragedy and regressive hypnotherapy.

create consistent records at regular intervals. During its creation the various band members had been working on different projects – Fafara had launched his own label and was keen to produce more bands, as well as write his own music. So with *Dark Days* fading fast from view Coal Chamber gave up trying to outrun the rest of the nu-metal pack. Fafara quickly resurfaced with **Devildriver**, a vehicle he reckons is the sound of the future. And Roadrunner have whipped out *Giving The Devil His Due* (2003), a career retrospective including plenty of rarities and remixes.

Coal Chamber
1997; Roadrunner

Korn et al had already got under way by this point and Coal Chamber are playing catch-up. Nevertheless, this is a crunchingly heavy set boasting a nice line in angst.

ALICE COOPER

Born February 4, 1948, Detroit, US

*"I am the biggest shark out there …
I am like one of those old, wise Great
Whites that sits at the bottom waiting
for the little ones to get tired and then
crunch!" Alice Cooper*

Of all the rock artists of the last three decades, **Alice Cooper** – born **Vincent Furnier**, the son of a preacher – ranks among the most important and influential. Chief among his enduring creations was the modern style of shock rock – a theatrical penchant for gross-out horror and misanthropy which would provoke predictably hostile reactions from the moral guardians of the day, and eventually be used as the blueprint for hell-raisers such as Marilyn Manson.

In the beginning, way back in 1965 while living in Phoenix Arizona, Cooper started his career in a band called the **Earwigs**, playing cover versions with school friends. The following year they changed their name to **The Spiders** and, with **Glen Buxton** (guitar), **Michael Bruce** (guitar/keyboards), **Dennis Dunaway** (bass) and **Neal Smith** (drums) along for the ride, they scored a major hit in their local area with "Don't Blow Your Mind". A move to LA in 1968 prompted yet another name change to **The Nazz** until they discovered that there was already a band of that name – featuring a young Todd Rundgren – already touring. In the end they decided to call themselves Alice Cooper – supposedly the name of a seventeenth-century witch conjured up during a ouija board session – referring to both the band and Cooper himself. Then came their first step in the right direction: they linked up with Frank Zappa and his manager Shep Gordon who signed them to his Straight label. But even though they had promising management behind them nothing could save their dodgy brand of 60s psychedelia. Two albums, *Pretties For You* (1969) and *Easy Action* (1970), were best forgotten – the group were dubbed the worst band in LA.

A move to Detroit in 1970 was just what they needed, and energized by the sound of the local scene – featuring the likes of the Stooges and MC5 – the newly inspired Alice Cooper signed to Warners, gave themselves a sonic overhaul and started to give their songs a visual component, a factor that would be key to their sudden rise to fame and notoriety. With producer Bob Ezrin directing their studio antics the first shot at conservative America was *Love It To Death* (1971); single "Eighteen" reached a respectable #21 in the charts and represented the first hit in what would prove to be a golden era for the band. This was raucous rock'n'roll with a satirical bite, a calculated stab at the morals and values middle America held dear. And at its heart was the rasping, sleazy presence of Cooper himself, by now plastering on the black eye make-up and utilizing various stage props – a guillotine and electric chair, as well as snakes, were early faves – to complement the shock value of the lyrics. *Killer* (1971) was more of the same and gave the fans classics such as "Under My Wheels", "You Drive Me Nervous", and the wantonly tasteless "Dead Babies".

The oldies hated it, but the youngsters loved it; sales sent the Ezrin-produced *School's Out* (1972) to #2 in the US and #4 in the UK charts, with the title track becoming a global teen anthem. This was the peak period of the band's popularity and they weren't going to stop churning out the tacky, trashy, black-hearted rock until every teenager was a convert. *Billion Dollar Babies* (1973) was an inspired piece of apocalyptic theatre, trampling all over the decadent ideals of the 70s, with Coops taking his anger out on baby dolls on stages across the US. More hits followed – "Elected", "Hello Hurray" and "No More Mr Nice Guy" all guaranteed Alice prime chart action. And even though things faltered a tad with follow-up *Muscle Of Love* (1974), *Alice Cooper's Greatest Hits,* released the same year, pulled together pretty much all the singles in one handy package of hilarious, dirty, driving rock.

By this point, however, Cooper sensed that the winning formula might soon be on the wane. So far the band's songwriting abilities had yielded an array of timeless classics; better to change tack while on a high. Amazingly to

The man in the centre of this picture is the godfather of shock rock … no, seriously.

COURTESY OF SPITFIRE RECORDS

some, the change came with Cooper ditching the band, adopting the band name as solely his own and hiring a backing band consisting largely of musicians who had played with Lou Reed, as well as a couple of session players who had helped out in the past. *Welcome To My Nightmare* (1975), produced yet again by Bob Ezrin, was a bona fide masterpiece, with the scattergun approach to gross-out subject matter abandoned in order to focus neatly upon a central horror concept, with actor Vincent Price providing narration. The album would also yield one of Cooper's best-loved, most often covered hits in the ballad "Only Women Bleed".

By the time of *Alice Cooper Goes To Hell* (1976), however, the rot had started to set

in. The album was acceptable, though by no means spectacular, and years of hard living and boozing were having a serious effect upon Cooper's health, which inevitably led to a deterioration in the quality of subsequent records: *Lace And Whiskey* (1977), *The Alice Cooper Show* (1978), and *From The Inside* (1978) – the lyrics of the latter inspired by Alice's spell in a psychiatric hospital recovering from alcoholism. As the 80s loomed matters worsened: *Flush The Fashion* (1980), *Special Forces* (1981), *Zipper Catches Skin* (1982), which failed to chart, and *Dada* (1983) – his last recording for Warners – were simply lacking in spark, wit and, above all, the wicked persona of Alice as he had been in the 70s. And then he vanished from view altogether in the mid-80s, presumably to perfect his golf swing.

It wasn't until he was hooked in to provide "He's Back (The Man Behind The Mask)" for the soundtrack to slasher movie *Friday The 13th Part VI* that a deal with MCA was struck and the *Nightmare Returns* tour was launched. The accompanying album, *Constrictor* (1986), was far from brilliant, but Cooper's career was buoyed by the fact that the 80s had spawned literally dozens of glammy acts who owed him a debt of gratitude: Twisted Sister, Mötley Crüe, WASP and Lizzy Borden, for example. *Raise Your Fist And Yell* (1987) was only marginally better, but his growing profile and the long-standing appeal of his back catalogue led to a new stage show and various festival appearances, including Reading.

The real commercial return occurred in 1989 with a signing to Epic and a collaboration with ace songwriter/producer Desmond Child. *Trash* (1989) was an MTV-friendly *tour de force* featuring smash hit single "Poison", which went to #2 in the UK and #7 in the US, his first single to chart there for nearly a decade. The album itself underlined Alice's celebrity status with famous names queuing up to join in; **Jon Bon Jovi** and Richie Sambora were there, as were most of **Aerosmith**. While the return to popularity can only have pleased long-standing fans, *Trash* wasn't exactly as nasty as the title suggested; rather it was a polished and sleek set of tunes aimed directly at the mass market. If there's one thing Cooper has learned over the years it's how to fit into the prevailing tastes of the day; call it cynicism, or common sense, but it was a survival trick that would help him well into the 90s and beyond.

The star turns came thick and fast with *Hey Stoopid* (1991) – **Slash**, **Ozzy Osbourne**, **Steve Vai**, **Joe Satriani**, **Nikki Sixx** and **Mick Mars** all chipped in – and Alice popped up in hit teen comedy *Wayne's World*, as did the track "Feed My Frankenstein". *The Last Temptation* (1994) arrived at a time when grunge was killing off the last vestiges of hair metal and, though the album's sound was harsh enough, over the next few years it was the compilation *Classicks* (1995), live effort *A Fistful Of Alice* (1997), and the gargantuan four-CD rarities blow-out *The Life And Crimes Of Alice Cooper* (1999) that kept the product flowing.

When finally Alice emerged once more it was with a renewed sense of purpose. In a post-Columbine climate Cooper knew exactly what targets to skewer – *Brutal Planet* (2000) once again showcased an artist able to reinvent and reshape his sound, this time to capitalize on the aggressive downtuned crunch of nu-metal. One of the stand-out cuts, "Wicked Young Man", picked through the fall-out of the horrific shootings. It was gory, blood-spattered and very heavy even for Alice, a formula that was convincingly repeated on *Dragontown* (2001).

Two years later, with nu-metal on the wane and old style garage rock back in vogue, Cooper opted to return to his roots – *The Eyes Of Alice Cooper* (2003) revved into sight. A triumph of minimalism, the simple makeshift studio set-up and live session work gave the whole album a vibrant and edgy feel that appealed to long-standing fans a touch baffled by Alice's experiment with nu-metal brutality.

⊙ Billion Dollar Babies
1973; Atlantic

Grotesque, glammy, and out to shock, Alice and the band were on top form. Along with a clutch of hits this one contains the dubiously titled "Raped and Freezin'", which just goes to show that taste never even entered the equation in the 70s.

⊙ Welcome To My Nightmare
1975; Atlantic

Alice minus his band but coming up with a terrific album helped by producer Bob Ezrin. Its creepy cartoon horror made it an instant classic.

⊙ The Life And Crimes Of Alice Cooper
1999; Rhino

If you can afford it then why not get fat on some Alice rarities? Four CDs worth of nasty, era-defining rock'n'roll. It's gotta be done.

⊙ The Eyes Of Alice Cooper
2003; Spitfire

The man returns to a more garagey sound and scores a hit. Possibly the best album he's done for a long while – raw, aggressive and packed with memorable tunes.

CORROSION OF CONFORMITY

Formed Raleigh, North Carolina, US, 1982

When it comes to setbacks and missed opportunities **Corrosion Of Conformity** could write a book about their experiences. Despite the frustrations, however, their reputation as one of the pioneering rock bands of the last twenty years remains very much intact. Chief among the accolades heaped upon this lot is their early fusion of hardcore punk and metal back in the 80s, when the scenes were largely separate and to cross over was considered sacrilegious.

Formed initially around high school buddies **Woodie Weatherman** (guitar), **Reed Mullin** (drums) and, most of the time, **Mike Dean** (bass), the early versions of COC were notoriously unstable. These three would prove to be the most common features in a history riddled with personnel changes.

In the early 80s the band were known as a hardcore punk outfit: short, punchy songs perfect for slamming in the pit and boasting serious, politically slanted lyrics. Their first foray into recording, the raging Black Flag-esque *Eye For An Eye* (1983), involved vocalist **Eric Eycke** bellowing his way through almost thirty brief but solid songs, which hinted vaguely at the kind of Black Sabbath worship that would inform their later career. The *Six Songs With Mike Singing* EP, released a couple of years later, witnessed the departure of Eycke leaving a trio to record *Animosity* (1986), before adding **Simon Bob** (vocals) for *Technocracy* (1987). The latter two albums on Metal Blade Records had sealed their position as one of the premier heavy bands bringing hardcore attitude to the metal masses.

It was, however, with *Blind* (1991) that they suddenly hit upon the right formula. Having taken time out to reassess their direction the band had added **Pepper Keenan** (guitar, ex-**Graveyard Rodeo**) and

Karl Agell (vocals). Dean had fallen out with the band following a disagreement over touring details and been replaced by **Phil Swisher**. The socially aware lyrics were still occasionally present but it was the gleaming polish of classic metal riveted to their youthful punky aggression that really hammered home. The key to the breakthrough was the revolutionary anthem "Vote With A Bullet" with Keenan's muscular southern drawl on lead vocals. The result was a snarlingly heavy Sabbath-esque album that garnered major critical praise and a sudden upswing in the kind of support slot they could comfortably land; touring with the likes of Soundgarden, for instance, did them no harm at all.

However, there was to be a glitch in their run of luck. The band were having major disagreements with their label, Relativity, and this, coupled with arguments over musical direction, scuppered what progress they had made. Agell was sacked and Swisher followed, the two of them heading off to form the heavy southern rock band **Leadfoot**. Keenan assumed lead vocals and the only bassist they could be sure of was Dean, so he was reinstated.

Things picked up again and the group's transformation into a full-blown metal band was well under way. If *Blind* was their calling card then *Deliverance* (1994), released on Sony, truly kicked the door in, with "Albatross" and "Clean My Wounds" commanding airtime on rock stations and the latter earning some valuable MTV rotation. Keenan's raucous yet soulful vocals and impeccable songwriting, coupled with the relentless and dirty, southern-tinged groove of the music had given the band their first hits. And Keenan's love for the sounds of the south led to him taking a little time the next year to contribute to Phil Anselmo's **Down** side-project put together during his time away from Pantera.

Back in the COC camp, moves were afoot to catapult the band to the next level; the album to do it was *Wiseblood* (1996). This developed upon the classic metal flavours of its predecessor with a terrific line in grungy guitar sounds and a passionate heart. It was enough to gain a support slot with Metallica – 'Tallica's **James Hetfield** had also provided backing vocals on "Man Or Ash" – allowing COC to wow some of the biggest crowds of their career. In fact, some metal fans, somewhat disgruntled by the Metalliboys' new direction with the freshly released *Load*,

preferred the gnarlier style of COC over the headliners. Such was the undeniable grit and integrity of the new album that "Drowning In A Daydream" was nominated for a Grammy award in the Best Metal Performance category.

And then it all began to crumble when COC were dropped by Sony. After some of the most incredible leaps forward, the band were back in the wilderness. This was a situation that was eventually resolved when they signed to Sanctuary, but it wasn't until 2000 that they got a record into the shops. *America's Volume Dealer* was the next step in their transformation, taking the fire of *Wiseblood* but developing the songwriting to create catchier and slightly more commercial nuggets of super-heavy melodic rock. Alongside the classic COC-sound of cuts such as "Who's Got The Fire" and "Diablo Blvd.", laidback numbers like "Stare Too Long" sounded as if they could have been written on a southern porch with the sun setting on the bayou – it was as though Lynyrd Skynrd had dropped by for a studio jam. Casting a backwards glance to their punk roots the European version of the album also threw in the thrashy swear-fest of "Rather See You Dead".

The follow-up was *Live Volume* (2001) recorded in Detroit, the Motor City vibe inspiring a classy performance from the band. Although it seemed that COC were, at last, back on track, things were put on hold as Keenan joined the reactivated Down for a far more involved period of writing and touring. A new COC album, *In The Arms Of God* is expected in 2005 along with a tour supporting Motörhead.

 Blind
1991; Relativity

Heavy and punky until now, this set marked a new period of development for COC. Their love of Sabbath shines through.

Deliverance
1994; Sony

By now the sounds and flavours of the 70s are really creeping into the mix. A little Deep Purple here, a bit of Skynyrd there. This one contains some of their earliest hits in "Albatross" and "Clean My Wounds".

 Wiseblood
1996; Sony

A nice'n'dirty guitar tone can go a long, long way and COC are masters of the filthy riff. A tight sound and better production, along with Keenan's seasoned drawl make this essential.

CRADLE OF FILTH

Formed Ipswich, UK, 1991

" ... the front has a rather happy looking devil fucking a nun. He looks quite chuffed with himself." Dani Filth on COF's line in T-shirts

Not many bands court controversy with the unfailing accuracy of this quintessentially English, black metal outfit. Right from their inception, with the line-up of **Dani Filth** (vocals), **Paul Ryan** (guitar), his brother **Ben Ryan** (keyboards), **John Pritchard** (bass) and **Darren** (drums), there was something uniquely different about **Cradle of Filth**'s approach to the darker side of metal. Three demos, respectively titled "Invoking The Unclean", "Orgiastic Pleasures" and "Total Fucking Darkness", showed a band coming to grips with gothic imagery and the vampire myth. They aspired to writing full-blown operatic pieces drenched in blood and darkness, a goal they would achieve a little way down the line after their debut *The Principle Of Evil Made Flesh* (1994) on Cacophonous Records. An album named *Goetia* was recorded prior to this effort but unpaid studio bills resulted in the master tapes being wiped.

The underground success of the debut was doubtless due to the band's quite unusual sound, and a fortuitous association with the burgeoning black metal scene of the early 90s, with its Scandinavian practitioners garnering plenty of negative headlines for their notoriously pyrotechnic and murderous adventures. Cradle remained distant from such distasteful events but the attendant shock waves helped their rise no end. During this period the line-up shifted a number of times, finally settling down with drummer **Nicholas Barker**, guitarists **Paul Allender** and **Stuart**, keyboardist **Damien** and **Robin Graves** on bass.

Preceded by the mini-LP *Vempire (Or Dark Faerytales In Phallustein)* (1996), *Dusk And Her Embrace* (1996) was a full-blown gothic epic of bloodcurdling proportions, released on Music For Nations and featured yet another new guitarist, **Gian Piras**, replacing the departed Allender. The music was fully realized thrash-opera topped off with Dani Filth's trademark eardrum-popping screech – the singing equivalent of steel talons being dragged across the

blackest of blackboards. Song titles included such gems as "A Gothic Romance (Red Roses For The Devil's Whore)" and "Beauty Slept In Sodom", betraying the band's wide and various influences from H.P. Lovecraft to Diamanda Galas, from Nietzsche to Hammer horror. It was blackly romantic, knowingly cinematic, charged through with highly wrought emotion and blood-spattered drama.

The band, now dressed as leather-clad S&M vampires, complete with ashen corpse face paint, were keenly aware that the best way to market themselves was with a nifty line in T-shirts. To call the designs offensive would be an understatement. The "Vestal Masturbation" T-shirt, for instance, features a semi-naked nun pleasuring herself, whilst the back boldly states "Jesus is a Cunt". Needless to say, the garment became one of their bestsellers. In interviews, too, they went out of their way to offend everyone, from environmentalists to church groups. They were clearly having fun, though Damien left to be replaced by **Les 'Lecter' Smith**.

By the time of *Cruelty And The Beast* (1998) – a concept album based on the grisly story of

Dani Filth: "I would like to thank Satan and all his little helpers for this award."

75

sixteenth-century noblewoman Countess Bathory, who would preserve her beauty by bathing in the blood of virgin girls – the Filth's style was firmly established. Sweeping gothic orchestration and passages of blistering thrash metal carried some of Dani Filth's most outrageously ornate and over-the-top lyrics. Such was their growing notoriety at this stage that they became the subject of an unintentionally humorous documentary in the BBC's *Living With The Enemy* strand, while month by month some new incident would result in press coverage. One marvellously farcical situation resulted from a photo shoot in the Vatican, when police armed with submachine guns took exception to Dani Filth's "I (heart) Satan" T-shirt and Lecter's customary vicar's dog collar. When questioned about these faux pas in the holy city, one of the band stated that they played "evil music", and a tour laminate featuring a semi-naked woman crucified on an upside-down cross was produced to prove they were in a metal band. Not exactly past masters at diplomacy, this attempt to diffuse a potentially dangerous situation failed and the band were questioned for an hour by the outraged authorities.

These fun and games aside, the band's musical mission continued with a vengeance. The *From The Cradle To Enslave* EP was unveiled in 1999 and allowed the band to indulge their cinematic whims by making a much-hyped video with cult horror director **Alex Chandon**. The horrific, blood-drenched mini-epic was issued in censored and uncensored forms on the *Pandaemonaeon* (1999) video, along with live footage of the band playing to a packed Astoria theatre in London.

The next full album *Midian* (2000) was based loosely upon horror writer Clive Barker's *Nightbreed* story and also featured *Hellraiser* horror actor Doug Bradley's ethereally spooky Cenobyte vocal contributions. By this point the band's notoriously fluid line-up had changed again to include Gian Piras (guitar), **Martin Powell** (keyboards), **Adrian Erlandsson** (drums) and Paul Allender (guitar), the latter back in the band after several years off being a family man. Robin Graves eventually left in 2001 to pursue other goals in life (to be replaced by ex-**Anathema** bass player **Dave Pybus**) while his bandmates busied themselves with a couple of cunningly punning titles – *Bitter Suites To Succubi* (2001) and *Lovecraft And Witch Hearts* (2002) – both compilations of sorts intended to plug the gap while the Filth

prepared to release their first full-blown major label atrocity on Sony. A live album *Live Bait For The Dead* (2002) whipped out by Snapper Music and another DVD titled *Heavy, Left-handed & Candid* (2002) provided a little distraction while the band toiled away in the dark recesses of their rehearsal dungeon perfecting the new material.

Signing to a major smelled to some like a sellout but the arrival of *Damnation And A Day* (2003) was preceded by the video for the single "Babalon A.D." – inspired by Pier Paolo Pasolini's highly controversial and often banned film *Salò* (based on 120 Days Of Sodom by the Marquis De Sade) – and was an intriguing taste of another loose concept album. With Sony's big bucks behind them Cradle were able to indulge in all manner of excess to bring their diseased vision to fruition, including a trip to Budapest to use a 40-piece orchestra and a 32-voice choir. It was the most elaborate and accessible Cradle album to date with slightly shorter, more economical songs and catchier melodies lurking beneath the evil riffing and fully orchestrated mayhem. And with the new album came the addition of yet another bad-taste T-shirt to the forever-expanding catalogue. "The back print reads 'Get Thee Behind Me, Satan', while the front has a rather happy looking devil fucking a nun. He looks quite chuffed with himself," chirped a very happy Dani Filth.

Aware of the credibility gap – a black metal band on a major label just seemed wrong – the band soon announced that they would release their next opus on Roadrunner, a far more metallic label all round. Incredibly, with touring and promotion done, including an appearance at the Donington Download festival – helped by second guitarist **James McKillboy** – the Filthy ones almost immediately set to work on *Nymphetamine* (2004), the title inspired by the "druggish, beast-like addiction to beautiful, classical women," according to the band.

Cruelty And The Beast
1998; Music For Nations

Don't expect subtlety, hit singles or poppy melodies; this is dark, savage, painful black metal played with frightening intensity and a complete disregard for prevailing musical trends.

Lovecraft And Witch Hearts
2002; Music For Nations

One of the best COF compilations available, combining favourites with rare tracks and remixes. Gory and great.

CREED

Formed Tallahassee, Florida, US, 1994; disbanded 2004

"My upbringing was very strict...I first heard Led Zeppelin in 1994 because rock'n'roll wasn't allowed in the house. My dad used to say that electric guitars were the devil's music. One day my parents woke up and I wasn't there ..."
Scott Stapp

Genius songwriters with a gift for tapping into the human soul, or chancers who struck upon a formula and milked it for all it was worth? With **Creed** you were in one camp or the other; the songs either struck a deep and resonant chord or simply sounded like any one of several bands capitalizing upon the Seattle sound of the late 90s. Whatever your stance, Creed were undeniably a runaway success, even if the music prompted some critics to comment that the last thing the world needed was another Pearl Jam.

The phenomenal rise of the band can be traced back to a chance meeting of old school friends **Scott Stapp** (vocals) and **Mark Tremonti** (guitar). Stapp's strict Christian background had brought him into major conflict with his ultra-religious parents who weren't happy with him pursuing a career in music. The conflict provided plenty of material for deep, soul-searching lyrics, which Tremonti set to the kind of dreary, heavy rock grind that had made bands such as Alice In Chains so popular. The group – which for a while was bizarrely called **Naked Toddler** – was completed by **Brian Marshall** (bass) and **Scott Phillips** (drums); it was this line-up that set about creating the songs that eventually turned up on *My Own Prison* (1999).

In reality *My Own Prison* had begun life a couple of years earlier as a self-financed release which sold astonishingly well. The album attracted the attention of Wind Up Records, who distributed through Sony, and the tapes were handed over to veteran studio man **Ron St Germain** to remix. The sonic overhaul gave the band their very first multi-million seller. Of course, it took a little while for the momentum to build, but radio stations just couldn't get enough of Stapp emotionally immolating himself on the likes of "Torn", "One", "What's This Life For" and the title track.

It was the kind of success story record companies love – provided the band can deliver more. Fortunately for Creed their next album, *Human Clay* (1999), exceeded all expectations, topping the US charts and eventually selling over ten million copies, helped along by Grammy-winning number one hit single "With Arms Wide Open" – a very serious little tune penned by Stapp upon learning that he was to become a dad. Stapp's sombre spiritual musings – the singer is a major Jim Morrison fan – obviously appealed hugely to a US audience who could tune in to his inner turmoil; the effect wasn't quite so marked in the more cynical UK.

Now established as the biggest band in the States, Creed took on all the usual trappings of stardom, including the bodyguards. "I've gotten death threats from right-wing Christian groups who think I'm leading their sons and daughters to hell, and Satan worshippers who think I talk about God too much in my music," he told the press. And then came the really fun stuff, such as the verbal fisticuffs with Limp Bizkit's Fred Durst and Marshall having a go at Pearl Jam during an interview. Marshall soon left to pursue other projects and the band soldiered on with **Brett Hestla** as a live replacement.

The loss of Marshall altered the band's direction not one jot as Tremonti handled the bass parts on *Weathered* (2001), an album featuring possibly one of the worst examples of cover art ever – the band's faces being chiselled out of

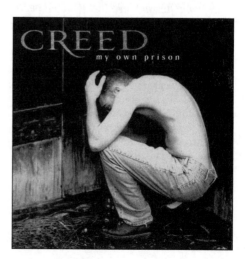

the trunk of a tree. The hit singles kept flowing and the album sold obscenely well, although things weren't going well for Stapp. He was unable to tour for a while after a car crash, and when fit again, personal problems seeped over into his performances. The most infamous instance occurred at a concert in Chicago in December 2002 when the singer appeared to be so intoxicated that he could barely stand or sing. Fans were so angered by the singer's sloppiness that they took him to court. They failed to win their case, but amazingly Stapp tried to justify his behaviour by saying he was making a dramatic gesture, intended to symbolize the turmoil of his private life.

All things considered it came as no surprise when the band folded. Not long after, Tremonti, Marshall and Phillips reappeared with new singer **Myles Kennedy** in **Alter Bridge**. Stapp eventually emerged with "Relearn Love" on the soundtrack to *The Passion Of The Christ*.

⦿ Human Clay
1999; Wind Up

Their debut of relentlessly serious songs is packed with hits. Stapp's rich and husky delivery gives the lyrics a spiritual gravity matched only by Tremonti's monolithic guitar work.

CROWBAR

Formed New Orleans, US, 1990

"Y'know, there's supposed to be a certain inaudible bass sound that'll make you shit and piss yourself – if we could just achieve that it would be great! We could sell Crowbar diapers at the gigs!" Jimmy Bower

Heavier than an astrophysics lecture, Crowbar are a fine example of the Louisiana sludge metal sound, a depressing and draining combination of stoner groove, cataclysmic doom and scorching metalcore. The fuzzed out tone of Sabbath runs deep within the veins of this formidable, monolithic crew. They sound so damned heavy that they don't so much write songs as weld them together from sheet steel and pig iron.

Chief architect is founding member **Kirk Windstein**, the larger-than-life guitarist/ vocalist who pens riffs vaster than even his impressive frame – and that's saying something. The combined weight of the band and all the equipment required to nightly erect such a towering wall of sonic angst is an awesome sight indeed.

Joining Windstein for the first grindingly heavy album, *Obedience Through Suffering* (1992), were **Todd Strange** (bass), **Kevin Noonan** (guitar) and **Craig Nunenmacher** (drums). It was released on the Grindcore label, an apt home for the band; the riffs thundered with the momentum of plate-tectonics and the drumming nailed it all home with unerring precision. Meanwhile, Windstein's tortured howl spat out the lyrics as though they were poison in his mouth. This was a formula that the band largely stuck to over the years, each subsequent album bringing new levels of refinement to bear upon the gut-level metal.

The self-titled follow-up released in 1993 included such aural batterings as "Existence Is Punishment" and "I Have Failed", proving, if anything, that Windstein was a fount of invention when it came to expressing how miserable he felt. It was the kind of sorrowful dirge metal that went down particularly well with a crowd intent on kicking up a slow-moving but unstoppable mosh. The live experience was captured on the mini-LP *Live + 1* (1994).

The next full-length album, *Time Heals Nothing* (1995), was basically business as usual except that the slightly higher number of speedier tracks, verging sometimes on thrash, brought a welcome relief from the usual plodding sludge. The occasional variation in Windstein's vocals – away from the caustic, often two-dimensional bellow – provided the kind of killer contrasts that enhanced the overall power of the songs.

However, the bigger news of the same year was Windstein and Strange's involvement with **Phil Anselmo**'s side-project, **Down**. When the surprise success of Down had subsided, Windstein turned his attention to *Broken Glass* (1996) – created with the aid of new guitarist **Sammy Pierre Duet** and new drummer **Jimmy Bower** (also a member of Down) – though by then, problems with their label Pavement were growing beyond the point of tolerance. So, after the *Past And Present* (1997) compilation the band moved on to Mayhem for the excellent *Odd Fellows Rest* (1998), the title inspired by the famous cemetery in New Orleans.

Crowbar: Who ate all the gumbo?

By the time of *Equilibrium* (2000) **Sid Montz** had taken over from Bower, whose many projects in and around the New Orleans metal scene were keeping him more than busy. Again the band had shifted label, this time to Spitfire/ Eagle, though nothing much had changed in Windstein's basic approach, except that the group had somehow been inspired to cover **Gary Wright**'s famous song "Dream Weaver". It certainly was a strange end to yet another gloomy collection.

Ever the constant in a fluid line-up, Windstein found himself with another new rhythm section, consisting of **Jeff Okoneski** (bass) and **Tony Costanza** (drums) for the self-explanatory *Sonic Excess In Its Purest Form* (2001). The only respite from the skull-cracking thrashers and plodders was the understated and minimal beauty of "In Times Of Sorrow". And then all went quiet on the Crowbar front; Windstein helped write a new Down album and then went on tour with it, which took the best part of three years.

Re-forming Crowbar for a new album began with Windstein as a one-man band before bassist **Rex Brown** (ex-**Pantera** and Down) and original drummer Nunenmacher (taking time off from **Black Label Society**) joined in the funereal fun to create Lifesblood For The Downtrodden (2005).

Past And Present
1997; Pavement

As good a place as any to sample early Crowbar. Windstein's powerful songwriting combined with the bone-crunching delivery make this one hell of a compilation.

Odd Fellows Rest
1998; Mayhem

Downtuned and doomed, this is one of the band's best latter-day albums packed with insanely heavy riffing and a mood of brooding dejection.

Equilibrium
2000; Spitfire/Eagle

Melodic, complex and stunningly melodramatic, this album turns depression into an art form. The likes of Linkin Park might think they can do angst but this is the real deal.

THE CULT

Formed Bradford, UK 1982;
disbanded 1995; re-formed 1999

The Cult aren't so much a band as the artistic vision of howling wolf child **Ian Astbury** and six-string shape-thrower **Billy Duffy**. Their name has become synonymous with outrageous, bombastic, arena-bothering

COURTESY OF SPITFIRE RECORDS

mega-rock, equal parts theatrical Native American mysticism and full-on leather-trousered machismo – all heavy metal clichés and glorious air-punching choruses. But it wasn't always like that.

Astbury had spent part of his youth in Canada and witnessed the plight of the Native Americans first hand. Consequently, he wanted to create a band reflecting his philosophical concerns. **Southern Death Cult** were born, a jangly twangly goth-punk hybrid who managed to whip up a storm of good vibes and positive critical feedback. But they didn't last long – Astbury shortened the name to **Death Cult** and ditched the entire band for a new line-up, including **Jamie Stuart** (bass), **Ray Mondo** (drums) and one Billy Duffy (guitars). Duffy had played with **Theatre Of Hate** and **The Nosebleeds** and arrived as a fully formed songwriter, the perfect foil for Astbury's lyrical flights of fantasy. Signed first to Situation 2 and then Beggars Banquet, they managed a couple of well-received singles in 1983 before trimming the name even further to become The Cult and acquiring a new drummer in **Nigel Preston**.

When *Dreamtime* (1984) arrived they had refined their approach by trying to remove any extraneous gothy fat to push their sound further towards the rock end of the spectrum. It was a risky move after being darlings of the alternative scene but a natural one, providing far more possibilities. The ghosts of Morrison and Hendrix were lurking within in the grooves of *Dreamtime* but the fusion of Astbury's spiritual yelping and Duffy's guitar lines had yet to reach a convincing critical mass. True ignition was achieved with *Love* (1985), produced by **Steve Brown** and featuring **Mark Brzezicki** on drums, Preston having been sacked for erratic drug-induced behaviour. At last they had hit their stride with a clamorous but mystical sound, chiming guitar lines accompanying war dance vocals in a sparkling collision of 60s psychedelia and big rock values. The shimmering "Rain" and stomping "She Sells Sanctuary" both went Top 20 and the album went Top 5 in the UK, though the US had still to fall in a big way for the Astbury/Duffy rock nexus.

Plans to repeat the success led to some frustrating sessions. Knowing they had to make a bold, brash statement the group decamped to New York in 1986 with a view to remixing their work with producer **Rick Rubin** – Astbury thought Rubin's cutting edge success with the Beastie Boys and Run DMC made him the ideal man to work with. In the end they decided to re-cut the entire record as a full-force, granite-fisted metal opus: *Electric* (1987). A greasy, open-throttle cover of "Born To Be Wild" represented the biker spirit of the 60s and elsewhere on the album The Cult did a damn fine job of borrowing a few tried and tested tricks from AC/DC and Led Zeppelin. Drumming of a vast, Bonham-esque nature – this time provided by **Les Warner** – anchored epic blues guitar licks, with singles "Wild Flower" and "Lil' Devil" owing more than a drink to Angus Young; Rubin had persuaded Duffy to strip away the effects-heavy sound he was used to and the results were beautifully lean and mean. The latter two songs, coupled with the killer swing of "Love Removal Machine" ensured healthy chart action and even the US was gradually getting hip to Astbury's lupine love-in – the album featured some of the singer's most inspirationally ludicrous lyrics. It would take a support slot with Bill Idol and then a headlining tour with Guns N' Roses in support to get things truly moving Stateside, but the opportunity was open for their return album – if the band could survive that long. The sudden success was leading to severe pressure within; Astbury was in love with rock'n'rollness and his behaviour was becoming increasingly degenerate – this included trashing stuff, not least the drum kit on a nightly basis, with the band eventually having to pay the bill for their lead singer's antics.

Barely together as a unit, they decided to cancel the Japanese leg of the tour before things were pushed beyond repair. They then ditched everyone, including Warner and their management, and moved to Los Angeles with a view to cracking America. And that they did in triumphant style with *Sonic Temple* (1989), produced by **Bob Rock**, despite the fact that news that Astbury's father had cancer was pushing the volatile vocalist closer to self-destruction. In the studio drums had been provided by session player **Mickey Curry**, but the live job went to **Matt Sorum**, with the group promoting what amounted to a mono-lithic slab of incredibly catchy radio-friendly metal. It was polished into world-beating shape by Duffy's expansive arrangements and Rock's unerring ear for the commercial – there was not a single duff track to be found.

The incendiary driving rock of "Fire Woman", string-laden "Edie (Ciao Baby)" about Warholian starlet Edie Sedgwick, scorching "Sun King" and epic "Sweet Soul Sister" all paid the charts a visit; the album went to #3 in the UK and Top 10 in the US. A stint supporting Metallica led to their own world tour but throughout, a chasm between Duffy and Astbury was widening; Astbury was frequently in an alcoholic stupor and the old cliché of travelling in separate tour buses seemed the only way to get themselves through it all. To make matters worse the recently married Stewart had already decided to quit.

As an antidote to the excessive madness, Astbury decided to direct his energies into a project reflecting the positive aspects of the music business. He organized the Gathering Of The Tribes festival in October 1990, with a wildly varying bill including Public Enemy, Soundgarden, Ice T, The Charlatans and Iggy Pop.

Despite the insanity of the previous tour, Astbury and Duffy were still able to write together – though the relationship was often highly strained – and 1991 brought *Ceremony* with Charlie Drayton (bass) and Mickey Curry back in the studio again. It was basically *Sonic Temple* trimmed of huge rock production values. Inevitably, though it sold relatively well, the band had fallen victim to their own success; they could only go down after the high of the previous album.

A compilation, *Pure Cult* (1993), preceded the release of *The Cult* (1994). In the meantime alternative metal had virtually killed off radio rock of the *Sonic Temple* variety, so when Duffy and Astbury finally felt they could stand being in each other's company they had to take things in a totally different direction. With the aid of Bob Rock once more and the addition of **Craig Adams** (bass) and **Scott Garrett** (drums) they opted for a stripped-back production, heavy on the bass and drums with Astbury's voice at the fore. It was a modern, state-of-the-art album but by this point, with long locks shorn and the landscape a hostile shade of grunge, it was just a matter of time before they called it a day, which they did in 1995.

And so it stayed until the late 90s; Astbury formed the **Holy Barbarians**, while Duffy went off to form **Coloursound** with the Alarm's **Mike Peters**. And then, in 1999 The Cult pulled themselves together for a tour of the US, which eventually led to *Beyond Good And Evil* (2001). By now grunge had given way to the dour and angst-filled sound of nu-metal, so in tune with the zeitgeist the album featured not only Astbury in full spiritual yelping mode but a smothering wall of down-tuned super-heavy riffing. It wasn't exactly classic Cult but it was a damn sight closer to their heyday sound than their last studio album had been – and a welcome return to some kind of form.

Love
1985; Beggars Banquet

Hippy sentiments set to tripped-out psychedelic rock studded with great choruses and an undercurrent of violence.

Electric
1987; Beggars Banquet

The Cult want to be Led Zeppelin, pure and simple. There's nothing goth about this collection of biker anthems. Zip up the leathers and get your legs astride the wolf child's Harley.

Sonic Temple
1989; Beggars Banquet

Unbeatable. Could this be the perfect modern metal album? Huge hooks, huge riffs, acres of leather, Astbury teetering on the edge amid the exploding guitars. Sublime.

D4

Formed Auckland, New Zealand, 1998

Hearing **D4** for the first time it would be easy to mistake them for a Detroit band. So strong and vital is their strain of diesel-injected garage punk that they come across more as a primal force than just another rock'n'roll band.

Formed by guitarists **Jimmy Christmas** and **Dion**, who had spent half their lives hanging around local recording studios picking up tips and tricks, the band went through a few line-up shifts before the addition of **Vaughan** (bass) and **Beaver** (drums) brought some measure of stability to their frenetic guitar squall.

Gigs at local clubs and pubs allowed them to build a sizeable following while their debut EP (released in 1999) secured some all-important airplay for tracks such as the thrashing "Come On!", which soon became a favourite on student radio. With a healthy buzz growing, support slots with the likes of the Hellacopters and Fu Manchu brought their scuzzy rock agenda to the masses, allowing them to tour Australia and Japan before playing the main stage at the Big Day Out festival in Auckland.

After only two years of hyperactive self-promotion various songs were demoed in late 2000 resulting in the New Zealand release *6Twenty* (2001); it was greeted with ecstatic reviews. It would be another year before the rest of the world officially got to hear this succinct 13-track adrenalized assault, showcasing some of the band's finest qualities, chief among them being the ability to play at two speeds: fast and faster. Like Motörhead playing the MC5, or AC/DC channelling the spirit of the Stooges, they mashed together the chaotic live energy of their favourite bands – outfits such as The Dictators, The Dead Boys and Ramones. The set featured three covers: Johnny Thunders' "Pirate Love", Guitar Wolf's "Invader Ace" and New Zealand punk band The Scavengers' "Mysterex"; there was no mistaking where this group were coming from, with Dion and Jimmy's shared vocal yells battling valiantly with the speedfreak riffing. Of their own tunes, standouts included "Rock'n'roll Motherfucker", "Heartbreaker" and the excellently sleazy single "Get Loose".

More singles followed, not least the strutting "Ladies Man", while performances in the UK and at the South By Southwest shindig in Austin, Texas, set them up as one of the antipodean bands most likely to clean up in the resurgent wave of good old fashioned rock.

 6Twenty
2002; Flying Nun/Infectious

The energy levels stay high throughout this smokin' slab of raw power. From the snotty attitude of punk to the loose sleaze of garage rock, it's all here for your delectation.

DANZIG

Formed Los Angeles, US, 1987

Black metal can mean hyper-speed thrash metal delivered with the sulphurous whiff of hell about it, or, in the hands of **Danzig**, a

sound akin to AC/DC providing the soundtrack to a black mass.

The diminutive, grimly tattooed and musclebound **Glenn Danzig** began his occult-loving career trajectory fronting seminal horror punks the **Misfits** in the late 70s and early 80s, where he indulged his love of B-movie schlock and cartoon violence. After taking the band to its logical conclusion he turned his attentions to a slightly more metallified direction with **Samhain** – meaning 'summer's end' – still dwelling lyrically on all things dark and creepy, but with a subtle twist of the satanic. Both bands enjoyed a level of success but remained essentially underground, cultivating a suitably weird audience of goths and punks – it was devil music for spooky kids of the night.

By 1987, however, Danzig felt it was time to take the music in another direction, so with guitarist **Johnny Christ** and bassist **Eerie Von** (both from Samhain) and renowned hardcore punk drummer **Chuck Biscuits** (ex-Black Flag, Circle Jerks, DOA) and a new deal inked with Def American he set about creating *Danzig* (1988). Kicking off with the spiralling evil groove of "Twist Of Cain" it was a brutally effective, if relatively simplistic vehicle for the moody singer's pagan and satanic musings. Glenn Danzig's evil Elvis croon and yelp had been fused to a series of economical and churning heavy blues riffs. And with his stock riding high due to Metallica having covered a couple of early Misfits tunes – "Last Caress" and "Green Hell"– the band supported Hetfield, Ulrich and co while they promoted *...And Justice For All*.

Where the first album had been rather basic and bare in the arrangements department, *Danzig II – Lucifuge* (1990) was a far more satisfying effort. Sure enough there were plenty of straightahead black-hearted rockers in the mould of the debut, but tunes such as "Blood And Tears" introduced elements of dark romance, while the loping and sinister "Killer Wolf" and "I'm The One", with its bluesy acoustic slide guitar, played up to the satanic Elvis image. The best was yet to come, however, with *Danzig III – How The Gods Kill* (1992). Wrapped in suitably disturbing

Glenn Danzig: Smell the glove, baby.

artwork, provided by HR Giger, it took the desire to experiment even further with lusher arrangements and a bleak atmosphere of doomed romance pervading the entire set. Standout cuts included the sultry title track and pounding "Dirty Black Summer". The same year found Danzig, in typical maverick style, releasing *Black Aria*, a classical album based upon the fall of Lucifer from heaven. Meanwhile, *Thrall – Demonsweatlive* (1993), a part-live/part-studio effort, made no bones about Danzig's musical heritage with a cover of the classic Presley track "Trouble".

At this point, ironically, it was a live version of "Mother" which broke the band into the mainstream with bizarre consequences. The lean and driven rock of the cut was over half a decade old and somewhat at odds with the direction the group were heading with *Danzig IV* (1994). With confusion in the air, the album proved to be something of a disappointment for new fans who expected more in the mould of the single, while older fans were reminded of just how tough Danzig could sound.

With more industrial-flavoured bands gradually coming to the fore Danzig took notice and pulled together a new band – **Joey Castillo** (drums), **Joseph Bishara** (keyboards/programming) and **Josh Lazie** (bass) along with contributions from guitarists **Mark Chaussee** and **Jerry Cantrell** (**Alice In Chains**). The aim was to incorporate cutting edge noise-mongering into a searing guitar-heavy attack. The result – *Danzig 5: Blackacidevil* (1996), released on Halloween – was doomed to failure. The songs weren't strong enough and it seemed as if Danzig, in his singular desire never to make the same album twice, was losing sight of just who his fans were. In addition, in some strange and twisted label dealings, Disney ended up as the company ultimately responsible for controlling Hollywood Records, the label to which the band were signed. The story goes that they didn't much appreciate the Danzig image and so didn't push the record.

Now in limbo, but not having learned his lesson, Danzig took three years to return with *Danzig 6:66 Satan's Child*, yet another delve into chilling industrial metal. Only the bluesy closing track "13" came anywhere close to echoing the finer timbre of the earlier albums. It was a heavy work-out and most fans just couldn't be bothered to pump those satanic cyber-steroids with the same conviction any longer. *Live On The Black Hand Side* (2001) at least incorporated the later, more clinical sounds with the burning analogue passion of early material. But with *Danzig 777: I Luciferi* (2002) and *Circle Of Snakes* (2004) the frowning crooner was back on more familiar ground and utilizing a traditional guitar, bass and drums line-up once more.

● Danzig
1988; Def American

AC/DC and Black Sabbath figure large in the occult scheme of things here. Dripping with menace and darkness, the songs have groove and bite even if it is all a little two-dimensional.

● Danzig II – Lucifuge
1990; Def American

More sensual and organic sounding than the debut. Danzig exercises his bluesy bellow on songs that sound like they have been properly crafted rather than simply bolted together.

● Danzig III – How The Gods Kill
1992; Def American

Arguably the best of the early albums, with oodles of atmosphere and a bleak gothic gloom hanging heavily over proceedings.

THE DARKNESS

Formed London, UK, 2000

There was, for many heavy music fans of a certain age, a golden period for metal: the 1980s. It was a decade of denim, leather, spandex and ridiculously big hair. Men wielding guitars were rock gods and fun was the be all and end all; nothing was too over-the-top when done in the name of entertainment. This era, however, came to a sudden grinding halt when grunge appeared. High-octane musicianship came a poor second to misery and angst; plaid shirts became the new fashion and all the hairspray jockeys who had enjoyed huge popularity began to feel a distinct chill blowing around their tightly trousered lunch boxes. For around a decade this sorry state of affairs persisted until a British band who didn't give a damn about musical trends and fashions, and working under the unlikely name of **The Darkness**, appeared on the scene.

The beginnings of The Darkness can be charted back to the unremarkable Suffolk town of Lowestoft where brothers **Justin** (vocals/guitar) and **Dan Hawkins** (guitar) grew up enjoying heavy music of a distinctly 80s variety and playing in covers bands. As the 90s kicked in they moved to London to get involved in the music business. They hooked up with **Frankie Poullain** (bass) to form **Empire**, a short-lived outfit lacking in both direction and conviction; the more indie-ish style of music just didn't suit anyone involved. Empire crumbled but the

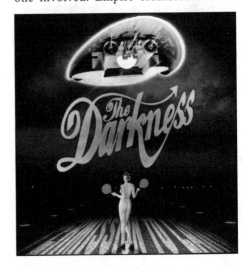

desire to rock was still strong and Dan persuaded Justin to both play guitar and put his amazingly shrill vocals at the forefront of their next project. They chose the most inappropriate name they could think of and thus was born a modern rock phenomenon, but not before Poullain was invited back on bass and old friend **Ed Graham** was seated behind the drums.

The time spent rethinking their creative direction had resulted in a band that was as focused on image as it was on the music, which drew on a myriad of 70s and 80s rock and metal. Their first UK gig took place at the Camden HQ club in early 2001 and the impression they made was astonishing. Word immediately began to spread about the band that time forgot. Graham and Dan Hawkins wouldn't have looked out of place in the line-up of AC/DC circa 1977, while Poullain sported an unlikely porn star moustache reminiscent of spacey guitarist Uli John Roth and was developing an unhealthy obsession with bandanas; centre stage, however, was the flamboyant presence of Justin Hawkins who drew as much comment for his tiger-skin catsuits as his ability to rip out guitar solos; he was a visual cross between Freddie Mercury and David Lee Roth. The fans loved it, while critics couldn't work out if this was all some sort of cunningly crafted practical joke. This cynical observation wasn't helped by the band's inbuilt sense of fun and irony – true, they looked like they had wandered in from a 70s fancy dress party but they rocked like the proverbial bastards. Their US debut was in the same year and took place during the South By Southwest music festival at Maggie Mae's in Austin, Texas.

Those who dismissed The Darkness's progress as some freak aberration suited only to touring the cabaret circuit were soon presented with physical recorded evidence of the band's ability to pull off some amazing studiobound pyrotechnics. The *I Believe In A Thing Called Love* EP was released in the summer of 2002 – the title track, backed with "Love Is Only A Feeling" and "Love On The Rocks With No Ice", raising more than just a knowing little smile. The EP sold out of its limited pressings and both Radio 1 and Xfm picked up on the band. In February 2003 the band released the expletive-riddled "Get Your Hands Off My Woman" and narrowly missed the Top 40, but they did earn themselves Single Of The Week in Kerrang!. The UK's metal fans were quickly catching on, however, and "Growing On Me" reached #11 in the singles charts while the album *Permission To Land* (2003) debuted at #2.

As a first album *Permission* was perhaps overly reliant on previously available material – it featured many of the songs already released on singles – but there was no denying the exuberantly dynamic and notably vintage flavour to the proceedings. The cover art said it all really – a spaceship being waved in to land by a naked woman in high heels. Opener "Black Shuck" rolled in on Angus Young-like guitar licks before bounding into a tongue-in-cheek tale about a supernaturally beast-like dog, and "Get Your Hands Off My Woman" appeared in all its potty-mouthed glory. There was even time for some genuine Zippos-in-the-air balladry in the form of "Love Is Only A Feeling".

By this point The Darkness were basking in the glow, despite the undercurrent of criticism that they were more reminiscent of Spinal Tap than a band with real longevity. Whatever the naysayers muttered, however, nothing could alter the fact that The Darkness were one of the must-see bands on the summer festival circuit. And when "I Believe In A Thing Called Love" was rereleased it went to #2 in the singles chart, followed some months later by their bid for the Christmas #1 slot with the smirk-inducingly titled "Christmas Time (Don't Let The Bells End)". They didn't quite make it, but early 2004 found the band capitalizing with mid-paced rocker "Love Is Only A Feeling".

All this chart activity and near-constant touring inevitably made the award-dishing machinery of the music and entertainment industry grind into action, even though The Darkness were – shock, horror – a rock band. They walked away with several Brit Awards in 2004, for Best Group, Best Rock Act and Best Album. Cue yet more rumblings of criticism from established acts and critics.

Joke band? Flash-in-the-pan novelty act? Or perhaps the next Queen? Only time will tell. For now there is no denying that it is a relief to experience modern rock drawing so extravagantly and successfully on a time when fun meant watching bizarrely dressed, hairy blokes strutting around a distant festival stage while bombed out of your brain on cider. And if it opens the heavily bolted door to more over-the-top mainstream metal then that can only be a good thing.

Permission To Land
2003; Must Destroy Music/Atlantic

An explosion of shamelessly borrowed riffs and licks it might be, but this album is packed with immensely catchy choruses and ridiculously overblown guitar solos. A sly sense of humour will have you chuckling while you dust off your old air guitar.

THE DATSUNS

Formed Cambridge, New Zealand, 1995

It's hard to believe that a country where sheep outnumber people could produce a band hailed as the force to save rock'n'roll. But that's exactly what happened when **The Datsuns**, originally named **Trinket**, decided to take the music they had been thrashing out for the best part of six years to the world.

The story starts unsensationally enough with a bunch of kids meeting at school and starting a band, eventually adopting the band moniker, in true Ramones style, as their surnames. In the mid-90s **Dolf Datsun** (bass/vocals) was caught up in the enthusiasm of the US pop-punk explosion spearheaded by the likes of Green Day and felt the urge to make some noise of his own. He grabbed his mate **Phil Datsun** (guitar) before they both approached the only kid in school with a drum kit, **Matt Datsun**, to be their sticksman. About a year later they hooked up with **Christian Datsun** (lead guitar), an older mate of Dolf's brother, who would prove to be the band's classic rock director. A self-taught musician, Christian had grown up marvelling at the vintage heavy rock vibes that could be found on slabs of dusty vinyl from charity stores. He wasn't doing much, so he reckoned he might as well enjoy some guitar mayhem and see where a little luck and dedication might take this new band.

They harboured a love of modern sounds but the writing sensibility of previous generations of rockers. A typical show would find them indulging in all the preposterous shape-throwing of yesteryear combined with the immediacy of garage punk; it was basic,

bluesy hard rock delivered with the venom of youth. So powerful was their toxic brew that they won their local Battle of the Bands competition in both 1997 and 1998. They set up their own label, Hellsquad Records, and at the turn of the millennium began releasing the occasional single. Needless to say, the loose'n'legless likes of "Supergyration" and "Fink For The Man" are now collectors' items.

As their reputation for Who-like live shows spread across New Zealand and Australia they began to set their sights, as AC/DC had before them, on Europe and the UK in particular. A handful of shows in early 2002 found the media salivating at the prospect of having yet another awesome band emerge from nowhere, proudly sporting the definite article. The Datsuns started their run of gigs on a shoestring and by the end found various labels falling over themselves to pick up their hotel bills. They eventually signed to Virgin satellite V2.

When *The Datsuns* (2002) finally emerged it was everything a classic rock fan could desire, combining the raw riffery of AC/DC with the arcane splendour of *Machine Head*-era Deep Purple, spiked with a healthy dose of punky brattishness. True to their rock ideals the Datsuns capitalized on their burgeoning fan base by touring relentlessly with like-minded bands such as The Von Bondies and The Hellacopters, and by spitting out snotty singles such as "MF From Hell" and "Harmonic Generator" – just two of the standout cuts from their fine debut.

The trusty retro metal formula was given another spin with "Blacken My Thumb" in early 2004 before *Outta Sight/Outta Mind* screeched into view in a hail of ballsy heavy rock riffs and greasy garage attitude.

The Datsuns
2002; Sweet Nothing/V2

Loud, raucous, unreconstructed blues rockers belted out with genuine fire and fury. Any one who remembers the first generation of heavy rockers will love this, as will those brought up with MTV-approved pop-punk.

Outta Sight/Outta Mind
2004; Hellsquad/V2

If the debut was their calling card then this one shoots to thrill with no small amount of style. They just plug 'em in and strap 'em on for a raw and raucous hoedown.

Death

Formed Florida, US, 1983; disbanded 2001

What better name for a metal band? Especially one concentrating so fixedly on the snuffing out of life? The sonic blood-letting career of mainman **Chuck Schuldiner** (guitar/vocals) is one of the most celebrated in the development of death metal as a thrash sub-genre. **Death** were the daddies of this hack'n'slay brand of guitar violence, and any-one with even the vaguest wish to count themselves as practitioners of extreme noise, from Carcass to Deicide, from Obituary to Cannibal Corpse, would count Schuldiner's unholy racket as a major influence.

At a time when bands such as Metallica and Anthrax were beginning to up the speed quotient of metal in general, Schuldiner had an altogether nastier, messier vision in mind. For a short while Schuldiner's nascent band went by the name of **Mantas** and featured **Rick Rozz** (guitar) and **Kam Lee** (drums) as part of an early line-up hellbent on creating as monstrous a thrash beast as possible. They went through the usual procedure of belting out live and demo tapes while searching for that ideal sound.

When Schuldiner finally got round to actually recording anything worthy of atten-tion, however, it was after a move to San Francisco, and with drummer **Chris Reifert**, his former bandmates having moved on to form **Massacre** in 1985. The product of Schuldiner's twisted imagination – and multi-instrumen-tal talents – was *Scream Bloody Gore* (1987), a brutal and disturbing slice of thrash that was both extremely primitive and highly addictive. The group of zombies on the sleeve quenching their thirst with goblets of blood said it all, as did the band's scythe-emblazoned logo. And for those who dared venture within the shadowy realm of Death there were songs such as 'Regurgitated Guts", "Zombie Ritual" and "Baptized In Blood" on offer. The legendary seeds of the Florida death scene had thus been sown.

His mission to kick start a record-ing career accomplished, Schuldiner headed back to Florida to re-recruit Rick Rozz (back from the dead, presumably), **Terry Butler** (bass) and **Bill Andrews** (drums) for the following year's *Leprosy* album. Little had changed bar the produc-tion, the blazing thrash display placing Death firmly at the vanguard of underground metal, which probably came as something of a relief to those a tad disappointed by Slayer's *South Of Heaven*, one of the most eagerly awaited thrash albums of the time.

By the time of 1990's *Spiritual Healing* Rozz had been replaced by **James Murphy** and hints of melody – nothing overtly hum-mable, mind you – were creeping into the mix, though Schuldiner was proving to be something of a single-minded operator when it came to the way Death functioned as a band. Amazingly Schuldiner pulled out of a proposed European tour leaving the other members to blunder on without him. Needless to say the critics were not kind.

It was at this point that any doubters had their mind's laid to rest: Death was Schuldiner's little monster and he was pre-pared to do whatever was required to make it a top-flight thrash unit for the 90s – and that included having what basically amounted to a revolving door line-up. *Human* (1991) was the first product of an all new line-up which was notable for the proficiency of drummer **Sean Reinert**. The technical and progressive power of the set made the primal bludgeon of their debut sound amateurish; but Schuldiner still wasn't happy. A compilation,

DEATH METAL

Trying to establish just what death metal is can be very confusing, a situation confounded by extreme metal's proliferation of sub-genres, all borrowing from each other's style. Here are the basics.

The term death metal really means an increase in the brutality quotient compared to thrash. 80s thrash metal was known for its speed and intensity, but it wasn't long before bands were incorporating more outrageous elements into the music to continually up the shock value. Generalizing hugely, death metal concentrated on morbid and gruesome lyrical matter (hence the hair-splitting sub-sub-genre of **gore metal**) and dispensed with some of thrash's more melodious aspects; throw in some incredibly fast blast-beat drum patterns and incorporate some growling vocals and you have death. Often dubbed 'cookie monster' vocals, after the children's TV series *Sesame Street*'s gruff-voiced, biccy-chomping character, the idea of the lead singer sounding thoroughly evil is a key aspect to a convincing death metal identity. Just to make things really confusing, none of these are hard and fast rules as bands are forever pushing the boundaries and never oblige by fitting neatly into a pigeonhole.

It is usually accepted that death metal became linked with specific locales and countries. In the US the Florida scene of the mid- to late 80s was a hotbed of deathly invention, with bands such as **Death, Morbid Angel, Obituary** and **Deicide** being representative of the sound; lyrically, Deicide could well be compared to black metal in that their stance is virulently anti-Christian, all of which shows how tricky it can be to tick off check boxes when defining a genre. The Florida sound is also often associated with the Morrisound studios where many of the leading death bands recorded their seminal albums.

Meanwhile, in the UK, among the chief pioneers of this music were **Carcass**, who brought with them, not only gore by the bucketload, but a hardcore punk sensibility. Their early albums, such as *Reek Of Putrefaction* and *Symphonies Of Sickness*, are acknowledged classics of **grindcore**, another confusing tag dreamt up to describe the racket produced by the legendary **Napalm Death**, who in turn were influenced by underground proto-grind bands such as **Repulsion** and **Siege**. To most ears there is little difference between grind and death bar their origin, especially as by the early 90s Napalm Death had moved in a more focused death metal direction; in other words, they began writing songs. This new sound was dubbed by some as melodic death metal. Just to illustrate the twisted cross-pollination effect taking place in the late 80s, the short-lived but influential **Terrorizer** boasted future members of both Morbid Angel and Napalm Death in its ranks.

Sweden was also getting in on the act, with early death metal acts such as **Carnage, Entombed, Edge Of Sanity** and **Dismember**. As the Swedish scene evolved in the early to mid-90s the bands gradually began to incorporate increasing amounts of melody – much as Carcass had done – along with more progressive touches. This created yet another style, often dubbed the **Gothenburg scene** (named, naturally enough, after the city where many of the bands were based), though it is probably fairer to describe it as Scandinavian death metal, given the number of bands and the pervasive, border-hopping sound.

rather weakly titled *Fate* (1992), helped plug the gap while another version of Death was being prepared. It was a worthy collection of tunes, but what the hordes were baying for was fresh blood.

The next rhythmic backbone of the unit included drummer **Gene Hoglan** (ex-Dark Angel). Now famed for his ultra-technical slamming style, Hoglan lasted for only two albums – the magnificently weighty *Individual Thought Patterns* (1993) and *Symbolic* (1995).

Death was then effectively put on hold while Schuldiner explored slightly more melodic climes with **Control Denied**, though the future line-up of the new band seemed to be interchangeable with output under the Death brand – guitarist **Shannon Hamm** and drummer **Richard Christy** featuring in both units. Bassist **Scott Clendenin** completed the new Death line-up which issued *The Sound Of Perseverance* (1998), once

Schuldiner had decided to put Control Denied on hold.

With his Death cravings satisfied, Schuldiner turned his attentions back to Control Denied, releasing the satisfyingly complex *The Fragile Art Of Existence* (1999) featuring **Tim Aymar** on more traditional metal vocals – a stark change in style compared to Schuldiner's usual vocal outpourings. That same year the legendary thrash-meister was diagnosed as suffering from cancer, which effectively resulted in Death issuing two live albums – *Live In LA (Death & Raw)* (2001) and *Live In Eindhoven* (2001) – basically to help pay for Schuldiner's medical bills prior to his untimely demise.

A legendary figure in the world of extreme metal, Schuldiner's legacy is a catalogue of classic, deathly delights which is sure to influence future metallers for years to come. Work had begun on a new Control Denied album, tentatively titled *When Machine And Man*

Collide; whether the remaining members will complete it for release remains to be seen.

◉ Scream Bloody Gore
1987; Combat

A cult classic, absolutely drenched in horror and gore. The lead provided by Schuldiner on this seminal slab of death metal would go on to influence just about every band in the genre.

◉ Human
1991; Relativity

By now they were largely eschewing the overt slasherama horror of their early work and concentrating on the horrors and fears of the mind. An essential slice of mid-period Death.

◉ The Sound Of Perseverance
1998; Nuclear Blast

A delightfully demented latter-day album brimming with insanely heavy riffing and Schuldiner's wild lead style. Lots of tunes about the pain of existence nailed firmly to a more progressive and complex approach – sadly it would be their last studio album.

DEEP PURPLE

Formed London, UK, 1967; disbanded 1976; re-formed 1984

Deep Purple: two words synonymous with classic heavy rock and all that implies – the excess, the glamour, the power, not to mention the sheer, ball-busting volume which bagged them a well-earned accolade from the *Guinness Book of Records,* crediting them with being the "loudest group in the world". As a band, they embody it all: the volatile artistry, the genius musicianship, the bust-ups and the reunions.

The band's inception dates all the way back to 1967 when former **Searchers** drummer **Chris Curtis** recruited guitarist **Ritchie Blackmore** and keyboard wizard **Jon Lord** to a band called **Roundabout**. Needless to say that outfit went the way of so many fledgling projects – straight to hell. With Curtis's departure in stepped **Ian Paice** (drums), **Nick Simper** (bass) and **Rod Evans** (vocals). Thankfully passing on the name Concrete God, they assumed the moniker

that would see them become one of the biggest heavy rock bands on the planet.

Basing their style around the sound of US band Vanilla Fudge, they produced four albums that, admittedly, sound pretty dated to modern ears. *Shades Of Deep Purple* (1968) was their first effort, preceded by a reworked version of Joe South's hit "Hush", which went Top 5 in the States. They weren't so much about heavy rock as 60s pop, what with Evans crooning in a Neil Diamond stylee – they even covered Diamond's "Kentucky Woman" for their next single. *The Book Of Taliesyn* (1968) and *Deep Purple* (1969) offered more of the same, while *Concerto For Group And Orchestra* (1970) was exactly that, a piece driven by Lord and Blackmore's love of all things classical. By this point Evans and Simper had been replaced by the turbo-lunged **Ian Gillan** and **Roger Glover**; the definitive line-up had been achieved and a rethink was in order.

The new direction harnessed a bombastic heavy blues thunder. The raw and majestic *Deep Purple In Rock* (1970) followed, giving them a hit single in "Black Night". As for the album's cover: the faces of the band carved Mount Rushmore-style set the seal on what lay within. It was a classic that relied on Gillan's marrow-curdling scream and penetrating range to propel the songs into heady realms well beyond the lighter material that had been peddled mere months before.

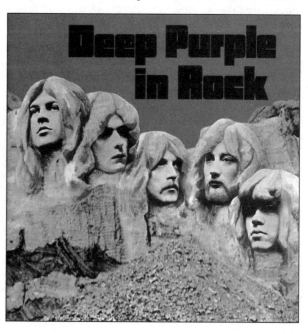

"Speed King" kicked off the record with a suitably zippy riff before spiralling off to explore the furthest regions of Blackmore and Lord's imaginations; "Blood Sucker" bounced along on a menacing blues guitar motif occasionally drilled through by Gillan's shrill shriek; the epic "Child In Time", clocking in at a marvellously excessive ten minutes plus, was an obvious highlight allowing yet more classically inspired progressive noodling. It was a formula that carried over to their concerts and formed the basis for lengthy instrumental duels and jams, Lord and Blackmore borrowing freely from all manner of sources – from nursery rhymes to Mozart and Bach.

Gillan headed off briefly to appear as the lead in *Jesus Christ Superstar* before *Fireball* (1971) appeared and injected a sense of humour into the straight-up progressive sound of ...*In Rock*. This was especially evident in "Anyone's Daughter" where Gillan's skill with off-the-wall lyrics and clever phrasing came to the fore. The improvement in production and strident growth in confidence found its perfect expression in what is generally regarded as one of the best heavy rock albums of all time: *Machine Head* (1972), which topped the UK charts for three weeks and went into the US Top 10. It featured some of the band's finest songs, including timeless slices of wildman rock such as "Space Truckin'" and the belting "Highway Star", while "When A Blind Man Cries" was a soulful and smouldering slowie. However, *Machine Head* will always be known as the album containing *that* song. Only "Stairway To Heaven" shares the same level of notoriety. Yes, we're talking about the most famous riff in metal – "Smoke On The Water". The song immortalized a now mythical incident during the recording of the album when the planned venue, the Montreux Casino (Switzerland), burned down. The result has become one of the most widely recognized soundbites of the last 30 years; the album was eventually completed on a mobile studio in the corridors of another hotel.

The Machine Head set yielded *Made In Japan* (1972), a revered and genre-defining live album. It captured the band at their peak as they ended an almost nonstop, three-year period of touring. They were a hugely successful unit, but inevitable rifts were forming. The fiery tension between Gillan, Glover and Blackmore came to a head following the release of the criminally underrated *Who Do We Think We Are* (1973). It launched with the strident "Woman From Tokyo", before heading off into Gillanesque territory with "Mary Long", the groovy "Rat Bat Blue" and ballsy "Smooth Dancer".

Gillan and Glover jumped ship to start solo careers and the band brought in the then unknown **David Coverdale** (vocals) and **Glenn Hughes** (bass, ex-**Trapeze**). Their next two albums, *Burn* (1974) and *Stormbringer* (1974), both went Top 10 in the UK and subsequent tours were successful, especially Stateside. *Burn* lived up to its title, Coverdale showcasing an impressive vocal style; *Stormbringer*, however, was anything but, the band's fire of old somewhat quenched by Hughes and Coverdale's penchant for lightweight funkiness. The infamously irascible Blackmore was none too pleased and quit to form **Rainbow**. **Tommy Bolin** took over for *Come Taste The Band* (1975), but it wasn't enough to stop the group collapsing. Tragically, Bolin's heroin habit led to his untimely demise after an overdose in late 1976.

The remaining members went off to start other projects with varying degrees of success – Coverdale, of course, eventually formed **Whitesnake** – while Deep Purple compilations and cash-ins kept popping up from time to time. And that's how things stayed until 1984 when the five members of the classic line-up couldn't resist the temptation any longer and re-emerged with *Perfect Strangers*, a strong comeback, given a boost by the cheeky single "Knocking At Your Back Door". *The Anthology* (1985) raided the back catalogue for the umpteenth time while the band worked on their next effort – *The House Of Blue Light* (1987).

Despite the fact that the band were making a go of it, there already seemed to be trouble brewing: during the subsequent tour Blackmore began refusing to play "Smoke On The Water". The decidedly ropy live album *Nobody's Perfect* (1988) kept the bandwagon rolling, but it was an unhappy unit that began the accompanying US tour. All obligations fulfilled, Gillan quit. Bizarrely, instead of this sealing the band's fate, Blackmore called on his old Rainbow singer **Joe Lynn Turner** to step in and record *Slaves & Masters* (1990), which is only recommended to incorrigible completists. The aberrant line-up didn't last for long; Gillan returned for *The Battle Rages On...* (1993), its title accurately describing Purple's situation. Blackmore seemingly couldn't stand being in the band with Gillan reinstated and he dramatically quit to reactivate Rainbow on the eve of a Japanese tour. His replacement for tour duties was genius guitarist **Joe Satriani**, who was eventually replaced by **Steve Morse** (ex-**Kansas**, ex-**Dixie Dregs**) for *Purpendicular* (1996) and *Abandon* (1998). The feeling of amped-up wildness was almost tangible on the new material.

The arena-sized touring continued, largely unhindered, into the new millennium with the band enjoying their seemingly never-ending popularity. The only change to this legendary unit was Lord bowing out to be replaced by **Don Airey** (ex-pretty much everybody!) by the time *Bananas* (2003) was released.

Deep Purple In Rock
1970; EMI

It's a much over-used description, but this really is a classic. From the iconic sleeve to the tunes within. Worth owning alone for the absurdly lengthy "Child In Time".

Fireball
1971; EMI

Another classic, this takes *...In Rock* and expands the textures and sound, improving things with a fuller production and more terrific songs.

Machine Head
1972; EMI

This set is the daddy of early-70s heavy rock. Among the belters and bluesy workouts you will find *that* riff driving *that* song. Rock would never be the same again.

Made In Japan
1972; EMI

It's worth picking this up in expanded form for all the extra tracks. Great fun, especially when Gillan cracks up during "Strange Kind Of Woman".

Who Do We Think We Are
1973; EMI

Criminally ignored, the internal pressures the band were facing overshadowed the music. There's plenty of quality material, especially the cracking "Woman From Tokyo".

Burn
1974; EMI

Some thought Coverdale wouldn't be able to replace Gillan. Well, he doesn't have quite the same power but his flexible yodelling is extremely confident.

Perfect Strangers
1984; EMI

It's almost as though they never went away. A logical progression from their 70s persona and helped by a clear and direct production.

Abandon
1998; EMI

Even with Morse in place of Blackmore, Purple are a tight and consummate band. This is the sound of a group that can write and record quality tunes with ease.

DEF LEPPARD

Formed Sheffield, UK, 1977

Emerging at the tail end of the 1970s, **Def Leppard** are without doubt one of the biggest rock bands in the world; their reputation was built upon multi-platinum albums, vast stadium-choking tours and, of course, their frustrating tendency to take an age to create each new album.

Joe Elliot's solo weightlifting spot always gets a good reaction.

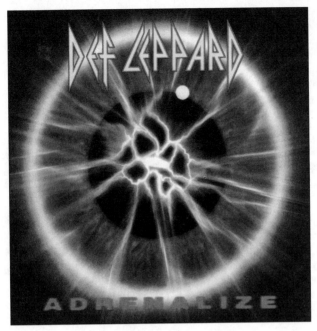

Over recent years they may have slipped increasingly into delivering something akin to soft metal, but it wasn't always so. The early line-up put together by **Rick Savage** (bass) included **Pete Willis** (guitar) and **Tony Kenning** (drums), a trio who went by the name **Atomic Mass** and who, as legend has it, spent much of their time rehearsing at their local comprehensive school. When **Joe Elliott** (vocals) entered the picture the band acquired the name Deaf Leopard and moved their rehearsals to a spoon factory; not surprising really considering Sheffield's reputation for cutlery production – metal of a different variety all together. The line-up needed more guitar fire power and **Steve "Steamin'" Clark** was the fella to provide it.

Inspired by classic artists such as T-Rex, Mott The Hoople, Thin Lizzy, Queen and David Bowie and with their reputation for a tightly rocking set gradually spreading, the next step was to get a record out. Before history could be made, however, Kenning was replaced by **Frank Noon**. *The Def Leppard EP*, more commonly referred to as "Getcha Rocks Off", was put together over two days and released in 1979 on their own Bludgeon Riffola label, the name inspired by a comment made by a journalist in a less than flattering review. Before they could make any more progress they had to deal with the small mat-

ter of acquiring a permanent drummer; **Rick Allen** was the skin pounder who got the job.

The EP sold out quickly and sessions for local Radio Hallam and John Peel made even greater waves, attracting the attention of Phonogram Records, who snapped up the band and re-pressed the EP before issuing "Wasted" as a single. The country's rock audience now fully primed, *On Through The Night* (1980) was produced by veteran Judas Priest knob twiddler **Tom Allom** and went into the UK Top 20. For a debut, it was an extremely assured and glossy piece of work, a result of their manic rehearsals and what would become an obsessive preoccupation with studio perfection. Gigs followed with AC/DC in the UK and support slots in the US with Judas Priest among others. They went down a storm in America, where fans couldn't resist the fresh-faced Elliott blasting out "Hello America". In the UK, however, their Stateside antics were perceived as some sort of sellout and instead of their 1980 Reading festival appearance being a triumph, all they got was a hail of bottles.

In turn, their next album, *High 'n' Dry* (1981) just made the Top 30 in the UK. In America, however, the classy production job provided by the sonic maestro himself **Mutt Lange** pushed them even closer to stardom.

The real breakthrough, however, came with *Pyromania* (1983). The sessions that went into creating this masterpiece of ultra-commercial metal were painful, the band constantly striving to outdo themselves and to meet Lange's stringent quality threshold. Willis, already shaky after their draining tour schedule, was the first to buckle in an alcohol-induced haze. His drinking was getting in the way of the band's progress and he was replaced by **Phil Collen** (ex-**Girl**). Clark was also drinking, but managed to keep his act together sufficiently not to hamper things. Despite all this the quality of the tunes was undeniable. The run-off groove of the record bore the etched legend "If you're gonna be a bear...be a grizzly" and sure enough the music sounded huge. "Rock Rock (Till You

Drop)" was an epic opener; "Rock Of Ages" rode in on a loose celebratory rap before erupting into a massive chorus; "Die Hard The Hunter" explored a demobbed soldier's disturbed state of mind; even the love songs had some bite to them rather than simply being slushy ballads. The only thing that kept *Pyromania* off the top slot in the US was Michael Jackson's *Thriller.*

Such a major success story required a sequel and the band had to come up with a new set of songs to rival their global headlining stature: this was where their nascent tendency to obsess over detail began to take control. Lange had burned himself out producing albums for Foreigner and the Cars, so **Jim Steinman**, famed for helping create Meat Loaf's *Bat Out Of Hell*, was picked. His style was diametrically opposed to that of Lange, which meant his days were numbered. With recording sessions now on hold the band took a break at the end of 1984, which turned into one of the most difficult periods they would ever face.

On New Year's Eve Allen was involved in a car crash that severed his left arm. Massively traumatized, but unbowed, the drummer vowed to play again. This was eventually achieved by using a special customized electronic kit allowing certain drum effects to be triggered via pedals. Meanwhile, the production of the new album ground on at an interminable pace, even with Lange back in the hot seat. Doubtless, one thing that encouraged the band immensely was the rousing reception they received – especially Allen, making his first public appearance – at the 1986 Donington Monsters Of Rock festival.

During the show a handful of new tunes were aired, but it wasn't until 1987 that *Hysteria* arrived and, true to its epic genesis, it brought with it the band's craziest period. It debuted at #1 in the UK chart but took a staggering 49 weeks to reach the top in the US. If the record label had been looking for a mine of hit singles, they couldn't have been more pleased: "Pour Some Sugar On Me", "Love Bites", "Armageddon It", "Animal", "Rocket" and 'Hysteria" all enjoyed some sort of major chart action.

The subsequent touring saw the band introduce their concerts-in-the-round to allow a greater number of people to experience the Leppard up close and personal – or as personal as several thousand fans crammed into aircraft hangar sized-venues could get. This was touring on the scale of a military

invasion and the spectacle was captured on the video *In The Round In Your Face* (1989).

So successful was the album that when the Diamond Awards – for albums that have shifted over ten million units in the US alone – were first introduced in 1999 *Hysteria* was one of the first to receive the accolade. At the time, however, the band were worrying whether it would sell enough to offset the record's expenses. Clark was feeling the pressure again and spent some time checking in and out of rehab. Despite attempts to get him on an even keel he was found dead at his Chelsea flat in January 1991 after a drinking binge with a friend; he had overdosed on a mixture of alcohol, painkillers and antidepressants.

There was much speculation as to who would fit in as the new guitarist. *Adrenalize* (1992) was put together without Lange or a replacement for Clark. With the album finally out veteran axe-slinger **Viv Campbell** was announced as the new addition. Having already made a very low-key club debut with the band he was formally introduced to the world during the Freddie Mercury Tribute Concert at Wembley Stadium in April 1992.

For the first time since their early days, the band actually managed to get another set out the following year, but only because they had been asked for a new song for the soundtrack to *Last Action Hero*. Pushed for time, they provided "Two Steps Behind", a B-side which suddenly turned into a Stateside hit, prompting them to bolt together Retro-Active – basically a clutch of rarities and B-sides given a polish.

But that didn't mean a new studio album would follow: *Vault – Greatest Hits 1980-1995* (1995) concentrated on their former incarnation's chart triumphs.

Somehow, the group had managed to survive the cull of 80s rock bands brought on by the advent of grunge – largely because they had won over such a large mainstream audience – but were now up against the forces of nu-metal. Their answer was the rather puzzling *Slang* (1996), with its tougher production sound.

Comfortable and assured of their place in the rock superleague, *Slang* was the kind of detour from which the Leppard could announce a return to their classic sound. Only it would take another three years before the frothy metal of *Euphoria* turned up. Those who had been turned on by *Pyromania* and *Hysteria* breathed a huge sigh of relief.

True to form another three years passed before *X* rode into town boasting an even slicker combination of ballads and relatively sedate rockers. The fact that the band were collaborating with people such as **Andreas Carlsson** and **Per Aldeheim** (the team providing tunes for popsters such as Britney Spears and 'N Sync) should give an idea as to the sound of big pop ballads such as "Unbelievable".

This is what the Leppard have always striven for from the moment they wrote "Hello America": to be the biggest mainstream rock band in the world regardless of what critics might think of them. They now have nothing left to prove.

⊙ On Through The Night
1980; Vertigo

There is a certain naive charm to these polished rockers. There are gloriously cheesy titles galore ("Rock Brigade", "Answer To The Master") and you can almost feel them searching for that elusive hit.

⊙ High 'n' Dry
1981; Vertigo

Enter Lange and the first inklings of global hugeness. Just check out the MTV-rotated "Bringin' On The Heartache" for epic grandeur.

⊙ Pyromania
1983; Vertigo

A classic, no question. Massive riffs, even bigger choruses. It might be ready for the radio but it still bounces with bags of energy.

⊙ Hysteria
1987; Vertigo

A world-beating pop-metal gem. Absolutely packed with hit singles and with a massive production sound.

⊙ Euphoria
1999; Vertigo

A pleasing late-era concoction, which has more in common with the 80s version of the band than what was to follow.

DEFTONES

Formed California, US, 1989

Of all the bands lumped into the loose and ever-expanding nu- and alt-metal scene, Sacramento's **Deftones** must be one of the most primally powerful and experimental. Somehow the band has taken a harsh and complex sound and turned it into a commercially viable proposition, while at the same time preserving their own genre-defying approach.

The band's story begins with school friends **Chino Moreno** (vocals), **Chi Cheng** (bass), **Stephen Carpenter** (guitar) and **Abe Cunningham** (drums) – who joined the band after the departure of their original drummer **John Taylor** – getting together to thrash out their adolescent angst at various neighbourhood clubs' pay-to-play nights. The band's sound was raw and pitched together everything from disparate hip-hop and punk influences to balls-out heavy metal.

Chief in shaping their direction was Moreno's love of 80s pop, which brought a dark and brooding quality to his vocal style and would eventually lead to the band recording cover versions of songs by Depeche Mode and Duran Duran. However, anyone looking for an overt chart-friendly pop angle would have been disappointed with the early Tones – this was the sound of anger and frustration tempered with a melancholic vibe.

The years of practising and local reputation-building eventually paid off when they were picked up by Maverick Records – Madonna's label. What had originally started as a bunch of mates making what they regarded as a fun noise was to turn into a scene-altering movement. In the post-grunge environment of the mid-90s, heavy music fans were ready for something that blew all the traditional metal clichés clean out of the water and for a while, following the release of *Adrenaline* (1995), it was difficult not to mention Deftones in the same breath as the likes of Korn. The album was brutally aggressive in places, with Carpenter's abrasive down-tuned riffing and Moreno's tortured vocals delivering the kind of extreme gratification the fans demanded. This was balanced by an ability to pull back from the edge of the emotional precipice with quieter, more intricately wrought passages. Also deep in the mix was the influence of the burgeoning screamo noisecore scene, which gave the Deftones an off-the-wall non-linear feel.

By the band's own admission, while the debut captured the nu-spirit of the time, it was a less than fully focused effort. The follow-up, 1997's *Around The Fur*, however, was much tighter – in short, it was a monster. The opening "My Own Summer (Shove It)" not only received heavy radio airplay but MTV picked up on the video which guaranteed that the Deftones had finally arrived. Likewise, songs such as "Be Quiet And Drive (Far Away)" proved that they could write more accessible and relatively melodic tunes alongside the real scorchers. By now the band's live appearances had become legendary, with Moreno pouring so much heart and soul into his performance that it was exhausting just to watch.

The superb *White Pony* (2000) – which saw the addition of **Frank Delgado** on turntables – was the sound of a band truly getting to grips with their muse. The rage and fire was still very much apparent but with a definite desire to make more of the arty and pensively ambient edge they displayed on previous efforts. The fact that the album was leaked onto the Internet during the period when the Napster music file-sharing controversy was at its peak didn't prevent the album from hitting the #3 position in the US charts and narrowly missing the Top 10 in the UK.

Just to confuse matters for the fans the album was later rereleased in the US with the addition of "Back To School", a song that wasn't finished when the band's release deadlines were looming. Elsewhere the song became the lead track on the *Back To School* (2001) mini-LP, leading a largely live tracklisting.

With *White Pony*'s astonishing range of emotion and power, it was hard to see what new tricks the band could assemble to top it. When *Deftones* (2003) arrived, however, the group exceeded all expectations. The sound was dense and claustrophobic, layers of melody shrouded in distortion and pain, Moreno's anguished vocals veering from a tormented shriek to a strange and eerie croon, his lyrics peppered with trademark cryptic abstractions. The set indicated that the Deftones were at the top of their game; it peaked at #2 in the US charts and #7 in the UK.

The strength not just of songwriting but artistic vision evident in the new album underlined just how far they had come since the first heady rush of nu-metal. With the sound of the nu gradually fading, the Deftones genre-bending tendencies had led them to pursue their own unique sonic agenda, allowing them to both stand apart from the crowd and still be viewed as pioneers on the alternative scene. Recently they have been working on a new album with producer, Bob Ezrin, due out in 2005.

⊙ Adrenaline
1995; Maverick

An amazing debut, though it's easy to understand the Korn comparisons. Thick, heavy and tormented, this still stands as one of the best examples of nu-metal.

⊙ Around The Fur
1997; Maverick

The anti-songwriting aesthetic of noisecore meets melody and down-tuned metal to produce a breakthrough album. Absolutely packed with pulse-pounding slices of malignant mutant noise.

⊙ White Pony
2000; Maverick

Artful and emotional, the Deftones are developing beyond the mid-90s alternative metal scene that spawned them to coin a sound unlike anything else in metaldom.

⊙ Deftones
2003; Maverick

Progressive, cryptic and ultimately challenging, the most gratifying aspect of this album is its ability to both charm and challenge in equal measure.

DEICIDE

Formed Florida, US, 1987

Deicide, Florida's most controversial metal crew, seem to exist solely to get up the noses of religious groups across the world. As mainstays of the death metal scene they have progressed little beyond the basic template of evil thrash metal with a virulently anti-Christian stance, making them one of the longest-running death metal bands, alongside the state's other purveyors of extreme chaos, Morbid Angel. In leader **Glen Benton** (bass/vocals) they have a frontman who knows very well how to whip up a media storm, whether it be in interview, through his deliberately blasphemous lyrics, or provocative album art.

deftones *around the fur*

Initially formed as **Amon** and heavily influenced by bands such as Black Sabbath, Venom, Slayer and Death, the Deicide line-up was completed by **Eric** and **Brian Hoffman** (guitars) and **Steve Asheim** (drums). Benton wanted the band to sound like hell on earth, so the obligatory underground apprenticeship was served honing their blastbeats and razor-sharp riffing while touting around two demos, "Sacrificial" and "Feasting The Beast". Eventually Roadrunner picked them up and packed them off to the studio to get the music of Beelzebub locked down on tape. The result was *Deicide* (1990), a death metal album with all the trimmings; gruff, unearthly vocals, plenty of speed and loads of Christian-baiting lyrics; all together a delightful combination when you added in Benton's penchant for branding an inverted crucifix on his forehead.

Just how did he get to sound so evil? Could it be that he was possessed by demons using his body as a vehicle to deliver their misanthropic message? The songs were, for the most part, short stabs of brutality pointing the way forward.

Next came *Legion* (1992), an album that is still considered by the satanic death cognoscenti as Deicide's best. It was even more vicious and blasphemous than their debut, and Benton capitalized on the band's notoriety – for chucking offal at the crowds, among other things – by claiming in press interviews to enjoy torturing animals. Not only were religious groups up in arms but the animal rights brigade too, the more extreme of whom wasted no time in issuing death threats. One group even, allegedly, planted a bomb at one of the band's gigs in Stockholm. They needn't have bothered because in another piece of media-baiting Benton claimed that he would commit suicide upon reaching the age of 32. Still, it all helped to massage the band's reputation as firebrand Satanists and cement their place in the death metal hall of infamy.

Amon: Feasting The Beast (1993) was basically a collection of old demos providing an insight into the band's shady history. The real meat was saved for their next offering, *Once Upon The Cross* (1995). The album's initial sleeve featured a disembowelled Christ upon the cross, autopsy-style. The protests were loud and vociferous. Publicity assured, the offending image was replaced with a bloody shroud, clearly with a crucified figure

beneath. All of which served to enhance the unrelentingly fierce attack of the songs, none of which deviated significantly from the patterns already laid out. In fact, for the discerning death metal fan *Serpents Of The Light* (1997), *Insineratehymn* (2000) and *In Torment, In Hell* (2001) offered more of the same beastly delights, all of them building infernally upon the band's early blueprint. Only *When Satan Lives* (1998) broke the flow of studio-based nastiness by providing a live document.

Come 2003 and Deicide's deal with Roadrunner ended with *The Best Of Deicide*, an album some critical wags suggested ought to be a very short affair. And then off they went to Earache for *Scars Of The Crucifix* (2004), an album which proved that when it comes to satisfying the death-loving hoards – if ain't broke, don't fix it.

Deicide
1990; Roadrunner

Very tight, very fast, very everything in fact. An evil little debut with Benton's vocals sounding particularly hair-raising.

Legion
1992; Roadrunner

Even heavier and more horrible than their debut, this for many is the best of satanic death, a distillation of pure hatred for Christianity and precision delivery.

Scars Of The Crucifix
2004; Earache

They still haven't got this anti-Christian thing off their chests. Blisteringly fast and driven with hell's own fury.

DIAMOND HEAD

Formed Stourbridge, UK, 1977

The story of **Diamond Head** is one of the most frustrating fragments of the history of the New Wave Of British Heavy Metal. Hugely influential and highly talented, the band were formed by schoolfriends **Brian Tatler** (guitar) and **Duncan Scott** (drums), who roped in **Sean Harris** (vocals) and **Colin Kimberly** (drums). Formed at a time when punk was ascendant, the band stuck to their guns and never deviated from their desire to become one of the best metal acts in the UK. They gradually built up a sizeable grass-roots following, making them one of the leading contenders in the rapidly evolving New Wave, alongside bands such as Def Leppard, Saxon and Iron Maiden. Key to their complex, urgent, driven sound was Tatler's undeniable gift for the monster riff. There was seemingly no end to the epic sounds the band's guitarist could pull off; complementing this raw bludgeon was Harris's high-pitched, almost sensual vocal delivery – a timeless, thrilling combination of sonic silk and steel.

Despite the constant gigging, and championing by *Sounds* magazine, the weekly bible of metal in the 70s – there seemed to be few takers among the major record labels. So in true DIY style they decided to do things independently. In early 1980 "Shoot Out The Lights"/"Helpless" was followed a few months later by "Sweet And Innocent"/ "Streets Of Gold". Their live reputation for electrifying shows had created an audience hungry for their vinyl output, but without major backing the singles shifted largely through word of mouth and the time they spent on the *Sounds* metal chart.

Created relatively cheaply, their first long player came untitled and packaged with white labels in a white sleeve. It was eventually dubbed, obviously, the "white album" and occasionally *Lightning To The Nations*, after its lead track. Now a highly collectable item, the quality and brilliance of the seven tracks within was staggering, with Tatler's instinctive sense of dynamics giving the tunes far greater range and depth than many of their contemporaries. There was doomy Sabbath grind in the classic "Am I Evil?" and the thunderous "Helpless", but the whole venture was leavened by a mercurial spirit that many compared to Led Zeppelin's. True, there were Spinal Tap moments, not least the nine-minutes plus of "Sucking My Love". But even when they pandered to metal cliché, Diamond Head were in a completely different league. Two more independent singles followed in 1981 – "Waited Too Long" and the *Diamond Lights* EP – before finally MCA stepped in.

At this point the band had an enviable media profile and plenty of material ready to go. So what did the label do? Instead of whipping out an album they chose to issue yet more singles and EPs, and sent the band out on tour. When, finally, *Living On ... Borrowed Time* (1982) arrived it had quality stamped all over it, but also contained several rerecordings of older tracks and production that dampened the spirit of the band's sound. Some put this down to the band's naivety in the studio and their inability to fight their corner when dealing with producer Mike Hedges.

More studio problems arose with the sessions for *Canterbury* (1983): both Kimberly and Scott departed to be replaced by **Merv Goldsworthy** and **Robbie France** respectively. Despite all this, the album was a stunning and bold statement, pretty much summed up by the stomping opener "Makin' Music". And this was no ordinary heavy metal. Acoustic flourishes, additional percussion, and lush backing vocals plus the band's progressive tendencies gave it a level of detail that delighted and flummoxed in equal measure (assuming the record played properly – a pressing problem meant thousands of early copies were faulty).

After an unconvincing opening slot at the *Donington Monsters Of Rock* festival the pressure really was on. Back in the studio work was started on a new set, *Flight East*, which was never completed because the group were dropped and then split. One of the most promising bands of the era had bitten the dust thanks to mismanagement and label incompetence.

Harris went off to work with guitarist Robin George, which resulted in a one-album project called **Notorious**, and Tatler formed **Radio Moscow**.

And so it would have stayed had it not been for a certain fanboy named **Lars Ulrich** and his little old beat combo **Metallica**, who covered "Am I Evil?", "Helpless", "It's Electric" and "The Prince" at various times. What's more the undeniable influence of Tatler's riffing can be heard throughout Metallica's heavily NWOBHM-influenced thrash debut *Kill 'Em All*. All this plus a compilation titled *Behold The Beginning* (1986), put together by Ulrich and Tatler, kept the Diamond Head reputation alive during the 80s.

Following an invitation by Metallica to jam through a couple of their old songs during the encores of a gig at Birmingham NEC, the impetus was clearly there for Diamond Head to have another go. In 1990 Tatler and Harris got back together with bassust **Eddie Chaos** and drummer `Karl Wilcox` but were reticent to use their old name, choosing to gig as **Dead Reckoning** before finally opting for their original moniker. *Death And Progress* (1993) arrived, featuring new bassist **Pete Vukovic** and a host of metal stars eager to help out, including **Black Sabbath** guitarist **Tony Iommi**, **Megadeth** guitarist **Dave Mustaine** and, naturally, Lars Ulrich. Diamond Head opened for Metallica at the Milton Keynes Bowl in the summer of 1993 and the show was captured on tape for *Evil Live* (1994).

But it would be a further seven years before Tatler and Harris rejoined forces to work on some acoustic material. In 2002 they were offered a headline slot at the New Jersey Metal Meltdown festival (their first ever US gig) and the level of interest in the band's music was such that they returned to the studio to record a new album, which is now awaiting the right deal for its release…

⊙ Living On … Borrowed Time
1982; MCA

There are some great songs here. Not quite the major label debut they needed but essential to anyone who values riffs raining down like bullets.

⊙ Death And Progress
1993; Castle

A cracking comeback album which sadly failed to capture the grunge addled imagination of the day.

⊙ The White Album aka Lightning To The Nations 2001; Castle

The reissue of their classic debut includes a whole bunch of excellent single tracks as well. The songs still sound as energetic as when they were first written.

⊙ The Diamond Head Anthology: Am I Evil? 2004; Castle

The number of Diamond Head compilations is huge but this is the best with a great cross-section of material and some fine sleeve notes.

DIMMU BORGIR

Formed Norway, 1993

Within the gloomy confines of the black metal scene many acts toil away beyond the reach of sunlight, where the embrace of the underground allows them to spew forth their venomous anti-Christian vitriol with arrogant abandon. For some, however, the sheer quality of their musicianship and professionalism marks them as the real contenders.

As black metal matures beyond the basic template of the thrashy 80s originators, the wave of acts influenced by the early pioneers in the 90s have taken the sound even further, perhaps not into the mainstream of rock but well within the radar of most metal fans. **Dimmu Borgir** – named after a particularly spooky area of bizarrely shaped lava flows in Iceland – are among the Scandinavian scene's most respected bands. Their name literally translated means "dark fortress", an apt moniker considering the incredibly dramatic and atmospheric brand of orchestral metal in which they specialize. Think Cradle Of Filth without the theatrical concepts and Hammer horror fixation and you'll be halfway to understanding their appeal, which has led to international tours, festival appearances and Norwegian Grammy awards.

The formation of an outfit as dedicated and focused as Dimmu Borgir required driven individuals. In this case it was the unholy triumvirate of **Shagrath** (drums/vocals), **Erkekjetter Silenoz** (guitar/vocals), and **Tjodalv** (guitar), who, steeped in the traditions of old-school black metal, had developed their skills in a number of underground thrash bands. They hooked up with **Brynjard Tristan** (bass) and **Stian Aarstad** (keyboards) and set about creating their first record, *Inn I Evighetens Morke*, a seven-inch EP which materialized in 1994 on the suitably sinister-sounding label Necromantic Gallery. For such a small-scale production it did remarkably well, selling out rapidly and providing a taste of the misanthropic delights the band were preparing for a full-scale debut.

As with their initial release *For All Tid* (1995) was sung in Norwegian, but provided a much broader canvas for their ambitious vision. The use of keyboards was vital to the kind of sound they were aiming for. While their run-of-the-mill thrash brethren were largely content to explore the brutal possibilities of headspinning guitar speed and hyperkinetic drumming, Dimmu Borgir wanted atmosphere, the more ominous the better. They also wanted a gothic sense of romance and black-hearted, satanic rage. All these vital components came from a cunning use of synths and effects and the ever-present influence of classical music. Soundwise, it might have been a touch primitive, but there was no escaping the sense of icy foreboding.

The orchestrally motivated grimness was honed with *Stormblåst* (1996). The album was a more fully realized set of tunes, the demonic screech of the vocals carried by assuredly powerful arrangements detailing not only the band's anti-Christian stance, but an almost cinematic, atmosphere of horror and brutality. The major upheaval, though one which was necessary for the continued development of the band, was that Shagrath and Tjodalv switched instruments, putting the more photogenic Shagrath firmly in the role of frontman.

With a new bassist, **Nagash**, and the blossoming black metal scene, the band were in the perfect position to move for- ward. The only thing hindering their progress internationally was the use of their mother tongue. The last thing they needed was to exclude potential fans, so the *Devil's Path* EP was something of an experiment with English, which finally made their infernal shrieking a touch easier to deci- pher. Notably they included a cover ver- sion of Celtic Frost's classic "Nocturnal Fear" – a blast from the past if ever there was one.

For some, the group abandoning their mother tongue smacked of selling out, especially in the tightly knit and purist cir- cles of the Scandinavian underground, but for Dimmu it was a case of evolve or die.

Dimmu Borgir model M&S's new menswear range.

Their flexibility thus established they upped the ante magnificently with *Enthrone Darkness Triumphant* (1997). So far their albums had been released on relatively small indie labels, but with their notoriety growing on an almost daily basis they were on the verge of a major breakthrough. In stepped Nuclear Blast, and a majestic production job provided by **Peter Tägtgren** (Hypocrisy's guitarist). It was a partnership that would provide the band with some of their best and most successful albums. Despite signing to a label famed for the brutal heaviness of its roster, the lyrics to "Tormentor Of Christian Souls" were conspicuous by their absence from the sleeve notes – apparently the evil nature of the words was too much for even a heavy metal label to contemplate publishing.

A stunning album and high-profile tours – such as the *Gods Of Darkness* trek across Europe undertaken in the company of Cradle Of Filth and Dissection – ensured that Dimmu had truly arrived, with the addition of guitarist **Astennu** allowing Shagrath to concentrate solely on fronting.

Despite the success, the band's line-up was still undergoing the occasional tweak; their 1998 *Dynamo* festival slot marked the first appearance of new keyboard player **Mustis**. The same year saw the release of *Godless Savage Garden*, a mini-album containing a couple of new cuts, live material and some favourites from previous albums. Although it was essentially a stopgap effort the set earned the band their first Norwegian Grammy nomination.

The time bought by *Godless Savage Garden* went into polishing the monstrous slayer of an album, *Spiritual Black Dimensions* (1999). The passion and power evident on songs such as "The Blazing Monoliths Of Defiance" and "Arcane Lifeforce Mysteria" underlined the huge leap forward the group had made in creating a layered, darkly beautiful and ornate wall of noise. The clean vocals provided by guest singer **Simen Hastnaes** (**Borknagar**) brought a new dimension to the carefully constructed tales of malevolent misanthropy. By the end of the year he had also become the band's new bass player.

By the time of the next album yet more line-up changes had occurred. Founding member Tjodalv had decided to forego the manic touring lifestyle to concentrate on being a family man. His replacement was former **Cradle Of Filth** drummer **Nick Barker** who had just completed a touring stint with Borknagar. Astennu's tenure in the band also came to an end and he was replaced by **Galder** of Old Man's Child notoriety. The first product of this thoroughly overhauled line-up was the fabulously tongue-twisting *Puritanical Euphoric Misanthropia* (2001), with the **Gothenburg Symphony Orchestra** providing the kind of full-blooded backing the band had been crying out for all along. The quality of the set was such that the band finally landed a Norwegian Grammy.

The *Alive In Torment* (2001) limited release mini-LP and *World Misanthropy* (2002) CD/DVD provided plenty of dark thrills and spills for dedicated followers, while the group worked assiduously on their next album, endeavouring to make it a worthy successor to their last studio effort. The result was *Death Cult Armageddon* (2003) which featured the **Prague Philharmonic Orchestra** providing the grandeur demanded by the songs. Needless to say it won a Norwegian Grammy in early 2004 and even made a dent on the *Billboard* chart, paving the way for the band to appear at Ozzfest as one of the few non-US bands. The tour saw the introduction of **Reno Killerich** as a replacement for Barker who was suddenly and inexplicably removed from the line-up.

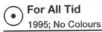

For All Tid
1995; No Colours

Their formative effort retains a certain charm and roughness. The aura of darkness is palpable as they concentrate on being as evil as possible.

Enthrone Darkness Triumphant
1997; Nuclear Blast

Gone are the Norwegian lyrics and instead the band's intentions are blasted out with crushing aggression and stunning clarity.

Spiritual Black Dimensions
1999; Nuclear Blast

Driven by the luscious keyboard arrangements the time changes will make your head swim while the thrashing guitar torment will make your eyes water.

Death Cult Armageddon
2003; Nuclear Blast

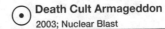

With orchestra in tow, Dimmu Borgir are unstoppable. The sheer scale of the material on offer is quite breathtaking.

DIO

Born July 10, 1942, New Hampshire, US

The little guy with the enormous voice, **Ronnie James Dio** is one of the longest-running artists in heavy metal today. His career reaches way back into the 1960s when he played bass in and fronted the **Electric Elves**. Needless to say, they were definitely not metal. Nor did they become anymore metallic when they changed into **Elf** for a handful of albums in the early 1970s.

Elf were reasonably successful, but Dio's first major break came when he was

recruited, along with most of his old band-mates, into **Ritchie Blackmore's Rainbow** where he recorded several classic hard rock albums and began to develop his soaring, operatic vocals and love of lyrics dealing with the mystical and fantastical – inspired by the young Ronnie's love of sci-fi and Arthurian legend.

In 1979, his connection with Blackmore severed, Dio tackled the unenviable task of filling in for Ozzy Osbourne in **Black Sabbath**. He stayed for two studio albums and the infamous *Live Evil*, during which period already inflated egos ran amok and Dio was eventually replaced by Deep Purple warbler Ian Gillan. By now his sword-and-sorcery fixation was seen as a trademark to which was added a penchant

for the ubiquitous devil horn salute. He took both of these lovable characteristics to his next project along with ex-Sabbath drummer **Vinnie Appice**, and it is at this point that Dio truly made his mark on the world of metal.

He and Appice took their time putting together a new band. First old Rainbow four-stringer **Jimmy Bain** was recruited, before they finally found their guitarist in the shape of ex-Sweet Savage member **Vivian Campbell**. It was the judicious selection of excellent musicians that ensured Dio would go on to eclipse the success of his old Sabbath cohorts for much of the 1980s, witnessed by the excellent *Holy Diver* (1983). A *tour de force* of melody and drama – legend has it that Dio decamped to Cornwall for a few days to stride around a few ruined castles for inspiration – the album set the mark for heavy metal in the 80s, creating a sound and dynamic that would propel the band to increasingly ludicrous and over-blown flights of fantasy; they could rip up a storm (witness opener "Stand Up And Shout"), they could bruise with precision (the crushing "Invisible" and "Shame On The Night"), and they could write with a keen ear for commercial melody (the parping keyboards of "Rainbow In The Dark").

The set's successor, *The Last In Line* (1984), which featured new keyboard player **Claude Schnell**, was equally classic and was assured a top-five placing in the UK charts.

By the time of *Sacred Heart* (1985), Dio was an arena-bothering, platinum-selling artist with an artistic vision to match. The albums so far had been complemented by stage sets inspired by the record sleeves, and the latter featured a dragon ... cue one of the most ridiculous concert spectacles of metal in the mid-80s: castles, duelling knights and Sir Ronnie James Dio fighting a huge dragon (named Denzil!) in the middle of it all. Call it rock'n'roll theatre, or just plain daft, it certainly gave the crowds their money's worth.

Soon after the band were involved in **Hear 'N' Aid** – the metal community's 1986 answer to Band Aid – Campbell decided to leave the group, having become somewhat disillusioned with their direction. His replacement was ex-Giuffria guitarist **Craig**

Goldy. The change made little difference to the band's sound or image, with live effort *Intermission* (1986) and *Dream Evil* (1987) gaining respectable chart placings on both sides of the Atlantic.

The period of acceptance and commercial success was about to come to an end, however; the records were selling and the stage shows were as gargantuan as ever, but the band, and Dio in particular, were in a creative corner. How can you keep rehashing the same ideas to keep the bandwagon rolling before the wheels eventually fall off? By the end of the 80s Dio found himself having to recruit an entirely new set of musicians: 17-year-old **Rowan Robertson** landed the job of guitarist; **Jens Johansson** (keyboards), **Teddy Cook** (bass) and **Simon Wright** (drums; ex-**AC/DC**). The result was one of the worst albums Dio ever put his name to: *Lock Up The Wolves* (1990).

After this debacle most fans wished someone would cage Dio instead. Here was one of metal's biggest stars flailing around without direction – where could he go? Answer: Black Sabbath, of course. All of which turned out to be another very bad idea. All those egos crammed into a studio produced the dull *Dehumanizer* (1992) and at a time when alternative rock was just starting to make things very difficult for metal's old guard.

Without a solid band line-up the rest of the 90s proved to be something of a trial for Dio. *Strange Highways* (1993) did little to boost his profile and *Angry Machines* (1996) was almost as bad as *Lock Up The Wolves* – the terrible artwork, featuring rampaging robots, didn't help matters at all. The decade was rounded out with the excessive *Inferno – Live In Line* (1998).

By the time of the new millennium Dio looked washed up; the albums weren't charting and nu-metal was giving artists like him a severe pummelling. And then the unthinkable happened: *Magica* (2000), an album that contained decent songs played by a band featuring Craig Goldy, Jimmy Bain and Simon Wright. Some of the old sparkle had returned, not bad going for what was basically a concept album.

Two years on and the strident *Killing The Dragon* had Dio back in familiar territory, but it was the magic of *Master Of The Moon* (2004) which indicated that the powerful new approach wasn't just a fluke.

Holy Diver
1983; Vertigo

An epic classic of 80s metal. Dio sounds assured and in total control. This has it all: big choruses, a sense of mystery and great big metallic guitars.

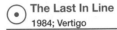
The Last In Line
1984; Vertigo

Never a man to abandon a formula while the punters are lapping it up, Dio dishes out a second helping of strident, melodic metal.

Magica
2000; Spitfire

It took a long time coming, but this is a return to the values of old, which can only be a good thing after the false starts of preceding years.

DISTURBED

Formed Chicago, US, 1997

In the realms of the nu, **Disturbed** are one of those rare bands who value melody as much as aggression; their grinding power is complemented by a natural ability to write annoyingly catchy, hook-laden metal.

The story of the band's rise in popularity depended upon them finding the right singer for the job. **Dan Donegan** (guitar), **Fuzz** (bass) and **Mike Wengren** (drums) had been knocking around the Chicago metal scene for quite a while, searching for the voice that would fit their brutal downtuned assault. They eventually found **David Draiman**, a singer with a singular voice and enough personal issues to provide lyrics for at least a decade of angst. Draiman's family background was one

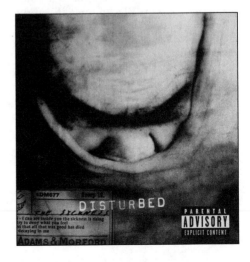

of religious conservatism against which he had rebelled with the ferocity of a caged rottweiler. He didn't want his life prescribed to him, he didn't like school – he was expelled from five boarding schools – and he certainly didn't want a safe respectable job. Big, bad metal was what he craved when he answering a classified ad for a singer. And it wasn't just attitude he brought with him. His vocal style veered from a throat-shredding roar to a bizarre shrieking, syncopated bark, allowing him to both deliver melodic hooks and indulge in a spot of machine-gun staccato rapping – this versatility made the band infamous on the club scene almost instantly.

A deal with Giant Records was inked at the peak of the nu-metal wave. Their debut album, *The Sickness* (2000), featured a corrosive clutch of economical riffs decorated with driving electronic squiggles and bleeps; Draiman's madman yelp was mixed well to the fore, stamping the band's identity home with the force of a hammer to an anvil. Tunes such as "Voices", "Stupify" and "Down With The Sickness" rapidly became concert faves – along with, oddly enough, a cover of Tears For Fears' "Shout". These shows usually kicked off with Draiman getting fried in an electric chair or struggling out of a cage. And then there were the hockey masks, boiler suits and straitjackets.

The same year a triumphant slot at Ozzfest – which would be reprised over subsequent years – led to serious levels of fan exposure and the debut going platinum.

Keen not to repeat the same formula for their follow-up, *Believe* (2002) was more of a tribute to the great names in metal. Reining in his desire to make angry animal noises, Draiman concentrated on projecting his voice with power and precision while the music was grander and more varied in scope than the simple guttural chug of much nu-metal.

The Sickness
2000; Giant

Animal cackling aside this is an eclectic but assured debut slotting in nicely alongside the latter-day wave of nu-metal acts to emerge from the States.

Believe
2002; Giant

Concentrating more on writing songs rather than vehicles for Draiman's wacky voice menagerie, this album sounds more capable and solid than their fiery debut.

Down

Formed New Orleans, US, 1995

" ... I try to be that behind-the-beat drummer barely catching the rhythm to fuck it up!" Jimmy Bower

There seems to be no stopping the former Pantera frontman **Phil Anselmo**. A man who likes to keep himself busy, the bull-throated singer has been involved in more projects than you can shake a stick at, and **Down** – a veritable metal supergroup if ever there was one – has been one of the more successful.

The group's goal was simple: to kick out some seriously heavy jams in the style of yesteryear. Big on groove and heavy of heart, the Down sound is classic depressed stoner metal, drawing on the darker, meaner side of life. Oh, and ridiculously vast quantities of weed.

Back in the mid-90s Anselmo got together with **Corrosion Of Conformity's Pepper Keenan** (guitar) and began writing some music that had nothing to do with his day job in Pantera. So successful was the vibe that it developed into a full-blown band completed by **Todd Strange** (bass) and **Kirk Windstein** (guitar) of **Crowbar** and Eyehategod's **Jimmy Bower** (drums). However, with no expectations as to where this extracurricular activity might lead, it was just an excuse for the band to get seriously ripped on whatever mind-altering substances they could get their hands on and grind out a vicious Sabbath-meets-southern-rock noise – it was swamp-doom of the highest order.

Such a line-up could hardly fail to produce something extraordinary and it soon became apparent that they had a real chemistry. The result was NOLA (1995), the title derived from New Orleans, Louisiana. Sludgier than the Mississippi delta and fierier than a mouthful of Tabasco, NOLA was an instant classic, Anselmo's troubled psyche spewing forth lyrics to aching stone-cold anthems such as "Bury Me In Smoke", "Lifer", "Rehab", "Pillars Of Eternity" and "Stone The Crow". Naturally there was also a tune dedicated to their dope-driven muse – "Hail The Leaf", the band's very own "Sweet Leaf".

Amazingly, given that the band managed only thirteen live shows, the album sold in excess of half a million copies. Seven years on

DOOM METAL

"And so in the sky shines the electric eye
Supernatural king takes the earth under his wing"

Little did **Ozzy** realize he had given us doom metal when he uttered these words to "Electric Funeral" over one of **Tony Iommi**'s most inspiringly heavy riffs. Of course, doom didn't spring fully formed from **Black Sabbath**'s blues-influenced heavy rock, but within the Ozzy-led period the seeds were sown of what would flourish into one of metal's heaviest subdivisions. The three elements are there – darkness, despair and depression. Not that the early Sabbath vibe had cornered the market in this sound; other bands such as **Pentagram**, **Blue Cheer** and **Iron Butterfly** – who can ignore the terrific riff to "Inna Gadda Da Vida"? – all brought elements to the table, even if some of them weren't particularly apocalyptic in their vision. It was, after all, just another form of rock'n'roll at the time.

Another key aspect to doom is the speed, or lack of it. During the 80s when metal had seemingly gone thrash mad there was an offshoot that took a far more funereal and magisterial tack, allowing the slothful riffing to create an atmosphere of unparalleled morbidity and, well, doom. This was the era of defining acts such as **Candlemass**, **St Vitus**, **The Obsessed** – lead bloke **Wino Weinrich** is revered as a doom luminary by many aficionados – and **Trouble**, among a burgeoning scene of bands who took their miserable metal very seriously. And who could argue with Sweden's Candlemass when they chose to call their debut *Epicus Doomicus Metallicus*? Doom – on an epic scale.

On into the 90s and a desire for experimentation led bands such as **Paradise Lost**, **Anathema**, **My Dying Bride** and **Cathedral** to take elements of early doom and fashion their own unique sounds. Paradise Lost incorporated aspects of death metal into their early doomy recipe, *Gothic* often cited as a landmark release. Likewise the early Anathema. Both bands have retained their inherent sense of melancholia but have gone in completely different directions. And then we have the incomparable Cathedral, perhaps one of the few acts to retain some bite. Even they have moved largely away from the slow plod of their nascent sound to incorporate a more groovy bounce and swagger.

and a sequel was issued, *Down II*. The logistics of getting everyone back together for a sequel were pretty tricky but during late 2001 the band convened in a barn, dubbed *Nodferatu's Lair*, in the middle of a swamp – in fact, on Anselmo's own acreage – and set about writing and recording in a marathon session that took just under a month.

The line-up had altered only slightly, Strange being replaced by Pantera's **Rex Brown**, but the sound was basically the same. The album was subtitled "A Bustle In Your Hedgerow…", a thank-you salute to Led Zeppelin; every now and then the spirit of Page and Plant would intercede (most noticeably on the closing epic "Landing On

The Mountains Of Meggido"), thanks to the ton of vintage equipment they had shipped in to create that authentic 70s sound.

Lyrically, Anselmo was back in soul-searching mood, tackling subjects such as his substance abuse. Among the scorching rockers, there were moments of soulful reflection, such as the dobro-inflected tearjerker "Where I'm Going" and the down-at-heel "Learn From This Mistake".

A far more comprehensive tour was organized this time round, but with live commitments completed the band went on hold to allow everyone to tackle other projects. Most notably Anselmo went back to **Superjoint Ritual**, though where he intends to go in the future in the wake of the shooting of Pantera guitarist, 'Dimebag' Darrell, remains to be seen.

NOLA
1995; Elektra

The sound of the south, Louisiana metal style. The influence of bands such as Black Sabbath and St Vitus hangs heavy over these huge, dope-fuelled grooves.

Down II
2002; Elektra

More of the same only executed with real intent. Anselmo dredges the depths for some troubled and troubling lyrics while his bandmates rip through some of the heaviest riffs this side of "Symptom Of The Universe".

DRAGONFORCE

Formed UK, 1999

In the recent dour shadow cast by nu-metal most bands bearing more traditional hard rock credentials have found themselves out of favour, forced to ply their axe-wielding trade more as curiosities. But now that nu-metal is beginning to die on its arse so those genres that had been eclipsed find favour once more. So it has been for power metal, the speedy, proggy more melodic cousin of thrash. One of the finest outfits practising such wildly over-the-top metal is London-based **Dragonforce**.

Originally formed around the nucleus of Hong Kong-born **Herman Li** (guitar), Englishman **Sam Totman** (guitar) and South African **Z. P. Theart** (vocals), and named **Dragonheart**, the main aim of this multinational outfit was to bring their ace musicianship to a genre much maligned in metal circles. Their name alone warned those with trendier tastes to stay away – a band influenced by classical music and powered by virtuoso tendencies and ludicrously pompous, chest-beating vocals. And, of course, all this was done fast, very, very fast indeed, with the line-up on their first demo recording completed by **Steve Scott** (bass), **Clive Nolan** (keyboards) and **Peter Hunt** (drums).

The quality of this self-produced five-tracker, recorded in a mere seven days and called *Valley Of The Damned*, was astonishing and with it the band excited sufficient interest to land them on tours with metal god Rob Halford and likeminded widdlers Stratovarius, as well as prompting over half a million downloads of the tracks from the Internet. They signed to Sanctuary Records and got down to recording *Valley Of The Damned* (2003), the album. The fantasy-fuelled lyrics and cover art coupled with the melodramatically theatrical nature of the music had critics hailing them as the next logical, evolutionary step for melodic power metal. By now they had changed their name to Dragonforce, to avoid confusion with another similarly named metal band, and brought in **Vadim Pruzhanov** (keyboards), **Didier Almouzni** (drums) and **Diccon Harper** (bass); additional parping keyboards were provided by Nolan once more.

While the blueprint for Dragonforce's music was definitely in the tradition of classic 80s

metal their delivery was nothing short of ferocious. Japanese metal magazine *Burrn!* had the group in the top three of their chart (pipped only by German speedmetallers Helloween and the new king of shock metal Marilyn Manson).

By the time of *Sonic Firestorm* (2004) the line-up featured new additions **Adrian Lambert** (bass) and **David Mackintosh** (drums). Again, the music pushed beyond the technical boundaries of the power metal genre and Dragonforce basically left the competition eating their dust as they out-parped and out-widdled them. Standout cuts included the strident opener "My Spirit Will Go On", while the prize for headbanging prog overkill went to "Soldiers Of The Wasteland".

With such a vast amount of musical skill at their disposal Dragonforce have travelled a very long way in a very short space of time to become one of the cutting-edge outfits in a genre that champions both melody and speedy aggression. Having set the bar so high, it's hard to know where they will go in the future. Whatever their next artistic move Dragonforce are sure to be making it at the speed of light.

Sonic Firestorm
2004; Noise

Neoclassical influences and incredible musicianship made this an instant hit. Proggy touches give the rampant power metal some cool twists and turns.

DREAM THEATER

Formed New York, US, 1987

What do you get when most of the members of a band meet up while attending Boston's renowned *Berklee School of Music*? With all that naked talent sloshing around the only adequate outlet has to be a prog outfit. **Dream Theater** have virtually become a byword for modern prog-metal, with a vast following of ravenous fans trading live tapes and snapping up their concept albums as soon as they hit the shelves. What's more the hunger to create is just too great to be channelled through Dream Theater alone; the number of side-projects – including **Liquid Tension Experiment**, **Transatlantic** and **Platypus** – is quite amazing.

In the mid-80s Dream Theater were known as **Majesty**, a vehicle for **Mike Petrucci** (guitar), **John Myung** (bass) and **Mike Portnoy** (drums) to practise their prog chops alongside **Kevin Moore** (keyboards). A demo was created with the help of singer **Chris Collins**, but it was when **Charlie Dominici** (vocals) joined that the band hit their stride. One name change and record deal later (with Mechanic Records) and the world's progheads finally had something substantial to get excited about. *When Dream And Day Unite* (1989) followed in the traditions of 70s prog but injected a major dose of butt-kicking metal into the equation, making something previously associated with whimsy and improbably long keyboard solos into a form of music that was actually thrilling to listen to.

Unfortunately, the strong debut proved to be something of a false start. The band fired Dominici and outgrew their small label almost as soon as the record was released. It took another three years before all the pieces were in place – new singer **James LaBrie** and a deal with Atlantic – for their masterful *Images And Words*, featuring the MTV fave "Pull Me Under". The strength of the album translated superbly to the live arena and the mini-LP *Live At The Marquee* (1993) was the first of many official concert recordings.

Awake (1994) turned out to be one of their heaviest studio efforts, possibly as a reaction to the darkness of grunge – the riff to "Lie" alone was a monster – but the success of the album was somewhat undercut by the loss of Moore, who went off to pursue a solo career. His replacement was **Derek Sherinian**, whose introduction to the fans couldn't have been more dramatic than with his contributions to *A Change Of Seasons* (1995). The title track was 23 minutes long and the remainder of the mini-LP consisted of a series of live cover songs – including tunes originally by Deep Purple and Led Zeppelin.

The high energy levels of their albums so far had earned them a certain reputation. Their next effort, however, took some getting used to. *Falling Into Infinity* (1997) swung in the opposite direction to *Awake*, the record label preventing the release of all the material the band had recorded. The result was disappointing and softer than what fans had been used to. It was a state of affairs that would be remedied a couple of years down the line by the band assuming control of their own output, but in the meantime the double album *Once In A Livetime* (1998) dished up some more con-

cert cuts while the various members spent time on their side-projects.

Metropolis Part 2: Scenes From A Memory (1999) – "Metropolis Part I" dated back to *Images And Words* – was the first fruit of the more creatively independent Dream Theater and featured new keyboard wizard **Jordan Rudess**. The concept behind the album was a sort of murder mystery thriller with the band pulling out all the stops to deliver one of their finest sets. It was a strong way to head into the new millennium and the momentum was maintained with the double album blow-out *Six Degrees Of Inner Turbulence* (2002) – featuring a 42-minute title track! – and the superb *Train Of Thought* (2003). The only blip occurred in 2001 when the triple album *Live Scenes From New York* was issued on September 11 with artwork featuring the New York skyline – including the Twin Towers – on fire. Needless to say, the artwork had to be quickly rectified. *Live At Budokan* (2004), however, arrived far more smoothly and came as both a triple CD and double DVD.

⊙ **Metropolis Part 2: Scenes From A Memory** 1999; Eastwest

Dream Theater sound cohesive and positively driven to create on this dramatic little beauty. The murder mystery angle plays upon the mercurial qualities of the human mind to make an album that is both intelligent and hard rocking.

DROWNING POOL

Formed Dallas, Texas, US, 1998

Drowning Pool's story so far is punctuated with great success and also tragedy of the kind that would halt the career of a less dedicated outfit.

The band's genesis came when drummer **Mike Luce** and guitarist **CJ Pierce** left their home town of New Orleans to hook up with bassist **Stevie Benton** in Dallas. Apart from an underground sludge metal scene New Orleans' reputation for blues and jazz made it a less than appropriate base for a metal band. Nu-metal was peaking during the late 90s and their sound fused elements of both old-school and nu-school metal; but they still lacked a singer, a voice to compete with and complement the tumultuous guitarts and rabid rhythms. **Dave 'Stage' Williams** was their man. He received his nickname from Pantera guitarist 'Dimebag' Darrell on account of his larger-than-life presence and aptitude for performing. The band's moniker followed when Benton recalled the name of the movie playing in the background when he had lost his virginity! A demo tape found its way to Atlanta metallers Sevendust and Drowning Pool were landed with their first support slot. Two years of touring provided them with a solid fan base. They then released *Sinner* (2001), having signed to Wind Up Records on the strength of heavy airplay on one of Dallas's biggest radio stations.

Williams' religious family background gave *Sinner* much of its lyrical bite, while his powerful roar worked to supreme effect on "Bodies". With its chorus chant of "Let the bodies hit the floor" it was specifically written to whip up a frenzied mosh wherever the band played. The single was the perfect accompaniment to TV wrestling and the video was one of the most frequently aired clips on MTV from a new band. So irresistible were the rough hewn charms of their piledriving metal that within six weeks the album had gone platinum.

The 2001 Ozzfest line-up had the band scheduled for an early morning slot on the third stage, but within a couple of weeks they had been promoted, and on a handful of dates they even took the main stage. Their steadily growing popularity ensured that 2002's Ozzfest would be even more successful for them as one of the main stage attractions. But then tragedy struck when Williams was found dead by his bandmates on August 14, 2002. The coroner reported that the 30-year-old singer had suffered from undiagnosed heart disease and that the cause of death had been natural.

Few bands recover from losing a lead singer under such circumstances and the group took their time in recovering from the shock of losing their friend. Later in the year they recorded "The Man Without Fear" with **Rob Zombie** guesting on vocals for the soundtrack to *Daredevil*. The remainder of their time was spent looking for a replacement. They found their man in Los Angeles tattoo artist **Jason 'Gong' Jones**, a singer with a voice similar, but not identical to Williams's. Jones officially

DRUMMER JOKES

In the world of metal, drummers traditionally come in for a lot of stick (excuse the pun) and often find themselves the object of ridicule … and who are we to argue? Here are some of the best drummer-bashing jokes around…

Q. "What do you call someone who hangs around with musicians?"
A. "A drummer."

Q. "Why do bands need roadies?"
A. "To translate what the drummer says."

Q. "What's the difference between a drum machine and a drummer?"
A. "You only have to punch the information into the drum machine once."

Q. "What's the difference between a drummer and a vacuum cleaner?"
A. "One of them you have to plug in before it sucks."

Q. "How is a drum solo like a sneeze?"
A. "You can tell it's coming, but there's nothing you can do about it."

Q. "What do you call a drummer who breaks up with his girlfriend?"
A. "Homeless."

Q. "How do you know when a drummer is at your door?"
A. "The knocking speeds up."

Q. "How can you tell if a drummer has been doing the crossword?"
A. "All the squares have been coloured in."

Q. "How many drummers does it take to change a light bulb?"
A. "Five. One to screw in the bulb and four to talk about how much better Neil Peart would have done it."

Q. "How many drummers does it take to change a light bulb?"
A. "Twenty. One to hold the bulb and nineteen to drink until the room spins."

joined the band in early 2004 and they wasted little time in getting album number two under way with the boisterous and belligerent "Step Up" earmarked to appear on the soundtrack to *The Punisher*.

It was a potent signal of what was to come with *Desensitized* (2004), which was

dedicated to their departed singer. With nu-metal generally acknowledged to be fading fast, any sonic trappings the band might have shared with the scene on their debut were shed fast and the more straight-ahead metal influences they had always harboured were proudly brought centre-stage. There were touches of Alice In Chains-like menace to the album's dark groove, but for the most part Jones's Anselmo-meets-Hetfield bark provided the focus to a set of songs thankfully devoid of the often tuneless chuggery of the nu.

 Sinner
2001; Wind-Up

Plenty of old-school nods punctuate this shreddingly heavy debut. "Bodies" has nothing to do with the Sex Pistols classic, being a rather more modern call to smash it up in the mosh pit.

 Desensitized
2004; Wind-Up

Recovering from their tragic loss this is a formidable return with Jason Jones's different vocal approach allowing the band to explore beyond the sound that defined their debut.

DRUMS: SOLOS AND BEYOND

The clichéd view is that drummers can't wait for their few minutes in the spotlight when they provide the soundtrack for a mass exodus to the bar. However, a terrific drum performance doesn't have to be a solo. An awesome drummer can provide a unique feel to a song whether it requires hyper-speed skin thrashing or a delicately judged and artistic approach. Some of the twenty performances below are of the solo variety while the rest are simply fantastic displays of skill within a typical song structure, but they're all guaranteed to inspire a sneaky spot of air-drumming.

"Heaven And Hell" (live) – **Keith Moon** *Live At Leeds* The Who 1970

"Rat Salad" – **Bill Ward** *Paranoid* Black Sabbath 1970

"The Mule" (live) – **Ian Paice** *Made In Japan* Deep Purple 1972

"Little Dolls" – **Lee Kerslake** *Diary Of A Madman* Ozzy Osbourne 1981

"Where Eagles Dare" – **Nicko McBrain** *Piece Of Mind* Iron Maiden 1983

"Hot For Teacher" – **Alex Van Halen** *1984* Van Halen 1984

"Shyboy" – **Greg Bissonette** *Eat 'Em And Smile* David Lee Roth 1986

"The Rhythm Method" (live) – **Neil Peart** *A Show Of Hands* Rush 1989

"Angel Of Death" (live) – **Dave Lombardo** *Decade Of Aggression* Slayer 1991

"Midlife Crisis" – **Mike Bordin** *Angel Dust* Faith No More 1992

"War Nerve" (live) – **Vinnie Paul** *Official Live: 101 Proof* Pantera 1997

"All Hail The New Flesh" – **Gene Hoglan** *City* Strapping Young Lad 1997

"Ytse Jam" (live) – **Mike Portnoy** *Once In A Livetime* Dream Theater 1998

"Drum Solo" (live) – **Vinny Appice** *Dio's Inferno: The Last In Live* Dio 1998

"Merkaba" (live) – **Danny Carey** *Salival* Tool 2000

"The Hollow" – **Josh Freese** *Mer De Noms* A Perfect Circle 2000

"People=Shit" – **Joey Jordison** *Iowa* Slipknot 2001

"Crusher Destroyer" – **Brann Dailor** *Remission* Mastodon 2002

"Drunkship Of Lanterns" – **Jon Theodore** *De-loused In The Comatorium* Mars Volta 2002

"Moby Dick" (live) – **John Bonham** *How The West Was Won* Led Zeppelin 2003

EMPEROR

Formed Telemark, Norway, 1991

Emperor are without doubt one of the most influential names in the murky underworld of Scandinavian black metal. They are widely regarded as pioneers of what would become the modern sound of malevolent metal, adding an interest in Norwegian folk heritage and classical music to the basic groove-print of blazing guitar lines and tornado-like drumming. Their seemingly alchemical ability to conjure up innovative permutations of menacing riffs and icily atmospheric passages often left their contemporaries slack-jawed with envy. What made them truly notorious, however, was their almost pathological hatred of Christianity. This hatred was elevated beyond the level of a mere philosophy of life and spilled over into criminal acts which – along with the activities of various other bands, not least Mayhem – garnered plenty of negative news coverage for the Norwegian scene.

The roots of Emperor's early outpourings can be traced to the brutality of the first thrash bands; the direction Emperor took the primal riffing and screaming, however, would mark them down as movers and shakers in the underground. The first line-up was a trio consisting of **Ihsahn** (guitar), **Mortiis** (bass) and **Samoth** (drums/vocals) who caused something of a stir with their "Wrath Of The Tyrant" demo. Beyond the fact that they were corpse-painted and satanic to the core there was little to distinguish them from

many of their compatriots, though it was certainly enough to attract the attention of the Candlelight label. Samoth shifted his attention to the guitar and **Faust** was recruited to pound the skins. Their first properly recorded material went onto an eponymous record along with music from fellow Norwegians **Enslaved**, released in 1993, also known as the *Hordanes Land* album. These four tracks along with the demo would later be collected on the *Wrath Of The Tyrant* compilation, an album strictly for completists and collectors, given the truly abominable sound quality of the demo songs.

Other than the amazingly accomplished nastiness of it all, there were already some unique aspects to the band's fledgling thrash; the vocals were typically chilling but the purple poetics of the lyrics penned by Mortiis also betrayed a pagan twist, rather than a plain, old-fashioned satanic one. The bleak landscape of Norway figured large in the scheme of things, usually as a springboard for leaps into fearsome infernal fantasy. The bassist, however, left the band early on to pursue his own agenda and was replaced by **Tchort**.

It wasn't until *In The Nightside Eclipse* (1994) that the full implications of their potential were first fully sampled. Extreme music would never be the same again. Their previous effort had contained only four compositions, whereas fans now had a full-blown album of nefarious nocturnal musings set to scorching riffs and spooky keyboards. But although the band were creating groundbreaking music, they were conducting themselves in a far from professional manner. The virulently anti-Christian sentiment was

EIGHTIES PROG ROCK

In the late 70s, after punk virtually wiped out any form of overblown rock, it seemed inconceivable that a genre such as prog could ever find a foothold again. However, the kids who had grown up listening to the first wave of bands were gradually forming their own groups and a new maturing audience was available as well as the oldsters from the first time round.

Key to the rise of these bands was a music press, especially *Kerrang!* magazine, who often featured them as just another part of the over-arching heavy rock universe. Into this receptive climate were born such neo-prog bands (as they were dubbed by some critics) as **IQ**, **Pendragon**, **Pallas**, and the quite magnificent **Twelfth Night**, who would have made much more of an impact had it not been for a distinct lack of interest from their latter record label Virgin. Nevertheless, albums such as *Fact And Fiction* (1982), the live *Live And Let Live* (1984), *Art And Illusion* (1984) and *XII* (1986) give a good flavour of how the band could handle both the long and the short of prog songs. Apart from a common musical heritage, another general characteristic shared by some of the new bands was a penchant for lyrics rooted in the personal and political as opposed to the more fantastical leanings of earlier prog.

Of all these acts, however, one stood out: **Marillion**. In an era when prog bands popped up on festival bills they appeared second from the top slot at the Donington Monsters of Rock in 1985 over such acts as **Bon Jovi** and **Metallica**. Fronted by the exceedingly tall and charismatic **Fish**, who borrowed a few face-painting tips from Peter Gabriel in the band's early days, they were a regular draw at London's Marquee club showcasing material from *Script For A Jester's Tear* (1983) and *Fugazi* (1984), glorious prog albums packed with lengthy multi-part tunes and the odd shorter effort. It was the full-blown concept fare of *Misplaced Childhood* (1985) – featuring the massive smash that was the poppy "Kayleigh", a song that was quite unrepresentative of their other works – and the part concept *Clutching At Straws* (1987), which launched them onto the festival and arena circuits of Europe and the UK, though America always eluded them. With Fish's departure the band brought in **Steve Hogarth** and continued to create some terrific music, not least the amazingly dramatic concept effort *Brave* (1994).

Despite the terminal unfashionability of prog in the style conscious UK, Marillion continue to plug away – *Marbles* arrived in 2004 – especially on the European continent and conduct much of their business using the Internet, likewise the various other bands. There is still a major demand for the neo-proggers; Twelfth Night's back catalogue has been reissued in various expanded forms on CD; Pallas issued *The Cross And The Crucible* in 2001; Pendragon released the *Acoustically Challenged* album in 2002; and IQ released *Dark Matter* in 2004.

---

spilling over into criminal deeds. Samoth found himself doing time for church burning, while Faust went the whole hog and ended up in prison for murder. It was antisocial behaviour on an epic scale, the kind of thing that the rock press and the media in general reported in full gory detail.

By the time Samoth was back in the fold the band line-up had mutated once again. They had a new bass player in **Alver** and drummer **Trym** (ex-Enslaved) had taken the place of Faust. The group then released the *Reverence* EP, which prefigured the almighty onslaught of the album that was to follow. When *Anthems To The Welkin At Dusk* (1997) arrived it was greeted as a watershed (or should that be bloodshed?) for the burgeoning black metal scene. By turns beautiful, bleak, savage and supremely misanthropic it was a blistering *tour de force* of innovation and extremity, exceeding listeners' expectations. In the UK *Terrorizer* magazine hailed the album as a masterpiece – certainly it was the kind of breakthrough that allowed the band to make some legendary live appearances around the world, helped out by the keyboard wizardry of **Charmand Grimloch**.

Now down to a basic trio – Alver didn't last long – the *Thorns Vs Emperor* split CD followed in 1999, before the full-length album *IX Equilibrium* pushed the boat out even further. It was as though Emperor were throwing down a challenge each time they came up with a new set. Increasingly orchestral in approach and relentless in its sonic viciousness it was a more technical-sounding album than its predecessor, an attempt to expand on ideas present in the *Anthems...* album.

Empirical Live Ceremony (2000), recorded at the LA2 in London in 1999, brought a taste of what the band could achieve in front of an audience, but the real meat lay within the riffery of the next studio effort, *Prometheus: The Discipline Of Fire And Demise* (2001). It was an album as majestic as its title suggested but it was also their last, Emperor choosing to bow out at the peak of their popularity – not for them the possibility of besmirching the band's name with mediocre material.

Two years on and *Scattered Ashes: A Decade Of Emperial Wrath* (2003) turned up as a reminder of what Emperor meant, the collection augmented by various rarities and remixes. Post Emperor the most prominent off-shoot has been **Zyklon**, featuring Samoth and Trym, whereas Ihsahn has concentrated on other projects, including **Peccatum**.

In The Nightside Eclipse
1994; Candlelight

This is where they started to get serious – intense, fast and thoroughly evil. Their progressive tendencies bubble away nicely, provoking them to take risks and carve a unique sound

Anthems To The Welkin At Dusk
1997; Candlelight

Better production helps this ambitious album hit home in true style. So ambitious are the band that it sounds almost like they are raising the bar for themselves with each successive track.

IX Equilibrium
1999; Candlelight

Where can you go when you have, seemingly, already peaked? Emperor throw in ever-increasing amounts of complexity and weirdness. Stunning.

Prometheus: The Discipline Of Fire And Demise 2001; Candlelight

A terrific title and another clutch of defiant black metal that pulls in a variety of off-the-wall experiments to bolster the onslaught.

Scattered Ashes: A Decade Of Emperial Wrath 2003; Candlelight

As good a place to start as any given that it contains a fair cross-section of the work. A nice fan release too, featuring rarities and extras.

ENTOMBED

Formed Stockholm, Sweden, 1989

"They've got some really good dirty movies on their bus!" Mikkey Dee on Entombed.

When it comes to Swedish death metal Entombed are one of the most enjoyable examples, having evolved and honed their sound over the years beyond the confines of the merely macabre and speedy. They are also one of the most prolific, in so far as issuing singles and EPs is concerned – the sheer number of cover songs they've recorded provides something of a headache for completists. Not only do they blast through versions of tunes made famous by bands as diverse as Bad Brains and Venom, this tight and belligerent metal crew are capable of a brutal and bludgeoning assault akin to a grungier, more satanic Motörhead or perhaps a sloppier, more rock'n'roll Slayer.

Heading back into the murky history of the late-80s Swedish thrash scene a band called **Nihilist** was toiling away at being as evil as possible, eventually producing three demos that almost clinched a deal. Unfortunately they disbanded before anything became of them; on the other hand, from the remains, Entombed were created. They banged out the *But Life Goes On* demo and managed to land a deal with Earache Records.

At this point the band's line-up was rather fluid, but included **L.G Petrov** (vocals), **Uffe Cederlund** (guitar), **Alex Hellid** (guitar) and **Nicke Andersson** (drums). Because of the somewhat insecure position of the band, when it came to recording their first album, *Left Hand Path* (1990), not only did Andersson and Cederlund have to share bass duties, but also they had to recycle old Nihilist songs because they didn't have enough new ones. Nevertheless, the quality of the album showed that they had something unusual to offer. Right from the beginning Entombed combined the power of thrash with something approaching horror existentialism. They baited religion and had death-fixated lyrics, but with a twist and always nailed to some terrifically bold riffing. Petrov's vocal style, in particular, with his impossibly gritty roar, gave the band a uniquely sadistic sound.

Petrov was duly sacked after clashing with Andersson. He was replaced by **Orvar Säfström** for the *Crawl* EP the following year but by the time *Clandestine* (1991) was due for recording it was actually Andersson who was at the mic. They had also acquired a new bassist in **Lars Rosenberg**. This odd game of musical chairs didn't prevent the new album being another hit with the death metal-loving cognoscenti. But things were about to get even more bizarre. The *Stranger Aeons* EP also featured Andersson's bellow but they had also recruited a new vocalist in **Johnny Dordevic** who was a technically better singer than either Petrov or Andersson. Dordevic's days in the band, however, were numbered and his replacement was…Petrov! He and Andersson might not have kissed and made up but at least they had patched things sufficiently for the gloriously guttural vocalist to return.

With Petrov back in the studio for yet another EP, this time titled *Hollowman*, the scene was set for one of their best-loved albums, *Wolverine Blues* (1993). They had

Emo

Another highly successful strain of punk is the curiously named emo, shorthand for emotional; in other words, a type of punk music with heart.

Emo is characterized by overwrought poetic lyrics centred on relationships, love, loss and disillusionment, usually delivered in a tremulous and plaintive vocal style, often making it sound as though the singer is about to burst into tears. Musically the melodies and rhythms are well defined, mid-paced and dramatic to underscore the singer's emotional torment. Visually, the band are nothing to write home about but the record sleeves usually feature abstract monochrome photos, giving the feeling that you are looking at some deeply personal pages of a family album; or rusted and decaying machinery; or some pretty flowers – basically, anything that conveys the idea that life is ephemeral and that we are destined to suffer broken hearts and harvest nothing but disappointment in our short lives. Happy stuff this is not. Fans usually pass the time buying satchels and wearing cardigans.

The popularity of bands such as **Jimmy Eat World**, **Get Up Kids** and **Taking Back Sunday**, to name but a few, can be traced back to the seminal **Fugazi**, the Dischord record label, and what is sometimes referred to as the Washington DC sound. Fugazi – part of whose lineage goes back to straight-edge pioneers **Minor Threat** and bands such as **Embrace** and **Rites Of Spring** – took the notion of hardcore, slowed it down and introduced more emotive, sung vocals. The sound was highly inventive and abrasive but over the years became diluted to create, essentially, a general indie-rock sound.

Another strain of punk, usually called post-hardcore, is also attributed to Fugazi. Post-hardcore is melodic but far heavier than emo, characterized by the fearsome energy of **At The Drive-In**, **Sparta**, **Quicksand** (who turned into **Rival Schools**, another emo band) and **Cave In**, again to name but a few.

been inching away from the confines of the genre for a while but now it was becoming a trademark. It was still good and thrashy stuff but elements of classic heavy rock and garage punk were creeping in. The result was slower, slightly more melodic riffing, revelling in some fiendishly heavy distortion and enhancing the impact of the songs through tight control of pacing and dynamics. Such a shift couldn't go without a tag, and the metal magazines dubbed it death'n'roll.

Although they had made a massive impact with *Wolverine Blues,* the spectre of label problems was beginning to haunt the band; they just couldn't get along with Earache anymore and began casting around for a new deal. In the end that meant they wouldn't get a studio album out for another four years. The dearth of material was punctuated by the *Out Of Hand* EP and "Night Of The Vampire" single (a split effort with **New Bomb Turks**).

The band finally returned with what is generally regarded as one mutha of a comeback: the superbly catchy, hellishly heavy *DCLXVI To Ride, Shoot Straight And Speak The Truth*, released on Music For Nations, and featuring new bassist **Jörgen Sandström**. The grit and grunt of *Wolverine Blues* had been liberally doused with axle grease and set on rails pointing straight to the heart of hell. It had it all: a crushing doom'n'death groove, fabulously raucous vocals, the spirit of old-school heavy rock and a creepy atmosphere of pungent evil, summed up by the eerie piano interlude, "DCLXVI", which could so easily have been lifted from *The Exorcist*. Not wanting to miss out on the fun, Earache cunningly slipped out an eponymously titled compilation at the same time.

Entombed – not your average boy band.

Yet another EP followed, *Wreckage*, and Andersson decided to leave to play full-time heavy rock of a more classic variety with his side-project **The Hellacopters**; **Peter Stjärnvind** replaced him. Maybe it was Andersson's departure that precipitated the change, or maybe they felt the death'n'roll formula was a little restrictive – whatever the reason, *Same Difference* (1998) took an unexpected twist away from the sound they had custom-built to their own requirements. This time they largely eschewed the smothering fuzz and sludge of their previous work for a more minimal approach, allowing the songs to breathe a little more. It was a bold experiment, but ultimately a failed one because the songs simply lacked the required degree of intensity – only Petrov sounded remotely dangerous, his fearsome yell still largely intact. Perhaps they felt it would be another watershed for them, a notion hinted at by the photo of the band sitting around a table on the back cover of the CD; it bore a suspicious resemblance to the picture of Metallica in a similar setting on the back cover of their *Load* album.

Speculation aside, if anyone wanted more of the old Entombed all they had to do was pick up a copy of *Monkey Puss* (*Live In London*), recorded during the Gods Of Grind tour of 1992, an album naughtily issued by Earache around the same time. The intriguing *Black Juju* EP (1999) had the fans somewhat placated but far more satisfying was *Uprising* (2000), a dirtier-sounding album with plenty of headbangworthy riffs jammed into every song. The ante was raised with *Morning Star* just a year later; it was as if the band were keen to make up for the odd detour of *Same Difference*.

Their next effort, *Sons Of Satan Praise The Lord* (2002), was a helpful trawl through the vaults, collecting together many of the covers they had recorded for their EPs and various compilations and tribute albums. There was so much material that they ended up issuing a double album including such priceless efforts as their take on Bob Dylan's "The Ballad Of Hollis Brown" and King Crimson's "21st Century Schizoid Man", alongside more traditional fare such as Motörhead's "One Track Mind" and Kiss's "God Of Thunder".

Decks cleared, *Inferno* blazed into life the following year, delivering more punchy death'n'roll. This was followed by *Unreal Estate* (2004), a CD/DVD live document capturing a performance given in 2002 at the Royal Opera House in Stockholm.

⊙ Left Hand Path
1990; Earache

The style of good old-fashioned death metal pervades this album, from the zippy riffing to Petrov's manic yelling. Already there are glimmerings of what Entombed might achieve.

⊙ Wolverine Blues
1993; Earache

This is where it really gets interesting. The gratuitously heavy and murky guitar tone provides a vintage heavy rock vibe accentuated by the more mid-paced arrangements.

⊙ DCLXVI To Ride, Shoot Straight, And Speak The Truth 1997; Music For Nations

Straddling the world of death and grungy garage rock with a huge amount of style, this album is simply oozing with classy ideas and massive chugging riffs. A classic guaranteed to blow your speakers.

⊙ Uprising
2000; Music For Nations

After the dead end of *Same Difference* this was a top-notch return to form. This is foot-to-the-floor metal right from the off.

⊙ Sons Of Satan Praise The Lord
2002; Music For Nations

A cool bit of fun and one that ought to help those poor souls trying to track down all the band's various releases and appearances. Worth it just to hear their rendition of "Amazing Grace".

EUROPE

Formed Stockholm, Sweden, 1982

There was a point during the mid-80s when bands such as **Europe** epitomized radio-friendly pop metal. While the seedy underbelly of metal was writhing under the sustained and increasingly violent assault of thrash in all its various guises, the commercial side of things was handled by bands with great hair and extremely white teeth. And Europe featured some of the best hair and teeth, belonging to none other than fluffy dreamboat singer **Joey Tempest**. His clear and proud vocals helped propel the band from relative obscurity to superstar status with *that* song, featuring a keyboard refrain at least as well known as, but completely lacking the vintage credibility of, "Smoke On The Water". "The Final Countdown" is one of those haunting tunes that refuses to die, a ubiquitous slice of uplifting commercial rock played at wedding reception discos, official sporting ceremonies and, well, any kind of event where a countdown is involved. Instead of ensuring their success for all eternity it became a limp-wristed albatross around their necks, the standard by which all their subsequent efforts were judged, which is a shame, because beneath the posing beat lay the heart of a decent hard rock band.

The roots of the band went back to the late 70s and a group named **Force** featuring **Tempest** as frontman, **John Norum** (guitar) and **Tony Reno** (drums). With the addition of **John Levén** (bass) in the early 80s they achieved a stable line-up and set about getting their first break, which happened when they won a rock talent competition. At that point they changed their name to Europe. The prize was a recording session and the result was an eponymous debut in 1983, which went into the Swedish Top 10. This was followed by *Wings Of Tomorrow* (1984), a decent enough melodic hard rocker. One line-up shift later – introducing **Mic Michaelli** (keyboards) and **Ian Haugland** (drums) – and the stage was set.

Within the wholesome and glossily produced grooves of *The Final Countdown* (1986) lay one of the biggest-selling singles of the 80s. "The Final Countdown" was a chart topper in the UK and a Top 10 hit in the US, boasting a massive drum sound and infectiously irritating keyboard riff at the expense of anything approaching the crunching heaviness of guitars. It was huge. So huge that nothing they did afterwards came close to its mainstream appeal, not even the gag-inducing wet ballad "Carrie".

By the time of *Out Of This World* (1988) they were worldwide superstars, though Norum had had enough and quit, to be replaced by **Kee Marcello**. The new album failed to match the stratospheric heights of its predecessor, while *Prisoners In Paradise* (1991) was released just as Seattle was starting to wipe the floor with poodle-haired rockers. Not even the lovely Joey's dazzling smile could save them. They folded to make way for a string of solo albums (most notably from Tempest) for much of the 90s. And then the unthinkable happened: Sanctuary Records stepped in and signed the old 1986 line-up to produce *Start From The Dark* (2004). Europe were back … the countdown had begun.

⊙ **The Final Countdown**
1986; Epic

What do you really need to know about this album other than that it contains "The Final Countdown"? Looking beyond the obvious, however, there are some enjoyably daft moments to be found in "Rock The Night" and "On The Loose".

EVANESCENCE

Formed Little Rock, Arkansas, US, 1999

Often the most successful bands are formed from a vision shared between just two individuals. So it was with this extraordinarily powerful goth metal outfit from the American Midwest. From a landscape not often associated with electronic melancholia, **Evanescence** sprang with the soaring, emotional vocals of **Amy Lee** and the crunching musical muscle of lead guitarist **Ben Moody**, who transformed Lee's piano-led tales of angst into riff-driven monsters. It was perfect for the MTV nu-metal generation.

The two met at summer camp while still teenagers when Moody heard habitual loner Lee playing Meatloaf's "I'd Do Anything For Love (But I Won't Do That)" on the piano. The classically trained Lee's combination of vocal and keyboard ability was potent enough for Moody to want to start a band, and while Lee was clearly very talented it would take a musician of Moody's sensibilities to shape the introspective lyrics into taut slabs of million-selling metal.

A few years down the line and **John LeCompt** (guitar), **Will Boyd** (bass) and **Rocky Gray** (drums) – the latter being the last person to join the band in 2002 – had been drafted in to form a touring unit. The early line-up also included keyboard player **John Hodges**. Early gigs around 2000 found the band working hard to define their live sound and touting a demo, a now out-of-print CD called *Origin*, and burning the odd CD EP for sale at shows. However, the major step towards success came with *Fallen* (2003), an album released on Wind-Up Records in the US.

Fallen was a polished slice of commercial goth metal. Emotive, beautiful piano melodies tinkled away plaintively, guitars gave the whole a spine of steel, while orchestral and electronic embellishments provided a brooding atmosphere. And in the middle of it all was Lee's rising, searing vocal performance articulating the pain of loneliness, lost love and spiritual issues which had the band corralled in with the Christian rock scene – though later they balked at their inclusion in various Christian music charts. Certainly, it didn't take a lyric sheet to reveal where the band were coming from.

Even if the likes of "Tourniquet" didn't appeal to the more secular listener, the formative experiences, insecurities and search for identity articulated by the 20-year-old Lee were gloomy enough to appeal to millions of teenagers, who may already have had a taste of Evanescence through their inclusion on the soundtrack to the *Daredevil* movie. The album featured two Evanescence tracks, "My Immortal" and hit single "Bring Me To Life", the latter basically being a duet between Lee and **Paul McCoy** of another Wind-Up band, **12 Stones**. McCoy's rapped contributions may well have been behind the band's early appeal in that it made them sound like a female-fronted Linkin Park. Whatever the reasons behind the success of *Fallen*, the album ended up going platinum in the US five times over and sold over ten million copies worldwide.

On stage, things were also becoming increasingly professional. Lee's individual sartorial style led her to design many of her own outfits and make-up and her growing penchant for stripy black and white tights, biker boots and little-girl-lost frocks and dresses quickly conferred upon her an iconic stage presence – a striking collision of feminine vulnerability and sexy grunginess.

In the end, however, the fact that Lee garnered much of the attention in the band may have been a factor in Moody suddenly leaving while in the middle of a 2003 tour. No reason was given for his departure and Lee continued the tour along with the other band members. Ironically, the fact that a good deal of the stage show was electronically enhanced meant that Moody's disappearance had little impact on their live sound.

Where Lee and her cohorts will head next without the writing talents of Moody remains to be seen. Certainly it was the guitarist's vision for the band that gave them their heaviness and bite and led to them being awarded two Grammys for Best New Artist and Best Hard Rock Performance. In the meantime Lee capitalized upon the band's touring partnership with labelmates Seether, and contributed vocals to their single "Broken" which was also featured on the soundtrack to the movie adventures of yet another Marvel comic book character, Punisher.

 Fallen
2002; Wind-Up/Sony

A powerful and emotional trip, this album sets various existential and spiritual ponderings to a storming metal backdrop of terrific grace and beauty.

EXODUS

Formed San Francisco, California, US, 1982; disbanded 1992; re-formed 1997 and 2001

This terrific, immensely influential thrash band never made the superleague, despite the fact that they were part of the West Coast scene that spawned the likes of Metallica, Slayer and Megadeth. Although they've suffered personal tragedy and been through the wringer of the music industry, they still want to make the music that drove them to strap on guitars in the first place.

Travelling back in time to the early 80s, the influence of hardcore punk and the New Wave Of British Heavy Metal was having a profound effect upon **Tom Hunting** (drums) and **Kirk Hammett** (guitar). They roped in **Gary Holt** (guitar) and gradually put together an early line-up of **Exodus**, which also featured **Paul Baloff** (vocals). They were speedy and intense, inching their way towards a style they could call their own and, along the way, impressing pretty much anyone and everyone who

Exodus: it could be you...

saw them. In fact, the fledgling **Metallica** particularly coveted Hammett's obvious skills as a lead guitarist. When **Dave Mustaine** was ousted from their line-up they invited Hammett along for the ride, and history was made – though that left one fine band without a lead guitarist. Hammett was eventually replaced by **Rick Hunolt**. With the addition of **Rob McKillop** (bass) the first vaguely stable line-up was in place.

For a while Exodus were at the forefront of the new, more vicious style of metal, but it wasn't until 1985 that they managed to issue their debut, which was released on Music For Nations in the UK. Bands such as Metallica, for instance, were already preparing their third album when this first slab of Exodus vinyl hit the shelves, the thrash bandwagon careering insanely forward, leaving behind those that couldn't keep up. Though it was late in coming and could have done with a slightly meatier production, *Bonded By Blood* – with a terrible sleeve depicting good and evil Siamese twins – was a thrash classic, aggressive riffs weaving an impressive wall of noise topped off by Baloff's bonkers barking. Highlights included "...And Then There Were None" and "Piranha", with the entire album rapidly achieving the status of a landmark release.

Even though the debut had at last delivered upon the promise of their formative years, reducing club PAs to smouldering piles of matchwood, they couldn't keep the band together. Baloff was replaced by **Steve Souza**, taking the group towards their most successful period. Souza had been a member of thrashers **Legacy** before they became **Testament**, so brought with him the requisite vocal style to push Exodus to the next level. The plaudits heaped upon the debut paved the way for *Pleasures Of The Flesh* (1987), a much better-produced album featuring such fine and feral brain-blasters as "Chemi-kill" (about politics, pollution and the environment) and "Parasite" (about, well, killer parasites really). Solos were fired off with deadly precision and the drumming was like an avalanche. This formula was

refined and deployed with equal conviction on *Fabulous Disaster* (1989). This set featured their infamous anthem on the bloody joys of the mosh pit, "The Toxic Waltz", and a decent enough plug through AC/DC's classic "Overdose". Less advisable was their cover of War's "Low Rider" – though it was nowhere near as bad as the one Korn would foist on metaldom a few years down the line.

Having spent enough time on the minimal budgets of Combat Records, Exodus forged ahead by signing to Capitol for *Impact Is Imminent* (1990) – with new drummer **John Tempesta** – while Combat saw fit to chuck out the decent enough live effort *Good Friendly Violent Fun* (1991) and *Lessons In Violence* (1992), a fairly solid "best of". The new studio album contained its fair share of razor-sharp riffing but didn't quite match the standard of their last efforts for Combat. The feeling that something was lacking pervaded *Force Of Habit* (1992) – with new bassist **Mike Butler** – by which time it looked as if Exodus were on the verge of splitting. With many of their early contemporaries now long-standing stadium-fillers it looked like they were battling the law of diminishing returns and would forever be trying to catch up. By the end of the year they had gone their separate ways.

There is, however, nothing quite like a nice bit of nostalgia and the reputation Exodus had earned as a formidably tight and

TEMPO OF THE DAMNED

deadly live crew, not to mention the legendary and influential status of the early albums, would not die. The fan clamour for a reunion was so strong that in 1997 the Baloff line-up (with another new bassist, **Jack Gibson**) reconvened in San Francisco to blast through a live set, drawing heavily on the material Baloff had had a hand in. Naturally, a live album of the event was released, *Another Lesson In Violence* (1997), but, although the seeds were sown for a rekindling of Exodus, the full re-formation didn't happen until 2001. However, tragedy struck in early 2002 when Baloff died of a massive stroke.

Determined to make a go of it, if anything as a tribute to Baloff, Steve Sousa was drafted back. In 2004 *Tempo Of The Damned* was hailed as a welcome return, the vintage Exodus twin-guitar rampage tempered by a modern approach to writing, the variation in pace making the compositions all the more powerful. However, this positive step forward was muted by Souza's sudden departure shortly afterward.

⊙ Bonded By Blood
1985; Combat

This is where it all started, a veritable thrash classic. An essential combination of wired riffing and sheer bloody-minded aggression – what more do you need to know?

⊙ Pleasures Of The Flesh
1987; Combat

A refinement of their debut. Torrents of molten guitar rain down as the band rip through a solid set of bona fide headbanging classics.

⊙ Another Lesson In Violence
1997; Century Media

Back together again, the live versions of some of these *Bonded By Blood* tracks sound better than the originals. They even dusted off an old Hammett-era tune: "Impaler".

EXTREME

Formed Boston, Massachusetts, US 1985; disbanded 1995

Sometimes the success of a band relies on that one special person, that secret ingredient X that creates a remarkable spark. In the case of **Extreme** that individual was Portuguese guitarist **Nuno Bettencourt** (ex-**Sinful**) whose amazing talent helped turn the band into one of the biggest names in rock during the early 90s. Though their success was launched largely on the back of the delicate, super-smoochy acoustic ballad "More Than Words" there was a great deal more to Extreme's make-up; touches of The Beatles, Cheap Trick, Queen, Van Halen and prog rock lurked within the songs, making them a whole lot more interesting to rock fans.

Back in the mid-80s **Gary Cherone** (vocals) and **Paul Geary** (drums) were members of **The Dream** who enjoyed a modest amount of success when their video clip for "Mutha (Don't Wanna Go To School Today)" won a competition on MTV's *Basement Tapes* programme. This minor coup, along with their eponymous six-track mini-LP, was about the sum of their achievements. With a change of name and the addition of **Bettencourt** in 1985 the standard improved dramatically, and when **Pat Badger** (bass) joined in 1986 the classic line-up was in place.

Despite their obvious talents – they seemed to be making a habit of winning local talent competitions – they still had to work out how to write some decent songs. Although their first official appearance on record had been "Play With Me" on the soundtrack to *Bill And Ted's Excellent Adventure* in 1988, it wasn't until winning an MTV video competition that they were signed to A&M. They spent far too long hiring and firing producers while trying to get their eponymous 1989 debut right, but when it arrived the most remarkable thing about the album was Bettencourt's playing, which soon resulted in his being lauded a guitar hero; it didn't take long for the guitar magazines to hail the new axe-pert or for the high-profile equipment endorsements to come rolling in.

The real breakthrough, however, occurred two years later with *Extreme II Pornograffitti*. The band's previous singles had been greeted with indifference but "More Than Words" – a favourite-in-waiting of mums the world over – became their first US chart topper and a #2 single in the UK. It was only held off the top slot by the equally slushy "(Everything I Do) I Do It For You" by Bryan Adams. The album was far more adventurous than the single, however, with socially aware lyrics popping up among those dealing with the search for love – it was an odd juxtaposition, with the airhead rock star photos of the band, all cowboy boots, leather

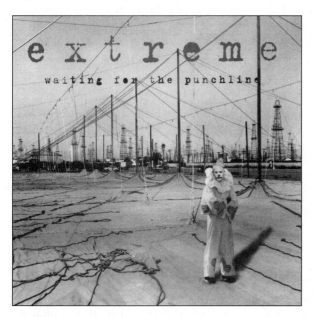

What finished them off was *Waiting For The Punchline* (1995), the band now featuring new drummer **Michael Mangini**. If the previous album puzzled some of the fans then the heavier, more basic production and generally more downbeat feel of the new one sealed their fate. For those that got where the band were coming from it was a sublime blend of mature musicianship and clever, searching lyrics – the sleeve art depicting a clown standing in a wasteland of electricity pylons said it all; the good-time 80s rock approach had been succeeded by the band's more troubled 90s, post-grunge concerns. By the summer of 1995 they had disbanded, though the obligatory career-ending compilation, *The Best Of Extreme: An Accidental Collision Of Atoms* (1998), was a while in coming.

Since then Bettencourt has gone on to release a string of solo projects – first *Schizophonic* (1997), then forming **Mourning Widows** and releasing an eponymous debut in 1999. This was followed by Mourning Widows' *Furnished Souls For Rent* (2000) before moving on to work as **Population One**. Meanwhile Cherone made the biggest post-Extreme splash by joining **Van Halen** for the ill-fated *Van Halen III*, which suffered a major critical pounding. Most recently he has been fronting **Tribe Of Judah**, the line-up including Mangini and Badger.

strides and nice hair, decorating the sleeve. As an antidote to the mellow "More Than Words" the cheerful Van Halen-meets-Chili Peppers metal of "Get The Funk Out", a distant cousin to Aerosmith's "Dude (Looks Like A Lady)", became a Top 20 hit in the UK. The chart-friendly aspect of the record was completed by another Top 5 US hit single in "Hole Hearted".

In 1992 they wore their influences literally on their sleeves when they turned in a staggering performance of Queen classics during A Concert For Life, the Freddie Mercury tribute event at Wembley Stadium. And, for a while they seemed unstoppable, picking up awards and making guest appearances on TV and radio – and then they released *III Sides To Every Story*. Musically it was an accomplished effort, but the proggy tendencies bubbling away beneath the surface began to take over, and dividing the tunes up into thematic sections – "Yours", "Mine" and "The Truth" – must have baffled those that just wanted more funky metal and lovely lilting ballads. It did well in the charts but when the single "Tragic Comic" – an acoustically inflected, lightweight rocker – only reached #15 in the UK, alarm bells must have been ringing.

⊙ Extreme
1989; A&M

Apart from the shocking hair and nightmare 80s fashions on the sleeve there are some fun singles to be found here, including "Kid Ego" and the early effort "Mutha". But the main draw has to be Bettencourt's skills with the six-string.

⊙ Extreme II Pornograffitti
1991; A&M

Forget that ballad for a moment and let the rest of the songs amuse and delight with their diversity and skill. The prog influences are there but don't swamp, making this a finely crafted blend of commercial hard rock and jaw-dropping technical chops.

FAITH NO MORE

Formed San Francisco, US, 1983; disbanded 1998

"... We basically like each other but we know each other well enough to hate each other too!" Billy Gould

Some may claim that **Faith No More** were responsible for spearheading much of what has passed for alternative metal over the last decade or so. With their roots in the Californian punk scene of the late 70s and early 80s there was always something wild and wilful about their approach to songwriting – their frankly bizarre clash of styles and attitudes. They knew how to funk it up, could chuck out rapping hits with ease, and rock with their own brand of corrosive metal. They were unique, often gloriously baffling and pioneering.

Back in the early 80s school friends **Billy Gould** (bass) and **Roddy Bottum** (keyboards) decided to get the latest in a series of bands off the ground with the help of **Mike 'Puffy' Bordin**, a drummer who had a penchant for thrashing the skins tribal style. Guitar power was eventually provided when **'Big Sick Ugly' Jim Martin**, was persuaded by his mate Metallica bassist Cliff Burton – also a chum of Bordin's – to audition for the band. All they needed was a singer, and they found one in the dreadlocked and frenetic **Chuck Mosely**. The disparate pieces were in place: Mosely was a bizarre frontman, they had a rhythm section heavy enough to

anchor a battleship, keyboards for a little class and melody and a guitarist with a very large Marshall stack, crazy hair and a love of strange spectacles. The combination was freakish, bordering on genius.

Their 1985 eponymous debut on the indie Mordam label was unlike anything previously peddled in the mainstream of metal. While big hair and spandex dominated at one end of the spectrum, thrash was blossoming at the other, and FNM were off with the crossover fairies, fusing rap with metal, hardcore punk and funk. They defied easy categorization, but got enough college radio stations behind them to build a cult following, which translated into a deal with London and the release of *Introduce Yourself* (1987). Key cut "We Care A Lot" was reworked from their debut album and became an alternative rap-metal anthem for the late 80s with a heavily MTV rotated video to boot, making them stars on the club scene and resulting in sell-out performances at the *Marquee* in London.

Despite the relative success all was not well. Mosely was deemed to be a loose cannon and was duly fired. The decision to replace him with singer **Mike Patton** would project FNM way beyond the celebrity of what was then deemed to be something of a novelty hit single to fully fledged superstars. Patton's background with way-out-there jazz-funk-death-metallers **Mr Bungle** made him perfect for the job of creating lyrics to what would be their watershed album, *The Real Thing* (1989) which eventually hit US #11 and UK #30. It was an album of breathtaking genius, combining the sublime melody of tunes such as "Underwater Love" with the power of classic metal in the shape of a cover of Black Sabbath's "War Pigs", a live favourite. They battered out terrifying death metal on "Surprise! You're Dead!" alongside a slew of hit singles: "From Out Of Nowhere", "Falling To Pieces" and "Epic", the latter providing yet another MTV-friendly hit. The cornerstone to the sudden improvement was Patton's charismatic persona, both live and in the studio; he was capable of wild child antics in public while at the same time easing his voice from a seductive croon to a demonic howl. With the album generating huge amounts of excitement in the rock press Patton pandered to his every sick and twisted whim for a laugh, egged on by his disbelieving bandmates; this was the era of the singer's infamous coprophiliac tendencies and strange, macabre hobbies such as collecting preserved foetuses and redundant body parts from pathology labs.

Live At Brixton Academy (1991) immortalized the heady rush of the band's live sound while they worked out what to do next; Patton briefly went back to record an album with Mr Bungle, while various accolades were heaped upon both the other various members of the group and their videos. The commercial success of *The Real Thing* had set a standard – which the band duly ignored to deliver *Angel Dust* (1992). Instead of remaking their landmark release they defied expectations with a work of terrifying range and dark wit. There was sinister metal in the distorted "Crack Hitler" and perverted "Jizzlobber", off-the-wall melody with UK top-ten hit "Midlife Crisis" and further rays of sunshine in the shape of "A Small Victory" and "Everything's Ruined". For the most part the set was a welter of brilliantly inventive and black-hearted bitterness, the arrangements providing as many hooks as Patton's superlative vocal performance. *Angel Dust* must surely rank as one of the most influential metal albums of the early 90s, going to #2 in the UK and #10 in the US; it defied the grunge juggernaut that was gaining momentum at the time and was a classic in a class of its own. The success of the album was sealed by an ever-increasing tour schedule and the surprise hit of "I'm Easy" – which made the UK Top 3 – a cover of the old Commodores song often wheeled out by the band as a live encore.

As so often happens, personnel problems brought the run of good fortune to an end: in Martin they had a guitar player who was becoming increasingly difficult to have around. His black-as-the-Sabbath demeanour and sound were perfect for the group, but the erratic behaviour was not. Hence Mr Bungle guitarist **Trey Spruance** helped out with the recording of *King For A Day, Fool For A Lifetime* (1995) and he was then replaced by **Dean Menta**. Despite the record hitting the UK Top 5, somehow the maverick magic seemed to have dissipated. The album raged and rocked in typical FNM style but it lacked the sheer diverse splendour of its predecessor and, as a result, rapidly dropped out of the charts, even though a couple of hits were gleaned from its far more hardcore grooves.

FNM appeared to have pushed themselves as far as they could go without letting off creative steam in other directions. Thus, Mr Bungle's *Disco Volante* made a very brief appearance in the charts and Bottum's *Seasick*, recorded with his side-project **Imperial Teen**, was released in 1996.

The following year the cheekily titled *Album Of The Year* was a major return to form for FNM, featuring a delightful array of potential classics, but that's exactly as they remained: potential classics. There were songs present that could have sat comfortably on *Angel Dust,* but it also seemed as if the band's days were numbered. Always game for a laugh they teamed up with 70s outfit **Sparks** for a version of "This Town Ain't Big Enough For Both Of Us" and then, only a few months after their album was released, FNM split in early 1998 leaving a legacy of brutality and beauty, ably summed up by the hastily churned out compilation *Who Cares A Lot? – The Greatest Hits* (1998).

Since then the various members have continued to work in the music business. Bordin remains a key player in **Ozzy Osbourne**'s band – in fact his desire to play away from FNM was alluded to as one of the causes of the split – while Gould has poured his energies into his eclectic Kool Arrow label. Patton dabbles with a variety of projects such as **Fantomas** and **Tomahawk** while also concentrating on his Ipecac label.

The Real Thing
London; 1989

This is where it all started. A collision of funk, rap, very heavy metal and Patton's weird love'n'death poetry.

Angel Dust
London; 1992

A disturbing and brilliant album that is both high on hooks and shot through with loathing, paranoia and Patton's unsavoury love of toilet business.

Album Of The Year
London; 1997

Could have lived up to its title had the momentum been there. Packed with some great dark tales chiselled out of Patton's strange predilections.

FASTER PUSSYCAT

Formed Hollywood, US, 1986

Close, but no cigar. That's one way of describing **Faster Pussycat**'s all too brief period punching a hole in the ozone layer alongside bands such as Poison and Guns N' Roses. Taking their name from the Russ Meyer flick *Faster Pussycat! Kill! Kill!* the fact that they sounded like a bad-ass bar room brawl with glitter bombs and guitars should come as no surprise.

The brilliantly named **Taime Downe** (vocals), **Brent Muscat** (guitar), **Greg Steele** (guitar), **Eric Stacy** (bass), and **Mark Michals** (drums) were a walking party zone on stage and they managed to capture the glitz and sleaze of their Aerosmith-meets-New York Dolls rock'n'roll on a nifty brace of albums before grunge tore up the trash rule-book in the early 90s. The first real taste of the band came with their charmingly degenerate self-titled debut in 1987, featuring all manner of

glammy gems, not least humorous odes to life in the fast lane such as "Bathroom Wall" and "Babylon". Downe had a voice that could scratch glass while the rest of the band made a virtue out of sounding like they had just spent the previous night rolling around in some Tinseltown gutter. Which they probably had.

One of their most memorable tours was supporting Guns N' Roses in the UK, though they were overshadowed by the unnerving popularity of the headliners. Their second album *Wake Me When It's Over* (1989) seems somewhat prophetic with hindsight because Seattle was preparing a massive and very rude wake-up call, just as this far more dense and heavy sounding album was proving that Faster Pussycat had more to them than pretty-boy pouts and a load of half-inched riffs. The only incident that really rocked the boat for the Pussycat was the departure of Michals, who was arrested on drugs charges. **Quiet Riot** drummer **Frankie Banali** helped out on the imminent European tour and was then replaced by **Brett Bradshaw**.

Third album **Whipped** (1992) couldn't have had a more ironic title – following its release the band were dropped by Elektra. They folded soon after. Years of new projects yielded very little in the way of material that could rival the old Faster Pussycat, so Downe re-formed the band in 2001 with Muscat and Steele alongside some new-found cohorts from **The Newlydeads**, one of his wilderness years outfits. Aside from the touring, a new CD appeared, *Between The Valley Of The Ultrapussy* (2001), which turned out to be a remix album with Downe taking a leaf out of Trent Reznor's book and giving some of the old songs an industrial sheen.

Faster Pussycat
1987; Elektra

This album arrived around the time of *Appetite For Destruction* but didn't do nearly the same amount of business. What it lacked in commercial appeal, however, it more than made up for with sheer nerve and some fine booty-shaking sleaze.

Wake Me When It's Over
1989; Elektra

"House Of Pain" was actually a top-thirty hit in America, helping this much better-realized set of songs go gold in the process. The band were trying to distance themselves from the over-the-top LA metal image of the mid-80s and actually succeeded.

FEAR FACTORY

Formed Los Angeles, US, 1990

Call them industrial metal, cyber metal or just a painful racket, there can be no doubt that **Fear Factory** were pioneers in the world of heavy metal, their music being a direct reflection of their obsession with technology. The results remain harsh and chilling and in the mid-90s their innovative stance influenced many bands that would go on to be branded with the nu-metal tag.

Influenced by the thrash explosion of the 80s **Dino Cazares** (guitar), **Burton C. Bell** (vocals) and **Raymond Herrera** (drums) first got their proto techno-metal to the public via a couple of **Bill Gould** (Faith No More)-produced tunes for the *L.A. Death Metal* compilation. The material was strong enough to get them signed to Roadrunner and their career as champions of computer-assisted metal got under way in brutal style with *Soul Of A New Machine* (1992). The early style was coloured with the crushing power of death metal, Herrera's drumming providing a stainless steel framework for Cazares' synapse-frazzling guitars and Bell's deathrattle vocals spitting out tortured sci-fi inflected lyrics which only occasionally ventured into clean and melodic realms. Crucially, the band were also experimenting with electronic flourishes and samples echoing industrial bands such as Nine Inch Nails, Ministry and Godflesh; it was cold, clinical and utterly mesmerizing in an all-senses-pummelled kind of way. Cazares handled bass duties in the studio but **Andrew Shives** was recruited for live work.

Embracing the notion of technology-driven metal, the band handed half a dozen tracks over to **Rhys Fulber** and **Bill Leeb** of **Frontline Assembly** for a spot of sonic re-engineering; the result was *Fear Is The Mindkiller* (1993). It was a pattern that would hold for their next two albums. By the time of *Demanufacture* (1995) **Christian Olde Wolbers** had taken over on bass and Fulber was providing keyboards in the studio as well as on stage, augmented by **Reynor Diego**. Another towering silicon-hearted monolith of circuit-encrusted metal, the album was given a radical reinterpretation on *Remanufacture (Cloning Technology)* (1997), some of the remixed songs virtually unrecognizable alongside the originals.

Their place secure as techno-metal pioneers, the way was clear for a spot of side-project work. Most notably, Cazares and Herrera were involved with death metal bandits **Brujeria** and Bell joined up with **Black Sabbath** bassist **Geezer Butler** in G//Z/R. Tangential creative desires sated, the Factory production line ground back into action again with 1998's *Obsolete*, a Fulber-produced concept album with distinctly *Terminator*-esque undertones which featured a series of screenplay interludes linking the story together in the lyric booklet. Their performance of "Edgecrusher" on *MTV Spring Break* heralded a step into the relative mainstream of metal and a cover of **Gary Numan**'s "Cars", featuring Numan trading vocally with Bell, was a radio hit. In addition, a slot on 1999's *Ozzfest* and their numerous appearances on soundtracks of films and computer games made the lead up to the new millennium the band's most successful period.

Fulber stayed on to produced 2001's *Digimortal*, their most melodic, though no less abrasive, sounding album. The synthesis of electronic and industrial metal was by now a seamless formula, but the album received lukewarm reviews and it was clear that all was not well in the Fear Factory camp. By 2002 they had effectively called it a day, a rift having formed between Cazares and the remainder of the band.

With the band indefinitely out of action Roadrunner began issuing whatever Factory-related material existed in the vaults; first up was *Concrete*, the band's previously unreleased first album, which had been recorded

in 1991 at **Blackie Lawless's** (WASP) studio with the aid of soon-to-be nu-metal producer extraordinaire **Ross Robinson** who worked there as an engineer. Several of the tracks had been reworked and rerecorded over the years but some were completely new to the fans. *The Hatefiles* compilation followed soon after.

Despite the fact that the band had claimed they were finished, it gradually became clear that they wished to continue – minus Cazares. *Archetype* (2004) featured Wolbers taking on guitar and bass for what was essentially a classic-sounding Fear Factory release, while they cast around and found a permanent bass player in the form of **Byron Stroud** (ex-Strapping Young Lad). The Factory was open for business once more.

⦿ Soul Of A New Machine
1992; Roadrunner

Brutal, cranium-splitting death-meets-industrial hybrid with a keen ear for electronic embellishment. One of the heaviest metal albums of that year.

⦿ Obsolete
1998; Roadrunner

A movie captured on CD. Heavy and caustic, the concept maybe a little clichéd, but the execution makes this one of their premium cyber experiences.

⦿ Digimortal
2001; Roadrunner

Satisfyingly melodic in places this is possibly their most successful combination of technology-driven noise and heavy metal.

FEEDER

Formed London, UK, 1995

Musical fashions can change in a most bewildering manner, but there will always be space for bands who can write good songs. **Feeder** are one of those rare entities that can combine crunching levels of heaviness with sweet and melodic hooks. With an impressive string of chart hits to their name they exude a mainstream pop appeal while at the same time convincingly maintaining their alternative credibility.

The key to Feeder's success can be laid at the door of South Wales native **Grant Nicholas** (vocals/guitar), a songwriter whose studio background enables him to direct the band's sound with great finesse. Nicholas had played in several bands back home in the early 90s and hooked up with **Jon Lee** (drums) in a group called **Temper Temper**. The two of them ended up in London keen to get things going for real and found **Taka Hirose** (bass) through the time-honoured process of scouring musicians' ads in the press. Armed with a bunch of would-be hits they signed to the Echo label and issued the *Two Colours* EP (1995), a highly collectable release that paved the way for the *Swim* (1996) mini-LP. Backed by a gung-ho touring schedule the album kick-started the band's career almost instantly, preparing both fans and critics for what would be an awesome full-length debut.

When **Polythene** (1997) arrived it was hailed as a revelation by the rock press and ended up being voted Album Of The Year by *Metal Hammer*. Imbued with the cool of grunge the music was overdriven and thrilling and shot through with a knowing pop sensibility; the set gave Feeder the first among many live favourites with the likes of "Descend" and "My Perfect Day". During the live shows that followed, the inclusion of new song "High" primed fans for what would become the group's first major hit single – previous efforts had just skimmed the Top 50 but "High" peaked at #24.

It was the kind of whirlwind debut that demanded an even punchier follow-up; *Yesterday Went Too Soon* (1999), mixed by **Nicholas** and **Andy Wallace** (famed for work on Nirvana's *Nevermind* and Slayer's *Reign In Blood*) upped the ante considerably. The major landmark, however, came with album number three. Singles from their second set had done reasonably well but the new "Buck Rogers" single bounced into the Top 5 on the back of a maddeningly catchy chorus. Its parent album, *Echo Park* (2001), debuted at #5 and rapidly went gold, the pop slant balanced against chewy slabs of granite guitar on the likes of "Choke" and "Bug".

At this point Feeder seemed to have it all, which made the sudden suicide of Jon Lee in early 2002 all the harder to comprehend. The group were shocked by the death of their friend, but *Comfort In Sound* (2002) confirmed that Feeder would continue, silencing the waves of speculation surrounding them. Considered their most mature album to date – and featuring **Mark**

Grant Nicholas – born under a bad sign.

Richardson (drums, ex-**Skunk Anansie**) – the sense of sadness was palpable in the lyrics which dealt with themes of loss and despair. The collection managed to turn disaster into a soulful triumph, the band celebrating the life and creative contribution of their friend and marking out a positive direction for the future – which was continued with their critically lauded *Pushing The Senses* (2005).

⊙ Polythene
1997; Echo

It's grunge, Jim, but not as we know it. This full-length debut takes the alternative spirit of grunge, borrows the huge guitars and injects a major dose of uplifting melody.

⊙ Yesterday Went Too Soon
1999; Echo

A fan favourite, this one. The Cold War spy movie concept made for an enigmatic series of CD sleeves but had little to do with the songs, which sounded even more assured than those on the debut.

⊙ Echo Park
2001; Echo

Worth checking out just for the massively enjoyable "Buck Rogers", this record trades off the lighter moments against some seriously heavy arrangements.

⊙ Comfort In Sound
2002; Echo

Emotionally bruised and battered by events, Nicholas and Hirose return with a diverse and powerful album.

FILTER

Formed Bay Village, Ohio, US, 1994

Over recent years the heavier end of the rock and metal spectrum has been dominated by nu-metal, the bastard son of rap and metal shot through with psychological poison and personal angst. So overwhelming has been its success that it has almost eclipsed the early 90s' take on extremity – industrial metal as expounded by outfits such as Ministry and Nine Inch Nails. From this stable came an at first little-known phenomenon called **Filter**, consisting basically of one man's vision and a massive amount of technical know-how, equipment, and a singular artistic vision – so much so that although Filter's base is industrial, it is almost impossible to really categorize their diverse and powerful sound.

Richard Patrick (vocals, guitars, bass, programming, drums) was a touring member of **Nine Inch Nails** and thus immersed in the possibilities inherent in electronic music. Having left the Trent Reznor regime Patrick hooked up with a like-minded musical adventurer named **Brian Liesegang** through a mutual friend. Ensconced in a small house in Patrick's home town of Bay Village, Ohio, they recorded what became *Short Bus* (1995), an album of breathtaking energy and sweeping soundscapes. It was a small but significant victory for the pair, who scored a respectable hit with "Hey Man, Nice Shot", which was picked up by alternative radio.

Though Liesegang left in 1997, Filter was very much an ongoing concern so Patrick set about consolidating his relatively modest success by putting together *Title Of Record* (1999), an album born from a period of personal torment for Patrick after the break-up of a relationship. At the time hip-hop was at the root of most bands' metal ragings but Patrick stuck to his industrial guns and the album was a diverse synthesis of fresh and dynamic electronic stylings and polished metallic splendour; it was the perfect middle finger salute to those who reckoned that Patrick had blown his creative wad on *Short Bus*. Chief in his success was finding musicians to complement his abilities, and the line-up featured guitarist **Geno Lenardo**, drummer **Steve Gillis** and bassist **Frank Cavanagh**.

This unit would grow stronger, the creative bond strengthened over a mammoth two-year and four-continent tour. With a staggering number of live shows to the group's name, Patrick was learning to relinquish some of the writing and control, allowing other ideas to seep into the mix. So when the band came to create *The Amalgamut* (2002) they really were a band and not just a bunch of hired hands performing for an artistic director. True to the idea of the band opening up, the theme of the record, if it could be said to have one, was the vast diversity of America's cultural heritage, an idea that Patrick had begun musing over during Filter's previous tour. Underpinning this notion were Patrick's hard-hitting lyrics, which included takes on the tragic Columbine school massacre ("Columind"), commonplace school violence ("American Cliché"), and the 9/11 terrorist attacks ("The Missing"). Softer textures could be found on tracks such as "The Only Way (Is the Wrong Way)" and "God Damn Me".

True to form, work on a fourth album progressed slowly but surely with ex-**Jane's Addiction** bassist **Eric Avery** helping out. At the time of writing it has yet to be released. Also, amid his Filter responsibilities, Richard Patrick has found time to team up with **Wes Borland** (ex-**Limp Bizkit**) and **Josh Freese** (**A Perfect Circle**) to form **The Damning Well**; their first effort, a song titled "Awakening", appeared on the movie soundtrack to *Underworld*.

⊙ **Short Bus**
1995; Reprise

A broad and imaginative slab of industrial noise, distinguished by Patrick's ability with a strong hook and melodic chorus.

⊙ **Title Of Record**
1999; Reprise

Four years on and the improvement is remarkable. As if the first album wasn't dynamic enough this record incorporates some truly sensitive touches with raging anger.

⊙ **The Amalgamut**
2002; Reprise

There's just no rushing some people. This took a year to write but the care that has gone into crafting the songs shows in its sweeping textures and moods.

FIREBIRD

Formed UK, 1999

It's odd to think that someone so steeped in gore and hardcore could then go on to create this vehicle for good old-fashioned blues-based heavy rock, but that's exactly what **Bill Steer** (guitar/vocals) did when **Carcass** was finally pronounced dead and buried in the mid-90s. Steer had been a member of political hardcore thrashers **Napalm Death** first and then moved on to help pioneer the melodic death metal sound of Carcass. This extreme career trajectory had taken him from the mid-80s to the mid-90s as Steer provided some of the heaviest, nastiest noise ever to emanate from the UK.

Beneath the iron-clad exterior, however, there beat the heart of a classic rocker. With the stench of Carcass gradually lifting, Steer took some time to reassess his priorities and decided that a complete change in musical direction was his main aim. He had been inspired to learn guitar after hearing some of the early greats such as Deep Purple and Led Zeppelin. Now it was time to go back to his roots, develop his playing style to include slide guitar and write some new songs.

He was offered a record deal in Japan as a solo artist but decided to form another band in the model of a vintage power trio, outfits such as Cream obviously providing the main

impetus. Joining him in the studio were old chums **Leo Smee** (bass, **Cathedral**) and **Ludwig Witt** (drums, **Spiritual Beggars**) and *Firebird* (2000) was the result. The set was a warm and soulful tribute to the great guitar-oriented grooves of the 70s. Everything from the album sleeve – a tastefully unclothed young lady in a strange, bird-like pose – to Steer's guitar tone reeked of the decade that style forgot. It was heavy and gloriously dirty sounding, fitting in nicely alongside the racket being churned out by US stoners such as Fu Manchu and Monster Magnet.

From there Steer deviated little from his original view, except to refine his songwriting. The critics had first been surprised and then delighted by the power and conviction of the debut, and the follow-up garnered yet more rave reviews. *Deluxe* (2001) utilized the same line-up and delivered yet more fabulously weed-heavy vibes with tunes such as "Hammer & Tongs" and 'Steamroller' positively swaggering into view, tatty pockets bulging with great riffs and ideas; the amazingly crunchy, loping slide riff to "Sad Man's Quarter" was also a major highlight; the frenzied mouth-harp thrash of the deliberately misnamed "Slow Blues" had to be heard to be believed. The only slight fly in the patchouli-smelling ointment was Steer's less-than-beefy voice, a bluesy yelper in the mould of a Gillan or a Rodgers could have worked wonders. However, Firebird was Steer's pyrotechnic little baby and there was plenty of material on offer to whet appetites for the live shows.

Clearly following the tenet of if-it-ain't-broke-don't-fix-it, Steer was hunting down yet more dusty old equipment for the inventively titled *No. 3* (2003). This time the line-up included **George Atlagic** (drums) and **Roger Nilsson** (bass, **Spiritual Beggars**), not that this meant any startling changes in approach. It was yet another masterclass in heavy rolling blues and blistering solos; the passion and professionalism of the delivery landed the group with several high-profile European tours alongside various stoner oufits, the live line-up including Steer's brother **Alasdair** on bass and **Alan French** on drums.

⊙ **Firebird**
2000; Music For Nations

Close your eyes and it could be 1972. Steer is a great guitarist and these songs are powered by both the blues and a mercurial spirit of invention. For guitar lovers everywhere.

⊙ **Deluxe**
2001; Music For Nations

Volume two in the saga of Steer's guitar fantasy. Plenty of blustering riffs to chew over and some fantastic soloing. It doesn't get better than this.

⊙ **No. 3**
2003; SPV

A change of label though probably not his underwear as Steer chugs through some of the crustiest heavy rock riffs since *Machine Head*.

FOO FIGHTERS

Formed Seattle, US, 1994

The **Foo Fighters** crashed spectacularly into view following the untimely demise of grunge godheads **Nirvana**. Few people realized that behind the Nirvana drum kit lurked a man of such prodigious musical talents. Prime mover **Dave Grohl** (guitar/vocals) played guitar well before he took up the drums, loved heavy rock and metal and had served time with a number of hardcore punk groups including the legendary **Scream**.

Throughout the rollercoasting nightmare of fame and fortune that was Nirvana's short glittering lifetime, Grohl nurtured a desire to create his own music. During periods off the road he took time out to write his own material; anyone lucky enough to have been on the ball in the early 90s would have been able to sample Grohl's songwriting on the highly collectible "Pocketwatch" tape recorded under the pseudonym **Late!**. The earliest official clue to his talents can be found as "Marigold", the low key B-side to Nirvana's penultimate single, "Heart Shaped Box".

Following the period of confusion and sadness after Cobain's suicide, Grohl decided to do what he had always wanted to do. In September 1994 he booked himself into a 24-track studio and like a one-man whirlwind created what would become the Foo Fighters debut release, in a mere seven days. The only thing he didn't play himself was a guitar part provided by **Greg Dulli** of the **Afghan Whigs** on "X-Static". Knowing that the only way forward was in a group, he set about recruiting **Nate Mendel** (bass) and **William Goldsmith** (drums) from short-lived Sub Pop hopefuls **Sunny Day Real Estate**. Meanwhile, old acquaintance **Pat Smear** (guitar), who had joined Nirvana on their final tour, was brought in to complete the line-up. Taking their name from the jargon used by World War II fighter pilots to describe UFOs, a new phenomenon was born; cool songs combined with supercool B-movie imagery.

To say that the curiosity generated by this new project was immense would be an understatement. The record company (Capitol) and media circus were positively salivating at the prospect of another band set to equal the majesty of Nirvana. The anticipation was such that first single, "This Is A Call", effortlessly tripped into the UK Top 5 in June 1995. Hugely commercial and floating on a rush of uplifting guitars and harmonies, it was a succulent slice of power pop-rock. Their debut UK gig at London's Kings College Union merely enhanced fans' expectations; in true punk style they ripped through a short and frenetic set showcasing the forthcoming album and leaving the crowd hungry for more.

Released on the Roswell label (to keep the UFO theme running), *Foo Fighters* (1995) was unleashed towards the end of June to near-universal acclaim. The dazzling brilliance of the first single was no fluke. Drawing on his early punk influences, Grohl had crafted twelve euphoric shots of hardcore melody and layered vocal harmonies.

F O O   F I G H T E R S

The lyrics were impenetrable gibberish but no one cared; it was the sound of the summer, leading many people to dub them the "hardcore Beach Boys". Naturally the Nirvana tag was wheeled out time after time as a reference point, but the ragged Foo Fighters sound owed little to the heavier, more troubled Nirvana vibe. Though often described as "grunge-lite", the group neatly sidestepped the Nirvana legacy; they were clearly a band in their own right with their own unique identity and a charismatic, multi-talented frontman.

The subsequent US tour was a major blast. Riding on the wave of enthusiasm and curiosity, the band were content to let things develop at their own pace allowing the weight of their individual reputations to drive things forward rather than rely solely on hype and Grohl's famous former gig. Late August brought them back to the UK for the Reading Rock festival and in a move that still defies explanation, they were booked to play the small overflowing Second Stage tent where eager fans squeezed themselves into every available space in the sweltering heat. Concerned for the fans' safety the band had to stop frequently to calm things down. The remainder of the year brought the release of two further singles ("I'll Stick Around" and "For All The Cows") and more very successful live shows.

At this point the band had come a long way on the back of what was, essentially, a collection of Grohl-penned solo material. The next stage was to prove they had the ability to go the distance, that their sudden rise was no fluke.

The first major hurdle they faced was finding a replacement for Goldsmith. Grohl played drums on all but two of the songs on the second album, *The Colour And The Shape* (1997), but they needed someone who would be able to undertake the gruelling tour schedule they had lined up. They finally settled on **Taylor Hawkins**, formerly of Alanis Morissette's band. As an exercise in consolidation the new album managed to avoid the trap of rehashing the glories of the debut and instead the band successfully experimented with a more dynamic range of material, spanning the familiar ("Monkey Wrench") and the absurd ("Hey, Johnny Park!").

During the European leg of the subsequent tour, rumours began to circulate that Smear was leaving the band after a backstage row with Grohl. The stories were dismissed by Grohl as "a bunch of Internet crap" but they persisted and on September 4, during the MTV Awards in New York, Smear bowed out and his replacement, **Franz Stahl**, was introduced.

Despite the blip encountered with Smear's departure, 1998 proved to be a highly successful instalment in the Fighters' career. Grohl indulged himself with a spot of movie soundtrack writing by scoring *Touch* with a little help from Verruca Salt songstress **Louise Post**. A contribution to the *X Files* movie soundtrack provided the band with a minor hit single but it was their assured appearance on the UK leg of Ozzfest that proved they had the staying power to maintain their position as one of the most popular post-grunge bands of the decade, a status underlined by their contribution to the *Mission: Impossible 2* soundtrack – a particularly rabid version of Pink Floyd's "Have A Cigar" recorded with **Queen's Brian May**. And then came 1999's superbly accomplished *There Is Nothing Left To Lose* album, and the addition of new guitarist **Chris Shiflett**. As well as some great singles, such as "Learn To Fly", the album spawned several hilarious videos that to this day regularly lighten MTV's daily diet of stodge. So successful was the combination of crunching rock and humorous visuals that both the album and promo clip for "Learn To Fly" landed Grammy awards.

More recently, the Foos have toured extensively, while Grohl has found time to drum for **Queens Of The Stone Age**, both live and on their *Songs For The Deaf*

album. The Foos own recording sessions were split in two in order to allow for this extracurricular activity, but the shift in gear led to a change of approach for the new album. Upon Grohl's return to the band many of the new songs were overhauled and rerecorded while a few new ones were added, many of the alterations instigated in a mere three weeks of frantic studio work. The *Orange County* soundtrack contribution, "The One", was a tantalizing taste of their new work at the end of 2001 and the Foos returned again in 2002 with *One By One*, another blinding slice of their own, unmistakeable brand of rock, featuring yet another guest spot by Brian May. Again they received a Grammy for their troubles, this time for "All My Life", which won in the Best Hard Rock Song category.

The stint with QOTSA was just one of the most high-profile collaborations for Grohl who has spent much of his non-Foos time lending a hand on a spectacular array of projects. He provided drums and guitar for Jack Black-fronted comedy duo **Tenacious D**'s eponymous debut album released in 2002; he played guitar on the cover of Neil Young's "I've Been Waiting For You", on **David Bowie**'s 2002 *Heathen* album; after meeting **Killing Joke** in New Zealand he agreed to provide the drums on their eponymous 2003 album.

Meanwhile, one of Grohl's earlier collaborations – writing and playing on "Goodbye Lament" on **Black Sabbath** guitarist **Tony Iommi**'s eponymous solo album of 2000 – provided him with the inspiration for **Probot**, a pure, unadulterated metal project. Grohl's opportunity to contribute had come at a time when he was writing extremely heavy material as an antidote to a promotional tour he had just completed, strumming out acoustic versions of "Learn To Fly" on various TV and radio shows. He needed to inject some rebellion back into his work after months of peddling lightweight renditions of one of the Foos most popular tunes. Iommi had roped in several guest vocalists to work on various tracks, so following a similar template Grohl began the ambitious and laborious procedure of contacting as many of his metal heroes from the 80s as he could to provide their own unique touches to his proposed scorching metal meltdown. When *Probot* (2003) arrived it was a heavyweight guitar worshipper's dream featuring a who's who of mainstream and underground metal, including **Lemmy**, **Lee Dorrian** (**Cathedral**), **Max Cavalera** (Soulfly), **King Diamond**, **Tom G Warrior** (**Celtic Frost**) and Cronos (**Venom**) among several others, as well as axework from former **Soundgarden** riffmeister **Kim Thayil**, and artwork from **Voivod** drummer **Away** aka **Michel Langevin**. And from one ludicrously heavy outing to another more industrial in flavour, Grohl has most recently been pounding the skins on Trent Reznor's new **Nine Inch Nails** album.

⊙ Foo Fighters
1995; Roswell/Capitol
___
Brilliantly paced and infectiously catchy, Grohl has proved to be an excellent songwriter and not just "that-drummer-out-of-Nirvana". Distortion, melody and attitude merge to make this one of 1995's most essential releases.

⊙ The Colour And The Shape
1997; Roswell
___
Nothing on here quite captures the heady brilliance of "This Is A Call" but the diversity of styles on offer are all pulled together into an agreeably melodic post-punk collection. A statement of intent proving that the Foo Fighters are here for the duration.

⊙ Nothing Left To Lose
1999; Roswell
___
Album number three kicks off with the pounding "Stacked Actors" (allegedly about a certain grunge actress and guitarist Grohl has had a few run-ins with) and blazes into the sunset on the rush provided by some of the band's best songs to date.

⊙ One By One
2002; Roswell
___
Effectively recorded twice, the overhauled songs range from the mellow and melancholy to the spit-fire furious. This is the sound of a band confident in their abilities and taking nothing for granted.

FOREIGNER

Formed New York, US, 1976

For a while during the 80s **Foreigner** were ubiquitous, their slick tricks with hooky melodies ensuring tons of chart action as ballads such as "Waiting For A Girl Like You" and "I Want To Know What Love Is" came to define FM radio rock *par excellence*. If you want immense lighter-waving ballads

then Foreigner are the band for you. Strictly speaking, however, this was only part of the story, because they were perfectly capable of belting out some tough (but highly tuneful) rockers as well. The combination of sublime melody, polished AOR chops and some ingenious songwriting made them one of the top groups of the last two decades.

The reason for the incredible melodic prowess of the band really comes down to the mundane fact that they were fantastic musicians. Rock veteran **Mick Jones** (guitar) had been knocking around in a variety of bands for over ten years and had worked with artists such as Jimmy Page, Jimi Hendrix and Humble Pie as well as being a member of **Spooky Tooth**. He gradually put the band together with multi-instrumentalist **Ian McDonald** (ex-**King Crimson**) and **Dennis Elliott** (drums). The three Brits were joined by Americans **Ed Gagliardi** (bass), **Al Greenwood** (keyboards), and the superb vocal talent of **Lou Gramm**, the mix of nationalities, naturally enough, leading to the Foreigner tag.

Soundwise they owed a great deal to the kind of melodic hard rock pioneered by the likes of Bad Company. From the off they couldn't help but land hit after hit. Their eponymous 1977 debut for Atlantic contained "Cold As Ice", "Feels Like The First Time" and "Long, Long Way From Home", Gramm proving to be a larynx technician of the highest order. The run was maintained by *Double Vision* (1978) and *Head Games* (1979), with the hits consistently building an undeniable head of steam, especially in the US where the record-buying public were seduced by their highly professional sound. During this period new bassist **Rick Wills** joined the band and their live profile grew as they played the California Jam II festival and Reading in the UK.

What really launched them into the super-league, however, was a team-up with **Mutt Lange**, who was making a name for himself as the premier rock producer extraordinaire. By now the line-up had been slimmed down by the departure of McDonald and Gagliardi, but the group's sound and fortunes grew exponentially. What Lange gave them was the kind of turbo-charged accessibility that would take them beyond the realms of mere hard rock and into the welcoming arms of 80s mainstream pop. What really made *4* (1981) a massive hit was "Waiting For A Girl

Like You", a big ballad even your granny could enjoy (their first Top 10 hit in the UK), although the album also contained such gutsy belters as the magnificent "Juke Box Hero", featuring some quite spine-tingling riffing, and the stomping "I'm Gonna Win". Keyboards were provided in the studio by **Thomas Dolby** but the balance with guitar and passionate vocals was what made the songs so strong.

Such a harmonization of the elements didn't exist with *Agent Provocateur* (1984), however. In the interim *Records* (1982), a greatest hits package, had kept their name in the limelight following some major touring, but back in the studio the desire to buff away any remaining roughness left over from their 70s incarnation was just too strong. The new album took production to new levels of perfection, a state of affairs immediately apparent to anyone who has heard "I Want To Know What Love Is", a chart-topping monster ballad that should have been released with a sick bag. The fact that it was preceded on the album by the almost equally slushy "That Was Yesterday" compounded the sugary overkill. The album didn't really come to life until the end of side one with the far rockier "Reaction To Action".

The sound of synths still ringing in his ears, Gramm headed off to record a solo effort, *Ready Or Not* (1987), but was back in the Foreigner line-up for *Inside Information* (1987), the hits still flowing, especially in the US with "I Don't Want To Live Without You" – you guessed it, another ballad.

It didn't take a genius to work out that Foreigner were past their best now. *Inside*

Information was altogether a weak set considering their earlier triumphs. This coupled with Gramm's growing disillusionment with the band's increasingly lightweight sound signalled the end as he threw himself into recording more solo efforts, while his co-writer Jones dabbled in production. Instead of letting things lie, however, Jones eventually found a new singer, **Johnny Edwards**, and put together *Unusual Heat* (1991). Predictably it was a huge flop.

Meanwhile Gramm was having a bad time of it with his new band **Shadowking**, featuring ex-**Whitesnake** guitarist **Vivian Campbell**. They managed one album and one gig, after which Campbell went off to join **Def Leppard**. Cue the Gramm and Jones reunion and *The Very Best ... And Beyond* (1992), a hits package plus three new songs. *Mr Moonlight* (1995) followed – the tour for which included a festival at a nudist recreation park where the band played for a totally naked crowd! But the glory days had faded to a mere distant twilight, a fact underlined by the seemingly endless hits albums that have popped up from time to time. Nevertheless, the touring continues with their 25th anniversary shows of 2002 being filmed for release as *25 All Access Tonight* (2004).

⊙ Foreigner
1977; Atlantic

A touch uneven but still packed with great songs, not least three hit singles. Gramm's voice is something of a revelation to say the least. The 2002 reissue includes four bonus tracks.

⊙ Double Vision
1978; Atlantic

They're finally hitting their hard-rocking groove here. Kick off track and US hit single "Hot Blooded" would be worth it alone, but fortunately the rest of the songs are equally strong. A melodic classic.

⊙ Head Games
1979; Atlantic

Much heavier-sounding this time round but without sacrificing the songwriting. Graced with one of the most puzzling sleeves in rock, depicting possibly one of the worst bathroom-inspired puns since UFO's *Force It*.

⊙ 4
1981; Atlantic

This is where it gets scary. Lange's legendary production style gives the band a flawless and radio-ready appeal. This has ballads and a fair share of rockers, making it an AOR classic.

FREE

Formed London, UK, 1968; disbanded 1973

It's odd to think that this powerful heavy blues outfit nearly copped the name **Heavy Metal Kids** at the behest of Island Records boss Chris Blackwell. The name they stuck with is far more evocative of the soulful and often beautiful rock songs they conjured up, making them one of the best examples of the way good old fashioned rhythm and blues permeated the hard rock psyche in the early 70s. When they finally hit their stride a little way into their career they found themselves suddenly turned into superstars – a state of affairs they found it hard to deal with, eventually leading to their split and, ultimately, tragedy.

Forming from a shamelessly R&B background **Simon Kirke** (drums) and **Paul Kossoff** (guitar) recruited first the velvet-and-steel voiced **Paul Rodgers** and then **Andy Fraser** (bass), it didn't take long for the fledgling unit to land a deal with Island. At the time they were all teenagers which presumably explains their label boss's enthusiasm for the inappropriate moniker. Straight from the off it was clear that the two major assets they possessed were Kossoff's brilliant riffing and fluid soloing plus Rodgers' golden tonsils; in combination the results were achingly emotional,

capable of stirring up everything from soaring elation to deepest despair.

Appropriately enough, their debut effort was dubbed *Tons Of Sobs* (1968), which did virtually nothing as far as the charts were concerned but introduced them to an audience immersed in the authenticity of the blues tradition. Their strength lay in smouldering live shows and their reputation grew at a grass roots level. The tough slog around venues in the UK and the US brought its rewards with eponymous album number two, which turned them into a Top 30 act in the UK in 1969. What really catapulted them to stardom, however, was the sunny riffy singles "All Right Now", with its spectacularly simple guitar refrain and instantly memorable chorus; it took the typical boy-meets-girl scenario of classic rock and expressed it in universally appealing terms. It was a smash hit single that would become one of the era-defining slices of 70s rock.

The accompanying album, *Fire And Water* (1970), was also a classic helped up the charts – narrowly missing the top slot – by the band appearing at the Isle Of Wight Festival. While "All Right Now" showcased their ability to pen hooky rockers the album was packed with great moments, including Kossoff's heroic pre-solo sustained note in the title track, Rodgers' aching vocals during "Oh I Wept", the plaintive piano refrain of "Heavy Load" and the loping nostalgia of "Remember". Each track boasted its own

unique character, making it an album of highlights, a *tour de force* of consistent songwriting and definitive performances. *Highway* (1971) followed but didn't reach the dizzying heights of its predecessor, though Free did enjoy another major hit with "My Brother Jake".

The new found fame, however, didn't sit well with the band. Internal pressures and their inability to reconcile commercial success with musical credibility weighed heavily upon them and so they split to pursue other projects; the label responded by issuing *Free Live!* (1971). Kirke and Kossoff got together with **Tetsu Yamauchi** (bass) and **John 'Rabbit' Bundrick** (keyboards) to record the obviously titled *Kossoff, Kirke, Tetsu And*

Rabbit (1971); Fraser formed **Toby**; and Rodgers formed **Peace** and supported Moot The Hoople.

The following year found the band regrouped and ready, but *Free At Last* was something of a disappointment compared to their previous work. A combination of problems were at the heart of the matter, chiefly Kossoff's growing drug addiction and the personality clash between Fraser and Rodgers. The latter resulted in Fraser leaving; the hole was plugged not by one new member but two, Tetsu Yamauchi and John 'Rabbit' Bundrick. The newly augmented line-up managed one last solid outing, *Heartbreaker* (1973), which contained one of their best songs in the drivingly heavy "Wishing Well", though by the time the record was released Kossoff had headed off to pursue a solo career and to form **Back Street Crawler**; it was a valiant effort to keep going after a spate of health problems but the drugs eventually got the better of him and he died in 1976 of heart failure while on a flight from Los Angeles to New York. His temporary replacement was **Wendell Richardson** of **Osibisa** but all Free managed were some live dates before officially folding.

Kirke and Rodgers went off to form **Bad Company** but that didn't stop the legacy of Free from being repackaged and re-released several times over. In particular "All Right Now" proved to be a perennial favourite apt to pop back into the charts whenever it was reissued.

Fire And Water
1970; Island

If you must own one Free album let it be this one. Moving, emotional and from the heart. And it contains their enduring major hit, "All Right Now".

Heartbreaker
1973; Island

It might not be the classic four-member line-up but there is some fine rocking to be enjoyed, including the bruising heavy blues of the title track and piano-driven mellowness of "Muddy Water". Oh, and the ace "Wishing Well".

FU MANCHU

Formed Southern California, US, 1990

For most people the 1970s was the decade without style, a wasteland of hideous fashion disasters and poor taste. But it

was also the decade of classic rock, Evil Knievel, skateboards, demolition derbies, custom vans and Cheech and Chong movies; in short it was the time when **Scott Hill** (guitar/vocals) was growing up. So when he came to start up a band it was only natural to delve into the good times of sun and fun, when hair was long and rock bands would lay waste with poly-decibel stadium-based extravaganzas featuring extended guitar jams and towering amplification. **Fu Manchu** is about all these things and more, making them a prime stoner band.

Of course, stoner is a lazy catch-all for branding any outfit with even a hint of Ozzy-led Black Sabbath to their groove, but Fu Manchu have never been about doom, rather they borrow the power and grind of the classic metal-from-Brum template, throw in a liberal dose of Blue Cheer superfuzz, a touch of Foghat boogie and inject it with their own unique Californian take on the decade that popularized spacehoppers. Few bands manage to combine their musical output so successfully with the look and feel of their artwork and graphics, but the synthesis of the visual with the aural is arguably what makes Fu Manchu such a long-lived and creatively fascinating outfit.

Alongside Scott Hill the earliest recorded incarnation of Fu Manchu featured **Ruben Romano** (drums), **Greg McCaughey** (bass) and **Glen Chivens** (vocals) on the stupendously hard-to-find "Kept Between Trees" single. A further clutch of singles and a line-up shift or two provided the classic *No One Rides For Free* (1994) album and a slightly more stable line-up featuring Eddie Glass (guitar) and Mark Abshire (bass). By the time of the following year's *Daredevil* album – featuring a dune buggy careering around a beach on the sleeve – **Brad Davis** had joined on bass. This line-up would remain solid for 1996's *In Search Of...*, a foxy lady poised to start a custom car race gracing the album's sleeve.

Each of these albums found Hill praising all that made the 70s fun – the cars, the girls, the vast quantities of weed – in his characteristically nonchalant, slacker vocal style. The band were striving for that killer combination of riff-laden nirvana and stylistic edge, and they achieved it with *The Action Is Go* (1997), though by now Hill had had enough of dealing with Romano and Glass, who left to form **Nebula** – a far more spacy and psychedelic take on stoner – and brought in ex-**Kyuss** member **Brant Bjork** (drums), and **Bob Balch** (guitar) from a local music equipment store. The excellent sleeve art featured cult 70s skateboard hero Tony Alva catching some big air, a huge set of headphones clamped to his Afro'd head.

On the live front, the best place to view Hill fronting his sludgy sonic warriors was on line-ups featuring bands with a similar classic guitar fixation and the Fus ended up supporting the likes of The Melvins, Clutch, White Zombie and Monster Magnet.

With a steady flow of new material for the fans, Fu Manchu turned into something of a touring behemoth, with only a couple of stopgap releases holding up their relentless pursuit of rock'n'roll on the road.

When *King Of The Road* (2000) screeched into view through clouds of burning rubber it was basically business as usual with Hill unearthing yet more 70s pastimes for lyrical exploration. *California Crossing* (2002), however, found them modifying their approach a touch. The sound was still as harsh as the content was kitsch, but under the guidance of producer **Matt Hyde**, who had worked with Monster Magnet, they decided to lay off the fuzz and speed somewhat and inject

COURTESY OF SPV RECORDS

Fu Manchu regret not packing their buckets and spades.

more melody. The end result was a little more like the radio-friendly sounds of the 70s, more Thin Lizzy and Cheap Trick than Sabbath. With the new album on the shelves Bjork decided it was time to go solo and ex-**Smile** member, **Scott Reeder** (bizarrely sharing the same name as an ex-member of Kyuss), stepped into the fold.

Naturally, a road beast like Fu Manchu must be heard live to fully appreciate the retro experience; hence *Go For It ... Live!* (2003) captured Hill and his powerchord-crunching co-drivers blazing through a few old favourites with no small degree of ferocity. And predictably, *Start The Machine* (2004), showed no let up in the studio either.

In Search Of...

Mammoth; 1996

Cars, girls, rock'n'roll; this one has it all. Hill drawls out his tales of gasoline and grass consumption over a thundering selection of taut, muscular riffs.

The Action Is Go

Mammoth; 1997

A new start for the band with Bjork and Balch on board. The subject matter is the same but it's attacked with even more relish than before.

California Crossing

Warners; 2002

A slight easing off in speed is detectable, though everything else is as fuzzed up and tough-sounding as before. Hill shines as a seasoned architect of the pummeling riff.

GILLAN

Formed London, UK, 1978

When **Ian Gillan**, whose voice defined **Deep Purple**'s classic early 70s period, headed off into the sunset, he was free to indulge himself in pretty much whatever he wanted. For a while this involved dabbling in a handful of non-musical projects – including running a recording studio and a country hotel – but it didn't take too long for the singer to get back to recording.

Gillan's first concerted effort bandwise was the **Ian Gillan Band**, but far from being a return to the kind of hard rocking that made Deep Purple so successful; they produced a string of distinctly funky, jazzy albums. *Child In Time* (1976), *Clear Air Turbulence* and *Scarabus* (both 1977) were fascinating sets absolutely bursting with ideas, but far too complex to satisfy on a gut level.

Things got seriously interesting for rock fans with the formation of **Gillan**. The singer retained keyboardist **Colin Towns** from his previous band and released one eponymous, Japan-only album in 1978 before overhauling the band to create what many fans consider to be the definitive line-up. **Bernie Tormé** (guitar), the bald and exuberantly bearded **John McCoy** (bass) and **Mick Underwood** (drums) joined Towns and Gillan to create some seriously fine hard rock albums during the late 70s and early 80s.

Mr Universe (1979) was the first product to grab the attention but the fun really started with *Glory Road* (1980) and *Future Shock* (1981). The records harked back to the tough and melodic heavy rock sound of Purple but were spiced up to compete with the New Wave Of British Heavy Metal; in short, the band had no problem competing with the kids who had grown up listening to Gillan's old band. Both *Glory Road* and *Future Shock* narrowly missed topping the UK charts, and singles such as "Mutually Assured Destruction" and the cracking "New Orleans" helped make them regular visitors to the *Top Of The Pops* studio. "Trouble" was their biggest hit (at #14 in the charts) but the B-side "Your Sister's On My List" was a fine example of the band's disarming tongue-in-cheek charm. They could rock your socks off and make you laugh as well; one of their best songs was the marvellous "No Laughing In Heaven", another top-forty hit.

Tormé was eventually replaced by future **Iron Maiden** guitarist **Janick Gers** and the live *Double Trouble* (1981) and *Magic* (1982) followed, the band's popularity riding high. Then, amid a welter of rumours regarding the re-formation of Deep Purple, the singer folded the band and turned up in **Black Sabbath** for *Born Again* (1983), a record that was thankfully better than the awful sleeve suggested. It was a team-up made in hell – not a good thing – and Gillan then headed off to rejoin Purple, leaving fans of his own band just the memory of an excellent heavy rock outfit.

The golden-tonsilled warbler spent much of the 80s and 90s bouncing in and out of Deep Purple, occasionally dabbling in one-off projects such as **Garth Rockett and the Moonshiners**, and **Rock Aid Armenia**. *Naked Thunder* (1990) was a touch more experimental than usual but *Toolbox* (1991) resurrected the old bluesy, heavy-rock sound with a new line-up of **Brett Bloomfield** (bass), **Leonard Haze** (drums, then ex-**Y&T**) and **Steve Morris** (guitar).

Mr Universe
1979; Acrobat

This narrowly missed the Top 10 in the UK when first issued. Great songs played with flair and passion with one of the best ever rock vocalists exercising his formidable power.

Glory Road
1980; Virgin

"Running, White Face, City Boy" and "Unchain Your Brain" are just two excellent reasons to crank this one up to eleven.

Future Shock
1981; Virgin

"No Laughing In Heaven" would be a novelty cut were it not for the fact that Gillan's talent with ludicrous lyrics stretches way back in time. This album is pacy, superbly played and ranks among the best British albums of the early 80s. A classic.

GIRLSCHOOL

Formed London, UK, 1978

America had The Runaways – an all-girl group, considered by some a mere novelty act – while the UK boasted the altogether more bruising **Girlschool**, who proved during the New Wave Of British Heavy Metal that it didn't take a surplus of testosterone to crank out some mean riffs. For a while they seemed unstoppable and then a series of iffy albums and some pure bad luck stifled their progress, causing them to disband in the late 80s. In a tenacious move, however, the band re-formed in the 90s and began to undertake tours across the UK, Europe and US.

Back in the 70s, school friends **Kim McAuliffe** (guitar/vocals) and **Enid Williams** (bass) put together an all-girl rock band called **Painted Lady**, but it was with the addition of **Kelly Johnson** (guitar/vocals) and **Denise Dufort** (drums) that the chemistry started to fizz. Like many of the bands of that era their brand of heavy rock was influenced by the spit and fire of punk, a sound that they channelled into their first single "Take It All Away", under the much better band name of Girlschool. The single got them noticed and they ended up supporting Motörhead in 1979, a break that would lead to their most successful period.

That old rock'n'roll rogue Lemmy took a shine to these bullet-belted youngsters and through his help – he set up a showcase attended by Bronze bigwig **Gerry Bron** – the group landed a proper record and management deal. Now signed with the same label as Motörhead they came up with *Demolition* (1980), produced by head studio knob twiddler **Vic Maile**. It wasn't exactly a classic – it was rather too rough and ready in the songwriting department – but it primed the metal-loving hordes for the much finer *Hit And Run* (1981).

The debut album had tickled the Top 30 in the UK but its follow-up charged straight into the Top 5, not least because of Girlschool's inspired collaboration with Motörhead on the highly amusing *St. Valentine's Day Massacre* EP. Issued under the name **Headgirl** the two bands gave the old Johnny Kidd classic "Please Don't Touch" a good going over down a dark alley with Lemmy's Rickenbacker, before turning their attention to "Bomber" (Motörhead) and "Emergency" (Girlschool). In the wake of their appearance on *Top Of The Pops*, *Hit And Run* really couldn't fail.

For the following year's *Screaming Blue Murder*, **Gil Weston-Jones** had replaced Williams. The album failed to hit the heights of *Hit And Run* in the charts and *Play Dirty* (1983) did nothing to halt the commercial slide, despite being produced by **Slade** duo **Noddy Holder** and **Jim Lea**.

A major rethink was in order but while the band worked out what to do next Johnson jumped ship; new recruits were **Jackie Bodimead** (vocals/keyboards) and **Cris Bonacci** (guitar). A change of label took them to Mercury – old home to the Runaways – and *Running Wild* (1985) which

was nothing of the sort, being an album tailored to US tastes. Bereft of any focus or direction they were seriously floundering by now. Bodimead left and they continued as a four-piece again. For some reason it was thought that another collaboration – this time with Gary Glitter! – might be the way to go, but then "I'm The Leader Of The Gang (I Am)" failed to do the business. After *Nightmare At Maple Cross* (1986) began to look like it was commercially dead in the water they soldiered on with *Take A Bite* (1988) – **Tracy Lamb** of **Rock Goddess** replacing the departed Weston-Jones – but soon the band folded.

Come 1992 and the band re-formed with new bassist **Jackie Carrera** for an eponymous comeback, just as grunge was hitting high gear. *Live* (1995) followed and the band kept going – with various past members flitting in and out of the line-up.

In 2002 the *21st Anniversary: Not That Innocent* album appeared and a couple of years later *Believe* (2004), with a more stable line-up: **Enid Williams** (bass/vocals), **Denise Dufort** (drums), **Kim McAuliffe** (vocals/guitar) and **Jackie Chambers** (lead guitar). More gigging followed.

Glam Metal

As the name suggests, what we are dealing with are bands whose image is as important as the music itself. The first glam bands appeared in the 70s, typified by the outrageously outfitted **The Sweet** in the UK and **Kiss** in the US. **Alice Cooper** enjoyed a brief dalliance with early glam (sometimes dubbed glitter rock), as did David Bowie, in heavily made-up, androgynous Ziggy Stardust mode, helping to sharpen up the genre's image and make it cool. At the other end of the cool spectrum **Slade** gave us fright-wigs and leftover tinsel – which is not surprising as one of their major hits was the eternally irritating "Merry Xmas Everybody". The emphasis of the music was largely on accessibility and hooks, which naturally enough took many of the best glam bands into the pop charts, even though they were actually delivering tuneful hard rock.

The 80s concept of glam took the basic tenets of the 70s version and amplified them. The hair was big – hence the parallel 'hair metal' tag – the outfits were flashy and ridiculous, but less fixated on pure glitter. With MTV a relatively new phenomenon hungry to latch onto the latest musical trends, these image-conscious bands found an ideal medium through which to reach millions, and bands such as **WASP**, **Ratt**, **Mötley Crüe**, **Cinderella**, **Poison** and **Twisted Sister** did just that. While the 70s scene had enjoyed something of a sexually ambiguous thrill through the vicarious exploits of bands such as the **New York Dolls**, the hard-rock-with-pop sensibilities of the 80s was resolutely hetero and the over-the-top image was matched by songs that were outrageously lewd and crude which led to the connected tag of cock rock. One of the most shocking tunes of the era, for the PMRC at any rate (see p.272), was WASP's "Animal (I Fuck Like A Beast)", but most bands preferred to go more for good-time party tunes than a violent assault on the audience's sensibilities with Poison's reliance on hooky choruses and ballads being a typical approach guaranteed to get plenty of airplay.

Of course, in a climate where pretty much all bands, bar the thrash outfits, boasted teased locks of some variety, many – such as **Whitesnake**, **Def Leppard** and **Bon Jovi** – were lumped into the hair metal category without being particularly glammy. Such pigeon-holing often went with a derisory attitude towards the music and some metal fans refused to regard anything so blatantly commercial as metal at all. All of which was ultimately academic when grunge came along and cut short the careers of all but the hardiest of glam and hair bands along with the prospects of the more overtly metal groups as well.

The Collection
2000; Castle

This double album provides an excellent cross section of the band's work with classic tracks from the early albums and their fantastic collaboration with Lemmy and the boys.

GOD FORBID

Formed New Brunswick, New Jersey, US, 1996

Regurgitating a formula is simply not in the nature of this behemoth of a band – not for them the technical speed of thrash, guttural roars of death metal, or naked fury of hardcore. No, when guitarist brothers

SEAN WRIGHT

God Forbid's dreaded Byron Davis.

Doc and **Dallas Coyle** began writing songs they wanted to take the essence of the different types of music they loved and twist them into a new kind of metal monster to stomp rival acts into the dirt. The duo grew up listening to bands such as Slayer and Metallica, but they wanted so much more than to simply rehash their sound.

Generous helpings of screamo hardcore came courtesy of **Byron Davis** (vocals), whose formidable lung capacity allowed not just man-on-the-edge wailing but precise, classic metal melodies, while the rhythm section of **Jon Outcault** (bass) and **Corey Pierce** (drums) displayed a technical interplay that permitted all manner of stylistic exploration – pure raging death stylings, plus old-school metal and brain-spinning speed in one energizing rush.

The band's first outing was 1998's *Out Of Misery* EP, on the independent 9 Volt label, providing a tentative taster of what was to come on *Reject The Sickness* (1999). As a debut album it was a storming affair, a harsh and abrasive statement of intent that toyed knowingly with melody but which did not succumb to the obvious tricks and clichés of metal songwriting. It was metal from the underground, with hardcore adding a frisson to the contemporary sound. Call it metalcore or just a refreshing change, the local New Jersey and New York metal stations pounded it to death on the airwaves until Century Media realized that there was something unique about this lot – and it wasn't just that they were four-fifths African American.

With such a galvanizing hell-for-leather approach to writing, **God Forbid** were one of a growing number of underground metal bands – such as Shadows Fall and Killswitch Engage – subverting the prevailing trend for down-tuned angsty nu-metal. They were proving to be a draw to both traditional metal

GOTH ROCK AND METAL

Goth was basically a late-70s off-shoot of punk. As the scene developed in the early- to mid 80s the overtly punk fashions began to incorporate increasing amounts of black while cultivating an air of theatrical glamour and darker, artier influences such as nihilism, the occult, Romantic literature, paganism and gothic horror – basically anything with a touch of the night to it. The focus was on the beauty of misery and an air of exquisite and resigned doom.

From this morass of influences came the dominating crossover form of bands such as the **Sisters Of Mercy**. What made them palatable to rock fans was their overt embracing of rock star values. *Floodland* (1987) was created with the aid of **Meat Loaf** collaborator, **Jim Steinman**, producing key tracks for an opulent, majestic feel, while *Vision Thing* (1990) was almost a metal album, its towering, riff-driven groove a joy to behold. **The Mission**, on the other hand, splintered away from the Sisters Of Mercy in the mid-80s and brought their latent Led Zeppelin influences to the fore on *Children* (1988), which was produced by Zep's **John Paul Jones**. Meanwhile the **Fields Of The Nephilim** brought bold cinematic menace to the game. Their vision was fully realized on *The Nephilim* (1988), an atmospheric masterpiece of barely restrained violence and shimmering beauty, owing as much to the intensity of **Motörhead** as any arty pretensions.

The goth influence on modern metal is extremely strong, from the fashion sense, to lyrics and artistic outlook. Part of the goth culture of the 80s gravitated towards industrial music with the result that aspects such as sexual fetishism figure largely in the music of such key artists as **Nine Inch Nails** and Marilyn Manson. Manson masterfully uses everything from leather and rubber to a spooky celebration of freakish, all with a highly literate sense of perversity. NIN's **Trent Reznor** meanwhile, revels in the dark side of the human psyche; fetishistic themes of pleasure in sexual degradation and slavery figure high on his list of song topics and videos.

Away from the overtly industrial metal backdrop the dark side of goth sensuality is plain to see in the music and image of black metallers **Cradle Of Filth**. The band drip with the theatrical trappings of goth, from the overt use of blood-and-sex Hammer horror to the leather-clad vampire myth that informs their image. For **Type O Negative**'s Pete Steel, on the other hand, it's all a bit more straightforward – he just seems to be totally in love with death and decay. While *October Rust* (1996) is distinctly autumnal in tone, *World Coming Down* (1999) is positively funereal. Steele's vocals often seem weighed down by the nihilistic pointlessness of it all and yet burn with passion; which is also what **HIM**'s **Ville Valo** manages to pull off with a winning combination of morbidity – the imagery of death is littered throughout the songs – and melancholic fire.

Doom metal also has a strong affinity with goth. Early albums by acts such as **Paradise Lost, Anathema**, and **My Dying Bride** display a strong gothic streak. Ethereal female vocals are sometimes incorporated to produce a ghostly counterpoint to the standard male vocals, a pioneering experiment pulled off by **Celtic Frost** back in the mid-80s. This yin and yang approach to metal is still used to great effect by a variety of bands, with **Lacuna Coil**, **Tristania** and **Theatre Of Tragedy** among the many to turn the experimentation into a major feature.

fans and to those looking for cool and new aural thrills way beyond those provided by Limp Bizkit and Korn.

Having signed to Century Media the road was clear for the band to bring their own brand of noise to the world. *Determination* (2001) boosted the somewhat rougher sound of their debut, with intelligent and barbed lyrics providing a cerebral counterpoint to the primal ferocity of the music. Naturally, a massive amount of touring, with bands such as Opeth, Cradle Of Filth and Mushroomhead, as well as their own headlining gigs in the UK, introduced them to a vast number of potential fans. In the same year *Out Of Misery* was re-released in expanded form, a sweaty fistful of tunes recorded live at CBGB's taking the running time up to that of a full album.

What new fans had discovered in *Determination* would be exceeded with *Gone Forever* (2004), a far more cohesive set of songs. The influence of the contemporary Swedish death metal scene could be felt, the duelling guitars of classic metal were all present and correct, the throat-shredding power of hardcore was there.

With such an accomplished album to their credit quite where God Forbid intend to take their everything-including-the-kitchen-sink approach to metal next remains to be seen.

◉ Gone Forever
2004; Century Media

It might have the whiff of death metal about it but this is a quantum leap beyond the genre. Melodic and cathartic in equal measure this is the sound of raw emotion laid bare against a huge backdrop of guitars. It will leave you breathless.

GRAND MAGUS

Formed Stockholm, Sweden, 1996

Of all the so-called stoner bands riding the resurgence of interest in down and dirty guitar thunder, this classic trio are one of the best, playing what they have dubbed "Black Magick Rock". Shades of the occult fused to a spine of old-school metal make **Grand Magus** a truly worthwhile prospect.

Back in the mid-90s **JB** (guitar/vocals) put the band together with **Fox** (bass) and **Iggy** (drums). JB had spent time playing in little known bands such as **Cardinal Fang** and **Supermouth**, with little success. The trio first played under the name **Smack**, trying to forge a reputation for themselves on the live circuit. Iggy was soon replaced by **Trisse** who saw an advert placed outside an anniversary showing of Deep Purple's *California Jam* concert. A rock-solid line-up now in place, their first demo was recorded in 1999 which led to a split single with fellow Swedes **Spiritual Beggars**, Grand Magus offering up "Twilight Train". The single eventually attracted the attention of Rise Above Records, the label dedicated to doom and stoner metal, set up by **Cathedral** mainman **Lee Dorrian**. They could not have wished for a more suitable home. By now they had already changed their name in order to better sum up their sound and direction. Within a couple of months of signing they were in the studio recording their eponymous debut, which rapidly garnered rave reviews from rock magazines across Europe.

Within the smouldering embers of *Grand Magus* (2001) there was a blues sensibility which brought to mind the classic riffery of Deep Purple and the fuzzy, bass-heavy horsepower of Black Sabbath. At the centre of their vintage groove was JB's impressive and throaty bellow, which so impressed Spiritual Beggars' **Michael Amott** that he asked the frontman to provide vocals for *On Fire* after the departure of singer Spice and tour Europe with them – which he did before returning to his own band.

Grand Magus, in turn, set about proving themselves on a variety of tours playing with the likes of Electric Wizard, Sloth and Terra Firma, bands among the *crème de la crème* of doom. All of which may have had some effect on the developing band because *Monument* (2003) was definitely heavier and darker than their debut, arcane themes evident in titles such as "Summer Solstice" and "Baptised In Fire". Yet again the critical clamour was overwhelmingly positive, making the album one of the underground metal successes of the year.

Grand Magus
2001; Rise Above

A superb debut of super-heavy blues rock. It's no wonder JB was half-inched by Spiritual Beggars to provide vocals – his soulful bellow is exceptional.

Monument
2003; Rise Above

Darker and even heavier than their debut, there is more of a doom flavour to this earth-shaking occult-driven opus.

GREAT WHITE

Formed Los Angeles, US, 1982

A tight and powerful live unit concentrating more on sound than the hair metal mentality that engulfed the West Coast, this lot peaked at the tail end of the 80s and then promptly fell victim to grunge. They didn't possess the invention or the solid, mainstream fan base necessary to ride out the storm of 90s alternative rock.

Heavily influenced by the greats of yesteryear, not least the mighty Led Zeppelin, **Great White** first issued their self-financed **Don Dokken**-produced debut mini-LP *Out Of The Night* in 1982 and caused enough of a stir to attract the attention of EMI America. The line-up at the time featured **Jack Russell** (vocals), **Mark Kendall** (guitar), **Lorne Black** (bass) and **Gary Holland** (drums); over the years the most constant factors would be Russell's amazingly Robert Plant-like wail and Kendall's incisive guitar style as other members came and went.

Their major label debut was an eponymous album issued in 1984; it was solid enough but did nothing sales-wise, resulting in the band being dropped, despite tours with Whitesnake and Judas Priest. Bouncing back in 1986 with *Shot In The Dark*, first released as an indie effort and then reissued on Capitol, they put the false start behind them and powered on, with new

drummer **Audie Desbrow** and guitarist **Michael Lardie**. *Once Bitten* (1987) was a melodic and assured follow-up which nearly cracked the US Top 20 and *Recovery: Live* (1988) was a contractual obligation live set, which nevertheless rocked hard. But it was with *Twice Shy* (1989) that they really slammed into the charts. A cover of **Ian Hunter**'s "Once Bitten, Twice Shy" went into the US Top 5 and the album into the Top 10.

The band had arrived, but just couldn't maintain the momentum with the next two studio efforts, *Hooked* (1991) and *Psycho City* (1992). When the first grunge rumblings emerged from the northwest of the US they were among the first hard rock casualties. And in 1994 – now signed to Zoo Entertainment – they put out *Sail Away,* a rather uninspiring set of tunes. The slide downhill continued with *Let It Rock* (1996) and *Can't Get There From Here* (1999), although their Led Zeppelin tribute album *Great Zeppelin* (1999) at least allowed the band to show off their roots.

Since then Great White have slipped further into a hinterland of live albums and compilations, punctuated by touring. And in February 2003 a tragic event took place that would haunt both the band and the fans. Nearly a hundred people died – including guitarist **Ty Longley** – during a gig at a nightclub in Rhode Island when the band's pyrotechnics started a major fire.

Greatest Hits
2001; Capitol

One of several compilations out there, this album covers a good deal of material including live tunes and cover versions.

GREEN RIVER

Formed Seattle, Washington, US, 1984; disbanded 1988

Deep in the mists that hung over the early Seattle grunge scene lurked the origins of one of the key rock groups of the early 1980s – **Green River**. Their importance lay not in their ability to sell records by the bucketload (to put it simply, they didn't) but in that they were the great grand-daddies of grunge. Apart from producing several records that epitomized the sound of Seattle, they eventually split to form **Mudhoney** and **Pearl Jam.**

In the beginning there were **The Limp Richards, Mr Epp** and **The Ducky Boys**. All three bands churned out variations of hardcore punk influenced by British New Wave and American heavy metal. Typical of any burgeoning rock scene the personnel situation was extremely fluid, if not downright incestuous. However, two key players in all three bands were **Mark Arm** (guitar/vox) and **Steve Turner** (guitar) who created Green River in late 1984. They were joined by **Alex Shumway** (drums) and Montana-born skate-punk **Jeff Ament** (bass).

Green River's sound took in all the usual influences and then spat them back as shards of splintered, fuzzed-up punk. Add to this a taste for bizarre imagery in their lyrics and what you have is a beast that would later be named grunge. They were so impressive live that alternative-set darlings Sonic Youth would request their presence on the bill whenever they played the area.

The summer of 1985 saw the addition of another ex-Ducky Boy, **Stone Gossard** (guitar), allowing Mark Arm to concentrate on his vocals. The band had already been featured on a compilation called *Deep Six* (1985), but the group's first true solo effort was the mini-LP *Come On Down* (1985), released on the Boston-based Homestead label. From the opening title track to the closer, "Tunnel Of Love", the set captured the raw fury of the band's live sound. Following the release Steve Turner left the fold, and further down the line teamed up with Mark Arm again to form Mudhoney ... but that's another story. Taking on replacement **Bruce Fairweather** (guitar), this line-up remained constant during the following bouts of success and internal strife.

GRUNGE

In the same way that punk stomped all over the pomposity of 70s rock, so grunge is accorded the dubious honour of having killed off 80s metal, especially that of the hair variety.

Again, as with punk, it is very difficult to pinpoint how it got kicked into motion, or indeed what it really is or was. Most critics point to Seattle as being the place where a scene evolved in the mid-80s, fired by US hardcore but also steeped in earlier metallic traditions and 60s garage rock. The result was bands such as **Mudhoney** and **Nirvana** who produced thick, crunchy discordant noise displaying a love of vintage equipment – Mudhoney's *Superfuzz Bigmuff* (1988) was named after their favourite make of distortion pedal – and a disregard for what passed as the rock star image of the day. They were about slabs of cathartic, primal rock, the antithesis of what MTV was pushing at the time.

The channel by which much of the early examples of grunge arrived was the independent Sub Pop label, who specialized in issuing singles and EPs promoting bands from the Seattle area, such as **Soundgarden** and **Green River** – who would eventually lead into **Pearl Jam** and Mudhoney. Other bands on the label who defined the very loose and sludgy early grunge sound included **Blood Circus**, **Tad** and **Swallow**.

Nirvana's first album, *Bleach* (1989), also arrived via Sub Pop. It was dirge heavy, with a latent melodic edge that was later uncovered on *Nevermind* (1991). At this point it became clear that something extraordinary was about to happen. The grunge tag had yet to find common usage but journalists quickly coined the term 'Generation X' to describe the teen slackers for whom the new sound seemed to be tailor-made. The potential commercial gains to be made soon had record labels searching for the next big thing, leading to a wave of bands such as Pearl Jam and **Alice In Chains** going on to great success.

Many of the groups that achieved such amazing sales based their music very much on a classic rock template rather than the limited appeal of squalling noise and atonal riffing. What made them stand apart from the rock scene of the 80s was the serious and downbeat nature of the music and lyrics – drug addiction and emotional strife were nice, dark topics for exploration – and their anti-image, typified by flannel work shirts and grotty thrift store jeans.

Ultimately, what was important was that such music was identified with being alternative and therefore cool, tapping into the *Zeitgeist* for the early 90s. It rapidly became the rock you were allowed to like because, superficially at least, it had little in common with the hedonistic, macho, good-time rock of the previous decade. With the media now tuned in to broadcasting anything remotely dour-sounding, grunge really came to describe an attitude and a particularly miserable guitar tone and style. The doomed and desperate aspects of grunge, of course, helped set the scene for nu-metal.

June 1986 saw the band record their first EP for the now-legendary Sub Pop label but, due to a record label cash crisis, the record wasn't released until July 1987. *Dry As A Bone* (1987) was a distillation of the Seattle scene ethos and the distinctive Sub Pop sound. These five gut-wrenching tracks were arguably as important as Nirvana's *Bleach* in gatecrashing the collective rock consciousness; people finally began to notice Seattle.

Following this success they began work on an album, laying down a version of **David Bowie**'s "Queen Bitch" alongside their own material. However, by the time *Rehab Doll* (1988) had hit the shelves, conflict within the band had reached crisis point. Three records and three tours down the line they split. As Mark Arm tells the story, it was a typical conflict between art and commerciality; punk versus the major label deal. After a gig at LA's *Scream Club* tempers exploded – Arm wanted backstage passes for friends, Ament on the other hand had already given them to record company A&R men who didn't even bother to turn up. Arm accused Ament of abandoning their principles and split from the band.

This spectacular implosion resulted in the creation of three bands that have etched their identities even more deeply on the world of rock: the short-lived **Mother Love Bone**, **Pearl Jam** and Mudhoney.

Come On Down
1985; Homestead

As a taster of what was to come, this vicious six-track mini-LP is akin to a snapshot of the embryonic Seattle scene. Energy, distortion and alienated attitude make a classic example of the sound that would be dubbed grunge.

Dry As A Bone
1987; Sub Pop

This EP alone went a major way towards building Sub Pop's international reputation as the home of weird alternative rock. Uncompromising and angry, these five tracks mark an important point in the creation of a sound that would become a worldwide phenomenon.

Rehab Doll
1988; Sub Pop

The band had split by the time this came out, but it gave an indication as to where the various members would be heading. Containing mainly new material it also features a couple of tracks from previous releases ("Swallow My Pride" from *Come On Down* and "Together We'll Never" from a 1986 single).

GUNS N' ROSES

Formed Los Angeles, US, 1985

The level of mystique and myth surrounding **Guns N' Roses** is quite phenomenal. For a few years they were one of the biggest bands in the world, their reputation for bringing the archetypal rock'n'roll lifestyle alive on stage was unmatched – they were shockingly authentic and richly deserved their tag of "most dangerous band on the planet". The electric volatility, upon which they thrived, however, was also their undoing and after burning brightly the band almost fizzled out in the mid-90s under the weight of ego, recrimination and litigation. From the flurry of sackings and lawsuits vocalist **Axl Rose** emerged with the right to use the band moniker – but has yet to produce a new studio album.

Guns N' Roses formed in mid-1985 from the smoking debris of several rock bands floating around the scuzzier neighbourhoods of LA. **William Axl Rose** (vocals) had been chief screamer in **Hollywood Rose**, and an early incarnation of **LA Guns**; **Jeff Isabelle** aka **Izzy Stradlin** (guitar) had known Axl since 1979; **Michael 'Duff' McKagan** (bass) had played in dozens of local punk and hardcore bands. Meanwhile, **Saul Hudson** aka **Slash** (guitar) and **Steven Adler** (drums) had previously put together an outfit called **Road Crew**.

After only two days' rehearsal this line-up, which many still regard as the definitive Guns N' Roses, played their first gig at LA's Troubadour Club on June 6, 1985. Following this trial by fire they kicked off on the aptly named Hell Tour. Everything that could go wrong did: their transport broke down; only twenty people turned up to their first gig; and the rest of the tour was cancelled.

The shambles of their live performances was a direct reflection of their chaotic lifestyle and accounts of the band's early days have long since passed into rock-lore – they slept rough and hung out in all-night porn shops and strip-joints, and they got hammered on Night Train, a cheap wine they would immortalize on their first album. They eventually moved into a poky rehearsal room; "The Hellhouse", as it became known, was the venue for some of LA's wildest parties.

During the mid-eighties LA was experiencing the stirrings of a glam and sleaze revival and trashy rock was definitely en vogue. The Gunners rapidly became one of the hottest attractions on the scene, and landed themselves a residency (of sorts) at the Troubadour. Their sound was a Molotov cocktail of razored guitars and attitude. The Rolling Stones and Aerosmith were major influences, but then so was punk. On stage, they were one of the most unholy and anger-fuelled acts around. They were louder than AC/DC (allegedly), and their songs stank of life in the gutter – the guns, girls, vice and violence.

It was only a matter of time before the major record companies would sniff them out. In March 1986 the band signed to Geffen for a mere $75,000 but the money vanished immediately on debt and drugs. In December 1986, while hunting for a suitable producer, they unleashed a self-produced, limited edition EP, *Live ?!*★@ Like A Suicide* containing four tracks: tacky covers of Rose Tattoo's "Nice Boys" and Aerosmith's "Mama Kin", along with two originals, "Move To The City" and "Reckless Life". Its crackling fury and raw energy ensured that all 10,000 copies sold out within four weeks.

By the time they arrived in Britain, in June 1987, their venomous reputation preceded them – the tabloid press even suggested that they spent their spare time torturing animals! They played three nights at London's Marquee club, and although reviews were less than ecstatic their appearances were true to form; Axl tried to pick fights with hecklers, while Slash and Izzy staggered nonchalantly around the stage under the influence of something far stronger than Jack Daniels.

It was not until the release of *Appetite For Destruction* (1987) that the band proved their importance. From the shuddering riff and police-siren scream of opener "Welcome To The Jungle", to the closing swagger of "Rocket Queen", each song was nailed home with murderous precision, the clash of bluesy hard rock and punk creating an addictive amalgam. The album was studded with instant classics: "Mr Brownstone" was pure, shuffling sleaze; "Out Ta Get Me" was all paranoid posturing; and "Sweet Child O' Mine" proved they could write hit singles. Over the next couple of years nearly half of the record would garner some kind of major chart action. The cover – a reproduction of a Robert Williams painting of a robot raping a woman – caused even more controversy than the expletive-ridden songs. Only initial quantities were shipped with the original cover and subsequently the Gunners' cross logo was used. The album topped the charts in the US and went top-five in the UK.

Back in the States the band continued to serve out their apprenticeship supporting The Cult and Mötley Crüe. When they returned to the UK in October their intention was to support Aerosmith. Feeling indestructible when the headliners pulled out, they went ahead with the tour anyway, finishing with a near sold-out gig at the then Hammersmith Odeon.

Their return to the UK, in August 1988, saw them play second from the bottom on the Donington Monsters of Rock bill. Despite the presence of Iron Maiden and Kiss, however, it was Guns N' Roses that the fans really wanted. Sadly, far from the triumphant set everyone predicted, crowd control problems ended in tragedy; a mighty surge towards the stage resulted in two young fans being crushed to death. The band stopped their set in order to calm the crowd, but it was too late.

The release of G N' R *Lies* (1988) was more of a holding operation rather than a true follow-up; it comprised their first EP, plus four new acoustic numbers. The beautiful lilting melody of "Patience" soothed, while "Used To Love Her" was pure black humour, dubbed by some as misogynistic. But it was the final track, "One In A Million", which found the band unintentionally courting controversy again. Written from the point of view of a hick white kid arriving in LA, Axl made references to "niggers" and "faggots". This resulted in the band being slung off the bill of an AIDS benefit gig in New York but, as ever, the controversy did them no harm – the album charted at #22 in the UK, and #2 in the US.

Their move towards self-destruction continued. On the first night of the Rolling Stones' Steel Wheels tour Axl (in front of 83,000 people) threatened to quit if certain band members did not ditch their drugs collections. Axl's vitriol was aimed primarily at Slash who spent 1990 collaborating with several other artists while he broke his heroin habit, but Adler found it harder to wake from the nightmare. He went in and out of rehab three times and was eventually replaced by **Matt Sorum** (ex-**The Cult**). Also on board now was **Dizzy Reed** (keyboards) who had been a member of LA band **The Wild** when he first met Axl. The two new Gunners made their debut at the *Rock In Rio* festival, in January 1991.

The group shocked everyone in the spring by actually recording some new songs, something their detractors maintained would never happen. It was a gargantuan project as they wanted to issue around thirty new tracks on two separate volumes. But, not only did Axl's notorious mood swings make the process excruciating, he ended up hating **Bob Clearmountain**'s mixing. Everything had to be scrapped and started over with **Bill Price** (of Sex Pistols fame).

"You Could Be Mine" was released as a taster in July (it was on the *Terminator II* soundtrack), closely followed by *Use Your Illusion I* and *II* (1991). With both volumes sitting pretty at #1 and #2 in the *Billboard* chart, the reaction was phenomenal, as the press argued over the merits of one compared to the other. The band handled the ragers such as "Right Next Door To Hell" and "Perfect Crime" with poisonous conviction and cruised effortlessly with the honky-tonk

Guitar Heroics

To shred or not to shred? That is the question. The guitar as lead instrument is one of the cornerstones of heavy metal. The axe hero with legs astride, pealing out wailing solos is an archetypal and indelible image going back to the 60s when the template of American blues was redefined by a slew of imaginative musicians. It was the decade that produced key bands such as the **Yardbirds** featuring, at one time or another, the formidable prowess of guitarists **Eric Clapton**, **Jeff Beck** and **Jimmy Page**.

Of course, one of the most celebrated of 60s six-stringers was **James Marshall Hendrix**, aka **Jimi Hendrix**, whose work has been elevated to legendary status following his untimely death in 1970. Hendrix's rise to prominence took place in the latter part of the decade during which time he issued a string of classic albums – *Are You Experienced?* (1967), *Axis: Bold As Love* (1968), *Electric Ladyland* (1968) and *Band Of Gypsys* (1970) – featuring his unique approach to guitar playing. Immensely flamboyant and daring, his studio performances transcended the serious chin-stroking heritage of the blues. Live he would mangle his guitar, play it with his teeth and set it on fire, bringing a sense of theatre to the rock stage.

Beyond the timeless appeal of Hendrix, the 70s guitar hero was typified by the likes of **Deep Purple**'s **Ritchie Blackmore**, whose classical influences brought a new level of virtuosity to the role of the lead guitar. Meanwhile **Eddie Van Halen**'s interlude solo "Eruption" on **Van Halen**'s eponymous 1978 debut introduced a dazzling degree of flashiness to the art of lead widdling. Also notable for bringing classical and baroque styles to the table in the early 80s was **Ozzy Osbourne** guitarist **Randy Rhoads**. Guitar playing was becoming increasingly technical and speedy and the man who really upped the bombastic stakes was Hendrix-inspired Blackmore fan, **Yngwie Malmsteen**. The young Swedish shock guitarist literally ripped the lid off a movement that was simmering just below the surface when he debuted Stateside with **Steeler**, who issued an eponymous album on the home of guitar heroics, Shrapnel Records, in 1983. He then moved on to **Alcatrazz** before creating his own vehicle, **Rising Force**, and a grandiose solo career.

While metal bands such as **Judas Priest** and **Iron Maiden** espoused the twin duelling guitars approach, embedded within traditional song structures, Malmsteen's approach brought the focus to bear solely upon the prowess of the guitarist. Thus he helped to create the axe-shredding explosion of the 80s which went on to influence pretty much every aspect of metal that utilized melodic and blisteringly fast guitar playing, most notably power- and symphonic-metal.

With Malmsteen's rise came a wave of similarly talented players who threw everything from jazz-fusion to Bach into the mix. **Steve Vai** had been a member of **Frank Zappa**'s band and had learned much of his technique under the tutelage of **Joe Satriani**. While Satriani began to issue amazing albums such as *Not Of This Earth* and *Surfing With The Alien* in 1987, Vai had managed his first solo outing, *Flex-Able*, in 1984 before finding his diary full for much of the 80s playing with Alcatrazz, **David Lee Roth** and **Public Image Limited** before ending his run as star guitarist with a stint in **Whitesnake**. Shortly afterwards he resumed his solo efforts with the massively successful and diverse-sounding *Passion And Warfare* (1990).

While Steeler lasted only one album on Shrapnel, another notable guitars-in-yer-face band on their roster was the inimitable **Racer X**, featuring the awesome fret-frazzling power of **Paul Gilbert** who was a mere eighteen years old when *Street Lethal* was recorded in 1985. The incredible talent of **Tony MacAlpine** – not to mention his gravity-defying bouffant barnet – also first arrived via Shrapnel. His *Edge Of Insanity* (1986) album and its follow-up *Maximum Security* (1987) were pretty much glued to any self-respecting wannabe guitar hero's stereo. MacAlpine also helped out with keyboards on **Vinnie Moore**'s instrumental debut *Mind's Eye* (1986), on which he competed with the neoclassical guitarist, not just on the speed of playing, but also on who had the nicest, fluffiest hair.

Yet another one-time Shrapnel shredder of note is **David Chastain** whose work resides in a more song-oriented format. Under the band name of **Chastain** the key line-up of the 80s included the rather superbly named singer **Leather Leone**. Sticking with the more song-based formula, guitarist **Chris Impellitteri** also gave his surname, Van Halen-style, to his band, which at one point included ex-**Rainbow** singer **Graham Bonnet** in the line-up for 1988's *Stand In Line*. Their version of "Since You've Been Gone" has to be heard to be believed.

Once grunge hit the airwaves in the early 90s, it was all largely over for many metal acts. The tenaciousness of these much-maligned virtuosos cannot be discounted however, and the G3 touring showcase which began in 1996 has featured a diverse selection of talent over the years, including Yngwie Malmsteen, **Michael Schenker**, **Uli John Roth**, **Robert Fripp**, **Eric Johnson**, **Dream Theater**'s **John Petrucci**, Steve Vai and Joe Satriani.

blues on "Bad Obsession" and "Dust And Bones". But they lost the plot with the bloated ballads "November Rain" and two versions of "Don't Cry", while "Get In The Ring" was just childish ranting. Although two epics, "Civil War" and "Coma", proved to be outstanding cuts of focused quality, generally, it all lacked the lean, live feel of their debut and many felt one killer album could have been assembled from the two.

GEORGE CHIN/REDFERNS

Axl Rose – looking like he's just stepped out of a salon.

They blasted their way through songs by The Damned ("New Rose"), the Sex Pistols ("Black Leather") and The Stooges ("Raw Power") among others. Again, though, they seemed unable to make a move without causing trouble. The (arguably tasteless) decision to include "Look At Your Game Girl", an acoustic song written by the murderous psychopath Charles Manson, put them on the defensive again.

The controversy dragged on as the band fulfilled touring commitments with Brian May and Rose Tattoo. The following year saw precious little activity in the way of new material, save for the release of a cover version of The Rolling Stones' timeless "Sympathy For The Devil", which was recorded for the film soundtrack of *Interview With The Vampire*, starring Tom Cruise.

From this point the saga gradually turned into a rock'n'roll farce. Axl was assuming more and more control over the band and the months without new Gunners material turned into years. As time ground on, various members were dropped as the lead singer put together a new line-up and worked intermi-

Throughout the subsequent tour the pressures began to mount again with Axl's temperamental nature resulting in some shows being delayed for up to three hours. Whilst the performances were successful the band had gradually turned into a major organisation, a far cry from the stripped-down, hungry unit of previous tours. It was from this tornado of relentless stress that Izzy quit in late 1991, to rest and concentrate on his first solo effort *Izzy Stradlin And The Juju Hounds* (1992); he was soon replaced by **Gilby Clarke** (ex-**Kill For Thrills**). Duff also put together a solo project, released as *Believe In Me* (1993), but remained in the band.

Amid the touring, a covers album, *The Spaghetti Incident?* (1993), provided an interesting insight into the group's influences.

nably on the next album. Meanwhile, Slash's new outfit **Slash's Snakepit** managed two albums: *It's Five O'clock Somewhere* (1995) and the solid *Ain't Life Grand* (2000). Gilby Clarke released a number of solo efforts and formed **Col. Parker** with old time GN'R member Tracii Guns; **McKagan** threw himself into a whole host of bands and solo projects, ranging from the sublime to the utterly terrible. His own solo material was at best mediocre, as was the output from his band **Loaded**, and one of the worst albums he was involved with was *Mad For The Racket* (2000), put together under the name of the **Racketeers**, a supergroup consisting of **Wayne Kramer** (ex-MC5), **Brian James** (ex-Damned) and **Stewart Copeland** (ex-

Police). One of the better sets he had a hand in was the **Neurotic Outsiders'** eponymous album in 1996 with a line-up that included **Steve Jones** (ex-Sex Pistols), **John Taylor** (Duran Duran) and **Matt Sorum**.

As for Axl's efforts, very little was heard from his band until the tail end of the 90s. *Use Your Illusion* (1998) was a compilation culled from the previous two volumes, and *Live Era '87-'93* (1999) was a live 'best of' album that included a new song, "It's Alright", but was merely competent. The first truly new material arrived in the form of the underwhelming "Oh My God" on the soundtrack to the Arnold Schwarzenegger blockbuster *End Of Days* in 1999. Who was actually involved in the band, however, was open to conjecture given Axl's notorious habit of dispensing with people's services. Only Dizzy Reed seemed to survive the upheavals unscathed.

The band's first live performance for seven years took place in the small hours of New Year's Day 2001 in Las Vegas' House Of Blues. Naturally they took the stage late but, when they did finally show up, the line-up of Axl, **Buckethead** (so-called because he wears an inverted KFC bucket on his head), **Robin Finck** (ex-**Nine Inch Nails**), **Paul Tobias** aka **Paul Huge** (that's three guitars), Reed, **Brian 'Brain' Mantia** (drums, ex-**Primus**), **Tommy Stinson** (bass, ex-**Replacements**) and **Chris Pittman** (keyboards, ex-Replicants) worked through some old favourites before introducing a few new numbers from the band's forever-in-production album, *Chinese Democracy*. The band appeared at *Rock In Rio* 2001 and further tour dates were added; they even made it to Europe and the UK in 2002 after a series of delays and false starts. Since then, however, no album has been forthcoming. What did happen was a flurry of legal actions, much of it directed at Axl for loss of earnings – apparently the singer had been turning down lucrative soundtrack slots. In a rare united front Axl, McKagan and Slash also launched a lawsuit to try to prevent *Greatest Hits* (2004) from being released, arguing it would interfere with their future plans. They failed.

Another album, *The Roots Of Guns N' Roses*, came out in the same year and was credited to Hollywood Rose. The record showcased a series of demos created when the Gunners were known as Hollywood Rose with a different line-up, but including Izzy and Axl. Fans were treated to raw, remixed and touched-up versions of tunes such as "Shadow Of Your Love", "Reckless Life" and "Anything Goes" dating back to 1984 – a sleazy blast from the past.

The most convincing band to form in the post-classic-line-up era remains the super-group **Velvet Revolver**, featuring Slash, McKagan, Sorum, Slash's mate **Dave Kushner**, and vocalist **Scott Weiland** (ex-**Stone Temple Pilots**). They played their first gig in Los Angeles in June 2003 and their album *Contraband* (2004) was well received. As was to be expected, the songs sounded a lot like Guns N' Roses numbers fronted by a different singer, Weiland's gift for skewed poetics bringing a welcome twist to something that could so easily have drifted into parody.

Quite where Guns N' Roses will go remains to be seen. No album has materialized, and it's not clear who's in the line-up or who has played on the new tunes. This leaves one of the most significant and thrilling bands to emerge from the seedy clubs and dives of 80s LA the subject of much speculation and, dare we say, ridicule. Who knows when the next instalment of this rock soap opera will air?

Appetite For Destruction
1987; Geffen

A classic, foul-mouthed debut proudly flaunting its influences. The Gunners sound genuinely dangerous as they shamelessly recycle rock's scarier moments; derivative but frighteningly good.

Use Your Illusion I & II
1991; Geffen

Unfortunately, the over-indulgent production masks the energy of the songs and, at thirty tunes, some material fails to hit the mark. However, somewhere beneath the dross lurk some of the group's finest moments.

The Spaghetti Incident?
1993; Geffen

A patchy trawl through the band's personal record collections. It is, however, worth listening to Axl's hilarious attempt at an English accent on the UK Subs' "Back At The Farm" – next to this, Dick Van Dyke's chirpy chimney sweep in *Mary Poppins* sounds positively authentic.

Greatest Hits
2004; Geffen

There is so much more to this band, but for pure chart fodder this delivers in spades.

HALFORD

Formed 1999

Ask any classic metal fan who they regard as the archetypal heavy metal icon and they will more than likely reply, "vocalist **Rob Halford**". Halford stamped his identity on the world of metal through his commanding presence as lead singer of **Judas Priest**, a role in which he epitomized what a metal vocalist should be. From Priest's early hard-rocking origins, the flamboyant singer gradually adopted what would become his trademark leather-and-studs image and, as he became increasingly follically challenged, turned into a latter-day bullet-headed Metal God. And if he looked the part then his ball-busting shriek was the classic voice of metaldom; if Iron Maiden's Bruce Dickinson was a controlled air-raid siren then Rob Halford was a demented, leather-clad banshee.

Throughout the late 70s and into the 80s Priest established themselves as a world-ranking metal act, but, as is the way with wayward creative types, Halford was becoming increasingly disillusioned with the direction his bandmates wished to take. By the time of 1990's *Painkiller* Halford was ready to leave the band to explore other possibilities – a massive shock for disciples of the Priest – and on his way out sued their label, Sony, for restrictive practices.

First off came **Fight**, featuring **Brian Tilse** (guitars), **Jay Jay** (bass), **Russ Parrish** (guitars) and **Scott Travis** from Judas Priest on drums. Originally Fight had been a parallel project to Halford's day job, but he decided that the more extreme, brutal style of Fight was where his heart lay. The two Fight albums were tight and belligerent. *War Of Words* (1993) was a tough and solid metal outing, while *A Small Deadly Space* (1995) – with guitarist **Mark Chausee** replacing Parrish – had a slightly grungier aspect, making it less appealing to those who had developed a taste for the first record. The stop-gap *Mutations* EP in between is best forgotten, consisting basically of already-out-there *War Of Words* studio versions, live cuts and alternate mixes.

Despite their early promise Fight were not particularly long lived. Halford's fascination with the Pantera-esque sound of squealing feedback and technical riffing segued uneasily into a darker desire to emulate the artistic ideals of bands such as Nine Inch Nails. Thus, **Two** was born, first as a collaboration with guitarist **John Lowery** and producer **Bob Marlette**, but which then underwent something of a reinvention by **Nine Inch Nails** mainman **Trent Reznor**. The result was *Voyeurs* (1998). If Priest fans had at least had the consolation that Halford was still in a heavy metal band, this comfort disappeared as he smothered himself in a swathe of black eyeliner and pretended to be Nosferatu. He even ditched his classic metallic wail, opting for a moodier style. Two was altogether more industrial, electronic and dark in scope, leading most fans to assume that metaldom had lost a great talent. And confusing more conservative fans further, it was around this time that Halford decided to come out as gay.

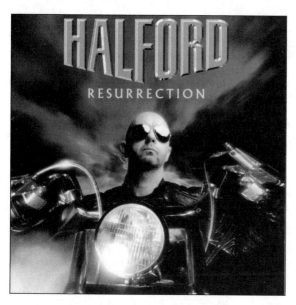

Needless to say, Two was neither a great critical nor commercial success, although it did clarify for Halford where his true musical proclivities lay. While the sexually charged S&M flavours of Two might have sated his desire for experimentation, in the end there was only one way forward: metal. Not just any old metal, but the heaviest, ballsiest metal possible.

The seeds were sown in 1998 and by 2000, eight years after quitting Priest, Halford launched his comeback, which was dubbed, naturally enough *Resurrection* (2000), featuring **Patrick Lachman** (guitars), **Mike Chlasciak** (guitars), **Ray Riendeau** (bass) and **Bobby Jarzombek** (drums). It was as though Halford had come home – the opening of the title track followed by "Made In Hell" was both a celebration of the music that had brought him stardom and a statement of intent. Coupled with the artwork that had Rob astride a motorbike – echoing his days on stage with Priest – it was as though the fans' prayers had been answered.

The effect was made all the more potent through a solid, dynamic production which teased the lethal edge of every riff while giving Halford's vocals full range to soar and growl with menace, not least on "The One You Love To Hate" which was written and performed with **Iron Maiden** vocalist **Bruce Dickinson**. The studio alchemy was re-created and trebled live when, during the subsequent touring both Dickinson and **Queensrÿche** vocalist **Geoff Tate** joined

Halford onstage in London. The world tour was captured on *Live Insurrection* (2001), which featured not only the new Halford tunes but material from Fight ("Into The Pit" and "Nailed To The Gun") and, of course, Priest cuts such as "Stained Class", "Jawbreaker", "Electric Eye" and "Breaking The Law", the band more than doing justice to the classics over a 94-show, seven-month long trek across twenty countries.

Most of 2001 was spent writing the follow-up to *Resurrection* with the band and production team remaining the same – after all, if ain't broke don't fix it. *Crucible* (2002) was worth the wait, and found the band experimenting with atmospherics, though the basics of tough riffage and Rob's chrome-plated scream remained unchanged. Once again, the artwork found Halford pandering to ideas of metallic deification; this time he swapped the motorbike for a gothic throne and the chains for a whip, though the leather and studs were still very much in place. Here was a man who simply did not care what people thought of him, a man confident of his place in the metal elite.

Despite the obvious power and invention of Halford the band, all was not right on the business side and, incredibly, by 2003 the amazing happened. Halford patched up his differences with Priest and with the classic line-up back in place, they began work on a new album.

Resurrection
2000; Metal-Is Records

The essence of heavy metal is captured right here on this album. Hi-octane headbanging brilliance from start to finish, this is a defiant and riotous selection of tunes.

Live Insurrection
2001; Metal-is Records

A faithful and spine-tingling collection of songs proving that Halford is one of the best vocalists alive. The Fight and Priest tunes crackle with energy and the Halford material is second to none.

Crucible
2002; Metal-Is Records

A more refined and theatrical set oozing power and atmosphere. It should come in a studded leather sleeve. Pure metal heaven.

HANOI ROCKS

Formed Helsinki, Finland, 1980;
disbanded 1985; re-formed 2002

Without this bunch of hairsprayed miscreants glam metal wouldn't have been quite so glamorous and bands such as Guns N' Roses wouldn't have had a clue how low to sling their guitars. They were so gloriously ramshackle and elegantly wasted that the world would have been theirs for the taking, were it not for a tragic turn of events in 1984.

The roots of these reckless sleaze rockers stretched back into the 70s Finnish punk scene to bands such as **Briard**, apparently the first Finnish punkers to record a single, **Pelle Miljoona** and **Maukka Perusjätkä**. By the early 80s the line-up stabilized with **Michael Monroe** (vocals, saxophone, harmonica), the brilliantly named **Nasty Suicide** (guitar), **Andy McCoy** (guitar), **Sam Yaffa** (bass) and **Gyp Casino** (drums). Not only could they strut live in a cocksure New York Dolls-meets-Rolling Stones manner, with Monroe occasionally parping away on saxophone, but they looked the part too; Monroe possessed possibly the finest set of cheekbones in rock. Their own inimitable style shone through on debut album *Bangkok Shocks Saigon Shakes Hanoi Rocks* (1981), a raucous bunch of tunes heavily influenced by the band's rough time trying to make it big.

Strangely enough one of the first times the UK got to sample the band was when they supported Wishbone Ash – a more incongruous combination would be hard to imagine. The band's reputation was spreading fast and album number two, *Oriental Beat* (1982), was almost unanimously lauded by the British rock press – McCoy's songwriting seemed to be improving with each session – and, of course, made them very big in Japan. The band relocated to London and found themselves at the centre of the action. However, the downside of this was their gradual slip into the grip of hard drugs, a trip from which it looked increasingly unlikely that their drummer would emerge alive. Casino's replacement was **Nicholas 'Razzle' Dingley**, an exuberant character who was desperate to join the ultimate rock'n'roll band. The story goes that he first pestered the band after a gig where they supported Lords Of The New Church; his persistence and attitude – he apparently threatened to break Casino's legs in order to get the gig – eventually got him the job. However, before he had the chance to appear on an album, *Self Destruction Blues* (1982) arrived, comprised of B-sides, demos and unreleased tracks.

Razzle finally made his debut on *Back To Mystery City* (1983), an exceedingly assured set produced by **Mott The Hoople** blokes **Dale Griffin** and **Overend Watts**. It was an album that had the band teetering on the edge of taking that all-important step into a whole new league. Overend Watts helped produce their live album *All Those Wasted Years* (1984), recorded at the famous Marquee club in London, but it was with their debut for major label CBS, *Two Steps From The Move* (1984), produced by Veteran knob twiddler **Bob Ezrin** (Kiss, Alice Cooper, Pink Floyd), that Hanoi were elevated to the next level. Sadly it was also their ticket to unforeseen disaster. They headed off to the States for a tour and in December 1984 ended up in Los Angeles where they partied hard with Mötley Crüe. Razzle went for a drive with Crüe singer Vince Neil and the intoxicated Neil lost control of his new sports car. Razzle was killed in the crash while Neil was unhurt.

Shocked and still grieving the band staggered on with the help of ex-**Clash** drummer **Terry Chimes** and *Rock 'N' Roll Divorce* (1985) was recorded live in Poland. The loss, however, was too great and the band folded, leaving the various members to pursue other projects.

Monroe made some of the highest-profile appearances over the subsequent years, with

plenty of compilations and reissues vying for fans' attention. In 2001, however, McCoy and Monroe toured Finland under the name **Hanoi Revisited**. From there it was but a short step to a reformation – with a new line-up featuring **Costello Hautamäki** (guitar), **Lacu** (drums) and **Timpa** (bass) – and a new album, *Twelve Shots On The Rocks* (2002). The band set about making up for lost time by touring much of Europe, Scandinavia and Japan. And by 2005 the line-up had changed again to include Conny Bloom (guitar, ex-Electric Boys) and Andy Christell (bass).

Two Steps From The Move
1984; CBS

The label wanted a hit single so the band recorded the old Creedence Clearwater Revival hit "Up Around The Bend". Producer Bob Ezrin and Mott The Hoople lyrics ace, **Ian Hunter**, share the writing credits with guitarist McCoy, making this an album with one hell of a pedigree.

Decadent Dangerous Delicious
2000; Castle

This is a cracking double-CD compilation of tracks spanning the band's 80s career, resplendent with great sleeve notes, featuring loads of magazine cuttings and tons of photos.

THE HAVNTED

Formed Gothenburg, Sweden, 1996

The Haunted: two words synonymous with the extreme metal elite, the name of one of the most important bands at the vanguard of what has been loosely dubbed the New Wave Of Swedish Heavy Metal. Put simply, The Haunted are one of the fastest, nastiest, most downright headbang-worthy of thrash metal outfits – perhaps only

Slayer can claim to have exceeded the manic ferocity of this lot on stage and in the studio. But it's a very close race indeed.

The Haunted were formed from the remains of another seminal thrash band, **At The Gates**. After forming in the very late 80s the latter issued a string of brilliantly named genre-defining albums – *With Fear I Kiss The Burning Darkness* (1992) was an early favourite – on labels such as Peaceville and Earache, culminating with the seminal *Slaughter Of The Soul* (1995). Initially they had been influenced by the death and thrash acts of the 80s, but as they progressed, an increasingly modern twist was added, bringing a pioneering level of polish and power to an old formula. At The Gates' days at the top of the thrash heap were numbered, however, leaving their drummer **Adrian Erlandsson** at a loose end. Ex-Séance guitarist **Patrik Jensen** suggested a spot of jamming and the sessions went so well that ex-At The Gates members (and twins) **Anders** (guitar) and **Jonas Björler** (bass) decided to join in. The new line-up might have lacked a name and a singer but Earache offered them a slot on an upcoming compilation album, giving them the impetus to get their act together. Ex-**Mary Beats Jane** vocalist **Peter Dolving** was soon recruited and with recording just a few days away The Haunted were born.

With the compilation album sessions behind them they took only a few more months to complete a brand new album – *The Haunted* (1998) – recorded at the same studios in Gothenburg where At The Gates had completed their swansong release. The power of the music was undeniable; from start to finish it was a blizzard of buzzsaw guitars and precision demolition drumming, with Dolving coming on like a rabid cross between Slayer's Tom Araya and Pantera's Phil Anselmo. The

HARD AND HEAVY ROCK

It's probably best to think of hard and heavy rock as being slightly different intensities of the same kind of music, that is, a form of rock played using guitar, bass and drums, rooted in the traditions of blues.

The blues quotient can vary, as can the subject matter of the lyrics and the image of the band, but basically we're talking about a bunch of bands all playing in the same ball park. Though it wouldn't be wrong to call, say, **Nirvana** a heavy rock band – because they were heavy and they certainly did rock – the term has taken on the baggage of acts from the 70s (**AC/DC**, **Led Zeppelin** and **Deep Purple** to **Aerosmith**, **Thin Lizzy** and **UFO** and 80s (**Def Leppard**, **Whitesnake**, **Guns N' Roses**, **Tesla** etc).

These groups can also be dubbed classic rock to indicate their origins, but that doesn't mean they are museum exhibits; many of these bands are still releasing albums and touring while the style is still inspiring new acts such as **The Darkness** and new rockers on the block **Silvertide** and **Tokyo Dragons**. As they say, the classics never die.

OLLE CARLSSON

You wouldn't want to be haunted by this lot.

extreme 'zines loved the disc and proclaimed the band one of the best newcomers on the scene. A UK support slot with Napalm Death in late 1998 added to the critical kudos.

At this point Dolving surprised everyone by jumping ship to pursue other musical interests – bizarrely, so the story goes, to get involved with country and western music! The Haunted remained a resolutely Stetson-free zone, however, and singer **Marco Aro** (ex-**Face Down**) took the mic for the next round of festival slots and prepared to front the band during their tour with thrash legends Testament. Before they could begin gigging with their heroes, however, The Haunted faced yet another problem: how to find a convincing replacement for Erlandsson who had departed to pound the skins for UK black metallers**Cradle Of Filth** . **Per Möller Jensen** (ex-**Invocator**) was the man for the job, at last providing a much-needed degree of stability, allowing them to capitalize on their growing US audience and to prepare for the next album.

When *The Haunted Made Me Do It* (2000) was unveiled it earned the band a Swedish Grammy for Best Hard Rock Album. Its inventive and intense tales of death, destruction and serial killers brought yet more dark thrash to the charts, both in their home country and across the US – in many territories it

was hailed as a groundbreaking departure from the usual deathly tripe dished out to extreme-music fans. The following year the band released *Live Rounds In Tokyo*, a tour document to keep the fans happy while they worked in the studio.

Their third album – *One Kill Wonder* (2003) – was almost completed without Anders Björler after he decided that resuming education was the way to go. Obviously, the lure of yet more hate and rage-fuelled lyrics set to a pulverizing storm of riffs and blastbeats was too great and the guitarist returned to contribute some of his most savage, yet melodic, work so far; the album was such a punishing affair that listening to its eleven songs hurtle past in a mere 38 minutes was like enduring a mosh pit in your front room. It was a formula taken to another level with *rEVOLVEr* (2004), featuring Dolving back home from the range and raring to rage. Aro was a great vocalist but there was no hiding the joy with which fans greeted the news.

The Haunted Made Me Do It
2000; Earache

A chilling and downright gruesome little thrash affair, all violent guitars and fearsome vocals.

One Kill Wonder
2003; Earache

Could it get any heavier? Evidently so. One of the essential thrash releases of the year, guaranteed to get heads shaking and mosh pits churning. A classic of the genre.

THE HELLACOPTERS

Formed Stockholm, Sweden, 1994

"I think of The Hellacopters as a cross between Cheap Trick and the Dead Boys, or Lynyrd Skynyrd and the Sex Pistols." Nick Royale

In the world of rock'n'roll the more things change the more some bands want to re-ignite the spirit of the past. It just seems a little odd that Sweden would produce so many bands borrowing wholesale from the likes of The Stooges, MC5, New York Dolls and just about any other down and dirty garage band you'd care to name. Such was the case, however, when **Nick Royale** (guitar/vox), **Kenny Håkansson** (bass), **Robert Eriksson** (drums) and **Backyard Babies'** lead guitarist **Dregen** decided to take on the world the old-fashioned way with a fistful of seven-inch singles.

Royale's day job at the time involved drumming for twisted metal crew **Entombed**, but the lure of snotty rock would gradually prove to be a greater draw as **The Hellacopters'** stock rose.

As momentum picked up, the four-man unit was in turn snapped up by the independent White Jazz label and the debut *Supershitty To The Max* (1996) emerged to almost unanimous praise. It was a rip-snorting, hi-octane sonic adventure recorded in a mere 26 hours with cues cheekily pinched from the band's many obvious US influences. And to reward those fans with turntables, they included "Its Too Late" on the vinyl version, a New York Dolls cover which was left off the CD. The following year found the band expanding their horizons by recruiting **Bobby Lee Fett**, aka **Boba Fett**, on piano and keyboards, giving a more honky-tonk revved-up Rolling Stones vibe for the second album, *Payin' The Dues* (1997).

By this time Dregen was feeling the pressure of splitting his time between two bands – besides, Backyard Babies were beginning to generate enough heat and excitement on their own to keep him more than busy. Something had to give – and it was The Hellacopters. It wasn't until early 1999 that **Robert 'Strings' Dahlqvist** stepped in to expand the line-up on a permanent basis, his more technically accomplished style giving the band a more complex and bluesy flavour. Before this however, *Grande Rock* (1999) emerged and proved to be yet another scorching slab of bad-boy boogie.

So far the template had basically involved speed and melody in equal measure but with the addition of Dahlqvist, the style of *High Visibility* (2000), was far more polished. This time recorded in three weeks – a relative eternity for a band that prefers life on the road over and above being cooped up in a studio – the album was a *tour de force* of intense melody and high impact delivery. What's more the album sleeve, featuring the various band members sporting impressive life-size angels wings, was inspired by an interview with Rob Tyner of MC5, who once said that musicians could be likened to angels who had come down to earth to spread joy and happiness.

Over recent years the vinyl-only rarities collection *High Energy Rock 'N'Roll* (2001) and the storming *By The Grace Of God* (2002) have kept The Hellacopters' name at the forefront of Swedish trash rock, not to mention the seemingly endless flow of seven- and twelve-inch singles, all of them featuring exclusive material. To help fans who couldn't track down all the songs popping up all over the place, two further huge compilations – *Cream Of The Crap! Vol.1* and *Vol. 2* (2002 and 2004) – pulled together a vast number of singles and non-album tracks.

Supershitty To The Max
1996; White Jazz

A berserk sprint through some of rock's sleazier, trashier moments. This is what New York Dolls might have sounded like with Lemmy in their ranks. Manic, driven, and 110 percent committed to the spirit of the music.

High Visibility
2000; Universal

A more professional production job makes this set of songs truly shine. Dahlqvist's blues-directed style certainly gives The Hellacopters' usual bluster a powerful bar-room swagger.

HELLOWEEN

Formed Germany, 1984

Back in the mid-80s when thrash was lighting up the metal underground with genuine flashes of creative brilliance, **Helloween** were greeted as yet another bunch of amazingly efficient Teutonic riff-merchants. They would, however, develop very quickly into highly influential power metallers, adding large helpings of melody and a progressive approach to a formula with lightning speed delivery at its heart.

The history of the band can be traced exhaustively back to the late 70s, but it was in the early to mid-80s that the line-up settled on **Kai Hansen** (guitar/vocals), **Michael Weikath** (guitar), **Markus Grosskopf** (bass) and **Ingo Swichtenberg** (drums), just as German groups such as Rage and Grave Digger were tooling up to take power metal to the masses. Helloween's first foray appeared on Noise Records, a self-titled mini-LP from 1985 which featured an exploding pumpkin on the sleeve. Although the imagery was more focused on horror, the use of a classic Jack O'Lantern would soon become their humorous trademark in a big way.

Their first full-length album, *Walls Of Jericho* (1985), had nothing to do with biblical ice cream manufacturers and everything to do with speedy metal. What they really lacked at this stage was a decent singer, which they found in **Michael Kiske**. The *Judas* (1986) mini-LP followed but it was the ambitious and driven *Keeper Of The Seven Keys Part I* (1987) that found the band at last tapping into their rich vein of talent. It was tuneful and tight, the closing epic title track taking the listener on a fantasy journey lasting nearly fifteen minutes – one of the first fully realized power metal classics had arrived. And the interior of the gatefold sleeve was plastered with cartoon pumpkins.

Having emerged into the mainstream of metal the band followed up with *Keeper Of The Seven Keys Part II* (1988). This was during a period of manic touring which found the band playing at the Donington Monsters of Rock festival, while their "Dr Stein" single just breached the UK Top 60, helping the album into the Top 30. During the touring Hansen decided to leave the band and **Roland Grapow** stepped in to replace him.

Recorded during the last bout of touring, *Live In The UK* (1989) kept fans happy while storm clouds loomed on the horizon. Convinced that Noise were the wrong label for them the band signed with EMI, thus starting a major court battle that eventually went against them, almost crippling them financially. To make matters much worse all the fighting had a detrimental effect on the music. *Pink Bubbles Go Ape* (1991) was on the receiving end of some serious criticism; any album that contains a song called "Heavy Metal Hamsters" is either a work of demented genius or just plain terrible and no prizes for guessing which in this case. Even the surreal sleeve – featuring a woman possibly about to kiss a kipper – was awful. The sleeve for *Chameleon* (1993) was positively mundane in comparison, looking like the result of a kindergarten fingerpainting exercise – it was the most exciting aspect of the entire thing.

With two middling-to-awful albums behind them and the yawning chasm of the unknown in front, the only thing to do was to get back to basics. New vocalist **Andi Deris** (ex-**Pink Cream 69**) and new drummer **Uli Kusch** (ex-**Gamma Ray**) were recruited and the newly revitalized band blasted back with *Master Of The Rings* (1994) on Sanctuary. Many fans reckoned it was their best studio album for quite a while. When *The Time Of The Oath* (1996) galloped into view they really couldn't believe their luck and the release of the double *High Live* (1996) was merely the steel cherry on top of a very heavy cake indeed. Sadly, the triumph was tempered by tragedy: the band's former drummer **Ingo Swichtenberg** committed

Keeper Of The Seven Keys
Part I

suicide – he had suffered from mental illness and had come to rely more on drugs and alcohol than on his medication.

The next few years saw various solo projects brought to fruition, though Helloween were themselves soon back in action with the excellent *Better Than Raw* (1998) and the rather odd *Metal Jukebox* (1999), which was exactly as the title suggested – a selection of cover tunes from a wildly eclectic range of artists, including the Scorpions, Jethro Tull, the Beatles, Faith No More and Abba. Back on track, *The Dark Ride* (2000) was the last album to feature Grapow and Kusch.

Treasure Chest (2002), a huge compilation set, was issued to keep things ticking over while the band sorted out new members and headed back to the studio. Holding on to a drummer proved to be a challenge – although Motörhead skin-thrasher **Mikkey Dee** helped out on *Rabbit Don't Come Easy* (2003); however, **Sascha Gerstner** (guitar) was a fine replacement for Grapow.

Keeper Of The Seven Keys Parts I & II
1987/1988; Noise

These two albums are prime examples of 80s power metal – all catchy melodies, blistering dual guitars and stampeding double kick drums. The songs crackle with energy and demand some serious air-guitar accompaniment.

Better Than Raw
1998; Sanctuary

This is a highly enjoyable power romp and features one of the only metal tunes in existence sung in Latin; the Weikath-penned "Lavdate Dominvm" (meaning "praise the Lord") has to be heard to be believed.

HIM

Formed Helsinki, Finland, 1996

For the uninitiated, heavy metal means chugging riffs, squealing guitar solos, thunderous drums and vocals projected from the bowels of hell. In this vision there is no room for subtlety, for poetry or romance. In the world of **HIM** (short for His Infernal Majesty), however, powerful music equates with not just brute force but melody that touches the soul and lyrics that describe the heart-rending sadness of lost love.

In 1996 singer **Ville Valo** was getting just a little bored working behind the counter of his father's sex shop and decided that it was time his visions of a future in the music industry became reality. To this end HIM were created, featuring **Lily Lazer** (guitar), **Mige Amour** (bass), **Zoltan Pluto** (keyboards), and **Gas Lipstick** (drums). As their bizarre and attention-grabbing handles would suggest, this was a band that made an impression almost instantly. And just like the heart-shaped pentagram tattoo that was rapidly adopted as their symbol, they got under the skin.

Key to Valo's image was the brooding style of Jim Morrison. It was towards his wasted poetic chic of magnetic melancholy that the Finnish singer aspired, as the band polished their demos and signed to BMG Finland. Very soon after, they released *Greatest Lovesongs Vol. 666* (1997) which went gold and spawned two hit singles in their homeland. The music was gothic, emotional and doomladen but steeped in melody – a fine, if slightly rough, trial run for what would be the album to really break them across Europe.

Razorblade Romance (2000) was recorded not once but twice, the second time with input from producer **John Fryer** whose credits included acts as diverse as Depeche Mode and Nine Inch Nails. Such broad reference points were perfect, however, for what HIM wished to achieve; this was music that displayed both electronic precision and loose grooves of passion.

Success across the Continent came almost ridiculously easily. Their single "Join Me In Death" topped the chart in both Finland and Germany for four weeks, going platinum in the latter. In the process they became the first Finnish band to achieve a #1 in Germany. Other standout tracks included the smothering, twisted romance of "Bury Me Deep Inside Your Heart", the chilling "Death Is In Love With Us" and a perfectly realized cover of Chris Isaak's "Wicked Game" – showing the confidence with which HIM could weave a bleak sonic shroud of instantly addictive sound from unlikely source material.

Follow-up album, *Deep Shadows And Brilliant Highlights* (2001), featuring new keyboardist Emerson Burton, found Valo exploiting his penchant for death and romance even further, a hearse with '666' painted upon its door adorning the centre pages of the lyric booklet. It was a charming and seductive album, its pop gloss giving the tales of perverse romance a warm and radio-friendly sheen.

HIM try to look nonchalent.

Its consummate professionalism, however, was eclipsed two years later by *Love Metal*. With combined sales of over two million albums to their credit, HIM were ready for something to truly make their presence felt. That came with eighteen months of songwriting followed by a soul-searching stint in the studio with **Hiili Hiilesmaa**, producer of the first HIM album – a studio maestro best noted for his work with the more uncompromising end of the metal spectrum, such as Sentenced and Moonspell. The tracks were then whisked halfway across the world to Scream Studios, Los Angeles – birthplace of Nirvana's "Nevermind" and Faith No More's "The Real Thing", trivia fans – to be mixed by **Tim Palmer** whose work with U2 had attracted Valo's attention. From the opening bittersweet torment of "Buried Alive By Love" to the closing epic "The Path", it was an album of sweet, soulful depth and fierce power. The video for the former single was directed by *Jackass* member **Bam Margera** and featured actress **Juliette Lewis** of *Natural Born Killers* and *Cape Fear* fame, giving an indication of the kind of high-profile fans the band were collecting along the way.

On stage their transformation from weirdly monikered goth-metal punks to a world-class act was quite astonishing. Three years previously Ville was a frontman in love with the glamour of death, a singer as much into pretty-boy posing as an icy purveyor of gothic romance. This time round the black-suited, chain-smoking singer was the epitome of smooth, understated cool.

In order to introduce fans to their back catalogue in as digestible a format as possible, the following year brought *And Love Said No... 1997-2004,* featuring a clever reworking of Neil Diamond's "Solitary Man" as well as a handful of rerecordings and new tracks.

Razorblade Romance
2000; BMG

A chilling and dramatic breakthrough album featuring amazing performances and an extremely catchy set of commercial goth-metal tunes. Stars in the making.

Love Metal
2003; BMG

Smooth, crooning, impassioned vocals and icy musical precision make this a hypnotic, addictive set of songs. Who ever thought doom romance could sound so appealing?

ICED EARTH

Formed Florida, US, 1984

The dedication of true believers in metal is second to none. Just as bands such as Manowar have stuck to their guns – or should that be axes? – and proclaimed death to false metal, so **Iced Earth** have never given up. In the face of changing metal fashions the band, driven onward hell for leather by guiding visionary guitarist **Jon Schaffer** (in a manner not dissimilar to bassist Steve Harris of Iron Maiden), have clung steadfastly to a power metal formula that has served them well year after year. When grunge was at its peak they actually dared to release concept albums; when nu-metal loped into view they indulged in ever more complex guitar heroics and histrionics. Seemingly ever the outsiders, their refusal to compromise has won them legions of dedicated fans and resulted in an impressive back catalogue of work, a tribute to sterling musicianship and good old-fashioned headbanging mania.

Even at the band's genesis as **Purgatory**, back in the thrash-driven past of 1984, it was a hard slog to get noticed. The nascent outfit's strivings for recognition on the live circuit around their home state resulted in numerous line-up shifts but served as a demanding arena to perfect their incisive style, influenced by Iron Maiden, Judas Priest, Metallica and countless thrash bands. What they – especially Schaffer – desired was professionalism, power and perfection. Three demos were cut over the years but it was a

name change around 1989 and a set of songs dubbed *Enter The Realm* that suddenly grabbed slippery record labels' attention. The tape was voted top demo in German magazine *Rock Hard* and very soon Iced Earth found themselves on Century Media.

With the line-up completed by **Mike McGill** (drums), **Gene Adams** (vocals), **Dave Abell** (bass) and **Randy Shawver** (guitar) their first Maiden-esque offering was *Iced Earth* (1990). There were plenty of galloping rhythms and terrific, chest-beating vocals – this was metal on an epic scale, although the production didn't quite match the artistic scope of the tunes. They tried to remedy this with *Night Of The Stormbringer* (1992) – with drummer **Rick Secchiari** and new singer **John Greely** – a concept album about a man whose faith fails him and he becomes a vessel for death and destruction on an apocalyptic scale. It was a bold move at a time when bands such as Alice In Chains and Pearl Jam were the new faces of heavy rock, but it demonstrated their sheer bloody-mindedness and determination, which paid off. The band's profile steadily grew across Europe.

With a gradual rise in fortune Schaffer began to realize that the deal they had struck with their label wasn't quite as generous as it could have been and so asked for a better cut of the royalties. Unsurprisingly the label said no. So the band went on strike. For nearly three years no shows were played and no music was recorded until the label relented.

The fury and frustration of this period came through clearly on their next effort,

Burnt Offerings (1995), which had new recruit **Matt Barlow** roaring, growling, shrieking and wailing like a siren on what was their heaviest – and some fans believe their best – album. There was also yet another new face on drums, **Rodney Beasley**. Songs sped past at a whipcrack lick, wicked time changes made the head spin and the closing track, "Dante's Inferno", was true to its mythic title, a sixteen-minute brimstone and bombast journey through the circles of hell. It was shamelessly progressive, symphonic and operatic in scale.

Seemingly unable to stick to a single sticksman, **Mark Prator** became the rhythmic driving force behind the next magnum opus, *The Dark Saga* (1996). Schaffer had the idea that Iced Earth could provide the soundtrack to the movie of hit comic book *Spawn*. The result was another concept album, this time based on **Todd McFarlane's** infamous demonic hero. The renowned comic artist even provided the album's cover art.

Days Of Purgatory (1997) followed, the title referring to the band's pre-Iced Earth existence; rather than provide any new material they went into the studio and cherry-picked some of their best material from the early years and then rerecorded parts, chiefly the vocals and rhythm sections.

Schaffer then relocated from Florida to Indianapolis and only Barlow remained in the line-up alongside new bassist **James MacDonough**. So when *Something Wicked This Way Comes* (1998) appeared much of it was recorded with the help of various guest musos. It was an opportunity to expand and experiment, and within the metallic grooves

there were flute, piano and mandolin adding a little softness to what was yet another ambitious outing.

Alive In Athens (1999) was an indication of their popularity across Europe – they still couldn't get arrested in the States – a sizeable three-CD effort recorded over two nights with two very different set lists, the idea being to combine as much of their back catalogue as possible. In order to address the band's relative low profile at home the limited edition *Melancholy* EP was put together with the aim of promoting some of Iced Earth's more accessible ballads to American radio. In the end the label didn't push forward with the plan; instead fans were tantalized with a rarity that was snapped up at low cost and went on to exchange hands for considerably more – until it was reissued a couple of years later with even more material on it.

With his **Demons & Wizards** side-project – a collaboration with **Blind Guardian** singer **Hansi Kürsch** – out of the way Schaffer concentrated on the next album. And what better subject than horror films? *Horror Show* (2001) wasn't exactly a concept album, more a themed effort, utilizing the additional efforts of **Larry Tarnowski** (guitar), **Steve DiGiorgio** (bass) and **Richard Christy** (drums). Far from being a take on modern *Scream*-style ironic horror, the songs harked back to the monsters of old – werewolves, vampires, Jekyll and Hyde, the *Creature From The Black Lagoon* and Frankenstein's monster all rose from the shadows for a quick power metal turn. Perhaps inadvisably they also included a cover version of Iron Maiden's "Transylvania" and included a song of their own about the *Phantom Of The Opera*!

While the album was one of Iced Earth's most enjoyable, touring plans fell apart when a proposed US trek with Judas Priest was cancelled because of the terrorist attacks on New York. In the end the band toured Europe again, but an important chance to promote themselves to a receptive American audience was lost.

In an effort to appeal to new fans that might not be aware of their previous material the band released *Dark Genesis* (2002), a five-CD box set. Their first three albums were included as was the band's *Enter The Realm* demo and a *Tribute To The Gods* CD, a collection of cover versions – naturally enough including Iron Maiden and Judas Priest songs, as well as tunes by Black Sabbath, Blue Öyster Cult and AC/DC. Not only that, but believing in providing fans with more bangs for their bucks, all the previously available material was remixed to improve sound quality and everything was repackaged with new artwork.

Such a glorious blow-out did at least divert attention away from the band's internal strife. Schaffer was presented with one of the biggest problems in Iced Earth's career: in Barlow they had a superb vocalist, but one who was going to quit after the next album. Hence the band had half-hearted performances from their lead singer who wouldn't be around to sing the new songs live anyway. The solution came in the shape of **Tim Owens**, former **Judas Priest** vocalist, who had previously discussed working on a side-project with Schaffer. Priest had announced that they would be reuniting with their original singer Rob Halford so Iced Earth quickly snapped up Owens. It was his incredible warbling that graced *The Glorious Burden* (2004).

In response to the new album Iced Earth's old label quickly bolted together a passable compilation, *The Blessed And The Damned* (2004).

⊙ The Glorious Burden
2004; SPV

In something of a departure from the usual, the theme this time is military history and specifically the US Civil War in the marathon 32-minute closing trilogy of tunes grouped together as "Gettysburg (1863)".

In Flames

Formed Gothenburg, Sweden, 1993

One of the pioneers of what is sometimes referred to as the Gothenburg sound, **In Flames** are a thundering thrash outfit who have developed into one of the most inventive metal bands to emerge from Scandinavia. Incorporating a great, old-school sense of melody and songwriting with deathly stylings, the band also took on the progressive tendencies of power metal – a style which has pointed the way forward for many of the so-called New Wave Of American Heavy Metal bands such as Shadows Fall.

The group formed from the splinters of various bands plying their trade in the metal underground of the early 90s. With a somewhat fluid line-up the band nevertheless managed to record a demo and land a deal with indie Wrong Again Records, resulting in the album *Lunar Strain* (1994). The *Subterranean* EP followed, consolidating the underground success of the band and leading to a deal with Nuclear Blast Records. So far they had garnered some serious attention but needed to stabilize their line-up.

The Jester Race (1995) was the breakthrough with the line-up of **Anders Fridén** (vocals), **Jesper Strömblad** (guitar), **Glenn Ljungström** (guitar), **Björn Gelotte** (drums) and **Johan Larsson** (bass). Fridén was a vocalist capable of some truly blood-curdling sounds, and, tempered by the duelling guitars, the result was compelling enough for the band to start winning over international audiences, including Japan. However, the sudden upswing in popularity meant greater commitments, something which Ljungström and Larsson were unable to guarantee. They had a hand in the *Black Ash Inheritance* EP and *Whoracle* (1998), but left afterwards. There was nothing else for it: some serious re-engineering was in order. Gelotte was given back his guitar (he had been a six-stringer before thrashing the skins) and **Peter Iwers** (bass) and **Daniel Svensson** (drums) plugged the gaps left in the rhythm unit.

The outcome couldn't have been better. *Colony* (1999), engineered, mixed and produced by Gothenburg-sound maestro (and **Dream Evil** guitarist) **Fredrik Nordström** was a triumph, leading to an ever-broadening fan base across the globe and a string of tours. *Clayman* (2000) saw the band experimenting a touch more, with less complex arrangements and cleaner vocals – rather than the usual demon-with-his-left-nut-caught-in-a-vice screaming and growling, though with *Reroute To Remain* (2002) the changes really did seem to flummox some of the fans. In the interim, between the two releases, fans only had *The Tokyo Showdown* live album to keep them going.

The *Trigger* EP in 2003 provided a handful of interesting remixes but the real meat arrived with *Soundtrack To Your Escape* (2004), which largely eschewed the Maiden-esque qualities of earlier albums for a heavily downtuned but characteristically accessible chug, embellished with electronics. Again, it was an album that divided the fans, with

In Flames (Anders Fridén kneeling).

Industrial Metal

Music of an industrial bent has come a long way since Dada-inspired performance art and **Throbbing Gristle** launching their Industrial Records label in the mid-1970s. The idea among such artists was to be as provocative as possible, challenging the norms of popular music and culture by colliding with them head-on in a welter of distorted electronic noise, taped loops and clattering percussion. This was often accompanied with disturbing imagery and totalitarian iconography to create a deliberately controversial aesthetic, as hard to swallow as the cacophonous noise music. As synths and electronic sampling became increasingly incorporated into the sound during the 80s, bands began to experiment more with dance-oriented beats and outfits such as **Cabaret Voltaire** actually began to enjoy some success.

As industrial began to fragment into confusing sub-genres, acts such as **Skinny Puppy**, **KMFDM**, **Frontline Assembly**, **Laibach** and **Front 242** came to prominence while a distinct rock influence began to pervade the scene. Major names in modern industrial metal, such as **Ministry** and **Nine Inch Nails**, are rooted in the dancier, club sound of the 80s but have pushed their sonic envelope to increasingly incorporate more aggressive rock guitar elements, a twist of punk and a good helping of rock'n'roll songwriting.

Nevertheless, the visual aspects remain largely unchanged, with dark and menacing imagery in both artwork and lyrics being the order of the day. For the contemporary metal fan, the likes of **Marilyn Manson**, **Al Jourgensen** and **Trent Reznor** represent the relative mainstream of industrial music, while the purist in search of a more extreme (and authentic, they would argue) fix will probably be revelling in the release of Throbbing Gristle's *TG24* (2003) limited edition box set, a 24-CD marathon of live performances.

long-standing devotees lamenting what they regarded as unnecessary changes, while those new to the group embraced the melodic intensity. The seal of approval on their experimentation came in the shape of a Swedish Grammy in early 2005.

The Jester Race
1995; Nuclear Blast

Call it the Gothenburg sound, call it melodic death metal, call it Susan if you like – this is powerful stuff drawing on a heap of influences and creating one of the fans' favourite albums. This is the kind of record virtually guaranteed to wreck your neck.

INCUBUS

Formed Calabasas, California, US, 1991

What is alternative rock? Are we talking grunge? Nu-metal perhaps? Or how about rap-metal? For **Incubus** it is all these things and more. They love to be uncategorizable in a world that loves to label. Formed by high-school mates **Brandon Boyd** (vocals), **Mike Einziger** (guitars), **Alex Katunich**, aka **Dirk Lance**, (bass) and **José Pasillas II** (drums), the band went through their birth throes in that ubiquitous and traditional womb of rock and metal, the humble urban garage. Some years were spent honing their live skills and building up a fan base on the Californian club scene, but for the most part they were searching for a sound that they could call their own.

From the early to mid-90s, while the music scene was in thrall of grunge, big-hair bands were on the wane and the likes of Faith No More and Red Hot Chili Peppers were on the rise. And when *Fungus Amongus* (1995) emerged it was a rough-and-ready amalgam of funk, rock, metal and wilful weirdness that merely hinted at what Incubus would go on to produce. Likewise the *Enjoy Incubus* mini-LP – also featuring DJ Lyfe. Released on the Immortal label, the set showcased a band with a singer whose vocal style came uncomfortably close to that of Faith No More crooner Mike Patton and a guitarist keen to make like the Chili Peppers' John Frusciante.

Much better and far more accomplished was *S.C.I.E.N.C.E* (1997), which ironed out the wrinkles and gave the band a much smoother, groove-oriented sound. Splashes of funk were off-set with driving riffage and spiky turntable shrapnel. Meanwhile, Boyd was beginning to really flex his lyrical muscles by encompassing a more intellectual world-view than would your average rock star. A staggering two years of touring followed during which Incubus shared the stage with the cream of both the new and the old school, including Limp Bizkit, Ozzy Osbourne, Black Sabbath and Korn, among others, on the Family Values tour of the US.

When Incubus eventually sprang back with a new album it proved to be their break-through. The title of *Make Yourself* (1999) alluded to the general direction of the lyrics which encouraged fans to shape and control their own destinies – not exactly an original message, but light years ahead of the girls, booze, and angst peddled by other notable artists. Boyd had also progressed immeasurably as a singer rather than remaining simply a vocalist who indulged in some snappy rapping. The overall success of the album was also, doubtless, down to a sterling production from **Scott Litt** and the introduction of **DJ Chris Kilmore**. A slot on 2000's Ozzfest ensured the album was still floating buoyantly in the charts a year later.

The next logical step was for Incubus to ditch the studio environment and apply the free-spirited approach to life they espoused to their own recordings. Hence *Morning View* (2001) was recorded in a Malibu mansion with breathtaking views of the ocean – beauty to feed the creative spirit. A fluid exercise in musical invention, *Morning View* was the band's most fully realized take on their artistic vision to date. The album also garnered them a neat fistful of hit singles in "Wish You Were Here", "Warning" and "Nice To Know You".

Despite the superlative musicianship evident on *Morning View* it soon became clear that all was not quite so beautiful within the band. Katunich was replaced by new bassist **Ben Kenney** for their next album, *A Crow Left Of The Murder* (2004), the title intended to indicate the band's desire not to be seen as part of the pack. It was an apt title. The creative direction the band had been pursuing had taken them ever further from the loose alternative pool they had originally been lumped into, and far from lying back and accepting their success, the new album was aggressive and uncompromising. Sure enough there were some smooth moments but what was evident from Boyd's lyrics was his anger and confusion at the state of the world. "Pistola" described the artist's pen as "the patriot's weapon of choice"; the single "Megalomaniac" laid into the vagaries of politicians and leaders; "Talk Show On Mute" took a swipe at the banality of American television. The sound was heavier and more driven, the tone a challenge to those people who thought of the band as solely a feel-good groove machine.

Make Yourself
1999; Immortal/Epic

Poetic, positive and powerful, Incubus finally take all their disparate influences and create something cohesively dazzling.

Morning View
2001; Immortal/Epic

A spontaneous-sounding album, absolutely dripping with melody – the rocky bits rock very hard and the relaxed bits are quite gorgeous. Most accomplished.

InME

Formed Brentwood, Essex, UK, 1996

It is very tempting to liken this UK-based trio to Aussie superstars Silverchair when you realize that they are barely into their twenties and signed their record deal in 2001 when they were mere teenagers. Setting the age issue to one side, however, it's the music that's important and **InMe** display a staggering level of maturity when it comes to freaking out with guitars. In the short space of time that they have been in the rock spotlight they have been heralded as saviours of Britrock, been nominated as Best British Newcomers at the 2002 *Kerrang!* Awards, as well as gracing the cover of the magazine twice. And that's quite apart from making a respectable dent on the charts and a huge impression on the live circuit – for just three fresh-faced lads they make one helluva racket.

Unlike the aforementioned Silverchair, InMe, originally named **Drowned**, were not suddenly handed huge quantities of success by tapping, however innocently, into the prevalent sound of the times – in the case of the Aussies it was grunge as practised by Pearl Jam and Alice In Chains. **Dave McPherson** (vocals/guitar), **Joe Morgan** (bass/backing vocals) and **Simon Taylor** (drums) were lifelong friends and had played in a number of bands during their school years. They came together back in the mid-90s and developed their style at their own steady pace. Writing impressively dynamic songs, they avoided pandering to nu-metal fashions and stuck to exploiting the power of a killer riff and good old-fashioned fistbanging choruses. Having won a few band competitions their ambitions grew. But their step up was the result of sheer luck rather than the outcome of bombarding record labels with demo tapes – they tried that and were ignored for their troubles. The story goes that equipment problems at a London gig delayed their set by a few minutes and a

SCARLET PAGE

InMe prepare to do the 'Scaramoosh' bit.

label rep keen on seeing the next band on the bill caught just the last couple of songs of their set. The rest is history.

Some months down the line the band were ready to unleash a brace of singles. The naggingly catchy "Underdose" was the first slab of nervous energy to emerge and hit the UK charts at #66; the tense and chugging "Firefly" debuted at #43; and the solid'n'punchy "Crushed Like Fruit" fared even better, climbing to #25 in the charts. What's more, their debut UK headline tour was a sellout. On the back of this success came support slots with Puddle Of Mudd and Hundred Reasons. And all of this without an album in the shops.

When *Overgrown Eden* (2003) arrived it was everything promised by the singles and more. Veteran metal producer **Colin Richardson** saw to it that the set was polished and professional but without losing one iota of youthful energy. McPherson's volatile, cracked vocals crooned and soared over a tumultuous swirl of belting riffs, his lyrics hinting at unimaginable levels of inner discord and sorrow – almost every song contained mentions of pain, death and suicide, par for the course in modern metal. And of course the album's overall anguished and twitchy vibe owed a big nod to Nirvana. The lamenting tone of the words driven home by the ferocious delivery rocketed the debut to #15 in the charts. Vast amounts

of touring followed – including a number of festivals – before the band jetted out to Los Angeles to record their follow-up, *White Butterfly* (2005).

⊙ **Overgrown Eden**
Music For Nations; 2003

Call it neo-grunge if you like but this trio whip up a veritable storm of classy, pained and primal rock with consummate ease.

Iron Maiden

Formed London, UK, 1976

"I started dressing as Sherlock Holmes, complete with walking stick and deer stalker. I also took to wearing a false beard and going into pubs ordering pints of beer." Bruce's reaction to the tedium of touring in the 80s.

Iron Maiden are without doubt one of the biggest, most popular and astutely marketed metal bands in the world – we're talking multi-platinum-selling platters accompanied by world tours of heroic proportions and ridiculous amounts of merchandising. Not a year seems to go by without some sort of

DEAN KARR

Iron Maiden: carrying the torch of the NWOBHM.

Maiden-related album release to keep the faithful happy, and that must be one of the band's secrets to longevity: a following carefully cultivated over the years and a dedication to keeping the fans contented.

The mid-70s wasn't exactly the best time to launch a metal band. Punk was just about to lay into the bloated behemoths of dinosaur rock, so from a commercial point of view it was a venture almost certain to fail. To **Steve Harris** (bass), **Dave Murray** (guitar), **Doug Sampson** (drums) and **Paul Di'anno** (vocals) the creation of Iron Maiden – named, naturally enough, after the medieval torture instrument – was the start of a crusade to keep metal alive. Far from indulging in musical excesses, however, Maiden were lean and driven; speedy riffing and Di'anno's gutter-level – dare we say punky? – bawling earning the band a decent grass roots following as they played in pubs such as The Cart And Horses in Stratford (their debut venue), The Bridge House in Canning Town and, of course, the Ruskin Arms in East Ham. Such was their fervour and youthful zeal that they rapidly came to be one of the bands most likely to break out from the gathering New Wave Of British Heavy Metal, so dubbed by *Sounds* magazine – if only they could get a record deal. With no labels showing an interest Maiden followed the route of so many other NWOBHM bands and self-released a set of demos as the *Soundhouse Tapes* EP, which was championed by DJ Neal Kay. By 1979 the EP was available via mail order and the

band had gained a focused manager, the soon-to-be-legendary, **Rod Smallwood**. Finally, following the recording of a couple of songs for the *Metal For Muthas* compilation they signed to EMI.

With the amount of work already put into creating a following, things took off faster than a galloping Harris bass-run in 1980. One quick line-up change – the addition of guitarist **Dennis Stratton** and new drummer **Clive Burr** – and "Running Free" was the first of many hit singles; when the band were invited to play *Top Of The Pops* they refused to mime and so became the first act to play live on the programme since The Who in 1972. Meanwhile, their eponymous debut album rocketed in to #4, featuring their ghoulish, shock-haired mascot Eddie gracing the sleeve; this was to be among the first of Eddie's appearances both in the Derek Riggs-designed artwork and onstage (usually a roadie with an Eddie head on!). Years of honing the material had given them some bona fide stage faves: "Phantom Of The Opera", a lengthy tune with an instantly memorable riff, the rampaging title track and "Sanctuary", which was released as a single with a sleeve depicting Eddie, bloody knife in hand, kneeling over the body of then-Prime Minister Margaret Thatcher. She was to get her revenge on the sleeve for "Women In Uniform" as she waited in ambush for Eddie with a submachine gun.

As soon as the chart assault began so did Maiden's mission to take metal across the globe; they supported Judas Priest in the UK, played the Reading Festival with UFO and travelled across Europe with Kiss. Maiden had, as they say, arrived.

By album number two, *Killers* (1981), Eddie was looking less like he'd stuck his fingers in a live socket and more like a demonic headbanger – brandishing a hatchet, the business end of which was dripping with blood. And they had replaced Stratton with **Adrian Smith**. The production provided by **Martin Birch** was light years removed from the rawer sound of their debut and gave even second division Maiden tunes such as "Genghis Khan" – historical figures being just one of the many inspirations for some of the band's more absurd efforts – a power that the loopy lyrics really didn't deserve. Much better were crackers such as "Wrathchild" and "Murders In The Rue Morgue". By now chart placings were a dead cert for both albums and singles, with Maiden spreading their ambitions further abroad to Japan and the US. It wasn't called The Killer World Tour for nothing.

The be(a)st, however, was yet to come. Di'anno, possibly the most volatile band member, was replaced by **Bruce Dickson** (former singer with **Samson**), whose voice was soon likened to an air-raid siren. His impressive multi-octave range and his athletic stage presence gave Maiden real stadium potential, which was finally realized with *Number Of The Beast* (1982), a polished and energized classic metal set, buzzing with energy and visceral vitality. Tracks such as the daft "Invaders" and "Gangland" rubbed up against real gold such as "Children Of The Damned" and "Hallowed Be Thy Name". The real guts of the album, however lay in the duo of "Run To The Hills" and "Number Of The Beast"; the former went Top 10 and the latter Top 20, propelling the album into the top slot as the Maiden machine geared up for the Beast On The Road world tour.

This was the start of Maiden's golden period of the 80s, where hit albums spawned hit singles and were followed by huge sell-out tours, with vast amounts of equipment and stage sets being carted from venue to venue and assembled by a crack troop of road warriors. This was metal on a

grand, epic scale. A natural follow-up to *Number...* was *Piece Of Mind* (1983). By now Burr had been replaced by **Nicko McBrain** (ex-Trust) and the line-up settled into a world-beating groove, with the new album providing plenty of new stage faves. Top of the picks included "The Trooper" and "Flight Of Icarus" – both hit singles – and the stonking "Die With Your Boots On".

The production that complemented *Powerslave* (1984) was even more ambitious than for the band's previous ventures and found them heading to the Eastern Bloc, to South America for the first time – they played Rock In Rio in front of around 200,000 fans – and playing five sold-out shows at Radio City, New York. They also become the first act to sell out four consecutive gigs at Long Beach Arena, California.

Musically, Maiden had branched out even further than before. They had always been a cut above the competition in the songwriting stakes – the classic duelling axes powering through cleverly structured melodies – but their progressive tendencies were surfacing now on the immense "Rime Of The Ancient Mariner", complete with creaking ship's timbers and spoken-word narrative revisiting Coleridge's original poem. Both the dog-fighting "Aces High" and apocalyptic "Two Minutes To Midnight" were much more bite-size and gave them yet more chart-hogging fodder.

Marking the end of a stunning run of albums, *Live After Death* (1985), recorded during the band's stint at Long Beach ("Scream for me Long Beach!") captured the full lunatic splendour of the World Slavery Tour on double album and video.

The next effort, *Somewhere In Time* (1986), in keeping with the sci-fi Eddie-as-futuristic-bounty-hunter/*Bladerunner* theme of the sleeve, found the band using the latest equipment – guitar and bass synths – on some tracks to create a distinctly different feel from that of previous albums. The sound wasn't as prominent as on, say, Judas Priest's *Turbo*, but the change was enough to irritate some fans who wanted more of the same old Maiden. Nevertheless, "Wasted Years" and "Stranger In A Strange Land" made respectable forays into the charts.

Sticking to their guns Maiden kept the synths and added a concept storyline for *Seventh Son Of A Seventh Son* (1988) which yielded a whopping four hit singles and sat in the #1 slot in the album charts, confirming the band's stature as the premier UK metal band. Just to underline this fact they played to over 100,000 fans at the Donington Monsters of Rock festival and then toured the festival around Europe.

Such a frenetic and intense period of activity must take its toll, however, and Maiden were not immune. First off was **Adrian Smith** who had been working on material for his first solo effort under the name **ASaP**; he left in 1990 to be replaced by **Janick Gers** (ex-**Gillan,** ex-**White Spirit),** and a member of Bruce Dickinson's band when the lead singer was working on his own solo material. Dickinson was also branching out while Maiden took a break. Inspired by the books of Tom Sharpe he penned his comic novel *The Adventures Of Lord Iffy Boatrace*, he was ranked seventh in the country as a swordsman and invited to join the Olympic fencing team and his *Tattooed Millionaire* solo album made a

decent impact on the charts – as did the series of Maiden singles reissued as double-disc gatefold packages.

The taste of solo success would have its own effect on Dickinson but not before *No Prayer For The Dying* (1990) debuted at #2 in the UK, and *Fear Of The Dark* (1992) debuted at #1. A back-to-basics collection, *No Prayer...* lacked that vital spark necessary to make a classic. It didn't help that boys-own action fare such as "The Assassin", "Run Silent, Run Deep" (with Dickinson trying to make lines such as "A cunning fox in the chicken's lair" sound serious) and "Tailgunner" sounded rather tired. Or that "Mother Russia" had some of the most ridiculous lyrics ever to afflict a Maiden song since "Alexander The Great". The album did, however, feature the band's first ever #1 single, "Bring Your Daughter ... To The Slaughter", a song originally written by Dickinson for *Nightmare On Elm Street 5:*

Iron Maiden's Steve Harris.

ROSS HALFIN

The Dream Child and intended for his solo debut. Harris was so taken by the tune he insisted it be saved for the next Maiden album.

Fear... likewise lacked any real killer cuts though the return to a sound reminiscent of their earlier albums was welcome, especially the more inventive and progressive instrumental passages, proving they were a band as capable of experimenting with dynamics as they were of piling on the bombast. That's not to say it didn't boast any hits; "Be Quick Or Be Dead" was a #2 hit and "From Here To Eternity" did well enough. The problem could be summed up in one word: grunge. The Seattle sound was gradually razing to the ground the careers of many a traditional metal band and Maiden were suffering too.

To make matters infinitely worse Dickinson decided to leave and pursue a solo career, robbing them of their signature vocals, a sound as characteristic as Harris's rampant bass and Murray's guitar leads. *A Real Live One* and *A Real Dead One* (both live sets) plus *Live At Donington* (1993) were to be his last Maiden outings.

The man eventually chosen to take on the enormous task of becoming the voice of one of the biggest bands in the world was ex-**Wolfsbane** yelper **Blaze Bayley**. "Man On The Edge" re-launched the band promisingly enough and *The X Factor* (1995) had its moments, but as with Judas Priest trying to replace Rob Halford, there was a sense that the band were having to re-establish themselves and inevitably there were those for whom the Blaze years were a loss. Bayley acquitted himself with no small

amount of skill and aplomb; already a seasoned frontman he knew exactly how to work an audience.

Best Of The Beast (1996) was a self-explanatory compilation, a stopgap before *Virtual XI* (1998) which did well enough in the UK – #16 in the chart – but, like its predecessor, it barely raised a fist, let alone a yell, in the US. Meanwhile, Dickinson had also been experiencing diminishing returns and in early 1999 the band announced his return to the fold, along with Adrian Smith, giving the band a triple-guitar attack.

The following year *Brave New World* was hailed as a mighty return to form. The set featured a stunning epic in the shape of "Dream Of Mirrors", while "Blood Brothers" was swept along with full orchestral accompaniment and "Nomad" dripped with atmosphere.

Rock In Rio (2002) gave a taste of the revitalized band in front of an enthusiastic South American crowd, before *Dance Of Death* (2003) confirmed that Maiden were back at the top of their game.

Number Of The Beast
1982; EMI

This is where Maiden really got it right. From the inspired Eddie-controlling-the-devil sleeve to the timeless title track, this album punches hard and mean – Dickinson sounds like he's been in the band forever.

Dance Of Death
2003; EMI

There's no duff material present and every tune boasts flair and imagination in spades, especially "Paschendale", an epic eight-and-a-half minutes about one of the bloodiest battles of World War I.

JANE'S ADDICTION

Formed Los Angeles, California, US, 1986;
disbanded 1991; re-formed 2001; disbanded 2004

A more precise embodiment of alternative rock it would be hard to find. Confrontational, arrogant and pretentious, **Jane's Addiction** turned all these aspects of their sound into virtues through the simple fact that they were a fantastic band. First formed as the mutant offspring of **Perry Farrell's** (vocals) demented imagination after leaving his first band **Psi-Com**, Farrell set about fulfilling his personal vision of rock as art. When he recruited **Dave Navarro** (guitar), **Eric Avery** (bass), and **Steve Perkins** (drums) from the pool of talent that is the LA club scene, he consciously chose from the city's alternative musical elite. And in so doing he created one of the most alien, yet credible, groups of the last two decades. Menacing and beautiful by turns, they defied classification as they spewed out their acid-tinged fix of metal, rock, punk and funk.

Their mission to corrupt and enlighten began with *Jane's Addiction* (1987), a live affair on the Triple X label. It succinctly displayed their unique live fury; songs such as "1%", "Whores" and "Pigs In Zen" were drug-fuelled splinters of a frenzied whole. Early performances reflected their desire to create an artistic, hedonistic experience. Their first manager was a prostitute who would greet punters topless; inside was a freakshow carnival of transsexual strippers, fire-eaters, snake-dancers and sleazy porn

flicks – it was a total mind-trip topped off by the band's skull-crushing, hypnotic presence. They were the essence of true alternative rock'n'roll, the toxic twin to the mainstream preening and posing of the LA cock-rock scene. Farrell commanded the stage like a malign stick-thin insect, while together, the band exuded an intense androgynous cool.

Exceeding the promise of the live debut, however, was their full major-label debut appearance, *Nothing's Shocking* (1988), released on Warner Brothers. It was nothing short of a terrifying classic. Everything about it, and the band's attitude, was intended to subvert established norms. The cover featured a sculpture of naked Siamese twins (modelled on Farrell's girlfriend, Casey Niccoli) with their heads on fire. Initial quantities were issued in ribbed rubber sleeves intended, perhaps, to protect the innocent while signalling to those on the same wave-length of the sonic perversions within.

Seductive opener "Up The Beach" was simply beguiling and dropped the unwary listener into the crashing pandemonium of "Ocean Sized". Everything about their sound was huge; the rhythms looped and mesmerised, the guitars scorched, and Farrell's processed staccato vocals echoed and shimmered throughout. Instant classics such as "Had A Dad" and "Mountain Song" were balanced by lighter psychedelic touches such as "Summertime Rolls", and the acoustic "Jane Says". Meanwhile, the anti-conformist funk of "Idiots Rule" featured Flea (**Red Hot Chili Peppers**) in the horn section. This was a record of danceable, dark, brooding perfection. The songs were about sex, death, love, and sheer heart-stopping, murderous fury and Farrell's inspiration came as much from real life as his (and the others') well documented use of drugs. Farrell saw narcotics as a creative tool, and himself as a modern-day psychonaut "exploring chaos".

The charged and unpredictable live shows matched the violent, mystical atmosphere of the album. Farrell magnetized audiences with his shamanistic poise, and baited them with vitriolic insults. Meanwhile, the others would assail each song at full, soul-tearing volume.

The band's second studio effort, *Ritual De Lo Habitual* (1990), was equally astonishing. An enchanting Mexican girl introduced the first song; translated, her words were, "Ladies and gentlemen, we have more influence over your children than you do...". As with the previous artwork, they fell foul of the censors. Farrell had created yet another sculpture, this time of himself and two women lying naked on a nuptial bed, surrounded by occultish trinkets and icons representing the Santarian religion (a belief system incorporating voodoo). The cover was banned and Farrell designed a plain white cover with the First Amendment printed on it; a comment about freedom of speech.

Aside from this skirmish with the forces of conservatism, the music opened up another artistic battlefront with a breathtaking, corrosive fix of incandescent noise. Scalding numbers like "Ain't No Right" nestled up against fragile moments such as "Classic Girl". The album's outstanding cut, though, was the rolling progressive rush of "Three Days", a ten-minute-plus epic of emotive passion. Sales of *Ritual...* in the first week alone outstripped those of *Nothing's Shocking*.

With critical and commercial plaudits flowing in it looked as though the group would effortlessly enter the major league of stadium rock. However, tensions within the

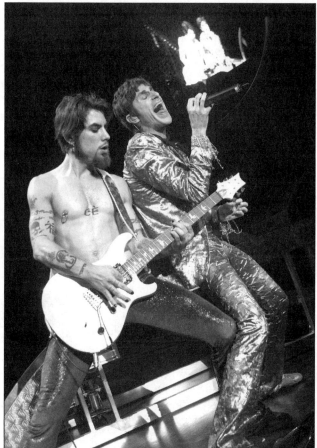

Ferrell and Navarro competing for the centre of attention.

band, which had previously been a source of dynamic creativity, were growing unchecked. They had openly admitted that they were far from being best friends, and at the outset the spark of conflict had given them a vital edge. Now, the substance abuse was adding to the problems as well.

Farrell announced that he had achieved all he wanted with the group, that he wanted to explore other artistic avenues, and had persuaded Warner Brothers to fund his next art project, a film entitled *The Gift*. Nevertheless, the final performances of the band were just as majestic as before, with the stage set drenched in trinkets and supernatural symbolism. The UK leg of the tour in 1991 saw them at their blood-curdling best. The Brixton Academy and London Marquee Club shows were particular high points, the band delaying their appearance on stage just long enough to have the crowd howling in

COURTESY OF CAPITOL RECORDS

anticipation before tearing into a set of unparalleled beauty and ferocity.

Taking the alternative agenda further, Farrell instigated the first Lollapalooza Tour in 1991, featuring a diverse bill of supporting bands including Ice-T, Henry Rollins, and Living Colour. The cracks were definitely showing during the first date in Arizona when the band were so wasted that they could barely play. Being shambolic was one thing, but no one predicted that they would self-destruct so publicly. The encores were a disaster; Navarro's amps failed, Farrell goaded him, and in front of an amazed crowd the axe-man tried to fell Farrell with his guitar, but failed. A punch-up ensued and the two had to be held apart. The final few gigs were, fortunately, a return to their previous brilliance.

With Jane's Addiction seemingly consigned to the history books Farrell and Perkins resurfaced in Porno For Pyros while Navarro began work on solo material, formed Deconstruction with Avery and turned up in the Red Hot Chili Peppers. Avery eventually went on to form Polar Bear.

None of these projects, however, matched the level of excellence exhibited by Jane's Addiction and over the years fans were tantalized by the possibility that they might re-form. And then it happened. Navarro joined up with Porno For Pyros to record "Hard Charger" for the soundtrack to Howard Stern's *Private Parts*. It proved to be such a blast that they re-formed to tour, with Flea on bass. A compilation of live tracks, demos and rarities, *Kettle Whistle* (1997), arrived as well, but the reunion was a short-lived affair.

Nevertheless, curiosity aroused and with the temptation tough to overcome, the various members still felt there was life in the ornery beast yet. So they reconvened to play the second Coachella Valley Music & Arts Festival in 2001 and then their own live dates with Porno For Pyros bassist Martyn LeNoble. Writing for a new album began in 2002 with legendary producer Bob Ezrin (Pink Floyd, Alice Cooper, Kiss) at the helm and new bassist **Chris Chaney** in the ranks. The result, *Strays* (2003), was an amazing return to form, as though the split over a decade earlier had never happened. Navarro's guitar lines were just as crystalline and dazzling as before and Farrell's idiosyncratic poetry still teetered on the edge of abstraction and outrage. A full tour followed, but, just as all great bands should, Jane's Addiction

bowed out once more, again leaving their audience wanting more.

⊙ Nothing's Shocking
1988; Warner Bros

Art-rock at its scariest. An essential studio effort where the band show great versatility and a knowing confidence.

⊙ Ritual De Lo Habitual
1990; Warner Bros

Music with as much colour and style as the perverse cover art; "Three Days" is worth the admission price alone. A recording of awesome consistency and terrifying depths.

⊙ Strays
2003; Warner Bros

Absolutely and utterly indispensable – it's just as though they never went away. This is studded with gem after gem.

JET

Formed Melbourne, Australia, 2002

The fact that this four-piece named themselves after one of Paul McCartney's biggest post-Beatles hits should give a clue as to the era they favour above all for inspiration. Next to the likes of the Casanovas, the Vines and the Datsuns, Jet are one of the most heavily classic rock-oriented bands to emerge from the club scene Down Under.

Brothers **Nic** (guitar/vocals) and **Chris Cester** (drums/vocals) formed the heart of the band alongside **Cameron Muncey** (guitar/vocals) and **Mark Wilson** (bass). The vibrancy of the Antipodean rock scene had already

attracted the attention of various record labels, and when the *NME* gave the thumbs up to Jet's "Take It Or Leave It" single, it seemed a dead cert that someone would pick up on their shameless evocation of AC/DC riffage and Stonesian swagger. If it was retro and heavy these guys loved it, making them the total antithesis of everything grunge had stood for.

They soon signed to Elektra and released their debut EP, *Dirty Sweet* in 2003, the title borrowed from T-Rex – there definitely seemed to be a pattern forming. The EP was basically a bunch of demo recordings spruced up, the rawness of the sound adding to the band's ragged sonic charm. It provided breathing space for a spot of touring and for the band to begin the recording of their first album, which was interrupted so that they could support the Rolling Stones.

When *Get Born* (2003) appeared in a haze of half-inched heavy blues riffs and gutter-snipe attitude, the world's rock press nearly went into meltdown hailing the band's genuine hard rock credentials. "Are You Gonna Be My Girl" – a tune which Marilyn Manson has been known to soundcheck with – won the Best Rock Video category at the MTV Awards in 2004 and ended up being used on Apple's iPod commercials in the States, while Vodaphone used it in Europe. "Hold On" was used in *Spiderman II* and the band won six Aria awards, Australia's equivalent to The Brits – they were nominated for seven but didn't win in the Biggest Selling Album category because *Get Born* hadn't been out long enough.

Get Born
2003; Elektra

You'd be forgiven for thinking you had fallen into a time warp with this crusty little collection of hard rocking tunes. Everything from the Faces' cheeky strut to Angus Young's string-bending heroics finds a home here.

JOURNEY

Formed San Francisco, US, 1973; disbanded 1987; re-formed 1996

Next to Foreigner, the 80s AOR airwaves were ruled by the melodic stadium-filling monster that was **Journey**. Massive, catchy choruses wedded to tastefully played guitar

lines was their stock in trade, helping them to rack up an indecently large number of hit singles and platinum albums. They folded at their peak to pursue solo careers but reunited nearly a decade later to continue in the much-changed musical landscape of the mid-90s.

Considering the type of rock this lot are associated with it might come as a bit of a shock to learn that they started off in the early 70s as a jazz-rock combo. The main-spring behind the music was **Neal Schon** (guitar) who had played with Latin rock legend, Carlos Santana, after nearly ending up with Eric Clapton in Derek And The Dominos. Journey's early career – featuring the albums *Journey* (1975), *Look Into The Future* (1976) and *Next* (1977) – was heading nowhere and the label CBS gave the band an ultimatum – get a decent singer or get the chop. This led to the recruitment of **Steve Perry**. With the new singer's sensitive, yet dynamic, vocals in the mix the line up of Schon, **Gregg Rolie** (keyboards), **Ross Valory** (bass) and **Aynsley Dunbar** (drums) were in business. The new, cohesive melodic rock sound was perfect for radio and "Wheel In The Sky" became their first modest hit, ushering in *Infinity* (1978). **Steve Smith** replaced Dunbar for *Evolution* (1979) and *Departure* (1980), the era of their biggest hit single yet, "Lovin', Touchin', Squeezin'"; the song went into the Top 20 but the best was yet to come.

Captured (1981) was a decent enough double live album but *Escape* (1981) was the band's crowning achievement, with **Jonathan Cain** replacing Rolie. It topped the charts in the US and went Top 40 in the relatively hard-hearted UK where Journey's awesomely polished adult-oriented sound was starting to make inroads. "Who's Crying Now" and "Open Arms" became their biggest hits yet, both going Top 5, the perfectly tailored choruses providing ideal fodder for FM stations still pumping out Boston's "More Than A Feeling". Next album, *Frontiers* (1983), nearly gave them another US chart-topper, held off the top slot by Michael Jackson's *Thriller*; it also almost went into the Top 5 in the UK.

By now, however, the band's desire to indulge in solo projects was starting to get the better of them, sapping some of their momentum. In addition both Smith and Valory were fired. As a result *Raised On Radio* finally arrived in 1986 with the help of **Randy Jackson** (bass) and **Larrie Londin** (drums). Despite its less than smooth creation the album was hailed by *Kerrang!* magazine as the band's best after *Escape*.

On a high note Journey called it quits in early 1987; Schon and Cain went off to form **Bad English** with John Waite and Perry kept working on the solo material. *Greatest Hits* (1988) was the inevitable chapter-closer on a story which picked up again in 1996 when the *Escape* line-up reconvened for *Trial By Fire*. Amazingly, considering the impact of alternative rock and grunge, the album peaked at #3 in the US. Unfortunately, illness precluded Perry from taking part in any live dates so the band were prevented from touring the album. *Greatest Hits Live* (1998) followed but it became clear that Perry's illness was going to be a serious impediment. So by the time of *Arrival* (2001) the line-up had been revised to include new singer **Steve Augeri** (ex-**Tall Stories**, **Tyketto**) – whose first appearance on record with the band had been "Remember Me" on the *Armageddon* soundtrack – and drummer **Deen Castronovo**. The band's sound had also been tweaked somewhat – a heavier direction had the guitars packing a far greater punch amid the well-honed melodies. The fresh approach was developed further on the 2002 *Red 13* EP, the band's first release on their own independent label, Journeymusic.

Escape
1981; CBS

A soft-rock classic if ever there was one. Perry's vocals are smooth yet muscular, the keyboards parp away with real class and Schon's guitar work is exemplary. No wonder it kept clocking up the platinum discs.

Greatest Hits
1988; CBS

A fine spread of 24-carat chart-botherers, including a couple of gems plucked from soundtracks.

JUDAS PRIEST

Formed Birmingham, UK, 1969

"You have to evolve or the sands of time will cover you up." Glenn Tipton

Surely one of the definitive metal bands in the world, **Judas Priest** emerged from the smoke of the industrial heartland of the UK in the early 70s, and proceeded to create many of the aspects of metal that would go on to become clichés in the hands of lesser practitioners. They have the twin-duelling axes, the hair-raising vocals and the leather-clad image; they are every inch the metal gods.

The roots of Priest trail as far back into the Midlands club scene as 1969 when the band were doing the rounds churning out cover versions. Led Zeppelin and Deep Purple were shortly to go huge with their turbo-charged blues and Sabbath were not far off from scaring the hell out of the record buying public with their eponymous debut. The 70s would be an ideal environment for Judas Priest to flourish but they still had to get their line-up sorted out. From the original band **K.K. Downing** (guitar) and **Ian Hill** (bass) were the only two to survive from the clubbing days; soon the addition of **Rob Halford** (vocals) and **John Hinch** (drums) would give them the impetus necessary to make it to the studio; over the coming decade, however, the band would find themselves chopping and changing drummers regularly. The crucial ingredient was second guitarist **Glenn Tipton**, giving them the ability to develop some sizzling six-string interplay – all of which was singularly lacking in their debut *Rocka Rolla* (1974) which snuck out on Gull Records. The label lacked the clout to push the band far, which was just as well because the songs really weren't up to much.

The real breakthrough quality-wise came with album number two, *Sad Wings Of Destiny* (1976), featuring **Alan Moore** on

Judas Priest in the 80s.

drums. It gave the band timeless classics such as "Tyrant", "Victim Of Changes" and "Ripper", the latter giving Halford ample opportunity to indulge in some deliciously nasty lyrics. They clearly had the potential but lacked a decent record deal. That eventually came with a signing to CBS/Columbia and *Sin After Sin* followed (1977) – this time with **Simon Phillips** behind the kit – a modest UK chart success peaking at #23. Again, packed with great tunes such as the ballad "Last Rose Of Summer", their cover of Joan Baez's "Diamonds And Rust" and classic "Dissident Aggressor", it should have done better than it did, but the production job provided by ex-**Deep Purple** bassist **Roger Glover** fell short this time round. And they still couldn't hold onto a drummer: Phillips was soon after replaced by **Les Binks**.

A maiden US tour in the summer of 1977 laid the foundations for the coming years and a double whammy of *Stained Class* (1978) – featuring the classic slow-building "Beyond The Realms Of Death" – and *Killing Machine* (1978) made decent forays into the UK album charts, helped by the band's ever-toughening stage look. The whip-wielding Halford had been pushing his image to the extreme – the band actually cancelled a tour of Germany when the increasingly S&M attired singer was banned from using his

whip by the promoter. By this point, in a musical landscape littered with the corpses of rock bands slain by punk, Priest needed something to push them into a league of their own. That arrived with their first true hit single, "Take On The World" which went to #14 in the UK. *Killing Machine,* promptly retitled *Hell Bent For Leather* – they couldn't have chosen a better title by this point – had the band's cracking revamp of Fleetwod Mac's "The Green Manalishi (With The Two-Pronged Crown)" bolted onto it and was issued in the US. Softened-up metal fans were then blasted with *Unleashed In The East* (1979), a live album recorded during one of the band's Japanese jaunts where they commanded some suitably sizeable crowds. It was the band's first outing with producer **Tom Allom** and was so successful – the album was jokingly referred to as *Unleashed In The Studio* because of the number of overdubs and tweaks polishing the sound – that the working relationship lasted for much of the coming 80s. The record gave Priest their first ever Top 10 album in the UK.

By now Halford had taken to arriving on stage astride a Harley Davidson; the band now needed a killer album to cement their standing as one of the great British metal acts. That album was *British Steel* (1980), featuring **Dave Holland** on drums. From the sleeve art depicting a British-made razor blade, to the ripping songs within, it was a ball-busting breakthrough. "Living After Midnight", "United" and, of course, "Breaking The Law" – the latter the quintessential riffmongous headbanger – all assaulted the singles charts. It was enough to get them on the bill of the first Monsters Of Rock festival in 1980, second only to headliners, Rainbow.

By contrast *Point Of Entry* (1981) was something of a puzzle compared to its bullet-belted, spike-studded, gas-guzzling predecessor. Instead of putting the pedal to the metal and leaving everyone standing it was almost relaxed in comparison. Only "Heading Out To The Highway" and "Solar Angels" came anywhere near the excitement levels of *British Steel*. It wasn't a mistake they repeated with *Screaming For Vengeance* (1982), a top-twenty stormer in both the UK and the US. The heavy-duty menace of "You've Got Another Thing Coming", the cyber-surveillance chugger "Electric Eye" and enervating rush of "Riding On The Wind" were just three outstanding cuts from an album that positively crackled with gymnastic riffing, blazing solos and a modern, sporty metal production that made *Point Of Entry* sound geriatric in comparison. This was the start of Priest's reign as one of the top metal

bands in the world during the 80s; the demand for the band throwing shapes decked out in the most ludicrous leather excesses available was quite astonishing, especially in the US where they spent much of 1983 touring their cowhide clad butts off.

Defenders Of The Faith (1984) found the band even further down the hard-and-fast route; "Freewheel Burning" was a murderous open-highway thrasher but the infinitely more sinister "Love Bites" and the self-explanatory "Eat Me Alive" had the moral guardians up in arms, especially in America where the band were about to find themselves embroiled in the kind of morale-sapping legal shenanigans that plagued Ozzy Osbourne's 80s career.

After a lengthy break Priest played Live Aid in Philadelphia before embarking on recording their next album. In December of 1985, however, events would take place that would plague Priest for the remainder of the decade. Two troubled teenagers shot themselves, apparently after listening to *Stained Class*. One survived and died three years later after a drug-induced coma. The band were sued by the parents who blamed them for inducing the teenagers to try to take their own lives through subliminal messages hidden in the music. In 1990 the judge rejected the claim.

The pressure of the impending court case not withstanding, Priest continued with business as usual. Not wishing to stagnate, *Turbo* (1986) featured a drastic change in the Priest sound – the use of guitar synths. It was a move employed by several bands who thought that strangely mangled guitar noises were preferable to good old-fashioned overdriven distortion. And to many fans, messing about with synths was akin to sacrilege, especially for a band like Priest. As a result *Turbo* got something of a mixed reception when it first bleeped and shuddered over the horizon.

Far more satisfying was *Priest... Live!* (1987) which presented the *Turbo* material in the context of the band's huge Fuel For Life tour of 1986. The next studio album contained a fairly frightful cover of Chuck

Berry's "Johnny B. Goode"; the remainder of *Ram It Down* (1988) did exactly what its title suggested. It was possibly the heaviest thing they had ever recorded, smoking with ire and bloodshot bad attitude; the screeching "Heavy Metal" was about as bombastic an anthem as any extreme metal fan could desire.

It was a direction continued with *Painkiller* (1990), an album not so much propelled as rocketed forward by new drummer **Scott Travis** (ex-**Racer X**). Travis's hyperspeed style gave the title track a fantastically heavy, thrashy edge. And just in case fans weren't sure of what they were going to get, there were tracks such as "Leather Rebel" and "Metal Meltdown" on offer. It looked as if Priest's position as kings of metal was unassailable – and then came the near-fatal blow. Halford decided to leave the band to pursue his side-project, **Fight**, and eventually go solo.

Picture the scene: one of the biggest metal acts in the world suddenly bereft of their outrageous, charismatic frontman, and at a time when grunge was killing off 80s metal. It would take a good while for the band to recover from this mighty blow. The man to replace Halford's big shoes was **Tim 'Ripper' Owens**, a singer who could pull off a remarkable Halford-style impression. The record labels had been quick to spew forth with the customary best-of compilations, sensing the band were done. Indeed, it was touch and go for a while, with hopes of a recovery complicated by the emergence of a whole new generation of nu-metal bands. When Priest stormed back with *Jugulator* (1997) it was a stupendously heavy piece of metalwork. The song titles said it all: "Blood Stained", "Dead Meat", "Death Row", "Decapitate" and "Brain Dead". The guitars were a downtuned cliff-face of gleaming steel and it all sounded deadly serious compared to their older material. Needless to say, fan support was split and it came down to *'98 Live Meltdown* (1998) to prove that Owens was a match for Halford's supernatural scream.

While they could clearly cut it live Priest found themselves having to lay the groundwork for a

return from the edge of oblivion. Vast amounts of touring followed and *Demolition* (2001) took the ultra-heavy sound even further. But the album lacked that vital spark necessary to interest anyone but the most rabid fans.

Ultimately, Halford, somewhat disenchanted with his lot as a solo artist, rejoined the band in 2003, but Owens soon moved on to **Iced Earth** – his last album with Priest was *Live In London* (2003). After a decade out of the band Halford's return was seen as an opportunity for Judas Priest to reclaim their mantle as one of the UK's greatest metal bands. The first fruit of the new era was the incredibly accomplished *Angel Of Retribution* (2005), with Priest effectively picking things up from where they had been left with *Painkiller.*

British Steel
1980; CBS

The speedy thrash of "Rapid Fire" launches this classic before heading into the martial march of "Metal Gods" and anthemic "Breaking the Law" – not bad going for just the opening three songs. The rest are just as powerful, making this a must-have.

Metal Works '73-'93
1993; CBS

This is a very tidy double-album compilation covering the Halford period of the band, making it a perfect springboard from which to explore the joys of Priest.

KID ROCK

Born Romeo, Michigan, US, January 17, 1971

The Kid, aka **Robert Ritchie**, is one of a kind. The fedora-wearing, cigar-chomping entrepreneur is one of the few artists to harness rap and rock in a shockingly convincing manner, in a career that has taken him from the blue-collar 'burbs of Detroit to the top of the celebrity rock pile. In the process he has sold shedloads of records – his breakthrough album *Devil Without A Cause* (1998) recently won a Diamond Award for ten million sales in the US alone – and with the aid of his **Twisted Brown Trucker** band, featuring the vocal talent of the iconically diminutive **Joe C**, created a genre all of his own: bling metal.

Anyone who experienced **Kid Rock**'s early years must have had an inkling that he would become a star. During the 80s he was a music sponge, absorbing a huge variety of sounds and influences, from Johnny Cash and Lynyrd Skynyrd, to Run DMC and Whodini. There was nothing that he wouldn't listen to, taking on board the possibilities and potential for his own music. This magpie mentality, coupled with an admiration for the unashamed playboy lifestyle championed by rap stars, naturally led to him spinning the wheels of steel and rocking basement parties in his neighbourhood.

These early experiments led to a one-off deal with Jive Records, a debut album and instant notoriety. *Grits Sandwiches For Breakfast* (1990) contained "Yo-Da-Lin In The Valley", an early controversial hit single with oral sex the subject matter. The skirt-chasing Kid talked it like he walked it, and his tongue-in-cheek ode to cunnilingus led to a university radio station being fined thousands of dollars for airing the risqué rhymes.

A similar tale followed "Balls In Your Mouth", a naughty little tune on *The Polyfuze Method* (1993) – following a new deal with Continuum Records – which landed yet another college radio station in very hot water. This was the kind of publicity it was impossible to buy and the Kid capitalized wholesale on his

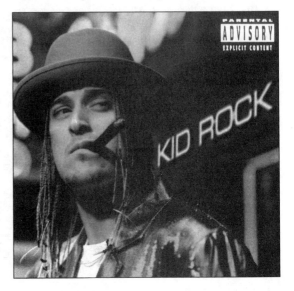

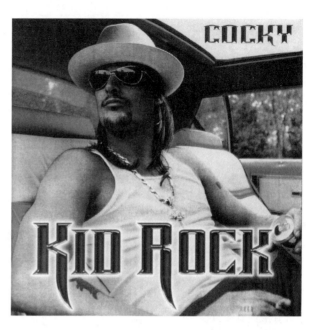

bad-boy image – he rapidly became renowned for his salty swear-fest raps coupled with metallic samples. One more effort was released by the label, the mini-LP *Fire It Up* (1994), but it was becoming increasingly clear that they didn't understand where the Kid was coming from or where he was going.

Concentrating upon his own Top Dog label, *Early Mornin' Stoned Pimp* (1996) took the funk'n'metal rap formula even further; it was clear the next album would be a watershed. When *Devil Without A Cause* (1998) arrived through a deal with Lava/Atlantic the whole world took notice and the metal community could no longer afford to ignore the Kid's burgeoning talent. With the Twisted Brown Trucker band now a firm fixture of Kid Rock's sound, he had crossed over from the realms of hip-hop, via metaldom, and was reaching for the stratosphere. There were a couple of reworked tunes from his previous effort, the beats were heavier and more inventive, the riffs eminently headbang-worthy and the rhymes even closer to the bone – even the Kid's pal **Eminem** turned up on the appropriately titled "Fuck Off". He was a bad-ass, foul-mouthed exhibitionist and he didn't care who knew it. What's more, it was a lifestyle that had landed him with a genuine mega-hit album.

The interim was a period of whirlwind activity. *The History Of Rock* (2000) came out, an album of reworked and remixed tracks alongside a few rarities. Also, he and the TBT band supported Metallica on their Summer Sanitarium tour, and, to prove that they had really arrived, the Kid and Joe C were immortalized on *The Simpsons*. Sadly it was also the year Joe C, a sufferer of Celiac disease, died of natural causes brought on by his long-term illness.

Cocky (2001) was yet another hit album – much bigger in America than in the UK, as was the case with his previous studio effort – with an awesome array of heavy rock samples and beats. Though it didn't quite scale the heights of *Devil...* it nevertheless marked a period when Kid Rock was rarely out of the headlines, whether it was for the duet with **Sheryl Crow** on "Picture" – which became

a huge hit – or his relationship with Pamela Anderson. Then, of course, there was the Kid's offshoot career in the movies.

His place in the upper echelons of America's entertainment business secured, he returned in 2003 with an eponymous studio album and another US hit single in the form of "Feel Like Makin' Love", a cover of the vintage Bad Company hit. Originally Crow featured on the song, but she and Kid Rock mutually decided that another duet so close on the heels of "Picture" would not be a good idea, so the vocals were removed.

Doubtless the duet version of this hard-rock classic will appear sooner or later. In the meantime, Kid Rock's self-indulgent mission to be the number one American bad ass continues.

 Devil Without A Cause
1998; Top Dog/Lava/Atlantic

This album makes his previous material sound like he was just warming up. The Twisted Brown Trucker band bring a real live feel to the songs, which feature a fine line in profane poetics. A crossover classic packed with laughs and plenty of headcracking metal. You have to believe him when he claims to be the Bullgod.

 Cocky
2001; Lava/Atlantic

Not quite as commercially successful as his breakthrough album, but positively heaving with terrific ideas and much guitar action. Some people might think that the Kid has gone soft with "Picture" but the tables are turned with the sweary country and heavy rap-rock hybrid of "Midnight Train To Memphis". Great stuff.

KILLSWITCH ENGAGE

Formed Boston, Massachusetts, US, 1999

Musicians with vision often find themselves shifting from one band to another trying to assemble combinations of like-minded individuals. So it was with **Mike D'Antonio** (bass), main songwriter of metalcore bruisers **Overcast**, whose swansong LP *Fight Ambition To Kill* (1997) is regarded as a landmark classic in underground circles. When Overcast disbanded in 1998 he began a quest to find personnel for what would become one of the heaviest and most technically proficient metal bands to emerge from the US. Two members of **Aftershock**, **Adam Dutkiewicz** (drums) and **Joel Stoetzel** (guitar), joined up first, followed by **Nothing Stays Gold** vocalist **Jesse Leach**. D'Antonio came up with the name and they set about fusing their hardcore punk influences to a solid metal framework. Key to their early sound was the influence of bands such as noisy screamo legends Converge, whose infamously nonlinear and emotion-laden approach to songwriting has launched a thousand copyist bands. **Killswitch Engage**, however, took the innovative approach and began adding dashes of the melodic Gothenburg sound to shape something unique and progressively powerful.

The band quickly garnered a reputation for themselves as support act on an In Flames tour and were quickly picked up by Ferret Records, home to bands with an unstraightforward approach to heaviness. Their self-titled debut emerged in 2000, a record that was both emotionally raw and brutally pummelling. The inventiveness of the band's writing merely hinted at what they would be capable of given a bigger budget, but at the heart of the album's success was the production job provided by **Dutkiewicz**. He would go on to fill the same role in the studio for the next two albums, as well as acting as second guitarist.

It was inevitable that such an imaginative band would eventually break away from their underground roots and the move came with a signing to Roadrunner Records in 2001, home to such artists as Slipknot, Type O Negative and Soulfly among many other cutting-edge modern metal acts.

Their second album, *Alive Or Just Breathing* (2002), was nothing short of a quantum leap forward. Leach was developing into an extraordinary frontman, his roaring vocal delivery taking the best of hardcore and death metal stylings and forging a new, altogether more ferocious, beast. Meanwhile, the music was white-hot with attitude and technical brilliance – thundering percussion driving forward intricately heavy riffing, drawing on elements of thrash and old-school heavy metal – it was a record that would give Slayer a run for their money in the brutality stakes. And just to show that they were still in touch with their previous work they re-engineered both "Vide Infra" and "Temple Of The Within" from their Ferret debut. Killswitch Engage were living up their name and proving to be a shock to the system – despite the aggressive nature of the music, these were songs with largely positive lyrical messages at heart, emotional and spiritual explorations of the human condition.

All would not pan out well, however, after the record's release. Leach quit the band via email, citing personal and health reasons. Had the Killswitch been flicked off permanently? Not a chance. True, the news was a shock, and awful to the newly burgeoning outfit, but the metalcore underground is nothing if not capable of rising in support. **Blood Has Been Shed** vocalist **Howard Jones** stepped up to the challenge and eventually brought with him BHBS drummer **Justin Foley**. He replaced former sticksman Tom Gomes in October 2003, just prior to their slot on the MTV2 Headbangers Ball.

At first fans were unsure whether Jones' voice would be a good enough substitute for Leach's titanic lung power, but with a string of triumphant live shows behind them, including Ozzfest, any doubts were soon put to rest. The real test would come in the studio, however, when writing for their third album was under way and new material was being shaped.

If anything Jones' abilities surpassed all expectations when *The End Of Heartache* (2004) was released. The artwork featured a greying, desiccated heart driven through with nails held in blood-drenched hands – another design provided by bass player D'Antonio who also works as a graphic artist and who put together the images for all the band's albums. The techniques of the previous set had led them to record what many critics were hailing as some sort of modern metal masterpiece. This was at once vicious and beautiful, aggressive and nurturing; the guitars sounded crisp, histrionic, raging, the melodies were epic and Jones was exceptional at the mic, delivering classic death rasps and clean, soaring passages, reminiscent of Faith No More's Mike Patton – utterly in command.

With such a compelling clutch of albums in so short a space of time Killswitch Engage rightfully deserve the accolades heaped upon them.

 Alive Or Just Breathing
2002; Roadrunner

It might sound like emotional anguish set to a scorching metal score and largely it is. Lyrically positive and musically innovative this album simply roars past, spitting up more ideas in one song than some bands cram onto whole albums.

 The End Of Heartache
2004; Roadrunner

By turns incredibly beautiful and face-rippingly aggressive, Killswitch's new vocalist Howard Jones brings greater range to the band's powerful sonic tirade.

KING DIAMOND

Formed Copenhagen, Denmark, 1985

Any self-respecting fan of screaming axes will already be familiar with the King's output through the highly influential **Mercyful Fate**. Coming on like a satanic Alice Cooper – by all accounts the supernaturally talented singer (real name Kim Bendix Petersen and an ex-footballer to boot!) was inspired to adopt his infamous face paint after experiencing Alice's live shows in the mid-70s – the idea was to create a convincingly evil, shock rock character to deliver some overtly infernal and extremely inventive metal tunes. **Mercyful Fate**'s early career lasted for one EP and two very fine albums – *Melissa* and *Don't Break The Oath* – before musical differences split the band and the King headed off to pursue a solo career in 1985.

From the Mercyful Fate line-up the King took **Michael Denner** (guitar) and **Timi Hansen** (bass) and added **Andy LaRocque** (guitar) and **Mikkey Dee** (drums). The singer's inhuman vocal range meant that the new

band were instantly recognizable to fans of the late Mercyful Fate. The first effort from the new line-up was the cheeky "No Presents For Christmas" single, the sleeve featuring the King in full make-up posing beside a stuffed reindeer – very scary indeed. The real meat, however, arrived with *Fatal Portrait* (1986) which, although it wasn't a million miles from the sound of Mercyful Fate, had more classic metal to it rather than speedy thrash. The indicator as to where the band were heading, however, came in the opening brace of songs which formed a neat little horror story. It wasn't quite a concept album, more a testing of the waters and a welcome change from the straightforward demonic stuff.

Having made a successful debut it was time for the band's mist-shrouded masterpiece, *Abigail* (1987). A full-on concept album, it focused on creepy gothic horror complete with cryptic prophecies, evil ghosts, reincarnation and insanity. Set to a suitably atmospheric metal backdrop the whole thing worked beautifully, which is more than can be said for *Them* (1988), which had its moments of mercurial madness but lacked the dark charm of *Abigail*. It did, however, sell well and nestled in the Top 90 of the US chart, no doubt helped somewhat by MTV picking up on "Welcome Home". The album also marked the beginning of a series of line-up shifts, during which LaRocque remained the only constant factor.

It was perhaps this rise in profile that set up the next notable episode in the King's career. A mini-LP, *The Dark Sides* (1988) pulled together a few rarities which were

King Diamond: "putting on The Ritz".

unremarkable in themselves; this time it was the King's make-up on the sleeve that would win him some publicity – but for the wrong reasons. Kiss bassist Gene Simmons felt that the King's look was just a bit too close to his own and slapped a lawsuit on the malevolent moustachioed warbler. In the end the matter was resolved out of court, but the King had to get his make-up tips from elsewhere.

The next album attempted to capitalize on the success of *Them* by being a sequel titled simply *Conspiracy* (1989). By now, however, it seemed like the blood of gothic horror was running a little thin and *The Eye* (1990) – with its nun-bothering witchcraft plot – didn't do so well, a situation not helped in the least by Roadrunner Records' ambivalent attitude to the band. Tour support was not forthcoming, so *In Concert 1987: Abigail* (1991) and the Mercyful Fate/King Diamond split compilation *A Dangerous Meeting* (1992) were little more than ways to fulfil their contract and move on.

Doubtless this fallow period helped prompt the re-formation of Mercyful Fate, but that didn't end the King's solo efforts. Instead the ravenous metal hordes got twice as much, with the singer keeping both strands of his career running in parallel. The first King Diamond album of the new period appeared on Metal Blade and was spookily titled *The Spider's Lullabye* (1995), a chilling tale of marrow-curdling phobia and, of course, gruesome death.

Upping the ante some-what was *The Graveyard* (1996) which touched upon incest in a mad sto-ryline concerning escaped lunatics, corrupt politicians and premature burial. In comparison *Voodoo* (1998) was something of a depar-ture, combining zombie myth with the usual blend of demonic possession and black magic.

The new millennium found the King forging ahead with *House Of God* (2000), and a couple of diversions – the *Nightmares In The Nineties* (2001) compilation, along with blast from the past, *King Diamond And Black Rose: 20 Years Ago, A Night Of Rehearsal* (2001), definitely one for the collectors – before opting to resurrect the ghosts of former glories by whipping out *Abigail II: The Revenge* (2002).

Despite the revisiting of one of King's best-known storylines with *Abigail* II, the band couldn't tour the album – again, due to lack of label support. Not that this has deterred him from continuing his horror crusade. His latest offering, *The Puppet Master* (2003) – including (shock horror!) a romantic twist in the tale – was counted by some fans as a return to form, considering that much of his output since the reforma-tion of Mercyful Fate has been a little uneven. Despite this somewhat bumpy period the King's influence cannot be underesti-mated, and his contribution to cult metal was acknowledged when **Foo Fighters** mainman **Dave Grohl** put together his **Probot** project and got King Diamond to sing on "Sweet Dreams".

Abigail
1987; Roadrunner

Generally considered to be the King's best concept effort, don't expect this to be drenched with blood. Rather it's an atmospheric horror story that relies more on gothic twists and turns to deliver its shocks.

Conspiracy
1989; Roadrunner

They're back again, those wicked spirits, in a sequel to *Them*. Cue lots more madness and murder. A nice and macabre little number, it gets a little patchy after this one.

KING'S X

Formed Springfield, Missouri, US, 1981

This classic power trio are without doubt one of the most creative and musical heavy rock bands on the planet. When they play it comes straight from the heart and with dazzling conviction, though the sound they make is next to impossible to categorize. Bass heavy riffs and oh-so-sweet Beatles-y vocal harmonies are artistically layered to give the effect of being lovingly pummelled with honey-coated knuckledusters.

The incredibly stable line-up of **Doug Pinnick** (bass/vocals), **Ty Tabor** (guitar/vocals) and **Jerry Gaskill** (drums/vocals) had been making music for quite a number of years – as **The Edge** and **Sneak Preview** – before attracting the kind of attention that would secure their place in metal history. Originally they met when students but it was a move to Houston, Texas in the mid-80s and a hook-up with one **Sam Taylor** that gave them the all-important push. Taylor was an extremely astute businessman who had been responsible for running the ZZ Top empire; his chief claim to fame was the production of the famously bearded ones' "TV Dinners" video. With Taylor on their side as mentor and Svengali they couldn't fail. They eventually secured a record deal with Megaforce and Atlantic Records after a showcase gig in New York, and with Taylor acting as co-producer they set about creating their first masterpiece.

When *Out Of The Silent Planet* (1988) appeared it met with enthusiastic public praise, the band being hailed as one of the brightest hopes for metal in the coming decade. The title was taken from the first book of a C. S. Lewis science-fiction fantasy trilogy, a perfect encapsulation of the futuristic sound of the music and the band's spiritual lyrical

King's X laying down some tracks.

outlook. Their Christian ideals were fairly obvious from a glance at their lyrics but they always maintained that they were a band that happened to be comprised of Christians rather than a Christian rock band. The positive perspective of the lyrics aside, what made the debut so astonishing was the quality of the songs. They were quite simply stunning. Economic in construction they were nevertheless built for maximum impact; Pinnick's bass was a seismic rumble contrasting beautifully with his bluesy gospel-tinged lead vocals, Gaskill's percussion provided a solid rhythmic spine to the tunes, while Tabor's stripped-back riffs and fluid solos gave the whole thing a vibrant live feel. The approach was clearly that less is more. The result? A debut of tight and powerful, harmony-packed songs without an ounce of fat. The only tiny fly in the ointment was the band's dodgy haircuts; suffice to say, the Lord forgives all things, even mutant mullets.

The formula was repeated with even greater success – though thankfully minus the rampant barnets – with their second effort *Gretchen Goes To Nebraska* (1989). Richer in tone than the lean and wiry workouts of the debut, the spiritual quota was maintained by an abstract Christian tale penned by Gaskill and reproduced on the inner sleeve. Meanwhile the songs contained inventive structures and effortless hooks; songs such as the fans' favourite "Over My Head" (with some awesome screaming from Pinnick), the nostalgic "Summerland" and the jaw-dropping "Pleiades" were among the best.

Faith Hope Love (1990) maintained the high quality and "It's Love" managed to secure the attention of MTV, having a more commercial spin than the band normally gave their songs. Meanwhile *King's X* (1992) proved to be the last album where Taylor provided guidance – one of the standout cuts being the raucous "Junior's Gone Wild" originally included on the soundtrack to *Bill And Ted's Bogus Journey*. While *Faith Hope Love* was shaping up to be one of their best-selling albums, their eponymous follow-up seemed to be all together more cerebral and difficult to crack, probably due to the band's progressive tendencies getting the better of them. The songs were no less mighty than before, but they demanded more work to unravel their intricacies.

1994 saw the band light up the stage at Woodstock and *Dogman* emerged on Atlantic, a set of songs with an altogether darker twist. The split with Taylor, in effect their unofficial fourth member, had come about because of creative differences, and the direction they were now taking was to forge a much tougher sound. They had been formidably heavy to begin with but hitching up with renowned producer **Brendan O'Brien**, responsible for albums by Pearl Jam and Stone Temple Pilots, accentuated the abrasive qualities that had lurked in check on earlier albums – witness "Go To Hell" which is almost a hardcore punk song. *Ear Candy* (1996), however, was something of an enigma in that it veered away from some of the outright heavy bombast they had made their own.

By now the years of critical acclaim, tours with AC/DC, Pearl Jam and Faith No More, but scant commercial reward seemed to be taking their toll and they left Atlantic with *Best Of King's X* (1997). A deal was struck subsequently with Metal Blade and *Tape Head* (1998) arrived to satisfy the faithful, as did *Please Come Home...Mr Bulbous* (2000), the Beatles-like harmonies flowing freely and the riffs slamming like concrete sumo wrestlers. *Manic Moonlight* (2001), meanwhile, saw the band expand their already wide dynamic range by adding loops and samples. *Black Like Sunday* (2003), on the other hand, was something of a departure. The band had created their own label, Brop!, and dusted off some very old songs from the 80s period before they became King's X. This was followed by *Live All Over* (2004), a double-album of killer gig material.

Beyond the trio's ventures there are plenty of extracurricular activities which often involve much prog-rock-influenced noodling. Of note are albums by **Poundhound** (Doug's baby) and **Jughead**, **Platypus** and **The Jelly Jam** (Ty's little experiments), though pretty much anything bearing their names is sure to be worth investigating.

Out Of The Silent Planet
1988; Megaforce/Atlantic

A fabulously bassy riff monster and one hell of a debut. Pinnick's soaring vocals are clear and soulful, while the music is virtually uncategorizable, featuring elements of the Beatles, Black Sabbath and gospel. Incredible.

Gretchen Goes To Nebraska
1989; Megaforce/Atlantic

Sprawling arrangements, incisive guitar solos and another terrific bass sound make this a favourite among fans. Includes the brilliantly funky "Over My Head".

Faith Hope Love
1990; Megaforce/Atlantic

A hat trick. Capitalizing on the experiments of their first two albums *FHL* continues with the clever songwriting and slick hooks. Heavy, positive, and maddeningly uplifting.

KISS

Formed New York, US, 1972

"I have to admit I've never been a Kiss fan. How they ever got away with 'I Was Made For Loving You' and we got fucking hammered for '1916', I'll never understand..." Lemmy on Kiss

Kiss are a not just any old heavy rock band. They are a highly influential, modern musical phenomenon, a multi-platinum act with a legendary past and possibly the biggest merchandising catalogue of any band ever. This overtly commercial aspect of the Kiss rock machine has led critics to suggest that this four-piece would do just about anything to keep the cash flowing in, and certainly the band have done little to dispel such criticisms, especially during the 90s when their reunion got into full swing. In fact, it is possible to dissect the Kiss career into an Elvis-style three-part summation: the hungry 1970s, the solid-if-unspectacular 80s, the bloated and excessive Las Vegas-inspired 90s.

In the beginning there was a band called **Wicked Lester**, the line-up of which featured

the two key and constant players in the history of one of metal's most celebrated bands. **Paul Stanley**, aka **The Starchild**, (guitar/vocals) and **Gene Simmons**, aka **The Demon**, (bass/vocals) had very ambitious ideas for creating the ultimate rock group. Picking up **Ace Frehley**, aka **Space Ace,** (lead guitar/vocals) and **Pete Criss**, aka **The Catman,** (drums/vocals), the line-up began experimenting with a theatrical, face-painted look that took them a while to perfect. In the meantime they made their first live club appearance in January 1973 (to an audience of between four and ten people, according to different versions of the tale!), moving up to support Blue Öyster Cult at the end of the year. This was just the start of what would become a massive rollercoasting schedule of touring and recording that would see the band reach the heady heights of rock stardom by the mid-70s.

With dedicated management and a record deal through the new Casablanca Record label, "Nothin' To Lose" was their first single and *Kiss* (1974) was their debut album, the sleeve for which looked remarkably similar to the Beatles' *With The Beatles*. This first album was home to some classic Kiss tracks – "Strutter", "Cold Gin" and "Black Diamond" – but it did little to break the band. Neither did the follow-up *Hotter Than Hell* (1974), although the distinctly Oriental flavour of the sleeve primed the Japanese market perfectly for when the band hit their stride.

The next album, *Dressed To Kill* (1975), was the one to truly kick things off. The production was more polished and contained what was to become their first major hit single, "Rock And Roll All Nite", though it was the live version from the excellent *Alive!* (1975) that really did the business by going to #12 in the US charts. *Alive!* itself went into the Top 10. From this point Kiss fever propelled the band from being a mere curiosity with potential, to a pyrotechnic-wielding, arena-filling, leather-clad, eight-legged monster. From kids' school lunchboxes, through band-endorsed vintage wines, to ladies underwear, the following years would bring a veritable avalanche of merchandising goodies – as well as some classic albums.

In an effort to consolidate their success the band turned to **Bob Ezrin** (fresh from his triumphant work on Alice Cooper's *Welcome To My Nightmare*) to produce their next

A Kiss and a cuddle.

studio effort. *Destroyer* (1976) was a loose concept album centred around the band's alter egos and contained their biggest hit yet – the slushy ballad "Beth", penned and sung by Criss went to #7 in the US. For a while it seemed the band could do no wrong. *Rock And Roll Over* (1976), *Love Gun* (1977) – home to the hilarious "Plaster Caster" – and the magnificent *Alive II* (1977) were duly trundled out and devoured by a public that had now taken Kiss to their hearts. Sure, they lacked the danger of their formative years but they were now huge – even featuring in their own Marvel comic book printed with the band's own blood mixed into the red ink – though the desire to maintain the same level of mainstream success would lead to some bizarre and disastrous decisions.

The first, frankly cheeky, idea was to issue four eponymous solo albums in 1978 along with *Double Platinum*, a compilation album. The latter was packed with prime Kiss, the former were not. And then things really did start to go weird. Criss was growing increasingly fed up with the band's direction and began to suffer from the excesses of the rock lifestyle. Already under pressure to keep the platinum albums rolling in and with disco in the ascendant the band decided to go more pop. *Dynasty* (1979) and *Unmasked* (1980) became the first of Kiss's albums to really lose the plot. "I Was Made For Lovin' You" from the former was a hit but was basically a disco track; the latter album endured the ignominy of only going gold, a major indication of how Kiss were slipping under. Problems with Criss had got to the point where **Anton Fig** had deputized for him during the *Dynasty* tour and the same thing happened during the creation of *Unmasked*. Criss's role was soon filled more permanently by **Eric Carr**, aka **The Fox**.

Incredibly, the band then decided that their next project ought to be another concept album and turned to their old buddy Bob Ezrin to help out. *(Music From) The Elder* (1981), with its fantasy storyline, was supposed to be fully realized in a film, but did so poorly that Kiss promptly shelved it. Out came *Killers* (1982), a compilation including some new tracks, and new album *Creatures Of The Night* (1982). During this period Frehley was the next line-up casualty and he was replaced by **Vinnie Vincent**.

The next move was to ditch the make-up, the general feeling being that the band were

entering a new era. The first album to feature Kiss minus the kabuki-style greasepaint was *Lick It Up* (1983), an album given a fresh spin by their new lead guitarist's fiery technique. At last they had taken a gamble that paid off, but keen to hold onto the new lease of life the continuing collaborations with outside songwriters, most notably **Desmond Child**, resulted in a rash of solid, safe and overtly commercial albums during the 80s: *Animalize* (1984), *Asylum* (1985), *Crazy Nights* (1997), *Smashes, Trashes & Hits* (1988, a remixed compilation) and *Hot In The Shade* (1989) all slotted neatly into the 80s paradigm of fist-pounding heavy rock without scaring off the fans, though the latter effort was very dull compared to earlier fare. Finally their line-up seemed to be settling down once more; Vincent had lasted just one album, as had his replacement **Mark St John** who had bowed out due to illness, but **Bruce Kulick** fitted easily into the Kiss set-up.

During the 80s Simmons had become somewhat distracted by acting, managing and producing, but refocused his attention on Kiss as the band entered their second decade. Sadly the band lost Carr to cancer on November 24, 1991 (the same day Freddie Mercury died), so the hit single success of their cover of **Argent's** "God Gave Rock'n'Roll To You" from the soundtrack to *Bill And Ted's Bogus Journey* was something of a bitter-sweet triumph. Carr's replacement was **Eric Singer**. The band's first full studio album of the decade was the Bob Ezrin-produced *Revenge* (1992), but it would be their last for quite some time as the Simmons-Stanley axis decided to issue compilations and live efforts. *Alive III* (1993) was a highly acceptable addition to their live legacy; *MTV Unplugged* (1996) was an interesting acoustic trawl through their back catalogue featuring the old line-up, which was billed as a reunion. And as soon as a permanent re-formation seemed certain, all future plans to develop the band's sound in hitherto unexpected directions were put on hold – to milk the nostalgia angle.

You Wanted The Best, You Got The Best (1996) was a live compilation cobbled together from previous releases, plus a tiny handful of unreleased songs; *Greatest Kiss* (1997) was yet another hits compilation; *Carnival Of Souls: The Final Session* (1997) presented the songs that had been completed prior to the reunion and, interestingly, had an almost Seattle-like dour and heavy grunge vibe. The actual reunion album, *Psycho Circus* (1998), was mediocre at best, with a handful of decent tunes, but no one cared because it was all just an excuse for one of the biggest comeback tours in rock history, which just seemed to go on and on and on. Kiss back in their make-up and costumes of the 70s could sell just about anything – and they did: a huge box set appeared in 2002 as did *The Very Best Of Kiss*, followed by *Symphony: Alive IV* (2003). This was yet another live effort, this time recorded in Australia with the Melbourne Symphony Orchestra who performed in full Kiss make-up, though Frehley had by now been replaced by **Tommy Thayer** (ex-**Black 'N' Blue**). Come 2004 and Criss was replaced again by Singer for yet more touring, with Simmons and Stanley seemingly unable to stop while the punters were still willing to buy into the myth. And even when the band finally ceased spitting fake blood and firing off the glitter bombs, fans had all the expos and conventions to attend. Will Kiss ever really die? Was that the sound of a Kiss casket creaking open again?

Double Platinum
1978; Casablanca

There are a ridiculous number of Kiss compilations available and this one packs in a whole bunch of goodies from the 70s. Lascivious and libidinous, this was the decade of some of their best songs.

Alive III
1993; Mercury

The previous live efforts are great too, but, for a set that includes a few of their better 80s tunes, this one captures plenty of the excitement Kiss generate on stage. Sure it's cheesy, but Kiss were never about anything other than simple, good-time party rock.

KITTIE

Formed Ontario, Canada, 1996

An ironic moniker if ever there was one. This all female nu-metal crew have nothing in common with fluffy little fur bundles. Put it this way, if there are still any male metalheads out there who doubt that women can rock as hard as blokes they should cop a caustic earful of this lot. Considering their tough-girl image it's somewhat amusing that the band's inception was in a school gym class when **Mercedes** **Lander** (drums) first met **Fallon Bowman** (guitar/vocals) and they decided to get a band going with **Morgan Lander** (vocals/guitar). The Silverchair tunes they used to jam are a long way from the churningly heavy sound they eventually settled on. Certainly the level of angst and the raw nature of the music is a damn sight closer to *Bleach*-era Nirvana – another band upon whose early material they cut their performing teeth.

As is often the way, the fledgling band went through a few personnel ructions – bassist **Tanya Candler** was replaced by **Talena Atfield** – but it made little difference to the ferocious assault they dealt out on their debut platter, *Spit* (2000), and a few months later on the *Paperdoll* EP. The rage emanating from every track was awesomely harsh on the ears, allowing them to slot comfortably among the Deftones and Korns of the nu-metal scene. Lyrically, the targets included misogynistic men, abusive relationships and a never-ending search for identity – those being the sunnier aspects of the torturous tales recounted.

Their debut having gone gold, Bowman bowed out prior to the recording of *Oracle* (2001), the stresses of touring being the apparent cause of her departure. Minus one, **Kittie** the band still turned in another stomping album, thus effectively silencing the naysayers. However, there was no denying that nu-metal as a genre was gradually running out of steam and in order to stay ahead of the game the band would have to evolve fast.

When *Until The End* (2004) arrived the gradual move away from nu-metal had begun with half the band having changed; **Lisa Marx** (guitar) and **Jennifer Arroyo** (bass) were the new members, helping to bring a little more range and variety to the usual Kittie formula. The songs were a touch more tuneful – though without sacrificing the heaviness – with Morgan's vocals being given more space to breathe and allowed to develop a sort of PJ Harvey-style spookiness.

The new Kittie was emerging. Where this takes one of the heaviest female metal acts remains to be seen.

Spit
2000; Artemis

A striking debut with a toxic level of pulse-pounding mania throughout. It's a bile-fuelled trawl through the kind of emotional and mental garbage most people would prefer to keep under wraps.

KORN

Formed Bakersfield, California, US, 1993

"It's just a fuckin' devious and dirty business, man. You're gonna get fucked. That's the first thing any band should know. It just depends how you wanna deal with getting fucked."
Jonathan Davis

A band such as **Korn** could never have existed without grunge. Among the pioneers of the alternative metal explosion of the mid-90s, Korn combined metal and hip-hop with the anti-rock stance of grunge, to create a fresh angle on a familiar sound, eventually dubbed nu-metal. The trail blazed by bands such as Faith No More set a precedent for Korn's formula. And in turn Korn have become one of the most influential nu-metal bands on the music scene, helping to kick-start not only Limp Bizkit's career but inspiring hundreds of far less worthy, baggy-trousered pretenders who confuse downtuning and yelling about an unhappy childhood with rock'n'roll entertainment.

The original line-up consisted of **James 'Munky' Shaffer** (guitar), **Brian 'Head' Welch** (guitar), **Reginald 'Fieldy' Arvizu** (bass) and **David Silveria** (drums), all of them members of California band **LAPD**. It wasn't until singer (and bagpipe torturer) **Jonathan Davis**, who worked by day in a mortuary, joined from local band **Sexart** that Korn began their controversial career.

The early days involved the band working as pizza chefs, furniture movers, and cleaners whilst working on a demo. In Davis they had someone who wasn't afraid to use personal stories of trauma and abuse in his lyrics, and when this hard-hitting subject matter was combined with the band's downtuned sound the result was extremely powerful. The music was brutal, yet its rage and rhythmic pulse saw them dubbed unimaginatively as funk metal,

while Davis's unusual style varied between singing, rapping and breathless shrieking.

Aside from the music this lot were very conscious of their image and of being seen as street cred. Decked out in all the latest flashy Adidas gear and signed to Epic's Immortal imprint the band produced *Korn* (1994).The underground buzz they created grew steadily but it took tours with Ozzy Osbourne, Megadeth, and Marilyn Manson to eventually send the album platinum – for many fans this album remains the pinnacle of Korn's achievements, its unpretentious blend of personal pain and monster riffing energy having yet to be bettered. Less sonically palatable and more disturbing, not least because of Davis's bagpipe playing, was *Life Is Peachy* (1996) which was a more instant success, producing a hit in "No Place To Hide". Other notably unpleasant tracks included such sing-a-long ditties as "Porno Creep", "A.D.I.D.A.S" (All Day I Dream About Sex) and a thorough mauling of the War classic "Low Rider" complete with Davis on bagpipes.

By the time of *Follow The Leader* (1998), featuring cover art by hot comic artist Todd McFarlane (creator of *Spawn*), and hit singles "Got The Life" and "Freak On A Leash", Korn were truly secure at the vanguard of nu-metal, which was reflected in the fact that the album debuted at #1 in the *Billboard* chart.

Fittingly the new record featured star turns by **Fred Durst** (**Limp Bizkit**) and **Ice Cube**, as well as **Cheech Marin** of Cheech and Chong infamy, and embraced everything from hip-hop to funk in its surge of fractious sound.

At the top of their game, Korn also set about securing their legacy by instigating the Family Values Tour, taking its cue from Lollapalooza but including a broad swathe of modern metal and hip-hop acts; the first tour resulted in an eponymous live album. Not only did they make their mark on the US tour circuit but the band also threw themselves into creating their own label, Elementree.

By the end of the decade Korn had decided that a new direction was needed to prevent stagnation. The result was *Issues* (1999), recorded with the band fresh from a triumphant set at Woodstock '99 and with cover art provided by a fan competition winner. This time the hip-hop elements were largely dispensed with in favour of a more straight-ahead pounding, and just like its predecessor the album debuted at #1 in the *Billboard* chart.

The nu-metal onslaught was by then galloping at full speed, and by the time of *Untouchables* (2002) it seemed that they could do no wrong, again minimizing the hip-hop to concentrate on downtuned grunt. The set was intense, threatening, polished, and guaranteed to annoy parents everywhere. However, it also took two years and a massive $4 million to record. Not only that, but the money poured into achieving such a huge and dynamic sound, guided by perfectionist producer **Michael Beinhorn**, had robbed the music of its spontaneity – Davis's tormented lyrics sounding rather hollow and unconvincing amid the expensive sonics.

It soon became clear that for all its finesse *Untouchables* was a financial failure. Vowing not to repeat the same mistake *Take A Look In The Mirror* (2003) was completed much more quickly – largely using a mobile studio while touring on Ozzfest – and without a big-name producer overseeing the process. The result was raw and suitably nasty, but still lacking the freshness of their debut.

Whether or not Korn can regain the ground lost though their recent studio indulgences and the loss of Welch, who departed in early 2005 after becoming a Christian, remains to be seen. And with the release of such a safe album as *Greatest Hits Vol.1* (2004) the question is: do they still possess the same hunger

and originality as when they first started out, now that they are comfortable millionaires? Time will tell.

Korn
1994; Immortal/Epic

Sludgy, nasty heavy metal replete with lyrics covering all manner of unsavoury topics. No hit singles, just plain old-fashioned raging throughout.

Follow The Leader
1998; Immortal/Epic

Displaying a hitherto unsuspected sense of dynamics, the big production job made Korn one of the biggest alternative bands to cross over into the mainstream consciousness.

KREATOR

Formed Essen, Germany, 1983

During the 80s, while the US spewed forth the likes of Slayer, Metallica and Anthrax, there was a similar cacophonous thrash revolution taking place in Europe. Germany was a hotbed of aggressive metal, with bands such as Sodom, Destruction and **Kreator** cranking out a hellish racket every bit as primal and focused as that emanating from the States. Kreator are one of the few bands remaining from this heyday still producing convincing material, though their attempts at broadening their sound have sometimes been less than successful.

Known originally by the name **Tormentor**, the band recorded the *End Of The World* demo and landed a deal, appropriately enough, on Noise Records. With the line-up of **Mille Petrozza** (guitar/vocals), **Jürgen 'Ventor' Reil** (drums/vocals) and **Rob Fioretti** (bass) firmly in place, Kreator rapidly set about proving that whatever was emanating from the US, they could pull off just the same level of extremity – if not more.

The impact of the band's first three albums was extraordinary. The precision and scorching speed of *Endless Pain* (1985) and *Pleasure To Kill* (1986) had the band ranked alongside Slayer in the guitar violence stakes. In fact some aficionados rated Kreator's frankly berserk attack more highly than anything penned by Messrs Araya, King and Hanneman; the lyrics covered subjects as diverse as death, nuclear war, naked aggression and the hypocrisies of

COURTESY OF **SPV R**ECORDS

Kreator reaching out to their fans.

religion, while the sonic bludgeon was so intense fans were in serious danger of losing teeth. The *Flag Of Hate* EP was the last release to feature the basic trio line-up with second guitarist **Jorg Tritze** joining in the fun on *Terrible Certainty* (1987).

The 1988 *Out Of The Dark ... Into The Light* EP featured a handful of live tracks but the band rounded out the end of the 80s with two more studio-based efforts, *Extreme Aggression* (1989) and *Coma Of Souls* (1990), the thrash genre providing a seemingly endless pit of inspiration. The only real change occurred with **Frank Gosdzik** replacing Tritze, which turned out to be a bit of a problem for Kreator. Over the years the songwriting had improved as had the sense of dynamics, but with pure thrash on the wane and the shadow of grunge looming, Kreator needed to evolve. The new album, aptly titled *Renewal* (1992) – signalling the band's attempt to change – was recorded at the legendary Morrisound Studios in Florida, and found the band experimenting with industrial vibes and trying to whip up an air of menace without always going for the throat. It was a gamble, which didn't completely come off; fans of old were puzzled while the fresh sound failed to grab the imagination of new listeners.

By the mid-90s Petrozza was the only original member left, with **Christian Giesler** (bass) and **Joe Cangelosi** (drums) coming on board for *Cause For Conflict* (1995), Kreator's least successful period, with the band now signed to Gun Records. The addition of **Tommy Vetterli** (guitar, ex-**Coroner**), replacing Gosdzik, and the return of Ventor raised expectations for *Outcast* (1997) but the album failed to set the world alight.

After their next effort, *Endorama* (1999), released on Drakkar, Kreator decided to re-introduce some measure of the old ferocity, the mature and experimental phase having achieved, at best, mixed results. In came **Sami Yli-Sirniö**, replacing Vetterli, for the **Andy Sneap**-produced *Violent Revolution* (2001), followed by the slamming *Enemy Of God* (2004).

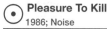

Pleasure To Kill
1986; Noise

The title says it all. If you think that Slayer had the thrash market sewn up in the 80s then this feral, force-ten tornado of insanely fast riffing should disabuse you of any such simplistic notions.

189

Kyuss

Formed Palm Desert, California, US 1990

Long before Queens Of The Stone Age assumed the mantle of the thinking man's stoner outfit there was the mighty **Kyuss**. Of all the bands that through their death throes gave birth to those who would go on to greatness, this heaving behemoth of primal metal is one of the most influential and fondly remembered. They managed only four albums – but what albums they were! – each outing marking a development in writing and invention that would spur an almost hysterical level of devotion from the converted, and set them up even after their demise as stoner pioneers.

The formative days of the band can be traced way back to **Katzenjammer** and then **Sons Of Kyuss**, the name apparently inspired by a character from *Dungeons And Dragons*. They were days of long and nerve-frazzling generator parties where the band – guitarist **Josh Homme**, vocalist **John Garcia**, bassist **Nick Oliveri** and drummer **Brant Bjork** – would haul all their equipment out into the parched desolation of the southern Californian desert and jam until dawn, entertaining a whole bunch of friends they had roped along for the ride.

Their first album, *Wretch* (1991), bore stylistic similarities to the sound of bands such as Soundgarden, a certain Sabbathy gloom to the riffing and a classic tripped-out metal vibe. Kyuss were, however, from the middle of nowhere rather than the hip and happening nexus of grunge, so *Wretch*'s basic but powerful groove was ignored. One person who did get where they were coming from was **Chris Goss**, singer/guitarist of **Masters Of Reality**. To him the fuzz'n'filth reminiscent of Blue Cheer and the pronounced psychedelic undertones were raw materials to be shaped and nurtured. He would rapidly become known as the band's fifth member and help produce what is often lauded as Kyuss's definitive work, *Blues For The Red Sun* (1993). It was strikingly innovative and sumptuously heavy, harking back to an era of massive effects pedals and monster amplification. Far from wallowing in nostalgia, however, a punky attitude brought a neat and modern twist to the material. The critical success of *Blues...* helped land the band unbelievable support slots with artists such as Danzig, Faith No More and Metallica and for a while they seemed to be destined for greatness, a band years ahead of their time.

Unfortunately, a series of events would set the band on a less than auspicious course. With their next effort, *Welcome To Sky Valley,* already recorded, their label, Chameleon, went bankrupt and around the same time they got rid of their manager and lost their drummer. Bjork's replacement was **Alfredo Hernandez**; Oliveri had already been replaced by **Scott Reeder** (ex-Obsessed). The band's signing to Elektra was to prove to be something of a challenge. The label simply didn't know what to do with their new acquisition. These were scuzzy, desert-rat rockers, sonic warriors with a love of noise and an ear for invention; they just didn't fit into a marketing department's idea of rock. So when *Welcome...* hit the shelves it didn't shift units because the label didn't know how or where to push them.

Disheartened by the lack of response to the music Kyuss managed *...And The Circus Leaves Town* (1995), before splitting. Homme was so deflated he apparently didn't touch a guitar for months before an invitation to help out **Screaming Trees** on tour inspired him to start writing. He eventually turned up in **Queens Of The Stone Age** shortly afterwards... but that's another story. In 2000, a strange little Kyuss coda popped up in the shape of *Muchas Gracias – The Best Of Kyuss*, which, in perverse fashion, was actually more a compilation of singles B-sides rather than a collection of hits.

⊙ Blues For The Red Sun
1993; Chameleon

This is a plush tribute to the spirit of the desert which was an inspiration for the album's monstrous vastness and depth. Elemental in its approach and forged in the white-hot heat of jam sessions, the songs are refreshingly inventive and draw on a sense of tradition and eclecticism.

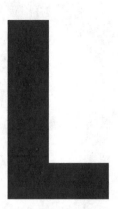

LACUNA COIL

Formed Milan, Italy, 1996

Unlike Germany, Italy has produced very few world-class metal bands, but if **Lacuna Coil** are anything to go by then they're obviously opting for quality over quantity. The band – whose name means empty spiral, a vague, poetic comment on their view of life – worked their way up from a shaky start to become a major global act, one of the first Italian metal bands to actually make an impact on America.

The band originally went under the moniker of **Ethereal** and ended up on Century Media after recording a two-track demo as a calling card. Unfortunately the name was already taken so they had to change it. Heavily influenced by classical music and opera, the band aimed to create lush orchestral arrangements with a distinctly gothic flavour. This was anchored by the crunch of guitars and decorated with **Cristina Scabbia**'s melodious singing voice as a counterpoint to **Andrea Ferro**'s more primal vocal style. It was a synthesis of the bitter and the sweet, the introspective lyrics dwelling on relationships and romantic, existential angst. It was an ambitious experiment, and not one that was entirely successful to begin with.

The line-up of **Scabbia**, **Ferro**, **Claudio Leo** (guitar), **Raffaele Zangaria** (guitar), **Marco Coti Zelati** (bass) and **Leonardo Forti** (drums) recorded their six-track eponymous debut in late 1997 which was released in early 1998. Their nascent sound was sufficiently driven and novel enough to garner plenty of metal media attention, especially as Scabbia combined supermodel looks with her powerful vocal style.

However, while on tour supporting labelmates Moonspell – during the months between recording sessions and the release date – the inexperienced bunch had succumbed to the pressure and nearly disintegrated mid-tour. So by the time the album was on the shelves the band had been through a line-up shift: a new, more stable drummer, **Cristiano 'Criz' Mozzati**, replaced Forti while **Cristiano Migliore** became their new guitarist.

With a solid line-up and a decent debut to tout, 1998 was a whirlwind of touring activity including a slot at Germany's huge Wacken Open Air festival before heading off to the studio again to record their first full-length album. When *In A Reverie* (1999) arrived it fulfilled all the promise of their mini-LP taster, though new second guitarist **Marco 'Maus' Biazzi** was appointed too late to feature on the new album.

The groundwork already established, the Coil embarked on a punishing tour schedule. Playing before huge European crowds ravenous for drama and passion the band were now fired up for their next studio foray. The *Halflife* (2000) mini-LP featured a cover of **Dubstar**'s "Stars", the fascinating "Senzafine" and instrumental experiment "Trance Awake".

One headlining tour later (including a sell-out gig in London) and the band were back in the studio for *Unleashed Memories* (2001),

Cristina and the boys are back in black.

on which their existential musings reached fever pitch. They had already become one of the most popular goth metal bands in Europe but the US provided a real challenge. They needed a record which oozed class and majesty and this they achieved in *Comalies* (2002), an album with a glittering commercial sheen to its heart of darkness. With similar bands such as Evanescence on the rise and an audience already tuned in to the angst of nu-metal, they couldn't fail.

Teamed up with bands such as Type O Negative and Danzig, Lacuna Coil felt the momentum gather during 2003 as they toured the States. "Heaven's A Lie" was released as a single and rapidly began appearing in the speciality charts; "Swamped" followed and repeated the same feat. The major breakthrough came with being hand-picked by Jack and Kelly Osbourne to appear on the Ozzfest bill in 2004 – the first Italian band to appear at the festival – helping them become the biggest-selling act on their label and possibly the biggest commercially successful Italian rock band of all time.

⊙ **Comalies**
2002; Century Media

The album's mood is one of soul-searching torment and despair, with Scabbia's sweet vocals the fiery focal point. In order to celebrate over 100,000 sales of *Comalies* in America an expanded version of the album added an entire

second disc of video clips and bonus tracks, some of them from acoustic sessions performed on US radio.

LAMB OF GOD

Formed Richmond, Virginia, US, 1994

Lamb Of God defy easy categorization, their progressive tendencies leading them to challenge and subvert the very music they love. Within their furious sonic meltdown can be heard elements of thrash, old school, hardcore punk, and math metal (see p.223). While their uncompromising stance might sound like the stuff of nightmares, their superlative musicianship and technical proficiency have made them into one of the most formidable metal bands to break free of the US underground in recent years.

Prior to becoming Lamb Of God the band was known as **Burn The Priest** and consisted of friends who had met while at university in Virginia. They began by recording a couple of split seven-inch singles with some other local acts before collecting the various tracks, adding a couple of bonus songs, and releasing them as *Sevens And More* (1998).

At the time the band comprised **Randy Blythe** (vocals), **John Campbell** (bass), **Abe**

Spear (guitar), **Mark Morton** (guitar) and **Chris Adler** (drums), a quintet who had the relentless professionalism of, say, Def Leppard but without the pop aspirations. They were about precision, power and politics, with lyrics centred around social commentary and the individual's place within and without society. It was a cerebral stance matched by the complexity and labyrinthine direction of the music. All these qualities were evident on their first proper album *Burn The Priest* (1998) released on the Legion label, a fearsome collection of tunes made all the more extreme by Blythe's manic screech. The somewhat oblique lyrics – the band weren't going to make it easy – meant the listener had to fight for every ounce of meaning.

With an album to their name, they began touring and replaced Spear with Adler's brother **Will**. Around this time they changed their name to **Lamb Of God** and sought to perfect their anti-songwriting approach with *New American Gospel* (2000), which appeared on Prosthetic Records. The only concession was Blythe's improved vocals, which had progressed from being excruciating to merely unintelligible, otherwise it was another scorching call to arms. Such an impenetrable sound demanded the attentions of an expert noise-smith and for their next effort they got one of the best – **Devin Townsend**, the man behind the aural monstrosity that is **Strapping Young Lad**. The result was the coruscating *As The Palaces Burn* (2003), a thick and crunchy slab of pummelling metal, driven by Adler's hyperactive drumming. It was just the kind of album to take the band to the breakthrough level; major labels were already interested and they ended up on Epic Records, who re-released the already critically lauded album in 2004.

The *Terror And Hubris* DVD – featuring interviews, live footage and promo clips – was issued as the band began working on their major label debut. The summer of 2004 saw Lamb Of God become one of the must-see acts at Ozzfest, building the sense of anticipation surrounding the release of their next record. *Ashes Of The Wake* (2004) was a more sinuous but no less muscular sounding album, highlighting the band's penchant for invention.

⊙ As The Palaces Burn
2003; Prosthetic

You won't find any verses or choruses here. Devin Townsend's production makes Lamb Of God sound truly scary. The number of riffs unleashed is quite incredible, while the unerring delivery and relentless momentum make sometimes exhausting listening.

LED ZEPPELIN

Formed London, UK, 1968; disbanded 1980

Where would rock'n'roll be without this mythical band of musical magpies? It's possible to have some epic arguments about who created heavy metal and the blame is often laid at the door of this lot. Put the suggestion to vocalist **Robert Plant**, however, and he would more than likely tell you where to get off. And quite rightly. **Led Zeppelin**'s contribution to rock was a constantly evolving experiment, rooted in the tradition of heavy blues while taking in sundry other influences, including folk, hippy psychedelia, funk and soul. The result was one of the world's most celebrated and influential rock bands whose music still sounds as amazing today as it did way back in the 70s.

The band's origins lay in Brit blues outfit **The Yardbirds** and their guitarist **Jimmy Page**. When the band split, Page, already an ace session man, decided to create **The New Yardbirds**. When first bassist **Chris Dreja** opted out, another session veteran **John Paul Jones** (bass/keyboards) joined up. Casting around for a singer, Page and band manager, the legendary **Pete Grant**, homed in on one Robert Plant, frontman for the brilliantly named **Hobbstweedle**. It was Plant who suggested that the line-up be completed by his mate, **Band Of Joy** drummer, **John Bonham**. With everything in place the four-

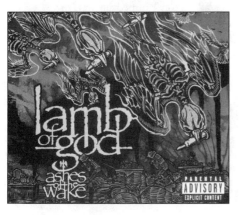

piece snapped up a record deal with Atlantic, recorded their debut album in a mere two weeks, and then completed some Scandinavian dates already booked under the New Yardbirds moniker. After they changed their name to **Led Zeppelin** – from Keith Moon's phrase to describe a terrible performance: "Going down like a lead zeppelin" – the band debuted at Surrey University on October 15, 1968.

By December they were in the US supporting Vanilla Fudge and MC5, almost instantly gaining rave reviews for their live performances. So electrifying were they live, that when they played with Iron Butterfly the headliners refused to go on, feeling they couldn't compete with the new Brits on the block. This assured start ensured that *Led Zeppelin* (1969) was a hit on both sides of the Atlantic, reaching #6 in the UK and #10 in the US. Produced by Page, it's not hard to understand why the debut fared so well; the playing is tight and urgent, the guitars deliver with both delicacy and scything power, and Bonham's drumming nails home the riffs with ruthless energy. On top of it all was Plant's hackle-raising, priapic wail. All subsequent albums would either top the charts or reach #2, a feat achieved in the UK without the aid of singles releases.

The amazing response to the debut was repeated with *Led Zeppelin II* (1969), the band working the heavy blues mojo for all it was worth on classics such as "The Lemon Song" and the fabulously un-PC "Whole

Lotta Love". By now they had become one of the hottest bands on the planet. Ridiculous sums were offered – and sometimes turned down – for live performances, and the records sat in the charts for months.

The first real surprise came with *Led Zeppelin III* (1970) and its largely acoustic leanings, although the change of style was tempered by one or two characteristically riffy efforts – not least the stunning opener "Immigrant Song". However, the sheer quality of the songs ensured that even those who were initially perplexed were eventually won round. There were no shocks with the following year's *Led Zeppelin IV*, aka *Four Symbols*, save that neither the band's name nor the album title featured anywhere on the sleeve. Sure "The Battle Of Evermore" was folky in origin (with additional vocals from **Fairport Convention**'s **Sandy Denny**), and "Going To California" had an almost ethereally light arrangement, but these were the antidotes to the strutting likes of "Black Dog" and "Rock'N'Roll", and the stiflingly heavy "When The Levee Breaks". And then, of course, there was one of the most famous songs ever written, the brilliantly structured "Stairway To Heaven" with its ballad-like verses and scorching lead break.

The strenuous effort not to repeat themselves took Led Zeppelin to the *Houses Of The Holy* (1973), and its odd experiments with reggae and funk with "D'Yer Mak'er" and the frankly bizarre "The Crunge". Where the album excelled, however, was in the eerie "No Quarter" and the stunning "The Rain Song"– one of the most beautiful and laid-back songs in rock. Period. Once again, the album title was not on the sleeve, though perversely the song "Houses Of The Holy" turned up on *Physical Graffiti* (1975), a double album released on the band's newly created Swan Song label. This was without doubt their crowning achievement: a sprawling collection with room for both the masterful whimsy of "Down By The Seaside" and bruising blues-rock epics like "In My Time Of Dying". The accompanying live shows at Earls Court (which sold out in a matter of hours) were among the longest ever played by the band, clocking in at over four hours.

Mick Gold/Redferns

Robert Plant.

The following year produced *Presence*, an album created while Plant was still in a wheelchair, following a serious car crash while holidaying with his wife. It also saw the release of the rockumentary, *The Song Remains The Same*, featuring footage filmed back at Madison Square Garden in 1973. With its insipid fantasy sequences, and a soundtrack that fails to capture the raw splendour of the band, the film is somewhat lacking as a concert document.

While the trauma of the car crash was bad enough, Plant was dealt another blow when his young son died in 1977. Both he and the band were devastated and effectively disappeared for two years. Their return was marked by *In Through The Out Door* (1979), and their first UK concert in four years at the Knebworth festival. A European tour took place the next year but their appearance in West Berlin was their last. A further disaster struck during rehearsals for a US tour at Page's home: after a night of heavy drinking, Bonham was found dead on September 25 having choked in his sleep. Led Zeppelin were no more.

A posthumous collection of demo recordings called *Coda* arrived a couple of years later, but by then the remaining members had launched their own projects. Jones went into production; Page formed **The Firm** with **Bad Company**'s **Paul Rodgers**; Plant launched a successful solo career and dabbled with the **Honeydrippers** (also featuring Page). And that's how it stayed until the Live Aid concert in 1985 when Phil Collins filled the drum slot. Although they regrouped for a couple of other one-off occasions (Atlantic Records' 40th anniversary bash in 1988 and Jason Bonham's wedding in 1990), the band was effectively laid to rest as a touring and recording entity.

The Zeppelin back catalogue, however, was another matter entirely. The new decade began with Page remastering old material for the *Led Zeppelin* box set and *Remasters* (both 1990), before appearing with **Whitesnake**'s **David Coverdale** on the *Coverdale/Page* (1993) album. In the same year *Box Set II* and *The Complete Studio Recordings* appeared. Page and Plant then tickled everyone's expectations with some Eastern-flavoured reworked Zep tunes and a few new songs on *No Quarter* (1994), followed four years later by the frustrating *Walking Into Clarksdale* (1998), a new set of songs 'un-produced' by

Steve Albini. Far more interesting was the self-explanatory *BBC Sessions* (1997), a double live album that at last gave fans some real rarities to chin-stroke over. This was in contrast to the rather pointless *Early Days* (1999) and *Latter Days* (2000), compilations which basically rehashed the *Remasters* material. What really underlined the enduring legacy of the band's importance was *How The West Was Won* (2003) and the *Led Zeppelin* DVD (2003), which contained nearly four hours of live film footage from various sources, all painstakingly restored.

Physical Graffiti
1975; Swan Song/Atlantic

All metal fans should really own every Zeppelin album, but if it has to be just one then this double extravaganza is it. Consistently brilliant, it showcases the different aspects of the band perfectly: from the gentle "In The Light" through the ripping "Custard Pie" and the epic and mystical "Kashmir" to the stomping sounds of "Trampled Under Foot". Sheer, indisputable genius.

How The West Was Won
2003; Atlantic

It's amazing to think that for a band that excelled live, Zeppelin didn't have a proper gig document to their name. Then Page stumbled across the tapes for this triple album while trawling through the archives, and the results are superb. Recorded way back in 1972, highlights include "Dazed And Confused" (over 25 minutes of it) and an epic version of "Whole Lotta Love". Along the way, the band throw in a fine selection of blues classics. Indispensable.

LIMP BIZKIT

Formed Jacksonville, Florida, US 1994

You might expect a band formed in the conservative Deep South of America to trade in the sort of laidback rootsy rock made famous by the likes of Lynyrd Skynyrd, but the story of **Limp Bizkit** is extraordinary precisely because of their efforts to stretch the rock envelope. In fact, the rise of Limp Bizkit, with it's emphasis on aggressive metal stylings welded securely to rap's street-level credibility, has been instrumental in focusing attention on those disparate bands all loosely lumped into the nu-metal camp. While bands such as Slipknot have gone on to emphasize the thrashier, more metallic end of the spectrum, bands like Limp Bizkit reflect the colourful rap side of things.

Still, none of this was apparent in the early 90s when **Fred Durst** was wallowing within the confines of his middle-class upbringing. Though his family background suggested a God-fearing kind of guy, within him was the urge to create the devil's music. Undistinguished as a scholar, he spent some

limp bizkit presents

PARENTAL ADVISORY EXPLICIT CONTENT

chocolate st★rfish and the hot dog flavored water

time in the navy before becoming a tattoo artist – biding his time as he put together his first band.

His most significant early outfit proved to be **Malachi Sage**, where he met **Sam Rivers** (bass), whose cousin, **John Everett Otto** (drums), was soon to join the like-minded pair. Otto knew of a young artist, **Wesley Louden Borland** (guitar), who was also frontman of a local metal band called **Goatslayer**. Borland's joining allowed Durst to ditch guitar and concentrate on fronting, something for which he clearly had a gift. A band seemed to be forming which merged the power and ferocity of metal with the style and sass of hip-hop; Durst indulged his penchant for foul-mouthed ranting and Borland brought a trademark theatricality to their shows through his love of weirdly coloured contact lenses, body paint and bizarre outfits.

Their first major break came not through any musical effort, however, but through Durst's day job as tattoo artist. Rising stars Korn happened to be passing through town and their love of needlework meant that Durst ended up befriending two of the band.

A tape eventually ended up with Korn producer Ross Robinson who loved the music and began talking them up in the industry. The ball had finally started to roll.

Their first national tour found the Bizkit opening for now-defunct hip-hoppers House Of Pain during which time they befriended **DJ Lethal**. With HOP stuttering towards their demise, Limp Bizkit eventually gained their turntablist in 1996. This, and the studio help of Ross Robinson, was to make them into stars.

Three Dollar Bill Y'All$ (1997), released on Interscope, contained all the stylistic elements that would appeal to the late 90s MTV generation: tough riffs, plenty of expletives and a readily identifiable vein of angst. But it sold poorly at first, largely because it confused the conservative, format-led US radio industry by being neither metal, nor rock, nor rap. The radio stations needed something familiar and that came in the shape of "Faith", a cover of George Michael's solo hit. The band had been knocking this around for a few years but when Michael was arrested for lewd behaviour in a public lavatory Limp Bizkit's version took on a previously absent sense of irony. As their first hit it launched an inevitable bout of touring.

The gigging would serve them in good stead for when *Significant Other* (1999) emerged. The band were now leaner and much meaner-sounding, the record carefully crafted with a radio-friendly polish, and a host of guests, from **Korn's Jonathan Davis** to **Stone Temple Pilots' Scott Weiland**. Weiland had acted as vocal coach, tuning up Durst's rather rough approach to the mic. Rather surprisingly, Durst was also made a senior vice president at Interscope around this time.

Taking a tip from the best, Durst then decided to emulate The Beatles, U2, and other classic rock luminaries, by playing a series of impromptu rooftop gigs around the US in order to advertise their new record. The plan didn't always work – they were usually stopped by the cops a few songs into their set – but it was enough to kick the record into the upper reaches of the *Billboard* chart, leaving the likes of Ricky Martin and the Backstreet Boys standing. Limp Bizkit had arrived – big-time.

The release of *Chocolate Starfish And The Hot Dog Flavored Water* (2000) marked Limp Bizkit as megastars, with hits such as "Take A Look Around" – from the soundtrack to *Mission: Impossible 2*. Durst himself had become a tabloid celebrity and the idol of a generation of disaffected, media-savvy youth.

The next couple of years, however, would prove to be something of a trial not just for Durst but the entire band. Borland had always been a character way too large and wacky to be contained by the Bizkit machine; in a move that had critics rubbing their hands with glee, he left Durst and company in order to release an album from his **Big Dumb Face** project, and generally pursue other avenues of musical creativity. With such a lot riding upon the search for a suitable replacement it seemed that Durst really hadn't a clue where to start. In a move that could be interpreted as cynical, *New Old Songs* (2001), featuring remixes of fan favourites, was released. While it gave people a taste of the Bizkit filtered through the abilities of a number of other artists, it also diverted attention from the circus that was the great guitarist search.

The band began work on a new album with a number of different six-stringers involved, including **Al Jourgensen** (Ministry), **Page Hamilton** (Helmet), **Brian 'Head' Welch** (Korn). Even Durst had a go. In the end ex-**Snot** guitarist **Mike Smith** was chosen and all previous recordings were abandoned in favour of starting afresh.

Before any new music could hit the shelves, Durst found himself in the media spotlight for his rather public involvement with pop starlet Britney Spears, as well as for the usual round of stories detailing temper tantrums and general rock star bad behaviour. In 2003 Limp Bizkit were scheduled to headline the Donington Download festival but failed to show up, instead playing a free gig in London's Finsbury Park by way of an apology. Durst also managed to lose a little weight and develop something of a Nirvana fixation, which included having a tattoo of Kurt Cobain.

Finally *Results May Vary* (2003) was released, with "Eat You Alive" as the first single, and never was there an album title more accurately named. A cover of The Who's "Behind Blue Eyes" was quite awful,

while tracks such as "Let Me Down", the funky "Red Light – Green Light" and "Head For The Barricade" contrasted the band's old sound with the more experimental "Underneath The Gun" and "Take It Home". Smith had slotted in very convincingly, though there was no denying that Durst was the only eye-catching individual left in the line-up.

Three Dollar Bill Y'All$
Interscope; 1997

Rough-and-ready, this is a genre-defining album. Durst is limbering up the bad-boy image that will serve him in good stead over subsequent albums.

Significant Other
Interscope; 1999

Fred really lets rip on this one, with the polished production giving the band's already powerful sound that little extra boost. A professional and imaginative album.

Chocolate Starfish And The Hot Dog Flavored Water Interscope; 2000

A mega-album from a mega-band. Packed with anger, angst and ace musicianship this one has it all.

LINKIN PARK

Formed Southern California, US, 1998

Rap metal has come a very long way since Mike Patton rhymed his way through the Faith No More mega-hit "Epic" in 1989. It would take almost another ten years before the synthesis of rap and rock would hit the mainstream in such a way as to dwarf the efforts of the pioneers and provide a fresh success for the vast umbrella genre known as nu-metal.

Linkin Park's story starts unassumingly enough with school buddies **Rob Bourdon** (drums), **Brad Delson** (guitar), and **Mike Shinoda** (MC/vocalist) sharing ideas and dreaming of musical superstardom. **DJ Joseph Hahn** eventually entered the equation and **Xero** was born, although the name **Hybrid Theory** would soon follow. As soon as Arizona native **Chester Bennington** joined as frontman and focal vocalist, everything fell into place and Linkin Park was born. Of course, no one would touch them with a barge pole at this stage and the band spent some time as gigging regulars around Los

Angeles while being turned down by various record companies. No one, it seemed, could see the appeal of their streamlined, angst-ridden metal, featuring Bennington's massive singing voice and Shinoda's street-savvy style of rapping. It wasn't until Warner Bros signed the band in 1999 that the wheels were set in motion.

Within a few months they were in the studio recording their debut album. When *Hybrid Theory* (2000) emerged – named after their earlier incarnation – no one knew it would prove to be such a monster-selling album. In the UK alone the album spawned five hit singles, peaked at #4 in the album charts a full year after its release, and spent a massive 60 weeks in the Top 40. In the US it became the biggest-selling album of 2001 and the second biggest seller around the world. The band was also nominated for various Grammys and won the category of Best Hard Rock Performance for "Crawling", their profile no doubt raised by an extremely punishing touring schedule that put them on stage over 300 times during 2001.

By 2002 they were officially massive. So what did they do? They bided their time by issuing the *Reanimation* (2002) remix album, which put them at the mercy of an army of DJs and producers. The album was packaged in a very arty manner with the tracklisting giving their song titles a modern (and irritating) text message style twist: "Paper Cut" became "Ppr:Kut", "Cure for the Itch" became "Kyur4 th Ich", "Crawling" became "KRWLNG". The results of this latest effort were hit and miss.

If the fans had been a touch put out by the remix package, *Meteora* (2003) was a return to the blueprint laid down by their debut – if it ain't broke, don't fix it clearly being the order of the day. The only change in the Linkin Park camp was the official addition of **Phoenix Farrell** on bass. The album's title had been inspired by the cover of a travel magazine they'd seen, featuring a cluster of Greek monasteries perched atop inaccessible mountain peaks: in Greek, *meteora*. The band loved the idea of the otherworldliness inspired by both word and image and decided it fitted perfectly with the music they were creating. The songs, while following closely on the heels of *Hybrid Theory*, provided some positive spin on their trademark searching introspection.

Summer 2003 found them on the road again as part of the massive Summer Sanitarium tour, playing alongside Metallica and several of their nu-metal contemporaries. Meanwhile autumn brought *Live In Texas* (2003), which was fairly self-explanatory and kept the Linkin Park devotees more than happy until *Collision Course* (2004). This set followed in the vein of *Reanimation* and saw the band team up with hip-hop star Jay-Z to rework tunes from both parties – keeping fans both bemused and perplexed until their next studio effort arrives.

⊙ Hybrid Theory
Warners; 2000

Take equal parts of metal and rap, fuse them together with epic production and you get this glossy debut studded with hit singles. A perfect point from which to take over the world.

⊙ Meteora
Warners; 2003

Back to the debut for inspiration, this album is chock-full of big riffs, smooth beats and silky rapping.

LITTLE ANGELS

Formed Scarborough, UK, 1987; disbanded 1994

For a while it looked as if **Little Angels** might steal some of the praise being heaped upon the melodic hard-rock bands emerging from the States. During the early 90s – until grunge happened – they were certainly touted as one of the UK's most promising young bands as they racked up hit singles and soldout the Hammersmith Odeon on their first major headlining tour in 1991. But like so many bands coming to prominence during the late 80s they just didn't have the momentum behind them to weather the inexorable changes of the following years.

Toby Jepson (vocals), **Bruce** "No, for the thousandth time I'm not moonlighting from Maiden" **Dickinson** (guitar) and **Mark Plunkett** (bass) met while at VIth form college and formed the rather unfortunately named **Mr Thrud**. Bruce's brother **Jimmy** soon joined up on keyboards and various drummers came and went until **Dave Hopper** stuck around long enough to record *The '87* EP for the indie Blue Strike Records. Finally, using the Little Angels moniker, the *Too Posh To Mosh* (1987) mini-LP followed on Powerstation, while among the band's early triumphs was a slot supporting Guns N' Roses at the Marquee when the legendary sleaze rockers made their UK debut.

The following year found the band consolidating their early work by signing to Polydor and preparing their debut album. **Michael Lee** replaced Hopper before the *Big Bad* EP tickled the lower reaches of the singles chart in early 1989. *Don't Prey For Me* (1989) followed and displayed the band's amazingly adept way with huge hooks and choruses, showing influences ranging from Def Leppard to Queen. By the summer of 1990 they were firmly ensconced in the charts with "She's A Little Angel" peaking at #21, helped along by an appearance on *Top Of The Pops*.

The exuberant naivety of their debut was replaced with a far more knowing and focused set of songs on *Young Gods* (1991) and the only blip in their seemingly unstoppable rise was the sacking of Lee for secretly auditioning for The Cult; he was soon replaced by **Mark 'Rich' Richardson**.

The venues and bills kept getting bigger – Wembley Arena with Van Halen, Milton Keynes Bowl with Bon Jovi – and their third album *Jam* (1993) topped the chart. By 1994, however, the cracks were showing. While the world was in the grip of grunge and reeling from the shock news of Kurt Cobain's death, *Little Of The Past* marked the end of the band. The various members went off to do their own things. The Dickinson brothers formed **b.l.o.w.** although Bruce's more lasting contribution to British music has been the creation of the Brighton Institute of Modern Music, the UK's very own rock school where aspiring youngsters can learn from their heroes. The sight of Little Angels' very own axe-pert in a suit and tie has to be seen to be believed.

 **Little Of The Past**
1994; Polydor

This is a tidy little compilation of rockers, displaying oodles of invention and a fine ear for great pop hooks. "She's A Little Angel" must rank as one of their finest efforts.

LIVE

Formed York, Pennsylvania, US, 1988

Without grunge **Live** would never have taken off, but to compare them to the morose musings of the Seattle sound would do little justice to their headlong and uplifting rush of melody and emotion.

The history of the band winds way back to the mid-80s and an outfit called **First Aid**, featuring **Chad Taylor** (guitar), **Patrick Dahlheimer** (bass) and **Chad Gracey** (drums). By the late 80s key mainman **Ed Kowalczyk** (vocals/guitar) had joined up and they became **Public Affection**, under which name they produced a cassette-only album called *The Death Of A Dictionary* (1989). These days this much-sought rarity changes hands for ridiculous sums of money, but at the time it was intended for sale at the band's shows for just a few dollars.

The rather pretentious album title was just a precursor to the arty and sometimes overly serious direction the band would take with Kowalczyk at the helm. One change of name later and the band signed to Radioactive Records just as Nirvana and their ilk were beginning to make some major waves. All that was alternative in rock suddenly became *de rigueur* and Live's melodic but driven sound was perfect for radio stations looking for something other than Poison and Mötley Crüe. What's more they had some substance to their lyrical stance. *Mental Jewelry* (1991) was produced by **Jerry Harrison** (ex-**Talking Heads**) and inspired by the philosophies of Jiddu Krishnamurti.

It wasn't until 1994's *Throwing Cooper*, however, that Live would tap into the post-grunge *Zeitgeist*, allowing Kowalczyk's impassioned and spiritual muse full flight. The rather earnest "I Alone" became a heavily rotated clip on MTV helping the album top the US charts. The band were never quite as popular in the UK but during the 90s there were few acts to touch the levels of hysteria they could generate when releasing an album. The follow-up *Secret Samadhi* (1997) was one of the most eagerly anticipated releases of the decade and threw yet more progressive twists and turns into their already unique style of songwriting. Despite the sometimes clunky and po-faced lyrics it topped the US charts again, though a hat trick eluded them with the release of the far superior *The Distance To Here* (1999). However, a top five placing is nothing to be sniffed at.

Maybe it was the unrelenting heaviness and over-reaching poetry of the songs, maybe they fell foul of the fickleness of rock fashions, but *V* (2001) and the terribly punning *Birds Of Pray* (2003) failed to hit the spot commercially, though the songs still displayed a near flawless sense of invention and dynamics. *Awake: The Best Of Live* (2004), a greatest hits CD and DVD package followed and tempted fans with "We Deal In Dreams", a previously unreleased track from the *Throwing Copper* sessions.

⊙ **The Distance To Here**
1999; Radioactive

Ed's voice soars and the riffs tumble forth like an ultra-melodic avalanche. This is one of those albums with an uplifting vibe so bright it almost dazzles. The band indulge in songcraft as intricate and complex as the incredible sleeve art.

LIVING COLOUR

Formed New York, US 1984; disbanded 1995; re-formed 2000

One of the most musically adventurous and talented bands of the late 80s and early 90s, **Living Colour** found themselves loosely lumped in with outfits such as Faith No More and Red Hot Chili Peppers because they had a bit more funk than usual to their hard-rocking make-up. In reality this highly versatile Afro-American four-piece could play almost any style of music they chose, and quite often they did, combining shamelessly metal chops with hardcore punk, jazz-rock noodling with funk, all in the space of one album. They were about everything from Chuck Berry to the Ramones, from Parliament to AC/DC.

Taking the band's name from the NBC TV pronouncement "this programme is brought to you in living colour" guitarist **Vernon Reid** – a founding member of the Black Rock Coalition – brought together **Will Calhoun** (drums), **Muzz Skillings** (bass) and **Corey Glover** (vocals) with a view to fusing a variety of seemingly disparate styles into a tightly rocking whole. It was an immensely ambitious vision but, given that the various members were music college graduates, the raw talent was there to be shaped and directed.

Key to the band landing a deal was the patronage of a certain **Mick Jagger** who clocked them ripping it up in supreme style at CBGB's in New York in 1986. He invited them to contribute on his *Primitive Cool* album and produced two demos which eventually enabled them sign to Epic Records. Jagger also produced some of the tracks that graced their fantastically assured debut *Vivid* (1988) which tore into the American Top 10 with a vengeance. It was as though the musical heritage of America had been compressed into a handful of rock songs. Hanging on Reid's finely controlled finger flinging, and a rhythm section of stunning precision and steely proficiency, was a mix of funk, blues, jazz, punk and metal. And all of it was cohesively shaped into pulsing nuggets of rock, with Glover's ranging and soulful vocals musing on a variety of socially aware lyrics. "Cult Of

Living Colour's Vernon (left) and Corey.

Personality" was self explanatory, as was "Open Letter (To A Landlord)", while "Which Way To America?" dissected the American Dream from the perspective of a black American. It was the first of these, however, that opened up possibilities for the band by going to #13 in the US singles charts in 1989. This prompted the first of the awards to arrive – an Elvis Award for Best New Band and no less than three MTV awards presented to them by their buddy Mick – which assured them of a timely support slot with the Rolling Stones on their US Steel Wheels tour.

When in the following year "Cult Of Personality" nabbed them a Grammy for Best Hard Rock Performance, there seemed to be no end to the accolades heaped upon them. By now combining charity appearances with their own commitments they managed to play the Reading Rock Festival and record a new album, *Time's Up* (1990). It was yet another off-the-wall *tour de force* with more of a solid hard-rock feel than their eclectic debut, and the awards continued to flood in.

Yet amid the welter of critical back-slapping sales didn't match those of their debut, and within the band personality frictions were interfering with the creation of their next album. In the end 1991 resulted in the *Biscuits* mini-LP plugging the gap while the

band sorted themselves out. This ultimately meant Skillings leaving in 1992 to be replaced by **Doug Wimbish** for *Stain* (1993), an album that had to compete with the rising tide of alt-metal and grunge. Unfortunately *Stain* made even less impact than its predecessor and this, coupled with the various members pursuing solo projects, resulted in the band splitting in 1995. The *Pride* compilation was whipped out hastily and all seemed done and dusted, until Calhoun gave Reid a call in December 2000 inviting him to check out a little side-project featuring the other members of the band. Pretty soon a comeback gig had been booked at CBGB's. A little touring, and working through four album's worth of music, occupied the next couple of years, but eventually *Collideoscope* (2003) emerged on Sanctuary and proved to be every bit as edgy, inventive and tough as their three previous efforts. Sensing there was still a potential market their old label dipped into the vaults and produced *Live At CBGB's Tuesday 12/19/89* (2005).

 Time's Up
1990; Epic

More determined and focused than their debut, this album spawned some of their best-loved songs. "Love Rears Its Ugly Head", "Type" and "Elvis Is Dead" are just three of the highlights of a set that is relentlessly and consistently powerful.

LOVE/HATE

Formed Los Angeles, California, US, 1986

A prime example of a band who should have made it but didn't, **Love/Hate**'s period of notoriety was painfully short but studded with moments of near-genius hard rock. The band's history can be traced back to the mid-80s and a rather odd sounding musical beast known as **Dataclan** – an outfit closer to Duran Duran than, say, Motörhead. Going exactly nowhere, they underwent a little personnel shake-up and made a concerted effort to rock like madmen. The line-up of **Jizzy Pearl** (vocals), **Jon E. Love** (guitar), **Skid Rose** (bass) and **Joey Gold** (drums) dubbed themselves the "stoopidest band in the world" and made a heroic bid for stardom by getting signed to CBS and recording one of the most astonishingly rabid debut albums ever. *Black Out In The Red Room* (1990) was the result of years of frustration and constant songwriting, and of ploughing through the L.A. club scene regardless of negative reactions. The anger and total focus of the band was filtered through the late-80s hedonistic hard-rock prism of copious boozing and drugs, creating a beast that was born of glam metal but possessing little of its effete preening and posing. When Love/Hate took the stage they were head-cracking, heavy-rock nihilists ready to sacrifice themselves completely to the moment, to crash and burn every night while striving for the ultimate high on their own thuggish terms.

"Why Do You Think They Call It Dope?" ended up on MTV and Love/Hate suddenly found themselves playing arenas with AC/DC, while the UK rock press embraced their balls-out craziness. Unfortunately, the US wasn't quite so receptive and when Nirvana suddenly appeared it became clear just what an impossible task lay ahead. They might have been a damn sight heavier than many of their L.A. rock contemporaries but they sure as hell weren't alternative enough to survive unscathed. *Wasted In America* (1992) was a spectacularly well-titled album, the band by now renowned for their party-hard attitude, but while it was a storming effort there was no holding back the inevitable. The record label dropped them in 1993 which meant *Let's Rumble* (1994) – an album featuring new guitarist **Darren Householder** – had to be funded by Rose flogging his sports car, and the record eventually hit the shelves via RCA in the UK and Caliber in the US. During this period Love returned to the band but by now their career seemed to be in a tailspin. Their next album, *I'm Not Happy* (1995), was the sound of a band completely without direction.

Pearl was so depressed by the entire situation, he needed time out, and on album number five, *Livin' Off Layla* (1997), **Mark Torin** of **Bullet Boys** stood in for him. It was still something of a mess. Finally, *Let's Eat* (1999) – without Rose as chief songwriter – was the last gasp from a band that should have split on a high note years earlier. From the wreckage Pearl made the most high-profile comeback; he tried his hand at writing short stories and ended up singing in both **L.A. Guns** and **Ratt** and recording his own solo material.

Black Out In The Red Room
1990; Columbia

There's sex, drugs and rock'n'roll in lethal quantities, making this one of the most promising debuts of the early 90s. Rose's songwriting is hard and efficient, and Pearl's feral snarl succinctly sums up the band's attitude. Damn near a classic.

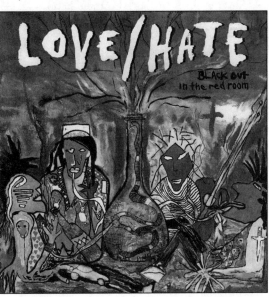

LYNYRD SKYNYRD

Formed Jacksonville, Florida 1965; disbanded 1977; re-formed 1987

The most legendary of southern hard-rock bands, **Lynyrd Skynyrd** – named after their high school gym teacher, Leonard Skinner, who was forever telling them to cut their hair – founded their reputation on a triple guitar attack and some terrific solos, not least the masterpiece that graces one of their most famous songs "Free Bird". They epitomized a downhome style of playing, but rose above their roots to become a major concert draw in the 70s. What stopped them from becoming true megastars was a tragic plane crash which put the band out of action for several years.

Originally formed at high school, the band didn't latch onto their wacky revenge moniker until 1970, though it took another three years and various line-up changes before their glorious debut on MCA Records, *Pronounced Leh-nerd Skin-nerd*. One early incarnation of Skynyrd featured future **Blackfoot** mainman **Rick Medlocke** on drums, but by the early 70s the band comprised **Ronnie Van Zant** (vocals), **Gary Rossington** (guitar), **Allen Collins** (guitar), **Ed King** (guitar), **Billy Powell** (keyboards), **Leon Wilkeson** (bass) and **Robert Burns** (drums). The sound was steeped in moonshine, deep-fried to a crisp and served up with a generous helping of hot sauce. Already renowned as a hard-living and dedicated touring outfit it didn't take much effort for the hits to start flowing. "Sweet Home Alabama" – their riposte to Neil Young's

Lynyrd Skynyrd.

GEMS/REDFERNS

"Southern Man" – went into the US Top 10 in 1974, while the marvellous album *Second Helping* (1974) really launched them into the big league.

Much of the mid-70s was taken with touring and a brace of fine albums – *Nuthin' Fancy* (1975), *Gimme Back My Bullets* (1976) and the live *One More From The Road* (1976) – plus the odd line-up change that brought in **Artimus Pyle** (drums) and **Steve Gaines** (guitar) for Ed King. The band were clearly on the ascendant but their next album, *Street Survivors* (1977), would almost be their last. Shortly after the record was released the band's tour plane crashed into a Mississippi swamp. Van Zant, Gaines and his sister Cassie (one of their backing singers), along with personal manager Dean Kilpatrick, were among those killed. The sleeve for the new album, a photo showing the band surrounded by flames, was quickly revised but the band ended there and then.

Skynyrd's First And Last (1978), a collection of unreleased material followed, as did compilations *Gold And Platinum* (1979) and *Best Of The Rest* (1982). It was another ten years, however, before Skynyrd reappeared for a tour, with Ronnie's brother **Johnny Van Zant** on vocals; the result was live album *Southern By The Grace Of God* (1987) and a rarities collection *Legend* (1987).

It wasn't until the 90s that the re-formed band really began hitting their stride again, with a string of tours and solid if unspectacular albums. In the mid-90s **Rick Medlocke** rejoined on guitar (Rossington, Powell, and Wilkeson were by now the only remaining original members) and Skynyrd went on to record the fine *Edge Of Forever* (1999). *Christmas Time Again* (2000) was as dire as the title suggested, but *Vicious Cycle* (2003) and *Thyrty* (2003), an anniversary compilation, proved that there was still plenty of energy left in this quintessential good-time band.

Thyrty
2003; Sanctuary

A fine spread of classic hard rock is represented here. Disc one contains some of their most essential early- to mid-70s recordings, while disc two delves into their later career. You can almost smell those illicit stills...

MACHINE HEAD

Formed San Francisco, US, 1992

"We're all digging deep into ourselves and bringing it out whether it's fuckin' beautiful or whether it's fuckin' hideously ugly…" Robb Flynn

Twisted, brutal and apocalyptically heavy, **Machine Head** are the evolutionary link between late-80s thrash metal and the 90s nu-wave. Led by vocalist/guitarist **Robb Flynn**, the band strive with each successive album to bring some new degree of extreme aural mayhem to their basic downtuned chuggery. Over the years they have delivered albums of breathtaking confidence; they've misfired a couple of times too, but when they bounce back it's always with a renewed desire to be the biggest, nastiest metal predator on the block.

Back in the 80s Flynn had been a member of Bay Area archetypal thrashers **Vio-lence**, but his master plan for Machine Head was quite different. In the early 90s grunge was king and a new pattern for metal was developing, building upon the speed of old but incorporating a grinding and downtuned quality to the riffing. The sound had to be oppressive, atmospheric, impassioned and, above all, heavy on an epic scale with vocals teetering on the edge of insanity. So, when *Burn My Eyes* (1994) arrived on Roadrunner Records – featuring the line-up of **Logan Mader** (guitar), **Adam Duce** (bass) and

Chris Kontos (drums) – it revealed just how effectively Flynn and Machine Head had tapped into the metal *Zeitgeist*. The album was hailed as a cutting-edge masterpiece, the aural equivalent to a good going-over with a concrete baseball bat.

Burn My Eyes was an almost instant smash. It went Top 30 in the UK and was a hit in Europe where the band were chosen to support Slayer – thus laying the groundwork for what would prove to be an invaluable level of support outside their homeland. The band's scrabble to the top of the mid-90s metal heap was also aided by the surprise appearance of "Old" in the UK's Top 50.

Inevitably, with a success on their hands their instinct was to repeat the formula. *The More Things Change…* (1997) featured **Dave McClain** on drums, but otherwise it was almost business as usual. The album went Top 20 in the UK, but as a whole the record paled in comparison to their first offering.

Shortly afterwards, the first major ructions in the line-up occurred when Mader left to be replaced by **Ahrue Luster**. The departure of such a long-standing founding member prompted Flynn into penning lyrics about betrayal and frustration for the next album, *The Burning Red* (1999). In interviews Flynn admitted that songs such as "I Defy", "Exhale The Vile" and "Devil With The King's Card" reflected the sense of devastation in losing Mader. Produced by upcoming nu-metal guru **Ross Robinson,** who stripped away the old layers of sonic grime, the vibe of the album was less cluttered and leaner than their previous effort. The band's admiration of hip-hop informed such tunes as

"Desire To Fire" and "From This Day", while "Silver" actually had Flynn singing. The refocusing of their writing was a necessary move, but one which upset long-time fans expecting *Burn My Eyes II*. Even more disturbing was the band's hamfisted mashing of the Police's classic pop hit "Message In A Bottle".

After the stylistic changes of their last album, the disappointing *Supercharger* (2001) suffered a lack of cohesion, despite some storming moments. But in any case the record was launched just weeks after the terrorist attacks of 9/11, when the media were wary of broadcasting anything unsuitable. The album's first single was "Crashing Around You", with a promo clip featuring the band playing in front of a massive projection of the San Francisco skyline aflame.

With the band's stock at an all-time low in the US, *Hellalive* (2003) at least revealed that the material from their last two studio efforts could sound powerful in front of thousands of fans. Despite this the band were almost dropped by their American label, and *Through The Ashes Of Empires* (2003) was released first in Europe and then in the States. This collection of songs recalled the urgent invention of their debut and underlined their determination to ignore everything but their own desire to make loud and frightening metal. New guitarist **Phil Demmel** – an old bandmate of Flynn's from his Vio-lence days – had replaced Luster and the positive atmosphere in the studio had contributed to their new-found impetus. The songs were long, complex and hot with the kind of riff-savvy fire that had endeared them to the fans ten years earlier.

⊙ Burn My Eyes
1994; Roadrunner

A classic that ushered in a new era of guitar violence. Downtuned, aggressive and angry beyond imagining, this album set the benchmark for extreme metal. Flynn's caustic roar cuts through the maelstrom with lyrics based upon pretty much anything that has pissed him off.

MAGNUM

Formed Birmingham, UK, 1973

No one plays pomp rock quite like Magnum. These Brummie rockers began

· On a Storytellers Night ·

with a quirky almost prog sound and rapidly developed into one of the UK's best melodic hard rock bands of the 80s and early 90s.

Anyone familiar mainly with their late-80s and early-90s hits such as "Days Of No Trust", "Start Talking Love" and "Rockin' Chair" might find it surprising that the band's first single (which flopped) was a cover of The Searchers' "Sweets For My Sweet" in early 1975. After this release the band's line-up settled down to **Bob Catley** (vocals), **Tony Clarkin** (guitar), **Colin 'Wally' Lowe** (bass), **Kex Gorin** (drums) and **Richard Bailey** (keyboards).

With a clutch of much fierier rock tunes recorded in demo form, the band signed to Jet Records, a move that would get their music to the masses but also create problems. *Kingdom Of Madness* (1978), recorded a couple of years prior to its release, only hit the shelves as the UK was reeling from the punk explosion – not the ideal context for Clarkin's hard rock with hooks and a nice line in twiddly keyboard frills. Still, the band were game and sheer good fortune landed them a support slot on Judas Priest's Sin After Sin tour. *Magnum II* (1979) and the live *Marauder* (1980) followed, with the latter making the album charts Top 40, but it was the addition of new keyboard player **Mark Stanway** that gave Magnum the extra boost. The next step up was *Chase The Dragon* (1982), another album delayed by record label dithering which, nevertheless, peaked at #17 and provided the band with several live classics, including the emotive "Soldier Of The Line" and "Sacred Hour".

The self-produced *The Eleventh Hour* (1983) turned out to be their last album for Jet Records. On tour with Ozzy Osbourne in the US, the band failed to make much impact and what little enthusiasm the label still had for them began to wane. Such was the mutual disenchantment, that years later the band admitted that they had considered pretending to split in order to get out of the deal. The period that followed didn't help matters as rumour and fact collided to produce utter confusion. Stanway ended up touring with Phil Lynott's **Grand Slam**, before replacing his replacement; rumours spread that Catley might be the new vocalist in Black Sabbath; and Gorin was replaced with **Jim Simpson**.

Amazingly, despite the likelihood of splitting, the band regrouped and produced one of their strongest albums yet, *On A Storyteller's Night* (1985). This was the prelude to their most successful period, and although **Mickey Barker** replaced Simpson, it slowed them up not one bit. Opening the Donington Monsters Of Rock festival in 1985, their subsequent signing to Polydor provided them with just the kind of support that had been missing up to now. *Vigilante* (1986) was produced by **Queen's Roger Taylor** and allowed them to tour as headliners; *Wings Of Heaven* (1988) peaked at #5 in the UK album chart, and *Goodnight L.A.* (1990) reached the Top 10. Despite this run of good fortune, however, record label politics meant that after releasing the live album *The Spirit* (1991) they would need to find a new home. *Sleepwalking* (1992) emerged on the trusty Music For Nations and *Rock Art* (1994) appeared on EMI, but the band had been dealt a fatal blow and things never really picked up again. A farewell tour was arranged and live album *The Last Dance* (1996) was touted as their last ever recording.

Clarkin, who needed a break, worked as a producer and formed **Hard Rain** with Catley for just two albums, *Hard Rain* and *When The Good Times Come*. Catley also tried his hand at some solo work. Hard Rain was then put on hold and it looked as if Magnum might reform. New bassist **Al Barrow** was added for *Breath Of Life* (2002) – an album that got the thumbs up from as unlikely a source as *Q* magazine – and by the time of *Brand New Morning* (2004) the band had roped in the services of **Thunder** drummer **Harry James**.

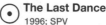

The Last Dance
1996; SPV

Magnum always excelled at live performances and often their concert recordings do greater justice to the songs than the studio versions. This double CD covers material from their debut right up to the hits. Can't say fairer than that.

YNGWIE J. MALMSTEEN

Born Stockholm, Sweden, June 30, 1963

Ask any metal fan about manic axe-shredders and you can bet your bullet belt that Mr **Malmsteen** will top the list of usual suspects. Epitomizing the flashy school of neoclassical metal, Malmsteen rose to prominence in the 80s when a sudden wave of guitar heroes and blistering instrumental albums pushed things to the outer limits of sanity. Famed for his technique and awesome virtuoso style, Malmsteen is a finger-flinger extraordinaire whose popularity was severely dented by grunge and also by the fact that people soon realized that – while he could spank a plank like a man possessed – he was in no danger of writing even a single memorable song. Hugely popular in Japan almost from the outset, Malmsteen has proved to be exceptionally tenacious, and he continues to tour and release albums which are voraciously consumed by guitar fans worldwide.

The story of Malmsteen's rise to the pinnacle of guitar mania goes back to when he was inspired by the likes of Jimi Hendrix and Deep Purple's Ritchie Blackmore. Malmsteen just couldn't get enough of the classical Blackmore style, admiring his volatile genius and all round expertise. Hence, much of the 70s were spent perfecting his own style and playing in bands such as **Powerhouse** and **Rising Force**. However, nothing happened with the demo tapes he put together until one made its way to Mike Varney, a writer for *Guitar Player* magazine and head of Shrapnel Records. Varney suggested Malmsteen head out to Los Angeles and record something for Shrapnel. That turned out to be an album with **Steeler**, featuring vocalist **Ron Keel**.

Malmsteen played with Steeler for only a short while, deciding to leave when he realized he was the most talented individual in the band – an indicator of the level of his ambition. He turned down the opportunity to join up with various high-profile rockers – including, apparently, Ozzy Osbourne – and hitched up with ex-**Rainbow** vocalist **Graham Bonnet** in **Alcatrazz** with whom he recorded *No Parole For Rock'N'Roll* (1983) and *Live Sentence* (1984). His love of the solo and his rapidly expanding ego led him to jump ship yet again. Striking out on his own, he created **Yngwie Malmsteen's Rising Force**, a vehicle dedicated to himself which helped kick-start the wave of instrumental metal albums on which speed and technique would be highlighted above all else.

Now signed to Polydor *Rising Force* (1984) charted in the US even though it was basically just tons of speedy fretboard thrashing, as in fan fave "As Above So Below". Incredibly, the album was nominated for a Grammy. Already huge in Japan, his next move was *Marching Out* (1985), which had some vague attempts at songwriting, including the risible "I Am A Viking". However, the six-string-loving hordes were not put off by such ludicrous fare and got their reward with the likes of "I'll See The Light, Tonight". *Trilogy* (1986), featuring a sleeve depicting Malmsteen battling a dragon with his guitar, continued with the frenetic finger-picking. Now incredibly dated, this album has provided the faithful with plenty of histrionic solos to air guitar to.

The following year saw Malmsteen almost despatched to Valhalla when he suffered a serious car crash. For a while it looked like damage to his right hand might render him unable to play, but he recovered and set about creating one of his most commercial efforts in *Odyssey* (1988). Aided by the professional vocals of former Rainbow singer **Joe Lynn Turner**, the album went Top 40 in the US and Top 30 in the UK. Despite the more accessible nature of the material Turner and Malmsteen didn't get along and the singer departed after *Trial By Fire: Live In Leningrad* (1989).

Eclipse (1990), marked the end of what had been an amazing run of luck for both Malmsteen and 80s rock in general. The *Collection* (1991) compilation was followed by *Fire & Ice* (1992) but suddenly the whole *raison d'être* behind the Malmsteen style was questioned as anti-heroic grunge took hold. Crashing from a major label deal to a series

of indies and Music For Nations he released a string of records – *The Seventh Sign* (1993), the Japan-only *I Can't Wait* EP (1994) and *Magnum Opus* (1995) – and took to touring places where he was revered; in other words Japan, where he undertook a 17-date tour in the mid-90s.

Inspiration (1996) was a set of cover tunes from bands that got Malmsteen strumming away in the first place. Needless to say the number of Blackmore-aided compositions far outweighed those from any other artists. *Facing The Animal* (1997) had Malmsteen back with his own material but *Concerto Suite For Electric Guitar And Orchestra In E Flat Minor Op.*1 (1998) – shades of Deep Purple's own early career concerto, perhaps? – finally articulated his classical influences. *Live!!* (1998) provided a snapshot of the Facing The Animal tour before the heavy, and more palatable, *Alchemy* (1999). *War To End All Wars* (2000) was an inauspicious way to herald the new millennium and encapsulated all the negative aspects of Malmsteen's career; leaving aside the terrible lyrics, the awful stab at reggae on "Black Sheep Of The Family", not to mention the general lack of decent songs, the production (by Yngwie himself) made the entire thing sound like a piss-poor demo. Fortunately for fans the *Concerto Suite Live* (2002), featuring the New Japan Philharmonic, was much better.

Having weathered both grunge and nu-metal by retreating and regrouping, Malmsteen now went on the attack with *Attack!!* (2003), his love of exclamation marks getting the better of him yet again. *The Genesis* (2003) album had nothing to do with dusty old prog rock and everything to do with his very early recordings, the irony-free, self-regarding title indicating Malmsteen's perspective on his own career. But this was a mere diversion compared to his attempts to gain a foothold in the US again, aided in no small way by an invitation to join the prestigious G3 tour, a guitar virtuoso's showcase, featuring Joe Satriani and Steve Vai. Meanwhile, Japan – that stronghold of Malmsteen fanatics – was treated to the *Instrumental Best Album* (2004) followed closely by *Unleash The Fury* (2005).

⊙ Rising Force
1984; Polydor

A guitar rises from the flames on the sleeve … prepare yourself for riffs, licks and solos previously thought impossible – Eddie Van Halen eat your heart out. It's incredible, influential stuff to be sure, and thankfully features little in the way of vocals, given the Maestro's inability to write decent lyrics of any kind whatsoever.

⊙ Marching Out
1985; Polydor

If you fancy a chuckle check out "I Am A Viking", a song that makes Dio sound like a poet. The words might be daft but there's no denying the man's skill at producing supernatural guitar sounds, making this the powerhouse album of guitar-shredding *par excellence*.

Manowar

Formed New York, US, 1980

Death to false metal! – This is the battle cry coined by these man-mountains in their crusade to bring True Metal to the world – whether we want it or not. The result of reading too many Conan the Barbarian comics, Manowar came into existence as the vision of one **Joey DeMaio** (bass). Legend has it that this one-time roadie for Black Sabbath found a like-minded soul in **Ross 'The Boss' Friedman** (guitar) backstage at Newcastle City Hall; DeMaio was working for Sabbath whilst Friedman was a member of support act **Shakin' Street**. Back in New York they recruited **Eric Adams** (vocals) and **Donnie Hamzik** (drums) into their heroic quest to expunge wimpy music from the face of the earth.

Theirs was the sound of testosterone and machismo run rampant, of leather, chains and instruments wielded as weapons. In the hands of Ross The Boss a guitar became an axe, a bloody one that he would grind with meticulous relish, while DeMaio famously possessed a bass guitar adorned with so many switches and controls it was affectionately dubbed 'The Enterprise'. Meanwhile, the thunderous output from the bass amps eventually earned the menacing title 'The Black Wind'.

With former Kiss manager Bill Aucoin behind them *Battle Hymns* (1982) polarized metal supporters: you either became an instant convert to the band's zealous pursuit of epic volume, or you thought that four blokes singing about Vikings and swords was cheesy in the extreme. But the album is worth listening to, even if it's simply to enjoy Orson Welles's ripe and dramatic voice-over

for the track "Dark Avenger". With its fantasy battle imagery and deadly serious approach, *Battle Hymns* remains a classic example of unreconstructed metal in its purest form.

Dropped by their first label, they brought in a new drummer in the formidable shape of **Scott Columbus** – a sticksman of such strength that a custom-built steel kit had to be made to endure the pounding. They then inked a new deal with Megaforce, using their own blood, and an era of furry loincloths, leather strides and bare chests was launched with *Into Glory Ride* (1983). Were these guys for real? You bet – there wasn't even a hint of irony to their poly-decibel onslaught. Ridiculously loud and proud of their uncompromising vision, the second stage of their career was truly under way. *Hail To England* (1984), recorded in a mere six days, was immensely heavy and dedicated to the Army of the Immortals, those who had bothered to turn up for the first tour. A rapid follow-up, *Sign Of The Hammer* (1984), spawned their major classic and succinct mission statement "All Men Play On 10", the correct volume setting for True Metal.

The next album did not emerge for another three years as the band toured solidly, headlining in Europe and performing as many support slots as possible in the US, not that easy since only the mighty Motörhead were unafraid of being blown away by them. *Fighting The World* (1987) was still as awesomely over the top as when the band first started, and the Spectacle Of Might tour saw the band go down in the Guinness Book of World Records as the loudest band ever, a record they would break themselves a few years down the line during their Secrets Of Steel tour, with an ear-mashing 129.5-decibel show in Germany.

Unfortunately *Kings Of Metal* (1988) was to be Friedman's last album, a set which featured DeMaio unleashing a blistering bass solo called "Sting Of The Bumble Bee". The gloriously excessive nature of the album also included travelling to the UK to record "The Crown And The Ring (Lament Of The Kings)" using the 100-voice, all-male Canoldir Choir.

Finding a replacement for their departed guitarist seemed a Herculean task, but a mean hombre going under the moniker of **Death Dealer** (we kid you not) stepped into the breach. Dave Shankle, as he is known to his

COURTESY OF SPV RECORDS

Manowar: Leathers are compulsory in Valhalla.

mum and dad, appeared on the next album. Along with the introduction of the rampaging **Rhino** (aka **Kenny Earl**) on drums for *The Triumph Of Steel* (1992), DeMaio and his sonic barbarians collectively presented their raised middle fingers to the grunge phenomenon. Their answer to metal falling out of favour was to record a 28-minute opening track, "Achilles, Agony And Ecstasy In Eight Parts" based on Homer's *The Iliad*.

Hell Of Steel (1994), a passable compilation, kept their dedicated following going while they forged their next opus, *Louder Than Hell* (1996). By now Death Dealer and Rhino had left to be replaced by **Karl Logan** and a returning Scott Columbus. The gargantuan double-live helping of *Hell On Wheels* (1997) was followed by live effort *Hell On Stage* (1999) as the band switched record labels again, from Geffen to Nuclear Blast. But even with a new record deal there was no hurrying the band along and *Warriors Of The World* took another three years to create.

Most recently, the band have been reissuing remastered silver editions of their early albums, bringing a new clarity and power to their classic grooves, and continuing with their live video series – the latest, *Hell On Earth III* (2003) was their most ambitiously over-the-top package yet.

Beware all those who mock the warriors of True Metal; Manowar are far from finished. They will return – the holy war against False Metal is a timeless and never-ending crusade.

Battle Hymns
1982; Liberty

Stand aside you weak and feeble rabble and make way for the awesome majesty of Manowar – meat-eating, axe-wielding, womanizing saviours of metal.

Triumph Of Steel
1992; Atlantic

The fight goes on. Words alone cannot convey the sheer metallic nature of this magnificently overblown, stupendously heavy, utterly focused album.

MARILYN MANSON

Formed Fort Lauderdale, Florida, US, 1990

"A normal white teenager doesn't have a support group other than Marilyn Manson." Marilyn Manson

Few bands of recent years have been controversial by design: the notoriety which so many groups crave as a means to shift lack-lustre records often comes by accident. Not so with Mr Manson and his ghastly crew, for whom the antagonization of conservative elements in American society was an integral part of the band's make-up. The result has been to sell vast quantities of albums, but such is the ubiquitous nature of Manson's celebrity these days that it is not necessary to tune into the music to experience the man's demonic charms – so wholesale has been the commercial exploitation of the Manson brand that one is just as likely to see him pop up in a computer game, as to appear on MTV.

Following a sickly childhood and an exclusive Christian education the young Ohio-born **Brian Warner** became fascinated by heavy metal. Working as a writer contributing to a Florida music paper and indulging in poetry readings, he also dabbled with a few no-hope bands and shaved off his eyebrows. He then took all his frustrated rage and channelled it into the creation of **Marilyn Manson** (vocals), the self-styled 'God of Fuck'. Initially called **Marilyn Manson and the Spooky Kids**, the star-crossed serial-killer line-up was completed by **Daisy Berkowitz** (guitar), **Twiggy Ramirez** (bass), **Madonna Wayne Gacy** (keyboards) and drummer **Sara Lee Lucas**. Members that jumped ship before the band took off but deserve a mention just for their truly marvellous names are **Zsa Zsa Speck** (keyboards), **Gidget Gein** (bass) and **Olivia Newton Bundy** (also bass).

The concept was simple: to see just how far America could be shaken to its foundations by a band supposedly distilling and reflecting back all of the country's moral cancers. Early recordings were EP cassettes sold at gigs and included such glorious titles as the *Meat Beat Cleaver Beat* and *Grist-O-Line*. The band's freaky live show ensured a strong local following almost instantly and

earned the band the accolade of Band Of The Year at the 1993 South Florida Rock Awards.

A key player in the band's ascendancy at this time was **Trent Reznor** of Nine Inch Nails who offered a support slot to Manson's fast-developing schlock horror show. He also asked Manson to be the first to sign to his new Nothing Records label and was also involved in producing and partly shaping the early Manson releases. The band's debut, *Portrait Of An American Family* (1994), owed a great deal to the likes of underground goth weirdos Alien Sex Fiend and industrial-noise pioneer Jim Thirlwell (aka Foetus), but, Manson admitted, the writing and appearance of the group at this time were too cartoonish for the kind of outrage he was trying to provoke. By now the band were named simply after their frontman.

By the time the *Smells Like Children* (1995) mini-LP arrived as a stopgap production, America was finally waking up to the full gaudy horror of Marilyn Manson. They scored an MTV hit with a cover of the Eurythmics' "Sweet Dreams" and suddenly Manson's surgical-corseted, bloody-bandage chic was invading every American home. To complete the degenerate image, a single pale contact lens gave his leering visage an extra twist of the knife. Such cod-horror theatrics were nothing new to the generations who had witnessed Alice Cooper at his peak, but predictable waves of hysteria came from fundamentalist religious groups, the main target for Manson's vicious lampooning. He was instantly dubbed a child-molesting, drug-abusing son of Satan which, naturally, made him even more attractive to the fans. The satanic part at least was correct – Manson had been made a priest of the Church Of Satan by its founder Dr Anton LaVey in late 1994, allowing him to use the title Reverend.

After the recording of the concept album *Antichrist Superstar* (1996) there was a line-up change, with replacement members **Ginger Fish** (drums) and **Zim Zum** (guitar) joining the Manson family. The new album had all the focus that their debut lacked and brought with it a live show guaranteed to offend middle-American sensibilities. At one point during the show the venue would be transformed into a mock Nazi rally; red, white and black flags bearing the international shock hazard symbol would appear while the band donned steel helmets and Manson demanded audience worship. Nothing new to David Bowie or Pink Floyd fans (the album even features a 'wormboy' character) but such coarse irony made Manson a wanted man on every redneck fundamentalist's hit-list. The group were banned from various towns as undesirables; ironically when the banning orders were challenged in court many of them were lifted.

As a practised manipulator of the press and public opinion Manson knew that a change of image could only be a good thing as the band launched full-scale into a period consolidating the commercial success of the preceding two years. With the release of *Mechanical Animals* (1998) – a Top 10 hit in the UK and the band's first #1 in the US – Manson was no longer the bizarre-looking spawn of Satan; suddenly he adopted a scary, cold female android look which meshed seamlessly with the new approach to the writing. Outrage was still very much the name of the game, but an obvious softening had occurred in the sound – the band by now featuring guitarist **John 5** (aka **John Lowery**) – which was occasionally compared to the kind of glam electro-dabbling David Bowie had indulged in twenty years earlier.

Marilyn applies his eyeshadow in a centrifuge.

Shock tactics and a killer live show – the sound of which was captured on *The Last Tour On Earth* (1999) – assured Manson acres of press coverage. The real challenge, however, was to maintain interest in what Manson saw as a strong artistic direction with lyrics reflecting observations on the world around him; simply arousing feelings of revulsion would be an easy and pointless victory. With *Holy Wood (In The Shadow Of The Valley Of Death)* (2000), a record created in the wake of the Columbine school shootings tragedy, Manson found himself the target of vilification because the two young perpetrators of the massacre were allegedly fans of his music; conservative elements branded him as somehow complicit in the blood-letting. Naturally, these events provided more than enough material for Manson to create an album focusing on the degenerate and contradictory values at the heart of American society. He later turned up in an interview talking eloquently about the mental state of the country in Michael Moore's documentary about American gun culture, *Bowling For Columbine*. What Manson has demonstrated so well up to now is how, in the MTV culture that passes for a modern music scene, cheap sensationalism and outrage are the lifeblood of rock'n'roll.

It was only a matter of time before Manson's showbiz aspirations led him to dabble in the movies, doubtless inspired by his own music video forays and a love of cult films and film-makers. He turned up as a transvestite dominatrix alongside Macaulay Culkin in *Party Monster* – not a huge leap from his appearance as a porn star alongside Twiggy Ramirez in David Lynch's *Lost Highway* (1997) – and in 2004 he appeared in *The Heart Is Deceitful Above All Things*, an Asia Argento movie in which Manson starred alongside Peter Fonda and Winona Ryder.

Prior to this celluloid excursion, however, Manson set about preparing another album, this time steeped in the imagery of 1930s Berlin. Working with renowned Austrian artist Gottfried Helnwein, the new look encompassed mock Nazi regalia and an overall feel of camp and cinematic menace. The album, *The Golden Age Of Grotesque* (2003) – featuring **Tim Skold** in place of the departed Twiggy – was widely acclaimed as one of the best the band had created, with a suitably wild Grotesk Burlesk stage show, featuring scantily clad and prosthetically disfigured female dancers. Much of the album's success was down to the songwriting prowess of the band members, not least John 5 who was credited with co-writing thirteen of the fifteen songs that sent the album to #1 on the *Billboard* chart – which made it all the more puzzling when Manson sacked the guitarist. But then Manson has always been a law unto himself, whether it's ending up in court for rubbing his crotch on a security guard's head during a gig, shredding the Bible in front of a rabid crowd or for sudden bouts of violence both on and off stage.

After this slice of moral-majority-baiting, Manson threw himself into a host of other activities. This included approving a range of wind-up toys in his image and exhibiting his own watercolour paintings, before preparing *Lest We Forget: The Best Of* (2004) – a self-explanatory compilation featuring the single "Personal Jesus", a cover version of the Depeche Mode hit.

Antichrist Superstar

1996; Interscope/Nothing

Do we laugh at him, or allow Mr Manson to take us for a ride? Marilyn is obviously unafraid to flaunt his influences, but that aside, behind the goth-shock treatment lurk some excellent tunes, particularly the glam-metal stomp of "The Beautiful People".

Mechanical Animals
1998; Interscope/Nothing

Anyone who thought *Antichrist Superstar* was a neat bag of tricks might be a tad disappointed with this. In reality, however, the writing is much better and the album provides a more cohesive listening experience. Never has shock rock sounded quite as accomplished as this.

MEAT LOAF

Born Dallas, Texas, US, September 27, 1951

Everything from Texas is huge, so the cliché goes, and **Meat Loaf** aka **Marvin Lee Aday** is no exception. The biggest voice in rock started off in the late 60s dabbling with psychedelic rock but the Texan's thespian tendencies then led him to acting roles. He appeared in Broadway musicals such as *Hair*, and as Eddie in the film *The Rocky Horror Picture Show*. It was during the 70s that he made his foray into making albums, when he teamed up with female singer **Stoney** (aka **Cheryl Murphy**) with whom he issued *Stoney And Meatloaf* on the Rare Earth label.

In 1976 Meat Loaf helped **Ted Nugent** out with vocals on his *Free For All* album, but it was a role in **Jim Steinman**'s musical *More Than You Deserve* that cemented one of the most famous music writing partnerships of the last three decades. In Meat Loaf's powerful voice Steinman had found the perfect way to deliver his wildly over-the-top songs and their collaboration was to catapult Meat Loaf to stardom. The classic *Bat Out Of Hell* album roped in the talents of Utopia guitarist **Todd Rundgren** (who also produced), **Roy Bittan** (keyboards) and a whole host of other instrumental and vocal talent – including **Ellen Foley** – to create an anthemic modern hard-rock opera, packed with deliciously overblown arrangements and fabulously tongue-in-cheek lyrics. The album didn't exactly smash its way to the top of the charts but as singles such as "You Took The Words Right Out Of My Mouth", "Paradise By The Dashboard Light" and the ultra-melodramatic title track became hits, the album sold and sold. The touring that accompanied the release ensured that the record crossed over into the mainstream to become one of the top-selling albums of all time.

Meatloaf: "I'll scream and scream and scream until I'm sick!"

The effect it had on Meat Loaf, however, was detrimental. Suddenly cast into the limelight he found it increasingly difficult to cope and his health suffered. The delays caused meant that the follow-up collaboration with Steinman, *Dead Ringer* – with Rundgren no longer in the picture – didn't appear for four years. **Cher** was the featured female vocal talent on the title track and the album, although topping the UK chart, noticeably suffered through the loss of momentum.

The subsequent 80s albums – *Midnight At The Lost And Found* (1983), *Bad Attitiude* (1984) and *Blind Before I Stop* (1986) – all had their moments but without Steinman providing his larger-than-life material, the songs just didn't have the necessary edge. The return to form came in 1993 when Meat Loaf reunited with Steinman for *Bat Out Of Hell II: Back Into Hell*, a US and UK chart topper and home to #1 single "I'd Do Anything For Love (But I Won't Do That)". The rest of the decade saw Meat Loaf take on more acting roles, not least in the darkly funny *Fight Club*, while still issuing albums such as *Welcome To The Neighborhood* (1995), *Live Around The World* (1996), *The Very Best Of Meat Loaf* (1998) and, most recently, *Couldn't Have Said It Better* (2003).

⊙ **Bat Out Of Hell**
1977; Epic

A stone-cold classic. Every track is a winner, featuring histrionic rock-opera action throughout and the performance of Meat Loaf's life. If your record collection doesn't include this then something's wrong.

MEGADETH

Formed San Francisco, California, US, 1983

"Fuckin' dealin' with Dave Mustaine will make you a true man!" Jonathan Davis from Korn

A far more technically accomplished thrash unit than many of their contemporaries, **Megadeth** brought a virtuoso edge to a genre more usually associated with brutal bluster than finesse. Starting out as a bunch of snot-nosed kids corralled together by guitarist/vocalist **Dave Mustaine** they gradually evolved into an elite metal outfit able to garner Grammy nominations and shift millions of albums.

When Mustaine was suddenly ejected from the fledgling line-up of **Metallica** after a drunken run-in with guitarist James Hetfield, his new-found ambition was to match and exceed his former bandmates' success. After reading an electoral pamphlet on the dangers of nuclear armaments, Mustaine thought 'megadeath' – a hypothetical quantity describing the body count after a nuclear attack – would make a perfect band name. So (after dropping a letter) Mustaine had a vehicle for his own eclectic style of riffing, and snarling vocal delivery. One of the first members he recruited was bassist **Dave Ellefson**, who would prove to be the one constant through the various stormy line-up changes. **Lee Raush** was the drummer and **Greg Handevidt** the second guitarist, but neither lasted long and during the upheavals **Slayer** guitarist **Kerry King** helped out during live dates, including their first gig. More permanent replacements – a loose term during Megadeth's early days – were **Chris Poland** (guitar) and **Gar Samuelson** (drums).

Signed to Combat Records, the band set about recording *Killing Is My Business ... And Business Is Good* (1985). The story goes that when the label gave the band some money for recording purposes, they spent half of it on drugs before they had even entered the studio. As a result they only kept their producer on for half the allotted time, leaving the album with plenty of spit but not nearly enough polish; it was raw, bitter and angry, just like Mustaine.

"Rattlehead" gave them a vicious little anthem all their own and for a laugh they dabbled with an evil cover of Nancy Sinatra's "Boots". "Mechanix" was almost identical to Metallica's "Four Horsemen", given that Mustaine had written the original riff, but the words were entirely different. However unfocused their debut was the band were at the vanguard of the growing thrash movement and ended up signing to Capitol Records for *Peace Sells ... But Who's Buying?* (1986), a far more satisfying chunk of speedy metal. They might not have looked like mean-spirited thrashers, but the contents were nasty – especially the blood and gore of "Black Friday". Conversely, the outstandingly chunky title track displayed Mustaine's ability to pen socially aware lyrics as well as the fun

Dave Mustaine earns some extra cash busking.

metal stuff, and pointed the way forward for some of the band's more outstanding moments. Internally, however, this was not a happy outfit, and they made a less than auspicious headlining appearance at the Hammersmith Odeon, plagued by equipment failure and Mustaine's fiery temper.

It was rapidly becoming clear that apart from Ellefson, Mustaine regarded the other musicians as little more than hired hands, and by the time of *So Far, So Good … So What!* (1988), Poland and Samuelson were history, replaced by guitarist **Jeff Young** and drummer **Chuck Behler**. This album was an extension of the driven rush of its predecessor, with songs that were inventively arranged and poundingly heavy. There were two classics in the shape of the emotional "In My Darkest Hour" (written after the death of Metallica bassist Cliff Burton in 1986) and the defiant "Hook In Mouth", which sank its teeth into the Parents Music Resource Centre (PMRC) and other organizations dead set on censorship. The band saw the album as a hasty rush job, however, put together in a haze of drink and hard drugs

with a less than sympathetic production (there was a lot of reverb, especially on Mustaine's vocals). That didn't stop it from being their first real chart success, climbing into the Top 30 in the US and also in the UK (aided by a gutsy hit single cover of the Sex Pistols' "Anarchy In The UK"). The band also put in an appearance playing at the Monsters Of Rock festival at Castle Donington in the same year.

Despite the growth in profile, narcotics were blowing a hole in both the band's potential and their bank balance. *So Far, So Good…* featured a song called "502", police code for driving while under the influence, and in a case of life imitating art, Mustaine was arrested for exactly this and forced to clean up. But not before Jeff Young and Chuck Behler were fired. Clearly Megadeth were teetering on the edge of self-destruction and for a while it looked as if Mustaine's attempts to outdo his old Metalli-pals had been scuppered through rock star excess. The one positive aspect of this period was the band's cover version of Alice Cooper's "No More Mr Nice Guy" for the soundtrack to Wes Craven's horror flick *Shocker*. It was the start of the band's regeneration and the single reached #13 in the UK.

On the look-out for new members again, Mustaine brought in ex-**Cacophony** guitar wizard **Marty Friedman** and drummer **Nick Menza**. Already a very technical-sounding band, Friedman's fluid guitar heroics gave them even more of a surgical edge. *Rust In Peace* (1990) was the birth of the new modern Megadeth, brimming with melody and directed aggression, replacing speed with a more considered approach. It made the Top 10 in the UK and a more modest Top 30 in the US, boosted by an excellent production from **Mike Clink** who had helped Guns N' Roses make *Appetite For Destruction* an immense success. The album gave them two live favourites in "Holy Wars…The Punishment Due" and the sci-fi conspiracy theory-inspired "Hangar 18", supposedly the location in an ultra-secret military base where the remains of aliens are kept hidden. Making up for lost time Megadeth found themselves on a super-heavyweight bill on the Clash Of The Titans tour on both sides of the Atlantic, alongside the likes of Slayer, Anthrax and Testament.

Rust In Peace, however, proved to be just a prelude to *Countdown To Extinction* (1992), which resolutely out-charted its predecessor. Metallica had just gone huge with their 'black' album *Metallica,* and Mustaine had his own success story at last – though Megadeth were no way as ubiquitous as his former band. Musically, *Countdown To Extinction* was highly accessible and exhibited their most inventive writing; "Sweating Bullets", for instance, drew on blues and jazz for its gloriously stuttering riff and structure.

Despite the success, the pressure of recording and touring led Mustaine to break his new found sobriety and nearly kill himself with a Valium overdose. Some months down the line, and now much calmer, he did the almost unthinkable and allowed Megadeth to share a bill with Metallica at the Milton Keynes Bowl. Diamond Head were also on the bill, and Mustaine later lent a hand on their *Death And Progress* album.

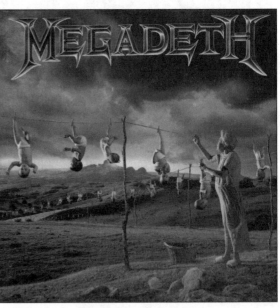

Incredibly, the trials and tribulations of kicking addiction didn't prevent the band from moving on to yet another triumphant album, *Youthanasia* (1994). This time it was the cover art that whipped up controversy. The sleeve depicted an elderly woman hanging babies out on a washing line, an obvious visual metaphor for the world's youth being hung out to dry. The album was banned in Malaysia and Singapore where the art was deemed to be in poor taste, likewise some shops in Germany and Canada refused to stock the record. That didn't stop it from heading to #6 in the UK and #4 in the US. The *Hidden Treasures* (1995) mini-LP pulled together a stopgap collection of cover versions and soundtrack odds and sods, and Mustaine collaborated with **Fear**'s **Lee Ving** on their **MD.45** project, before the band's next major change.

Megadeth had been heading on a melodic trajectory since the early 90s and *Cryptic Writings* (1997) and its follow-up *Risk*

(1999) – the latter with new drummer **Jimmy DeGrasso** – saw the band fully embrace the idea that glossily produced, largely radio-friendly fare, was the way to go. The albums had their fair share of powerful tunes, but, ironically, there was little sense of danger; the vicarious thrill of Megadeth's serrated riffing was subsumed beneath a welter of studio effects and smooth mixing. Far from boosting Megadeth into the realms of Metallica's success, both albums seemed to alienate much of the band's core support. To top it all Friedman left the band in early 2000 to be replaced by **Al Pitrelli**.

By the time *The World Needs A Hero* (2001) arrived the band had changed their management and label to Sanctuary. According to Mustaine, the guiding voices suggesting they should tone things down had been left behind, and as a result the new album was more in the vein of *Rust In Peace* and *Countdown To Extinction*. As if to welcome back fans disgusted by their former less aggressive transgressions, they even penned a tune called "Return To Hangar". Unfortunately events took a drastic nosedive in early 2002 when Mustaine injured his left arm and hand, making it impossible to play guitar. Megadeth called it a day shortly afterwards and the lacklustre *Rude Awakening* (2002) live album was their apparent swan song.

No one really believed that Mustaine would be out of action forever and sure enough, having recovered, he resurrected Megadeth for *The System Has Failed* (2004), though the line-up was noticeably bereft of Ellefson with whom relations had become strained. The surprise addition was old-time associate Chris Poland who helped out in the studio.

⊙ Peace Sells...But Who's Buying?
1986; Capitol

This remains one of the band's best albums. Aside from the usual metallic occult subject matter chewed over in "The Conjuring" and "Bad Omen", they also have a go at mangling Willie Dixon's "I Ain't Superstitious".

⊙ Countdown To Extinction
1992; Capitol

This album boasts some of Megadeth's best writing and most politically aware lyrics. The title track is inspired by environmental concerns about the future of the planet; "Architecture Of Aggression" explores the nature of global conflict; and "Foreclosure Of A Dream" takes a jaundiced look at America's economy.

MERCYFUL FATE

Formed Copenhagen, Denmark, 1981

Along with bands such as Venom, Danish madballs **Mercyful Fate** must be counted among the guilty for giving many future thrash acts that all-important infernal pitchfork prod in the direction of Old Nick. Next to the likes of the aforementioned Geordie hellraisers and Celtic Frost, this lot helped give black metal its deadly nightshade allure. They have the requisite twin-guitar riff engine, a pounding rhythm section and a wildly theatrical lead singer, the infamous **King Diamond** who doesn't mind how daft he looks on stage so long as he is making an impact. The chief weapon in their satanic arsenal, however, is the King's incredible vocal range. Imagine Rob Halford on steroids times ten – now you're beginning to get the picture. We're talking about a supernatural wail that can bring down a rampaging rhino at a hundred feet. Then, of course, we mustn't forget to factor in the black-and-white face paint (which looks particularly odd with the King's moustache peeping through), the jet-black cape and his bone

crucifix mic stand. Quite a magnificently diabolical sight.

The story goes that the King aka **Kim Bendix Petersen** was marking time in a little-known band called **Black Rose** before joining up with **Hank Shermann** (guitar) of punk band **Brats**. With the addition of **Michael Denner** (guitar, also of Brats), **Timi 'Grabber' Hansen** (bass) and **Kim Ruzz** (drums) Mercyful Fate were all set to rejig and spew out their diet of classic Sabbath and Priest riffs in the form of chuggingly heavy shards of progressive, aggressive proto-thrash. Demos notwithstanding, the first taste of the band arrived in the shape of their highly collectable eponymous EP, also known as the *Nuns Have No Fun* EP, its sleeve a crude depiction of a black mass complete with a bare-breasted young woman (a nun?) astride a crucifix.

Raw though the first effort was, what followed set the standard for underground metal of the early 80s. First came *Melissa* (1983), a crunching collection of tuneful and inventive riffs with the King's insane falsetto telling tales of nefarious dealings with the devil and dalliances with other demonic forces of the night. It was a masterpiece of such proportions that when Metallica came to put together their *Garage Inc* double album in 1998 they included a Mercyful Fate medley comprised of tracks from *Melissa* – "Satan's Fall", "Curse Of The Pharoahs", "Into The Coven" and "Evil" – plus "A Corpse Without Soul" from the debut EP. *Melissa* was followed by the remarkable *Don't Break The Oath* (1984), another landmark release, heavy with the occult and laden with the King's wild banshee vocals.

Despite the rave reviews for this double whammy, that old chestnut of musical differences stopped them in their tracks. The chief problems were the King's lyrical predilections, which rarely ventured beyond hailing the point-tailed fella downstairs, and the fact that Shermann thought they ought to bring in a more commercial, melodic sound. The King left with Denner and Hansen to form **King Diamond** and enjoyed a decent run of solo albums, while Shermann formed **Fate**. *The Beginning* (1987), a compilation album (combining their first EP plus some live BBC material), drew a line under Mercyful Fate's early period.

Eventually Shermann and Denner – the latter no longer a member of King Diamond – got together in a project called **Zoser Mez**, which precipitated the reformation of Mercyful Fate with all the original members except for Ruzz. The *Return Of The Vampire* (1992) rarities collection appeared and then a proper studio album, *In The Shadows* (1993) on Metal Blade Records. For the recording, Ruzz was replaced by **Morten Nielsen**, though **Metallica**'s drummer **Lars Ulrich** turned up as a special guest on the final track "Return Of The Vampire" (1993). Thus it was pretty much business as usual except that the King now provided a little more lyrical variety. Instead of overtly satanic musings his efforts concentrated on creepy horror, choosing to describe supernatural vignettes and tell stories more in the style of the concept albums he had just spent five years writing.

With new drummer **Snowy Shaw** already in place for *Time* (1994), the next new addition was **Sharlee D'Angelo** (bass). Following the limited edition *The Bell Witch* mini-LP, the King settled into a regular pattern of recording albums both with Mercyful Fate and under his own name, making him one of the most prolific artists in modern metal. *Into The Unknown* (1996), *Dead Again* (1998) and *9* (1999) followed, with the Mercyful Fate line-up eventually settling down to include **Mike Wead** (guitar) and **Bjarne T. Holm** (drums).

Maybe it's the seemingly relentless flow of material from the King over recent years, but the albums have lacked some of the fierce originality that used to mark them out as so special.

Metal Ballads

The power ballad as it's often referred to, seems like a contradiction in terms, but some of the most popular metal tunes – or should that be the ones calculated to have some sort of chart appeal? – are ballads designed to get crowds swaying with lighters held aloft. Most mainstream bands have had a go at penning a soppy melody or two, as a quick glance through the vast rock love-song compilation album sections in most record stores will prove

Aerosmith are a band who specialize in making their female fans go all doe-eyed and many of their albums feature a slowy or two, though most people will know them for tunes such as "Angel" and massive hit "I Don't Want To Miss A Thing". Poodle-permed, tight-trousered rockers **Whitesnake** are also known for their love of all things sentimental with one of smooth crooner **David Coverdale**'s finest smoochy efforts being "Is This Love?". In fact the 80s and early 90s saw perhaps the widest proliferation of wimpy rock tunes, more often than not tied in with some suitably MTV-friendly promo clip from bands such as **Foreigner** ("Waiting For A Girl Like You", "I Want To Know What Love Is"), **Def Leppard** ("Hysteria", "Love Bites"), **Extreme** ("More Than Words"), **Bon Jovi** ("I'll Be There For You", "Never Say Goodbye"). The list goes on: **Scorpions** ("Still Loving You", "Wind Of Change"), **Mötley Crüe** ("Home Sweet Home"), **Poison** ("Every Rose Has Its Thorn", "Something To Believe In"), and **Guns N' Roses** ("Don't Cry", "November Rain", and, of course, "Sweet Child O' Mine"). Even progressive metallers **Queensrÿche** joined in ("Silent Lucidity").

Most of these ditties are gently rocking lurve tunes, but wind the clock back to the 70s and the calibre of love songs was often astonishing. Scots outfit **Nazareth** enjoyed a hit with "Love Hurts" while even shock rocker **Alice Cooper** managed a big hit with "Only Women Bleed", one of his oft-covered softies. Meanwhile, **Thin Lizzy**'s **Phil Lynott** was a master when it came to ballads: "Don't Believe A Word" and "Still In Love With You" are among his greatest songs and suffer not a jot from schmaltz. And then we have what some consider to be **Led Zeppelin**'s greatest rock ballad – "Stairway To Heaven", though "Rain Song" comes closer to the ballad recipe and is an extraordinarily beautiful piece of music.

The really interesting ballads, however, come from those not normally associated with the style. **Metallica**'s "Nothing Else Matters" was a huge hit despite sounding nothing like Metallica – only **Hetfield**'s growling delivery gives it away. Getting slightly weirder, the madman of metal **Ozzy Osbourne** has been known to come over all sensitive; among his best from the 80s are "Goodbye To Romance" and "So Tired". Pushing the boat out further, titanic metallers **Judas Priest** showed early on that they could muster up a decent amount of emotion with the oft-overlooked "Last Rose Of Summer" – imagine **Rob Halford** warbling about flowers and the changing of the seasons. And then we come to **Motörhead** and the Jack-and-coke snarl of **Lemmy**. Even the Lemster can manage to bring a tear to the eye: one of the 'Head's most diverse albums, *1916*, contains the sad, cello-accompanied war tale of the title track, while "Love Me Forever" brings a characteristic sinister twist to the usual lighters-in-the-air formula. Perhaps oddest of all and seemingly way out of character is one of **AC/DC**'s earliest tunes, "Love Song", from the Aussie version of *High Voltage*; imagine **Bon Scott** trying to get his usually sleazy tonsils around a bunch of slushy lyrics. Quite unnerving.

That, and the general lack of support from the label, explains the failure to make any great leaps forward. That said, Shermann, Denner and Holm have taken an interesting sideways step to form **Force Of Evil** with **Iron Fire** vocalist **Martin Steene** and King Diamond bassist **Hal Patino**. Of course, the side-project lacks the King's barking-mad vocals, but is still solidly rooted in modern metal – with a twist of the Mercyful style of old.

 Melissa
1983; Roadrunner

Apparently Melissa was the name given to the skull mascot the band used to take on stage with them. Quite a suitable name considering the satanic but tuneful thrash the band were peddling. This is a classic bursting with great riffs and the King's inhuman vocals.

 Don't Break The Oath
1984; Roadrunner

More bonkers shrieking from the King and more hooky riffs and blistering solos. The lyrics are gloriously over the top, but then what else would you expect?

ℳETALLICA

Formed San Francisco, US, 1981

"We don't mind you throwing shit up at the stage, just don't hit our beers – they're our fuel, man!" James Hetfield

Though synonymous with the term 'heavy metal', **Metallica** have over the years consistently blurred the boundaries between mainstream rock and the extreme end of the metal spectrum with shots of melody and mixers of aggression.

As with most fledgling bands, their initial line-up was very fluid. In October 1981 Danish-born **Lars Ulrich** (drums) recruited **James Hetfield** (guitar/vocals) through a classified ad. With **Lloyd Grant** on guitar, they recorded a version of "Hit The Lights" for the *Metal Massacre* compilation album. Grant didn't last long, but the addition of **Dave Mustaine** (guitar) and **Ron McGovney** (bass) brought stability to the line-up.

Following the recording of their legendary seven-track demo, *No Life Till Leather*, McGovney was replaced by bell-bottom jeans aficionado **Cliff Burton** (bass) from fellow Bay-Area thrashers **Trauma**. Mustaine in turn quit after a series of bitter clashes with Hetfield and Ulrich in early 1983, going on to form **Megadeth**, and was replaced by **Kirk Hammett** (guitar; ex-**Exodus**). Things settled down.

Finding fresh momentum after all the infighting, the band wasted no time in directing their energies into their initial release, *Kill 'Em All* (1983). This was a true heavy metal album with a sleeve that proclaimed 'Bang that head that doesn't bang'. The songs ran the gamut of metal clichés – life on the road, war, death and violence – but the overall sound was energizingly fresh. There was even a spot of virtuosity in the form of Burton's bass solo, "(Anaesthesia) Pulling Teeth".

The early promise was confirmed with their second release, *Ride The Lightning* (1984). Fleming Rasmussen's production, which harnessed their original aggression, heralded the group's sonic trademark: a thick, heavy crunch in the rhythm guitar department augmented by Hetfield's vicious growl. The opening track, "Fight Fire With Fire", lulls you into a false sense of security with a mock-classical intro, before plunging head-long into a cauldron of relentless, speeding guitars. Metallica took another sure step towards world domination by signing to Def Leppard's management, Q-Prime.

Clearly on a roll, the band released what is generally regarded as their masterwork in 1986. *Master Of Puppets* hit #29 in the US charts and #47 in the UK, all without a single promotional video or hit single. With Rasmussen again producing, they took the winning formula of their previous effort to its logical conclusion. The bludgeoning opener, "Battery", had a classical intro, while "Welcome Home (Sanitarium)" was their token mellow number. There was even another instrumental in the shape of the sublime "Orion". For six months, the band supported Ozzy Osbourne on the huge Ultimate Sin tour. They seemed invincible, and even when Hetfield broke his wrist skateboarding, they continued with roadie **James Marshall** playing while Hetfield sang. However, tragedy struck on the Scandinavian leg of their own world tour, when their tour bus crashed and Burton was killed.

Remarkably the band regrouped within a couple of months, taking on the less flamboyant **Jason Newsted** (bass) from thrash band **Flotsam & Jetsam**. Wasting little time, the remainder of the tour was completed before the band launched into their next off-the-wall project, jamming on cover versions of their favourite British metal songs in Ulrich's garage. The result of the sessions, *The $5.98 EP – Garage*

Days Re-Revisited (1987), featured stripped-down vibrant versions of bone-crunchers by Holocaust, Diamond Head, Budgie, Killing Joke and The Misfits. The EP was a significant landmark not only because it landed them chart positions (when all they intended was to have a bit of fun after some serious touring) but because it show-cased the kind of music – late-70s and early 80s New Wave Of British Heavy Metal – that had inspired Ulrich to put together the ultimate metal band.

The next album, . . . *And Justice For All* (1988), saw the Metallica bandwagon thunder on: it entered the UK chart at #4, and stayed in the US chart for a year. Unfortunately, a truly bizarre production sound shoved the drums so far to the front of the mix that the bass was reduced to a wallowing rumble. This was compounded by overly complex arrangements, robbing the songs of their immediacy. Despite the criticisms, the band showed that they were capable of re-creating their former glories in the shape of "Dyer's

James Hetfield boasts about last weekend's fishing trip.

DARREN EDWARDS

METALCORE

Are they punk or are they metal? Another sub-genre impossible to pin down, metalcore involves a quaking fusion of hardcore and heavy metal, though without the by-product of extreme speed. Instead there is room for some steel-riveted mid-paced chugging, often referred to as 'mosh parts', designed to whip the crowd into a frenzy. Bands such as **Madball**, **Hatebreed** and **Sick Of It All** excel in this field.

Another vital component to the extreme heaviness is a vocalist capable of stripping flesh from bone with the power of his voice alone. Often the vocals are completely unintelligible, a shame because, lyrically, the topics often centre upon politics, social commentary and identity.

A trait among some bands is an adherence to nonstandard song structure, effectively eliminating the usual verse-chorus pattern. This complex nonlinearity makes for some dizzying dynamic invention and almost jazz-like craziness – hence the related tag of 'math metal' or 'mathcore' – with bands such as **The Dillinger Escape Plan**, **Converge** and **Mastodon** among the growing number using this approach.

Often what confuses matters is the image. It is quite likely that a metalcore band will look more like a hardcore outfit – short-hair, tattoos, maybe sporting skatewear – than a classic metal combo. Then again, just to really twist things, the sound is so malleable that it's possible for a band to display metalcore elements and yet sound more metal than hardcore. In other words, the sound covers a wide spectrum, with bands such as **Killswitch Engage** and **Lamb Of God** sitting more towards the metal end – with their thrashier sound and nods to the more melodic old school of metal.

Eve", "Harvester Of Sorrow" and the monumental "One".

As record sales soared, the Bay-Area boys were awarded Grammys for Best Metal Performance in 1990 (for "One") and 1991 (for a cover of Queen's "Stone Cold Crazy"), then with the arrival of *Metallica* (1991) the group made a leap into the rock superleague. By recruiting **Bob Rock** as producer, they turned out an album which had a clean, commercial edge but still appealed to veteran fans, even if Rock's penchant for string arrangements turned the already slushy sentimentality of "Nothing Else Matters" into elevator music. Largely mid-paced and somewhat lacking in the speed and aggression of yore, the new record nevertheless contained one of their all-time fan faves in the shape of "Enter Sandman", its pile-driving riff the inspiration to thousands of bedroom guitarists.

The following three years brought an extensive touring schedule, including a tastefully titled live box set, *Live Shit: Binge And Purge* (1993), and a prolonged period in the studio putting together their next magnum opus, *Load* (1996). This was melody-metal supreme with Hetfield re-staking his claim as the genre's best contemporary practitioner. It was released to hugely positive reviews – "the only heavy metal band that adults can listen to without feeling their IQ diminishing", said one grateful critic – and met with predictably huge sales. *Reload* (1997) was more than a sequel thrown together from leftovers and while it had its patchy moments, it was, on the whole, a satisfying

plateful of swaggering, cranium-caving badness. What turned off some of their most devoted followers was the accompanying change in image; the decision was taken to give their street-level credibility an alternative spin and nowhere was this more painfully evident than in the arty photography gracing the CD booklets.

Having decided that they would avoid indulging in binge bouts of recording followed by vast stretches of touring, the band opted for a more productive schedule following the *Load* sessions. Therefore almost exactly one year after the release of *Reload* they knocked out *Garage Inc.* (1998). The double album consisted of the previously long-deleted *Garage Days* EP plus a whole host of other B-side cover versions, while the second disc contained a clutch of newly recorded covers from artists as diverse as Thin Lizzy and Nick Cave. The sound was rawer and more spontaneous, making for a welcome change from their often anal studio dabbling. But to keep the *Load* albums firmly on the agenda, a state-of-the-art concert video, *Cunning Stunts* (1998), was released directly afterwards. And then it all went a little pear-shaped – at least as far as the average heavy metal fan was concerned. With bank balances bulging once more the band decided that it would be a great idea to reinterpret their live set with full orchestral support. To this end conductor/composer **Michael Kamen** was recruited along with the San Francisco Symphony Orchestra for a blast through the Metalli-repertoire, complete with sweeping

Metal Movies

Rock and metal songs feature on plenty of soundtracks but there are few movies that use rock and metal as the basis of a story. Nevertheless, search hard and some interesting titles pop up. These films aren't exactly classics but some of them come damn close...

Trick Or Treat (1986)
Directed by Charles Martin Smith; starring Marc Price, Tony Fields
Taking its cue directly form the concerns of 80s metal – backwards masking, the moral majority out to demonize the music and so forth – this messy amalgamation of horror and comedy is far from perfect. It does, however, boast a cracking soundtrack and features amusing appearances from **Ozzy Osbourne** and **Gene Simmons**.

Bill And Ted's Excellent Adventure (1989)
Directed by Stephen Herek; starring Keanu Reeves, Alex Winter
Arriving just as hair metal was about to bite the dust, this bodacious movie provides unreconstructed rock fare for kids who like to play on eleven. Reeves and Winter are perfect as the lovable dopey heroes who travel through time trying to do their history homework.

Bill And Ted's Bogus Journey (1991)
Directed by Peter Hewitt; starring Keanu Reeves, Alex Winter
Hipper and funnier than the first outing the two leads are almost completely overshadowed by the superb character of the Grim Reaper cheekily pinched from Ingmar Bergman's *The Seventh Seal*. This is worth watching just for the marvellous scenes where the heroes have to challenge the scythe-wielding one to a series of games.

Wayne's World (1992)
Directed by Penelope Spheeris; starring Mike Myers, Dana Carvey
Schwing! Along with Bill and Ted, Wayne and Garth are responsible for coining some of the most enduring 90s rock phrases. The plot is nothing to get excited about but the execution is rarely less than ludicrously charming, hinging almost entirely upon Myers' excellent performance.

Airheads (1994)
Directed by Michael Lehmann; starring Brendan Fraser, Steve Buscemi, Adam Sandler
How do you get your band noticed? Hijack the local radio station, of course. With water pistols. This film contains some of the sharpest, funniest lines ever penned for a metal movie, even if the end result isn't quite a master-piece. And remember Lemmy *is* God.

Still Crazy (1998)
Directed by Brian Gibson; starring Stephen Rea, Billy Connolly, Jimmy Nail, Bill Nighy, Timothy Spall
Scripted by veteran British comedy writers Dick Clement and Ian La Frenais this movie is both extremely funny and features well fleshed-out characters. The storyline about a band that reunites long after their glory days are past isn't exactly original but the performances are spot on and the music is excellent.

Detroit Rock City (1999)
Directed by Adam Rifkin; starring Giuseppe Andrews, James DeBello, Edward Furlong
With a title like that, this movie can only be about one band: **Kiss**. Or rather about the lengths their fans would go to in the 70s to get to a show. It's not as funny as it could be but features some neat little in-jokes and references Kiss-ophiles will enjoy spotting.

Almost Famous (2000)
Directed by Cameron Crowe; Starring Billy Crudup, Kate Hudson, Patrick Fugit, Frances McDormand
Crowe wrote the script as well as directed. After all, the story is based upon his own past as a teenage writer for *Rolling Stone* magazine, the first band he ever toured with being the Allman Brothers. Fugit plays the young William Miller given an amazing break to launch a career as a rock journo and it's in the fine details of the drama that Crowe shows his deft touch as director.

Rock Star (2001)
Directed by Stephen Herek; starring Mark Wahlberg, Jennifer Anniston
This movie is something of a lost opportunity. Based upon the story of ex- **Judas Priest** singer **Tim Owens**, who got the job after featuring in a Priest tribute band, this promised much. In the end the script settles for a love story with a painfully predictable plot. Still, the music is good and the gig scenes are exciting enough.

School Of Rock (2003)
Directed by Richard Linklater; starring Jack Black
Black playing loser Dewey Finn is nothing short of amazing in this comedy. The premise is thin – Finn accidentally lands a job in a school where he actually finds his calling – but it's all carried off with such wit and reverence for rock that the result is hilarious. The school kids are a revelation too.

strings while the conventionally amplified Hetfield and co. did their best to drown out everyone in the process. The mixed results could be sampled on *S&M* (1999).

After that, the cracks began to appear: Newsted departed in early 2001 and Hetfield eventually ended up in rehab. All of which slowed down the recording of their next album. In the end producer **Bob Rock** handled the bass playing and even ended up sharing writing credits, rather than it simply being the James and Lars show (as had been the case for much of the band's career). Another change came in the style of production which was more ragged and raw than the usual overly detailed approach. The resulting *St Anger* (2003) surprised many fans and critics alike. If their previous studio efforts had been akin to a gleaming Ferrari, *St Anger* was like a greasy, turbocharged wrecking truck, throbbing with menace beneath the hood and about as subtle as a punch to the throat. Unfortunately, possibly influenced by the more stripped-down and economical approach of nu-metal, there was a distinct lack of variety, most notably, guitar solos. Appearing to be different just for the sake of it, it also didn't help that the snare drum sounded like Lars was banging on a rusty radiator with a piece of lead piping. Still that didn't stop it from topping charts pretty much the world over, though like *Load* and *Reload* its appeal was somewhat limited.

With a new-found urgency to their game Metallica recruited ex-**Suicidal Tendencies** and **Ozzy Osbourne** bassist **Rob Trujillo** to fill the hole in their ranks. Once again they hit the road in spectacular style while the *Some Kind Of Monster* documentary – filmed during the *St Anger* period – gave the fans a warts-and-all perspective on the world's biggest metal band.

⊙ Ride The Lightning
1984; Vertigo

The first glimmerings of greatness. Big fat riffs, delivered with technical precision. Hetfield's vocals sound meaner and more mature. Definitely a spandex-free zone.

⊙ ...And Justice For All
1988; Vertigo

Surely the prizewinner in the 'Most Complex Riffing' category. It consists of mainly Hetfield/ Ulrich tunes with so many parts they're in danger of disappearing up their own backsides. High points include the two hit singles "Harvester Of Sorrow" and "One".

⊙ Metallica
1991; Vertigo

Big rock production values made this slick and predominantly mid-paced – nonetheless, a landmark metal release of the 90s.

⊙ Load
1996; Vertigo

You want doomy metal? Ace-heavy balladry? A lone acoustic ballad? Metallica show they can do the lot better than anyone around.

⊙ Garage Inc.
1998; Vertigo

Forget about tracking down those elusive B-sides and grab this double album. When the covers work, this is splendid stuff, and even when they don't (check out the unintentionally hilarious version of "Whisky In The Jar") it's still tons of fun.

⊙ St Anger
2003; Vertigo

Gone is the anal sonic meddling, and in comes speed and snarling aggression once again. Hetfield sounds incandescently livid for much of this album, but what happened to Lars's drum sound and Kirk's guitar – did he forget to plug it in?

MINISTRY

Formed Chicago, US, 1981

Along with Nine Inch Nails, the adventures of **Al Jourgensen** (vocals/guitar/ programming) as **Ministry** have become synonymous with industrial metal. Their abrasive, intense and clattering sound, featuring not just huge, processed guitars but a wall of electronic and computer-generated mayhem, influenced scores of artists. As well as this, the political nature of the lyrics have earned the band a reputation as something of a major countercultural force. Jourgensen's dissatisfaction with US politics, and especially George W. Bush, prompted him to align with various organizations dedicated to removing the president through the ballot box.

It wasn't always this serious, however, because Ministry's roots lie in 80s synth pop, the *With Sympathy* (1983) album bearing little resemblance to the furious noise that would be released a few years down the line. The next experiment was *Twitch* (1986) which at least hinted at the direction Jourgensen would take; he also worked on numerous side-projects, including the

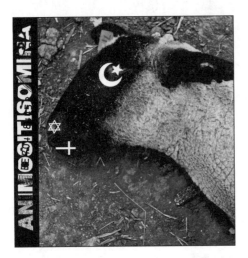

Revolting Cocks, Pailhead, Acid Horse, PTP, 1000 Homo DJs and Lard. The real breakthrough occurred with the addition of Paul Barker (bass/programming) along with a few of Barker's cohorts from the Blackouts. *The Land Of Rape And Honey* (1988), released on Sire Records, was the start of the revolution, an unholy combination of guitar, machine and ear-scalding distortion. The new focus was pushed even further with *The Mind Is A Terrible Thing To Taste* (1989); the

dance-based influences were still there but subverted to propel dark spirals of guitar and twisted vocals.

The live mini-LP and video, *In Case You Didn't Feel Like Showing Up* (1990), provided a taste of the band's live show but it was little more than an amusing distraction while Jourgensen planned his next move. This was a stroke of genius called "Jesus Built My Hotrod", a single featuring a brilliant gibberish vocal line from **Butthole Surfer, Gibby Haynes**. While the single introduced Ministry to the MTV generation there was even more industrial fun to be found on *Psalm 69: The Way To Succeed And The Way To Suck Eggs* (1992) which went into the UK's Top 40 and to #27 in the US. Ministry had officially arrived and would capitalize on their new level of notoriety by touring with Sepultura, the Red Hot Chili Peppers and playing Lollapalooza.

Incredibly, with the scene set for more platinum-selling aggro-metal, no Ministry album appeared for another four years. There were stories about bust-ups, legal problems, Jourgensen's heroin habit, and general discord. The Revolting Cocks managed *Linger Fickin' Good … And Other Barnyard Oddities* in 1993, and Jourgensen

MODERN PROG ROCK AND METAL

Beyond the continuing careers of the 80s prog acts, bands professing a love of convoluted musicianship and conceptual themes are still popping up. Among the best of these are Sweden's **Flower Kings**, America's **Spock's Beard**, the UK's exceptional **Porcupine Tree** – who lie somewhere in the grey area between space rock, prog and various other categories – and the supergroup **Transatlantic**, composed of members of **Dream Theater**, the Flower Kings, Marillion and Spock's Beard.

Canada's premier rock export, **Rush**, have a long history of overtly progressive albums and are still touring and releasing records to great acclaim. Sometimes also referred to as art rock, this genre identity describes bands who would otherwise be relatively tough to define. The weird and experimental **Tool** display progressive flourishes without resorting to crazy keyboard-bothering antics and toured with King Crimson in tow, providing an interesting clue about their musical proclivities. Canada's **Voivod** evolved from a thrash band into a strange metallic beast spewing jazzy riffs while attempting to channel Pink Floyd; likewise the epic melancholy of Swedish metal depressives **Opeth**, who have worked with Porcupine Tree's Steven Wilson.

Invoking the term prog metal, as opposed to simply rock, conjures up a definite cluster of bands whose musicianship is both faultless and more aggressively intense, which sometimes allows a bleed over both into and from power- and symphonic-metal. America's **Symphony X** are among those producing powerful material – really getting up to speed with V (2000) – and the long-running **Savatage** evolved rapidly from a straightforward metal band into a full-blown concept act. Of all of them, however, there are generally three groups named by fans as key players: **Queensrÿche, Dream Theater** and **Fates Warning**.

Queensrÿche are acknowledged as one of the most commercially successful prog metal acts, their *Operation: Mindcrime* (1988) and *Empire* (1990) albums being among their best. Dream Theater's take on prog is more akin to the vintage 70s notion in that theirs is a sound that features some truly jaw-dropping instrumental passages and keyboard work as well as over-arching themes and narratives. American metallers Fates Warning began life as a Maiden-esque sounding band before letting their imaginations run away with them on albums such as *The Spectre Within* (1985), *Awaken The Guardian* (1986) and *No Exit* (1988), the latter containing the eight-part, 21-minute epic "The Ivory Gate Of Dreams".

dabbled in some production work, but it was altogether a missed opportunity. When Ministry finally got themselves sorted, *Filth Pig* (1996) arrived to less than ecstatic reviews; crushing martial guitars ruled this time round at the expense of the usual samples barrage, but what killed it for most fans was the plodding pace. *Dark Side Of The Spoon* (1999) appeared after yet another period of silence following another diversion with Lard. And while it fared better than *Filth Pig,* the album again failed to ignite the same level of interest as *Psalm 69.*

At this point Ministry parted company with Warners, who issued *Greatest Fits* (2001), and signed to Sanctuary who promptly released the live *Sphinctour* (2002) album. With George W. Bush in the White House presiding over America's new climate of fear, Jourgensen and Ministry turned in *Animositisomina* (2003), feeding off the same rage that informed *Psalm 69* (recorded while Bush Sr. was president). The same level of anger was focused on *Houses Of The Molé* (2004), which was recorded without Barker but with a whole new crew of Ministry noise-smiths in tow. With a presidential campaign under way, Jourgensen's anger with the US political system seemed unquenchable, giving fans of old the kind of warm glow only rebellious, industrial-strength metal can achieve.

⊙ Psalm 69: The Way To Succeed And The Way To Suck Eggs
1992; Warners

Ministry had been building up to this masterpiece for a few years. A record that positively seethes with creative anger, prompting Jourgensen to joke in interviews that he does his best work when there are Republicans in the White House.

MISFITS

Formed Lodi, New Jersey, US, 1977

Though strictly speaking not metal, the Misfits are, nevertheless, one of those legendary bands whose influence has spread far and wide, their horror punk schtick inspiring the likes of Marilyn Manson, Rob Zombie and, of course, Metallica. In fact, the latter's cover versions of "Green Hell" and "Last Caress" on their 1987 *Garage Days Re-revisited* EP were responsible for promoting the Misfits at a time when the band were out of action and locked in various legal battles. Their popularity had previously been at a largely cult level, a following cultivated through the release of highly collectible seven-inch singles, EPs and a tiny handful of albums. Of course, by the time Metallica bashed out their cover versions, Misfits's prime mover **Glenn Danzig** (vocals) had moved on to **Samhain**

The Misfits – available to hire for childrens' parties.

MICK HUTSON/REDFERNS

227

and his own solo career – even so the Misfits remain the epitome of punk cool.

In the late 70s the Misfits line-up was extremely volatile, but it eventually settled down when Danzig teamed up with **Jerry Only** (bass). One of their longest serving drummers was **Arthur 'The Goog' Googy** and their most reliable guitarist turned out to be **Doyle**, Jerry's younger brother. With a name taken from Marilyn Monroe's last film, and a fixation with B-movie horror flicks, 1950s sci-fi and early rock'n'roll, the Misfits revelled in monsters and gore, while other punk bands simply railed against the system. Club gigs were booked, rehearsal sessions were played and the band worked at establishing themselves by issuing releases on their own Blank label which later became Plan 9, named after *Plan 9 From Outer Space* – one of the worst sci-fi movies ever made. "Cough/Cool" backed by "She" (1977) was the first record of many, including the *Bullet* EP, "Horror Business" and the twelve-inch *Beware* EP.

In 1979 they adopted their famous Crimson Ghost mascot – taken from a 1946 US adventure serial in which the Crimson Ghost was a villainous character with a skeletal face – who began popping up on record sleeves. But their first real album didn't arrive until 1982 when *Walk Among Us* gave the faithful something more than just a two-minute fix of catchy riffing and Danzig's over-the-top howling in Evil Elvis style. At this point the band had also perfected the ghoul look, complete with sunken eye make-up and slicked forward devilocks. The *Evilive* mini-LP and *Earth A.D./Wolfsblood* followed in 1983 and suddenly it was all over. Compilations such as *Legacy Of Brutality* (1985) appeared as Danzig went off to form **Samhain**, while the others hung up their tattered black leathers and wondered what to do next.

It's a little-known fact that Jerry and Doyle briefly dabbled in metal by forming **Kryst The Conqueror**, utilizing the vocal talents of **Jeff Scott Soto**, best known for singing in the band of guitarist, Yngwie Malmsteen. Apparently an album was recorded but only an EP was released in 1990. In the meantime legal wranglings were going on as the brothers tried to reach a settlement with Danzig over the use of the Misfits name.

Eventually some agreement was reached and the Misfits were reborn in 1995 with a line-up that included **Michale Graves**

(vocals) and **Dr Chud** (drums). *American Psycho* (1997) arrived through Geffen (after some live shows), though the sound was a lot slicker and calculated to appeal to the mass market. Having switched to Roadrunner Records, *Famous Monsters* (1999) shamelessly worked through songs involving just about every movie and comic book horror character they could think of. *Cuts From The Crypt* (2001) dished up some interesting rarities and demos from various recording sessions, but *Project 1950* (2003) was basically a sorry collection of 50s cover versions supposedly showcasing the band's roots. By now Jerry Only was living up to his name as the sole remaining original member, the other positions now taken by **Dez Cadena** (guitar, ex-**Black Flag**) and **Marky Ramone** (drums).

⦿ Legacy Of Brutality
1985; Caroline

Walk Among Us is great but this compilation of biting punk rock and shock tactics should tell you all you need to know about the band that had such a profound effect on generations of punks and metalheads.

MONSTER MAGNET

Formed New Jersey, US, 1989

"An off-duty police woman came on the bus once, drunk and medicated, wanting sex. She scared the hell out of us ... We're screaming 'Call the cops!' and she's screaming 'I am the cops...!'"
Dave Wyndorf on groupies

At the forefront of the movement dubbed 'stoner rock' you'll find the incomparable **Monster Magnet**, led by leather-trousered, devil-whiskered, arch space cadet **Dave Wyndorf**. Having released a number of singles and albums while trying to launch his career into orbit, Wyndorf was an already established, if relatively unsuccessful, musician when the Magnet were formed in 1989. Steeped in everything from the trashy rock ethic of The Stooges to the imponderable drone of space-rock stalwarts Hawkwind, Wyndorf (**guitar/vocals**) had a unique vision which was finally realized when he assembled **Tim Cronin** (vocals), **John McBain** (guitar),

Monster Magnet with the 'leather-trousered, devil-whiskered, arch space cadet' Dave Wyndorf (seated).

Joe Calandra (bass), and **John Kleiman** (drums). Their first feedback-soaked psycho-rock outing was a self-titled mini-LP released in 1990.

Afterwards Wyndorf decided to take the spotlight and lead singer duties, a move which allowed him to indulge his wild'n'dangerous rock persona without hindrance. The band then focused on their first full-length album for independent label Caroline. *Spine Of God* (1991), a raw and rolling slab of punk-suffused psychedelia, was followed by the space-jamming mini-LP *Tab* (1992). Having attracted the attention of A&M, McBain was then replaced by **Ed Mundell** and the band concentrated on creating what would become the titanic *Superjudge* album. Released in 1993, it finally proved that Monster Magnet's very own chauffeur-driven UFO had landed. Gone

were the more self-indulgent, jam-oriented and feedback-inspired trimmings, to be replaced by a leaner more metallic and riff-based power. Even with the excesses stripped away the band still sounded like an outfit trapped in an alarmingly psychedelic time-warp. While the music had a toxic charm all its own, the band continued to look like a bunch of stoners who had accidentally wandered in off the street and into the studio.

As perpetual outsiders – with an accompanying fashion sense – Wyndorf and crew continued towards their rendezvous with the mothership at warp factor nine, pausing only to polish their production efforts for 1995's *Dopes To Infinity*. Nestling within the stoned-out grooves of that particularly heavy record was the band's first major hit single "Negasonic Teenage Warhead", a song with the requisite weirdness and appeal to break

229

the band into the wider public consciousness. Despite this, the albums themselves were simply not selling well enough, even though the critical reaction was good, so Wyndorf slunk into hotel-room exile in Las Vegas to reshape the band's direction. Who knows what stellar deities visited Wyndorf during this period, or what substances proved to be an inspiration, but from the nonstop glitter and neon of Sin City the quintessential retro-glitz of *Powertrip* was born (1998). This sleek and glamorous album positively bulged with Wyndorf's customary tales of cosmic strangeness, helped by the addition of guitarist **Phil Caivano**. Gone were the ragged T-shirts and ripped jeans and in came black leather, evil shades and an attitude acknowledging their status as avenging prophets of galactic rock, a fact celebrated by standout cut "Space Lord" on which Wyndorf proclaimed himself to be the king of the cosmos. The single, plus the title track, was supported by videos which used styles more prevalent in hip-hop promos, thus enhancing the band's visual appeal significantly. This was no bad thing, considering the ravages their excessive lifestyle had heaped upon them so far.

At last the band were on a sustainable course – presumably with the controls set for the heart of the sun – and the formula was refined and repeated to greater success with *God Says No* (2001), a stunning *tour de force* released through Polydor. Wyndorf's new-found role as chief space cadet had him standing legs akimbo sporting leather strides with a shiny chrome cod-piece and brandishing a vicious-looking bullwhip (the black-as-death shades go without saying). If their pre-

vious effort had been a watershed then this gave Wyndorf's usually bombastic writing a welcome edge of levity. The title track was a laidback interstellar cruise; "Kiss Of The Scorpion" focused on a 60s Hammond-fuelled vibe; "Gravity Well" took the spirit of Led Zeppelin's "Black Country Woman" and pulled it backwards through a black hole; and the single "Heads Explode" was an MTV-aimed sonic supernova.

Unfortunately, being stuck on a major label, with all its attendant marketing and business baggage, didn't suit Wyndorf at all, and it wasn't until with *Monolithic Baby* (2004) on the more downscale SPV label that he launched the Magnet once more. In the meantime he busied himself working on the soundtrack to the motorcycle madness flick *Torque*. *Monolithic Baby* was recorded with stalwarts Mundell and Caivano, **Jim Baglino** (bass) and **Michael Wildwood** and **Josh Freas** on drumming duties, (with **Bob Pantella** taking over in the live arena). All the standard trademarks were present, but Wyndorf made more of his formative influences this time round by including "The Right Stuff", originally by Robert Calvert of Hawkwind infamy, and the Unicorn track, "There's No Way Out Of Here". Of course, the original numbers were topped through with the regulation levels of venom and attitude, and the whole exuded a leanness and hunger that reinforced the band's status as long-established purveyors of monumental metal.

⊙ Dopes To Infinity
1995; A&M

A space rock collection of quite impeccable credentials, this boasts the titanic "Negasonic Teenage Warhead". Simply sublime, baby.

⊙ Powertrip
1998; A&M

The ultimate stoner trip – and then some. When Wyndorf tells you he's a freakin' Space Lord you have no choice but to believe him.

⊙ God Says No
2001; A&M

Sleek, streamlined, stunning; Wyndorf pulls together a gloriously over-the-top acid-fuelled psychedelic binge of colossal proportions. This is your gateway to the stars – essential.

⊙ Monolithic Baby
2004; SPV

Despite the long break Wyndorf and his motley bunch of space cowboys can do this drone metal thing with consummate ease. A terrific and mean return to the fray.

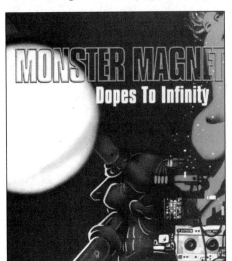

MONTROSE

Formed San Francisco, California US, 1973; disbanded 1977

For a short period in the 70s one of the finest heavy rock bands to emerge from the sunshine state was this four-piece, featuring the slamming six-string talents of one **Ronnie Montrose**. Montrose had carved out a small niche for himself as a session player for a variety of artists such as Van Morrison and Herbie Hancock, but when it came to his own work he envisioned something far more visceral.

Calling on the services of his old buddy **Bill Church** (bass), and unknown quantities **Sammy Hagar** (vocals) and **Denny Carmassi** (drums), Montrose set about creating what would become one of the finest early metal albums to emerge from the US. The guitarist had already met **Ted Templeman** – who would go on to produce Van Halen's greatest albums – enlisting him to twiddle the knobs on the debut album.

With hindsight the combination of talent really couldn't fail. The 1973 eponymous album was a monster of rock from start to finish and contained absolutely no ballads. It was just chiselled riff after riff, a sizzling guitar work-out featuring possibly the rockingest opening trio of tracks ever to grace a heavy rock album: "Rock The Nation", the Hagar-penned "Bad Motor Scooter" (check out Ronnie making like a souped-up gas-guzzler with his six-string) and "Space Station No. 5".

The album didn't exactly take the charts by storm, but the band raged back with a new bassist in **Alan Fitzgerald** and another fistful of ballsy, bluesy metal entitled *Paper Money* (1974). The title track and "I Got The Fire" stood out as obvious bruisers, but the whole album was a work of brilliance, positively smoking with dirty licks and Hagar's demented alley-cat yowl.

They almost scored a hat trick with *Warner Bros. Presents Montrose!* (1975), but some of the tracks fell just a little short of terrific. By now Hagar had gone solo – he and Ronnie had experienced a clash of egos – and been replaced by **Bob James**; the band had also added **Jim Alcivar** (keyboards), thus expanding the sound but losing some of the hunger of the early material. Also lacking was Templeman's magic touch as Montrose him-

self took over at the desk. *Jump On It* (1976) was a much better stab at recapturing the raw power that crackled through the debut, but was somewhat overshadowed by the dodgy sleeve – featuring a close up on a pair of bikini briefs – which gave the title track a whole new and unintended meaning.

Despite the attempt to get back on track, it rapidly dawned on Ronnie that it was impossible to re-create something by endless tinkering. The band folded, but it wasn't the end of the guitarist's career, although he never created anything quite so instinctively metallic ever again. Relaunching himself under his full name in the late 70s, he then reunited with Denny Carmassi to form **Gamma**, producing four albums with the band. Of his later work the album *Mean* (1987) marked a return to rock, but disciples of shameless guitar heroics still regard the early Montrose albums as the real thing. And with good reason.

Montrose
1973; Warners

A genuine, grade-A heavy rock classic. Hagar is a howling party machine on vocals and Montrose takes no prisoners in his never-ending search for truly filthy guitar tones.

Paper Money
1974; Warners

Another amazing album rammed with great songs. A touch more diverse-sounding than the debut, this is nevertheless a vital and vigorous follow-up.

GARY MOORE

Born Belfast, Northern Ireland, April 4, 1952

As far as axe heroics go **Gary Moore** is one of the best. Far from indulging in the flash and empty shredding of so many less considerate players, he is renowned for his searing and incisive style, though for much of the 90s and into this decade his output has been blues-oriented rather than the bluesy heavy rock of the 80s.

The early 70s was the time in which Moore really began to feel his way towards a style he could call his own. He recorded two fondly regarded albums with **Skid Row**, before dishing up one of his own, *Grinding Stone* (1973), with the **Gary Moore Band**. During this period Moore got to know **Phil**

Lynott and it was with Thin Lizzy that he first made a major impact, initially as a replacement for Eric Bell early on in Lizzy's career, then as a substitute when Brian Robertson left, before making a significant contribution on *Black Rose (A Rock Legend)* .

Meanwhile he had recorded *Back On The Streets* (1978), featuring a version of the Phil Lynott/ Thin Lizzy tune "Don't Believe A Word", while the 1979 top-ten hit "Parisienne Walkways" (guest vocals provided by Lynott) fixed him in the minds of the rock world as the bloke who made his guitar wail with passion. It was precisely the kind of signature work that would define his performing identity for years to come.

Before embarking on his most metallic period he released an eponymous album with his band **G-Force** in 1980. It was in 1982, however, that Moore's career as a solo hard rocker was forged with *Corridors Of Power*. A reaction to the Cold War and the shadow of nuclear destruction, *Victims Of The Future* (1984) also featured some truly blistering guitar work and a modest hit single in "Empty Rooms". True, Moore was never much of a natural vocalist but he made up for it with the kind of guitar magic that sent shivers down the spine and demanded some serious tennis racquet action. The live album *We Want Moore* (1984) provided a sample of what Moore's live show was all about, but anyone who doubted his amazing gift for riffs and fluid solos only had to make their way to Donington Monsters Of Rock in 1984 to catch him ignite the stage with his six-string pyrotechnics.

The roll continued with "Out In The Fields" which teamed Moore up with his old Thin Lizzy buddy Phil Lynott for a rousing anti-war rampage, which charged all the way up to #5 in the UK charts, the duo appearing on TV wearing scarlet military tunics. The album *Run For Cover* (1985) also featured the Lynott-penned "Military Man", but it would be the last truly heavy outing for Moore. *Rockin' Every Night: Live In Japan* (1986) effectively drew a line under the rock era.

Never satisfied with sticking to one sound for too long Moore decided to explore his Irish heritage for a couple of albums – *Wild Frontier* (1987) and *After The War* (1989) – before heading straight for the blues, and a string of quality albums which really had very little to do with heavy rock or metal. He

returned with some heavier material on 2002's *Scars*, featuring **Cass Lewis** (bass, ex-**Skunk Anansie**) and **Darrin Mooney** (drums, **Primal Scream**). The album and DVD *Live At The Monsters Of Rock* (2003) were captured when the power trio provided support on Whitesnake's 2003 tour. The following year, however, Moore returned to the bluesy sound with *Power Of The Blues*.

⊙ Victims Of The Future
1984; Virgin

OK, so Moore isn't a natural vocalist but his feisty guitar work more than makes up for it on this cracking album.

⊙ We Want Moore
1984; Virgin

As far as Moore live albums go – and there are a few knocking around – this one is pretty good. It kicks off with "Murder In The Skies" and includes Gazza getting all emotional with "Empty Rooms".

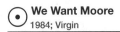

MORBID ANGEL

Formed Florida, US, 1984

The epitome of the Floridian death metal sound, **Morbid Angel** are one of the most technically proficient and uncompromising bands currently pushing at the boundaries of the genre. Influenced by bands such as Death and Slayer they have taken the basic thrash template and completely twisted it into their image, bringing precision and passion to a music usually obsessed with simply being as evil as possible. So influential has their contribution been to the development of underground metal, that in 1999 *Rolling Stone* counted Morbid Angel among the top ten most important metal bands of all time.

Ever the perfectionists, the band – then a trio – recorded, then abandoned, their debut album in the mid-80s because they were unhappy with the result. A quick line-up shift later and **Trey Azagthoth** (guitars), **Pete Sandoval** (drums), **Richard Brunelle** (guitars) and **David Vincent** (vocals/bass) materialized in a cloud of sulphur with the masterful *Altars Of Madness* (1989) on Earache, recorded at the legendary Morrisound studios in Tampa, Florida. Almost at a stroke the band had placed themselves at the forefront of a genre oozing with slime-ridden reprobates vying for the crown of sonic pestilence. What set them

above their peers was an intelligence and artistic vision that made their thrash not just nasty but downright toxic, and their overt occult leanings – much of their lyrical ideas being spawned by Azagthoth's unusual religious beliefs – never masked their sheer power and economy. Azagthoth was an axe shredder with a style all his own and the riff-mongering was of such titanic and speedy proportions it made many of their peers sound like rank amateurs. And then there was Sandoval's drumming which set the standard for blitzkrieg bombast.

Next up was *Blessed Are The Sick* (1991), a record now considered to be a classic of deathly thrash. In production terms it surpassed their debut for clarity and energy and also featured Vincent at his bloodcurdling best, his vocals seemingly transmitted from the lungs of hell. Then in early 1992 *Abominations Of Desolation*, their first studio demos recorded way back in 1986, finally saw the light of day. Continuing to give albums titles in alphabetical order – was this the method to their madness? – meant that *Covenant* (1993) came next, a groundbreaking album which challenged the received wisdom as to what constituted death metal. The band's stature was further boosted by global touring and recognition from the mainstream labels; in the US the album was released via Giant, an affiliate of Warners. But by this point Brunelle had left to be replaced by **Erik Rutan** for *Domination* (1995).

Entangled In Chaos (1996), produced by Azagthoth and recorded during their European tour of the same year, showcased the band as a supertight thrash unit eminently capable of reproducing their studio excesses in a live context. Moving on through the alphabet and you get to the tongue-twisting

Formulas Fatal To The Flesh (1998), featuring a new line-up, with Vincent and Rutan out and **Steve Tucker** was in on bass and vocals. Stripped down to a trio Azagthoth handled all the guitar parts and allowed himself full licence to experiment. When the album was reissued in 1999, *Love Of Lava* – basically most of the inventive strangeness of Azagthoth's guitar solos distilled onto one disc – was included as a bonus CD (only 5000 copies were made).

With Rutan back in the band *Gateways To Annihilation* (2000) continued to delve into occult lore and Azagthoth's own peculiar philosophical perspective, as well as providing a spot of guitar synth. Musically it was a refinement of the style they had spent so much blood and sweat developing since the beginning.

Like a death metal yo-yo Rutan was gone from the band by the time of *Heretic* (2003), an album with an underlying theme rooted in numerology; everything from the artwork to the timings between songs and the actual number of tracks was imbued with occult significance.

⦿ Blessed Are The Sick
1991; Earache

This is very scary stuff indeed. Azagthoth's guitar histrionics are simply jaw-dropping in their audacity, which makes the blasphemies and horror all the more threatening.

Mortiis

Born Skien, Norway, July 25, 1975

"So I'm standing there in front of a big audience with my pants down and a small little dick sticking out and I'm like this is the worst day of my life. Which it was." Mortiis on the perils of live strip shows.

Mortiis has been dubbed everything from a freak, to a troll, to a visionary; he has been ridiculed, lauded and treated as a circus sideshow. One thing is for sure: as an artist he's way out there, and is about as eccentric as they come.

As far as careers go, the experimental multi-instrumentalist – real name **Håvard Ellefson** – has had something of strange run.

PAUL HARRIES

Mortiis doesn't feel human until he's had his morning coffee.

He first came to prominence with black metal pioneers **Emperor** back in the very early 1990s and was a member of the inner circle of the extreme Scandinavian metal scene. During that time, inspired by the mythology of both his homeland and the dark fantasy of books such as The Lord Of The Rings he began experimenting with the prosthetic make-up that would eventually become his trademark. Just as Emperor were beginning to make some progress he decided to leave and strike out on his own.

Rumours began to circulate about how the wacky musician, who lived halfway up a mountain, would commune freely with the spirits of the forests. Some thought he was stark raving bonkers, others thought he was a genius, as the alter ego he had created for

himself – by now fully realized with prosthetic pointy ears and a beak-like nose – seemed to take over. Accessorizing with some truly bizarre bat wings and black leather, Mortiis had transformed himself into a creature who wouldn't have looked out of place in the armies of Sauron.

The 1990s saw him release a string of largely instrumental, synth-based albums: *Født Til Å Herske* (1993), *Ånden Som Gjorde Opprör* (1994), *Reiser Av En Dimensjon Ukjent* (1995), *Crypt Of The Wizard* (1996) and *The Stargate* (1999). They appealed to a largely underground fan base who admired Mortiis' commitment and hated the mainstream. Mortiis' first UK performance, for instance, took place at the Whitby Goth Festival in 1997, where he was carried onto the stage in a coffin and performed much of his set behind a white back-lit sheet, stepping out in front every now and then to pretend to suck blood from an obligingly prostrate young lady.

By the late 1990s he had signed to Earache Records and gradually shifted away from instrumentals to a more darkwave, goth pop direction; *The Smell Of Rain* (2001) owed as much to the bleaker moments of Depeche Mode as to the industrial vibe of Nine Inch Nails. Fans of old largely hated it, but the musical progression summoned legions of new followers intrigued by the man who looked like a walking advert for a Halloween costumier. A huge amount of touring and writing followed and by the time of *The Grudge* (2004), Mortiis had assembled a stable band: **Levi Gawron** (guitar), **Asmund Sveinunggard** (bass) and **Leo Troy** (drums). The more industrial metal focus landed him with his first minor hit single, the title track of the album peaking in the UK charts at #51. Mortiis had become the toast of the rock press, a genuine maverick metaller.

The fact that the prosthetics have now become somewhat more economical in appearance, looking as though he has a mask stitched to his face, suggests that a Kiss-like unmasking might not be an impossibility. Quite where Mortiis will go next, however, is anyone's guess.

⊙ The Grudge
2004; Earache

This is way more accessible than the pointy-eared one's early ambient battle soundtracks. The gothic overtones are still present but filtered through a more industrial muse and cranked out with great swathes of guitar.

MOTHER LOVE BONE

Formed Seattle, Washington, US, 1988; disbanded 1990

Mother Love Bone were yet another much-hyped group hailing from the Seattle area who would have gone on to world-conquering highs were it not for a tragic twist of fate. Their place in metaldom is secure, however, because their demise led

to the creation of some of Seattle's finest contributions to the world of heavy rock.

Following the demise of bruising rockers **Green River**, **Stone Gossard** (guitar), **Bruce Fairweather** (guitar), and **Jeff Ament** (bass) set about the task of creating a new outfit and along the way recruited **Greg Gilmour** (drums). But their final addition, **Andrew Wood** (vocals), was their ace and joker rolled into one.

While Green River had been spewing out their furious fragmented sounds, much attention had been paid to another local group, **Malfunkshun**, fronted by Wood. Malfunkshun's sound can best be described as an explosion of punk and over-the-top 1970s glam rock; Wood could often be seen wearing outrageous silver suits and platform-soled motorcycle boots. The man considered himself to be a total rock star, even if no one else did. This blend of extreme influences and Wood's rock star persona twisted Mother Love Bone into something unique.

Though Wood was far from being a perfect singer, his presence on record cannot be underestimated. His lyrics were daring, bizarre and overblown, but he had a vision and shaped the band's sound accordingly. The first studio outing issued on Mercury, the *Shine* EP (1989), has his personality firmly stamped on it. These six outstanding cuts aroused a huge amount of interest, and were quickly followed by their first full-length album, *Apple* (1990), with lyrics reflecting Wood's larger-than-life rock star persona. Not to be outdone, the rest of the band matched the lyrical hyperbole with a huge hard rock sound that wouldn't have been out of place in the 1970s, rocking out with full guitar histrionics on tracks like "Come Bite The Apple" and laying down a gentler groove on "Man Of Golden Words".

Following a promotional tour the future looked extremely promising. However, just as *Apple* was due for release in March 1990, the band's ascent was cut short by Wood's death after an accidental heroin overdose. After such a crippling blow the remainder of the group elected to disband, although a measure of their achievement can be gauged from the fact that the beautifully swirling "Chloe Dancer/Crown of Thorns" found its way onto the soundtrack of Cameron Crowe's Seattle-based romantic comedy *Singles*. The saga does not end here though.

Following Wood's untimely death, his close friend **Chris Cornell** of **Soundgarden** began work on the **Temple of the Dog** tribute project using various members of Mother Love Bone and Soundgarden, and the then unheard of **Eddie Vedder**. This was, of course, the beginnings of **Pearl Jam**, but as they say, that's another story.

Shine
1989; Stardog Records/Mercury

Curiously lumped in with the Seattle sound, this six-track EP boasted strong melodies and classic songwriting. Wood was proving to be a twisted genius with his lyrics while the rest of the band created a musical backdrop of equal grandeur.

Apple
1990; Stardog Records/Mercury

Wood continues his self-mythologization, and the big fat production sound means that the songs sometimes verge on operatic metal. The interest whipped up by the quality of the release marked the band out for future success.

Mother Love Bone
1992; Mercury

As a posthumous release, following the huge success of Pearl Jam, this is hard to beat. It features a double-CD compilation of the band's previously released material along with the unsanctioned inclusion of the unreleased "Lady Godiva Blues".

MÖTLEY CRÜE

Formed Los Angeles, California, US, 1981

It's been said a hundred times before but that doesn't make it any less true: when it comes to sex, drugs and rock'n'roll **Mötley Crüe** are way up there in the premier league. They didn't so much write the book on archetypal bad-boy behaviour (much less read it) – they chainsawed it in half and torched it with napalm. In their time they did it all: marrying *Playboy* centrefolds, nearly killing themselves and others around them, and allegedly taking every kind of narcotic known to man. Throughout the 1980s and into the 90s Crüe needed no instruction on how to live up to the self-destructive image of pouting rock stars. They just got on with it, influencing a whole generation of glam metal.

It all started way back in 1981 when ex-London member **Nikki Sixx** (bass) decided he needed a fresh start in trying to break into the LA music scene. He recruited **Mick** **Mars** (guitar) after spotting the six-stringer's advert for a band in a local paper; he picked up **Tommy Lee** (drums) through a mutual acquaintance; and **Vince Neil** (vocals) was discovered fronting local scene fixtures **Rockandi**. Together they became Mötley Crüe, their umlauts as excessive as their lipgloss-and-spandex image. The plan was simple (if indeed it could be called a plan): to rock the world, to sell millions of records, and to sleep with as many groupies and take as many drugs as possible. Not necessarily in that order, though preferably all at the same time. And they set about accomplishing their goals with an enthusiasm bordering on monomania. Needless to say, they were soon well known not just to the denizens of LA clubs such as the Starwood, Troubadour and the Whisky A-Go-Go, but to the local constabulary as well. Their early shows involved such ridiculous and crude sub-Alice Cooper-esque theatrical spectacles as decapitating mannequins and setting each other on fire, all set to a ribald, sleazy soundtrack of punky trash metal. They looked like Kiss crossed with the New York Dolls and adhered to the kind of offstage manifesto made infamous by Steven Tyler and Joe Perry, the so-called Toxic Twins of Aerosmith. Crüe's act was hugely derivative, but no one cared when it was all so enthrallingly, tackily entertaining.

This (barely) walking nightmare of bad behaviour, doubtless kept upright only through copious applications of hairspray – the term 'hair metal' was pretty much invented for them – managed to record *Too Fast For Love* (1981), a raw collection of demos. They released it on their own Leathür label and shifted twenty thousand copies before it was picked up by Elektra Records. Which was a good thing because, with the record label bankrolling them, the Crüe could really show the world how to party. But not before their debut was polished somewhat and rereleased to capitalize on their newly expanded audience.

With the aid of producer **Tom Werman** the next move was *Shout At The Devil* (1983), an album that took their nascent sleaze metal aesthetic and bolted a sub-satanic, postapocalyptic theme on top. It was ridiculous but classic stuff. Their cover version of the Beatles's "Helter Skelter" was terrible, but there was little to fault in the thumping anthemic title track, the vicious "Bastard",

Mötley Crüe proudly show how many chords they've mastered.

and the one–two punch to the throat of "Knock 'Em Dead Kid". Not to mention the rest of the tightly produced selection of goodies, many of which would become immoveable live favourites. Naturally, around this time the band began to attract the attention of the Parents Music Resources Center (PMRC), a right-wing pressure group intent on stamping out fun of the heavy metal variety for good. The Crüe were firmly in its sights for much of the 1980s though the band regarded this more as a badge of honour than a threat.

At this point the Crüe were given one of their biggest breaks: they found themselves as support act to Ozzy Osbourne who was promoting his *Bark At The Moon* album. Playing to huge arenas across the US took the band to wholly unvisited areas of America, where the good folks simply didn't understand what was about to hit them. However, with such frenetic activity around such a volatile band it was perhaps inevitable that disaster would strike. This happened in spectacular and tragic fashion in December 1984, when a tanked-up Vince Neil crashed his car in LA. The accident killed his passenger Razzle, the drummer of upcoming glamsters Hanoi Rocks, effectively ending their career and putting Neil in front of a jury; Crüe were mad, bad and now literally dangerous to know. Amazingly Neil got off relatively lightly, with a short custodial sentence and community service, and the band's follow-up album, *Theatre Of Pain* (1985) was dedicated to the memory of Nick 'Razzle' Dingley. Maybe it was due to the shock they had received but, creatively speaking, it was one of their weakest records. That didn't, however, stop their cover of Brownsville Station's "Smokin' In The Boys Room" from becoming a hit, or indeed the ballad "Home Sweet Home" – a song dedicated to life on the road – from becoming an MTV fixture.

Far more convincing was 1987's *Girls Girls Girls,* which narrowly scraped the top slot in the US album charts and which featured such classics as "Wild Side" and, of course, the storming title track celebrating the band's love of strip joints and, well, girls. The accompanying tour, however, not only featured Lee's amazing upside-down drum solo, but had the upcoming Guns N' Roses in support. A couple of years down the line the relationship between the bands would erupt

in a long-running feud, much to everyone's enjoyment – there's nothing quite like a good spat between intoxicated rock stars. Far more seriously, at this point the various members' epic consumption of narcotics almost brought their careers to another premature end. Sixx overdosed on heroin and was effectively clinically dead for several minutes before a shot of adrenaline directly into his heart revived him.

The brush with death inspired Sixx to pen "Kickstart My Heart" one of the standout tracks on 1989's *Dr Feelgood*, a slick MTV-friendly package which topped the US album charts and made the Top 5 in the UK. Producer **Bob Rock**'s knack for obtaining muscular studio performances took the now relatively sober band's more rough'n'ready sound and moulded it into a machine of sleek power and economy. There were delicate touches of slide-guitar, bar-room boogie piano, and colourful stabs of brass. Neil's brash vocals, in particular, were buffed to create choruses of genuine air-punching quality. Just to underline the star quality of the production, backing vocals were provided by the likes of **Steven Tyler** (**Aerosmith**), **Robin Zander** and **Rick Nielsen** (**Cheap Trick**), **Skid Row** and even **Bryan Adams**.

Crüe were at the top of their game and, just in case anyone had missed out on any of the previous ten years' worth of hellraising, *Decade Of Decadence* (1991) pulled together some of their more convincing moments and even threw in a cover of the Sex Pistols' "Anarchy In The UK".

Having survived ten years of near-death experiences, in the end it was good old-fashioned musical differences that brought them stumbling to their leather-clad knees. Neil had already been dabbling with the occasional side-project and he was eventually ousted in 1992, replaced by ex-**Scream** vocalist **John Corabi**. The seismic nature of this upheaval was to put Crüe on the back foot for much of the next decade, even though they set up their own label, Mötley Records, and eventually gained the rights to their entire back catalogue.

The advent of grunge had almost killed off the kind of overblown spectacle Sixx and his peers were used to delivering. The result of this shift in musical taste was *Mötley Crüe* (1994) where fans had to get their heads around a heavied-up, more contemporary sound and Corabi's voice at the mic. Standout track, if there was such a thing, was single "Hooligan's Holiday", but all in all it was a diversion best forgotten.

With a less than auspicious solo career behind him, and Crüe struggling to maintain any form of credibility, Neil was brought back into the fold for *Generation Swine* (1997), which had its moments but failed to hit the halcyon heights of their 1980s glory days. *The Best Of Mötley Crüe* (1998) was duly trundled out, along with a host of live, compilation and reissued and remastered studio albums to remind everyone just how good the band could be. But it was 2000's *New Tattoo* – featuring, appropriately, a cover of the Tubes classic "White Punks On Dope" – which found them at least sounding like they were having fun again, although it was a somewhat muted return to some kind of form. By now, drummer Tommy Lee, bored with the music and having had numerous run-ins with Neil, had opted to start a less-than-likely rap metal career with **Methods Of Mayhem**. So sitting behind the kit was veteran ex-**Ozzy Osbourne** drummer **Randy Castillo**. Sadly Castillo was too ill to take part on the tour promoting the album and he died in 2002.

More recently the band seemed to be relying increasingly on compilations – most notably *Loud As Fuck* (2003), and the tastelessly titled box sets, *Music To Crash Your Car To Vol 1* and *Vol 2* – to keep their name in the limelight. For a while, with Sixx working on his **Brides Of Destruction** project as well as writing for other artists, and Tommy Lee putting the brakes on a reunification, students of the hellraising rock'n'roll lifestyle had to

study the band's salacious book, *The Dirt*, to get their fix of Crüe-related insanity; it features input from all the members and boasts moments of both incredibly ugly stupidity and near genius.

Ironically it was *Red, White & Crue* (2005), yet another compilation, that heralded the revitalization of their career. The double-CD greatest hits set was released as the precursor to the band's reunion world tour and debuted in the *Billboard* chart at #6, setting the scene for a full-on global assault, a piece of news that was greeted with the same degree of astonishment as Vince Neil's VH1-sponsored facelift. Despite the years of excess, the miraculous fact that they had all somehow evaded the Grim Reaper, meant that the Crüe legend was assured at least a couple more gory chapters.

Dr Feelgood
1989; Universal

Slick and commercial, Bob Rock's production takes the Crüe's raw power and channels it into nuggets of memorable party metal. Worth it just to hear "Kickstart My Heart".

Music To Crash Your Car To Vol 1
2003; Universal

If you can afford it, pick this one up. It contains everything from the original mix of their first album right through to *Girls Girls Girls* as well as a whole bunch of rarities and demos.

MOTÖRHEAD

Formed London, UK, 1975

"I woke up once and found that someone had buried me in the garden. They'd stuck me in the flower bed then put the flowers back on top again ... I think that all happened on vodka ... or possibly Special Brew." Lemmy

One of the most single-minded and intense rock bands to strike fear and loathing into the hearts of clean-living folks the world over, Motörhead were the creation of bass-playing, gravel-throated **Ian 'Lemmy' Kilmister**, the son of a vicar. A self-confessed "speed freak", Lemmy spent much of his youth kicking around in various bands (**The Rockin' Vickers**, **The Motown Sect**) and roadie-ing for the likes of Jimi

Motörhead do their zombie routine.

Hendrix and Pink Floyd. Following a four-year stint with psychedelic rockers **Hawkwind** from whose ranks he was fired, the next logical step was the creation of his own band. Taking the name from a Hawkwind song he had penned himself – his original choice of Bastard was deemed to be commercial suicide – Lemmy bolted Motörhead together in 1975 with **Larry Wallis** (guitar) and **Lucas Fox** (drums).

Brazenly displaying their love of blues and boogie, the initial line-up produced only one album, *On Parole* (1979), recorded in 1976 but held back by a hesitant record label. After a less than impressive under-rehearsed slot supporting Blue Öyster Cult at the Hammersmith Odeon, which resulted in some terrible press, the line-up changed. Fox and Wallis were replaced by **'Fast' Eddie Clarke** (guitar) and **Phil 'Philthy Animal' Taylor** (drums) to create the definitive 'Head line-up. The result was a string of classic albums and notorious live performances. First *Motörhead* (1977), then *Overkill* and *Bomber* (both 1979) delivered muscular, deadly

rock'n'roll, screaming disrespect for authority figures and the status quo ("Lawman", "All The Aces", "Talking Head"), while their first minor hit arrived as a cover of The Kingsmen's "Louie Louie" in autumn 1978. It's hard not to believe Lemmy when he claims to have invented thrash metal when listening to the likes of "Overkill" and "Bomber" hurtling past at a whiplash lick. In the nihilistic punk landscape of the late 1970s, the band found themselves in the unique position of being accepted by both long-haired rockers and spiky-headed punks.

Ace Of Spades (1980) showed Lemmy and the boys at the peak of their powers in a rock scene reeling under the onslaught of the New Wave Of British Heavy Metal. Its title track (a hit single) was a cut guaranteed to make your teeth rattle and your nose bleed, whilst the rest of the set celebrated the staples of the rock'n'roll life: women in "Jailbait", the road in "(We Are) The Road Crew" and general antisocial mayhem in "The Hammer". To complete their cartoon outlaw image, the cover showed the band clad in spaghetti-western-inspired bandit-black leathers. The classic follow-up, *No Sleep 'Til Hammersmith* (1981), recorded on the Ace Of Spades tour, careered into the UK charts at #1 and captured their sound more fully than a dozen studio albums could have done. Fan favourites such as the grinding "Capricorn", "No Class" – with a boogie riff borrowed from ZZ Top's "Tush" – and the Hell's Angels anthem, "Iron Horse"/"Born To Lose" were spat out at relentless, paint-stripping volume. The whole band played as tightly as a clenched fist, while Lemmy threw his head back and sang as though he had had razor blades washed down with meths for breakfast.

Motörhead seemed unstoppable, and an unholy liaison with **Girlschool** produced the appallingly mixed but hugely successful *St Valentine's Day Massacre* EP. The roll did not last and *Iron Fist* (1982) did not match the metallic brilliance of their previous efforts, due mainly to the flat production, provided in part by Fast Eddie. He soon departed to form **Fastway**, and **Brian 'Robbo' Robertson** (ex-**Thin Lizzy** and **Wild Horses**) was drafted in to take over guitar duties. *Another Perfect Day* (1983) was glossier, and Robertson's playing brought a hint of subtlety, space and melody to the usual terminal head-spin of rioting guitars. Unfortunately, Robertson was never truly accepted by the fans, as his approach failed to capture the warts-and-all glory of old Motörhead. Coupled with personality clashes in the band, his stay would be a short one.

Lemmy re-formed the band with two new guitarists, **Michael 'Wurzel' Burston** and **Phil Campbell**, and Philthy moved on to be replaced by **Pete Gill** (ex-**Saxon**). A new era dawned: the double compilation album *No Remorse* (1984) contained twenty classics and four new cuts, including the rolling thunder of "Locomotive" and the gonzoid "Killed By Death". In true Motörhead style, limited quantities were released in a tasteful, gold-embossed, black leather sleeve. Pete Gill remained for the release of the bellicose *Orgasmatron* (1986) and the band's Donington Monsters Of Rock festival appearance, but Philthy returned to the fold for *Rock 'N' Roll* (1987) and the long-promised second live volume, *No Sleep At All* (1988) – the latter proudly displaying the legend "Everything Louder Than Everything Else". The new

material was solid but lacked the necessary evil spark; the band seemed to be treading water.

A new management team and a move to Los Angeles, however, produced *1916* (1991). With the bastard breakneck boogie of "Going To Brazil" and the bloodshot rattle of "Make My Day", the band were back on gasoline-guzzling form again, with some interesting experimental touches provided by songs such as "Love Me Forever", detailing a very twisted love affair, and the creepy "Nightmare/The Dreamtime". In fact, it was one of their gnarliest efforts since their inception, helped largely by having a cracking set of tunes produced with just the right degree of muscle and clarity. In an unprecedented show of sensitivity, the title track featured a cello backing Lemmy's cracked voice as he told the tragic story of a young soldier's life cut short.

After Philthy's second departure in 1992, **Mick Brown** (better known as **Mikkey Dee**) took over on drums. The 1990s saw the band recording a slew of albums that all had outstanding moments, but mostly they were business as usual. *March Or Die* (1992) was the sound of the band sticking to a formula while *Bastards* (1993) was a fearsome slice of 'Head, but one which ended up being criminally overlooked because it was issued on ZYX, a German label best known for dance music. *Sacrifice* (1995), *Overnight Sensation* (1996) and *Snake Bite Love* (1998) careered along convincingly without any particular highlights, though in interviews Lemmy consistently aired the view that he believed that line-up

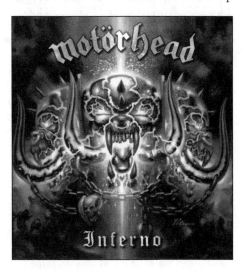

was far more professional and powerful than any past incarnation of the band. As it happens, with *Overnight Sensation* the band reverted to a trio with the departure of Wurzel. *We Are Motörhead* (2000) arrived with a particularly metallic version of the Sex Pistols' 'God Save The Queen' nestling among some of their best songs to date, though its follow-up *Hammered* (2002) was somehow less venomous-sounding in comparison. In order to celebrate 25 years of hellraising, *The Best Of Motörhead* (2001) pulled together some of the band's best-loved tracks and provided them in remastered form – never before had these classics sounded so good. In addition, the *25 & Alive: Boneshaker* DVD captured a 25th anniversary show with guests such as Brian May, 'Fast' Eddie Clarke and Doro Pesch joining Lemmy and co on stage.

Live, Motörhead, remain unique: not many rock bands of recent years can come close to the adrenaline rush and red-eyed savagery of full-force Motörhead; *Everything Louder Than Everyone Else* (1999) and *Live At Brixton Academy: The Complete Concert* (2003) were worthy additions to the band's growing collection of concert documents, but didn't come close to the jaw-dropping quality of the reissued double-CD version of *No Sleep 'Til Hammersmith* (2001), featuring seventeen rollicking unreleased classics in addition to the original running order.

Underlining the fact that by now Motörhead were something of an institution the band were invited to play a one-off gig at London's Royal Opera House in Covent Garden in February 2004. It was a perfect prelude to the release of *Inferno* (2004), a stonking and ornery slice of rock nirvana, Lemmy's bass riffs ripping through the mix like a dog with its arse on fire, making it easily their best album since *1916*.

Ace Of Spades
1980; Castle Communications

No-holds-barred, no-frills rock'n'roll, this showcases the best of their early period. The re-released version includes a number of hard-to-find bonus tracks, making it even more indispensable.

No Sleep 'Til Hammersmith
1981; Castle Communications

Setting the standard for rock live albums, this contains proven crowd-pleasers throughout. Lemmy and the boys have rarely sounded this dirty and incisive on record. As with the other early album rereleases, this version contains a number of excellent bonus tracks. A lesson in how to make something great even better.

Orgasmatron
1986; Castle Communications

An excellent comeback album after a fallow period. Lemmy sounds truly warty, while the title track has become a grinding live favourite.

1916
1991; Epic

Another outstanding album, particularly for the diversity of material. The title track is surprisingly moving, and elsewhere ("Love Me Forever", "Nightmare/ Dreamtime") the band experiment with arrangements and production techniques to great effect.

MUDVAYNE

Formed Peoria, Illinois, US 1996

" ... the music isn't just about being angry ..." Ryknow

The vast, empty stretches of America's Midwest might seem like a strange place for metal to flourish. But then again, the fact that there isn't much there for kids to tap into might explain it. Certainly the lack of normal prospects spurred on a certain masked nine-piece from Des Moines to become one of the biggest nu-metal acts of the last few years, and the same is true of this similarly challenging four-piece from some six hours down the highway in Peoria. And, as seems to be the way with these things, Slipknot did play a role in their rise, though musically **Mudvayne** are some distance from the churning thrash of their fellow sonic extremists.

Mudvayne came together with the express purpose of messing with people's heads on pretty much every level. For a start they were known as **sPaG** aka **Matt McDonough** (drums), **Gurrg** aka **Greg Tribbett** (guitar), **Kud** aka Chad Gray (vocals) and **Ryknow** aka **Ryan Martinie** (bass) – the usage of daft nicknames intended not just to protect the identities of the guilty but to enhance the band's otherness. They also had a very childish sense of humour. Influenced by the songwriting style of 1970s progressive outfits such as King Crimson, the technical

the concepts behind their album, which was named after the pharmacological term for the lethal dosage level of a substance that would kill fifty percent of test subjects, the analogy being that their brand of art-metal was packed with deadly, challenging ideas. The album opened with "Monolith", named after the jet black obelisk in Stanley Kubrick's *2001: A Space Odyssey*, and the rest of its tracks were peppered with audio snippets reiterating their commitment to artistic and intellectual evolution.

"Any good work of art will appeal to different types of people," explained sPaG. "In that way the work is more human. I would like to think that for the fourteen-year-old kids who want to listen to some heavy groove music it's not necessary to understand some of the more intellectual ideas. I wouldn't like to think we intentionally alienate any market. The, for lack of a better term, deeper levels are present for anyone that has the initiative." Granted, Mudvayne appeared a little pretentious compared to their nu-metal peers, but it did make a refreshing change to have a greater depth brought to what was essentially brutal and cathartic noise.

Their position as one of the more innovative and musically adventurous metal bands now sealed, *The Beginning Of All Things To End* (2001) appeared. It contained their self-produced debut along with some bonus tracks, as a means of bringing new fans up to speed and foiling bootleggers. *The End Of All Things To Come* (2002) followed soon after – along with the band changing their names to **Chüd**, **Güüg**, **R-üD**, and **Spüg**, just for the hell of it. The album revealed their efforts to mature and make their music a touch more melodic, rather than a fiendishly constructed torrent of riffs and jagged time changes. Sure enough, the oddball structures were still there – "Trapped In The Wake Of A Dream" was written in mindboggling 17/8 and 11/8 time – but the presence of producer **Dave Bottrill**, a man experienced in working with both King Crimson and Tool, helped push the band into slightly more open creative waters. And this time round Kud was actually singing some of the time too. The follow-up, *Lost And Found*, (2005) finally saw the band ditch the wacky image and nicknames to concentrate fully on the music.

thrash of Megadeth and the jazzy, math-metal approach of Swedish weirdoes Meshuggah, the Mudvayne sound was harsh, often atonal, scattered with odd time signatures and suffused with a general sense of the bizarre. Kud's vocals ranged from out-and-out nu-metal screaming, to semi-rapped machine-gun banter. Beneath them were downtuned, sludgy guitars and a rhythm section that could stop on a dime and instantly head off into deep tangential waters.

With the intention of getting themselves a record contract, the band recorded a demo album *Kill, I Oughtta* (1997) but it took a crossing of paths with Shawn 'Clown' Crahan of Slipknot at a music showcase in Chicago to clinch a deal; the percussionist was later credited as being 'executive producer' on their Epic debut *L.D. 50* (2000). Crahan's involvement may have pushed wary A&R people in the right direction but, with an album in the bag, it was the success of their subsequent shows with Slipknot that properly won Mudvayne a receptive audience across the US.

Both Slipknot fans and the media were quick to pick up on similarities between the bands, though in reality the only thing they had in common was a desire to be as heavy and extreme as possible. The comments were doubtless encouraged by Mudvayne's love of outlandish dress and make-up, all four of them having adopted warpaint and fitting personae to complement their daft nicknames. Mudvayne were keen to press home

L.D. 50
2000; Epic

Pretentious nu-metal anyone? Challenging, abrasive and very scary, the musical proficiency and confrontational lyrics make this a very bitter pill to swallow.

The End Of All Things To Come
2002; Epic

More assured, more open, and most importantly, more melodic, though without compromising on the band's vision. This is heavy beyond most people's endurance, but this time around you're more likely to remember the choruses.

MURDERDOLLS

Formed Des Moines, Iowa, US 1995

It would be hard to imagine any member of Slipknot making music that didn't sound like the advent of Armageddon, but if you didn't know it you would be hard pressed to realize that the **Murderdolls** is actually Slipknot drummer **Joey Jordison**'s very own little baby. Well, OK, it's more like Rosemary's Baby, but the point is that while Slipknot have been lumped in with the nu-metal crowd, the Murderdolls hark back to more old-fashioned rock'n'roll values. Their sound isn't a million miles from Marilyn Manson jamming on classic Mötley Crüe songs, with a lethal dose of the Misfits' horror punk thrown in for good measure. And we mustn't forget the influence of the godfather of shock rock himself, Alice Cooper.

The band's history goes back to the mid 90s when Jordison (guitar) and the excellently named **Dizzy Draztik** (vocals) formed the **Rejects** – later becoming Murderdolls – who performed during Jordison's downtime from Slipknot. When Slipknot took off in a big way Jordison put away his 'Dolls and went off to play drums in a boiler suit and kabuki mask. During 2001 and into 2002, however, while Slipknot were taking time off, Jordison resurrected his other band and revamped the line-up, pulling in **Static X** guitarist **Tripp Eisen** and bass player **Wednesday 13** from **Frankenstein Drag Queens From Planet 13**. Jordison and Wednesday 13 met for the first time when they entered the studio but hit it off so well that the latter ended up singing lead vocals while the vast bulk of the music was played by Jordison.

In the end, with *Beyond The Valley Of The Murderdolls* (2002) nearing completion, Eisen felt he couldn't commit full-time to a project that would interfere with his work in Static X and bowed out. However, at this point a full Murderdolls line-up was coalescing, completed by **Acey Slade** (guitar), **Eric Griffin** (bass), and **Ben Graves** (drums). They were glammy, trashy and ghoulish in a horror B-movie kind of way, like the Halloween-loving distant cousins of Twisted Sister – in fact a fab little ditty called "Twist My Sister" nestled alongside tunes such as "B-Movie Scream Queen" and the excellent "Dressed To Depress". The rock press championed them and they scored a hit with a cover of Billy Idol's "White Wedding" which peaked at #24 in the UK charts. The sight of the band on the usually squeaky clean *Top Of The Pops* was truly something to behold.

However, with Slipknot swinging back into action in late 2003, Murderdolls were put on hold. Wednesday 13 signed a solo deal with Roadrunner and recorded *Transylvania 90210: Songs Of Death, Dying And The Dead* (2005), an album in the same vein as both the Murderdolls and his previous band – that's to say, more cartoon horror punk and metal drawing heavily on trash TV and B-movies.

Beyond The Valley Of The Murderdolls
2002; Roadrunner

Not exactly groundbreaking but great fun all the same; Jordison's brainchild is one mean hard-rock fix. This album spits and snarls and revels in gore, but what do you expect when frontman Wednesday 13 watches nothing but slasher flicks?

MY DYING BRIDE

Formed Yorkshire, UK 1990

In the mist-shrouded, gloomy netherworld of doom metal, the UK's **My Dying Bride** are among the best and most fastidious practitioners of depressive dirges. Way back in the early 90s, alongside Anathema and Paradise Lost, My Dying Bride were considered one of the true pioneering doom bands. But while their contemporaries have gradually moved away from their early sound, MDB have continued to hang like a particularly menacing thundercloud over the more extreme metal scene.

Influenced by the death and thrash metal of the 80s, MDB first materialized in 1990 with darkness in their hearts and a desire to produce the most miserable music imaginable. After six months of rehearsals and writing, their legendary *Towards The Sinister* demo appeared followed by their first seven-inch offering, "God Is Alone". The latter was primal stuff, with harsh and hellish vocals riding atop a storm of brutal and jagged riffing, punctuated by the occasional slow passage. Soon the line-up of **Aaron Stainthorpe** (vocals), **Calvin Robertshaw** (guitar), **Andrew Craighan** (guitar), **Ade Jackson** (bass) and **Rick Miah** (drums) attracted the attention of Peacville Records and their first proper EP, 1991's *Symphonaire Infernus Et Spera Empyrium* was on its way, followed by *As The Flower Withers* (1992).

The quality of the production on the album may have been somewhat coarse but there was already a sense of the classic doom aesthetic about everything the band were doing. The vocals were still growled and there were still thrash sections here and there but the nascent ability to create darkness through sloth was beginning to seep through, helped immensely by the experimental addition of violin, courtesy of **Martin Powell**. A degree of subtlety and a more sedate atmosphere pervaded their hymns of depression, some of which lumbered on well past the eight-minute mark. The album's artwork was created by graphic novel artist **Dave McKean**, famed for the dark imagery of his photographic collages.

The *Thrash Of Naked Limbs* EP in 1992 cemented their place in the European doom underground and Powell was recruited as a full-time member by the time of *Turn Loose The Swans* (1993), which saw the band make a leap forward in terms of composition. The avant-garde spirit of acts such as Celtic Frost was clearly in the air, as keyboards, violin and female vocals combined to create a chilling soundscape of icy, emotional despair. And the use of clean semi-spoken vocals brought another dimension to the depression, with Stainthorpe's almost stately delivery bringing a sense of bowed majesty to the album.

Yet another EP, *I Am The Bloody Earth*, preceded *The Angel And The Dark River* (1995), six epic tracks of erotic and sinister doom embellished with gothic touches and a glorious sense of the utterly maudlin. And the songs averaged around nine minutes in length, allowing fans to absorb every shade of black. MDB were very clearly the UK's chief purveyors of misery yet were more popular with audiences on the continent who were happy to wallow in their tortured shadow; the band made several European festival appearances including the famous Dynamo festival in Holland. A support slot with Iron Maiden also introduced them to new, more mainstream metalheads across Europe while the cunning *Trinity* album was in fact a repackaging of their EPs, allowing those who had missed out to sample the band's earlier sound.

The next couple of years brought touring commitments with fellow UK doomsters Cathedral (though theirs was a more tongue-in-cheek love of morbidity) and the Finnish outfit Sentenced. In the US they supported Dio while promoting their fourth album, *Like Gods Of The Sun* (1996). Unfortunately illness forced Miah to quit the band soon after and he was replaced by **Bill Law**. Powell also decided to leave at this point, signalling a period of relative weirdness for both the band and the fans. The result was the decidedly odd *34.788%...Complete* (1998), the title of which was inspired by a strange dream of Jackson's in which he was told that a certain percentage of man's time on earth had already been used up. Everything on the album seemed designed to baffle – from the music, which featured strange electronic touches, to the artwork, with its sci-fi close-up of a withered spider.

The record proved a critical success because it succeeded in pushing the genre barriers in hitherto unexplored directions. But with a new drummer, **Shaun Taylor-Steels** (ex-**Anathema**), and new guitarist **Hamish Glencross** (ex-**Solstice**), *The Light At The End Of The World* (1999) was a move back into more familiar territory, without the fussiness of the previous album's production.

As befits a band with such a varied back catalogue the next two years saw the pulling together of two compilations of rare material – *Meisterwork I* (2000) and *Meisterwork II* (2001) – before *The Dreadful Hours* (2001) emerged to great critical reaction. The following year brought two live packages: *For Darkest Eyes* was a combination of promotional videos and live concert footage with

Aaron (seated) sulks because no one told him about the dress code.

the band in full tormented meltdown, while *The Voice Of The Wretched* was a traditional live CD.

The band's most recent album *Songs Of Darkness, Words Of Light* (2004) has sealed their title as godfathers of British doom metal, being a lush and complex fusion of bleak poetry, emotional tension and sheer grandiose noise, helped along by new keyboard player **Sarah Stanton**.

As The Flower Withers
1992; Peaceville

This is not as refined as later works but it's strong on creativity and invention. The band push themselves in hitherto unexplored directions and already the heady stench of doom hangs heavy.

NAPALM DEATH

Formed Birmingham, UK, 1982

The name **Napalm Death** is legendary in the world of extreme music; those two words have become synonymous with a genre they helped pioneer: grindcore. It's nasty, it's brutal, it's downright hard to listen to, and has influenced countless imitators who are intoxicated by the sheer blasting speed of it all.

The band's origins were rooted in the anarcho-hardcore punk scene of the early 80s. As the line-up evolved and got its act together they began to make serious enough waves for Earache Records to take an interest, leading to the sessions that went into creating their classic debut, *Scum* (1987). The creation of *Scum* was far from straightforward, however. It was put together in two sessions, nine months apart with a line-up that was still unstable. Those involved were **Justin Broadrick** (guitar), **Nik Bullen** (bass/vocals), **Lee Dorrian** (vocals), **Bill Steer** (guitar), **Jim Whitely** (bass) and **Mick Harris** (drums). Broadrick and Bullen were from an earlier incarnation of the band, so when their involvement with the recording was done they left.

Scum was to have a major effect over the coming years. No one had heard anything quite so primitive and savage before. The speed at which these politically charged anti-songs were delivered was astonishing – some of them were mere seconds long and the infamous "You Suffer" was literally over in a second. The runoff groove of side one was etched with the legend "whirlwind holocaust" which summed it all up quite effectively. Of course, thrash metal had been around for a while but it was the complete punky disregard for the rules that made Napalm Death into hardcore heroes right from the off. The following year brought new bassist **Shane Embury** and a head-spinning consolidation album, *From Enslavement To Obliteration* (1988). This line-up lasted until the *Mentally Murdered* EP, after which Dorrian left to form **Cathedral** and Steer went off to concentrate on **Carcass**. **Mark 'Barney' Greenway** (vocals), **Jesse Pintado** (guitar) and **Mitch Harris** (guitar) then stepped into the fold for *Harmony Corruption* (1990), an altogether more disciplined and song-based approach akin to death metal. The aggres-

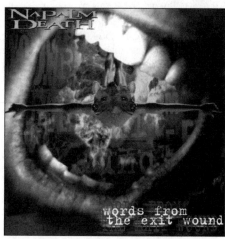

sion levels were still way off the scale, Greenway's vocals were every bit as unintelligible as before and the radical political agenda was still in place, with "Extremity Retained" a broadside directed at critics who dared to suggest that the band were just creating an unholy racket.

Death By Manipulation (1991) was a very useful compilation that pulled together a whole host of tracks from various singles and EPs, before the band went through one more shift and brought in **Danny Herrera** to replace Mick Harris for *Utopia Banished* (1992). Over the next few years Napalm Death became one of the most heralded extreme bands on the face of the planet taking their blastcore style on the road for several tours while a steady stream of records was released: a typically volatile cover of the Dead Kennedys' "Nazi Punks Fuck Off" graced an EP; *Fear, Emptiness, Despair* (1994) pushed the envelope with a more modern production; the *Greed Killing* EP laid the groundwork for *Diatribes* (1996). And then came an amusing and confusing game of musical chairs. Greenway fell out with the band and ended up singing on an **Extreme Noise Terror** album. Meanwhile ENT's singer **Phil Vane** ended up in Napalm Death, but before any more recording took place Greenway was reinstated for the very fine *Inside The Torn Apart* (1997).

Words From The Exit Wound (1998) was their last album for Earache; they then signed with Dreamcatcher and continued their career of sonic terrorism with an EP of roots cover versions, *Leaders Not Followers*, followed by *Enemy Of The Music Business* (2000) and *Order Of The Leech* (2002). Earache finally got round to issuing a double album of key tracks and rarities, *Noise For Music's Sake* (2003), before the band ripped back into action with the gloriously indulgent full album *Leaders Not Followers: Part 2* (2004) on Century Media. This was followed by *The Code Is Red… Long Live The Code* (2005).

Noise For Music's Sake
2003; Earache

There is just so much Napalm Death music out there it's virtually impossible to construct a reasonable compilation. That said, this is a fair attempt spread across two discs with Earache having access to the bulk of their bulging back catalogue. Collectors will relish the second disc of rarities and live tracks.

NAZARETH

Formed Dunfermline, Scotland 1969

The fact that rockers such as Axl Rose and Michael Monroe rate this outfit would recommend further investigation, but even without such high-level endorsements **Nazareth** are a force to be reckoned with. They have been releasing albums for over thirty years and are still at it. One reason for this seeming indestructibility lies in their roots as a covers band **The Shadettes**. In order to make it on the club circuit they had to learn hit tunes fast and this discipline helped hone their skills and repertoire. The result was that when **Dan McCafferty** (vocals), **Manny Charlton** (guitar), **Pete Agnew** (bass) and **Darrell Sweet** (drums) went professional, some of their best-loved, chart-bothering material would be Nazzed up versions of other people's songs.

Their first couple of albums *Nazareth* (1971) and *Exercises* (1972) marked the beginning of their most prolific and successful period and they truly hit their stride when "Broken Down Angel" went Top 10. The classic *Razamanaz* (1973) album showcased their own unique brand of catchy heavy rock, all brisk rhythms with McCafferty's whisky'n'nicotine drenched vocals. *Loud'N'Proud* (1973) and *Rampant* (1974) kept the riffs coming thick and fast, "This Flight Tonight" (a Joni Mitchell tune from the former) providing yet another hit. But Nazareth weren't successful everywhere: *Hair Of The Dog* (1975) failed to chart in the UK even as the band were becoming superstars in America on the back of their cover version of the Everley Brothers' "Love Hurts". The single went Top 10 and the album went Top 20; Guns N' Roses would later cover the title track on their *The Spaghetti Incident?* album. Likewise *Close Enough For Rock'N'Roll* (1976) did very little in the UK but the US loved it.

Play'N'The Game (1976) – apparently very big in Canada – and *Expect No Mercy* (1977) were gradually veering towards a heavier sound, but by now Charlton reckoned the guitar front needed expanding to make things more inventive. So **Zal Cleminson** of **The Sensational Alex Harvey Band** pitched in his lot for *No Mean City* (1979) and *Malice In Wonderland* (1980), though he left when financial pressures at their then label,

Mountain, put the band on hold for a while. For *The Fool Circle* (1980) keyboard player **John Locke** helped out on some tracks. Guitarist **Billy Rankin** was eventually added to increase the guitar firepower again; witness the energetic *'Snaz* (1981) live album.

By now, however, the studio albums were beginning to become more experimental, throwing in elements of soul and funk, leading to a rash of records during the 80s which sounded like the band couldn't quite focus. After *Sound Elixir* (1983) Rankin left to go solo and Nazareth headed towards the confusing *Snakes'N'Ladders* (1989), which led to Charlton leaving the band. Rankin briefly returned, though he was soon replaced by **Jimmy Murrison**. The far rockier *No Jive* (1991) and *Move Me* (1994) found the band embarking on serious amounts of global touring – sporting a new keyboard player in **Ronnie Leahy** – before they signed to SPV for *Boogaloo* (1998). They toured with vintage heavyweights Uriah Heep and seemed to be back on track again until Sweet suddenly died of a heart attack. Devastated, the band regrouped and brought in Agnew's eldest son **Lee** on drums. More touring ensued and a packed gig at Glasgow's Garage resulted in the live *Homecoming* (2001). With Leahy's retirement the Naz were back to a four-piece, still undertaking world tours three decades after it all began.

Razamanaz
1973; Castle

Arguably the best of their early efforts, this album kicked them into orbit and turned 1973 into their year. "Bad, Bad Boy", "Broken Down Angel" and the cracking title track make this one great heavy rock album.

ΠICKELBACK

Formed Hanna, Alberta, US 1996

One of rock's huge success stories of recent years, **Nickelback** are a band that have managed to stay true to their original sound and shift millions of albums, taking them from humble beginnings as a four-piece trekking around Canada in the back of a van, to arena-filling, chart-hogging, radio-clogging grunge metallers.

For all their amazing commercial success Nickelback's start was as modest as they come. While vying for fame they had to take what jobs they could to pay the bills – the band name came from the change given back to customers when they worked at Starbucks. Chief writer, guitarist and vocalist **Chad Kroeger**, his brother **Mike** (bass), cousin **Brandon Kroeger** (drums) and **Ryan Peake** (guitar) got their act together and decided that a move to Vancouver would be immensely more helpful than trying to cultivate a following out in the prairies. With a few thousand dollars borrowed from the Kroegers' stepfather they took the classic DIY route by recording first the *Hesher* EP followed by *Curb* (1996).

"When you listen to it you can hear our style is slightly immature; it hasn't fully developed. You can hear us learning on tape," explains Mike Kroeger, trying to describe the band's first steps in the studio. From their new base they set about touring their butts off, crossing the vast distances between Canadian cities in the back of a van. "We progressed on cross-country tours which is gruelling. Essentially you have about 7000 km of road across Canada – a lot of driving. Look at the maps and you'll see how far apart the cities are and those drives in the winter time are a real treat!"

Curb was an effective calling card and within its slightly lumpen grooves can be seen the glitter of grunge gold. The prolific Chad had far better songs lined up for *The State* (2000) – featuring new drummer **Ryan Vikedal** – which was independently released at first and then picked up by Roadrunner Records after "Leader Of Men" proved to be a major radio hit. Whether by design or happy accident Nickelback had struck upon a fantastically sweet combination of melodic, grungy metal and earnest, though somewhat bitty and vague, lyrics – all delivered in Kroeger's powerful, throaty croon. It was perfect for US and Canadian radio stations already in tune with similar-sounding acts such as 3 Doors Down and Creed – a hint of classic rock and a whole lot of Pearl Jam-like bombast minus the guitar solos.

"Leader Of Men" ensured that *The State* sold in huge quantities but Nickelback truly arrived as an unpretentious, global album-selling machine with *Silver Side Up* (2001), a record produced by **Rick Parashar** (Pearl Jam, Alice In Chains). To say that this was a monster would be to undersell it; at this point Nickelback became synonymous with

COURTESY OF ROADRUNNER RECORDS

Nickelback hanging out.

mind-bending sales statistics. The album went gold or platinum several times over across ten countries, then came the Grammy nominations, *Billboard* awards and Junos (Canada's equivalent to the Grammys).

Kroeger's writing had now become more focused, and the melodic quality of the hard-hitting tunes more than satisfied those hungry for hummable angst. Nickelback were everywhere, prompting critics to lambast them for plodding unoriginality and fans to scoop up anything with their name on it – hence their decision to reissue *Curb* for the completists in 2002.

The next year *The Long Road* (2003) arrived preceded by "Someday", a weepy single about a relationship break-up on which acoustic refrains and a soaring chorus allowed Kroeger's cracked vocals to strain plaintively. It marked yet another hit. Largely interchangeable with their earlier material, the songs on *The Long Road* were a tad harder, with Kroeger's lyrics sounding more accessible this time round. Platinum sales assured, Nickelback followed the long road around the globe promoting the album. In spite of their success, in January 2005 Vikedal quit the band; he was replaced by Daniel Adair.

Silver Side Up
2001; Roadrunner

This is radio grunge of the slickest order. "How You Remind Me", "Too Bad" and "Never Again" ensured that the band got a huge amount of coverage in 2002, the troubled but insanely catchy "How You Remind Me" grabbing an obscene amount of airplay.

NIGHTWISH

Formed Finland, 1996

Fancy a bit of gothic film-score metal? **Nightwish** are the band for you. Combining progressive power metal, orchestral music and opera, with a strong element of drama and atmosphere plus a dash of brooding paganism and dark magic, they have become one of the biggest bands in Europe. You don't so much listen to Nightwish as immerse yourself in their shamelessly romantic fantasy world. Such is the band's success, that in 2003 singer **Tarja Turunen** was invited to meet Finland's president.

The concept behind Nightwish came largely from **Tuomas Holopainen** (keyboards). He was joined by **Erno Vuorinen** (guitar), **Jukka Nevalainen** (drums) and, finally, their ace in the hole, the strikingly beautiful and classically trained singer **Tarja Turunen**. As an initial four-piece they had it all – enviable music expertise and a talented and photogenic front person. Getting things going in the mid-90s, however, required a bit of juggling, as the various members were caught up in national service and higher education. Nevertheless, a deal with Spinefarm was struck and *Angels Fall First* (1997) emerged as the first of their forays into the realms of gothic epics. The single "The Carpenter" became their first top-ten single

THE NEW WAVE OF BRITISH HEAVY METAL

Of all the periods through which modern heavy metal has progressed, one of the most influential has been dubbed the **New Wave Of British Heavy Metal** (often shortened to **NWOBHM**). In much the same way that grunge has been credited for killing off the air-brained excesses of 1980s hair metal, back in the late 1970s punk was busy doing exactly the same thing to more traditional rock bands. Monster rock acts such as Led Zeppelin and Black Sabbath had come to define a largely stadium-centric rock experience and had succumbed to the trappings of stardom, transporting these now huge acts way beyond the vital energy of early gigs staged in smaller, sweatier venues. So when punk reared its snotty head on the UK's music scene many fans were immediately drawn to its essentially DIY ethos and rebellious fuck-you attitude; the established rock dinosaurs' days were numbered, especially from the music critics' point of view.

Heavy metal was far from crushed into nonexistence, however. It simply mutated to survive and emerge blinking through the dry ice and post-gig carnage to survey the damage. While the trendy music magazines were chasing after the next Sex Pistols a loose groundswell of activity was growing on the metal front. Across the UK young metal bands were taking the blueprints laid down by the past masters and injecting their own style. At the grass roots level metal was becoming faster, more exciting; there was nothing cumbersome or lumbering about this new brand of metal – in fact, though some of its practitioners may have balked at the suggestion, metal had become slightly 'punked up' in so far as the energy levels and sheer adrenaline rush were prime ingredients. Also, rather like on the punk scene, most bands who were strapped for cash were happy to issue small quantities of self-financed and self-produced singles and albums, with the result that NWOBHM collectors can spend very happy lifetimes chasing down ultra-rare vinyl.

Key bands were outfits such as **Praying Mantis**, **Angel Witch**, the **Tygers Of Pan Tang** and **Samson**. Naturally the scene also produced some of the longest-running standard-bearers in the world of metal. **Iron Maiden** are one of the biggest heavy metal bands in the world, while acts like **Def Leppard**, **Motörhead** and **Saxon** are still going strong.

What elevated the New Wave Of British Heavy Metal to the status of one of the key moments in metal history, however, was its effect on future stars, not least a certain little Bay-Area thrash band called **Metallica**. Drummer **Lars Ulrich**'s love of NWOBHM drove him to put together an outfit of similar style, economy and power; Metallica's first studio album, *Kill 'Em All*, is nothing if not a thrashy tribute to UK bands such as **Diamond Head**. As if the connection really needed spelling out, the B-side to their 1984 "Creeping Death" single featured Diamond Head's classic chugger "Am I Evil?" and **Blitzkrieg**'s "Blitzkrieg"; three years on and their *Garage Days Re-Revisited* EP featured covers of tracks by **Holocaust**, **Budgie** and Diamond Head, firmly stamping the term NWOBHM onto the metal world's collective consciousness.

in their home country and the album nearly breached the Top 30.

Second album *Oceanborn* (1998) was a definite step towards the notion of widescreen metal. They had added **Sami Vänskä** (bass) and in the studio they brought in a string section. This time they scored a #1 single with "Sacrament Of Wilderness" and *Oceanborn* went into the Top 5. Not only were they making a huge impression at home, but across Europe – most notably Germany – they were rapidly heading for the top. Such was their profile that they almost ended up representing Finland in the Eurovision Song Contest. Fortunately, that honour went to someone else and the band had to make do with the Finnish chart-topping *Wishmaster* (2000) and a successful world tour.

The *From Wishes To Eternity* (2001) live DVD and *Over The Hills And Far Away* EP – the title track a cover of a Gary Moore tune – gave the fans plenty to keep them amused, even as the band was on the verge

of splitting. In the end Vänskä was replaced by **Marco Hietala** and *Century Child* (2002) became their second album chart-topper, complete with orchestra and choir.

The style evident on *Century Child* was taken to its logical conclusion on their most

ambitious album to date, *Once* (2004), which over the summer hit the top slot in *Billboard*'s Eurochart. Expertly penned by Holopainen, it often sounded like a sprawling movie score, the galloping metal complemented by the classical expertise of the orchestra and chorus of the Academy of St Martin-in-the-Fields. Highlights included "Creek Mary's Blood", their attempt at a colossal *Dances With Wolves*-type symphonic metal soundtrack, and the ten-minute masterwork "Ghost Love Score". Predictably, while Nightwish picked up a variety of Finnish music press awards, Turunen's first solo single, "Yhden Enkelin Unelma" ("One Angel's Dream") topped the Finnish charts and went gold in the process.

Once
2004; Nuclear Blast

This sounds truly vast, a stunning combination of streamlined metallic power and refined classical influences. Hietala provides tougher male vocals to balance Turunen's sweet clarity and the songs simply defy convention, displaying more imagination in just a few bars than some bands can muster over an entire career.

NILE

Formed Greenville, South Carolina, US 1993

Iron Maiden dabbled with ancient Egyptian myth on *Powerslave* but this incredibly proficient death metal outfit have made a career out of it, gradually perfecting a blend of historically rooted, H.P. Lovecraft-inspired horror and sizzling thrash rifferama. The result is a genre all their own: pyramid metal, complete with sleeve notes to explain what in the name of Horus is going on in the songs.

It's amazing to think that the torrent of mayhem unleashed by **Nile** was originally down to the trio of **Karl Sanders** (guitar/vocals), **Chief Spires** (bass/vocals) and **Pete Hammoura** (drums/vocals) who began their trips back in time to the land of the Pharaohs on two independent releases, the *Festivals Of Atonement* (1995) mini-LP and the *Ramses Bringer Of War* EP from 1997. Sanders was still perfecting his cookie-monster roar and, although played fast, the music had yet to shift into hyperdrive. Already evident, however, was the use of instrumental interludes to evoke an atmosphere of ancient magic and ceremony.

After their label went bust Nile signed to Relapse Records and the three tracks from their *Ramses* EP were reworked to far greater effect on their proper debut album, *Amongst The Catacombs Of Nephren-Ka* (1998). They took their Middle Eastern folklore-infused metal on the road with Morbid Angel, to whom they bore some sonic resemblance, and made their European debut at the Dynamo festival in 1999.

In The Beginning (2000) brought together their first two releases so fans could get their hands on the by now long-deleted material; this gave the band time enough to decipher a few more hieroglyphics and ancient scrolls in order to fuel the dark fantasies of their next album, *Black Seeds Of Vengeance* (2000). Highlights of this were the eerie "Libation Unto The Shades Who Lurk In The Shadows Of The Temple Of Anhur" and the searing "Masturbating The War God". So focused and intricate was the attack that it seemed almost a shift towards symphonic death metal. By now **Dallas Toler-Wade** (guitars/vocals) was a member and the additional firepower provided plenty of flexibility to experiment further.

The use of ancient scriptures as the basis for songs was taken to new and inspired extremes with *In Their Darkened Shrines* (2002) and its epic four-part title track (ancient Egyptian prog death, anyone?). Once more the line-up had shifted to include **Tony Laureano** (drums) and **Jon Vesano** (bass/vocals), though the former was eventually replaced by George Kollias and the latter left just as *Annihilation Of The Wicked* (2005) was released.

In Their Darkened Shrines
2002; Relapse

Streamlined, brutal and utterly compelling, the avalanche of riffs and blastbeat drumming is truly amazing. The title track recounts the tale of a rebellious serpent cult trying to overthrow the rule of the Pharaoh. So now you know.

NINE INCH NAILS

Formed San Francisco, California, US 1988

There are few artists that can truly say they influenced a generation of music-makers but the man behind **Nine Inch Nails**, multi-instrumentalist **Trent Reznor**, most certainly can. Through a combination of luck, harnessed to a prodigious amount of talent and an ear for a good commercial hook, Reznor's emotionally tortured and tortuous outpourings have pushed industrial metal firmly into the limelight. As a result, he has primed modern metal lovers for the likes of Marilyn Manson and a whole host of bands keen to give their music a harsh and dissonant edge.

Ironically, the young Reznor got one of his first gigs in the 80s with an AOR band called **The Innocent**. However, his real fascination lay in early industrial sounds, so when he had gathered sufficient funds to record a demo, he began creating music focused towards the darker end of the spectrum. The music, created entirely by himself, attracted the attention of several labels and he ended up signing to TVT Records – a decision that he would come to regret and which would influence much of his mid-90s output.

With *Pretty Hate Machine* (1989) it soon became clear that Reznor was a man capable of plumbing the depths of the human psyche through the incisive application of sound, his one-man sonic assaults cutting like an electronic scalpel straight to the soul. The album festered away in the lower reaches of the charts, racking up sales on the back of singles such as "Sin" and "Head Like A Hole" and building up Reznor's reputation for virulent angst. On the live front Reznor recruited a band to get the point across; among those hired early on were **Chris Vrenna** (drums) and **Richard Patrick** (guitar), who eventually went on to form **Filter**. The band ended up supporting artists such as The Jesus & Mary Chain and Guns N' Roses (Axl Rose was reportedly a big fan) but with the latter support slot, they found that their distinctly un-hard rock didn't convince the more straight-ahead rock crowds. They finally found their live home on the first Lollapalooza tour in 1991, the first taste of grunge creating an environment where alternative sounds could flourish.

By now NIN's debut had grown into a hit for the label who duly began to interfere with Reznor's vision, thus precipitating a lengthy legal battle as he tried to extricate himself from the contract. While he struggled with TVT he set up his own Nothing label which would have distribution through Interscope. Finally able to get a new record out, *Broken* (1992) was a mini-LP that built on the more intense and organic racket of NIN's live sound but which went much further in its quest for extremity than their debut. The pent-up fury Reznor felt after his tussle with TVT seeped into the fibre of the recording. And then there was the controversy surrounding the video for "Happiness In Slavery", which featured S&M performance artist **Bob Flanagan** supposedly being tortured to death by a machine. The video was, of course, banned and *Broken* was followed shortly after by a remix disc suitably titled *Fixed*.

As if all this wasn't shocking enough Reznor's next outing, *The Downward Spiral* (1994) was a masterpiece of degradation and

Nine Inch Nails' Trent Reznor.

NINETIES POP PUNK

By far one of the most significant developments in 90s rock was the pop punk explosion. Melody was always a feature of early punk and it was to the greats that many bands turned for inspiration.

Rancid appeared in the early 90s championing a sound not a million miles from a heavier **Clash** and with a taste for ska to boot. Over the years they maintained a level of credibility and success by incorporating real tunes with a decent quota of aggression. But the real increase in popularity came with **Green Day** and **The Offspring**, who took their cue from early bands such as **Stiff Little Fingers** and **The Damned**, but with a lighter touch. Green Day scored a smash hit album with *Dookie* (1994), likewise The Offspring enjoyed a breakthrough with *Smash* (1994). This resulted in a glut of similar-sounding bands as the major labels scrambled to sign anybody capable of stringing together some upbeat chords and sing-along harmonies. The upshot was yet more chart-friendly punk in the shape of **Blink 182**, who broke through with 1999's *Enema Of The State*, and more hit albums from the likes of **Sum 41** and **Good Charlotte**, all clearly aimed at young pop fans, who were also ready to buy records from the likes of **McFly** and **Busted**.

The commercial success (sell-out?) of such bands is something of a bone of contention in punk circles, as the music that was supposed to be the epitome of rebellion in the late 70s has become a packaged commodity – with the music industry calling all the shots.

misery recorded in the Hollywood mansion where actress Sharon Tate was murdered by the Manson family. The clash of metal and machine was starker and more painful than ever, particularly on the *Closer* EP which gave Reznor a hit (complete with censored video) with an X-rated chorus. The album glowered away in the UK Top 10, narrowly missing the #1 spot in the US. Reznor rounded off a busy year by producing the soundtrack to Oliver Stone's *Natural Born Killers*. An album of remixes, *Further Down The Spiral* (1995), deconstructed Reznor's trademark bile into further poisonous permutations.

So staggering was the impact of *The Downward Spiral*, it was hard to see where NIN could go next. Before the next album came a spate of production work. Reznor worked on **Marilyn Manson**'s *Antichrist Superstar* album, the self-styled 'God Of Fuck' being one of the artists signed to his Nothing label. He also put together the soundtrack to David Lynch's *Lost Highway*, for which he also contributed "The Perfect Drug", and he worked as producer on **Rob Halford**'s **Two** project. All the while he also toiled away on perfecting his next bout of industrial terrorism which arrived a full half-decade after his last full-length album – in the meantime, the only titbit for fans was the double-video package *Closure* (1997).

On *The Fragile* (1999), a sprawling double album clocking in at over one hundred minutes, Reznor gave his muse full rein, with songs spanning a variety of moods, from the haunting to the bleakly nihilistic. A remix album, *Things Falling Apart* (2000), was fol-

lowed by *And All That Could Have Been* (2002), a live package of material gathered while on tour. Reznor, in typical fashion, then took his sweet time over recording *With Teeth* which arrived to great fanfare in (2005).

The Downward Spiral
1994; Nothing

This is not a happy record. It is, however, extremely intense. For starters check out the title track, the profanity-strewn "Closer" and "March Of The Pigs". This is filth and psychic grime turned into music. Essential.

NIRVANA

Formed Aberdeen, Washington, US 1986; disbanded 1994.

Like nearly every other musical icon from Elvis to Jim Morrison, **Kurt Cobain** had a psyche that was too big for one body. A mass of contradictions, he behaved like a passionate fan but hated being the object of adoration; he endlessly baited his audience, but became the symbol of an age; he was not a particularly talented guitarist, but a songwriter of genius with the ability to capture the torment of the human condition in a few abstract lines of poetry and jagged blasts of squalling noise. His distillation of the early 90s *Zeitgeist* helped create the sound that would become known as grunge, a wave of angst-driven music that would almost completely extinguish the excesses of 80s rock.

The embryonic **Nirvana** formed in late 1986 in the trailer park, limbo-hell of Aberdeen, Washington, eight miles from Seattle. Comprising Cobain (guitars/vocals) and **Chris Novoselic** (bass), they went through a succession of drummers before finding a suitable hard-hitter in **Chad Channing**.

Encapsulating the repressed rage and alienation of Seattle's youth, they rapidly became an act to watch out for. Novoselic, a wild and lanky player, had a penchant for hurling his bass around stage, while Cobain developed a taste for trashing equipment in true nihilistic style. Altogether they churned up a heavy, thrumming, pop sludge that took in influences as diverse as Aerosmith and the Butthole Surfers.

Having garnered the interest of the hip Seattle label Sub Pop, they recorded their first single in June 1988. "Love Buzz" (a sonically bastardized Shocking Blue cover version) was the epitome of the grunge sound; thick and claustrophobic with stabs of near-smothered melody.

Bleach (1989) followed soon after and cost a mere $606 dollars to record. As the band were broke at the time, the money was coughed up by new member **Jason Everman** (guitar). Far from a perfect debut, *Bleach* showed the band trying hard to balance their influences against their label's perceived hipness. Cobain's lyrics were thrown together very quickly, but it was his vocal style and phrasing that turned the minimal verses into catchy hooks; "About A Girl" was unashamedly melodious, and acted as a lighter contrast to the spare genius of "School" and the leaden crush of "Blew".

A full US tour allowed the band to hone their live technique to near perfection: if it was a great gig they would destroy their equipment through sheer euphoria; if it was a poor gig they would destroy everything in a fit of frustration. As few gigs fell into the ordinary category they spent a lot of time making repairs. About this time tensions were growing with Everman, whose overt metallist tendencies grated with the others and he departed soon after.

Down to a three-piece, they continued touring after the release of the *Blew* EP (1989). Conditions on their European tour

PAUL BERGEN/REDFERNS

Nirvana – the fathers of grunge.

were abysmal, however, with Nirvana and fellow-tourists Tad crammed into a minuscule tour bus – all 6' 7" of Novoselic and 300-plus pounds of Tad front man Tad Doyle. Never having experienced total good health, Cobain's already crippling stomach problems got worse and he retreated behind a wall of sleep. Rome proved to be their nadir when a paranoid Cobain suffered a near breakdown on stage.

Over the next few months their bad luck with drummers continued; Channing left and his replacement **Dan Peters** lasted exactly one gig, although he was involved with writing the bass-heavy "Sliver". At the time **Dave Grohl** (drums) was a member of explosive hardcore band **Scream**. His power and precision were so impressive that it soon became obvious that they had found the vital, dynamic third member they had been searching for. With their fan base growing, Cobain was confident that their next record would be a milestone production. They finally settled on Geffen for a deal, but as they waited during the interminably grey depressing winter of 1990 Cobain began taking heroin.

Little did Cobain realize what he would be unleashing over the coming months. With the release of the classic *Nevermind* (1991) it soon became clear that records would be classified as pre- or post-Nirvana. The songs were superb: the scathing "Smells Like Teen Spirit" bizarrely owed a debt to Boston's "More Than a Feeling", while "In Bloom", "Lithium" and "Come As You Are" were all instantly memorable stabs at targets as disparate as macho male values and social conformity. The disturbing acoustic "Polly" and the confessional whisperings of "Something In The Way" complemented the intensity of "Breed" and the hardcore punk of "Territorial Pissings". **Butch Vig**'s production and **Andy Wallace**'s mixing rendered their previously plodding sound into a glistening and sleek beast ready to take on both commercial radio station playlists and the charts.

Somehow Nirvana, and particularly Cobain had unwittingly filled a musical gap. They took a hard-headed, punk-influenced artistic stance and fused it to a more mainstream-oriented hard rock sound; somewhere in this mix Cobain was voicing the emp-

tiness felt by the youth in the cultural vacuum of 90s America. The media would soon coin a catch-all phrase to sum up this so-called slacker phenomenon: Generation X.

Suddenly it was not just alternative kids who were tuning in, but everyone including those they positively despised: the jocks, the misogynistic metalheads, the racist, homophobic rednecks. Nirvana were appalled by their broad appeal, and none of their new found audience seemed to appreciate the degree of hate they inspired in their new idols. Their success drove them to extremes of obnoxiousness; they felt indestructible, and tried to infuriate and alienate their audiences by being as openly offensive as possible: Cobain would wear dresses, they would kiss each other on stage and equipment was destroyed even before their sets were finished.

In early 1992 Cobain married Hole's Courtney Love and immediately provided the press with a rich seam of conjecture as stories of her pregnancy and apparent hard drug consumption hit the papers. With Cobain's new and controversial wife on the scene the air of edgy doom about the band seemed to become amplified and focused. Amid rumours of the band's impending self-destruction through heroin and health problems, Nirvana turned in a fevered performance at the Reading Rock Festival. Cobain turned the rumours inside out by arriving on stage dressed in a white hospital gown, and being pushed in a wheel chair. By the end of the set the stage was a no-man's-land of

howling feedback and splintered fragments of the band's abused equipment. Towards the end of the year *Incesticide* (1992) was released and drew together much of their earlier material that had been available only on rare releases and bootlegs. A similar and very-hard-to-find release, *Hoarmoaning* (1992), was prepared for the Japanese market.

The studio follow-up to *Nevermind*, *In Utero* (1993), was recorded by Steve Albini, famed for his raw, honest approach to production. Geffen hated the result because it lacked the metallic polish of its predecessor. Although melodies were still in evidence they were buried under a ragged, thicker sound – a blend of *Bleach*'s smothering bludgeon and *Nevermind*'s diamond-hard swirl of guitars.

The subsequent tour saw **Pat Smear** (guitar), of seminal punksters the **Germs**, join the band to fill out their live sound. However, the European leg of the tour nearly brought tragedy. Cobain had managed to give the impression of control, but in March 1994 he almost died in Rome as a result of a toxic cocktail of depressants washed down with alcohol. It was back in Washington on April 5 that Cobain finally succeeded in taking his own life, to the disbelief and utter, miserable confusion of those left behind. His songwriting and performing genius was commemorated on the hushed and reverential MTV *Unplugged In New York* (1994) session, recorded in late 1993. The band worked their way through a delicately poised set of covers, and with the swamping howl of amplification removed, Cobain's voice is veiled in pained emotion.

From the remains of Nirvana, Dave Grohl is the only member to produce any significant new music; he created the **Foo Fighters**, for which he recruited Pat Smear. Meanwhile, after a protracted break from the scene, Novoselic turned up in 1996 with new band **Sweet 75**, though this and his subsequent work have remained relatively low-key.

While the *Unplugged* set showed the band at their quietest, the 1996 *From The Muddy Banks Of The Wishkah* set should come with a set of ear protectors. This was the Nirvana that took on the world: a primal, angry and extremely loud band. At last, with a live recording of "Smells Like Teen Spirit" speeded up to full throttle to balance the sweet depression of "Pennyroyal Tea", there was a document of this three-headed monster, standing tall and roaring.

A lengthy hiatus preceded a compilation album simply titled *Nirvana* (2002), featuring one new cut, "You Know You're Right", with rumour suggesting that there were other unheard gems lurking in the vaults – ample material for a box set. The possibility of such a project tying up the loose ends created by Cobain's untimely demise had long been mired in wrangling between the remaining members of the band and Cobain's widow, Courtney Love. Further fuelling the speculation was the publication of *Journals*, material culled from Cobain's own notebooks detailing lyrics and his own peculiar songwriting processes. The book split the fan community; some condemned it as a cynical cash-in, while others welcomed it as a means of shedding light on Cobain's unique creativity. In late 2004, however, the holy grail three-CD and one DVD collection of *With The Lights Out* finally gave people what they wanted by delving into the band's archives to deliver a whole range of goodies, from demos and outtakes, to rare live performances.

⊙ Nevermind
1991; Geffen

Slick rock production meets grunge. Cobain's songwriting is assured and scathing. A defining moment in rock music, and a yardstick it would be judged by in the future.

⊙ In Utero
1993; Geffen

Not an instant classic, but more honest in feel due to the scuzzier production. The lyrics are coloured with images of disease and sickness, an expression of the pressures felt by the band.

⊙ Unplugged In New York
1994; Geffen

The band show their influences by jamming on covers by artists as diverse as David Bowie and Leadbelly. Original material is delivered with a clarity and rare emotional power; "Pennyroyal Tea" has never sounded so ethereal and cleansing.

⊙ From The Muddy Banks Of The Wishkah
1996; Geffen

If *Unplugged* sounds funereally depressing then this is the antidote – full-volume renditions of several Nirvana classics.

⊙ Nirvana
2002; Geffen

This handy collection contains some of their most stunning songs. The fact that it leaves off plenty of others provides lots of fuel for fan arguments over the tracklisting.

TED NUGENT

Born Detroit, Michigan, US, December 13, 1948

"I remember when we covered 'Cat Scratch Fever' years ago and Lemmy said 'Ah Phil, it's no good I can't sing these fuckin' lyrics'…" Phil Campbell on Ted Nugent

When it comes to all-out gonzoid heavy rocking entertainment there are few out there who can touch the self-proclaimed "Motor City Madman". With his Gibson Byrdland seemingly grafted to his person – the cover of 1980's *Scream Dream* depicts his arms morphing into guitars – **Ted Nugent** is as red-blooded and fiery as axe heroes get. Also renowned for his mighty gob – he definitely needs no amplification when on a roll – about the only thing that eclipses his status as a fabulously hairy heavy rocker is his reputation for outrageous opinions. For the uninitiated this unflinching alpha male is an anti-alcohol, anti-drug, gun-loving, pro-hunting son of the Wild West, his right-wing politics often earning him more publicity than his guitar playing. It's impossible to avoid his motor-mouth ranting, as anyone who has witnessed his bonkers live shows will confirm – if you don't get mown down by his blitzkrieg six-string pyrotechnics then his self-aggrandizing rapid-fire between-song banter will surely finish you off.

The Nuge's axe-slinging antics started at around the age of eight, three years after he started bow-hunting – a skill that would allow for some crazy flaming-arrow antics on stage – and led to him joining an impressive array of bands during his early years, among them **Lourdes**, the **Royal High Boys** and **Cobo Hall**. It was with the **Amboy Dukes**, however, that he first came to prominence, the band specializing in ridiculous amounts of jamming. Nugent gradually took control of the band; he renamed them **Ted Nugent & The Amboy Dukes** before making plans, in the early 70s, for the solo career that would bring him a brace of platinum-selling albums.

First came a campaign of over-the-top self-publicity where he challenged various guitar-slingers of the day to on-stage widdling and feedback battles. Among his adversaries were Iron Butterfly's Mike Pinera, MC5's Wayne Kramer, Mahogany Rush's Frank Marino and Mountain's Leslie West. Then, as Ted Nugent's Amboy Dukes issued *Call Of The Wild* and *Tooth, Fang & Claw* – titled naturally enough after Nugent's love of blood sports – the band folded, leaving the man himself to pursue his solo quarry. He retained the Dukes' bassist **Rob Grange** and brought in **Derek St Holmes** (guitar/vocals) and **Cliff Davies** (drums), took on Aerosmith's management and signed to Epic for his 1975 eponymous debut. "Just What The Doctor Ordered" and "Motor City Madhouse" said it all; the album was a white-hot, guitar-worshipping party from start to finish replete with sizzling solos and Nugent's, er, unique lyrical slant on relationships with the fairer sex.

It was the beginning of the period of Nugent's greatest popularity, and he wasn't afraid to let people know it. The first album stayed in the US charts for 62 weeks yielding a modest hit single in "Hey Baby", but it was the following year's rip-snorting *Free For All* (featuring guest vocals by **Meat Loaf**) that really sank its fangs deep and refused to let go, becoming his first million-seller. The leather loincloth-wearing, caveman-bearded Nuge now had the cracking title track, "Dog Eat Dog", "Turn It Up" and "Street Rats" to add to his live repertoire of gonzo rock'n'roll; by now his shows regularly kicked off with Nugent swinging Tarzan-style onto the stage – he was cockier than ever and completely unapologetic about his passion for performance.

The only thing he really lacked at this stage was a genuinely massive hit single. That arrived with his next album, *Cat Scratch Fever* (1977). The title track became his first US top-thirty hit while the album went to #17. The previous year had brought him to the UK for his debut performance at the Reading Festival and shortly prior to the launch of the third album he returned for a full tour, his reputation as a libidinous axe-wielding maniac helping the album reach #28 in the UK.

Double Live Gonzo! and *Weekend Warriors* (both 1978) proved to be his last truly great albums. The former captured terrific versions of songs from his first three albums while his fourth studio effort was decent enough, though the limelight hogging ringmaster's rough-and-ready attitude towards his fellow band members had brought about major line-up shifts: St Holmes was replaced by **Charlie Huhn** and Grange was replaced by **David Hull**, who was then replaced by **Walter Monahan** for *State Of Shock* (1979). By now, however, the quality of the writing was suffering.

The aforementioned *Scream Dream*, despite its freaky sleeve, was patchy, with only the opening "Wango Tango" and the title track

THE NU WAVE TAKES THE RAP

The wave of grunge that helped sweep away much of the more traditional metal elements of the 80s left something of a vacuum in the 90s. Inevitably other styles gradually plugged the gap; chief among them was so-called **nu-metal**, one of the music industry's success stories of the last decade.

Occasionally also called **rap metal**, the more general nu-metal term encompasses a multitude of styles with hip-hop being the point of origin. The collision with the rap tag is understandable but it is more useful to think of rap metal bands as chiefly using rap-style vocals in conjunction with more recognizably old-school metal. Nu-metal, however, incorporates rapping as just one of several facets and any nu-metal spotter would be listening out for the following characteristics.

Lyrically nu-metal takes some of its cues from grunge and deals much of the time with angst of one kind or another; vocally the tales of inner turmoil and emotional hardship are delivered in anything from a clean, but melancholy, singing style to a guttural hardcore roar; if the vocalist can throw some rap and hip-hop stylings into the mix, so much the better.

The generally downbeat nature of the lyrics and vocals requires a musical accompaniment of equal power. Hence the riffing is downtuned for maximum bottom-end aggression and most of the complexity and tunefulness of traditional metal is jettisoned in favour of a churning and brutal rhythmic attack. One other fundamental point, though there are the odd exceptions, is that there are no guitar solos. Nu-metal frowns upon such wanton displays of fun and ego; this is catharsis music, a chance to take part in an explosive therapy session and nothing must distract from the oppressive misery of it all. This simplification of sound is one of the main criticisms voiced by nu-metal detractors.

Rhythmically the drums and bass bring an element of funkiness and usually incorporate hip-hop break beats. Some bands even utilize a DJ; **Linkin Park**, **Slipknot**, **Limp Bizkit** and **Deftones** are among those that bring "turntablizm" to the equation.

Quite how such a synthesis of disparate elements took place is always tough to pin down, but bands such as **Rage Against The Machine** and **Faith No More** must be counted among the pioneers. Back in the 80s, rap was seen as something of an oddity when bolted onto metal, but with outfits such as the **Beastie Boys** riding high in the charts and tunes such as Faith No More's "We Care A Lot" breaking down barriers the potential was always there. While FNM were eclectic in style, Rage Against The Machine revelled in a more focused hip-hop sound emulated purely through a rap vocal-led guitar/bass/drums setup. The missing link in all this, it could be argued, was the unhinged vocal style of FNM singer **Mike Patton** who could swing from a croon to a roar without breaking into a sweat, allowing the band to smash genre taboos almost at will.

In the alternative-loving 90s bands such as **Korn** and Deftones emerged among the first wave of nu-metallers. Not only did they sound different, but they looked different when compared to more traditional metallers, adopting a skateboarding and sportswear-led image appealing directly to the youth of the day. By the end of the decade the metal scene was choked with similar-sounding bands, guitars downtuned below the knees of their anti-fit jeans, ranting and wailing about what a terrible time they had in school. From this morass of cookie-cutter angst only a handful of bands stood out as offering anything beyond the generic noise; chief among these was **Slipknot** whose emergence and rapid domination of the metal scene in the new millennium signified the peak of the genre's popularity.

coming anywhere close to Nugent's previous highpoints; meanwhile *Intensities In 10 Cities* (1981) was a live album of largely new material that only really had its fantastic title going for it.

Yet more line-up shenanigans resulted in St Holmes returning to the band, but even a new deal with Atlantic couldn't halt the slide – *Nugent* (1982), *Penetrator* (1984), *Little Miss Dangerous* (1986) and *If You Can't Lick 'Em ... Lick 'Em* (1988) were vastly underwhelming. Maybe it was all the guest contributors that made these sound so unfocused, even though the latter featured a couple of Nugent's typically inspired titles in "Separate The Men From The Boys, Please" and "The Harder They Come (The Harder I Get)".

The fact that his profile was dwindling as a solo artist, at least as far as studio albums were concerned, presumably led to his next move. He largely abandoned the wildman of rock schtick and formed **Damn Yankees** with **Tommy Shaw** (guitar; ex-**Styx**), **Jack Blades** (bass; ex-**Night Ranger**) and **Michael Cartellone** (drums), an outfit specializing in super-smooth AOR tailor-made for FM radio. The result was two huge-selling albums and a major hit single in 1991 when "High Enough" hit #3 in the US.

It wasn't until 1995 that any new studio material appeared but when it did *Spirit Of The Wild* tried damn hard to recapture the power of Nugent's heyday. For those unconvinced by the new stuff, the 90s brought a plethora of compilations and expanded reissues allowing for plenty of value-added nostalgia, especially the *Live At Hammersmith '79* (1997) album. *Full Bluntal Nugity* (2001) captured Nugent's thirteenth annual Whiplash Bash on New Year's Eve 2000 at the Palace Of Auburn Hills in Detroit – it was a shameless, one hundred percent overdub-free celebration in classic style, and a perfect lead-in to *Craveman* (2002). The set featured such Nuge nuggets as "Wang Dang Doodle" and "My Baby Likes My Butter On Her Gritz".

Naturally, the albums were complemented by plenty of live shows and Nugent's neverending campaigns supporting those interests close to his all-American heart – he even played a gig for 500 US servicemen in Iraq in June 2004. Then there were his many business projects, one of which involved publishing a cookery book titled *Kill It And Grill It*.

Cat Scratch Fever
1977; Epic

The title track is a classic as is the brilliantly titled "Wang Dang Sweet Poontang" – just listen to that guitar wail. This is about as romantic as Ted ever got.

Great Gonzos! The Best Of Ted Nugent
1981; Epic; Reissued 1999

This album was great when it was first released over twenty years ago, but with "Yank Me, Crank Me" and "Homebound" added, plus one new song, "Give Me Just A Little", the reissue tops it for essential Nugent.

OPETH

Formed Stockholm, Sweden, 1990

Opeth are unique: a progressive death metal band. Though perhaps that label really doesn't do justice to the influences and complexities that make up their blend of gloomy atmospherics and soaring melodies. Like Paradise Lost their lyrics are inspired by the existential pains of the human condition, but developing a fitting soundtrack for their subject matter has led **Opeth** to ever more meandering and convoluted song structures.

Key to Opeth's sound is their chief song-writer **Mikael Åkerfeldt** (guitar/vocals). The first album that Åkerfeldt bought was Iron Maiden's *Number Of The Beast* but as the 1980s progressed he became increasingly fascinated by thrash and especially death metal – anything that had a little of the occult to it. Bands such as Morbid Angel, Death and the twisted weirdness of Voivod all contributed to his early interest in writing music. However, by the early 1990s the guitarist felt that ordinary death metal – the speed, the blastbeats, the guttural roar – was somewhat limiting. With writing partner **Peter Lindgren** (guitar) on board the duo were joined by **Johan DeFarfalla** (bass) – who replaced early Opeth bassist **Stefan Guteklint** – and **Anders Nordin** (drums). With a solid line-up in

place they stripped away pretty much all but a few stylistic elements of death metal – blast-beat drumming was out of the question. Åkerfeldt interpolated clean vocals into the traditional deathly grunting, while twin-guitar harmonies and acoustic interludes gave Opeth an identity all their own. As for the lyrics, they eschewed the typical death metal predilection for gore in favour of a vast sense of emptiness and emotional anguish.

They quickly attracted the attention of Candlelight Records. *Orchid* (1995) was born, the brilliant floral sleeve hinting at the unusual metal sound within. The majority of the seven songs clocked in at between ten and fifteen minutes in length – this was

marathon misery metal at its finest. A similar pattern was followed on *Morningrise* (1996) and the cheerfully titled *My Arms, Your Hearse* (1998). The critical and relative commercial success of the former meant an immediate rise in profile, gigs with old heroes Morbid Angel and a European tour with UK black metallers, Cradle Of Filth. The consolidation provided by the latter album placed them firmly within a league of their own; no one else could sustain the same level of invention and majestic morbidity.

One line-up shift later – introducing **Martin Mendez** (bass) and **Martin Lopez** (drums) – and the newly revamped Opeth was ready to take on a new millennium of extreme metal with *Still Life* (1999) on Peaceville Records. For some bands the gradual rise in popularity might have resulted in a trimming down of the progressive excesses and a penning of more accessible tunes, but once again Opeth turned in a sumptuous set of captivating and melodic torment – each tune a fully fledged melodrama.

With such a weight of critical approval the band were only a power chord or two away from their master opus, which was nurtured by producer **Steven Wilson**, the mainman behind progsters Porcupine Tree. With the label machinery of Music For Nations behind them, *Blackwater Park* (2001) was, like Metallica's *Master Of Puppets,* Opeth's very own masterpiece, an extraordinary, autumnal sounding album, populated by the ghosts of painful memories and brittle, whispering intimations of decay and death. It was a massive leap forward for their credibility, landing them with several European festival dates as well as their own headlining tour of Europe and their first US tour.

Interestingly, the success of *Blackwater Park* did not see the band resting on their laurels. Rather they set themselves a bigger challenge: to record two albums back to back in the same time that it took them to record the last, and to do something quite different stylistically. One set would be heavy and the other a complete departure, a largely mellow and acoustic affair. *Deliverance* (2002) was an amazingly tight effort, with the band's musical prowess hammering home compositions of

brutal precision and unnerving complexity, leavened occasionally by their tried-and-tested acoustic interludes. So powerful was the songwriting that they were awarded a Swedish Grammy for Best Rock/Metal Act. And one year later the counterpart album *Damnation* (2003) displayed a distinctly non-metal aspect to Åkerfeldt's writing – sweeping and grandiose with an almost crystalline beauty to the songs, the album could almost have been mistaken as a mainstream effort, were it not for the chilling spectre of doom hanging over it.

⊙ **Blackwater Park**
2001; Music For Nations

This really is a breakthrough, a gothic masterpiece of mood, tension and superb musicianship. Steven Wilson's expertise in producing sumptuous and complex music brings out the best in Opeth's meandering and funereal approach to songwriting.

ORANGE GOBLIN

Formed London, UK, 1995

This grimy retro metal outfit harks back to simple times, when denim and leather were the only sartorial choices open to rockers and when festivals were fuelled on shed-loads of scrumpy and weed. Far from being mere stoner throwbacks, however, **Orange Goblin** are capable of harnessing

ORCHESTRAL METAL

At first orchestral metal may appear to be an oxymoron – this combination ought to be a recipe doomed to failure, but over the years this obscure branch of metallic experimentation has resulted in some fascinating live and studio-bound albums, even if the results haven't always been even.

So, who is to blame for the idea in the first place? Way back in 1970 **Deep Purple**, casting around to find direction, released *Concerto For Group And Orchestra With The Royal Philharmonic Orchestra*. The album wasn't great and it wasn't particularly metal – in fact, they pretty soon abandoned the idea for straight-ahead rock – but it did kick off the decade in which the **Electric Light Orchestra** would make a string of incredibly successful albums featuring orchestra and choir.

Come the era of the guitar hero and power metal in the 80s and the gates were wide open to classical influences as a whole slew of metal bands began experimenting with progressive orchestral arrangements, though few actually used full-blown orchestras preferring to keep things relatively small-scale. In among the classically influenced guitar mayhem bands such as **Celtic Frost** stood out for their willingness to push the thrash metal envelope; *Into The Pandemonium* (1987) was an avant-garde masterpiece featuring a string section and operatic female vocals to give a morbidly gothic flavour to the music, an experiment that would influence greatly the development of black metal, a genre often described in symphonic terms. Indeed, one of the UK's biggest extreme bands, **Cradle Of Filth**, used a 40-piece orchestra and 32-voice choir on their *Damnation And A Day* (2003) album.

When it came to a full interaction between band and orchestra, however, the man most metallers would call in was composer **Michael Kamen**, who sadly died at the end of 2003. Kamen's successes in scoring films led him to work with artists as diverse as **Aerosmith** – most notably on their orchestral version of "Dream On" for MTV's tenth anniversary celebrations – and **Queensrÿche**, for whom he arranged strings and choir on their classic concept album *Operation: Mindcrime* (1988). His biggest metal-related work, however, arrived when **Metallica** decided that a symphonic adaptation of their oeuvre was the way to go, resulting in 1999's *S&M* live album featuring the San Francisco Symphony Orchestra. The album was a critical success despite the fact that it didn't really work as a Metallica record.

Hot on the heels of the Metalliboys came **Scorpions** in 2000 with *Moment Of Glory* and the Berlin Philharmonic Orchestra. Old favourites were recast with strings and it was altogether more melodically convincing than Metallica's effort, even if it made the Scorps sound like they ought to be pensioned off.

The prize for the most ludicrous example of orchestra and metal in tandem, however, must go to **Kiss**, for whom there is no such thing as going over the top. Their *Symphony – Alive IV* (2003) featured the 60-piece Melbourne Symphony accompanying them on ten tracks – while wearing full Kiss make-up.

incredible horsepower both live and in the studio.

Back in the mid-1990s the Goblin were known as **Our Haunted Kingdom**, a band with a penchant for psychedelia and big, bruising Sabbath riffery, making them ideal gigging partners for bands such as Mourn and Electric Wizard. During one of these gigs they were spotted by Cathedral frontman Lee Dorrian, who so enjoyed the band's 1970s-flavoured doom metal that he signed them to his Rise Above label. So with the line-up of **Ben Ward** (vocals), **Martyn Millard** (bass), **Joe Hoare** (guitar), **Pete O'Malley** (guitar) and **Chris Turner** (drums) the band began their career as one of the UK's finest purveyors of vintage metal, at a time when grunge was fading and nu-metal was just stepping up to the gate. They released only one song as Our Haunted Kingdom, "Aquatic Fanatic" – a split seven-incher with Electric Wizard – before becoming Orange Goblin.

The Goblin's first full-length album was the fabulous *Frequencies From Planet Ten* (1997). "Song Of The Purple Mushroom Fish" gave a fair indication of what chemicals the band ingested for breakfast; the likes of "Lothlorian" and "Saruman's Wish" gave an even bigger clue as to where these guys were coming from. *Time Travelling Blues* (1998), however, largely dispensed with Tolkein, looking instead to H.G. Wells and John Carpenter's *Dark Star* for sci-fi inspiration. Meanwhile, the female biker astride a chopper pictured on the sleeve was giving the middle finger to all those who didn't get it. Although plenty of people *did*, leading to support slots with the likes of US stoners Unida and Queens Of The Stone Age.

Continuing the biker metal theme, *The Big Black* (2000) sleeve showed an unclothed and ghostly biker chick, reclining on her roadhog against a background of the Milky Way. The songs were tighter and heavier than before, the twin-engine turbo fury of Hoare and

O'Malley's riffing a joy to hear, the layered thunder driving along songs such as "Hot Magic, Red Planet" and "Alcofuel" with a reckless abandon, recalling Motörhead at their most relentless. Clearly a band that liked the occasional thirst-quenching ale, the hidden track at the end consisted of a sequence of phone messages recorded when Ward was completely trollied, and made for a very amusing booze-soaked finale.

2002's *Coup De Grace* continued to display the band's love of crazy visuals. This time the album's sleeve recalled a classic EC horror comic, featuring a creepy and ghoulish crypt-keeper type wielding an axe (painted by cult artist Frank Kozik). For help on the music front, John Garcia (**Unida**, ex-**Kyuss**) was brought in and contributed vocals to "Made Of Rats" and "Jesus Beater". The leap forward in quality – aided, no doubt, by another former Kyuss man, bassist **Scott Reeder** on production – meant the band finally made it to America for their own headlining tour, and played some sold-out dates in Los Angeles and New York.

The rise in their fortunes, however, couldn't tempt O'Malley to stay; he headed off for a more sedate career in art, which meant that *Thieving From The House Of God* (2004) found them reduced to a four-piece. The album emerged to rave reviews across the British rock press – hardly surprising given that the new material succinctly summed up the uncompromising mega-metal stance the band had been peddling for nearly a decade.

⊙ **Time Travelling Blues**
1998; Rise Above

Biker metal at its finest. You can almost smell the gasoline and burning rubber as they open the throttle and blaze through these songs. There is nothing even remotely subtle about this album. Gargantuan riffs forged from space debris and bits of crashed UFOs avalanche upon you without mercy. Immense and glorious.

OZZY OSBOURNE

Born Birmingham, UK, December 3, 1948

"What can you say to Ozzy that he doesn't already know? 'You're a bad ass, you're still alive and you still rock!'" Nick Oliveri (ex-Queens Of The Stone Age) on Ozzy.

Ozzy Osbourne is a heavy metal icon. Period. Few performers come even close to the Ozzmeister's reputation for lunacy and rock'n'roll carnage. Coming to prominence fronting Brum metallers **Black Sabbath**, he quickly established formidable appetites for drugs and boozing which would affect the way much of his career panned out. Not only that, but with his bandmates he defined the sound of heavy metal and sold millions of records around the globe. After leaving Sabbath, Ozzy's career went on to outstrip his former bandmates' efforts while producing a string of classic, and not so classic, solo albums. Lately, due largely to the MTV series *The Osbournes*, Ozzy has stepped beyond the confines of being simply a barking mad rock star to become a bona fide mainstream celebrity.

When Ozzy departed Black Sabbath in 1979 the world knew only of his efforts writing with **Tony Iommi**, **Geezer Butler** and **Bill Ward**. He was a singer whose identity, though larger than life, was still inextricably linked to the definitive line-up of a world-famous group. He needed musicians around him who understood his strengths and he needed direction and focus; without these things his solo career could have quickly gone off the rails. Initial plans to utilize guitarist **Gary Moore** and bassist **Glenn Hughes** hit the skids early on, but the unit he formed with **Bob Daisley** (bass; ex-**Rainbow**), **Lee Kerslake** (drums; ex-**Uriah Heep**) and **Randy Rhoads** (guitar) would prove to be legendary.

Key to Ozzy's early success was the stellar talent that was **Randy Rhoads**. The guitarist had played on the first two **Quiet Riot** albums, but his abilities extended well beyond rock to encompass classical and blues influences, while his playing style was technically astonishing. In short, Rhoads was the kind of guitar hero Ozzy needed.

Having signed to one-time Sabbath manager **Don Arden**'s Jet Records label, the scene was set for *Blizzard Of Ozz* (1980). This was a true classic heavy metal album that would map Ozzy's direction for years to come and which, even now, forms the backbone of virtually every set list of his. The opening salvo of "I Don't Know" and "Crazy Train" (still live favourites today) kicked the album off in roaring style, Rhoads nailing every single riff with blistering, jaw-dropping proficiency. Rhoads also provided a sweet little classical interlude called "Dee" which served as an introduction to the stormingly heavy classic "Suicide Solution", with lyrics about alcoholic oblivion. **Don Airey** (ex-Rainbow) provided the ominously grandiose keyboards to kick off "Mr Crowley", written, unsurprisingly, about infamous occultist Aleister Crowley, while "No Bone Movies" and "Steal Away (The Night)" featured some superb, fluid bass runs complementing the frenetic guitars. One of the outstanding epics of the album, however, was "Revelation (Mother Earth)". Full to overflowing with menacing classical flourishes, and topped off with doom-laden lyrics about impending nuclear and environmental holocaust, it was balanced against the earlier softer ballad "Goodbye To Romance". There was not a duff track to be found. The band aired their wares at the Edinburgh Nite Club during the Edinburgh Rock Festival in August 1980 and both "Crazy Train" and "Mr Crowley" achieved reasonable chart placings while the album went to #7.

The US reaction was similarly ecstatic. The album stayed in the charts for two years, fuelled by some punishing tour schedules and Ozzy's inability to avoid outrage and controversy. One particularly infamous incident occurred when Ozzy, growing somewhat bored during a meeting in Los Angeles with assembled record label executives, decided to bite the head off a dove that was intended to be part of a media stunt. Needless to say, the original idea didn't involve orally decapitating feathered creatures of any kind.

Second album *Diary Of A Madman* (1981) followed soon after. Ozzy had recruited **Rudy Sarzo** (bass) and **Tommy Aldridge** (drums), though the songwriting and performance credits should have included Kerslake and Daisley who had left to join Uriah Heep. Often overlooked as a follow-up, the album didn't quite match the stature of Ozzy's solo debut but did contain some fantastic songs all the same. Again, the first two songs on the album – "Over The Mountain" and "Flying High Again" (a subject Ozzy was very familiar with) – would both become live staples, while the voodoo-inspired horror of "Little Dolls" featured some wonderfully menacing tribal drumming.

The subsequent US tour, however, would go down as one of the most exciting in rock history. The reaction to the newly revamped Ozzy was nothing short of incredible and the spectacular show was augmented by the appearance of a dwarf who was introduced onstage as 'Ronnie', a none-too-PC dig at the diminutive singer Ronnie James Dio, who had replaced Ozzy in Sabbath. And again Ozzy seemed incapable of avoiding trouble. In another notorious incident in early 1982 during a show in Des Moines, Iowa, Ozzy picked up what he thought was a toy bat, hurled onstage by a member of the crowd, and bit it. It wasn't a toy. In fact it was very much alive and it bit Ozzy back. After the show the singer reportedly had to endure several rabies shots. In yet another scandalous tour incident, a drunken Ozzy was arrested in San Antonio, Texas for urinating on the Alamo monument – while wearing one of his wife's dresses.

What followed a few weeks down the line would almost scupper Ozzy's career entirely. While travelling across Florida the occupants of the tour plane decided it would be great fun to dive-bomb the tour bus. Unfortunately things went too far and a wing tip clipped the vehicle, bringing the plane to the ground in a horrific fireball. The pilot, the tour's hair-stylist and Randy Rhoads, who had all been on board the aircraft, died. This event more than any other would haunt Ozzy for the rest of his career. Without the prodigiously talented guitarist, Ozzy was lost, though **Bernie Tormé** (ex-**Gillan**) was drafted in to complete the tour.

Guitarist **Brad Gillis** stayed with Ozzy long enough to record the live *Talk Of The Devil* (1982), a collection of Sabbath tunes intended to act as a spoiler to Black Sabbath's own forthcoming live album. A permanent guitarist was found at last in the shape of another incredibly talented six-string pyro-technician, **Jake E. Lee** (ex-Rough Cutt), shortly before Ozzy made another vastly significant move: he married Sharon, daughter of Don Arden, and she took over from her father as Ozzy's manager (Ozzy had been

married before but left his wife Thelma Mayfair in 1981). This close bond between him and his management would prove to be a double-edged sword. Sharon understood what was needed to keep Ozzy on an even keel – an altogether less intense work schedule – but she clashed with her father over various business decisions. Many rows later and after family tensions reached breaking point, Sharon gained full control over Ozzy's future career path, enabling him to gradually gain some control over his drug and booze dependency.

When *Bark At The Moon* (1983) was released on Epic – with Daisley back on bass and helping with production – the fans were treated to the sight of their hero in full lycan-thropic disguise, looking barking mad on the sleeve. The music was much tougher sounding with a distinctly metallic flavour pervading

FIN COSTELLO/REDFERNS

Repent all ye sinners for the Ozzman cometh.

the entire album, as opposed to the more classically oriented moods Rhoads had previously conjured up.

Come 1985 and the ghost of Sabbath past reared its head, as all four original members were reunited to perform for one day at Live Aid in Philadelphia, despite Don Arden's attempt to claim a huge amount in damages from Ozzy for getting together with his former bandmates. The performance was less than spectacular and the same could be said of *The Ultimate Sin* (1986), with the new rhythm section of **Phil Soussan** (bass; ex-**Wildlife**) and **Randy Castillo** (drums; ex-**Lita Ford**). Despite the more workmanlike metal on offer, and the whiff of nuclear obliteration ever-present in the lyrics, *The Ultimate Sin* would prove to be one of Ozzy's best-selling albums, doubtless helped by the MTV video for single "Shot In The Dark". The triumph of headlining the Donington Monsters Of Rock festival, however, was offset somewhat by having to deal with a lawsuit claiming that the lyrics to "Suicide Solution" had caused a teenager to kill himself. The case was eventually dismissed.

The threat of legal action was constant through the 1980s as Ozzy became one of several high-profile rock targets for the highly influential conservative Christian groups that were proliferating. In an inspired bit of parody, the year 1987 saw Ozzy make an appearance as a fundamentalist preacher in the heavy metal horror movie *Trick Or Treat*. Despite this minor highlight there was no getting away from the fact that his relationship with guitarist Jake E. Lee had run its course, and that Ozzy would soon have to search out fresh talent. But not before the release of the superb *Tribute* live album which basically showcased Randy Rhoads' tenure in the band. It was a bitter-sweet set underlining the extent to which Rhoads was missed by both Ozzy and the fans.

The search for a new guitarist resulted in **Zakk Wylde** stepping into the ring. His shaggy blond locks and distinctive black-and-white target guitar made him a prominent fixture on stage; there was also more than a passing resemblance to Rhoads. *No Rest For The Wicked* (1988) was another hit album with old writing partner and bassist Daisley back in the band; for subsequent live dates, however, **Geezer Butler** was tempted to rejoin his old Sabbath mate.

Despite the continuing popularity and commercial success, Ozzy's old instabilities were still bubbling just under the surface. In August 1989 Ozzy played the massive Moscow Music Peace Festival alongside Mötley Crüe, Bon Jovi, the Scorpions, Skid Row and Cinderella, raising money to tackle alcohol and drug addiction in Russia and the US. But personal alcohol-related disaster followed just a few weeks afterwards: Ozzy was charged with threatening to kill his wife. While the charges were dropped and the two were reconciled it seemed that the marathon of legal problems would never end, as yet more parents of suicidal teenagers filed lawsuits which would be eventually dismissed.

The only product released in 1990 was the so-so *Just Say Ozzy* mini-LP, presumably to keep people interested while Ozzy got his act together again. The next full-blown Ozzy extravaganza came in the form of *No More Tears* (1991), this time with musical input coming from both **Mike Inez** and **Lemmy** of **Motörhead**. It was possibly one of Ozzy's least sparkling efforts but by this point the constant touring and pressure had taken their toll; he had nothing left to prove and felt that the time had come to call it a day. What were to be his last live dates in 1992 included a set by Black Sabbath who he had invited along as special guests, though **Dio** refused to be involved.

It would have been a spectacular way to say goodbye. He was awarded a star on the Rock Walk on Sunset Boulevard, and anyway, grunge was killing off the careers of most 1980s metal bands. The only Ozzy album of any significance for a period of nearly three years was *Live And Loud* (1993), while the records continued to sell in platinum-rewarded quantities. Ozzy was awarded a Grammy for Best Metal Performance for "I Don't Want To Change the World", and the Kudos Award at the first ever *Kerrang!* awards.

In the end it seems that all Ozzy really wanted was a very long holiday, because *Ozzmosis* arrived in 1995 along with a full Retirement Sucks tour. The album was, again, rather a disappointing affair with even more outside writers being drafted in to provide the tunes. Yet nothing could stop the Ozzmania, especially with the advent in 1996 of the Ozzfest, a touring festival capitalizing on the growing nu-metal scene. There was also a distinct sense of anticipation in the air regarding a possible Black Sabbath and Ozzy reunion, which finally came off in December 1997 with two historic shows at the National Exhibition Centre in Birmingham. *The Ozzman Cometh* (1997), a compilation featuring both solo and Sabbath material, and *Reunion* (1998), recorded during the dates with Black Sabbath, kept things rolling.

By the time of *Down To Earth* (2001) – which saw a large number of songwriters again chipping in – the albums had definitely lost their edge. It was a stronger album than the lamentable *Ozzmosis* but it lacked the individual flair and danger of the earlier efforts. Still, this ought to have come as no surprise, because the world was witnessing the creation of Ozzy Osbourne the celebrity. There were invitations for dinner at the White House, a chance to play before the Queen at the Golden Jubilee celebrations, the launch of *The Osbournes* series on MTV (one of the single most successful TV shows of recent years) and regular appearances on chat shows. The man who had been hounded by moral guardians for corrupting the youth of the day with his heavy metal anthems and drunken ways was now a member of the entertainment establishment, so much so that *Live At Budokan* (2002) and most recently *The Essential Ozzy Osbourne* (2003) slipped by without alerting much interest.

In a rather bizarre move, the controversy surrounding the reissues of both *Blizzard Of Ozz* and *Diary Of A Madman* indicate perhaps how far the Ozzy business machine has distanced the man from the fans. For a long time Daisley and Kerslake had been in dispute with Ozzy over unpaid royalties. As a result of this the decision was taken to re-record their instruments using the services of bassist **Rob Trujillo** and drummer **Mike Bordin**, an act of sacrilege to most fans. Imagine what the first two Led Zeppelin albums might have sounded like without John Bonham and John Paul Jones!

In late 2003 Ozzy's continuing quest for world domination was put on hold when he was very badly injured in a quad-bike accident on his Buckinghamshire estate. Recovery was slow but, thankfully, sure and in early 2005 he eventually gave the world a four-CD box set dubbed, naturally enough, *Prince Of Darkness*. It was packed with everything from rare live tracks and demos to a disc of somewhat bizarre collaborations – not least with hip-hoppers **Wu Tang Clan** and the muppet, **Miss Piggy** – and another disc of cover versions. Ozzy worked with guitarists such as **Alice In Chains'** Jerry Cantrell and **Moutain's** Leslie West to record a variety of his fave songs originally written by artisis as diverse as **The Beatles**, **Buffalo Springfield** and **King Crimson**.

⊙ Blizzard Of Ozz
1980; Epic

Every metal fan should have this classic – but only the version with Kerslake and Daisley playing. Seek it out. The reissue is just not the same.

⊙ Diary Of A Madman
1981; Epic

It's often overlooked in favour of Ozzy's debut but this is another masterpiece – though again, only the version with Ozzy's old rhythm section.

PANTERA

Formed Dallas, Texas, US, 1981; disbanded 2003

For years **Pantera** were one of the premier extreme metal bands in the world. Ugly, twisted and supremely heavy they were true predators of metal, capable of vicious intensity and an unrelenting groove that their peers could only dream of. With their purgatorial, titanic sound they were the inspiration to hundreds of copyists, all of whom tried to appropriate their platinum-selling power. What's more, to the uninitiated, it appeared that Pantera had emerged as fully formed heavyweights at the start of the 1990s. The truth, however, was rather more grisly and disturbing...

Having played together in their high-school jazz band of 1980, brothers 'Diamond' Darrell (guitars) and **Vinnie Paul Abbott** (drums), plus **Rex 'Rocker' Brown** (bass) formed the original Pantera with **Terry Glaze** (vocals/guitars). In those days they were very much of the tacky, glam-influenced school – poodle-perm hair, dubious spandex trousers and Kiss-type anthems. For the curious, the period can be sampled on *Metal Magic* (1983), *Projects In The Jungle* (1984) and *I Am The Night* (1985). Although each album was progressively heavier than the last, they were still light years away from their later blistering sound.

Glaze departed in the late 1980s and for a while **David Peacock** took over. But it wasn't until he was replaced by the wild **Phil Anselmo** that the band began mutating into the Pantera of today. Their last flirtation with 1980s-style metal came with *Power Metal* (1988), which went some way towards marking out their future career path. Recorded at Vinnie Abbott's father's studio, the album was mixed and marketed by the band themselves and, despite the extremely cheesy cover art ("We looked like dorks"), it managed to shift 35,000 units.

Having finally attracted the attention of a major label, the band signed to Atco, and everything fell neatly into place. Ditching the glam and the cock-rock posturing, the band went for a distinctly more aggressive image and a stripped-down heavy sound. *Cowboys From Hell* (1990) was a forearm smash of an album, with Anselmo's powerful voice teetering on the edge of mania. The riffs on "Primal Concrete Sledge" and "The Art Of Shredding" gave established bands like Metallica a run for their money, while "Shattered" sounded remarkably like modern Judas Priest, with Anselmo hitting some painfully high notes. With a dedicated fan base ready to lap up their new fierce sound, success was assured for their steroidal power groove.

With the help of **Terry Date** in the studio, *Vulgar Display Of Power* (1992) established Pantera as being among the extreme metal vanguard. The band's assertively muscular stance was again borne out on tracks such as "Fucking Hostile" and "Mouth For War". The guitar sound often edged towards meltdown, and the drum attack was so crushing that it quickly became evident why Vinnie Paul was known as 'The Brick Wall'.

By the time of *Far Beyond Driven* (1994) they had pushed their sound even further.

Dimebag Darrell grinds his axe.

putting together **Down**, a brutal and thundering side-project featuring various members of **Crowbar** and **Eyehategod**.

Having taken a well-deserved break from the mayhem of live shows and recording, the band stepped back into the heavyweight arena with possibly their most savage offering to date. *The Great Southern Trend Kill* (1996) was an album of towering stature, psychotic mood swings and battering rhythms. The all-out rattling speed that had characterized their previous efforts was still in evidence, but the band had tempered their approach with mellower textures in "Suicide Note Pt. 1" and the doom-laden "Floods". The black vibes emanating from Anselmo's lyrics hinted at his growing drug problem, the effects of which nearly floored the band before they could capitalize on their powerful new work. Just months after the album was released Anselmo overdosed on heroin after a gig in Dallas and was dead for five minutes before being revived. Amazingly, the tour wasn't cancelled and Anselmo took to the stage in San Antonio a couple of days later.

In 1997 *Official Live: 101 Proof* came storming out to show just how hard'n'heavy the band could be in the live arena. Having been out of action for such a long time, the band even made an appearance on the UK leg of the Ozzfest rock festival, alongside other heavyweights such as Slayer and Soulfly. However, for a variety of reasons – not least rumours of personnel issues with Anselmo – it took three years to get *Reinventing The Steel* into the stores. Whereas the *Trendkill* album had been relatively inventive and diverse, the new material opted largely for searing, straight-ahead fury. But, rather than trying to re-establish themselves amid all the fresh-faced nu-metal bands stealing their thunder and trademark heaviness, Pantera's focus shifted to a flurry of

The trademark sonic squeals were ever-present while the whole thing had an unrelenting over-the-edge atmosphere in its tales of hate, fear, paranoia and brutalized existence. Perhaps realizing the unsuitability of his name, it was at this point that 'Diamond' Darrell became the equally unlikely 'Dimebag' Darrell.

The summer of 1994 heralded an appearance at the Donington Monsters of Rock Festival, the inevitable packed touring schedule, and the recording of an old Poison Idea song ("The Badge") for the soundtrack to the film *The Crow*. With *Far Beyond Driven* having gone platinum in the US, the band took the opportunity to indulge themselves with a variety of solo projects and guest appearances. 'Dimebag' Darrell provided guitars for **Anthrax**'s *Stomp 442*, while Anselmo was instrumental in solo activity, most notably from Anselmo. His **Down** and **Superjoint Ritual** projects got back into full swing, allowing him to indulge himself in a more sludgy, doomy style of stoner metal.

In 2003 the inevitable career-ending best-of compilation was bolted together – *Reinventing Hell: The Best Of Pantera* (2003). Pantera had folded, or rather they had splintered – the guys didn't disappear gracefully. While Anselmo busied himself with Superjoint Ritual the Abbott brothers put together **Damageplan** with **Patrick Lachman** (ex-**Halford**) on vocals and **Bob Kakaha**, aka **Bob Zilla**, on bass. The result was the solid *New Found Power* (2004), the sleeve depicting the four-piece strolling nonchalantly away from a monstrous explosion detonating behind them.

From poodle-rockers to behemoths of the metal scene, Pantera's transformation was totally successful and uncompromisingly deadly. As one of the hardest and heaviest bands in the world, their influence on the metal scene cannot be underestimated. Such was their legacy that for a while fans held onto the hope that they could somehow patch up their differences and re-emerge even stronger than before. Such a faint possibility was destroyed, however, by a tragic turn of events on December 8, 2004 when Damageplan were playing a club gig in Columbus, Ohio. Dimebag Darrell was one of four people killed by a gunman who appeared on stage during the band's first number, began arguing with the guitarist and then started shooting. The shooter was also killed by the police during the incident so the motivation behind his actions will never be truly known, though there were suggestions that he was a disgruntled Pantera fan who took the dissolution of his favourite band very personally and to a homicidal degree.

Needless to say, the incident left the metal community and fans utterly stunned and the memorial service that took place a few days later featured many prominent musicians – including Zakk Wylde and Eddie Van Halen, though notably not Anselmo – celebrating Dimebag's life. Anselmo was apparently barred from the service in light of his continual feuding with the deceased guitarist; it certainly didn't help that *Metal Hammer* magazine had coincidentally published an interview with Anselmo, conducted months earlier, in which the vocalist had said that Dimebag ought to be "beaten severely". A devastated Anselmo

issued a press statement after the shooting in which he claimed to love Dimebag as a brother despite all the arguing; he also added that the incident had led him to question his own direction in life and that he was done with music for the time being. All of which draws a very sad line underneath the career of one of metal's biggest bands. Where this leaves the individual players remains to be seen.

⊙ Cowboys From Hell
1990; Atco

From the roots of a glam band grew a mad and mutated monster. The album positively bristles with jagged riffs and solid rhythms. Clearly influenced by 1980s thrash, it took the standards of the genre and forged a vicious new sound for the 1990s.

⊙ Vulgar Display Of Power
1992; Atco

Even more foul-mouthed and antisocial than their major-label debut, this album simply rages.

⊙ Far Beyond Driven
1994; Atco

Dark and brooding, the band continued to explore the outer realms of the metal genre. Anselmo's vocals veer between a claustrophobic intensity on tracks such as "Becoming" and a more sinister spoken style on the twisted love song "Good Friends And A Bottle of Pills". Fearsome stuff.

⊙ The Great Southern Trend Kill
1996; Atco

Just when it seemed that things couldn't get any nastier or heavier... Anselmo sounds like he is on the verge of madness, while melodic guitar solos interweave with some of the harshest, most menacing riffs ever recorded.

⊙ Official Live: 101 Proof
1997; Eastwest

A raw, clattering live outing produced by Vinnie Paul and 'Dimebag' Darrell which predictably concentrates on the guitar and drum sound at the expense of Rex Brown's sub-bass rumble. It features two new studio tracks, "Where You Come From" and "I Can't Hide", penned after Anselmo's near-fatal overdose.

PAPA ROACH

Formed Vacaville, California, US, 1993

"Rock'n'roll keeps me alive!" Coby Dick

No one could accuse Californian nu-metallers **Papa Roach** of not paying their dues. For seven years, prior to inking

PARENTS MUSIC RESOURCE CENTER

Heavy metal by its very nature has always courted controversy. The whole point of the music is to be outrageous, exciting and entertaining. Wherever there are people trying to have fun, however, there will be those for whom the 'fun' violates some kind of moral standard and if those people happen to be the wives of various congressmen and senators then they will probably be in a better position than most to try to impose their views on things.

Back in the mid-1980s, at the height of the Reagan administration, metal artists such as **WASP, Twisted Sister, Mötley Crüe, Ozzy Osbourne** and **Judas Priest** were at the top of their game. Soon, however, they and many others would be hounded by the creation of the **Parents Music Resource Center**, the membership of which included **Susan Baker** (wife of Treasury Secretary James Baker), **Nancy Thurmond** (wife of Senator Strom Thurmond) and **Tipper Gore** (wife of Senator later to be Vice President Al Gore). The *raison d'être* of this committee was simple. They believed that many of the ills apparently afflicting American society could be traced to the influence of popular music, particularly heavy metal and rap music. Heavy metal, it was claimed, encourages drug use, violence, criminal behaviour and suicide.

Their plan was to introduce a labelling system to warn parents of explicit content, despite the fact that this would violate the first amendment rights of the artists, a state of affairs alluded to by opponents of the move. The PMRC nevertheless pushed for this while the Record Industry Association of America (RIAA) resisted.

On September 19, 1985 the US Senate Commerce, Technology and Transportation Committee began an investigation into the content of rock music and various artists including **Frank Zappa**, **Dee Snider** (Twisted Sister) and **John Denver** were called as witnesses. Ultimately the RIAA decided to give in before the hearings had even finished and the result was what some called the "Tipper sticker". Of course, the commercial and legal implications were immense. Various chain stores refused to stock such stickered records and some politicians wanted outright bans or jail sentences for anyone caught trying to sell these albums to children.

Over the years, however, this extreme reaction to the content of heavy metal music has lessened, and metal and rap have continued to grow in popularity. Nevertheless, the RIAA still encourages labelling of explicit content.

their major-label deal with Dreamworks, they plied their trade around their home state. They honed their rap/metal interface by supporting legions of bands, from Suicidal Tendencies to the Deftones – their diverse approach to rocking out making them ideal gig mates for a wide variety of acts. And while they maintained the gigging marathon they kept the stream of self-produced albums and EPs flowing for the fans until, at the turn of the millennium, they found themselves up there with Limp Bizkit and Korn as chief delegates of the nu-wave of heavy metal.

Winding back the clock to the early 90s, school friends **Jacoby Shaddix** (vocals), **Jerry Horton** (guitar), **Dave Buckner** (drums), and **Will James** (bass) were taking on influences from a number of artists and bands, citing Faith No More (singling out vocalist Mike Patton in particular) as their heroes. They went through the usual rounds of talent competitions and traumas, getting established in their home territory of north California through their DIY approach. The years from 1994 to 1999 saw the band produce an impressive array of outpourings. *Potatoes For Christmas* was a mini-LP from 1994, followed by *Caca Bonita* the following year. In 1996 **Tobin Esperance** stepped in when James could no longer commit to the band and the

next year their first album appeared, *Old Friends From Young Years*, recorded for a mere $700. With a huge groundswell of support building, the album found favour with local radio and the band upped the level of their professional profile by releasing another couple of EPs, *5 Tracks Deep* (1998) and *Let 'Em Know* (1999). By this point Papa Roach had a sizeable catalogue of material, had supported several major-league bands in their area and had plenty of fans, who took to referring to them as P-Roach for short. They could no longer be ignored by the major labels, and Dreamworks stepped in.

Despite the major-label bankroll behind them *Infest* (2000) seemed to just appear out of nowhere on the album charts, hitting the Top 10 in the UK after peaking some months earlier at #5 in the US. It was a stunningly commercial nu-metal set, the timing of which was impeccable, with Fred Durst and co. mercilessly mashing metal and rap together. The music scene was easily seduced by Papa Roach's patented slick and melodic riffing topped off by Shaddix's trick of dropping rhymes with ruthless efficiency before letting the vocal chords rip on a particularly potent chorus or two. Around this time, Shaddix adopted the cringeworthy pseudonym of **Coby Dick**. The formula was so sweet and simple it would have been almost embarrassing, were it not for the fact that, live, Papa Roach simply slayed. On a stripped-down stage set, the band typically clad head to toe in black, they played with live-wire ferocity; Shaddix's manic stage persona was intense and, on occasion, he would get so worked up that he would actually vomit.

With such a monster album to their name, a follow-up was inevitably going to be a problem. Do the same thing again and you risk sounding stale, especially if the mood of the moment shifts unexpectedly; try something new and you risk alienating the fans who have been there from the start. Sensing that the nu-metal bubble might be straining, even if it had yet to burst, the band opted to stretch their creativity with *Lovehatetragedy* (2002). Its sleeve art, bizarrely, pictured a baby wearing headphones and throwing the devil horn salute, intending to symbolize the band's rebirth... or something. In a distinctly irony-free Spinal Tap-style publicity stunt the band actually played a rooftop gig promoting the launch of the record, alongside a giant inflatable doll of said new-born rocker. Thankfully this was a freak aberration and the blow-up baby was sent to its heavy metal crèche soon after.

Only one song on the new album – "She Loves Me Not" – had any affiliation with rap-metal (ironically, it had been left over from the previous album because it had sounded just a touch too rock), with the remaining tunes allowing full rein for Shaddix, by now no longer a Dick, to vent his spleen in a more traditional manner – by singing. The album was written largely on the road while the band were suffering from the pressure of being propelled from minor-league wannabes to stage-razing superstars,

meaning the songs were more emotionally driven than previously. In many ways all this made *Lovehatetragedy* a far more interesting album than its genre-bending predecessor.

Whereas *Infest* had largely been a uniform pounding, the new album allowed the band to extricate themselves from a sound that was rapidly ageing, and so reinvent themselves. It was a move they had to make, but one they ended up paying for: the album was a relative flop compared to its predecessor. The evolution continued with *Getting Away With Murder* (2004), an album that featured strong, melodic vocal lines from Shaddix and a greater sense of freedom in the songwriting, especially on the more ballad-like single "Scars".

⊙ Infest
2000; Dreamworks

This features the MTV fave "Last Resort", an ode to potential suicide. Shaddix's turbulent upbringing provided him with a fair few issues to get off his chest, his lyrics covering everything from a miserable childhood, to getting royally ripped.

⊙ Lovehatetragedy
2002; Dreamworks

The energy levels are high throughout with particular peaks being the towering, majestic menace of "Black Clouds", its companion piece of misery "Decompression Period", the emotionally masochistic fugue (and live favourite) "Walking Through Barbed Wire", and Shaddix's defiant call to arms "Born With Nothing, Die With Everything".

PARADISE LOST

Formed Halifax, Yorkshire, UK, 1988

"I always remember a song called 'Enchantment' from Draconian Times. People read all kinds of deep, meaningful things into that and later I asked Nick (Holmes) 'What was all that about then?' And he said 'Oh, it's about wanking!'" Greg Mackintosh

Paradise Lost are one of those bands that seem to have greater success on the Continent than they do in their home country, a curious situation given the sheer quality of the metal they produce. They have always strived to progress and, as such, defied critics and small-minded fans who always scream sell-out when confronted by change. From death'n'doom roots to melodic electro-metal,

PASTIMES

When not on the road or cooped up in a studio how exactly do these hellraisers let their hair down?

Iron Maiden frontman **Bruce Dickinson** is well known as something of a metal renaissance man. Not only does he present TV programmes and his own BBC radio rock show, he also writes novels (the adventures of Lord Iffy Boatrace, to be precise) – although he is probably best known for being an expert swordsman and commercial pilot. **David Lee Roth** likes to climb mountains – check out the sleeve to *Skyscraper* to see Roth in action – sometime **Jane's Addiction** bloke, **Perry Farrell**, likes to wax his board and indulge in a little surfing.

While some prefer to keep animals – **Roger Daltrey** with his trout farm, **Slash** and his snakes – there are those who like to blow holes in them. The most famous hunter would have to be the wildman of rock **Ted Nugent**, whose ability as a marksman and bow-hunter is part of his stage show.

Leaving the macho types to sharpen their bowie knives there are rockers of a more sensitive disposition as well. While **James Hetfield** is out stalking deer his drumming buddy **Lars Ulrich** has cultivated a reputation as something of a fine-art connoisseur. He has built up a collection of work by Asger Jorn and Karel Appel as well as Jean-Michel Basquiat whose *Profit 1*, a thirteen-foot long-haired portrait of a voodoo warrior, went under the hammer at Christie's in New York for $5,000,000 in 2002. And then there are those who like to create their own canvas: the world's oldest schoolboy, **Angus Young**, likes nothing more than to paint landscapes, while the self-proclaimed 'God Of Fuck', **Marilyn Manson**, has recently exhibited his paintings. His first gallery show, named after his *The Golden Age Of Grotesque* album, featured fifty pieces, painted with a child's watercolour set and a 1920s mortician's kit, used to make-up the faces of cadavers. Far more in character is his interest in taxidermy and his collection of prosthetic limbs.

There are many other collectors out there: UFO's **Pete Way** likes to collect model trains, Anthrax chap **Scott Ian** is a well-known fan of comic books, while **Ozzy Osbourne** has a strong interest in Nazi memorabilia, but no longer has any – he sold his collection to **Lemmy**. The **Motörhead** frontman has been an avid collector of Nazi memorabilia for years, concentrating on design, artistry and workmanship – mainly ceremonial daggers, knives and swords. Another collector of the sinister is **Jimmy Page**, whose fascination with Aleister Crowley led him to buy the Scottish estate, Boleskine House, former residence of the notorious diabolist. Of a more gruesome bent, singer **Mike Patton**'s time in **Faith No More** saw him develop a nice line in preserved human organs and fetuses. Kiss's **Gene Simmons**, on the other hand, is lucky that his day job meshes neatly with his chief passion: he loves collecting money.

---

the one aspect that has remained constant is the fact that they sound thoroughly, supernaturally miserable; there is no gripe too small for them to turn into a melancholy masterpiece.

The story of the band's formation can be traced back to a chance meeting between **Nick Holmes** (vocals) and **Gregor Mackintosh** (lead guitar) in a pub. Holmes remarked upon Mackintosh's jacket, which was decorated with a Kreator logo, this being the heyday of 80s thrash metal. Common metal fanboy ground established, the duo became the writing nucleus of the band, completed by **Aaron Aedy** (rhythm guitar), **Steve Edmondson** (bass) and **Matthew Archer** (drums). Two demos, *Drown In Darkness* and *Frozen Illusion* followed, with the band proudly displaying their love of Black Sabbath, goth rock and thrash before they were snapped up by local underground label Peaceville Records in 1990.

The imaginatively titled debut album *Lost Paradise* (1990) – the sleeve shot showing the band hanging out in a cemetery looking mean and moody – was something of a mixed bag. The album contained flashes of

inspiration that set them apart from other fledgling bands; they were already incorporating female vocals to balance out Holmes' deathly roar, while the dynamic changes of pace marked them out from ordinary thrashers. However, the good points were somewhat undercut by a less than sparkling production job.

Any production problems, however, were ironed out by the time of *Gothic* (1991). At the time it was hailed as a classic of extreme metal, albeit one with an understanding of melody, lush string sections and yet more ethereal female vocals – making it a relatively accessible experiment in gloom and introspection. Europe now beckoned.

Now signed to Music For Nations, *Shades Of God* (1992) was produced by **Simon Efemey** (who had worked previously with Pantera and the Wildhearts) who took the band further in a melodic direction without compromising on the brute crunching power of the guitars or the grandiose and sedate pace of the rhythms. Their *As I Die* EP was chosen as Single Of The week by Metallica on MTV Europe – a fine endorsement.

While their previous album had given them a killer encore tune in "As I Die" the real leap forward took place over the period of *Icon* (1993) and its storming follow-up *Draconian Times* (1995), featuring new drummer **Lee Morris**. By this point huge European festival audiences were a staple of their touring schedule and Holmes was using his true singing voice rather than bowing to the pressure of their death metal roots. *Icon* shot into the album charts across Europe and even the UK couldn't resist *Draconian Times*, which actually charted at #16 when it was released at the height of Britpop; incredible as it may seem even *Q* magazine included it among their top 50 albums of 1995. Of course, there were the odd mutterings of sell-out from those who liked their metal to stay in its own little ghetto, but the overwhelming response was that their gamble had paid off.

World tour accomplished, the band wanted to take their symbiotic relationship with depression and misery even further. They craved the clinical detachment and emotional isolation afforded by electronics and industrial embellishments. It was a radical move, even for a band that had a reputation for relentless progression, but *One Second* (1997) was the logical conclusion, an album of icy atmospherics and chilling robotic rhythms. Of course, the Continent loved it – *One Second* went Top 20 across ten countries, and Top 40 in the UK.

A signing to EMI's Electrola label led to an even more extreme departure; some critics accused the band of forgetting to plug in their guitars for *Host* (1999), so all-pervasive was the wall of electronica, but the compositional brilliance of the tracks displayed a band keen to satisfy themselves creatively. Besides, anyone horrified by *Host* must surely have been placated by *Believe In Nothing* (2001) and *Symbol Of Life* (2002), the latter produced by long-time Fear Factory collaborators **Rhys Fulber** and engineer/mixer **Greg Reely**. Having edged out along the cybergoth precipice as far as they wished to go, they applied the chugging guitar riffs once more, achieving a stunning balance between digitally-enhanced moping and mid-paced metal.

So creatively satisfying was the latter album that Fulber and Reely helped produce *Paradise Lost* (2005) featuring new drummer Jeff Singer (ex-**Blaze** and **Kill II This**).

⊙ Draconian Times
1995; Music For Nations

This collection was a real breakthrough. Highlights include "Forever Failure", "Hallowed Land" and "The Last Time", where the band really show off their ability to write gargantuan goth paeans to misery with real style and panache.

⊙ One Second
1997; Music For Nations

Some hated this bold departure, but most fans realized that this was where the band had been heading all along. It sounds almost as though Depeche Mode were masquerading as a metal band.

PEARL JAM

Formed Seattle, Washington, US, 1990

The genesis of **Pearl Jam** was rooted in chance and tragedy. **Stone Gossard** (guitar) and **Jeff Ament** (bass) had both been members of seminal grungers **Green River**, and later **Mother Love Bone**, with ex-**Malfunkshun** member **Andrew Wood** on vocals. When Wood died of an overdose, his long-time friend **Chris Cornell** (of **Soundgarden**) put together a tribute project called *Temple Of The Dog* (1991). Gossard, Ament, and new recruit **Mike McCready** (guitar) were roped in, as was **Eddie Vedder**

POMP ROCK

Exactly the kind of thing likely to make thrash fans turn green around the gills, **pomp** is the beaming melodic love child of smooth and lush AOR and twiddly-diddly prog rock.

The tag obviously comes from the deprecating view that such music was pompous in the extreme, but for many fans it's a badge of affinity worn with pride. At its peak in the 70s and 80s the phenomenon was very much an American movement that would quite often be lumped in with prog, though its sound is really distinctive enough to warrant a fluffy little category all of its own. Just think of **Yes** at their most ludicrously inflated crossed with a band such as, say, **Boston** or **Journey**, creating a sound that was basically a very commercial hard rock take on British and European prog. Heavily keyboard-oriented and decorated with epic and emotional vocals, the result was more complex and overblown than straightforward melodic rock and was represented by a plethora of highly talented bands whose period in the limelight and subsequent fall from view brings tears of nostalgia to the eye of many a pomp aficionado.

The longest-running and most successful UK band with pomp leanings is **Magnum**, and from Germany **Zeno** are worth mentioning if only because their guitarist, **Jochen 'Zeno' Roth**, was the younger brother of renowned guitarist Uli John Roth. Across the Atlantic was where the real action was, however, and bands such as **Starcastle**, **Roadmaster**, **Aviary**, **Fairchild** and **Shotgun Symphony** all plied their harmony-laden trade with varying degrees of success. One band that should have made it very big indeed was the legendary **Angel**. The story goes that they were spotted by Kiss's Gene Simmons and signed up to the same Casablanca label as the famously face-painted ones, and then spent much of the 70s trying to break out of Kiss's shadow. The line-up featured one **Greg Giuffria** on keyboards who would go on to greater success solo and with **House Of Lords**. At the time the lack of commercial comeback was both puzzling and frustrating. The band specialized in huge, majestic melodies – best sampled on *Angel* (1975), *On Earth As It Is In Heaven* (1977), *White Hot* (1977) and *Sinful* (1979) – and they had a fabulously coiffed, glammy, virginal all-in-white image to go with the pristine power of the music; not only that but their albums also sported a nifty logo that could be spun through 180 degrees and still read the same upside down.

Far luckier were **Kansas** who peaked in the US with a couple of top-five albums in *Leftoverture* (1976) and *Point Of Know Return* (1977), but of them all it is **Styx** who are often regarded as being the daddies of pomp. During the early 70s their proggy style was largely ignored, but when they recruited guitarist **Tommy Shaw** in 1976 they suddenly hit their radio-friendly stride. *The Grand Illusion* (1977), *Pieces Of Eight* (1978), *Cornerstone* (1980) and the pomp concept album *Paradise Theater* (1981) made major inroads into the charts with the latter becoming a #1 hit in the US and a top-ten wonder in the UK.

who had provided some vocals for an instrumental demo tape put together by the others. He provided backing vocals on the project and a dual lead vocal on "Hunger Strike" with Cornell.

Once *Temple Of The Dog* was in the can **Dave Krusen** (drums) joined the other four. Flirting with different names on the way (Mookie Blaylock and Reenk Roink) they eventually settled for Pearl Jam – named after an allegedly hallucinogenic recipe belonging to Vedder's grandmother – and set about overturning the Seattle music scene.

By spring 1991 Pearl Jam had begun to play live shows in the area, supporting the likes of Alice in Chains. As the word about the Seattle scene spread, the band signed to Epic and their debut *Ten* (1992) was rushed out. Although it was recorded speedily it killed any media or marketing preconceptions of the Seattle grunge sound. It distilled the pain and attitude of the disaffected, but injected it with an electric, classic rock feel. Gossard and McCready's playing owed as

much to Jimi Hendrix as to any punk band. Vedder's lyrics and vocals carried a rare, raw emotion and the soaringly poetic "Evenflow", "Alive" and "Jeremy" took elements of his own traumatic childhood and transformed them into universal experience.

Just as *Ten* entered the US charts Krusen left to deal with personal problems and was replaced by **Dave Abbruzzese**. New studio sessions culminated in a rerecording of "Evenflow" while new tracks "State Of Love And Trust" and "Breathe" both ended up on the soundtrack of *Singles*, starring Matt Dillon, a romantic comedy based on the Seattle music scene. Three of the band even managed to make cameo appearances as part of Dillon's grunge combo Citizen Dick.

In February 1992 they prepared to hit Europe, but record companies didn't bank on the Seattle hype having reached the UK and so arranged for the first concert to be an A&R bash only. Hundreds of fans were literally left out in the cold. Although Vedder and Abbruzzese mingled outside to apologize, the media were less than kind. Reviews equated their driven sound with the creaking, rock dinosaurs of the 70s while Kurt Cobain fuelled the controversy by calling them a corporate band (conveniently forgetting their lengthy apprenticeships as members of some of Seattle's finest). The fans, on the other hand, could not have cared less; *Ten* outstripped *Nevermind* in the US metal charts and outsold it world-wide in 1992. To top off their success they made several high profile appearances: they supported The Cult at Finsbury Park, London; performed an unplugged set for MTV; and toured with Lollapalooza II.

A new album was planned for late 1992, but touring schedules slowed things to a crawl. Gossard kept himself fresh during the hiatus by working on *Shame* (1993) a product of his **Brad** side-project; it was a mellow, danceable mix of psychedelia and funk rhythms. In the summer of 1993 they provided support for Neil Young's European tour with the gig at Finsbury Park finding them tearing into soulful, breathtaking versions of old favourites along with fresh punk-inspired material; the high points were the new "Glorified G" and an expletive-ridden, vein-bursting rendition of "Leash". They joined Young for a powerful version of "Rockin' In The Free World", a song they reprised later in the year at the MTV Awards. A new and important alliance had been forged.

When *Vs* (1993) finally saw the light of day the fans' response was one of awe. It entered at #1 in the *Billboard* charts. It was a more consistently furious effort than their debut, with the guitars and rhythms raging more freely and Vedder displaying the full range of his vocal and lyrical diversity; songs of raw, blood-curdling anger ("Go", "Animal", "Blood") were balanced by mellower textures ("Daughter"). Overall, it sounded more caustic, accomplished and mature than *Ten*.

During this period the band were no strangers to controversy. They had always maintained that their fans were vitally important to them, and often went out of their way to

be as accessible to them as possible. This dedication to the public took a new turn in 1994. While continuing to tour, and make occasional appearances with Neil Young, they weighed in against the corporate might of the Ticketmaster booking agency, which they accused of raising ticket prices beyond the spending power of their younger followers. They were joined in their protest by such artists as REM, Aerosmith, and of course Neil Young.

Aside from this public-spirited crusade they also managed to record some new music. To show their faith in vinyl, *Vitalogy* (1994) was released first on record, and then CD which saw it rocket to the top of the *Billboard* charts. Tracks such as the searing "Spin The Black Circle" and the belligerent threats of "Not For You" delivered the usual doses of mayhem. However, tracks such as the pointless "Stupid Mop" and 'Bugs' dragged on the album's overall momentum.

Apart from McCready's **Mad Season** side-project – featuring **Alice In Chains'** **Layne Staley** on vocals – 1995 saw Pearl Jam's partnership with Neil Young flourish, their encore jams at shows together developing into the poignant, broad sweep of *Mirror Ball*

(1995). Recorded in a mere four days, the record was a potent blend of Pearl Jam's hard rock influences and Young's poetic meanderings, oiled with generous doses of teeth-

POWER TO THE PEOPLE

Yet another tricky-to-define metallic sub-genre, **power metal** can include a variety of basic building blocks. Chief among these is melody and copious speed, often characterized by blisteringly fast dual leads and riff work and a rhythm section capable of keeping things pumping along at a lung-busting gallop, often matched in majesty by chest-beating, hi-octane vocals; hence the **speed metal** tag which is sometimes used interchangeably. The bizarre result of all this unleashed energy is that the music can often sound almost happy, as opposed to the usual dark and menacing ambience conjured by most metal music.

The roots of the genre can be traced back to the vocals and guitar styles of bands such as **Judas Priest** and **Iron Maiden**, though the speed angle comes more from thrash metal of the 80s. Of course, the neoclassical influence of the 80s axe-shredders such as **Yngwie Malmsteen** plays a major role in the identity of many power metal bands, especially those who edge towards the more symphonic end of the spectrum. And just to make things really interesting there is usually a proggish element lurking in there as well; thus it's not unusual for power metallers to write lengthy songs in movements with plenty of fiendish tempo changes and an emphasis on fantastical lyrical fare.

One of the longest-running power metal bands is Germany's **Helloween** who started off more as a thrash unit and rapidly developed into one of the finest practitioners of heavy but melodic speed metal in the mid- to late 80s. For some reason Germany seems to excel in producing bands of this ilk, with **Rage**, **Blind Guardian**, **Running Wild** and **Gamma Ray** being among the many producing this kind of tuneful bludgeon. Scandinavia is also adept at producing some top bands, with the likes of **Nightwish**, **Stratovarius** and **Hammerfall**. Of course, the power metal phenomenon isn't restricted to Europe and Scandinavia ; the US's **Iced Earth** are at the top of their game, featuring ex-Judas Priest screamer **Tim Owens**, and the UK boasts one of the fastest new multinational outfits in the stunning **Dragonforce**.

grating, over-driven feedback. Unfortunately, in a fit of marketing pique, Young's record company refused to allow Pearl Jam's name to appear on the sleeve.

Meanwhile the band, true to their word, continued to make a stand against Ticketmaster by arranging an alternative tour taking in less-established venues. Progress was often hampered by enforced cancellations and security problems but when things went well, audiences were treated not only to Pearl Jam, but to Young jamming on songs from *Mirror Ball*.

The following year saw the band lose Dave Abbruzzese but gain **Jack Irons** and finally focus their attention on a new studio effort. *No Code* (1996) was steeped in the all-American tradition of garage punk, but instead of lunging headfirst into a soundscape of heaving guitars the songs marked out a more thoughtful approach. Opening track "Sometimes" was a slow burner and it wasn't until "Hail Hail" that things kicked off in familiar style. What the album lacked in pace it made up for in poise and moving, troubled lyrics. Overall, though, it received a less-than-ecstatic reception and the band turned back to what they knew best for *Yield* (1998) and the live opus *Live On Two Legs* (1998), straight-ahead hard rocking. The live album featured former Soundgarden

drummer **Matt Cameron** (replacing Irons) as part of the live setup, and he actually contributed to the songwriting on the next LP *Binaural* (2000). As ever it was a *tour de force* showcase of the band's subtlety and power, addressing both personal and social issues with a deft touch. Later that same year, as if to emphasize the band's punk credentials, they opted to release a series of 25 live bootleg CDs, all of them recorded, warts'n'all, during their European tour. So successful was the idea that they kept it going for subsequent tours.

2002 brought with it *Riot Act*, another blast of armchair politics and big guitars tempered by moments of laid-back sensitivity. *Lost Dogs* (2003) was a treat for the collectors, presenting a whole two CDs-worth of rare tracks stretching back over the band's entire career. Its release was complemented by the *Pearl Jam Live At The Garden* DVD, recorded at Madison Square Garden.

Pearl Jam remain one of the most dedicated rock bands around, both to their fans and their music. This much is evident in the amazing number of side-projects in which the band indulge when not Pearl Jamming: Gossard completed a solo album in 2001 titled *Bayleaf*, and Brad issued a third album, *Welcome To Discovery Park,* in 2003; Mike McCready put out an album with **The**

Rockfords in 2000; and Jeff Ament's **Three Fish** have managed two albums so far. As far as we know Ticketmaster's MD hasn't bought any of them.

⊙ Temple Of The Dog
1991; A&M

Though strictly speaking it's not pure Pearl Jam, the songwriting and musicianship tips over the line into the sublime.

⊙ Ten
1992; Epic

An inconsistent debut, but agreeably brooding and dark in places. It destroyed any preconceptions of what a Seattle band should sound like.

⊙ Vs
1993; Epic

Worthy, vital and powerful, shot through with a melodic core, pulsing with a feral, snarling attitude.

⊙ Vitalogy
1994; Epic

The band's love affair with punk continues with this roller-coasting release. Occasionally brilliant, this recording features the band making a stab at "Better Man", a song from Vedder's days with **Bad Radio**.

⊙ No Code
1996; Epic

More thoughtful and focused than its hit-and-miss predecessor. A controlled and emotive collection of rock songs that concentrate more on quality than high-octane thrills. Vedder takes most of the writing credits and it shows in the moody textures and introspective tone.

⊙ Live On Two Legs
1998; Epic

While the band's studio output has proved to be a touch uneven, Eddie and the boys still excel in the live context, as can be experienced in this taut and lean concert set. It even makes some of their less worthy tunes bearable.

⊙ Binaural
2000; Epic

Full-tilt tracks such as "Breakerfall", "Insignificance" and "Evacuation" ought to sate those who feel that the Jam have been easing off the gas pedal. Meanwhile the darker aspects of the collection benefit immensely from Vedder's ever-moody vocals.

⊙ Lost Dogs
2003; Epic

Are those rarities and B-sides eluding you? Fear not because this double album covers the whole of their career to date; none of these songs have ever found their way onto their studio albums.

PITCHSHIFTER

Formed Nottingham, UK, 1990

Pitchshifter are one of the UK's most uncompromising and experimental bands. In the eruption of noise that is a **Pitchshifter** album one is likely to hear everything from drum'n'bass and hip-hop, to scorching heavy metal and punk, via a deluge of samples and electronic shock tactics. The result is exhilarating, overtly anti-authoritarian and deliberately confrontational, placing them at the forefront of British industrial metal.

Brothers **JS** (vocals) and **Mark Clayden** (bass) started the band at the beginning of the 1990s. They combined their love of harsh vibes – as produced by bands such as Big Black and Swans – with their interest in technology to make brutal, distorted noise, designed to get feet jumping on club dance floors while making heads explode. With the aid of **Johnny Carter** (guitar/programming) they issued *Industrial* (1991) on Peaceville. It was raw and primal stuff – tunes such as "Skin Grip" and "Inflamator" were not for the fainthearted – as much informed by Dead Kennedys-style punk as the club underground.

Moving to Earache Records, the home of extremity, their next effort was the *Submit* (1992) mini-LP, made with the aid of **Stuart Toolin** on additional guitars. Harking back to the sloganeering of punk's heyday, the band would thrust mock propagandist leaflets upon the crowd at gigs while on-stage strobe-light levels would be set to kill, alongside a slide show which intensified the aural pounding. The band were about questioning everything, from the motives of politicians, multinational corporations and the news media, to the complacency of the music industry. They wanted people to think while crowd-surfing, to make fans' brains tick as their bodies were subjected to their industrial-strength pummelling.

The next major leap forward in their sonic agenda was *Desensitized* (1993). It was challenging, anarchic and sealed their position as top underground noiseniks. On the live front the addition of drummer **DJ Walters** brought a more organic feel to the regimented sound, which crackled with pneumatic precision and driven energy.

COURTESY OF PITCHSHIFTER

Pitchshifter's JS feels the love.

Always up for experimentation the band's next offering was *Pitchshifter Vs Biohazard, Therapy?, Gunshot – The Remix War* (1994), where the band let three of their contemporaries loose on their material to do their worst. The Pitchshifter juggernaut was unstoppable and one of the highlights of 1995 was their literally showstopping slot at the Phoenix festival. The mysterious appearance of a crop circle in the shape of Pitchshifter's instantly recognizable 'eye' symbol in an adjoining field preceded a killer set during which the crowd invaded the stage, resulting in the promoters pulling the plug.

By the mid-90s the band had pushed the industrial template to its limit and for their next journey to the studio planned another shift in style. *Infotainment?* (1996) plugged away at the usual political and social targets but the guitar factor had been increased as had the melody levels – Pitchshifter had become adept songwriters and not just maverick noise artists. In tune with their love of technology as a means of destroying barriers they included a huge number of samples on the CD to allow fans to construct their own efforts on computer.

The next shift in identity came with the addition of guitarist **Jim Davies** and *www. pitchshifter.com* (1998). Davies had just finished

helping the Prodigy record *Fat Of The Land* and was the natural choice for the skin-flaying levels of coruscating guitar the band wanted on their new album. In addition, their ever-ascending fortunes had landed them a deal with Geffen, a major label, at last. The single "Genius" (backed by their cover of XTC's "Making Plans For Nigel") made a modest chart appearance at #71 and primed the fans for the newly streamlined sound. A second single, "Microwaved", narrowly missed breaching the Top 50. The heightened exposure landed "Genius" with a *Kerrang!* award for best video and got them a valuable opening slot on the UK leg of Ozzfest.

Never satisfied with the state of their home country, the band next fired off their *Un-United Kingdom* EP, marking Davies' writing debut with the band. It sounded like the Sex Pistols jamming with Ministry, JS Clayden pulling off a remarkable Johnny Rotten-like sneering vocal; "Everything Sucks (Again)" merely underlined their level of dissatisfaction before an inflammatory cover version of Big Black's "Kerosene".

The more economical, guitar-packed and hook-laden approach prefigured Pitchshifter's most song-oriented album to date, *Deviant* (2000) on MCA, and a whole host of line-up shifts. Carter left, as did Walters, who was replaced on the album by **John Stanier** (ex-**Helmet**); on the live front **Matt Grundy** stepped in on rhythm guitar and **Jason Bowld** took over on drums.

A trek across America with Ozzfest behind them and Grundy decided to leave. After a lengthy gestation period *P.S.I.* (2002) emerged on Sanctuary. Sensing that they had taken Pitchshifter to its logical conclusion, the following year the band announced that they would be taking indefinite leave to explore other musical avenues. Their parting shot was *Bootlegged, Distorted, Remixed & Uploaded* (2003) on their own PSI Records imprint, a thank-you live album for the fans with a second disc featuring several remixes of popular tracks. According to the band this would be it for a long time – no shows, no albums, nothing. But the lure of the live adrenaline surge proved to be too much. A live DVD, *P.S.I.Entology* (2004), found the band only too keen to hit the road again for a short run of dates billed as DVD launch parties. It seems it's too early to write off the kings of the UK's alternative metal scene.

 Deviant
2000; MCA

You can actually sing along to this one, despite the spiky riffs and samples. One highlight is the guest appearance of *Jello Biafra* (ex-Dead Kennedys), adding his sarcastic ranting observations on modern life to "As Seen On TV".

 P.S.I.
2002; Sanctuary

Standing for "Pitch Shifter Industries", the sheer heaviness on offer is a clever move considering the nu-metal fashion for downtuned nastiness. Fortunately it's carried by the band's trademark grooviness, a peculiarly memorable collision of almost commercial melody and scorching power.

P.O.D.

Formed San Diego, California, US, 1992

While many of their nu-metal contemporaries come on like a heavy therapy session set to the sound of cement-mixer guitars, this four-piece from California are all together more positive. This could be because of the California sunshine, but is more than likely down to their Christian beliefs, though, like many bands espousing a spiritual outlook on life, they're often at pains not to be pigeonholed. Regardless of their lyrical proclivities it is impossible to deny the band's immense popularity, especially in the US where their indie origins have eventually led to appearances at Ozzfest and a Grammy nomination in the Best Hard Rock Performance category in 2002.

The early history of **P.O.D.** – which, incidentally, stands for Payable On Death – began in the usual way, with the band playing as many venues to as many people as possible. The line-up of **Sonny Sandoval** (vocals), **Marcos Curiel** (guitar), **Traa**

PROG ROCK

Considered by many as the starting point for pomp rock and modern prog metal, the distinct **prog rock** category has a long and illustrious history stretching back to the experimental 60s.

Most early prog rock was really a European and British phenomenon, probably due to the strong traditions of classical music present at the time, and the name obviously came from the notion that the music was progressive and hugely inventive. Thus the key elements were reflected in prog: the songs were, more often than not, very long and divided into movements, featuring virtuoso performances with an emphasis on complex keyboards. Throw in some clever time signatures and a penchant for wacky storytelling and fantasy-led concept albums and prog was, for a while, a critically lauded genre.

Early prog can in no way be confused with what became known as heavy metal, but in the 70s when genre distinctions hadn't become hard and fast it was perfectly possible to be a fan who would indulge in both **Black Sabbath** and **Emerson, Lake and Palmer**, for instance. The lighter side of prog was reflected in the output of such whimsical and quintessentially English acts as **Jethro Tull**, **Yes** and **Genesis**, while those who fancied more of a challenge could take on **King Crimson** or **Van Der Graaf Generator**. Meanwhile, a band such as **Pink Floyd** were really in a league all of their own, creating concept albums yet delivering their grandiose statements in a more bombastic, heavy rock style, largely devoid of excessive keyboard solos.

The more cerebral approach to rock pioneered by the early progsters naturally led to a second wave of artists who came to prominence in the 80s in a movement often dubbed **neo-prog**.

Punk And UK Hardcore (Influence On Metal)

Though far from being one of their best, **Guns N' Roses'** covers album *The Spaghetti Incident?* (1993) is an intriguing snapshot of the manner in which punk and hardcore – a more militantly aggressive form of punk – have affected the development of rock and metal. In the track listing no less than nine out of the twelve songs are either punk songs or come from the progenitors of punk. In the former category we have tunes originally written by the **Dead Boys**, **The Damned**, the **UK Subs**, **Fear**, the **Sex Pistols** and the **Misfits**, while in the latter we have numbers originally penned by **Iggy And The Stooges** and **The New York Dolls**. All this (and more) went into creating one of the most important bands of the 80s and early 90s.

Entire books have been written about the origins of punk, so generalizing hugely, its roots stretch back in the US to political garage bands such as the **MC5** and the outrageous raunch of Iggy And The Stooges, while in the UK critics often point to the UK pub rock scene and glam as sources of grass roots inspiration. Throw in a wild fashion sense and some basic chords – The **Ramones'** desire to get back to the power of 60s pop is a fine example of this minimal aesthetic in action – and you arrive at punk, the antithesis of the self-indulgent and self-important as played by the usual suspects: the Sex Pistols, The Damned and **The Clash** to name but a few. The Pistols, in particular, might only have recorded one album of any significance – *Never Mind The Bollocks* (1977) – around which much of their myth hangs, but they eventually became one of the most covered groups in rock. Aside from Guns N' Roses, dozens of stylistically different bands, including **Megadeth**, **Sepultura**, **Anthrax**, **Motörhead**, **Skid Row** and **Bush**, have covered their songs. Punk brought rebellion back into rock and stuck two fingers up at a music industry seen as complicit in neutering a form of music that should be street level and dangerous.

The common view is that punk killed rock and metal stone dead, but it's probably more accurate to say that its effect was more selective; some bands, most notably the huge arena-fillers, or dinosaurs as they were called, experienced problems, but the result was that the vitality of this back-to-basics form of music energized new bands and new movements, one of these in the UK being the **New Wave Of British Heavy Metal**, where punk's youthful disdain for tradition and its DIY attitude encouraged fresh new acts into the limelight.

As punk developed it inevitably splintered into a variety of sub-genres; the impact on metal of the slightly later, harsher sounding hardcore movement is also important. The belligerent and confrontational UK hardcore punk scene of the early 80s produced bands such as **The Exploited**, **GBH** and **Discharge**, who would have a profound effect on thrashers such as Sepultura and **Metallica**, while the anarchist leanings of bands such as **Rudimentary Peni**, **Crass** and **Conflict** fed into the creation of such bands as **Napalm Death**, the **Electro-Hippies**, **Extreme Noise Terror**, **Heresy**, **The Stupids** and **Doom**.

Daniels (bass), **Noah 'Wuv' Bernardo** (drums) really began to get their act together in 1993 as they began to prepare for their first album. The band's southern Californian background exposed them to Latin rhythms, reggae, hip-hop and, of course, punk and metal. All of these influences shaped their early recordings which were issued on their own Rescue Records label.

First came *Snuff The Punk* (1994), an outpouring that owed as much to Rage Against The Machine-style rap metal as it did to jazz and funk. The lyrics espoused a sort of street-level Christianity set to a soundtrack born of their blue-collar backgrounds. *Brown* (1996) followed and delivered more of the same, providing ample material for *Live At Tomfest* (1997), which showcased the band's developing rap and metal style. It was derivative but sufficiently well realized, and catchy enough to capture the imagination of Atlantic. Before their major-label debut, however, they fired off one more righteously independent release in the shape

of *The Warriors* EP – 'warriors' being the band's most hardcore followers.

Given a nice studio and a decent budget to play with, *The Fundamental Elements Of Southtown* (1999) erupted as a full-on nu-metal set, all downtuned guitars but upbeat, positive lyrics. The years of live shows and self-released albums had laid down a foundation often lacking in many bands signed long before they're ready. P.O.D., however, were very ready indeed. As the album went platinum they found themselves on tour with Ozzfest 2000 and popping up on many movie soundtracks.

The sudden explosion in popularity and the appearance on concert bills featuring many secular acts championing the rock'n'roll lifestyle had some of their more devout following accusing them of selling out. But the band maintained that their primary purpose was to rock as hard and often as possible – besides their undeniably growing profile was getting a positive message to many more people this way. This was certainly true when *Satellite* (2001) went into the *Billboard* Top 10. It was a life-affirming collection of tunes, crammed with incendiary rockers, not least the likes of the title track, "Boom" and "Set It Off", and a handful of interesting guest appearances; iconic **Bad Brains** vocalist **HR** popped up on the thrash'n'reggae workout "Without Jah, Nothin'", while superstar Jamaican toaster **Eek-A-Mouse** made an appearance on the super-smooth ragga rap of "Ridiculous". With Sandoval's rap-heavy style to the fore, the album very much underlined the multicultural nature of the band's individual backgrounds.

By the time of *Payable On Death* (2003) they had lost Curiel and gained **Jason Truby** (ex-**Living Sacrifice**), for an album that saw them shifting gradually away from the overt rap and metal sound for a more soaring, mainstream approach. Otherwise, it was another prime example of uplifting and melodic songwriting.

⊙ The Fundamental Elements Of Southtown 1999; Atlantic

Heavy, but with lyrics far removed from the usual angst and self-loathing associated with nu-metal. It's not hard to understand the mass appeal of these chunky slabs of diversely influenced noise.

⊙ Satellite 2001; Atlantic

A real breakthrough in sound and songwriting. P.O.D. make everything sound smooth and effortless as they cruise through funky rap-inflected metal and throw in a wide variety of alternative sounds for good measure. This is catchy and commercial heavy rock ideal for the MTV and Ozzfest generation.

POISON

Formed Los Angeles, US, 1985

Famed more for their outrageous image than anything else **Poison** were the epitome of glam. They were so heavily coiffed and madeup it wouldn't be too much of a stretch to suggest they were leaders in a genre entirely of their own making: ladyboy metal. That they managed to sell squillions of records is almost incidental to the fact that they were one of the craziest and ridiculously entertaining hair bands of the decadent 1980s, a period of metal that crystallized

everything these boys held dear: sex, drugs, and fun, fun, fun.

Originally **Bret Michaels** (vocals), **Bobby Dall** (bass) and **Rikki Rockett** (drums) had got together as three-quarters of a line-up playing gigs in their hometown of Pittsburgh. However, it was with a move way out west to the capital of hairspray abuse, Los Angeles, that they found their niche, and also one **C.C. DeVille** (guitar). LA was already a hotbed of sleazy rock'n'roll, boasting a scene crammed with bands doing impressions of the New York Dolls. Poison, however, had the balls and dedication to become kings of this particularly glammy hill.

By now a proficient and tightly honed live unit, the band unleashed *Look What The Cat Dragged In* (1986) upon a world already reeling from the onslaught of Ratt, Mötley Crüe and Twisted Sister. Already softened up for the kill, trash rock fans took the ludicrously slutty-looking blokes on the album sleeve to their hearts. This was pure bubblegum for the ears, from the street-savvy gutter anthem "Cry Tough" to the snotty closing teen-protest of "Let Me Go To The Show". Their ace in the hole was "Talk Dirty To Me", a US top-ten hit and MTV favourite, which sent the album into the Top 5.

There was more rock'n'roll slap'n'tickle in 1988 when the band released *Open Up And Say … Ahh!*. The album fell just one short of the top slot in the US and went Top 20 in the UK, while Bret and the boys revelled in their first US #1 single, the lonely-cowboy ballad "Every Rose Has Its Thorn" (Jon Bon Jovi has a lot to answer for). The song would go on to be immortalized in *Bill & Ted's*

Bogus Journey, in a priceless scene where the titular heroes must enter heaven by coming up with a pearl of wisdom – they choose the chorus of Poison's most famous ballad.

The hit singles kept flowing and Poison were happy to roll with it, their well publicised appetite for womanizing and hellraising reaching Olympic proportions along the way. *Flesh & Blood* (1990) was yet another smash album that shimmied its way almost to the top of the US chart. In the midst of this carnal carnival, however, the main protagonists were feeling the pressure and relations between Michaels and DeVille were rapidly going down the pan. The chain had well and truly been pulled when the two of them began a fist fight behind the scenes of the 1991 MTV Music Awards. No one knows who won, but it certainly wasn't the band: DeVille left to be replaced, eventually, by **Richie Kotzen**.

Swallow This Live (1991) papered over the cracks but by now the band's formula was looking staler than their make-up, especially in the stark light of grunge. No one wanted to have fun anymore, certainly not in the way Poison had been championing for the last five years. However, when *Native Tongue* (1993) arrived, it sounded like the band were actually taking themselves seriously in an effort to slot into the new rock landscape. No one got it. Sales of the new album were very disappointing and Kotzen's days were numbered, especially as he didn't really fit in with the group.

Guitarist **Blues Saraceno** was brought in to begin recording *Crack A Smile*, but the sessions were shelved when Michaels suffered serious injuries in a car crash. So instead of a new album, *Greatest Hits 1986–1996* (1996) was issued at the behest of their label, Capitol.

With the future of Poison looking decidedly dubious, the various members indulged in solo projects. Michaels hogged most of the attention with his new film production company, formed with his movie-star buddy Charlie Sheen. And then there was the infamous episode of the videotape featuring Michaels and Pamela Anderson doing the "unskinny bop" that grabbed tabloid headlines. Eventually, in 1998 it looked as if DeVille might rejoin the band, and in 1999 it became a reality for a tour.

Finally back in the studio, they put together *Crack A Smile ... And More* (2000) and then issued *Power To The People* (2000), a live album. In concert they guaranteed everybody a good time; the only thing that marred their regular US summer tour slot was when Dall had to have emergency surgery after injuring his spine on stage. Although they were back in action to support their new 2002 album *Hollyweird*, it turned out to be a major disappointment – the production and writing falling well below standard.

Look What The Cat Dragged In
1986; Music For Nations

Look at those gorgeous girls on the sleeve! Quite obviously airbrushed to make the lads look even prettier than they did in the flesh, the band photos let you know exactly what to expect inside. This is pure glam metal, rammed with loads of big-haired riff action.

Open Up And Say ... Ahh!
1988; Capitol

Their debut was all flash and this goes no further, but nonetheless it delivers ten tasty slices of Poison pie. Michaels yelps out the choruses like a horny Rottweiler while DeVille throws every shape in the book. And then some.

QUEEN

Formed London, UK, 1971

From *Wayne's World*, through Her Royal Highness's 2002 golden jubilee celebrations, to karaoke sessions the length and breadth of the country, the enduring popularity of this quintessentially eccentric British heavy rock band seems to know no bounds. Even after the untimely demise of their fabulously flamboyant lead singer, **Queen** go on, and have made regular visits to the charts with a seemingly never-ending string of CDs and DVDs.

The roots of Queen and her glorious reign lay in a band called **Smile**. **Brian May** (guitar) and **Roger Taylor** (drums) had managed one US-only single release under the name before adding one **Freddie Mercury** (vocals) and acquiring the world-conquering moniker, Queen. A handful of bass players later and **John Deacon** completed the line-up. While still dabbling in higher education or working, the various band members balanced their own activities with those of promoting the band, but the creation of a demo tape was about to set them on the road to stardom.

Some months down the line they secured a deal with EMI, recorded a session for the BBC and made their first appearance as Queen at the legendary Marquee Club in April 1973. Mercury had a little solo fun issuing a cover of the Beach Boys' "I Can Hear Music" (under the ace pseudonym of **Larry Lurex**) before the band released *Queen* (1973) and headed off on tour with Mott

The Hoople. As a debut *Queen* was less than stunning but one short cut, "Seven Seas Of Rhye", turned up reworked on *Queen II* (1974) and became their breakthrough single. Their debut seven-inch, "Keep Yourself Alive", had failed to do the business but when a David Bowie promo film was unavailable for *Top Of The Pops* Queen filled the slot and sent themselves into the Top 10; Queen would eventually come second only to the Beatles for scoring top-ten singles. The album eventually made #5 in the UK.

By now all the elements that would propel the band into the heavy rock superleague were in place, chiefly May's instantly recognizable guitar tone and Mercury's magnetic stage presence – the singer was without doubt the focal point with his preening, cocksure demeanour and ability to work a crowd. Then, of course, there were the black-and-white catsuits and ludicrous hairstyles. Queen were in their element, especially the camp Mercury who revelled in his role of rock'n'roll ringmaster.

With *Sheer Heart Attack* (1974) the band finally delivered an album they could work to the hilt. It was a record packed with superlative moments and some great hits ("Now I'm Here" and "Killer Queen") but the real coup was waiting in the wings. Mercury's outrageously pompous mock-operatic "Bohemian Rhapsody" on *A Night At The Opera* (1975) became their first #1 hit single, helped by a pioneering video clip, and became one of the most popular rock anthems of all time; the cross-sectional appeal of this stunning piece of work remains simply staggering. The album was also one of the band's finest, and also topped the chart. In comparison *A Day At The Races* (1976) was a rather patchy affair, possibly because the band produced it themselves, but most likely because the songs weren't so hot – apart from, of course, the fantastic rocker "Tie Your Mother Down". Supremely successful, by the mid-70s the band had started turning their attentions to a variety of extra-curricular projects and became tax exiles.

The disappointment of *A Day At The Races* aside this was the era of classic Queen and *News Of The World* (1977) gave the public two songs to rival Bohemian Rhapsody in the ubiquity stakes: "We Will Rock You" and "We Are The Champions". The latter became a lavish, over-the top set-closer on tour. Meanwhile "Bicycle Race" from *Jazz* (1978) boosted the fortunes of bicycle bell manufacturers the world over as fans bought up all spare stocks just so they could ring them during the song. And who was taking part in the "Bicycle Race"? Why, "Fat Bottomed Girls", of course. This was the era of the nude bicycle race stunt and the infamous single sleeve – a nude cycle-loving large-bottomed young lady who was ren-

dered more modest by the late addition of some teeny tiny bikini briefs. The risqué poster of the race that should have been packaged with the album ended up being largely distributed through mail order.

Live Killers (1979) was followed by *The Game* (1980) which spawned the excellent, though more dancefloor-oriented "Another One Bites The Dust"; this was their first album to feature synthesizers in the mix. The *Flash Gordon* (1980) soundtrack provided the band with their first opportunity to write music specifically for a film while *Queen's Greatest Hits* (1981) was a very fine compilation that handily pulled together most of their more desirable chart-bothering efforts. The diversion from heavy rock continued with the far less enticing *Hot Space* (1982), which found the band dabbling in all sorts of perplexing disco-flavoured experiments. It was a direction continued far more palatably with *The Works* (1984) which balanced its synth tendencies with some heavier guitar sounds. And then came the band's show-stealing appearance at Live Aid in 1985; to many Queen's performance was the highlight of the day as they rocked in a way some of their

Queen: "'Ere, Brian, how does this one go again?"

most recent albums had not. Subsequently however, *A Kind Of Magic* (1986), featuring tunes written for the film *Highlander*, although heavy enough in places, lacked the spark of ingenuity and urgency that fired their more off-the-wall brilliance in the 70s. Nevertheless, the band seemed more popular than ever now, a fact underlined by *Live Magic* (1987).

The final years of the band as a recording unit saw them immersed in their many solo projects as well as collecting innumerable accolades for their sterling career so far. Next offering *The Miracle* (1989) had its moments but there was nothing earth-shattering in its content; likewise *Innuendo* (1991), although the title track scored the band another #1 single. The years spanning these recordings saw a gradual build-up in the rumours focusing upon Mercury's failing health and even as *Greatest Hits II* began to settle down at the top of the charts, all attention was on the front man's mysterious illness. This was eventually revealed to be AIDS just shortly before he died on November 24, 1991.

The loss was so momentous that on April 20, 1992 the remainder of the band helped stage a huge tribute at Wembley Stadium dubbed "A Concert For Life", during which the rock glitterati – including Metallica, Def Leppard and Guns N' Roses among many others – celebrated the singer's life and music. The profits went towards raising AIDS awareness.

The years that followed found absolutely no let-up in the popularity of the band. They had become a heavy-rock institution and when *Made In Heaven* (1995) appeared – featuring Mercury's last recording sessions – it was another chart topper, followed by *Queen Rocks* (1997), a compilation that excised all the synths and lightweight material in favour of what Queen did best. And when *Greatest Hits III* (1999) arrived it concentrated on various collaborations and solo bits and pieces.

The more recent period sees the Queen-related releases continuing; later items include *The Solo Collection*, a Freddie Mercury box set; *The Platinum Collection* (2000); a reissue of *Live At Wembley '86* (2003); and a British release for the previously Japan-only *Queen Greatest Karaoke Hits*, Queen songs with Mercury's vocals mixed out – now you too can front your favourite band. And then there's the West End show *We Will Rock You* – but the less said about that the better. Amazingly, though the idea seemed impossible without Mercury, Queen have announced a tour for 2005 with **Free/Bad Company** vocalist **Paul Rodgers** fronting the band.

Sheer Heart Attack
1974; EMI

This is where Queen get really interesting. Glamorous and deadly, the band were hitting their stride with classics like "Killer Queen" and the truly fantastic hard-rock blitz of "Stone Cold Crazy". All guitar – no synths.

A Night At The Opera
1975; EMI

Yes, it contains one of the best-loved, most widely known rock tracks in history, but there's a lot more fun to be had here than just "Bohemian Rhapsody". Check out "Death On Two Legs (Dedicated to...)" and the whimsical "Seaside Rendezvous'. A classic.

News Of The World
1977; EMI

"I suck your mind, you blow my head" croons Mercury on the hot and steamy "Get Down, Make Love". Wacky, brilliant and studded with moments of genius, not least those tunes that get wheeled out during sporting events.

Live Killers
1979; EMI

Lots of their 70s material blasted out live. You really can't lose.

Greatest Hits I & II
1994; EMI

There are some odd exclusions – where's "Tie Your Mother Down"? – but for sheer chart magic this is hard to beat. From their more dancy and lightweight excursions to their slamming, heavy guitar sound this has it all. Well, almost.

QUEENS OF THE STONE AGE

Formed California, US, 1997

"If you don't like what you're playing yourself how in the hell is anybody else gonna get it?" Nick Oliveri on the band's philosophy.

Some bands achieve a legendary status once they have been consigned to the great outdoor festival in the sky, and so it was with proto-stoner outfit **Kyuss**, who blazed a trail of sludged-out riffs and gargantuan rhythms

through the collective rock psyche during the 1990s, before splitting up and eventually forming **Queens Of The Stone Age**.

After Kyuss imploded, **Josh Homme** headed up to Seattle to tour with the Screaming Trees while recording a number of singles with the likes of Soundgarden's **Matt Cameron** and Dinosaur Jr's **Mike Johnson** under the name **Gamma Ray** – which unfortunately also proved to be the name of a dodgy German metal band stuck 'in an 80s time warp. Homme then recruited former Kyuss drummer **Alfredo Hernandez**, along with a bunch of helpful mates, and adopted Queens Of The Stone Age as the band's name. They set about writing *Queens Of The Stone Age* (1998), which eventually emerged on the cool indie label Loosegroove. By Homme's own admission, the task this time round was to concentrate on songwriting rather than free-form jamming. The result was tight, almost surgically economical in places, but the focus on melody and power brought a welcome punch and groove to the previously more fluid Kyuss style. The album was hailed as an underground triumph.

At this point former Kyuss bassist **Nick Oliveri** left **The Dwarves**, in which he had played under the moniker **Rex Everything**, and joined Homme in Queens. He had also spent some of the interim messing about with his **Mondo Generator** project, which eventually yielded an album, *Cocaine Rodeo*

(2000), oddly enough featuring both Homme and former Kyuss drummer **Brant Bjork**. Needless to say, Kyuss fans were getting very excited at this point, but Homme chose to maintain his artistically free approach to music-making and continued to take part in other projects such as the various *Desert Sessions* albums released on Man's Ruin. Meanwhile, the Queens' momentum grew. These writing sessions – basically consisting of Homme corralling as many great musicians as possible into the Rancho de la Luna studio in the high desert town of Joshua Tree for extended jam sessions – would eventually achieve legendary status, and the influence of these sojourns can be heard throughout the Queens' work.

Heavy touring ensured that the band's next album was highly anticipated. When *R* (2000) appeared on Interscope it was immediately dubbed a masterpiece. **Dave Catching** (keyboards) filled the band's sound out and **Nicky Lucerno** and **Gene Trautmann** appeared on drums and percussion. R was towering, angular, and seriously groovy, its name taken from the 'R' rating, indicating 'Restricted' in the American film classification system, the category for movies of a more adult content. All of which made perfect sense when lead track "Feel Good Hit Of The Summer" consisted basically of the line "Nicotine, Valium, Vicodin, marijuana, ecstasy and alcohol...C-c-c-c-cocaine!!!!" screamed over and over. There was no need to guess what Homme and his buddies got up to when they indulged in a spot of rest and recuperation: their reputed love of partying very hard often providing some bizarre lyrical content. Witness such gems as 'Monsters In The Parasol', 'Leg Of Lamb' and 'Better Living Through Chemistry'. *R* also featured many big names: **Rob Halford (Judas Priest)**, **Chris Goss** (Masters Of Reality), **Mark Lanegan** and **Barrett Martin (Screaming Trees)** all brought their own unique touches to the overall feel, although the sound established with the debut was maintained – with warm and driving grooves being the order of the day.

The same structure was maintained for *Songs For The Deaf* (2002), which, coming after what had by now been hailed as a modern classic, was expected to be the greatest album of the year. Despite all this pressure, Homme and Oliveri just did what came naturally. They got a bunch of mates together, including the likes of **Casey Chaos** (**Amen**), **Mark Lanegan** – who by now had become a member of the band through his touring commitments with them, **Dean Ween** and **Dave Grohl** (**Foo Fighters**) on drums, and had a blast in the studio. The result was by no means a musical paradigm shift, but nevertheless rocked hard in the by-now-familiar Queens fashion: dirty, economical riffing, sweet harmonies, and a weird sense of humour, which made *Songs For The Deaf* essential listening.

Kicking back from his role in Queens, Oliveri concentrated on releasing another Mondo Generator effort, titled *A Drug Problem That Never Existed* (2003) while Homme had a bash at volumes nine and ten of his *Desert Sessions* and yet another side-project, the **Eagles Of Death Metal**, whose debut was *Peace, Love And Death Metal* (2004). Bizarrely, in this period, ructions within Queens resulted in Homme sacking Oliveri for vague reasons centred, ironically, around the latter's penchant for getting very badly wasted. As a result, for some critics, *Lullabies To Paralyze* (2005) lacked bite as Homme became the main songwriter for the band.

Queens Of The Stone Age
1998; Loosegroove/Roadrunner

A more song-oriented approach to the raw riffery of the 70s. Homme's vocals provide an eerily silky counterpoint to the groovy heaviness.

R
2000; Interscope

Working with long-time production collaborator Chris Goss evidently suits the Queens because this is the album that truly kicked them into the limelight. Weirdly experimental at times this is, nevertheless, a *tour de force* of both style and content.

Songs For The Deaf
2002; Interscope

Based around the old idea of someone tuning in a radio (yep, that old chestnut), though done with some style, this takes the notion of creative jamming to its illogical conclusion and delivers songs that are groovily catchy, featuring tons of disparate ideas.

QUEEnSRŸCHE

Formed Seattle, US, 1981

The northwestern American seaboard may be regarded as the birthplace of all things grungy, but back in the early 1980s, metal was the prevailing sound. Brit metallers Iron Maiden and Judas Priest were riding high with hit albums in the US, so it was natural for **Queensrÿche** to absorb these influences and model themselves on similar lines. Over the years they have become widely regarded as one of the most intelligent and progressive metal bands still cutting albums and touring.

Schoolfriends **Geoff Tate** (vocals), **Chris DeGarmo** (guitar), **Michael Wilton** (guitar), **Eddie Jackson** (bass) and **Scott Rockenfield** (drums) had all put in time in covers bands but decided the only way forward was to concentrate on their own material. Key to their sound was Tate's incredibly powerful and searing voice, the singer having studied opera for a while. They spent a good two years rehearsing and worked for a while under the naff name of **The Mob** before mashing together a couple of words from one of their favourite tracks, "Queen Of The Reich" – and doing that loveably daft 80s thing with umlauts. Famously, their *Queensrÿche* EP, which started off as a widely circulated demo tape, was their passport to an extraordinary career. Originally a self-financed release through their then manager's label, the popularity of the record led to 60,000 copies being sold and the band signing to EMI, who promptly rereleased the EP in order to make a dent on the charts.

Shamelessly basing their style on the big metal acts of the day, it would take a while for the band to find their own identity. On *The Warning* (1984), they weren't yet there. An unsuitable producer, a pushy label and a dreadful final mix crippled what could have been a cracking debut. Instead it was merely solid, with the occasional glimmer of class beneath the murk. It wasn't until 1986 that a strident, ballsy and refined metal album emerged from them. *Rage For Order* had a futuristic feel and was gloriously pompous in both range and execution, with clever songwriting touches. The album helped the band net an ever-widening cult following and a

Queensrÿche in all their mid-80s majesty.

EBET ROBERTS/REDFERNS

few live slots supporting Metallica. Publicity pics from the time are quite gruesome with the band wearing neo-modern shoulder-padded jackets, pouting in full glammy make-up and sporting absurdly teased hair. No doubt they were persuaded by the record company to project a sci-fi feel to their progressive metal, and they ended up looking like extras from a *Mad Max* movie. Not a good look for any band, even one from the 80s.

The ridiculous public image was soon ditched as the band took more control with the help of a new management team. Focused and fully charged with terrific ideas they next issued what many believe to be their finest album, the veritable masterpiece *Operation: Mindcrime* (1988). While their contemporaries were content to chuck out standard glam or thrash metal the 'Rÿche weren't about to conform. They had already been hinting at their progressive tendencies, and their new offering was a concept album complete with a full cast of characters and a hip political thriller plotline about a street kid called Nikki who is drawn into an evil assassination plot.

Europe loved it. America was slightly slower on the uptake. Nevertheless, the sub-Orwellian concept album gave them their first platinum-selling hit, success they were to repeat with its follow-up, *Empire* (1990). The mellow "Silent Lucidity" was a huge US hit single which went Top 10, pushing the album to do the same. Their efforts were rewarded with a slot on the 1991 Monsters Of Rock tour alongside Metallica, Mötley Crüe and Black Crowes, prior to the release of *Operation: Livecrime*, a live souvenir of the *Mindcrime* tour.

The next move the band made would come in 1994. The touring of the preceding years had taken its toll and they needed to take a break before reconvening for *Promised Land*. Amazingly, for a world taken over by grunge, there were still enough fans around wanting to hear Queensrÿche – albeit in a rather more downbeat mode – to send the album to #3 in the US charts and #13 in the UK.

However, over the next couple of years it became clear that the band were reaping diminishing returns. Not only had grunge trimmed their audience but nu-metal was gradually shifting perceptions of what metal ought to be. In this new climate the band decided to adopt a no-frills approach to their songwriting for *Hear In The Now Frontier* (1997), which arguably robbed them of their uniqueness. The album was a poor seller – not helped by the fact that their label went bankrupt and cut their tour support short. DeGarmo decided that it just wasn't fun anymore, so he did the unthinkable and quit in early 1998.

Minus one of their key writers and with a relative failure of a new album on their hands the 'Rÿche looked very shaky. They took on board long-time friend and producer **Kelly Gray** as DeGarmo's replacement but *Q2K* (1999) wasn't the return to glorious form that people had been hoping for – which may have been the reason for issuing *Greatest Hits* (2000) so soon afterwards.

A move to Sanctuary Records prompted a confusing batch of releases in its wake: *Live Evolution* (2001), a reissue of *Operation: Livecrime* and *Classic Masters* (2003); soon to follow was *Tribe* (2003) with DeGarmo back in the band, at least for part of the writing process, and with live albums seemingly being whipped out of thin air, *The Art Of Live* (2004), came shortly after.

⊙ Operation: Mindcrime
1988; EMI

They wanted to take a risk, to gamble on giving vent to their full-blown artistic vision and we got this, a timeless classic. The orchestral arrangements come courtesy of soundtrack composer *Michael Kamen*, while the metal quotient is as potent as the dramatically gripping plot.

⊙ Empire
1990; EMI

They had already proved they could hold together a sprawling concept album and with **Empire** they pared down their approach to concentrate on writing separate songs with intricate mood and structure. The result was nothing short of stunning.

QUIET RIOT

Formed Los Angeles, US, 1975

Were it not for some extraordinary luck, coupled with a little twist of fate, **Quiet Riot** would barely warrant a mention in metal history. As it stands, however, this heavy-rock crew are worth a note, partly because, over a short period, they sold a huge number of records – thus making metal a commercial pop commodity of interest to record labels – and also because of the personages that passed through their ranks.

The mid-70s incarnation of the band featured none other than the vastly talented **Randy Rhoads** (guitar). With Rhoads in the band the riotous ones managed two albums: an eponymous debut and *Quiet Riot II*, in 1978 and 1979 respectively. At this point Rhoads' skills on guitar were pretty much only appreciated in Japan where the band had managed to land a deal and built up a bit of a following with their more pop-oriented hard-rock sound. Elsewhere they had trouble gaining any ground.

Rhoads famously got a call to join **Ozzy Osbourne**'s band, so Quiet Riot, which also featured vocalist **Kevin DuBrow**, folded. Far from vanishing from view, however, DuBrow, undeterred, formed a band – first under his own name and then taking on the Quiet Riot moniker again – with a line-up which included **Carlos Cavazo** (guitar), **Rudy Sarzo** (bass) and **Frankie Banali** (drums).

There was nothing to suggest that the newly revitalized Quiet Riot would enjoy anything beyond the meagre success they had achieved so far, but all that was to change with *Metal Health* (1983). Incredibly, the album topped the chart in the US – the first metal album to do so – and sold in its millions. The sudden turnaround in fortune can be put firmly down to their sparky cover version of Slade's dyslexic classic "Cum On Feel The Noize" – with DuBrow's Noddy Holder-esque vocals great throughout – and also their nice line in stripy spandex. The record was a remarkable feat of riff re-engineering and went into the Top 5, but the band couldn't maintain the momentum.

They blazed back the following year with an attempt to copy their success of 1983, including the recording of another Slade cover version, "Mama Weer All Crazee Now", gracing *Condition Critical*. But it failed to ignite and things very quickly started to go pear-shaped. Tensions within the band began to rise and DuBrow began to portion out the blame. In one infamous interview he even began to slate the new upcoming rock bands. It didn't take long for the united front to crumble and Sarzo left. He eventually joined **Whitesnake** and was replaced by **Chuck Wright** for *Quiet Riot III* (1986) which got a thorough drubbing at the hands of the critics. By now things had deteriorated to the point that DuBrow was becoming impossible to deal with; legend has it that no one wanted to travel with him following a final tour date in Hawaii. Partly by accident, partly by design, he was abandoned at their hotel.

When the band returned for yet another eponymous effort in 1988 it was ex-**Rough Cutt** vocalist **Paul Shortino** who took DuBrow's place. Wright had also been replaced by **Sean McNabb**. The less said about this album the better. It was time to put everyone out of their misery.

The tale doesn't end here, however. In the early 90s DuBrow began working with **Cavazo** in a band called **Heat**. It wasn't long before they dusted down the old band name and lured back Banali for *Terrified* (1993), recorded with bassist **Kenny Hilary**. This was followed by *Down To The Bone* (1995), which, appropriately, was released on the Kamikaze label. Incredibly, given the personality clash between DuBrow and their old bassist, Sarzo was tempted back to resurrect the classic line-up. It may have seemed like a good idea but by the time of *Alive And Well* (1999) far too much time had passed. The

airwaves were saturated with alternative sounds and no one really gave a damn anymore. A new studio album followed called *Guilty Pleasures* (2001) but the band eventu-

ally fell apart again in 2003. Seemingly boasting more lives than a heavy metal feline they re-formed in 2004 and issued *Quiet Riot Live & Rare* in January 2005.

 Metal Health
1983; Pasha

A surprise smash hit bursting with fantastic, good-time heavy rock tunes. The title track is a fist-raising stomper as is their cover of Slade's classic, "Cum On Feel The Noize". Get that head banging!

QUIREBOYS

Formed Newcastle UK, 1985; disbanded 1993; re-formed 2000

First they were the **Choirboys**, then they were the **Queerboys** and finally they became the **Quireboys**, one of the UK's best-loved hard-rock acts of the late 1980s and early 90s. Their instantly identifiable, blues-harp honkin', ivory-tinklin', Faces-style bar-room boogie landed them with a decent clutch of good-time hit singles, but their template for unpretentious rock'n'roll fun simply couldn't last the battering dealt out by grunge.

Looking like they had dressed themselves during a blackout in a jumble sale, the line-up of **Spike** (vocals), **Guy Bailey** (guitar), **Ginger** (guitar), **Nigel Mogg** (bass), **Chris Johnstone** (keyboards) and **Nick 'Coze' Connel** (drums) began to make waves by regularly selling out the Marquee and by issuing singles "Mayfair" and "There She Goes Again" on Survival Records. They played the Reading Rock Festival in 1987 and supported Guns N' Roses at the Hammersmith Odeon. By the time of their deal with EMI, Ginger had been replaced with **Guy Griffin**, while Connel had been replaced with **Ian Wallace**. Wallace was in turn replaced soon after by **Rudy Richman**. Ginger went off to form the **Wildhearts**, but that's another story entirely.

Rod Stewart guitarist **Jim Cregan** helped produce *A Bit Of What You Fancy* (1990), the release of which was preceded by hit singles "7 O'Clock" and "Hey You". The sense

THE QUIREBOYS

THIS IS ROCK'N'ROLL

with Metallica's so-called 'Black' album. By the time the Quireboys' record was done Seattle grunge was the order of the day and, although the album was a great second offering, it stiffed. The band split shortly afterwards and for the next few years they toiled away on their own pet projects, until a writing session between Spike and Griffin yielded a demo that landed a deal with Sanctuary. With Mogg back in the band the Quireboys were resurrected with the addition of **Luke Bossendorfer** (guitar) and **Martin Henderson** (drums). *This Is Rock 'N'Roll* (2001) was the result, with **Keith Weir** providing the keyboards on stage.

A major bout of touring ensued, including dates supporting Alice Cooper on the 2002 Monsters of Rock tour, during which time **Jason Bonham** helped out on drums. The *100% Live 2002* (2003) album kept up the momentum and *Well Oiled* (2004), featuring new members **Paul Guerin** (guitar) and **Pip Mailing** (drums), followed on SPV. There were also more touring commitments, including dates with David Lee Roth and Whitesnake.

of fun exuded by the band on these charmingly straightforward songs was infectious, Spike's throaty rasp playing easily off the sleazy slide guitar and honky-tonk piano. For a while their #2 hit album was the Quireboys' ticket to major rock festival billings in the US and UK; in 1990 they made a memorable appearance at the Donington Monsters Of Rock in a touring schedule that took them from Japan to Los Angeles via Newcastle, the latter date a support slot with the Rolling Stones.

There were high hopes for a storming follow-up album. The band were looking to rope in **Bob Rock** as producer for *Bitter Sweet And Twisted* (1993) but Rock was busy

⦿ A Bit Of What You Fancy
1990; Parlophone

Yes, it sounds like the British answer to the Black Crowes – all Faces riffs and Rod Stewart bluster – but for good, honest rock entertainment you just can't go wrong with this. Goes down great with a bevy or two.

RAGE AGAINST THE MACHINE

Formed Los Angeles, US, 1991; disbanded 2001

Rage Against The Machine were a phenomenon, no question about it. While rap and metal had been bolted together before RATM, the combination was little more than a novelty. Then this four-piece erupted into the public consciousness in a welter of expletives, politically aware rapping and hip-hop stylings created exclusively on guitar. It was unique, attention grabbing and thrilling on a gut level. Their almost instant success provided a springboard for a career that wasn't so much about selling millions of records (which they did) as it was about raising public consciousness of a variety of social and political issues – from women's rights to protests against sweatshop labour. The band would play benefit shows and generally throw their weight behind as many worthy causes as possible – RATM had both a singer and a guitarist that came from politically active families which had instilled in them a radical sense of social justice. Critics accused the band of selling out by signing to an evil corporate entity (i.e. a major label record company), to which their response was that they wanted to spread the word as far, as wide, and as effectively as possible.

The line-up consisted of **Zack de la Rocha** (vocals), **Tom Morello** (guitar), **Tim Commerford** aka **Timmy C** (bass) and **Brad Wilk** (drums). Morello had been a member of **Lock Up** (not to be confused with the more recent death-metal supergroup of the same name), who had managed to release an album, during which time he had first met Wilk. So part of the chemistry was already in place before the confrontational de la Rocha gave the fledgling rock'n'roll revolutionaries their essential polemical drive. A twelve-track tape was recorded and sold at shows and through the band's fan club. Having shifted 5000 copies of what was essentially an entire album's worth of songs, a major label had to take notice. They ended up on Epic Records and set about making waves supporting Suicidal Tendencies and Porno For Pyros, and appearing at Lollapalooza, slotting in easily into the post-hair metal, alternative scene of the early 90s.

While the focused bedlam of the live shows was extraordinary, their eponymous debut album, released in 1992 was explosive. Preceded by the UK top-thirty hit single "Killing In The Name", which caused something of a controversy with its defiant refrain of "Fuck you, I won't do what you tell me!", the album was a relentless torrent of incisive fury. De la Rocha's boiling mad rhymes married to Morello's innovative, turntable-aping guitar licks and a neck-snapping rhythm section created infectious street-level anthems for bedroom anarchists around the globe. The album was an indisputable classic, and Rage were suddenly the coolest band on the planet, oozing the kind of credibility that even had pundits on serious arts programmes pondering their merits.

Far from capitalizing on this surge of popularity, however, the band spent the next four years or so playing live and fighting the power by supporting various political causes. In 1993 they famously took the stage at Lollapalooza III naked and gagged with duct tape in a silent 15-minute protest against censorship; each member had a letter scrawled on his chest to spell out P-M-R-C (Parents Music Resource Center), the right-wing pressure group.

The buzz built up for the arrival of *Evil Empire* (1996) was phenomenal and propelled the album to the top slot in the US charts and to #4 in the UK. Musically, it was more of the same though leaving such a long gap between releases inevitably led to a sense of anticlimax. The sense of righteous rebellion still came through strongly but the songs seemed a tad stale compared to the invigoratingly irate debut. But the disappointment was mitigated by yet more livewire gigging and campaigning. Money from various performances went to causes as diverse as Tibetan freedom and the campaign to free death row inmate Mumia Abu-Jamal. And anyone who had yet to experience Rage live got the chance to pick up their eponymous video package in 1997, which included gig footage, uncensored versions of their music videos, various non-album tracks and a superb reworking of Bruce Springsteen's "The Ghost Of Tom Joad". Fans wanting a slightly more esoteric live effort had to track down a copy of the Japanese release, *Live & Rare* (1997).

The follow-up to *Evil Empire* was far more cohesive and satisfying. *The Battle Of Los Angeles* (1999) found them topping the US charts again, their anger not dampened one iota. With tracks such as "Calm Like A Bomb", "War Within A Breath" and "Sleep Now In The Fire" it seemed as though the band could go on hacking and slashing at the belly of the Western capitalist beast until it was finally slain.

Unfortunately the stability of the band began to crumble over the next year and *Renegades* (2000), originally planned as a fun stopgap of cover versions showcasing the

band's musical roots, turned out to be their last studio recording. The artists whose music was given the Rage treatment included the Rolling Stones, MC5, Cypress Hill and Erik B and Rakim and the vibe of the album was quite different to the usual band offerings, which made it a somewhat odd note with which to sign off. De la Rocha headed off to experiment with straight-up hip-hop while the other three considered their next move. In the meantime *The Battle Of Mexico City* (2001) live DVD – the band had given outspoken support for human rights and democratic reform in Mexico – served up a highlight of the band's career. Another live album and DVD, *Live At The Grand Olympic Auditorium* (2003), presented the band's final live show of their career in 2000; the DVD included substantial de la Rocha stage banter and included bonus footage of the band's famous coup performing outside the Democratic National Convention in LA in 2000.

Following the demise of RATM, the most high-profile comeback featured the remaining three members, who joined up with ex-**Soundgarden** singer **Chris Cornell** to create **Audioslave**, a supergroup in the grand tradition. They took their sweet time jamming and writing and eventually released an eponymous album in 2002, preceded by the riff-monster single "Cochise". Fans wanting more rap rhymes were obviously disappointed, but for anyone with a love of classic heavy rock and bombastic vocals, Audioslave were the ideal combination of vintage metal and Morello's unmistakeably modern and idiosyncratic guitar work.

⊙ Rage Against The Machine
1992; Epic

The rap and metal combination wasn't new but Rage wielded it dedicatedly and uncompromisingly in a deadly onslaught. "Bombtrack", "Freedom", "Fistful Of Steel", "Township Rebellion" and, of course, the hypnotic and charged "Killing In The Name", with its straight-to-the-point refrain, make this a ranting, rampaging classic.

⊙ Evil Empire
1996; Epic

It took an age to get released and pales in comparison to the debut. But brushing any initial disappointment to one side, there are some great individual tracks, not least the opening "People Of The Sun" and hit single "Bulls On Parade".

⊙ The Battle Of Los Angeles
1999; Epic

This collection is a far better successor to their debut. The band sound like they are barely controlling their blitzkrieg of squealing riffs and lyrical ire. This is a glorious ram raid on what RATM see as the hypocritical values at the heart of Western democracy.

RAINBOW

Formed 1975, disbanded 1984; re-formed 1995; disbanded shortly after

Mention these archetypal heavy rockers to metal fans of a certain age and they will go misty-eyed remembering the fantasy-laden excess of it all. Bombastic, over-the-top and brilliantly gifted, Rainbow were responsible for some of the most commercial metal of the 1970s and 80s, starting off primarily as an album-oriented outfit and gradually spreading into more chart-friendly territory as they developed.

Key to the band's early success was the directing musical force of ex-**Deep Purple** guitar genius **Ritchie Blackmore** and the sword'n'sorcery-lovin' vocalist **Ronnie James Dio**. The story goes that Blackmore had become increasingly dissatisfied with the direction Deep Purple were taking. He didn't like the album *Stormbringer* and had contributed virtually nothing to the writing. He was annoyed at the band's refusal to have a go at "Black Sheep Of The Family" – a song by

Quatermass and one of his favourite tunes. So he nabbed all but the guitarist of moderately successful rockers **Elf** (including Ronnie James Dio) and set about recording the Quatermass tune with an idea that it might be a single. Dio shared his love of medieval styles of art and music, and the sessions went so well that they decided to extend them. The result was *Ritchie Blackmore's Rainbow* (1975), recorded with the help of producer **Martin Birch**, a collaboration that would continue over several albums. From the opener, "Man On The Silver Mountain", it was a solid gold classic. Blackmore's superlative guitar pyrotechnics underpinned Dio's early forays into fantastical lyrics, complete with his love of rainbows, which would soon become a ubiquitous motif. The album sleeve depicted a rainbow arcing over a fantasy castle incorporating a guitar into its structure.

Rainbow was a resounding creative success, but perfectionist Blackmore craved a more stable setup. So, retaining Dio, he replaced the rest of the band with **Jimmy Bain** (bass), **Tony Carey** (keyboards) and **Cozy Powell** (drums), a line-up many regard as Rainbow's definitive one. It was certainly the most consistently creative and brilliant. If the debut had laid out Blackmore's blueprint for medievalism, myth and stonkingly terrific rock'n'roll then *Rising* (1976) was a superb creation from a band at their peak. Its six tracks were finely crafted, most of them tipping the rock scales towards the epic, with Dio in his loopy lyrical element. "Tarot Woman" set the tone for the album's two closing eight-minute-plus set pieces – "Stargazer", complete with orchestral touches, and "A Light In The Black". The set was yet another classic.

Naturally, a line-up oozing such talent and credibility had to showcase their live credentials and many of the 1976 shows were recorded to compile *On Stage* (1977). It was perhaps a little premature to be wheeling out a live document but the album managed to capture some of the flavour of their mid-70s world tour, with a live version of Deep Purple's "Mistreated" clocking in at over thirteen minutes of guitar-twiddling brilliance.

Before the third studio album, however, Blackmore's penchant for hiring and firing musos resulted in bassist **Mark Clarke** (ex-**Uriah Heep**) replacing Bain for a few months, before **Bob Daisley** stepped in along with new member **David Stone** on keyboards. Despite this maestro-conducted game of musical chairs, *Long Live Rock'n'Roll* (1978) contained yet another cracking set of tunes with a belting opening title song and a fine rendition of "Kill The King" – which had previously featured as part of their live set and was first captured on *On Stage*. "L.A. Connection" was sprinkled with some tasteful ivory tinkling, while both "Gates Of Babylon" and "Rainbow Eyes" featured more orchestral dabbling in the vein of "Stargazer".

Despite the successful albums Blackmore just didn't seem satisfied with his lot. It was line-up shuffle time again, with only Powell remaining behind the drum kit. **Roger Glover** (ex-Deep Purple) stepped in on bass, co-writing and production, **Don Airey** took over on keyboards, and one **Graham Bonnet** was recruited as vocalist, after Blackmore failed to persuade his old Deep Purple cohort Ian Gillan to join the band. Dio left to join Black Sabbath and with him went much of the band's mystical flavour:

there were no more rainbows, no more wizards and no more magic. *Down To Earth* (1979) just contained driving, ballsy, heavy rock and provided the band with their first real singles chart action – "Since You Been Gone", a Russ Ballard-penned tune was a top-ten hit, while "All Night Long" was a

top-five smash. The mist-shrouded era of Dio had been blasted away by a gloriously modern approach, Bonnet's strident and rasping vocals bringing real grit to the catchy choruses of the hits – it was enough for the band to land the headlining slot at the very first Donington Monsters Of Rock festival in 1980.

Unbelievably, Blackmore still wanted to tinker with the setup. Powell had already left following their Donington appearance and Bonnet's taste in Hawaiian shirts made him a dead cert for the chop – he disappeared to pursue a solo career. Enter drummer **Bob Rondinelli** and the formidable vocal talent of **Joe Lynn Turner**. With Blackmore's eye seemingly firmly fixed on the mainstream, Turner provided – with his smooth and easy power – bags more of the required transatlantic appeal than Bonnet. Cue another monster single smash in "I Surrender", another Russ Ballard tune. It went to #3 in the UK and heralded the arrival of *Difficult To Cure* (1981), which also went to #3, an album moulded upon the polished hard-rock sound of bands such as Bad Company. The same pattern was followed for *Straight Between The Eyes* (1982); with Turner gradually sharing some of the writing credits the band were in danger of sounding more like Foreigner, were it not for Blackmore's classical influences and guitar virtuosity. This time round the casualty was Airey who went off to join **Ozzy Osbourne**; he was replaced by **David Rosenthal**.

When *Bent Out Of Shape* (1983) appeared the ultra-modern 80's sleeve pretty much severed any significant connection with the band's earlier efforts; they had swung from seminal orc-bothering hard rockers to a slick mainstream band with an eye on FM radio. This time a new drummer, **Chuck Bürgi**, was drafted in but the album lacked the sparkle or sword-wielding charm of Dio-era Rainbow; again, only Blackmore's idiosyncratic writing and Glover's strong production values prevented them from losing their identity entirely.

The gradual slide towards commercialism was halted only after both Blackmore and Glover were invited to rejoin Deep Purple. Rainbow bowed out during a tour of Japan, specifically two shows at the Budokan Hall, Tokyo, during which the band played a lengthy, rapturously received version of their arrangement of Beethoven's *Ninth*, "Difficult To Cure", featuring a full symphony orchestra, the entire spectacle illuminated by rainbow-coloured lighting. This version surfaced a couple of years later on the *Final Vinyl* (1986) rarities compilation along with the previously unreleased "Bad Girl".

And so it would have stayed had Blackmore not re-formed Rainbow for some gigging and an album in 1995. *Stranger In Us All* involved a completely new band with vocals handled by **Doogie White**; needless to say it is one of the less celebrated Rainbow offerings. Shortly thereafter one of rock's greatest guitarists decided that hey-nonny-nonny sixteenth-century folk music was the way forward and he began to pour his considerable string-bending powers into Blackmore's Night alongside his young vocalist partner **Candice Night**. Who would have thought the demon of the guitar would end up playing hurdy-gurdy?

◉ Ritchie Blackmore's Rainbow
Polydor; 1975

Not bad going for an album that started out as just a single. Dio's writing is the perfect match for Blackmore's classical and baroque leanings. The result is a storming debut, no question.

◉ Rising
Polydor; 1976

The definitive Rainbow album – a stone-cold classic and no mistake. Chestbeating vocals, oodles of ludicrous mystical nonsense and Blackmore widdling away in neoclassical mode in the middle of it all.

◉ Down To Earth
Polydor; 1979

Slick and commercial with Graham Bonnet's vocals a more than adequate replacement for Dio's golden tonsils. And then there are the hit singles, "All Night Long" and "Since You Been Gone".

◉ Difficult To Cure
Polydor; 1981

Joe Lynn Turner's arrival takes the band even further down the American FM rock route, albeit with some style and guts. The opening duo of "I Surrender" and "Spotlight Kid" take some beating.

RAMMSTEIN
Formed Berlin, Germany, 1994

For years anyone asked to describe German heavy metal would invariably mention such globe-trotting mega-acts of the 1980s as the Scorpions and, possibly, Accept. The 90s, however, brought a whole new dimension to Teutonic metal in the provocative, headline-grabbing, chart-topping **Rammstein** – the name literally translating as 'ramming stone' – a ram made of rock – which perfectly encapsulated the surging, battering power of the music.

An early incarnation of Rammstein consisted of **Richard Kruspe-Bernstein** (guitar), **Christoph Schneider** (drums) and **Oliver Riedel** (bass), working hard to formulate a new sound after Kruspe-Bernstein felt that his other band – the catchily named **Orgasm Death Gimmicks** – wasn't heading in the direction he desired. Eventually **Till Lindemann** (vocals) joined and the demo produced by this unit won a battle of the bands competition; the prize was studio time, marking the beginning for the outfit who would go on to redefine the face of modern German music. Guitarist **Paul Landers** needed no persuading to join his mates once he heard the nascent Rammstein sound and keyboard player **Christian Lorenz** supplied the necessary sound-effects wizardry that had thus far been lacking. The band began work on their first album.

When *Herzeleid* (1995) – meaning 'heart-ache' – was released, the effect in their home country was electric, and the record went platinum in several territories across Europe. Rammstein had struck upon the ideal package: a blistering brand of metal which layered regimented guitars on top of a pulverizingly pumping rhythm section. To top it off Lindemann was a formidable presence on stage – the singer had trained as an Olympic swimmer – and the *coup de grâce* was his rich and resonating, operatic baritone, singing in German. When they added elements of industrial, techno and German classical music, the result was not unlike listening to a combination of Front 242, Laibach, Ministry and Nine Inch Nails. This martial sound, coupled with the artwork – featuring all six band members looking buff and bare-chested in front of a gigantic flower – sparked off all

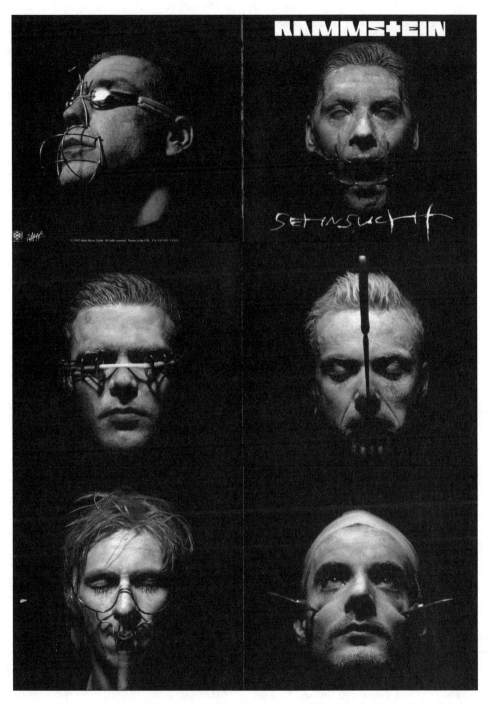

manner of media speculation about the band. Were they gay? Did this assertive display of German manhood indicate they were closet Nazis? Was this all just one big joke? Though the album artwork was adjusted for the US release, the band always denied any kind of deliberate political posturing. Nevertheless, their self-conscious image, when coupled with such strident lyrics, lent a fascinating mystique to everything they created. Their disavowals of any provocative intent were not always convincing: for instance, the video accompanying their cover version of Depeche Mode's "Stripped" used clips from Leni Riefenstahl's film of the 1936 Berlin Olympics, she being one of Hitler's favourite film-makers.

However, as their career progressed it became apparent that Rammstein did have a sense of humour, even if it was rather weird at times. Follow-up *Sehnsucht* (1997) – meaning 'yearning' – this time featured images of the various band members' faces wrapped in barbed wire and twisted metal, just the kind of thing to spark off rumours about the band's apparent predilection for violence and sadomasochism. While the music was as intense as ever, drawing freely upon their German heritage and modern industro-metal, they were becoming increasingly renowned for their spectacular live show. Lindemann had trained in the use of pyrotechnics and the event had become a literally incendiary affair every night as he would light himself up like a walking Roman Candle. Then there was the set piece "Bück Dich" during which Lindemann would reveal a massive strapped-on dildo, simulate sex with whoever was nearest and then spurt milk all over both the stage and the crowd.

With *Sehnsucht* given a US release in early 1998 the scene was set for a triumphant trek across America on the Ozzfest and Family Values tours, where crowds were stunned by their show, which included a spectacular array of pyrotechnics. One infamous incident occurred in Worcester, Massachusetts. When the priapic singer was feigning sex with the keyboard player, he was arrested in mid-flow as it were, for 'lascivious conduct' in public. They managed to get away with a small fine.

Needless to say, such antics guaranteed the band maximum media exposure and they became one of the few German acts to really break the US market, helped no end by their breakthrough single "Du Hast". This was some feat considering that, apart from the aforementioned Depeche Mode cover, they staunchly refused to dilute their approach by singing in English.

The next year brought the self-explanatory *Live Aus Berlin*, a smart move that showcased the band's live spectacle for anyone who had not yet seen Lindemann going up in flames. Their third full album, the stunning *Mutter* (2001), used the tried-and-tested services of producer **Jacob Hellner** again and the result was astonishing. The band pushed their

creative vision even further into the dark imaginings of their collective twisted mind. The cover depicted a baby preserved as a medical specimen in a jar and the band were photographed in similar poses within. The title track was an emotional, skin-crawling ballad with a streak of black humour, while the marching thunder of "Links 2 3 4" led to the accusations of militaristic fetishism being raked over again. It was gloriously baroque, pompous, excessively arty and absurdly ambitious and, of course, was their most successful album to date.

It took three years for *Reise Reise* to finally arrive but when it did all the trademark Rammstein tricks were in place – the wacky sense of black humour and disturbing imagery – plus a sense of gothic overload.

⦿ Herzeleid
1995; Motor Music/Universal

Six shirtless blokes standing in front of a huge flower? It must be an album of German industrial metal then. A stunning debut ideal for both the dance floor and the mosh pit.

⦿ Sehnsucht
1997; Motor Music/Universal

More of the same operatic excesses and gargantuan riffing, Till Lindemann's rolling German 'r's raising more than a smile. The ideal soundtrack to forge metal to.

⦿ Mutter
2001; Motor Music/Universal

It's all here: Wagnerian classicism, brutal guitars, crunching rhythms and weird tales of love, heart-rending loss, horror and sadness. Wonderful and strange stuff.

RAMONES

Formed Forest Hills, New York, US, 1974; disbanded 1996

Anyone doubting the validity of including these punkers in a book about metal should wrap their ears around Motörhead's "R.A.M.O.N.E.S." from *1916*. Or better still cast an eye over the various rockers who pay homage to Da Brudders' legacy on tribute covers album *We're A Happy Family* (2003) – Kiss, Metallica, Red Hot Chili Peppers, Marilyn Manson and Rob Zombie among several other artists get down and dirty with some great, catchy tunes. And that really is the key to the Ramones: they were a terrific rock'n'roll band over and above what genre pigeonhole they may have been thrust into – and their influence cannot be discounted.

With their family name in place – supposedly inspired by a Paul McCartney pseudonym – the gangly **Joey** (**Jeff Hyman**; vocals), **Johnny** (**John Cummings**; guitar), **Dee Dee** (**Douglas Colvin**; bass), and **Tommy** (**Thomas Erdelyi**; drums), dressed in their trademark tattered jeans and black leather jackets became a resident fixture at the legendary CBGB club, typically pumping out a half-hour set packed with around fifteen songs, pausing in between tunes just long enough for the "1-2-3-4!" count-in to the next one. Their songwriting style was inspired by the aesthetic of 60s pop but the delivery, with Johnny's speedy guitar lines and Joey's Noo Yoik sneer, was pure punk'n'roll. In 1976 they made their UK debut playing London's Roundhouse, bringing a taste of US punk to a scene that was about to explode with its own homegrown rebels.

Some argue that the Ramones were the first true punk band, but such trainspotterish debates are secondary to the music, and the 70s saw the band at its prime with *Ramones* (1976), *Leave Home* (1977) and *Rocket To Russia* (1977) banged out in the space of just

eighteen months. They were all snotty classics, the latter usually heralded as the most consistent and featuring such succinct pleasures as "Rockaway Beach", "Teenage Lobotomy" and "Sheena Is A Punk Rocker". *Road To Ruin* (1978) was also great but lacked that touch of brilliance present on its predecessors. It was the first album to feature **Marky** (aka **Marc Bell**) replacing Tommy, who wanted to be a producer. The group hadn't scored any major hits after their years of touring and the pressure was beginning to show.

As the decade ended the band appeared in **Allan Arkush**'s teen comedy *Rock 'N' Roll High School*, contributing a few songs to the soundtrack, before *It's Alive* (1979) became hailed as a definitive live statement. Their label, Sire, wanted to nudge the band towards more chart-oriented material and so the mythical **Phil Spector** was drafted in to produce *End Of The Century* (1980), though his 'Wall Of Sound' technique failed to make much impact. "Baby I Love You" became a UK top-ten hit, and the album peaked at #14 but that was pretty much it. The sound of the record was at odds with the usual Ramones minimal majesty and remains something of an oddity.

Into the 80s and things started to get messy. *Pleasant Dreams* (1981) and

HOWARD BARLOW

The Ramones were pioneers of punk karaoke.

Subterranean Jungle (1983) were back to the formula of old, but Marky left before the latter was finished and **Richie** (aka **Richard Beau**) ended up drumming on some of their less fondly remembered albums: *Too Tough To Die* (1985), *Animal Boy* (1986) and *Half Way To Sanity* (1987). They weren't out-and-out bombs, but they lacked really great tunes, a problem rectified with the compilation *Ramones Mania* (1988). They were now competing against waves of hardcore punk bands who themselves had been influenced by their gutsy sonic assault, and while albums such as *Too Tough To Die* were spiky enough, *Brain Drain* (1989) was definitely below par. By now Marky was back in the band but it was Dee Dee's turn to rock the boat; he left to become a rap artist and release solo albums, though he continued to contribute song ideas to the band. His replacement was **C.J.** (aka **Christopher Joseph Ward**).

The Ramones live reputation was as assured into the 90s as it had been in their heyday and their latter years saw a proliferation of live albums. *Loco Live* (1991), *Greatest Hits Live* (1996) and *We're Outta Here* (1997) were all solid Ramones, battle-hardened and irrepressible. The latter was recorded at their last ever gig, at the Palace in Hollywood in August 1996, and featured guest appearances by various members of Motörhead, Pearl Jam and Soundgarden. In the studio they managed three albums: *Acid Eaters* (1993) was a set of covers, the kind of thing a diehard fan might be interested in, while *Mondo Bizarro* (1992) and *Adios Amigos* (1994) were sets of originals, a far cry from the essential stuff of the 70s and even the 80s. Far more rewarding were the two huge compilations *All The Stuff (And More) Volume 1* and *Volume 2* (1990); even after their demise the compilations kept coming – *Hey Ho Let's Go!: Anthology* (1999) and *Loud, Fast Ramones* (2002) – retreading the past and dusting off rare mixes and edits.

In April 2002 the band were inducted into the Rock And Roll Hall Of Fame, though Joey never got to experience the tribute as he died of lymphatic cancer in April 2001. Dee Dee made it to the induction ceremony but died in June 2002, apparently of a drugs overdose. Johnny Ramone died of prostate cancer in September 2004. Ironically, the *Ramones Raw* (2004) DVD debuted at #5 in the *Billboard* video chart, the highest placing the band ever achieved during their entire career.

⊙ Hey Ho Let's Go!: Anthology
1999; Rhino

This is a sprawling double album complete with comprehensive booklet and liner notes. Though the first three studio albums and *It's Alive* will tell you everything you need to know, this selection of delinquent tales and buzzsaw rock'n'roll is pretty hard to beat for sheer breadth and depth.

RATT

Formed Los Angeles, US, 1983; disbanded 1991; re-formed 1997

If you're looking for 1980s thrills and spills then **Ratt** are the band for you. Never much troubled by things such as depth or complexity this sleazy, glam-metal outfit were all about sex, fun and day-glo spandex, though not necessarily in that order. Oh, and big hair. Next to Mötley Crüe, with whom they were pals, this lot had some of the best barnets on the Strip, all nicely teased and voluminous. They looked a little like Twisted Sister, only with better make-up and heels.

This trashy, glitzy outfit actually evolved from late-70s band **Mickey Ratt** – which at one point included the talents of future Ozzy

Osbourne guitarist **Jake E. Lee** – but it was the line-up featuring **Stephen Pearcy** (vocals), **Robbin Crosby** (guitar), **Warren DeMartini** (guitar), **Juan Croucier** (bass) and **Bobby Blotzer** (drums) that went on to become arena-bothering superstars in the 80s.

A self-financed eponymous debut was what really caught the hairspray generation's attention in 1983. Well, that and the stocking-clad legs of model and future Mrs David Coverdale, **Tawny Kitaen** on the cover. The songs were great, the legs were even greater, so great in fact that Kitaen also graced the sleeve of Ratt's Atlantic label debut *Out Of The Cellar* (1984). It sped into the US Top 10 on a rocket of smash-and-grab riffs and Pearcy's guttersnipe vocals, while "Round And Round" was the undemanding, flash'n'roll hit single clogging up the airwaves in late 1984. The band's team-up with producer **Beau Hill** would prove to be a very successful and relatively long-lived partnership.

They never made such major waves in the UK, although their peak period did bring them over for a slot at the 1985 Donington Monsters Of Rock festival, sharing the stage with the likes of ZZ Top, Bon Jovi and Metallica. Their second album *Invasion Of Your Privacy* (1985) delivered yet more of the same tacky tunes about lurve and went Top 10 in the US again; they even made a modest showing in the UK charts.

They weren't quite so lucky with album number three. So far the platinum sales seemed to be effortless; just snap together some sticky-fingered riffs, chuck in a blazing solo or two and a big chorus, then fire off the pyrotechnics. By the time of *Dancing Undercover* (1986) and *Reach For The Sky* (1988) the formula just wasn't hitting the same high points as before and Ratt seemed to be running out of ideas. *Detonator* (1990) saw the band make it into the new decade with a solid album but desperately in need of a revitalizing hit or two; even drafting in the chart-forging talent of **Desmond Child** couldn't keep them going.

Instead of soldiering on the band began to fragment and *Ratt N' Roll* (1991) was their kiss-off from the label as Pearcy headed off to form **Arcade** with **Cinderella**'s Fred Coury and eventually his own label, Top Fuel Records. In 1997, having weathered the storm created by grunge, Ratt reformed and released *Collage* (1997), followed by yet another eponymous effort in 1999, but neither album rekindled the kind of interest they had garnered in the 80s. Pearcy left again and lawsuits began to fly, battling over ownership of the Ratt name. Pearcy lost his claims and to date the band are still going with original members Blotzer and DeMartini joined by **John Corabi** (guitar, ex-**Mötley Crüe** vocalist), **Robbie Crane** (bass, ex-**Vince Neil**'s Band) and **Jizzy Pearl** (vocals, ex-**Love/Hate**). In a sad twist of the tale, in 2001 guitarist Robbin Crosby revealed that he had been suffering from AIDS contracted through heroin use; he died in the summer of 2002.

Ratt
1983; Music For Nations

Six tracks of prime sleazoid hard rock straight from the gutters of Los Angeles. Worth checking out just for the ace "You Think You're Tough".

Out Of The Cellar
1984; Atlantic

If you thought the debut EP was tacky you ain't heard nothing yet. These bump and grind anthems are an example of hair metal at its finest.

Invasion Of Your Privacy
1985; Atlantic

"Lay It Down" is one good reason to check this out. "You're In Love" and "Between The Eyes" are another two. As ever, there's a touch of pop to Ratt's steamy glam sound.

RAVEN

Formed Newcastle, UK, 1975

Among metal fans, who really care about such things, the debate about who really invented speed metal more often than not includes the merits (or lack thereof) of this bunch of Geordie headcases.

Formed back in the mid-70s by brothers **Mark** (guitar/vocals) and **John Gallagher** (bass/vocals), the initial line-up went through the usual formative shake-ups whilst they developed their sound – a none too inspiring heavy-metal racket. It wasn't until 1977 that they started to make some headway with a more stable line-up featuring **Paul Bowden** (guitar/vocals) and **Mick Kenworthy** (drums). At this point the band would play any time, any place, anywhere and one infamous occasion involved playing at a Hell's Angels outdoor rally. The band ended up playing "Born To Be Wild" five times in torrential rainfall before one of them had the bright idea of faking an electric shock so they could make their escape. So far they had gained a reputation for some inspired stage insanity and a lot of gear trashing.

By 1979 they became a three-piece with **Rob Hunter** joining them on drums. It was at this point that the true **Raven** identity was forged. John's lead high-pitched vocal style was undeniably unique while their adoption of extreme speed made them a standout act on the burgeoning New Wave Of British Heavy Metal scene. Getting a deal to record the single "Don't Need Your Money" for Neat Records in 1980 heralded the four-year period of their greatest success, during which they released *Rock Until You Drop* (1981), *Wiped Out* (1982), *All For One* (1983) and *Live At The Inferno* (1984), plus a handful of well-received EPs, not least the *Crash! Bang! Wallop!* EP. *All For One* was particularly noteworthy for the calibre of the songwriting and production quality and involved the input of **Udo Dirkschneider**, singer from German metal loonies **Accept**, and producer **Michael Wagener**. Raven described themselves as 'athletic rock' – even though they were arguably well ahead of their time as one of the earliest progenitors of the thrash movement.

Fed up with waiting for the rest of the music world to catch up with them they made what was, in hindsight, a very bad move. They relocated to the US and secured a deal with Atlantic in an effort to crack bigger markets. In order to achieve this they adopted a more melodic sound and released *Stay Hard* (1985), which did relatively well in the States but which had fans at home feeling somewhat bewildered at the change in direction. At a time when some of the biggest names in metal, such as Judas Priest, were experimenting with the possibilities of guitar synths and studio technology, *The Pack Is Back* (1986) reflected a similarly contemporary approach.

After *Life's A Bitch* (1987), possibly one of their heaviest albums, problems with Atlantic came to a head, Rob Hunter left to be replaced by **Joe Hasselvander** and they moved label to Combat/Relativity. *Nothing Exceeds Like Excess* (1988) was a return to their more abrasive signature sound but further problems and arguments with their label seriously hampered their progress, a situation from which they never really recovered.

A series of albums followed – *Architect Of Fear* (1991), mini-LP *Heads Up!* (1991), *Glow* (1994), *Destroy All Monsters – Live In Japan* (1995) and *Everything Louder* (1997) – which failed to set the world alight but were well-received by diehard fans the world over. The songs and spirit captured on *One For All* (1999) reminded the band so much of their heyday – probably because Michael Wagener was producing again – that they near-as-damn named it after their breakthrough album. Meanwhile *Raw Tracks* (1999) brought together a tasty number of rarities for the fans.

Despite what many believe about this band's demise they seem determined never to give in. The touring continues and a new album has been promised. Just to whet the appetites of the faithful, in late 2004 the band made available on the Internet a few tantalizing snippets of demos they were working on, though quite when the finished product will hit the streets is anyone's guess.

⊙ Rock Until You Drop
1981; Neat Records

This sounds pretty rough due to a distinct lack of production polish. Highly innovative for the period, this is a basic thrash metal blueprint.

⊙ All For One
1983; Neat Records

Much like the first, only with a more dynamic production job from Michael Wagener and Accept's Udo Dirkschneider.

RED HOT CHILI PEPPERS

Formed Hollywood, California, US, 1983.

Often imitated but never bettered (or even equalled), the **Red Hot Chili Peppers'** career started off shakily before the growing success of various alternative acts in the late 1980s, not least Faith No More, tuned rock and metal fans into the terrific possibilities to be had by adding huge bass lines and funky riffing to punk and metal. It was a tricky mixture and even the Chilis didn't get it right at the beginning. But in **Rick Rubin** they found a producer who could bring out the best in their off-the-wall songwriting and boost them towards worldwide stardom. Even though many of their peers have since folded or faded into obscurity, the Chilis have survived the various shifts in musical taste of the last twenty years and have just kept going – whilst getting better all the time.

These funky punksters were originally formed from the remains of the garage band **Anthem**, at the beginning of the 1980s. Led by **Anthony Kiedis** aka **Antwan the Swan** (vocals) and featuring **Hillel Slovak** (guitar), **Michael Balzary** aka **Flea** (bass) and **Jack Irons** (drums), they set about changing the face of rock in the only way they knew how: by blending thrashing punk and metal with the sublime, smooth funk sounds of the 1970s – and taking off their clothes.

The creation of their first release, *The Red Hot Chili Peppers* (1984), was a traumatic affair. Acquiring a speculative deal with EMI America, contractual obligations meant that **Jack Sherman** (guitars) and **Cliff Martinez** (drums) of **Captain Beefheart** fame were used for the recording sessions, while production was handled by **Gang of Four**'s **Andy Gill**. The result was flat and disappointing, completely failing to capture their brash pumping live sound. The only outstanding cut was the super-sleazy "Mommy, Where's Daddy?", a song replete with dodgy lyrics and a slow hypnotic bass riff. However, the album laid down the band's manifesto: sex, good times, a smattering of social conscience, and yet more sex. Live, they built their reputation through outrageous excess: the athletic Kiedis would indulge in stage-commanding acrobatics whilst Flea and Slovak would hip-grind their way through the set wearing nothing but sweat-soaked underpants.

Their second studio effort *Freaky Styley* (1985) was produced by none other than the Funkmeister General himself, **George Clinton**. This time the full line-up played and were augmented by a horn section featuring **Maceo Parker** and **Fred Wesley**, both veterans of James Brown's band, amongst others. The group hit their stride: the set had a fresher, sexier sound, with Kiedis developing his own rapping style, while the arrangements were far catchier than their debut. Their musical influences were apparent in the stonking cover versions, "If You Want Me To Stay" (Sly and the Family Stone) and "Hollywood, Africa" (The Meters) and, while the funk-punk polarity occasionally grated, the overall standard was much higher.

The next stage of the band's career saw them shamelessly hype their own notoriety with *The Abbey Road* EP (1988) announcing the infamous 'socks on cocks' era – the cover art was a brazen pastiche of the Beatles' *Abbey Road* sleeve, the important fact being that the group were stark naked save for socks covering their genitals. Images of the band were plastered everywhere. Pushing the boat out even further was the *Uplift Mofo Party Plan* (1988), which went one step beyond the mellowness of *Freaky Styley* by throwing in a major dose of metallic psychedelia aided by producer **Michael Beinhorn**. Not being a band to shy away from controversy the album contains the "Special Secret Song Inside". The need for a cryptic title becomes clear when the band all join in on the chorus of "I want to party on your pussy, baby!" Such lyrics posed a question that has dogged the band since their inception: are the Chili Peppers sexy or sexist? Whatever the answer, it did no harm to their profile, the song becoming a sweaty live favourite.

Just as the Chilis were enjoying the attention, the partying and mayhem were cut short when Slovak overdosed on heroin in June 1988. His death threw the band into turmoil. Extremely upset, Irons left the band and two new members were found: **Chad Smith** (drums) and **John Frusciante** (guitar).

Pulled back from the edge of self-destruction the funky monks put all their energy into *Mother's Milk* (1989), which they dedicated to the memory of Slovak. Perhaps reflecting the chaos of the preceding year the album sounded distinctly half-baked in places. Acknowledging their formative influences once more, there were covers of Hendrix's "Fire" and Stevie Wonder's "Higher Ground" and, as a tribute to Slovak, they included "Knock Me Down", expressing the pain of losing a close friend. Despite the rather fragmented nature of the songs, *Mother's Milk* proved to be the watershed they were looking for, with both "Higher Ground" and "Knock Me Down" becoming hits. They embarked on a European tour which further enhanced their reputation for outrageous live spectacles.

Despite their growing international profile, *Mother's Milk* proved to be their last outing with EMI. Snapped up by Warners, their next effort was the wonderfully titled *Blood Sugar Sex Magik* (1991), produced by **Rick Rubin**. Usually associated with the heavier end of the metal spectrum (Slayer, Danzig), Rubin helped to shape a more mature, more cohesive sound for the group and accentuated their innate sense of melody and ballad-writing – this was alongside the usual slices of excess and macho sexual prowess of course. The result was the sublime "Breaking The Girl" and tear-jerking drug tale of "Under The Bridge". The album peaked at #3 in the US and made the Top 30 in the UK. Not wanting to lose out on the success the Chilis were finally enjoying, EMI's *What Hits?!* (1992) pulled together a succinct collection of the band's more immediate tracks.

Although the band seemed to have finally found their niche, personnel problems began to surface again as touring pressures pushed Frusciante close to the edge (he had started to babble about "playing in colours" during interviews). His replacement, in June 1992, was **Arik Marshall** (guitar) who stayed with the band during the subsequent bout of summer festivals. However, after personality clashes, Marshall departed soon after, leaving a significant vacuum. They

finally settled on **Dave Navarro** (formerly of **Jane's Addiction**), his talent for melody and shuddering power complementing the hard-edged funk-punk'n'metal recipe.

EMI plundered the vaults once more for *Out In L.A.* (1994), an album cobbled together from live and studio rarities, while the band were engrossed in their next studio effort, *One Hot Minute* (1995). The strength of the songwriting was a testament to a band at the peak of their creativity, though Navarro's input produced a marked change in the band's dynamics which some fans found hard to accept. The album boasted the soulful mellowness of "Walkabout", the chaos of "Warped" and minimal acoustic track "Pea". It was a top-five hit in both the US and UK. Though *One Hot Minute* spawned hits in the shape of "My Friends" and "Aeroplane", one of the best tunes of this era was a cover version of the Ohio Players' "Love Rollercoaster" which found its way onto the soundtrack to *Beavis And Butthead Do America*, providing them with a UK top-ten hit in 1997.

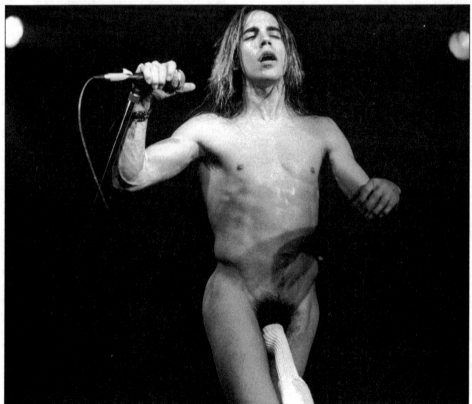

During the 80s Anthony Kiedis believed in travelling light.

Despite the obvious strengths of the record, Navarro's role in the band had always seemed just a little too strained to last and Frusciante, having ironed out his personal problems, was reinstated. *Californication* (1999) was a record simply dripping with succulent funk riffs and the requisite lewd'n'crude attitude that had made the band a byword for risqué entertainment. It became yet another top-five hit on both sides of the Atlantic, boasting some of the best songwriting the band had ever come up with, and heralding something of a renaissance following the shaky period of the mid-90s. Suddenly accolades began to pile up, not least a Grammy for Best Rock Song for "Scar Tissue", and they topped off one of their most successful periods by playing the huge Rock In Rio festival in January 2001.

The following year saw the expansive *Off The Map* DVD capturing the band in full live mode, with *By The Way* arriving shortly afterwards – proving that the Chilis' newfound energy and direction was no fluke. Again produced by Rick Rubin, the album was lauded by critics and loved by fans, its textured sound and range of styles providing a great sense of depth and spawning another major hit in the title track. The next year brought yet another *Greatest Hits* (2003) package – a special CD/DVD edition included fifteen videos and a whole host of fan-pleasing extras – celebrating their twentieth anniversary with style and most of their essential tunes from *Mother's Milk* onwards. Released simultaneously, *Live At Slane Castle* showed the band working over a massive crowd of 80,000 fans with extreme ease and a killer arsenal of eighteen hits.

And to follow up the *Slane Castle* DVD the band issued *Live In Hyde Park* (2004), their first official concert album, a double-CD set taken from their three-night summer stint, dishing up everything from cover versions to some new tunes. Meanwhile Anthony Kiedis put the finishing touches to his autobiography titled *Scar Tissue*, which was published in the autumn to extremely positive reviews, not least from heavyweight US news publication *Time* magazine.

Freaky Styley
1985; EMI

Smooth and soulful as they prove they really can cut a mellow groove. The use of a horn section adds colour to the proceedings while George Clinton's production gives the recording depth and a cool finish.

Uplift Mofo Party Plan
1987; EMI

Forceful and crude, they sound like the Beastie Boys in places with splashes of metal spicing up the psychedelic sex slant. Contains the notorious "Special Secret Song Inside" – clearly giving the finger to the moral majority.

Mother's Milk
1989; EMI

Chaotic clash of thrashy punk and heavy-handed funk. Contains the moving "Knock Me Down" and the furious tight rapping of "Magic Johnson". In total, though, the eclectic mix of material makes it less accessible.

Blood Sugar Sex Magik
1991; Warner Bros

Integrated, polished and accomplished; at last they sound truly together. Rick Rubin's crisp production and the inclusion of emotive ballads and sexy choruses make this a vital release.

Californication
1999; Warner Bros

Didn't like *One Hot Minute*? Fear not because Frusciante's genius turned this album into a huge hit and marked a return to form. Sexy, wise and powerful the songs cover all the funk'n'rock bases.

By The Way
2002; Warner Bros

It's hard to imagine a record superior to *Californication*, but this is it. Dazzling songs, lush arrangements and warm textures make this one of the band's best albums. Ever.

HENRY ROLLINS

Born Washington DC, US, February 13, 1961

Henry Rollins aka **Henry Garfield** can make you laugh with his spoken word performances, intrigue you with his self-published short stories, surprise you with his turns as an actor – and hurt you with his music. Not just intellectually and emotionally but physically, as he tears into his subject matter with the voracity of a tattooed pitbull. Henry wants you to reel with each body-slamming line and quake with every breeze-block riff. He doesn't so much sing as shout tunefully, exposing his world view for you to take or leave.

Rollins' career as a vocalist began when he joined hardcore punk heroes **Black Flag** back in the 80s. Black Flag's uncompromising sound made them hugely influential in

Henry Rollins and co wonder where they should put their new settee.

musical circles where anti-authoritarianism, aggression and extremity are valued; rock and metal, from grunge to thrash, owe a debt to the Flag's legacy. Records such as *Damaged* (1981) and *My War* (1984) positively dripped with confrontational lyrics born of Rollins' straight-edge lifestyle and progressive outlook while the music was as bellicose as the band's towering frontman.

When Black Flag disbanded in 1986 Rollins threw himself into spoken-word performances and began a solo recording career beginning with *Hot Animal Machine* (1987). He then put together the Rollins Band line-up of **Chris Haskett** (guitar), **Andrew Weiss** (bass) and **Simeon Cain** (drums) for a series of relatively low-key indie albums: *Life Time* (1988) was followed by *Hard Volume* (1989) and the live *Turned On* (1990).

The jazzy, funky metal and heavy rock Rollins was driving at demanded a bigger audience so a deal was struck with Imago for *The End Of Silence* (1992). The Rollins Band

played Lollapalooza in the early 90s, leading to an even bigger appearance at Woodstock in 1994 and the breakthrough album *Weight,* featuring new bassist, **Melvin Gibbs**. Rollins had streamlined his attack and the effect that it had was akin to being mown down by a velvet juggernaut. It narrowly missed the Top 20 in the UK. As the spoken-word albums continued to flow and the odd acting job popped up – look out for Henry in Michael Mann's *Heat* and David Lynch's *Lost Highway* – the band suddenly found themselves without a deal as Imago folded. It took three years for *Come In And Burn* to arrive on Dreamworks, but it was clear that Rollins wasn't getting off on the group's chemistry anymore.

He had been producing a band called **Mother Superior** and they impressed him so much that he recruited **Jim Wilson** (guitar), **Marcus Blake** (bass) and **Jason Mackenroth** (drums) to be the Rollins Band Mark II. *Get Some Go Again* (2000) and *Nice* (2001) were

fiery heavy-rock work-outs with great groove and power. Their release was complemented by *Yellow Blues* (2001) and *A Nicer Shade Of Red* (2001), issued on Rollins' own imprint 2.13.61; the albums included even more songs from the original sessions with the new line-up and, in the case of *Yellow Blues,* material that was intended to turn the single disc of *Get Some Go Again* into a double album, but which was left out by Dreamworks. The *End Of Silence Demos* (2003) and *Weighting* (2002), likewise, provided greater insight into the two earlier albums *The End Of Silence* and, you guessed it, *Weight*. And just to give fans even more muscular hard rock to chew over, *The Only Way To Know For Sure* (2002) album dished up some seriously loud live versions for comparison.

Weight
1994; Imago

Strap yourself in for some intense, cathartic and very heavy rock. It's a bit like entering a very intense therapy session and definitely the kind of inventive pummelling you won't forget in a hurry, especially the jazz metal of hit single "Liar" and the chugging "Icon".

ROSE TATTOO

Formed Sydney, Australia 1977

Not just a band but a full-on brawl waiting to happen, Rose Tattoo really do put the hard into hard rock. Imagine AC/DC's bluesy crunch with added slide guitar, delivered by a bunch of tattooed thugs who'd punch your lights out soon as look at you. If Guns N'

Roses were the world's most dangerous band then they had very good teachers in this lot.

Formed in the Sydney pub scene by the bald-headed **Angry Anderson** (vocals, ex-**Buster Brown**) and **Peter Wells** (slide guitar/vocals, ex-**Buffalo**) who wanted to create an honest-to-God, bone-breaking heavy rock machine, they recruited **Mick Cocks** (lead/rhythm guitar), **Geordie Leach** (bass, ex-**Buster Brown)** and **Dallas 'Digger' Royall** (drums, ex-**Buster Brown)**. Their reputation for lethal live shows and intense, no-messing, bad-boy boogie made them ideal material for Albert Productions: producers **Harry Vanda** and **George Young** gave their debut album *Rose Tattoo* (1978) a raw, street-level production job crackling with the kind of nerve-frazzling energy they gave AC/DC's classic *Let There Be Rock*. Home country hit "Bad Boy For Love" owed more than a few beers to the Young brothers' "She's Got Balls" and "Nice Boys" was to have a profound effect on Guns N' Roses who covered it on their debut EP. In short, it was a classic. It was eventually released across Europe in 1980, renamed *Rock'N'Roll Outlaw*, allowing the band to come to the UK for some stunning shows at the Marquee and a near-mythical appearance at the Reading Rock Festival in 1981.

The profile-boosting gigs meant that *Assault And Battery* (1981), another fine selection of grimy, sleazy tales from the gutter, made a decent dent on the UK charts, but nothing that was going to turn them into tattooed millionaires. The following year brought *Scarred For Life* (1982) featuring new guitarist **Rob Riley**, who replaced Cocks. Sadly, it was to be their last truly amazing album for quite a while because during the subsequent touring the band fractured under the pressure.

Anderson regrouped with Leach and brought in **John Meyer** (guitar), **Greg Jordan** (slide guitar) and **Scott Johnston** (drums) for the immensely disappointing *Southern Stars* (1984), which lacked the bristling fury of the early material. *Beats From A Single Drum* (1986) is best ignored – it was an Angry Anderson solo effort in all but name and contained the frankly baffling 1988 top-five ballad hit "Suddenly" which became known as the *Neighbours* wedding theme (the Aussie soap's golden couple, Scott and Charlene, tied the knot while Angry wailed away in the background). To

Rose Tattoo enjoy a cuddly moment.

GLENN A. BAKER/REDFERNS

see the former bad boy sing this tripe on *Top Of The Pops*, occasionally flashing his chipped front teeth, was a heartbreaking sight indeed. Angry didn't seem to be Angry anymore. He went off to develop a mainstream music career with a side order of TV presenting and acting; he appeared as King Herod in a production of *Jesus Christ Superstar* and took the role of Ironbar in *Mad Max III*.

The catalyst that really got them going once again was being asked by Guns N' Roses to support them during their 1993 Australian tour; only Royall was absent, the drummer having died in 1991 after suffering from the excesses of the rock lifestyle. The seeds were sown even though the band members went off to pursue different musical projects.

In 1999 they were invited over to Germany for some support slots and ended up playing the Wacken Open Air festival the following year, during which they recorded the live 'best of' *25 To Life* (2000) with a line-up featuring Riley, Wells and Anderson plus **Steve King** (bass) and **Paul DeMarco** (drums). The crowd was treated to the old knuckle-dusting magic and the band returned with some blistering UK shows in 2001 and the exceptional *Pain* in 2002, a natural follow-up to *Scarred For Life*.

⊙ **Rose Tattoo aka Rock 'N' Roll Outlaw**
1978; Albert

An incredible debut that sounds like a Saturday night ruck caught on tape. The album's masterpiece is the brutal gang war tale "The Butcher And Fast Eddy", Anderson's chilling delivery vying with Wells' and Cocks' menacing guitar lines.

DAVID LEE ROTH

Born Bloomington, Indiana, US, October 10, 1955

If you're looking for the quintessential metal showman, then look no further than the ex-**Van Halen** front man. A man who lives it like he sings it, there is no gap between the onstage and offstage **Roth** – he is a turbocharged, motormouthed party machine. And he knows how to rock. Hard.

There was no way to hide the Van Halen fans' trepidation when Diamond Dave upped and left Eddie widdling into thin air in 1985. The hyperactive Mr Roth needed action and his former bandmates just weren't cutting it. With a hit single, an excellent cover of the Beach Boys' "California Girls", and the cracking *Crazy From The Heat* mini-LP to his dazzling name Roth was ready to take on the world. None of the cuts on his first solo outing were even remotely metal, but songs such as "Just A Gigolo" "I Ain't Got Nobody", "Easy Street", "Coconut Grove" and the aforementioned Beach Boys classic dished up sun-drenched vistas and steamy tropical fun by the spadeful, as well as expanding on some of the excursions into different musical styles and cover versions he indulged in with his Van Halen cronies. In other words, it was all pure Roth right down to the hilarious videos, buxom blondes and day-glo spandex.

While the mini-LP was just a little bit of fun whipped up with the help of old Van Halen-producing stalwart **Ted Templeman** plus some crack sessioneers, *Eat 'Em And Smile* (1986) harnessed some elite musical forces in the execution of its party-hard manifesto. Roth brought in the bionic guitar genius of **Stevie Vai** (ex-**Frank Zappa** band, ex-**Alcatrazz**, former pupil of extraordinary six-stringer **Joe Satriani**), bassist **Billy Sheehan** (ex-**Talas**) and drummer **Gregg Bissonette**, and put together a killer team. In Vai, Roth had a musician every bit as technically gifted as Eddie Van Halen but with a dynamic flair all his own, and now there was a rhythm section that was tighter than a gnat's chuff. Then there were the songs: ten rambunctious, funny, hard-rocking nuggets of Templeman-produced technicolour genius. Roth's war-painted face on the sleeve said it all. There were the cover versions, of course – "That's Life", "I'm Easy" and a crunching revamp of the old Nashville Teens' "Tobacco Road" – but the original tunes sent the entire thing stratospheric. Roth's call and response dialogue with Vai's squealing axe preceding the band's tumble into sizzling US hit single "Yankee Rose" was one of the high points of metal that year. "Shyboy" reworked a Talas tune Sheehan was responsible for into a pummelling bass work out; "Ladies Nite In Buffalo?" had a sleazy *film noir* feel about it; "Goin' Crazy!" was an archetypal party anthem served up in patented Roth style, the musical equivalent of polished teeth and big, big hair. And that was just side one. MTV loved the videos, and the album went to #4 in the US and Top 30 in the UK.

It wasn't for nothing that Roth's unit became known as the **Yankee Rose Band**, and it was with this line-up, plus keyboard player **Brett Tuggle**, that they went on to record *Skyscraper*, with Vai and Roth producing. But Roth had had enough of aping the

spitfire axe-tormenting antics of his old outfit and wanted something lusher and more involving. The synth quotient was higher and the production was glossier, but only "Hot Dog And A Shake" possessed the same level of momentum as the songs from the debut. That's not to say that the album was tame. Far from it. It was all about cars, girls and big guitars – only with a little more thought and imagination in the writing and a little less fire and spontaneity. Some fans preferred the immediacy of the old stuff but that didn't stop the record going Top 10 in the US and just miss the same heights in the UK. It was helped no end by the singalong pop-metal of "Just Like Paradise", a petite and polished little number drenched in sugary sweet synths and boasting a wicked Vai solo at its heart. It was all ideal arena-filling fare and to complement the huge sounds Roth wanted dazzling eye candy to match. This was the era of the giant Roth surfboard and boxing ring, immense lighting rigs and ridiculous costume changes. It had to be big, it had to be bold.

Roth's third outing fared better in the UK charts – #4, as opposed to #18 in the US – with 'let's-build-a-cathedral-of-metal' producer **Bob Rock** at the helm. *A Little Ain't Enough* (1991) certainly sounded more like a 3am Jack-soaked fistfight in a two-dollar whorehouse than its slightly cleverer and less spontaneous-sounding predecessor. By now Vai was out of the picture and guitarists **Jason Becker** and **Steve Hunter** brought a more traditional double-edged axe attack to the sound of the album, which also featured Gregg's brother **Matt** on bass. It was bruising, stupendously over-the-top and good fun, though not a patch on Roth's debut. Standouts included the tongue-in-cheek romp of "Hammerhead Shark", the celebratory title track and smouldering blues of "Sensible Shoes".

While Roth was on the road, something was happening in a little ol', out-of-the-way town known as Seattle. The tour was a massive money-loser, for not only did Dave seem unwilling to stick to what he did best, but the whole big metal party was just about to run out of cheesy nibbles. It was a lose/lose situation and *Your Filthy Little Mouth* (1994) took the full force of the blow. First, there were no familiar faces apart from Dave's, though **Terry Kilgore** (guitar), **John Regan** (bass), **Ray Brinker** and **Larry Aberman** (both drums) acquitted themselves with some style. But the songs weren't up to much, veering through too many styles and trying to be too hip, against a grunge backdrop. "Cheatin' Heart Café" was a duet with country star **Travis Tritt** and was just embarrassing. "No Big 'Ting", with its reggae flavour, didn't work either. Only the saucy title track and sexy laid-back mellowness of "Sunburn" made any impression. Ultimately, Roth was too out of touch and not even his garish personality could help the new album. It was a huge flop.

With his fortunes on the wane and his Van Halen bandmates floundering, the faithful were clamouring for a reunion louder than ever in the mid-90s. And it seemed like it was going to happen. On the back of a couple of new tunes written with Eddie, it was announced that Diamond Dave would return for a 'best of' compilation album. But at the MTV awards in 1996, Dave, by all accounts, was behaving in his usual over-the-top, overbearing manner and Eddie, believing the comeback wouldn't work, shelved the plans. Never one to say die, Roth simply threw himself into his next recording project, after issuing his own *The Best* (1997) compilation. With the help of a variety of musicians, including guitarists **John Lowery**, Terry Kilgore and **Mike Hartman**, *DLR Band* (1998) was released on Roth's own Wawazat!! label. It was like listening to Van Halen swinging concrete boxing gloves, heavy like *A Little Ain't Enough,* but with less finesse. It was Roth's answer to the new musical climate and a welcome way to erase the memory of his previous album.

Despite this minor triumph Roth was still a long way from reclaiming any kind of glory and rumours persisted about a get-together with Van Halen, especially after *Van Halen III* had tanked. The story goes that in 2000 the old line-up got together for a spot of informal writing but nothing came of it, the stumbling block seemingly Eddie's reticence to rub egos with Roth once more.

Come 2002 and in a tantalizing and slightly Spinal Tap-ish manner Roth and Sammy Hagar agreed to sheath their barbed tongues and to go on the road together across the US. The tour was successful enough to add a second leg without even a new album to promote. Then Roth delved into the past and did what he does rather well. He recorded a bunch of cover versions for *Diamond Dave* (2003) with **Nile Rodgers** on guitar – clearly, Dave didn't blame *Your Filthy Little Mouth's*

failure on Rodgers' production job. A small handful of original tunes sat alongside reworkings of old Savoy Brown, Hendrix and Beatles tunes. It wasn't particularly heavy – in fact it was quite laid-back – but it was consistently enjoyable. For the subsequent tour, however, Roth really went back to his roots – he put together a band capable of driving home both classic Van Halen songs and his solo material and indulged in a purely greatest hits set. Was this a man dwelling on past glories and putting a brave face on defeat? Or is this just part of the Roth masterplan? Certainly, getting back together with Van Halen seems unlikely at the moment, seeing as Hagar has taken the singer's slot again recently. Whatever happens, rest assured Roth's irrepressible nature means he'll just keep going and going.

⊙ Eat 'Em And Smile
1986; Warner Bros

This album is the natural bridge between Roth's Van Halen days and his later outings. To all intents and purposes it follows the old VH blueprint of short, potent party tunes only this time with Roth completely in charge. Vai is a stunning replacement for Eddie and the entire thing is powered by an amazing degree of recklessness.

⊙ Skyscraper
1988; Warner Bros

Less in-yer-face and more of a cinematic, big rock experience. The production is lush, the synths more prevalent and the songwriting more considered, making this one of the quintessential stadium-pleasing albums of the late 80s.

THE RUNAWAYS

Formed Los Angeles, US 1975; disbanded 1978

O utrageous and well ahead of their time, The Runaways were the prototype for pretty much every all-girl rock band that followed, at a time when strapping on a guitar and firing off power chords was virtually an all-male preserve. They didn't make it big as a band but they did launch solo careers that are still going today.

The man behind this venture was the notorious writer, producer and entrepreneur **Kim Fowley**. He helped form the band with **Kari Krome**, who was set to be the band's singer but ended up contributing lyrics instead. The line-up, once it had stabilized, included **Cheri Currie** (vocals), **Joan Jett** (guitar), **Lita Ford** (guitar), **Jackie Fox** (bass) and **Sandy West** (drums). All the girls were sixteen years old, bar Ford, who was seventeen. Their ages, plus the brazen choice of lyrical subjects – not least their first single, the fantastically lascivious "Cherry Bomb" – almost instantly set off a wave of criticism that this was nothing but jailbait rock. The fact remained, however, that they were a terrific band. They were picked up by Mercury Records and their Fowley-produced eponymous debut landed in 1976, with Currie giving one of her best pouts on the sleeve.

The album made only a minuscule dent on the *Billboard* chart but it didn't stop the band from kicking up a storm live, with Jett and Ford cranking out smoking riffs and Currie sporting a basque and suspenders. These antics were a gift for the tabloids who got very hot under the collar when the band ventured over to the UK in 1976. The blend of no-messing heavy rock and teenage sexuality was revisited on *Queens Of Noise* – another chart flop – the first of three albums released in 1977. Some critics still couldn't see any merit in the band but the girls couldn't have cared less, because they were touring the world.

Inevitably such a novel group was bound to strike a chord in Japan and that's how *Live In Japan* (1977) came about. It was a raucous indication of the power these five teens could muster on stage but, behind the scenes, the pressure was already taking its toll. Fox was

the first to quit. She was replaced by **Vicki Blue**. And then Currie left to pursue a solo career. She released a couple of albums and popped up in the odd movie, including *This Is Spinal Tap*. (Her role, though cut in the original, is back in full on the DVD special edition of the classic rockumentary. Vicki Blue appears in the film too.) With Currie gone, Jett took over on vocals and the band put together *Waitin' For The Night* (1977). The scene was now set for the final internal ructions that would end the band.

Blue was soon gone and replaced by **Laurie McAllister**, while Ford and Jett were tugging the band in different directions. Jett was more punky rock'n'roll at heart, Ford was metal through and through. The tension was almost palpable when *And Now … The Runaways* (1978) was recorded and padded out with various cover versions. With Fowley seemingly no longer interested in them, they split; in 1987 he tried to restart the teen-girl rock phenomenon with a completely new line-up but no one paid any attention.

The most high-profile post-Runaways careers belong to Jett and Ford. The 80s saw Ford come back with *Out For Blood* (1983), *Dancin' On The Edge* (1984) and her most successful album in the US, *Lita* (1988). The latter provided a #8 US hit single in the form of "Close My Eyes Forever", a ballad duet with **Ozzy Osbourne**. Joan Jett, meanwhile, issued various albums but enjoyed her greatest success with *I Love Rock 'N' Roll* (1982). The album went to #2 in the US while the title

The Runaways soak up some rays.

track – originally performed by the Arrows – gave her a #4 hit in the UK and a chart-topper in America. With *The Hit List* (1990) Jett turned to classic rock tunes again to create an album composed entirely of covers.

⊙ The Best Of The Runaways
1982; Mercury

There are plenty of compilations out there but this one includes a good selection of tunes. There are a couple of decent live cuts present and, of course, it kicks off with the cracking "Cherry Bomb".

RUSH

Formed Toronto, Canada, 1968

It is tempting to look upon this Canadian trio as the professors of metal, purveyors of intelligent and thought-provoking songs shot through with the energy of huge guitars and amps going up to eleven. The 1970s were undoubtedly the era of some of their greatest albums – by the end of the decade they had been dubbed Official Ambassadors Of Music by the Canadian government – but even as the smoother sounding 80s bled into the proficient 90s and beyond, they were still capable of creating quality albums. Of course, maturity and their desire to progress as musicians mean all those youthful barbed edges are long gone, though they still tower over the vast majority of rockers.

Rush's genesis lay in the hard-rocking blues sound of the 60s. **Alex Lifeson** (guitar), **Geddy Lee** (vocals/bass) and **John Rutsey** (drums) came together as major fans of the Who, Led Zeppelin, Cream and the Yardbirds. Their first single was a cover version of Buddy Holly's "Not Fade Away", a little chunk of vinyl history that now commands absurd sums from eager collectors. This love of old time rock'n'roll would find its natural outlet over thirty years later with their roots covers album *Feedback* (2004). At the start, however, they couldn't get anyone to take the idea of a metal band from Canada seriously, so they formed their own Moon Records label. With the help of producer **Terry Brown** – a friendship that

would guide their career for many albums – they issued their eponymous debut in 1973, all driving heavy-rock riffs and Lee's almost Plant-esque, helium-fuelled yelp. It did so well that Mercury reissued it in 1974 but changes were afoot: Rutsey left to be replaced by **Neil Peart** and Rush's classic and still enduring line-up was in place.

Peart brought with him a love of science fiction and fantasy, an ability to pen a lyric and a virtuosity that allowed Rush to blossom into a fully fledged prog metal band. Rather than adopting the classical influences of many of their peers, however, a fluid and jazzy King Crimson-style complexity crept in. Songs were often structured in 'chapters' or 'movements', they were built around alien time signatures, and Peart's lyrics were marked by his bookish disposition. Their first effort in a more complex vein was *Fly By Night* (1975), the eight-and-a-half minute, four-part "By-Tor & The Snow Dog" at its heart. This was followed by the less artistically successful *Caress Of Steel* (1975), with its epic "The Fountain Of Lamneth" taking up the entire second side.

The follow up, however, was to be a classic. It was the era of Peart's astonishing handlebar moustache and the equally flamboyant *2112*

(1976) displayed all the energy that *Caress Of Steel* lacked, the lengthy title track being based upon novelist Ayn Rand's *Anthem*. It was a piece of fiery drama and great delicacy, perfect for their burgeoning live reputation which took them to the UK in 1977 for a series of sell-out dates. The release of concert document *All The World's A Stage* (1976) drew a pattern to which the band have largely adhered throughout their career: discounting compilation albums, they would issue four studio efforts followed by a live one.

While in the UK they headed over to Rockfield Studios in Wales to record *A Farewell To Kings* (1977), which contained the immense "Xanadu" and eerie sci-fi trip "Cygnus X-1". Unsurprisingly, the work they put into the UK meant the album went to #22 in the chart and also breached the Top 40 in the US. *Hemispheres* (1978) was to be their last truly major prog work-out; of its four tracks the title piece was one side long while the final one was the nine-and-a-half-minute "La Villa Strangiato", subtitled "an exercise in self-indulgence". *Permanent Waves* (1980) and the superb *Moving Pictures* (1981) both contained a single nod towards the long songs of their 70s career – "Natural Science" and "The Camera Eye" respectively – but they were now veering towards the economy of shorter tunes, albeit ones with cerebral lyrics. "Spirit Of Radio" was their biggest hit from this era, making #13 in the UK.

The live *Exit ... Stage Left* (1981) effectively drew a line under what the band had achieved so far. Synthesizers had already been part of the Rush equation for a few years but usually only as a tool for embellishment. Into the 80s, keyboards and technology came to dominate the band's sound, which retained the inventive playing but sacrificed much of their earlier gut-level power for the plushness and comfort of arena rock. *Signals* (1982) and *Grace Under Pressure* (1984) were beautifully crafted but relatively bland, the band by now having abandoned Terry Brown. Though this course was maintained by *Power Windows* (1985) and *Hold Your Fire* (1987), it all made a whole lot more sense live when sheer volume blew a massive hole through the stifling clinical studio production and let the songs breathe.

A Show Of Hands (1988) was their customary live set but *Presto* (1989), their first album for Atlantic, was a welcome return to a much brighter, harder sound. By now, however, the albums were coming less frequently – *Roll The Bones* (1991), *Counterparts* (1993) and *Test For Echo* (1996) were spaced out enough to allow room for Lifeson's side-project **Victor** – while the band were constantly striving for a balance between out-and-out rock and a desire to experiment.

Consequently when the triple-disc *Different Stages/Live* (1998) arrived with one CD dedicated to a Hammersmith Odeon show from 1978 it felt like a downpour after a drought.

The dawn of the millennium saw precious little action from the Rush studio but Lee issued his first solo project, *My Favorite Headache,* in 2000. It seemed as if the band had gone into hibernation. Rumours about retirement began to surface but the vast Rush machinery ground back into action for *Vapor Trails* (2002), the band having by now transcended the vagaries of rock fashion and settled into the niche they had been carving for a decade. They broke their familiar pattern by releasing another live effort, *Rush In Rio* (2003), as an album and a DVD, followed by *Feedback*. It was a chance for them to take their enormous arena-sized megaproduction on the road again to the delight of fans who thought the band might have had their day.

2112
1976; Mercury

This is a masterpiece, and we're not just talking about the drummer's epic soup strainer. The sci-fi extravaganza of the first side tends to overshadow the equally strong song-based second side. Here you'll find the classic "A Passage To Bangkok" imbued with the sweet fragrance of Mary Jane. Nuff said.

The Spirit Of Radio: Greatest Hits
1974-1987 2003; Mercury

There are some great Rush compilations out there – *Chronicles* and the huge *Retrospective I* and *II* – but this one is slightly more user-friendly. There's a good spread of songs here, and the limited edition version comes with a DVD.

Formed Tampa, Florida, US, 1983

This highly inventive and progressive metal outfit have never quite hit the big time, despite having constantly turned in intriguing albums during their twenty-plus years of existence.

Formed originally as **Avatar**, the band released the rare *City Beneath The Surface* EP in 1983 before changing their name. The line-up of brothers **Jon** (vocals/keyboards) and **Criss Oliva** (guitar), plus **Keith Collins** (bass) and **Steve Wacholz** (drums) were heavily influenced by British bands such as Iron Maiden and Judas Priest, giving their energetic early material a vital, power metal twist. Typical of this sound were *Sirens* (1983) and *The Dungeons Are Calling* (1984) mini-LP, the latter featuring the Maiden-esque "The Whip", a fabulously un-PC little number. *Power Of The Night* (1985) was their first album for Atlantic and was even better – altogether more focused and polished.

The shift to a major label brought with it pressure to hit some pay dirt, though their attempt to do so with the more mainstream melodic sound of *Fight For The Rock* (1986) – featuring new bassist **Johnny Lee Middleton** – was a step in the wrong direction and still the least favourite album among fans. Still, the record took the band to Europe and the UK for the first time, building their following prior to the release of *Hall Of The Mountain King* (1987). The album's producer was **Paul O'Neill**, who helped the band

exploit their progressive tendencies to create a majestic and grand metallic statement. He effectively became a member of Savatage over the coming years providing a major compositional hand in the studio, guiding them towards an increasingly complex and orchestral sound.

Chris Caffery was added as second guitar for what is generally regarded as one of Savatage's finest efforts, *Gutter Ballet* (1989), though he left soon after. The tempos were more varied, as was the songwriting, with keyboards and guitars integrating more fully than before. It was a mature and regal affair paving the way for the full-blown concept effort that followed, *Streets: A Rock Opera* (1991), based on a book by O'Neill.

At this point Jon Oliva began to develop voice problems so the band recruited **Zachary Stevens** (ex-**White Witch**) for *Edge Of Thorns* (1993). Oliva continued to write and provide keyboards for the band. Stevens' powerful vocals brought a more accessible hard rock edge to Savatage's sound, though the songs remained as uncompromising as ever. It was another quality album but the band had little time to reap the rewards – in the same year Criss Oliva was killed by a drunk driver.

The band decided that in tribute to their guitarist they would keep the group going; ex-**Testament** six-stringer **Alex Skolnick** was brought in for *Handful Of Rain* (1994). The next album, the concept piece *Dead Winter Dead* (1995) – featuring a revamped line-up of Chris Caffery, **Al Pitrelli** (guitar) and **Jeff Plate** (drums), was based upon the war in Yugoslavia. The band's taste for unusual concepts burgeoned with *The Wake Of Magellan*

(1997), the songs based around current affairs (not least the murder of Irish reporter Veronica Guerin) and a storyline concerning an old sailor's desire for a heroic death.

In 1996 Jon Oliva became one of the core members of O'Neill's brainchild, **The Trans-Siberian Orchestra**. They largely released orchestral rock Christmas albums, O'Neill's work with them during the last years of the decade running in parallel with his Savatage recording and touring commitments. This, plus the change of record label to Nuclear Blast, meant that *Poets And Madmen* didn't arrive until 2001 with Stevens having left due to family commitments and Pitrelli joining **Megadeth**; Jon Oliva provided vocals on the album but the band soon after recruited **Damond Jiniya**.

⦿ Gutter Ballet
1990; Atlantic

This is where Savatage bloom into the kind of band hinted at on *Hall Of The Mountain King*. The sound is massive and dramatic, a combination of operatic influences and prog metal, making this one of the band's best-loved albums.

Saxon

Formed Barnsley, England, 1979

Rejoicing under their original name, **Son Of A Bitch**, this outfit started out as an amalgamation of two bands doing the rounds in South Yorkshire during the mid- to late 1970s, **Sob** and **Coast**. Not surprisingly they had little success until they changed their name to **Saxon**, with a line-up featuring **Biff Byford** (vocals), **Paul Quinn** (guitar), **Graham Oliver** (guitar) **Steve Dawson** (bass) and **Pete Gill** (drums). They may have been a little late to spearhead the growing New Wave Of British Heavy Metal but they would soon come to embody some of its quintessential qualities.

They were picked up by Carrere Records and their debut, *Saxon* (1979), was unleashed on a metal scene that had hitherto experienced them only as a support act to the likes of the Ian Gillan Band and the Heavy Metal Kids, amongst a whole host of other rock acts. Several things made their debut hard to ignore: it featured some of the worst, most embarrassing cover art (a Saxon warrior wielding a blood-stained sword) ever to grace a chunk of vinyl and some of the

dumbest song titles and lyrics you could wish for in tunes such as "Stallions Of The Highway" and "Big Teaser".

They were not subtle by any stretch of the imagination, but they possessed an ability to pen melodic metal anthems with great ease. And at a time when Iron Maiden had their mascot, Eddie, and Motörhead were showing off their Bomber, Saxon had a lighting gantry shaped like a giant eagle, dubbed 'Biff's Budgie' by the roadcrew. Soon to follow was the classic *Wheels Of Steel* (1980) and its rapid follow-up *Strong Arm Of The Law* (1980) – they were genuine, 100-percent flame-grilled rockers from start to finish. These two efforts gave the band some of their most enduring stage favourites in the title tracks, as well as the hits "Dallas 1pm" and "747 (Strangers In The Night)". The following year brought the cheesy but indispensable *Denim And Leather*. It was at this point that Pete Gill injured his hand and was replaced two days before a major European tour by **Nigel Glockler**.

With 1982 came plans to crack the US, resulting in a series of insane dashes around the world culminating in the band touring America, flying back to the UK to play the Donington Monsters of Rock festival, returning to America for another show, then scooting back to Europe for a festival date in Germany. It was at this point that *The Eagle Has Landed* (1982) live album was released and consolidated their status as one of the most prolific and hard-working bands on the scene.

Subsequent albums *Power And The Glory* (1983) and *Crusader* (1984) were part of a

Saxon worship at the church of rock'n'roll.

concerted effort to build on their already established profile in America, but whilst the albums were relatively strong the band appeared to be smoothing their sound somewhat to appeal more to the mainstream. The mid- to late 80s brought a string of increasingly wimpy albums, honed to appeal to a mass market and MTV – *Innocence Is No Excuse* (1985), *Rock The Nations* (1986), *Destiny* (1988) and the live *Rock And Roll Gypsies* (1989). There were also some line-up changes as new bassist **Paul Johnson** stepped into the fold only to be replaced by **Tim 'Nibbs' Carter**. Meanwhile Nigel Glockler went off to play for GTR; he was replaced briefly by **Nigel Durham**, but then returned after GTR bit the dust.

The 1990s saw the advent of grunge and a purging wave of anti-metal sentiment. If Saxon had been viewed as a cliché before, they were now considered dead wood to all but the hardiest of rock fans. Somehow they weathered the nosedive in popularity with a continuing stream of releases: *Greatest Hits Live* (1990), *Solid Ball Of Rock* (1990), *Forever Free* (1992), *Dogs Of War* (1995) and *The Eagle Has Landed Part II* (1996) all emerged to little excitement in the UK but were presumably welcomed in European bastions of metal such as Germany, where irony-free titles were still welcomed with enthusiasm. Metal bands never die – they

just end up touring on the continent. During this period Graham Oliver inexplicably decided it would be a good idea to leave and reform Son Of A Bitch with Steve Dawson and Pete Gill. He was replaced by **Doug Scaratt**.

The next studio album, *Unleash The Beast* (1997), and subsequent tour went a long way to re-establishing the band in peoples' consciousnesses, helped, no doubt, by a general resurgence of interest in all things metallic; and just to remind the faithful what the band had sounded like at the start of their career, the *BBC Sessions* (1998) dusted off the tapes to some old Radio 1 *Friday Rock Show* sessions and their appearance at the Reading Festival in 1986. The following year brought another blast from the past in the release of *Live At Donington 1980*.

It was a real pleasure to once again experience a shamelessly unreconstructed rock band plying their trade, a feeling that extended to the band's two subsequent efforts, *Metalhead* (1999) and *Killing Ground* (2001), both of which found Biff and his hoary cohorts – the line-up now completed by Quinn, Scaratt, Carter and drummer **Fritz Randow** – resolutely firing on all cylinders. The albums sounded far heavier and more accomplished than their previous output, even though the lyrical subject matter still covered familiar bases.

In an unnecessary but fun revisionist exercise their next trip to the studio was to rerecord some of their old standards using state-of-the-art equipment and technology. *Heavy Metal Thunder* (2002) reworked tracks such as "Dallas 1pm", "Princess Of The Night" and "Wheels Of Steel"; a second CD contained crackling live tracks recorded during dates in the US in 2002. For a true live feast, however, the band had something special in mind: *The Saxon Chronicles* (2003), a double DVD of live footage from 2001's Wacken Open Air festival, plus promo clips and TV appearances.

Apparently unstoppable, the band returned in 2004 with another storming studio offering titled *Lionheart*.

⊙ Wheels Of Steel/Strong Arm Of The Law
1997; EMI

A stonking double-CD package of two classic metal albums, replete with eleven bonus live tracks. You can't go wrong with this one.

MICHAEL SCHENKER

Born Savstedt, Germany, January 10, 1955

There are axe heroes and then there is Michael Schenker. With a personality that is as volatile as his blazing guitar style he has had a hand in creating some of the hottest hard rock of the last three decades.

In 1973 Schenker was part of the Scorpions line-up that recorded *Lonesome Crow*, but was poached by Brit rockers UFO. From *Phenomenon* (1974) to *Strangers In The Night* (1978) he provided awesome firepower to such classics "Doctor Doctor" and "Rock Bottom". Personality clashes within the band, most notably with singer Phil Mogg, led to him taking his trademark Gibson Flying V to rock pastures new. Stopping only to help out the Scorpions on *Lovedrive* (1979), he formed the Michael Schenker Group by gathering around him a bunch of session players, including Don Airey (keyboards), Mo Foster (bass), Simon Phillips (drums) and Gary Barden (vocals). In 1980, with Rainbow bassist Roger Glover producing, the band created a dazzling eponymous debut of dextrous fretwork and *tour de force* hard rock manoeuvring.

It was a terrific start – a top-ten album no less – but Schenker needed an actual band rather than a bunch of hired hands. He retained Barden and drafted in old UFO mucker Paul Raymond (keyboards), Chris Glen (bass) and Cozy Powell (drums) for some hugely successful touring and album number two, *MSG* (1981). The UK audience were ravenous for whatever the hotshot guitarist could dish out and "Attack Of The Mad Axeman" said it all. The double whammy was transformed into a triumphant hat trick when *One Night At Budokan* (1982) went into the Top 5. Unfortunately, the line-up fractured after this run of luck and Schenker headed towards the mid-80s with uncertainty.

Assault Attack (1982), a decent enough effort, featured ex-Rainbow singer Graham Bonnet but the chemistry, such as it was, couldn't last. In the run-up to the band's appearance at Reading in 1982 Bonnet and Schenker enjoyed a frank exchange of views

before a warm-up gig and the singer was sacked; he went on to form Alcatrazz and employ his own fretboard wizards. Barden was brought back in, but there was no glossing over the instability. To top it all, *Built To Destroy* (1983) was a bona fide clunker suffering from mediocre writing and woeful production; it was remixed for the US market but the damage had been done. The live *Rock Will Never Die* (1984) was the most ironic title Schenker could have chosen for his next release.

It took another three years before Schenker returned with his eye set on a smoother, more commercial brand of hard rock. He had roped in the vocal talent of Robin McAuley (ex-Grand Prix, ex-Far Corporation) and the band were now going under the moniker of the McAuley Schenker Group. *Perfect Timing* (1987), *Save Yourself* (1989) and another album entitled *MSG* (1992) followed. The group toured with the likes of Bon Jovi, Def Leppard and Iron Maiden but the most exciting piece of work from this period to feature Schenker was the eponymous 1991 album created by supergroup Contraband, featuring Schenker, Tracii Guns (guitar, L.A. Guns), Bobby Blotzer (drums, Ratt), Share Pedersen

(bass, Vixen) and Richard Black (vocals, Shark Island).

They said it couldn't happen but the mid-90s saw the guitarist back in UFO for a major US tour and their *Walk On Water* (1995) album before releasing acoustic solo effort, *Thank You* (1995). He then managed to squeeze out *Written In The Sand* before heading out on the road again with UFO. The see-sawing between his own band and the latter characterized much of Schenker's work in the late 90s and into the next decade. He issued *The Unforgiven* (1999), *The Unforgiven World Tour* (1999) and the dire instrumental albums *Adventures Of The Imagination* and *Dreams And Expressions* (both 2000). Thankfully he also helped UFO out with *Covenant* (2000) and *Sharks* (2002), punctuated by his own hard-rocking *Be Aware Of Scorpions* (2001) and *Arachnophobiac* (2003). Meanwhile the **Schenker Pattison Summit**, featuring singer **Dave Pattison**, delivered a collection of classic covers, *The Endless Jam* (2004).

⊙ **The Michael Schenker Group**
1980; Chrysalis

Some might prefer the second album but as a statement of intent this classic is hard to beat. Schenker plays out of his skin and his sessioners rise to the occasion like the consummate professionals they are.

SCORPIONS

Formed Hanover, Germany, 1969

"If you think we're going soft and we're boring old farts we're here to kick your fucking ass and tell you we're still here ... " Klaus Meine

It's a little strange to think that Germany, a country where heavy metal seems to be perennially popular, has produced so few truly world-class rock acts. Newcomers Rammstein may have the upper hand at the moment but for classic axe-wielding posing, **Scorpions** are past masters, the period of their biggest successes having come during the heyday of metal in the 80s when spandex and big hair ruled. The stadiums of the world were rocked to their foundations by these unreconstructed riff merchants dishing up anthems laden with memorable hooks and power ballads of teary-eyed soppiness.

The early Scorpions consisted of **Rudi Schenker** (guitar/vocals), **Karl Heinz Follmer** (guitar), **Lothar Heimberg** (bass) and **Wolfgang Dziony** (drums) and went about trying to twist Pink Floyd's weird psychedelic dabblings into their own peculiarly Germanic notion of hard rock. It wasn't until Schenker passed singing duties on to **Klaus Meine** and recruited his own brother, **Michael Schenker**, as lead guitarist that the band began to vaguely resemble the Teutonic outfit that would one day ask the world "Do yew vahnt to rawk?"

Their first, unremarkable album, *Action* (1972), formed the soundtrack to the movie *Das Kalte Paradies* and was later dubbed *Lonesome Crow* overseas. Michael's six-string expertise couldn't fail to be noticed, however, and he was pinched by Brit rockers **UFO** who had recently lost Bernie Marsden. **Uli Jon Roth** stepped into the fold and a string of mid-70s albums – *Fly To The Rainbow* (1974), *In Trance* (1975), *Virgin Killer* (1976) and *Taken By Force* (1977) – charted the development of their sound from psychedelia to a more straightforward hard rock direction. Despite courting controversy in a variety of ways, not least by their growing taste for outrageous sleeve art – *Virgin Killer*, for instance, featured a naked pre-pubescent girl and a sheet of fortuitously positioned, cracked glass – they toured to only mediocre success. They were, however, big in Japan, hence the double live effort *Tokyo Tapes* (1978), which was the last long-player to feature Roth, who went off to pursue his Jimi Hendrix fixation with new group **Electric Sun**.

At this point UFO had had enough of Michael Schenker's drink and drugs habit and kicked him out straight back into the welcoming arms of his brother's band. He didn't stay for long but did manage to help Scorpions pen their breakthrough album, *Lovedrive* (1979). The bizarre cover art, featuring a woman on the back seat of a car and a man attempting to remove his hand from her breast, which is covered in bubble gum, resulted in the album being banned in the States. The band, however, survived the Americans' inability to comprehend the German sense of humour and lived to rhyme "fire" with "desire" another day. The classic line-up now included Michael Schenker's replacement **Matthias Jabs**, **Francis Buchholz** (bass) and **Herman 'The German' Rarebell** (drums).

Lovedrive conquered through sheer songwriting bravado. The mid-paced "Loving You Sunday Morning" was an exercise in tightly controlled melody; "Another Piece Of Meat" was forceful and speedy; "Coast

SCORPIONS BERLINER PHILHARMONIKER

MOMENT OF GLORY

increasingly protracted, and in this case *Savage Amusement* emerged a full three years later, yet continued to spawn hits. The band went on to tour with the Monsters of Rock festival in 1989 and performed in Russia for the first time. But it wasn't until 1990 that *Crazy World* made the Scorpions one of the biggest bands in the world. It contained a major hit single in the form of a Meine-penned tune about the reunification of Germany, "Wind Of Change" – featuring possibly the only example of whistling in a heavy metal song.

Ralph Riekermann (bass) and **James Kottak** (drums) were recruited and a steady stream of albums – *Face The Heat* (1993), *Live Bites* (1995), *Pure Instinct* (1996) and *Eye To Eye* (1999) – kept things ticking over, but the band became one of the many rock acts to fall victim to the winds of grunge sweeping through the music scene during the 90s. The latter album in particular was a misfiring attempt to modernize the band's sound and overhaul their image; out went the screaming axes and in came all sorts of production trickery, including sequenced percussion and computerized bleeps and blips. One major offender was single "To Be No. 1"; the only recognizably Scorpions aspect to the tune was Meine's vocal performance lurking beneath a mess of computerized drums and vocals. The accompanying video latched on to the Monica Lewinsky scandal surrounding President Clinton but any humour was lost on the fans who were presumably shaking their heads in disbelief.

This state of affairs was not helped by the band's somewhat odd decision to follow up with first a symphonic album featuring the Berlin Philharmonic Orchestra and then an acoustic effort – *Moment Of Glory* (2000) and *Acoustica* (2001) respectively – at a time when such moves were surely passé. Only a return to driving hard rock could prevent the gradual decline of this once heavyweight monster of a metal band, and that fortunately arrived in the shape of *Unbreakable* (2004), which dispensed with all forms of gimmickry and returned to the melodic

To Coast" was a nifty instrumental; and the closing triple whammy of "Is There Anybody There?", "Lovedrive" and "Holiday" was a sustained display of commercial metal at its best. It gave them a Top 40 placing in the UK and cracked the US Top 60. Suddenly the band's trademark flying V guitars and stripy spandex strides were everywhere and heralded a lengthy period of major worldwide success with *Animal Magnetism* (1980), featuring yet another weird cover with strange sexual connotations – a dog and a woman kneeling in front of a man with his back turned to the viewer ... go figure – and *Blackout* (1982). Each album beat its predecessor in the charts with the latter going Top 10 in the US and narrowly missing the same feat in the UK – even if the writing missed some of the hunger evident on *Lovedrive*.

Now that even the Americans were succumbing to the band's peculiar charms, it was *Love At First Sting* (1984) that made them into superstars as "Rock You Like A Hurricane" stormed on to MTV and brought double-platinum success. The album also contained the worldwide hit ballad "Still Loving You". *World Wide Live* (1985) was a testament to the band's huge popularity with the cover featuring their show-stopping feat of daring – the human pyramid.

When a band becomes truly successful the periods between albums usually become metal and power ballad formula of the group's glory days, albeit with suitably modern production.

Lovedrive
1979; EMI

An album of rude, politically incorrect, highly melodic hard rock. This was a defining moment in the band's history. And check out the cover art.

Animal Magnetism
1980; EMI

Yet another strange cover, but that doesn't detract from the intrinsic quality of the songs.

Love At First Sting
1984; EMI

A monster hit album, once again featuring a hard-rocking and extremely commercial selection of tunes.

SEPULTURA

Formed Belo Horizonte, Brazil, 1984

Surviving one of the most brutally policed countries in South America is no picnic but from their roots in Brazil's third largest city, **Sepultura** have developed from an enthusiastic, if generic, thrash band into a genuinely inventive and versatile international act, combining the cultural and rhythmic heritage of their homeland with the unabashed universally recognized power of metal.

Influenced by a range of styles from British punk through to extreme heavy metal, the original line-up came together in 1985, naming themselves after the Portuguese for 'grave'. The line-up of **Jairo T** (lead guitar), brothers **Igor Cavalera** (drums) and **Max Cavalera** (vox/rhythm guitars), and **Paulo Jr** (bass) wasted little time in emulating the conventions of the burgeoning thrash scene of the mid-1980s. Their first great adventure in a recording studio was a split project shared with another Brazilian band, Overdose. The *Bestial Devastation* EP (1985) was the result, and features every acknowledged cliché and touchstone of heavy metal, from the church-crushing devil on the cover to track titles such as "Antichrist" and "Necromancer".

The following year brought more thrash-by-numbers in *Morbid Visions* (1986). Recorded in seven days, the band were still firmly caught up in the bullet-belted, spikes and leather image of heavy metal. Soon after, Jairo T was replaced by **Andreas Kisser** (guitars) and a solid – some would argue classic – line-up was formed. Although the production values of the recordings improved in terms of clarity and overall ferocity, *Schizophrenia* (1987) suffered from yet more howling heavy metal clichés, and some truly terrible cover art. The set was mixed by veteran thrash producer Scott Burns, whose involvement in future recordings would see the creation of some of the band's finest moments.

It was not until *Beneath The Remains* (1989), their first album for Roadrunner, that the band's true potential was tapped. The increasingly powerful production accentuated the brutal speed of the twin-guitar interplay, whilst Max Cavalera's roaring vocals sounded truly bloodcurdling, with the political undertones of their previous material brought to the fore on tracks such as "Mass Hypnosis" and "Primitive Culture".

Sepultura had clearly survived the wave of 80s thrash metal on which they had surfed in and were pushing themselves beyond the restrictive confines of speeding guitars and jackhammer drumming. And as a measure of their growing international stature the band played before huge audiences at the Dynamo and Rock in Rio festivals of 1990. Gathering all their energy and momentum, *Arise* (1991) was their first album to be recorded outside

South America. They continued to experiment within the genre, constantly redefining their position; the music had grown in depth and the terse, fractured lyrics reflected feelings of hate, injustice, and righteous anger, Cavalera gradually finding his voice as a writer of powerful polemics.

By the time *Chaos AD* (1993) was released the band were heading towards inevitable greatness. With Andy Wallace at the production helm, they largely reduced their reliance on blunt speed and instead wielded their razor-sharp sense of outrage like a deadly weapon. Overtly political protest songs had replaced songs about demons. Each track oozed militant aggression; from "Refuse/ Resist" to "Clenched Fist" the album is a guttural scream of rage. Infamous punk agitator **Jello Biafra** provided lyrics for "Biotech Is Godzilla", while the world music instrumental "Kaiowas" (inspired by the memory of a Brazilian Indian tribe who committed mass suicide in protest against the government) pointed towards the paradigm-busting experimentation of what would follow.

The following year brought further acclaim and a continued rise in their fortunes as they appeared for the first time at the Donington Monsters of Rock festival. The result was, naturally, a performance of hair-raising intensity. Max Cavalera also took the opportunity to indulge himself with a side-project called **Nailbomb**, which also featured the talents of Fudge Tunnel's **Alex Newport**.

By now the band's sound had matured into a genuinely bowel-quaking rumble compared to their watery-thin early efforts; they were downtuned and distorted to a fearsome degree, helping to cement what would become the signature guitar tone for nu-metal. The next stage of their development brought more in the way of experimentation with traditional Brazilian instrumentation and tribal rhythms entering the mix. *Roots* (1996) was their most adventurous recording to date, gathering acclaim from a wide variety of critics. The band included more personal songs alongside the politics, with the overall theme being a return to cultural and musical roots. The album features a variety of guest appearances: **Carlinhos Brown** (famed Brazilian percussionist), the **Xavantes** (a Brazilian Indian tribe), **DJ Lethal** (House Of Pain), **Mike Patton** (then of **Faith No More**), and Jonathan Davis (Korn).

The album as a whole was a landmark in metallic innovation, a ground-breaking achievement that wrenched the group from the cosy confines of the specialist metal sections in record stores and into the welcoming embrace of the rock mainstream; they became the band of the moment, a distillation of the heavy music *Zeitgeist*, and favoured cover stars of the music press. From their adolescent background as a thrash band, Sepultura had successfully thrown off the chains of convention and matured into a fearsomely inventive outfit with a vibrant, honest approach to music, and a healthy disrespect for power and authority. *Roots* was such a breakthrough that Roadrunner issued it in a number of successive formats, featuring additional rare material to entice fans and completists alike.

Success, however, was a short-lived luxury as a tragic series of events turned Sepultura's future upside down. Just prior to the band's appearance at the Donington Monsters of Rock Festival Max Cavalera and his wife Gloria (also their manager) had to return to the US after receiving news of the death of Gloria's son. Naturally, the tragedy had a profound effect on the band's future. The result was a rift which grew between Max and the rest of the band; he was unhappy with their desire to tour later in the year whilst he and Gloria were still coming to terms with their loss. To add to the confusion the other three members suddenly fired Gloria a few days before Christmas. Max resigned, outraged at the band's treatment of someone who had supported them unconditionally for seven years.

What followed was a period of limbo where the remaining three members contradicted Max's version of events and stated that Sepultura were still an ongoing concern, despite the departure of their front man. What Sepultura would sound like without his trademark vocals and attitude was not clear. Max, however, merely threw himself into his work and began recording material with Californian cult heroes the **Deftones** as well as forming **Soulfly**.

From the ashes of Sepultura Mark I rose Sepultura Mark II. After what seemed like an interminable period of flux the remaining three members recruited the imposing figure of one **Derrick Green** to replace Max as the band's vocal roar. Standing at six feet plus, the dreadlocked Green lived up to his nickname, 'The Predator', in both stature, stage presence and vocal abilities. With a new member installed, they set about creating *Against* (1998), an album which took their previous ethno-metal dabblings and focused them in hitherto unexplored directions.

Sadly, the initial rush of excitement that greeted the band after their triumphant re-emergence gradually turned to indifference with *Nation* (2001). All the requisite stylings were in place, as was the band's healthy rebellious streak, but the momentum they had lost with Max's departure had left them with a monumental amount of catching up to do, a task hampered by a less than even release. As a result the group parted ways with Roadrunner.

To lose one's front man might be considered bad luck, but to be dropped by a record label as well might be deemed careless. Sepultura, however, are nothing if not fighters. Seemingly pushed into a corner, they kicked back hard with the ferocious *Roorback* (2003) on SPV, featuring their *Revolusongs* EP as a bonus with the early edition. The EP had been a Japan- and Brazil-only release of cover versions. They ripped their way through tunes by a variety of artists including Public Enemy, Jane's Addiction, Hellhammer and Exodus. The cover of U2's "Bullet The Blue Sky" was included as a bonus cut on later copies of *Roorback*. While the EP showed the progress Green had made in becoming the voice of Sepultura, *Roorback* was a clinching *tour de force* which largely dispensed with the mid-90s world music-infused thrash approach and instead concentrated on sheer head-removing power. The lyrics were uncompromisingly bleak, the music equally direct and menacing, making it their most accomplished post-Max effort.

Beneath The Remains
1989; Roadrunner

Their breakthrough album. A steamrollering collection of fierce time changes and blitzing guitar speed. The conventions of thrash metal are very much in evidence but the intensity of the music makes it a fine example of what could be done within the genre.

Chaos AD
1993; Roadrunner

The beginning of a hugely successful and experimental phase. They finally abandoned the heavy metal standards for a more political approach. The repeated chant of "We Who Are Not As Others" says it all. It also contains a stunning cover version of New Model Army's "The Hunt".

Roots
1996; Roadrunner

A sonic experience of monumental proportions. The use of traditional Brazilian instrumentation and the tribal atmosphere fuse effortlessly with the anger of the music. Check out the rattling Portuguese of "Ratamahatta", the instrumental interlude "Jasco" and the mantric chants of "Itsari" for examples of innovation and diversity. Sheer brilliance.

Roorback
2003; SPV

The title means "black propaganda; defamatory falsehoods published for political effect". What better, more cynical title could they have chosen for this screaming, bellicose return to form?

SHADOWS FALL

Formed Massachusetts, US, 1996

It was inevitable that as the nu-metal bandwagon slowed styles of music from the underground would gradually permeate the mainstream metal consciousness. Over the last couple of years the bands that had been treading a different, more shadowy path from those basking in the glow of commercial success have been coming to the fore, with the media dubbing these loose clusters of bands with tags such as the New Wave Of Swedish Heavy Metal, or the New Wave Of American Heavy Metal, in deference to the influential flurry of activity that took place in the UK towards the end of the 1970s.

If **Shadows Fall** – named after a comic book – have to be lumped in with a movement, then the New Wave Of American Heavy Metal is as good as any, though they do not share quite the same creative vision as, say, God Forbid and Killswitch Engaged – other than they seek to rock your teeth right out of your skull. While many of their labelmates – they currently reside on Century Media – and contemporaries count hardcore punk stylings in their make-up, Shadows Fall's lineage is a lot more straightforward, incorporating the trappings of the now classic Swedish death metal sound with progressive, intricate riffing and a distinctly European flavour, often reminding of Mercyful Fate and Diamond Head as well as the sound of other melodic but superheavy artists, not least early-days Metallica.

The group's early years were spent searching for an identity, the line-up having been put together by **Matthew Bachand** (guitar/vocals) and **Jonathan Donais** (guitar/vocals). With **Philip Labonte** (vocals), **Paul Romanko** (bass) and **David Germain** (drums) on board they released the "To Ashes"/"Fleshold" single in 1997 on Ellington Records. *Somber Eyes To The Sky* (1998), released on Bachand's own Lifeless Records, featured the first inklings of what the band were capable of, though what in effect had been issued was a bunch of demo recordings intended to secure the band a deal. Labonte eventually proved to be the weakest link – his desire to continue with overtly aggressive vocals set him at odds with his more experimental bandmates – and he was replaced by **Brian Fair** (ex-Overcast), a singer with a far more gymnastic set of vocal chords; Fair could handle not just death metal aggro, part of the nascent Shadows Fall signature sound, but clean melodic lines and hooks with ease. His voice provided the band with another instrument rather than simply being a mouthpiece for lyrics, an advantage which was amplified when Bachand and Donais's vocal efforts were layered in as well. It wasn't long before extreme metal label Century Media were showing a major interest in signing the band.

The singer's versatile larynx helped make *Of One Blood* (2000) something of a cult triumph. Metal radio stations in the States loved the band's thrashy roots and shameless guitar wizardy; the group were not afraid to widdle away with histrionic, guitar-hero solos while grounding the songs with solid, frantic riffing – it was the kind of metal that appealed not just to old-school fans but drew in younger aficionados of heavy music too. Such was the buzz of excitement around the band's progress that MTV recognized their potential with a *You Hear It First* feature. Of course, relentless bouts of

touring ensued and the band played shows with the likes of Kittie and kindred sonic souls King Diamond, In Flames and Nevermore. They even ended up at Japan's Beast Feast alongside Slayer and Pantera.

The band's stature was boosted immeasurably, however, with the release of *The Art Of Balance* (2002) featuring new drummer **Jason Bittner**. Up to this point the band had been working through older material – including the two tunes from their debut 7" single, which had popped up on both of their previous albums – but the new album provided the opportunity for fresh perspectives and experimentation. While Fair's positive lyrical slant was influenced by the ideas of unity and harmony, both spiritual and material, musically the band were shaping their output to be more challenging and diverse; the title track could best be described as a power ballad; meanwhile light instrumental passages

Shadows Fall's Brian Fair.

led into thunderous riff-storms, and harmonic vocals provided a counterpoint to the brutal death metal growling; it was a literal exposition of the album title, a balance between intricate beauty and technical aggression. They even threw in a cover version of Pink Floyd's "Welcome To The Machine", which emphasized the progressive side of their writing while adapting the tune to their epic thrash crunch – it was an odd but stylish way to round off a record of true quality.

With such a powerhouse of a record to promote it was inevitable that Shadows Fall would be at the vanguard of the next wave of metal acts to surge into the mainstream, which they did in style by running off with a variety of critical accolades and undertaking a barnstorming stint on 2003's Ozzfest, as well as an acclaimed slot supporting Iron Maiden at the Donington Download festival. It was a triumphant run-up to the release of *The War Within* (2004), which tore mercilessly into the *Billboard* Top 20.

⊙ The Art Of Balance
2003; Century Media

With most of the old material out of the band's system, this album basks in the glow of fresh invention and diversity. Streamlined duelling guitars joust atop a murderously precise rhythm section. Modern metal at its finest.

SILVERCHAIR

Formed Newcastle, New South Wales, Australia, 1992

The story of **Silverchair** is one of talent, barefaced cheek and plain good luck. The tale of their genesis is the stuff of Hollywood movies: three friends grow up listening to their parents' record collections, form a band when they are barely in their teens, and by winning a talent competition go on to solid platinum success.

Growing up in one of Australia's most industrialized cities, there seemed to be little else to do other than surf or play in a band to relieve the terminal boredom. Having been brought up on classic hard rock, **Daniel Johns** (vox/guitars), **Chris Joannou** (bass) and **Ben Gillies** (drums) formed a garage band, in the true sense of the term, at the tender age of twelve. Using equipment bought by their parents they played the only

kind of gigs they could get – street fairs and the like – pumping out cover versions of old songs by Black Sabbath, Deep Purple, and Led Zeppelin.

In June 1994 their fortunes took a sudden upswing. Having progressed to listening to Pearl Jam and Soundgarden, the band entered a national demo competition and out of 800 entrants they came first. They had lit the blue touch paper. Their song "Tomorrow" won them a session on Australia's national alternative station, 2JJJ FM, where the track was recut and entered the station's playlist. In a matter of months a four-song indie-label EP ("Tomorrow" plus "Acid Rain", "Blind" and "Stoned") gave them a gold-plated #1 single.

Shortly after, "Pure Massacre" – their second Australian single – followed "Tomorrow" into the charts, only missing the #1 slot thanks to the Cranberries. The situation seemed to have a momentum all of its own; *Frogstomp* (1995) was recorded in just nine days and effortlessly entered the Australian charts at #1; in the US it cruised into the Top 10. The three schoolboys had become rock stars with their parents as managers.

The album, a surprisingly mature-sounding debut, owed as much to the band's Seattle fixation as it did to their parent's record collections. The downtuned classic rock feel topped off with Johns's remarkable Eddie Vedder-style vocals led to obvious Pearl Jam comparisons. Without a doubt, in an unpretentious childlike way, they had tapped into the rock audience's craving for the familiar. On the other hand, while there was no denying the stunningly assured sound, the sometimes creaking lyrics betrayed the boys' lack of life experience.

With supreme ease the band suddenly found themselves in the world of professional managers, A&R men, corporate bullshit and huge international audiences. Among their many and varied live dates, they played the Big Day Out (the Australian equivalent of Lollapalooza) and the UK Reading Festival and ended up supporting the Red Hot Chili Peppers in late 1995. It was on this consolidation of their Stateside success that they experienced the audience confusion that has epitomized people's reactions the world over: how could it be that three sixteen-year-olds were responsible for the hit singles heard on the radio? The release of their follow-up, *Freak Show* (1997), confirmed that the band still owed a great deal to the spirit of grunge. Whilst their debut appropriated the Pearl Jam sound, the second often sounded eerily like Nirvana, from the choice of song titles ("Abuse Me", "Slave", "Freak") right down to Johns' uncanny Cobain-style vocals. The sometimes uncomfortable similarity led critics to ponder upon who they would sound like by the time of their third album. But such trifles didn't concern the Aussie fans, who sent three of the set's songs into the Top 10.

With criticisms that they were nothing but an Aussie grunge band still plaguing them the band made a conscious decision to alter their approach – *Neon Ballroom* (1999) sounded far more mature. The title was intended to signal the nineteen-year-olds' desire to combine classic and modern influences to create a whole new Silverchair sound. This time round Johns composed several of the songs as poems before adding any music, resulting in a far more convincing set of personal lyrics. Musically, the most noticeable change was the addition of orchestral passages; renowned pianist **David Helfgott** tinkled the ivories alongside the Sydney Symphony Orchestra on the epic "Emotion Sickness", while further keyboards were added by jazz pianist **Chris Abrahams** and Midnight Oil's **Jim Moginie**. Electronic embellish-

ments were provided by Aussie electronica artist **Paul Mac**. They even had backing vocals provided by the New South Wales Public School Choir.

The previous albums had been created during breaks from schoolwork, but having now graduated, the trio were free to concentrate fully on writing and recording. It took a full two months to complete, but the result was a plusher, more involving album than either *Frogstomp* or *Freak Show*. The collection helped the band become the biggest-selling Australian rock band of the 90s.

After a yearlong break during 2000 the band prepared themselves to play before the biggest audience of their career, 250,000 people at Rock In Rio 2001. It was one hell of a way to get into the spirit of their new material, which was just as grand in scale. New album *Diorama* (2002) sought to swamp the senses with its widescreen sound. The previous experiments with novel arrangements and orchestration were taken even further to create a truly expansive and colourful sonic experience. Some critics suggested that the new direction was heading dangerously towards MOR rock, that the new material was self-consciously soft and overly radio-friendly. Perhaps most bizarrely the band that had been lambasted for being too young were now considered to be old before their time.

Despite all the work that went in to creating their most ambitious album to date,

the band's plans for touring were seriously compromised by illness. Much of 2002 was lost while Johns was laidup suffering from reactive arthritis. When he recovered, however, Silverchair took to the road with a vengeance and a spectacular European tour in 2003 ended with a four-night sold-out residency at London's Shepherd's Bush Empire.

The Across The Night world tour provided them with material for *Live From Faraway Stables* (2003), an album and DVD that was released in Australia at Christmas.

Silverchair have confirmed that they will record at least another new album, even though Johns has expressed his desire to work full time on **The Dissociatives**, his collaboration with Paul Mac, which has so far yielded one album.

⊙ Frogstomp
1995; Murmur/Sony

Hugely derivative of the grunge scene, this does nevertheless contain some undeniably solid tunes and hooks. Despite the similarities to Pearl Jam, tracks like "Tomorrow" show a naive but talented approach to hard rock.

⊙ Diorama
2002; Atlantic

This was a huge leap forward for the band and Johns' writing had improved immensely. Van Dyke Parks, who has worked with the Beach Boys, directed orchestral arrangements while old hands Jim Moginie and Paul Mac turned up again to add to the expansive songs.

SKID ROW

Formed New Jersey, US, 1987;
disbanded 1996; re-formed 1999

Skid Row were one of the quintessential rock bands of the late 80s. In an era that favoured superficial preening and pouting over raw talent they had a knack for combining genuine melodic hooks and massive balls-out choruses with a gloriously heavy sound. In front man **Sebastian Bach** they had not only a charismatic poster boy but a singer with incredible lung power able to exude both emotion during the obligatory ballads and rage during the air-punching barnstormers.

The near mythical tale of Skid Row's rise involves one **Jon Bon Jovi** who was friends with guitarist **Dave 'The Snake' Sabo**. In their youth the two apparently agreed on a sort of mutual aid pact: whoever made it to the top first would help out the other. Sabo's partner in crime was (male) bassist **Rachel Bolan** and together they recruited **Scotti Hill** (guitar), **Rob Affuso** (drums) and, of course, singer Bach. At the time, Bach was a member of dodgy glamsters **Madame X** but truly found his vocation as the formidable motormouth behind the mic for Skid Row. He really was the band's trump card, a superstar in waiting, willing to play the role for all it was worth.

Thanks to their Bon Jovi connection, getting a record deal was a relatively simple process, but this wasn't just a ridiculously easy ride for a mediocre bunch of wannabes. Skid Row were a snarling whirlwind of commercially inflected anthemic metal and wayward punk. And they were far heavier hitters than their poodle-permed mentor. What's more they wrote terrific songs, as was ably demonstrated by their 1989 eponymous debut. It peaked at #6 in the US and spat out hit singles with almost obscene abandon. "I Remember You" was their token, lighters-in-the-air ballad, "18 And Life" articulated the fans' adolescent angst, while "Youth Gone Wild" was all flailing fists and one mutha of a monstrous chorus. Even so the UK was a tad reticent about this bunch and it took a storming support slot with Bon Jovi at Milton Keynes to get things started.

Coupled with the almost instant commercial success came a career in the media, Bach seemingly unable to stay out of the rock press headlines, more often than not for some sort of high-spirited lunacy gone wrong. In 1990, for instance, Bach was put on probation for injuring a fan by throwing a bottle into the crowd during a gig in Boston. Then there was the infamous T-shirt featuring a homophobic slogan and the much-publicized punch-up with Jon Bon Jovi, an incident which led to the revelation that, in return for the early helping hand, both Bon Jovi and guitarist Richie Sambora held the rights to Skid Row's publishing royalties.

Bach's way with expletives also got him into trouble in the UK while supporting Guns N' Roses. Brent Council had declared Wembley Stadium a foul-language-free zone but Skid Row played "Get The Fuck Out" anyway. At this point the band were promoting *Slave To The Grind* (1991), an album

COURTESY OF SPV RECORDS

Skid Row salute their fans.

that gave the world a middle-finger salute and refused to pander to the commercial excesses present on its predecessor; it also debuted in the *Billboard* Chart at #1, an unprecedented feat for a metal band. It was rammed with raging lyrics and supremely heavy riffing. Baffled fans who had expected some lighter material were disappointed, but Skid Row's daring and uncompromising decision to get nastier impressed those who previously thought the band were nothing more than Bon Jovi's lap dogs.

A compilation, *B-Side Ourselves* (1992), kept the fans going, but grunge was starting to wipe out 80s metal and *Subhuman Race* (1995) took an age to emerge and, when it did, it came with an even tougher sound. The bone-crunching aggression of the new album flummoxed everyone; the band had left it too long and failed to maintain their momentum either with regular output or a consistent sound. The pressure on the band was immense and they succumbed in 1996.

Bach went on to form the short-lived **The Last Hard Men** in 1996 (with **Smashing Pumpkins** drummer **Jimmy Chamberlin**), who only managed "School's Out", for the soundtrack to *Scream*, and the album *Bring*

'Em Bach Alive (1999). Meanwhile, Bolan issued *Dressing Up The Idiot* (1997) under the moniker of a project bizarrely dubbed **Prunella Scales**. All the while a mooted reunion seemed tantalizingly out of reach; but in 1999 news came that the band would be re-forming – minus Bach. The new line-up, featuring singer **Johnny Solinger** and drummer **Phil Varone**, supported Kiss during their 2000 farewell tour and began an arduous US schedule to restock their fan base prior to the release of *Thickskin* (2003).

Skid Row
Atlantic; 1989

Immense, crowd-pleasing metal. Tough and powerful but with a gleaming commercial edge, the songs on this eponymous effort introduce a band of consummate skill and verve.

Slave To The Grind
Atlantic; 1991

Gone is the saccharine of the debut and instead Bach gets to freak out over a blazing barrage of taut, angry riffing. Startlingly heavy at the time, it hasn't lost its power to shock and please.

Subhuman Race
Atlantic; 1995

Heavy, angry and taking absolutely no prisoners, this is the sound of a band reinventing themselves.

SKUNK ANANSIE

Formed London, 1994; disbanded 2001

"They're the best band to come out of England in ten years!" Lemmy on Skunk Anansie

For a while during the 90s **Skunk Anansie**'s venomous, corrosive brand of rock was a welcome antidote to the plodding clichés trotted out by lesser acts; not only that but they managed to rack up a respectable

number of hits along the way, making them one of the more commercially successful alternative heavy rock bands to have emerged from the UK in recent years.

Named after the black-furred, white-striped creature and a spider prominently featured in Jamaican folk tales ('Anansie'), they were snapped up by One Little Indian, after only their second gig. Not being a band to bother with last names, the line-up consisted of **Skin** (vocals), **Ace** (guitars), **Cass** (bass) and **Robbie** (drums). Right from the off they were a band that were striking both visually and sonically. Their sound was a hybrid of emotive soulful vocals and scathing metal, influenced by punk and funk, while sartorially their confrontational attitude was reflected in variations on army surplus chic. Skin could safely say that she was the only black female singer to ever shave her head and paint on a white stripe from back to front.

Their initial foray into the world of recording came in the shape of a Radio 1 session for the *Evening Show*. So impressive was their slot that Radio 1 released a track from the session as a limited edition 7" single; "Little Baby Swastikkka" came out on mail order only and sold out quickly. The song was typical of what would become the Skunk Anansie trademark; taut and angry, the lyrics were based on Skin's own experiences of racism – she had once seen some graffiti swastikas sprayed so low on a wall that they were clearly the work of a child. The group's first official record company outing was "Selling Jesus" in 1995, a nightmare pyrotechnic assault on the hypocrisies of religion. It reached #46 in the UK.

The summer brought the usual round of rock festivals, with performances at both Glastonbury and Reading – Skin looking more outlandish than ever with her ultra-cropped hair dyed electric blue, and a white cross daubed on her forehead. All this activity softened fans up for *Sunburnt And Paranoid* (1995). The songs were intelligent, lean and versatile while Skin's vocals shimmered with emotion and shuddered with rage. The lyrics covered everything from relationships ("Charity", "Pity") through to racism ("Intellectualise My Blackness") and sexual politics ("Rise Up"), with great finesse and a dramatic delivery. Clearly the caustic politics and no-holds-barred delivery appealed across the musical spectrum; not only did the album go Top 10 but the group were voted best new band of 1995 by *Kerrang!* readers.

In 1996 the band acquired a more stable line-up with **Mark Richardson** joining them on drums in time to record *Stoosh*. If the debut had bristled with a charming naiveté then the follow-up smoothed things over with a powerful production, though it did nothing to calm them down; the record kicked off with the in-yer-face "Yes, It's Fucking Political", but made space for moments of tenderness with hits such as "Brazen (Weep)" and "Hedonism (Just Because You Feel Good)".

The combination of commercialism and muscular metal was repeated on *Post Orgasmic Chill* (1999). Loops and samples peppered the usual blend of skewed rockers and big ballads, but it was gradually becoming clear that the Skunk were burning themselves out. The tours were successful, the hit singles seemed to come with ease but the lure of solo careers and the possibility of exploring other sounds was growing too great.

After a bout of touring the band members headed off to indulge their solo whims and by 2001 the unit had dissolved. Since then Skin has launched a solo career with the album *Fleshwounds* (2003), concentrating upon a cleaner and mellower songwriting approach; Ace returned with *Still Hungry* (2003), a rocky affair featuring a host of different vocalists including **Motörhead**'s **Lemmy** and **Benji** of Skindred; Cass turned up in **Gary Moore**'s band and on *Scars* (2002); meanwhile Mark went off to join **Feeder**.

⊙ Sunburnt And Paranoid
1995; One Little Indian

Caustic, vitriolic dissident rock; as a debut this is confident and musically assured. The lyrics are honest expressions of emotion while the musicianship is second to none.

⊙ Stoosh
1996; One Little Indian

The time spent on writing great songs shines through here. Whether they're lashing out with the riffs or letting the emotion get the better of them on the slowies, Skunk Anansie are never less than riveting.

SLADE

Formed Wolverhampton, UK, 1964

There's a lot more to this story than just "Merry Xmas Everybody". Joey Ramone was a fan, Kurt Cobain thought they were cool, even David Coverdale dug them for their glammy hard-rock stomp and guitarist **Noddy Holder**'s incredible vocals. For a while in the 70s it was impossible to switch on the radio without being assailed by Slademania; they were one of the UK's top-selling bands who landed hits around the world, except for the US, which remained resolutely stubborn to their Midlands working-class charm until the 80s. And then, just as they were going to support Ozzy Osbourne on the back of their American top-forty album *Keep Your Hands Off My Power Supply* (1984), bassist **Jim Lea** fell ill and the group had to bail out of the tour.

The charts statistics for **Slade** are quite extraordinary. But it wasn't like that when they started out in the 60s. **Don Powell** (drums) and **Dave Hill** (guitar) had started out in **The Vendors** before picking up **Lea** and **Holder** and becoming first **The N' Betweens** and then **Ambrose Slade**. Trimming the name further was part of a concerted effort to grab the public's attention. First they wore suits, then went for the skinhead look and finally settled on the glam-rock image just as the UK was getting used to the likes of T-Rex, Gary Glitter, and the Sweet. Under the guidance of manager **Chas Chandler** – he of Animals fame and one-time Jimi Hendrix manager – they became a veritable hit machine, regulars on *Top Of The Pops* and (according to teachers at the time) responsible for school pupils' inability to spell correctly, their first #1 being "Coz I Luv You" in 1971. All together they scored six chart-toppers and between 1971 and 1976 all their singles entered the Top 20.

They already had some albums under their belts, but *Slade Alive!* (1972) was their first major chart hit, narrowly missing the top slot. They really got going, however, with *Slayed?* (1973) which contained one of their finest hard-rocking good-time hits, "Mama Weer All Crazee Now". The 1973 *Sladest* compilation pulled together several of their single-only tracks and topped the charts, meanwhile *Old, New, Borrowed And Blue* (1974) topped the charts with new songs. The release of the *Slade In Flame* (1974) soundtrack, to their film of the same name,

really marked a shift in public tastes; its follow-up, *Nobody's Fools* (1976), only went into the Top 20. The record was tailored to please American ears and with punk just around the corner Slade suddenly found their sound out of favour on both sides of the Atlantic. The following year they suitably enough released *Whatever Happened To Slade*.

A series of poor business decisions meant that the rest of the 70s saw the band's profile slip almost to zero. They were, however, revitalized by a chance slot at the 1980 Reading Festival when, according to various critics, they stole the show. A Donington Monsters of Rock appearance in 1981 went down similarly well. "My Oh My" narrowly failed to hit the Christmas top slot in 1983, but the fact that earlier in the year Quiet Riot had scored a massive hit with Slade's "Cum On Feel The Noize" meant that Slade were at last earning some US recognition. They failed to capitalize on it but still managed to maintain a certain level of interest, even scoring a #21 hit with "Radio Wall Of Sound" in 1991. Amazingly they haven't yet called it a day and the band – minus Holder, who has moved into acting and broadcasting – are still touring internationally, while issuing the odd live album now and then.

⊙ Greatest Hits
1997; Polydor

Unashamedly pop, but only in that Lea and Holder wrote great hooky melodies, this excellent handful of rockers covers the band's major top-thirty hits from 1971 to 1991.

SLAYER

Formed Huntington Beach, Los Angeles, US, 1982

"Someone once asked me whether I used to pose in front of a mirror ... The closest thing I've ever done to that is stand in front of a mirror with a broom, fucking rocking out, pretending, just jamming out ... " Tom Araya

The name **Slayer** must surely be synonymous with thrash metal of the most intense and disturbing variety. No first-division heavy metal outfit has ever managed to so consistently produce records as compellingly brutal and fast. The writing nucleus of **Tom Araya** (bass/vocals), **Kerry King** (guitar) and **Jeff Hanneman** (guitar) was completed with **Dave Lombardo** on drums to form what is generally regarded as the classic line-up that made its debut in 1983 by contributing "Aggressive Perfector" to the *Metal Massacre III* compilation.

Already making a name for themselves locally as one of the fastest bands in the burgeoning thrash scene, Slayer were signed by the Metal Blade label before unleashing *Show No Mercy* (1984) and *Hell Awaits* (1985); 1984's *Haunting The Chapel* EP also provided a nice little diversion for the growing legion of extreme thrash fans, while *Live Undead* (1985), a minor addition to their oeuvre, only went to show that they could reproduce their deadly noisefest live without missing a beat.

If they managed to prove one thing with their first two genre-bending studio efforts it was that subtlety was not a watchword; each record was a scorching blast of satanic speed metal played with numbing technical precision and an obvious love of shock-tactic lyrics. Unfortunately, what merit there was in these recordings was lost in the abysmal production values; they did, however, prepare the world for what was to become their finest hour, or to be more precise 28 minutes. Teaming up with hip producer **Rick Rubin** they came up with *Reign In Blood* (1986), one of the most vicious and caustic metal releases of the genre's history. The production was crisp and clear for once, allowing the listener to fully appreciate the precise care with which each infernally tuneless guitar solo was delivered and the loving manner in which each tasteless line was growled. The album largely refined their previous agenda of satanic torture, death and carnage – "Piece By Piece", "Altar Of Sacrifice", "Criminally Insane"; they all rattled along with murderous relish. The key song, however, was opening track "Angel Of Death", which insensitively detailed the atrocities perpetrated by Nazi doctor Joseph Mengele. This opened the floodgates to a torrent of criticism. Indeed, the band's detractors positively revelled in accusing them of unsavoury political leanings; the fact that their fan club was named Slaytanic Wehrmacht and that the band's logo was emblazoned on an iron eagle didn't help, nor did their insistence on exploring other Nazi-related subjects on subsequent releases.

Follow-up studio outings *South Of Heaven* (1988) – no prizes for guessing what era of history "Behind The Crooked Cross" dealt with – and *Seasons In The Abyss* (1990) had more than a whiff of sulphur about them and saw Rubin reprise his powerful production job whilst the band experimented by slowing down occasionally to a mere brisk sprint; some of the band's most brutally effective tunes resulted from adopting a deliberate and insistent mid-paced chug, erupting into full-scale demolition riffing. *Live – Decade Of Aggression* (1991), an intense double album, boasted no overdubs but instead put studio favourites through the live shredder in an astonishingly brutal and definitive manner.

Despite their apparent inexorable ascent Slayer have always suffered from potentially self-destructive personality clashes and Dave Lombardo was the member upon which the tension focused. So when the drummer departed to form his own group, **Grip Inc.**, the band were left in the unenviable position of finding a permanent member who could replicate his power and technical proficiency. A few stand-ins came and went before **Paul Bostaph** took over for a notable period during which *Divine Intervention* (1994) was recorded and which also saw the bulk of the material coming from King. Each subsequent album had enjoyed improving chart positions, but this record marked a highpoint in their career; in the UK it went Top 20, as had *Seasons In The Abyss*; in the US though they had a genuine top-ten hit

Slayer's Kerry King.

MICK HUTSON/REDFERNS

on their hands. Ironically, as a record, *Divine Intervention* found the band suffering from a sense of stagnation; they were very much going through the motions. In the same year they also worked alongside **Ice-T** on a cover of the Exploited's "Disorder" for the *Judgment Night* soundtrack, a step that would prove to be prophetic when considering their next studio effort.

In a move that most other groups would deem to be commercial suicide, *Undisputed Attitude* (1996) was an all-out covers album of the punk and hardcore music that had influenced the group along the way. Originally intended to include songs written by artists such as Deep Purple, Slayer found that they could not re-create them without sounding 70s into the bargain; being unable to Slayerize these tunes they fell by the wayside leaving the more easily adapted and aggressive material. No sooner was this complete than Bostaph left, claiming that the band's style was too limiting, to be replaced by **John Dette**.

It took another two years before a major return to form for the band – with Bostaph back in the ranks again – in the shape of the mighty *Diabolus In Musica* (1998), which was followed by the even more inventively evil *God Hates Us All* (2001), proving, if anything, that Slayer had not lost their deliberately controversial touch. At a time when Slayer's contemporaries had evolved beyond all-out speed and violence, fans were heartened to find King and co still playing with the same venom that had fired them all those years ago.

While *Diabolus In Musica* sounded lean and ravenously hungry, *God Hates Us All* added a nice visual twist to Slayer's ever-growing catalogue of controversy; the sleeve depicted a Bible spattered with blood and driven through with nails, the band's logo branded on the cover. The album ended up on the record store shelves with a rather innocuous plain white insert decorated with crucifixes masking the offending artwork beneath.

Any major band with such a lengthy career indulges in the gluttonous blow-out of the best-of and rarities box set at some point and *Soundtrack To The Apocalypse* (2003) was an awesome creation. Fans could choose from the slimmed down standard version or a magnificently sinful five-disc edition in a nice big box.

Whether one regards them as basic, blistering white-noise merchants or the last true thrash band to produce commercially viable metal music, there can be no denying that Slayer are a singularly influential, unchanging and uncompromising unit.

Reign In Blood
1986; Def Jam

An offensive and extreme thrash album that has gone on to be one of the most influential heavy metal albums of the 1980s. Sheer, unadulterated speed from start to finish, most of the tunes clock in at around the two-minute mark. Quite long enough for some.

SLIPKNOT

Formed Des Moines, Iowa, US, 1995

"So we're putting on the suits and masks but we didn't realise we're parked right next to a very nice jewellery store! We put all this shit on and jump back in the van but before we can get outta there we're suddenly surrounded by cops with guns ..." Paul Gray

Call it thrash metal, call it rap, or call it nu-metal, for one of the main embodiments of this recent rock mutation look no further than **Slipknot**, these nine masked and numbered men who took a few disparate elements prevalent on the metal scene and bolted together a genuinely scary Frankenstein's monster.

Out in the vast conservative emptiness of middle America, in the heart of Iowa, some like-minded musicians were indulging their passion for metal – the more extreme the better. Which isn't surprising really considering that Des Moines was the town at the heart of Ozzy Osbourne's infamous bat-munching episode back in 1982. Since then the legend has grown and doubtless inspired **Sid Wilson**, #0 (DJ), **Joey Jordison**, #1 (drums), **Paul Gray**, #2 (bass), **Chris Fehn**, #3 (custom percussion), **James Root**, #4 (guitars), **Craig Jones**, #5 (samples), **Shawn 'Clown' Crahan**, #6 (custom percussion), **Mick Thomson**, #7 (guitar) and **Corey Taylor**, #8 (vocals).

Prior to their skull-caving, nine-man incarnation the band enjoyed the usual shifting line-up and produced one self-financed album, charmingly titled *Mate, Feed, Kill, Repeat* (1996), which currently changes hands on the Internet for silly money. Apparently no one in the band owns a copy. They tried in vain to get a proper deal and ended up being rejected by all the major labels; one executive at Epic records was heard to comment that if Slipknot were the future of music then he didn't want to live. There's no indication of what the person in question did when the band signed to Roadrunner Records in 1997 and producer **Ross Robinson** got his evil-genius hands on them in the studio.

When the band finally erupted into the metal consciousness they caused a major sensation with both their music and image,

Corey Taylor (right) wonders whether rain will stop play.

grabbing headlines and media attention as they exploited the twisted circus sideshow facet of their stage act. Each band member took a number instead of a name and they hid their identities further by donning identical boiler suits and adopting a stage persona reflected in a unique mask. Most readily identifiable were bassist Paul Gray in his pig mask and Shawn Crahan with his Clown mask. It was as though a bunch of lunatics had escaped an asylum via a Halloween jumble sale and somehow found their way into a studio. And when *Slipknot* (1999) crashed into the charts it proved to be a coruscating and accurate encapsulation of youthful frustration and alienation. The music took the basic thrash metal sound of Sepultura, all tribal rhythms and harsh guttural roars, and amplified it to a terrifyingly intense level, not least by having Joey Jordison's thundering drums augmented by two sets of custom percussion kits, both in the studio and on stage. Of course, Chris Fehn and Shawn 'Clown' Crahan didn't just pummel seven shades of shit out of their kits while playing live; the two of them acted as weird cheerleaders, throwing mocking and menacing shapes at the crowd.

It was heavy, it was ugly, it was utterly beguiling to teenagers who wanted something even more extreme with which to shock their parents and teachers. With maximum exposure guaranteed through a slot on the 1999 Ozzfest, the debut went to #1 in *Billboard*'s Heatseekers chart. A year and a half later they had toured the world and garnered accolades around the globe – in the UK, *Kerrang!* magazine voted them best International Live Act. They had taken the nu-metal phenomenon into the mainstream, alongside other breakthrough acts such as Korn and Limp Bizkit.

Consolidation came in the form of *Iowa* (2001). The anticipation surrounding the launch of the new album was even more intense than for their debut; record stores around the globe adjusted their opening times to allow rabid fans – lovingly dubbed 'maggots' by the band – to get their hands on the CD at the stroke of midnight on the day of release. After such a devastating arrival how would they top the aural insanity of *Slipknot*? What would these sickos from the middle of nowhere do next? Could they be even more offensive? Fans needn't have worried because *Iowa* was so grotesquely extreme it eclipsed pretty much every other heavy release when it hit the shelves, the band having opted to go for an almost death'n'black metal intensity. "People = Shit" opened with various band members screaming at the top of their lungs before a scalding blast-beat driven storm of guitars jack-hammered into the mix; following track "Disasterpiece" revelled in a lightning-fast hardcore death-punk chorus; "The Heretic Anthem" decapitated the rock star myth and paraded the blood-spattered head through the streets. The parental advisory stickers plastered on the CD cases really could not even begin to describe the expletive-strewn horrors that lurked within. A real symphony of sickness, it was harsh, brutal, and ridiculously over the top, being once again produced by Ross Robinson. Not surprisingly it rocketed to the top of most album charts around the world and middle-class teenagers out shopping with their mums on a Saturday morning could be seen wearing "People = Shit" hoodies and T-shirts. And naturally, slots on the Ozzfest and Pledge Of Allegiance tours beckoned.

Such a level of excitement can be tough for even the most consummate performers to maintain, and so it proved for Slipknot. *Iowa* may well have been more accomplished, but with the general feeling that nu-metal was running out of steam, it was hard to see where the nontet could go, and it was clear that they badly needed a break from each other. Joey Jordison took time out to work with another project, **Murderdolls**, a bunch of glam-tastic trash punkers who managed a UK hit with a cover of Billy Idol's "White Wedding". Meanwhile, Slipknot lead singer Corey Taylor concentrated on his **Stone Sour** project, and Shawn Crahan dabbled with the far more gently rocking **To My Surprise**. While time was taken with recording and touring these bands, the Slipknot faithful were treated to the *Disasterpieces* (2002) and *Welcome To Our Neighborhood* (2003) DVDs, the latter a rerelease of their 1999 home video.

With creative desires vented in other quarters, the band returned to the studio with famed producer **Rick Rubin** to create *Vol. 3: (The Subliminal Verses)* (2004), which turned out to be a surprise for anyone expecting yet another aggravated sonic pummelling. The violence levels were high but Rubin's input had drawn almost virtuoso performances from some of the band members, while experimental touches of cello, melody and industrial samples gave the entire album a more expansive and textured feel.

⊙ Slipknot
1999; Roadrunner

Take a generous helping of Sepultura, downtune even more, throw in a menagerie of drumming and let a bloke wearing a rubber mask shot through with devil's dreads scream over the top about his miserable childhood. Ah, bliss.

⊙ Iowa
2001; Roadrunner

More of the same only heavier. And with a black (presumably) satanic goat on the front. This album features one of the band's nihilistic slogans, "People = Shit", turned into a song. Nice.

SMASHING PUMPKINS

Formed Chicago, US, 1988; disbanded 2000

Smashing Pumpkins were in many ways the quintessential 90s rock band. Alongside the likes of Jane's Addiction – who they supported in their early days – they epitomized the alternative rock aesthetic, channelling the fury and spirit of punk into an arty and personal musical statement. With their capacity for astonishing heaviness coupled with great delicacy they were tailor-made for the Lollapalooza generation.

The band centred at first around **Billy Corgan** (guitar/vocals), **D'Arcy Wretzky**, who played bass, and originally a drum machine, until **James Iha** (guitar) and finally **Jimmy Chamberlin** (drums) came on board. A couple of singles followed, "I Am One" and "Tristessa", the latter on Sub Pop. The interest generated led to a deal with Hut Records and *Gish* (1991) was unleashed on an audience still coping with the fall-out of "Smells Like Teen Spirit". The Pumpkins looked completely unassuming but revelled

in a polydecibel assault more akin to the driving abandon of Perry Farrell and co. than the bleak bludgeon of Nirvana. Nevertheless, in Corgan they had an enigmatic and fiery focus, his reedy voice somehow weaving ethereally through the incendiary guitar bombast. On stage he liked to wear the odd dress and took to trashing live sets as the band set about touring with the likes of Pearl Jam and the Red Hot Chili Peppers.

The first album was recorded with Nirvana producer **Butch Vig** and they retained his services for *Siamese Dream* (1993). The preceding "Cherub Rock" single cracked the UK Top 40 heralding the band's most confident and successful phase. *Gish* sounded primitive compared to the unruly emotional forces gathered on the new album; the largely acoustic and string-laden top-twenty hit "Disarm" would have been accompanied with an appearance on *Top Of The Pops* were it not for the violent imagery of the lyrics. All together, the recording process had been so gruelling that the band were reported as being on the verge of splitting afterwards. Though few bands release rarities albums so early in their career, the compilation *Pisces Iscariot* (1994) kept the Pumpkin product rolling as the band became a star attraction on the Lollapalooza tour.

By this time Corgan had garnered something of a reputation as a prolific writer, and for *Mellon Collie And The Infinite Sadness* (1995) he pulled out all the stops to deliver a huge double album blow-out. Guided by Nine Inch Nails producers **Alan Moulder** and **Flood** the depth and breadth of material was simply amazing. Vig's tendency to polish the guitar sound to a sheen was replaced by a more ragged intensity allowing the individual character of each half of the set – subtitled "Dawn To Dusk" and "Twilight To Starlight" – to come through.

The band had rapidly become one of alt rock's biggest acts, especially as the new material had topped the chart in the US and gone Top 5 in the UK. But with greatness can come chaos, and the summer of 1996 found the band in the thick of controversy. Their touring keyboard player **Jonathan Melvoin** died from a heroin overdose just prior to the band headlining Madison Square Garden. Chamberlin was sacked for his drug abusing ways and the band quickly called in **Matt Walker** (drums, Filter) and **Dennis Flemion** (keyboards) to complete their touring commitments.

The *Zero* (1996) mini-LP followed, but it would be the last familiar piece from the Pumpkins for some time. While preparing the material for the new album, madness reigned and Corgan declared that rock was dead. Maybe the volatile front man hadn't come up with any good riffs because *Adore* (1998) stripped back much of the band's anger and replaced it with synths, samples and loops. It was baffling, something of a blip in the band's catalogue, which was rectified with *Machina/ The Machines Of God* (2000). The return to form wasn't quite so straightforward, however. Chamberlin had by now been reinstated – he had spent some of the intervening time drumming in supergroup **Last Hard Men** with ex- **Skid Row** singer **Sebastian Bach** and ex-Breeders guitarist **Kelley Deal** – but D'Arcy had decided to leave. Her replacement was former Hole bassist **Melissa Auf Der Maur** who, ironically, had originally been inspired to play after hearing the Pumpkins.

The new record combined the harsher electronic textures of *Adore* with greater use of guitar to create a far more satisfying balance of the traditional and the experimental. The publicity surrounding the band's final album wasn't as positive as it could have been, however. In a statement to the press the Pumpkins' new manager, Sharon Osbourne, said that she was resigning from her role for health reasons – Billy Corgan was making her sick.

Despite the decent final album, the band split soon after. Iha had already started a solo career in 1998 with *Let It Come Down*; Auf Der Maur eventually emerged with an eponymous solo debut in 2004; while Corgan retained Chamberlin and put together **Zwan**, featuring bass player **Paz Lenchantin** (ex-**A Perfect Circle**) among others. They managed one album, *Mary Star Of The Sea* (2003), and then split, which was a shame seeing as the acoustic cover version of Iron Maiden's "Number Of The Beast" on their single "Honestly" was quite refreshingly bizarre. Pumpkins fans had to make do with the greatest hits collection *Rotten Apples* (2001) and then *Earphoria* (2002), basically a compilation of rarities and live bits and pieces.

⊙ Siamese Dream
1993; Hut/Virgin

Equal part savage guitar onslaught and cloud-like hush, this set finds Corgan's bewildering lyrics nailed to a kind of metal that wouldn't seem out of place in a Victorian nursery.

⊙ Mellon Collie And The Infinite Sadness
1995; Hut/Virgin

Epic, sprawling and hugely ambitious, this album encompasses a myriad of moods and styles but retains a tight hold on the attention. This is the kind of record that rewards repeated listening, each delve into Corgan's world turning up unexpected gems.

8OIL

Formed Chicago, US, 1998

As nu-metal gradually chunders to a halt, bands which have always had more than a hint of authentic old-school metal to their make-up are edging into the limelight, and few come as heavy and mighty as **Soil**, a five-piece from Chicago.

Originally, Soil were formed as something of a side-project by **Adam Zadel** (guitar) and **Tim King** (bass) who were looking for a musical outlet apart from their more death-oriented outfit **Oppressor**, the name having been inspired by the song "Rot In Soil", from Entombed's *Wolverine Blues* album. They had **Tom Schofield** (drums) and **Shaun Glass** (guitar) in place already but lacked a suitably gutsy vocalist; then King heard **Ryan McCombs** on a compilation album of unsigned bands and knew instantly that he had found the ideal singer. With all the personnel in place and a whole bunch of songs all ready to go they dived straight in with their *El Chupacabra*

EP, issued in 1998. This was followed in quick succession by *Throttle Junkies* (1999), which was something of an oddity given that it was produced by infamous indie noise guru Steve Albini. Albini's standard studio aesthetic usually involves merely recording a band in a warts'n'all scenario, which didn't really suit Soil's everything-including-the-kitchen-sink riffing. Still, whatever the sonic shortfalls of their debut disc, not many people got to hear it because the record label folded shortly after the album hit the shelves, leaving Soil to pick up the pieces after the cruel false start.

It took nearly two years of hard slog and continual pressure – McCombs was living in the band's rehearsal space for much of the time – before *Scars* (2001) appeared on J Records to capitalize upon the band's relentless gigging. Drenched in attitude and positively bleeding terrific riffs the album was a distillation of all the hard knocks and setbacks suffered by the band. The frustration and negativity had been turned around and spat back out as surging, caustic metal, with McCombs' harsh growl vying with the churning riffs and wrecking-ball rhythms for the soul of each and every song. It helped land Soil on some of the heaviest tours trundling across the US at the time – they paid their dues with Rob Zombie, Ozzy Osbourne and Mudvayne, among many others, as well as taking a slot at Ozzfest. In total thirteen months of touring established Soil as one of the meanest and tightest bands on the circuit.

Next up the *Pride* EP gave a taster of what was to come, the stuttering and belligerent title track kicking off their next album, *Redefine* (2004). Whereas *Scars* had been about straightahead groove and barbed hooks, the new songs layered on the darkness with relish, touches of grungy suffering oozing up from the sludgy riffing, not least on the Alice In Chains-esque "Can You Heal Me", featuring McCombs doing an uncannily authentic impression of Layne Staley. It was a performance of great power which made the announcement a few months later that McComb was leaving due to family commitments all the more surprising.

⊙ Scars
2001; J Records

The quality is high throughout and break-out single "Halo", with its insistent melodic hook, is an obvious highlight. Elsewhere this set reminds occasionally of prime Machine Head, Pantera and Metallica, which must be a good thing.

SOULFLY

Formed Phoenix, Arizona, US, 1997

"Heavy music survives all the trends and stays strong." Max Cavalera

Soulfly are one of the few bands to truly push the boundaries of what is acceptable within the metal genre; their pioneering attitude to music and style can be laid at the door of founding member and key songwriter **Max Cavalera** (bass/vocals). Cavalera's career path has not been easy – he has been victim of both personal tragedy and music business strife – but the more he has been pushed around by outside forces, the more doggedly determined and uncompromising he has become.

The Soulfly journey began during particularly dark days for the dreadlocked frontman.

Having created the thrash-meets-world-music classic *Roots* (1996) with his former group **Sepultura**, Cavalera found himself ousted from the band he had started. Not only that but he had to deal with the death of his stepson at virtually the same time. Such a turbulent and troubled time might well have led to him hanging up his bass for good, but instead the result was a period of grieving that fed a tornado of creativity: Soulfly was born, the vehicle for Cavalera's tormented outpourings.

The first eponymous, **Ross Robinson**-produced album was released in 1998, featuring **Jackson Bandeira** (guitar), **Marcello D. Rapp** (bass) and **Roy Mayorga** (drums) as key players, and immediately catapulted the band into a flurry of Ozzfest-related activity. Inevitably, comparisons with *Roots* were made, but what was apparent was that amid the cathartic raging and roaring, Cavalera was gradually edging towards a sound

SOUTHERN ROCK

Take a little Delta blues, a touch of 60s psychedelia, plus a dash of outlaw country and add it to a basic hard-rock formula; the result is the phenomenon of southern rock. The bands of the era would often bedeck their stage sets with the confederate flag and generally celebrate all things southern, from moonshine to heading down Mexico way for a spot of hellraising.

Without doubt the peak period for this form of rock'n'roll was the 70s and 80s, and one of the major locales responsible for producing some of the best bands was Jacksonville, Florida. **Duane Allman** of the Allman Brothers Band is often accorded the honour of having brought blues slide guitar into the formula, making it a ubiquitous weapon in the southern rock armoury. One of the acknowledged giants of the genre was Lynyrd Skynyrd, who are still touring, having long since recovered from the 1977 plane crash that derailed their stellar career for a decade. Other successful practitioners include the hard-edged Blackfoot, who really started cooking in the late 70s with *Strikes*, plus **Molly Hatchet** and **.38 Special**.

While Skynyrd can be thought of as rootsier rockers – as indeed can the gospel-flavoured country-blues of **Black Oak Arkansas** – Molly Hatchet purveyed a more commercially polished and boogiefied sound. They looked set for the top, debuted with a single cover of the Allman's "Dreams I'll Never See" and were at their peak on the fine *Flirtin' With Disaster* (1979), but lost ground after losing frontman **Danny Joe Brown**. .38 Special boasted **Donnie Van Zant** – younger brother of Lynyrd Skynyrd singer Ronnie Van Zant – as front man and started off in a relatively authentic southern rock fashion on their eponymous 1977 debut before gradually introducing more straight-ahead melodic rock and AOR elements until they lost the plot completely.

While the UK enjoyed the bluesy boogie of **Status Quo** in their 70s heyday, arguably the titans of the sound were the US's ZZ Top who truly went global with their own brand of Delta-blues inspired rock in the 80s. While MTV allowed the likes of the **Georgia Satellites** a brief shot at the charts with their excellent 1986 eponymous major-label debut and singles such as "Battleship Chains" and "Keep Your Hands To Yourself", the kings of technology-driven, cyber-boogie were the two-thirds bearded trio from Texas. They were already a massive draw in the 70s, especially in the States, but their harnessing of deep-fried southern musical traditions to crisp, modern production sounds allowed them to cross over into the mainstream like no other southern band has managed since.

Since the success of ZZ Top the only southern-flavoured outfit to truly enjoy anything like mainstream acceptance has been the Black Crowes. The Crowes' style largely eschews commercial polish in favour of a more organic and rough-hewn sound going back to the jamming ethic and psychedelic rock of the 60s and 70s; as a result they have more in common with the pioneers of the original style. Considering music with a more metallic edge, US stoner bands sometimes feature southern vibes within their make-up, with the hillbilly menace of **Alabama Thunder Pussy** and crunching power of **Corrosion Of Conformity** being among the best.

that would stretch beyond the template he had created; he didn't want to be saddled with a static band line-up, so various guest stars were drafted in to bring different flavours to the thrash, which was also peppered with ethnic percussion and a variety of unusual instrumentation; **Chino Moreno** (**Deftones**), Benji (Skindred), and **Fred Durst** (**Limp Bizkit**), among others, brought their own unique qualities to the songs.

By the time of *Primitive* (2000) Cavalera had earned himself the title of the Bob Marley of metal, an idea underlined by the decision to have the album sleeve created by long-time Marley designer Neville Garrick. The studio line-up had shifted to include new drummer **Joey Nunez** and ex-**Snot** guitarist **Mikey Doling**, while the vocal guest turns came thick and fast: **Tom Araya** (**Slayer**), **Corey Taylor** (**Slipknot**), **Grady Avenell** (Will Haven), Chino Moreno (again) and, surprisingly, **Sean Lennon**. Of the latter writing collaboration Cavalera told the press: "That was definitely the most diverse moment on the record. I met him in Australia in 1999 doing the Big Day Out festival and we became friends. I found out he was a fan of what I do and he knew a lot about my music which surprised me at first, but then talking about stuff there were more similarities between what he likes and what I like; Sean wasn't so far away as people think

to work with me. It's just when you say those names together you go whoah!" The two collaborated on "Son Song", which was co-produced by Lennon, and dealt with living without a father from an early age, something both musicians had experienced. The mix of mellowness and aggression was one of the most unusual aspects of an album that pushed Cavalera's usual cocktail of political, social and spiritual concerns into areas that had listeners both delighted and perplexed.

Two years down the line and Cavalera was trying to defy expectation yet again with *III*. "I decided to do something totally different to the last record. The last one had a lot of different people on it, which I enjoy very much, but I thought about going a little more back to the roots of the past." he told the press. By now, the one thing fans could expect was to be regaled with an increasingly diverse selection of sounds and sure enough the basic, downtuned thrash was complemented by an Indian and Middle Eastern vibe.

The diverse manifesto continued on *Prophecy* (2004). The line-up this time included **Marc Rizzo** (guitar; ex-Ill Niño), and the combined bass skills of **Bobby Burns** (ex-Primer 55) and **Dave Ellefson** (ex-**Megadeth**) with Cavalera insisting that their respective nu- and old-school metal influences brought different qualities to the songs. And then there were the experiments with sheepskin bagpipes, Serbian gypsies, flamenco guitar and dub, not to mention the distinctly reggae touch of the crowned lion on the sleeve.

 Soulfly
1998; Roadrunner

The Ross Robinson touch brings a distinctly nu-metal sheen to the Sepultura-flavoured thrash, but this is Max's baby through and through. Grief, rage and emotional torment pour out in a torrent of raw, primal riffing.

 Prophecy
2004; Roadrunner

The world music stance makes this one of Cavalera's most interesting albums. The desire to experiment is strong but rooted in the epic bombast that made Sepultura into thrash gods.

SOUNDGARDEN

Formed Seattle, US, 1985; disbanded 1997

Alongside Alice In Chains, **Soundgarden** were among the more metallic representatives of the Seattle sound. All grinding atonal riffing and raving vocals they garnered both critical acclaim and represented a radical, though no less heavy, departure from the normal metal shenanigans of the mainstream.

The initial line-up consisted of **Chris Cornell** (vocals), **Kim Thayil** (guitar), **Hiro Yamamoto** (bass) and **Matt Cameron** (drums) and specialized in being as left of centre as it's possible for a metal band to be. Cornell's shrieking vocals complemented perfectly Thayil's squalling, feedback-driven style, all Sabbath doom and punk abandon. It was all viciously driven by a rhythm section fuelled by weird time signatures. This stormy psychedelic brew of metal and punk led to an early signing with the legendary Sub Pop and the release of various singles and EPs – "Hunted Down", "Screaming Life" and "FOPP" – during the period between 1987 and 1988. Of course, there was a distinct whiff of grungy change in the air at the time and various major labels were keen to tap into the raw potential lurking in Seattle's seamy underground scene. But Soundgarden chose the uncompromising route for their debut and issued the brazen *Ultramega OK* (1988) on the indie SST.

The early EPs had all been raw and manically driven slabs of surging noise and the band's debut offered more of the same, veering from spacy drone-metal to hardcore, punky thrashing. When finally they came to sign with A&M, their new masters got yet more in *Louder Than Love* (1989). They took their love of 70s hard rock and metal and pounded it almost beyond recognition in a welter of off-kilter melodies and man-on-the-edge screaming; it was a huge, menacing and utterly compelling expression of idiosyncratic songwriting, which largely seemed to baffle audiences.

Louder Than Love was the last recording featuring Yamamoto, who was first replaced by **Jason Everman** (ex-**Nirvana**) and then more permanently by **Ben Shepherd**. During 1990 Cornell and Cameron took part in the **Temple Of The Dog** project – recording an eponymous album as a tribute to

friend and musician Andrew Wood of Mother Love Bone, who had died of a drug overdose. This project also featured future **Pearl Jam** members **Jeff Ament**, **Stone Gossard**, **Mike McCready** and **Eddie Vedder**. For anyone disturbed by Soundgarden's love of shit-kicking noise, the heartfelt, purely emotional outpouring came as something of a revelation, but it was an exercise whose accessibility seeped through to Soundgarden's next album. The gradual change in sound from fiery but perverse metal to a more focused but no less edgy style gave *Badmotorfinger* (1991) just the impetus it needed to break through the confusion and appeal to the mainstream without compromising the group's integrity. It was a revelatory record that broke them into arenas the world over, helped along mightily by a support slot with Guns N' Roses.

Singles "Outshined", "Rusty Cage" and "Jesus Christ Pose" all charted with a vengeance, while *Temple Of The Dog* (1991) went to #5 in the US. The rise in profile also landed them a place on the soundtrack to Cameron Crowe's Seattle rom-com *Singles* with the breeze-block riffing of "Birth Ritual". Cornell also contributing a solo effort in the acoustic and markedly Zeppelin-esque "Seasons".

With *Badmotorfinger* rapidly going platinum, a 1993 tour with the man many were hailing as the godfather of grunge, Neil Young, preceded the awesome *Superunknown* (1994). While *Badmotorfinger* had featured more streamlined writing, the new album refined things further to include the laid-back psychedelia of "Black Hole Sun" and "Fell On Black Days", the percussive strangeness of "Spoonman" and the typically miserable "The Day I Tried To Live", which all charted. From Seattle noise-hogs to the elite of alt metal, Soundgarden's progress brought a neat crop of industry accolades, including a Grammy for "Spoonman".

The assured nature of their genius and consistently even output made the era of *Down On The Upside* (1996) all the more puzzling. The self-produced album was chock-full of Soundgarden gems – "Pretty Noose", "Burden In My Hand" and "Blow Up The Outside World" were singles of real quality – but somehow the whole was less satisfying, the cohesion and purpose of *Superunknown* now a muted and fading echo. Touring commitments completed, the band decided by mutual consent to call it a day in April 1997. Even though Soundgarden clearly had the individual vision to range well beyond the confines of a mere pigeon-holing tag, grunge, it seemed, was grinding to a halt and was carrying the band's fortunes with it.

Two years down the line and Cornell was the only member to launch an alternative career of real, high-profile note. His occasional introspective and powerful solo outings led to *Euphoria Morning* (1999), a mature and bleak collection of songs combining Soundgarden's more considered musical elements with his own skewed world vision. And come 2002 he popped up again as lead singer in supergroup **Audioslave** alongside three-quarters of **Rage Against The Machine**.

Louder Than Love
1989; A&M

Deliberately odd and wilful, Soundgarden sound gloriously pissed off, yet exude enough intelligence and humour to make this a classic of early grunge. Cornell's lyrics range from the oblique on "Ugly Truth", via the socially conscious on "Hands All Over", to the ironic on "Big Dumb Sex".

Badmotorfinger
1991; A&M

Gone are the squeals and feedback. In their stead comes bitter and twisted metal of a more economic and dark variety, bristling with barbed hooks and black intentions. Another classic.

Superunknown
1994; A&M

A world beater. Huge riffs, depressing lyrics and big fat choruses make this a triumph of invention and wit. The eclectic range of material propelled the album into the Top 5 in the UK and straight to #1 in the US.

SPINAL TAP

Given the legendary status of *This Is Spinal Tap* as a mock metal documentary – some critics dubbing it one of the funniest films of all time – it's odd to think that upon its release in 1984 it was a relative failure. It has many features in common with the British *Comic Strip Presents* creation *Bad News Tour*, but outstrips the latter TV production for sheer scale and scope. *Bad News* was concerned with the exploits of a terrible metal band setting off on their first tour whereas the Spinal Tap boys were stars once and are keen to recapture their glory

days, even though circumstances beyond their control render their comeback a total disaster.

The film was **Rob Reiner**'s directorial debut and he also played the role of documentary-maker Marty DiBergi. The hugely talented cast included **Michael McKean** (David St. Hubbins, vocals/guitar/manipulative girlfriend), **Christopher Guest** (Nigel Tufnel, guitar/amps that go to eleven) and **Harry Shearer** (Derek Smalls, bass/cucumber). The acute deadpan style of the production skewered not just some of the most ludicrous aspects of 70s and early 80s metal, but satirized the fickle nature of the fame game, giving the film far greater depth than if it had just consisted of a string of sketches. Some of the incidents in the movie were even based on real events, though sadly not the spontaneously combusting drummer. All of which is a touch ironic seeing as the origins of the idea date back to characters created for an American television comedy special from the late 70s called *The TV Show*.

The film was accompanied by an album, *This Is Spinal Tap* (1984), featuring such classics as "Big Bottom" – once covered by Soundgarden – and "Sex Farm". It wasn't until eight years later – during which time the film had gained a massive cult following through its video release – that the joke was revived when Spinal Tap played the Freddie Mercury tribute gig, dubbed A Concert For Life, at Wembley Stadium. In addition, the Tap also played the Albert Hall and the gig was recorded for later video release. Of course, another album was issued, *Break Like The Wind* (1992) – featuring guest appearances from **Slash**, Toto's **Steve Lukather**, **Joe Satriani**, **Cher** and **Jeff Beck** – and even a couple of charting singles, "Bitch School" and the brilliant "The Majesty Of Rock".

The Albert Hall footage turned up as part of *The Return Of Spinal Tap* video in 1999, with interwoven rockumentary-style cutscenes. It wasn't as funny and didn't reward repeated viewings but fans of the original film did finally get to see the special edition DVD version, which included loads of the footage that was trimmed for theatrical release in 1984. Mind you, for real aficionados of the inept Tap, the Holy Grail is the rumoured rough edits of the film. Much of it was ad-libbed by the cast and hours of film were shot before being edited down. There

Mick Hutson/Redferns

Nigel Tufnel breaks like the wind.

break to one **Fred Durst** of **Limp Bizkit** infamy.

The band's history began at a Christmas party when singer **Aaron Lewis** met guitarist **Mike Mushok**. The two decided to pool their talents with **Jon Wysocki** (drums) and eventually **Johnny April** (bass) to thrash through some of their darkest nightmares in as heavy a style as possible. They played their first gig in February 1995. Desperate to get some of their songs out to the people of New England, where they were garnering increasing waves of grass-roots level support, they decided to record *Tormented* (1996) for sale at gigs. Things could have ticked along quite nicely with the band getting precisely nowhere other than the handful of venues they could drive to, but then their buddies in Sugarmilk asked them along to support Limp Bizkit in Hartford, Connecticut.

At this point one might assume that baseball-capped Fred materialized in fairy-godmother guise, waved his magic wand and gave them a record deal. Except that that wasn't quite how things played out. In fact Durst hated them almost instantly and wanted them thrown off the bill. The reason? The artwork for *Tormented* featured a blood-spattered Bible impaled on a knife and a Barbie doll nailed to a crucifix. Like the music, the cover was a DIY job and pretty standard fare for a metal band, really. Durst, however, being a spiritual kind of guy, thought they were in league with Satan and made his feelings known in no uncertain terms, despite their protests and explanations as to the cover's symbolism. They could feel their big fat break going up in smoke. Maybe that inspired them to inject their frustrations even harder into their set; shortly after they had finished their slot, Durst reappeared and said they were one of the best bands he had seen over the last couple of years. After Mushok finally got some demos to him, Durst invited the band down to his base in Florida to work on their nu-material, and the rest, as they say, is history.

is, apparently, a bootleg version of the film clocking in at between four and five hours, but even that is as nothing compared to whisperings about a whopping ten-hour cut lurking somewhere in the vaults.

STAIND

Formed Springfield, Massachusetts, US, 1994

Anguished, miserable and able to sell millions of records with a single frown, **Staind** are one of nu-metal's more versatile frontline outfits, capable of both teeth-jarring heaviness and heart-melting sadness. And, in common with some of their baggy-trousered, wallet-chained peers, they owe their big

Stoner And Space Rock

Grindingly heavy and awesomely groovy with it, stoner rock owes its distinctive jamming style and sound to the formative era of heavy rock and metal back in the late 60s and early 70s. That and copious amounts of herbal relaxant.

The chief element that usually defines the stoner identity is a guitar style evocative of early **Black Sabbath**, though without the overly doomy twist which would send the music off on a related but slightly different course. Another aspect is the psychedelic edge and sci-fi/fantasy themes of the lyrics and artwork, a thread that leads back to early space rock outfits such as Hawkwind. These proto-typical space cadets and perennial free-festival favourites made a name for themselves back in the 70s with their strobe-laden hard rock thrum refracted through vast amounts of mind-altering substances and a taste for Michael Moorcock fantasy fiction. At times the line-up boasted anything up to ten people and their back catalogue is equally as excessive; any serious student of tripped-out metal will probably find any of the albums featuring **Lemmy** well worth investigating. For many fans the expansive and riffy *Space Ritual* (1973) offers the peak of space rock perfection, though *Warrior On The Edge Of Time* (1975), featuring Moorcock himself, is an extraordinary experience as well.

Any rock'n'roll astronauts out there wanting to get truly lost in space may also wish to dip into the freaked-out delights of the **Pink Fairies** – who shared the stage every now and then with Hawkwind, as well as lending them the odd musician – plus such German acts as **Amon Düül II**, **Can**, **Faust**, **Tangerine Dream** and those loveable pothead pixies, France's **Gong**. All things considered it wouldn't be way off the mark to describe space rock as basically hippie music fuelled on large quantities of psychotropic drugs, a big dose of krautrock and a barking mad line in electronic experimentalism. These days the space rock torch is carried in many forms, with the likes of festival veterans **Ozric Tentacles** sticking fairly closely to the original tenets, while **The Orb** and ex-Gong guitarist **Steve Hillage** (under the banner of System 7) provide an ambient/trance manifestation of the interstellar vibe. On the distinctly more guitar-led front, bands such as **Radiohead** and **Anathema** also reflect some of the mercurial majesty of space rock; the latter in particular owing a debt to early Pink Floyd.

During the 80s the Sabbath influence was most pronounced in the growth of the doom scene, but in the early 90s modern stoner took off in a major way with **Queens Of The Stone Age**-forerunners **Kyuss** – helped along by Masters Of Reality mainman **Chris Goss** as producer – whose legendary wilderness jam sessions led to the desert rock tag. While **Josh Homme** and his buddies were getting frazzled in the California sun, on the other side of the US, in New Jersey, **Dave Wyndorf** was powering up **Monster Magnet** for his own unique take on 60s and 70s psychedelia. As the US scene continued to thrive through the activities of bands such as **Fu Manchu** and offshoot **Nebula**, the sound took on its own unique twist in other locations around the globe, not least in the UK, with the likes of **Orange Goblin**, **Firebird** and **Sally**, and notably in Sweden from whence **Spiritual Beggars** (featuring the ever-busy guitarist Michael Amott) began delivering their own powerful brand of herb-laced metal, best experienced on *Ad Astra* (2000) and *On Fire* (2002).

With Durst and Bizkit's **DJ Lethal** serving as A&R and a new deal with Flip Records, Staind were in an ideal position to scale the depths of nu-metaldom. Durst co-produced *Dysfunction* (1999), a set of bruising down-tuned delights and introspective wailing. Lewis had previously performed many acoustic solo sets, which gave the band a sensitive edge lacking in most of their contemporaries; his versatile vocals even gave them radio hits in "Just Go", "Mudshovel" and "Home". A plethora of awards and gig slots followed during which they happened on yet more luck on the Family Values Tour 1999 when Lewis decided one night to play an acoustic version of an unfinished track, "Outside". Whenever the song had been played in the past he had just ad-libbed the lyrics, but the tune was captured on tape with Durst singing along as well – suddenly they had a #1 radio hit on their hands. The live version and a full-band version were included on *Break The Cycle* (2001), a record which consolidated their nu-metal credentials but provided all sorts of intriguing possibilities for future development with the band's continuing acoustic and mellow experimentations; songs such as "It's Been A While" and "Epiphany" stepped off the gas and delivered their soul-searching lyrics with greater delicacy.

Maybe they could sense the nu-metal bandwagon losing its way but the softer aspects of the music were stretched across *14 Shades Of Grey* (2003) – a kiss-of-death title if ever there was one – summing up perfectly the contents. If *Break The Cycle* had indicated the radio-friendly way forward then the new album really was the sound of the nu-metal kids growing up. Buffed and polished to perfection, the songs largely followed the acoustic verse-and-big-soaring-chorus formula with Lewis's lyrical public therapy sessions seemingly never-ending. Commercial success was assured even as the musical wave that had birthed them was diminishing.

⊙ Dysfunction
1999; Flip/Elektra

Lots of shouting, lots of gnashing of teeth, plenty of grinding riffs. The sense of personal misery hangs over the lyrics like a black cloud of doom.

⊙ Break The Cycle
2001; Flip/Elektra

Nothing to do with Lewis falling off his bike, though he would doubtless have crowbarred a painful childhood memory such as that into one of the tunes here. Less laboured than *Dysfunction*, with all sorts of plush mellow moments to be found.

⊙ 14 Shades Of Grey
2003; Flip/Elektra

Beautifully honed radio metal for the new millennium. This band never liked guitar solos, but the mid-paced precision of these tunes makes them irritatingly catchy.

Stone Temple Pilots

Formed San Diego, California, US, 1991; disbanded 2003

"Did we turn into a butterfly or from a maggot into a fly? It could have been either way." Scott Weiland

Stone Temple Pilots are one of those bands that could have had it all but instead blew away what potential they had for longevity. Ironically, the main cause of their dysfunctional career trajectory was also one of their chief assets: the unpredictable talent of singer **Scott Weiland**. They began their platinum-selling ascent as archetypal grungers and then headed for their messy collision with destiny having developed into a band truly capable of surprising both their fans and critics by attempting something different with almost every album.

Back in the early 80s Weiland and **Robert DeLeo** (bass) met at a Black Flag concert in Long Beach. They were from diametrically opposed musical backgrounds – Weiland from punk, DeLeo from hard rock – but discovered that they were both seeing the same girl, and when she left town they moved into her empty apartment. Together they created a band called **Mighty Joe Young**, which eventually became known as Stone Temple Pilots. In addition to Weiland and DeLeo, it featured drummer **Eric Kretz** and – a while later – Robert's brother **Dean** on guitar.

The band made a decision to steer clear of the Los Angeles corporate music scene and instead build up their technique and following in the clubs of San Diego – a tactic that says much about their attitude and direction. Despite such honourable intentions it is hard to ignore the fact that they were ploughing the same musical furrow as Alice In Chains and Pearl Jam, which probably explained the rapid interest from Atlantic Records, with whom they signed in spring 1992.

The depth of the band's experience shone through on their masterly debut album *Core* (1992). Years of practice, coupled with **Brendan O'Brien**'s superb production, shot them to seemingly overnight success. "Sex Type Thing", "Plush" and "Creep" became firm video and radio favourites, but the album boasted a diversity of styles, with lyrics telling stories of twisted romance and alienation. What was more, Weiland's ability to dip into a variety of characters added immeasurably to the album's emotional depth.

The touring began with appearances on the Lollapalooza second stage, support slots with Megadeth, and an appearance at the MTV Spring Festivities. Eschewing the mainstream course briefly, they turned down a chance to tour with Aerosmith, and upheld their alternative credentials by co-headlining

his continuing chemical dependency resulted in his being admitted to a rehab clinic, throwing touring and recording schedules into chaos. Nonetheless, the band's third album, *Tiny Music ... Songs From The Vatican Gift Shop* (1996), was masterful, and combined cutting lyrics (often about the shallowness of corporate rock) with a fresh and open retro sound; tracks such as "Lady Picture Show" had a distinct Beatles flavour. By the end of the year Weiland appeared to have his problems under some kind of control and the band set about recovering the time lost by embarking on a modest tour of the US. The fan reaction suggested that the Pilots hadn't lost much in the way of momentum.

After this, however, the band rarely enjoyed a decent run of good luck. Whilst Weiland dealt with his addiction problems the remaining members worked on their side-project dubbed **Talk Show** and produced an album, *Talk Show* (1997). This, however, stiffed and though Weiland appeared to be in control of his vices he was yet again caught with narcotics. Throughout all this confusion, however, he managed to record and release a fairly well-received solo effort.

Amazingly, after all the turmoil, the Pilots managed to reconvene long enough to create *No. 4* (1999), which at least proved that their desire to continue remained strong, even though it wasn't exactly their best work. In the meantime Weiland got his act together and sobered up, becoming a family man in the process, but was eventually diagnosed as suffering from bipolar disorder, which results in bouts of depression, a possible partial cause for his behaviour. In interview he also claimed not to be taking his medication because it interfered with his creativity. In an attempt to maintain some consistency and credibility they released a much better album in *Shangri-La Dee Da* (2001), once again trading off their love of the Beatles and bold, heavy arrangements.

Sadly, it was an album that was largely overlooked because of Weiland's inability to stay out of trouble, and though his contributions as an artist made the Pilots a grunge metal

a national outing with the Butthole Surfers. The next year brought yet more live engagements and appearances at benefits for women's pro-choice causes.

In August 1993, still apparently keen to straddle both the alternative and mainstream camps, they played two sell-out shows at New York's Roseland Ballroom, where they sported full Kiss make-up in reverent emulation of their childhood heroes. Slipping easily from the wilfully bizarre to the prestigious, they also recorded an *MTV Unplugged* session, as their avalanche of success led to accolades from the music press and broadcast media.

With *Purple* (1994), Stone Temple Pilots opted for a more spontaneous live sound, and the album was completed within a month. Like its predecessor, it bristled with a bewildering range of textures and emotions, ranging from the fluid melody of the hit "Interstate Love Song" to the ethereal "Big Empty", which appeared on the film soundtrack to *The Crow*. An instant #1 album in the US, it was followed by the usual prolonged bouts of touring, interrupted only by the recording of a version of "Dancing Days" for the compilation *Encomium: A Tribute To Led Zeppelin* (1995).

Things were confused for the band, however. Weiland had developed a drug addiction and had brushes with the law – he was arrested for possession of cocaine and heroin – and original in a sea of copyists it was ultimately his behaviour that made them untenable. The label, presumably sensing that they were going to get little joy out of the Pilots again, trundled out the obligatory compilation album, simply titled *Thank You*, in 2003.

Since then, ironically, it has been Weiland who has popped up with the highest-profile comeback working with former **Guns N' Roses** stars **Slash, Duff McKagan, Matt Sorum** and Slash's mate **Dave Kushner** in a supergroup called **Velvet Revolver**. Suitably enough, after contributing to a couple of movie soundtracks, they released *Contraband* in 2004. Who knows how long the honeymoon will last…

⊙ Core
1992; Atlantic

Leaving aside similarities with some of Seattle's finest, this boasts wicked riffs, unforgettable hooks, and a menacingly charismatic performance from Scott Weiland. An exceptional debut.

⊙ Purple
1994; Atlantic

More songs of love and emptiness, by equal turns harsh and sweetly melodic. The live production sound gives the songs a furious urgency and a more haunting dimension, while the ironic 'easy-listening' epilogue is extremely funny.

⊙ Tiny Music ... Songs From The Vatican Gift Shop
1996; Atlantic

Another lurch through a whole menu of musical approaches, ranging from whimsical 60s pop through to scalding straight-ahead rock.

SUPERJOINT RITUAL

Formed Louisiana, US, 2000

There is no end to the projects that **Phil Anselmo** has a hand in, but with the tragic demise of **Pantera** the raging vocalist has spent more time on **Superjoint Ritual** than anything else, including sludge metallers **Down**. It's fair to say that this beyond-extreme-metal outfit is now his primary concern, though quite where he intends to go with it in the future is open to question given the emotional turmoil created by the tragic death of Pantera guitarist, Dimebag Darrell, in late 2004.

The history of the Superjoint stretches way back into the 90s when they began rehearsing and writing as a basement band. However, with the future of Texas groove metallers Pantera looking increasingly shaky during the late 90s Anselmo chose to take the Superjoint above ground and show nu-metal what pure, white-hot unadulterated rage really sounded like. He took on the role of singer and guitarist in the studio alongside his buddy from Down **Jimmy Bower** (guitar) and **Joe Fazzio** (drums), plus **Michael Haaga** (bass).

The result was astonishingly heavy, taking the battering speed of thrash and injecting a lethal dose of hardcore punk noise for good measure. *Use Once And Destroy* (2002) became Anselmo's calling card as he put together a titanic live line-up featuring **Kevin Bond** (guitar) and **Hank Williams III** (bass), grandson of the country music legend. Far from pandering to the mainstream or trying to cultivate continuity with Pantera, Anselmo's aim was to create the kind of music that fired him up in the first place and that meant taking tunes such as "Everyone Hates Everyone", "Alcoholik" and "Fuck Your Enemy" to the fans clamouring for ever more potent sounds. The live show was captured on the *Live In Dallas, Tx* (2002) DVD.

The second album, *A Lethal Dose Of American Hatred* (2003), was even more caustic than the first and intended to be a patriotic statement, an unashamedly pro-American record; tunes such as "Personal Insult" epitomized the belligerent stance. Elsewhere it was a thundering rampage through the dark side of modern existence: the drugs, the hate, the filth and violence. The live shows were, of course, hellishly intense and the band's growing reputation landed them a slot on Ozzfest 2004. The DVD *Live At CBGB: Changing The Face Of Music Through Uncompromising Anti-Image* (2004), on the other hand, displayed the power of the band in a more intimate setting.

⊙ A Lethal Dose Of American Hatred
2003; Mayan

This is a prime example of migraine metal. Unrelentingly mean-spirited and bleak, this album is the stuff of nightmares. There are no tunes or melodies as such, just merciless, pounding noise and Anselmo screaming oblivion.

THE SWEET

Formed UK, 1968

Usually associated with the bubblegum glam pop of their singles hits of the early 70s, **The Sweet** were, behind all the glitz, really a striking hard-rock band. Just one listen to the blazing performance on the remastered *Live At The Rainbow 1973* (1999) – originally part of *Strung Up* (1975) – should confirm the fact.

They started off as **The Sweetshop**, then trimmed their name down and headed into the early 70s with the classic line-up of **Brian Connolly** (vocals), **Andy Scott** (guitar/vocals), **Steve Priest** (bass/vocals) and **Mick Tucker** (drums/vocals) looking like walking adverts for Bacofoil – we're talking glitter outfits of outrageous campness here. Kiss looked like undertakers in comparison. Teamed up with ace pop writers **Nicky Chinn** and **Mike Chapman** they delivered high-charting tunes such as "Funny Funny", "Co-Co" and "Little Willy". It was all about saucy seaside postcard innuendo and risqué fun, but the band wanted to beef up their sound and enjoy greater writing input. Thus

Chinn and Chapman came up with the heavier pop rock of "Wig-Wam Bam", their classic #1 hit "Blockbuster", the awesome "Ballroom Blitz" and "Teenage Rampage".

In 1974 *Sweet Fanny Adams* marked their gradual move away from the Chinn/Chapman style. A couple of tunes belonged to the latter but elsewhere the band were striking out as hard rockers with their own ideas. Likewise, *Desolation Boulevard* (1975) contained only two Chinn/Chapman compositions and The Sweet scored a self-penned hit of their own, the #2 charting "Fox On The Run". *Give Us A Wink* (1976) was a bona fide Sweet album with no external songwriters. The US beckoned and the band spent a good deal of time abroad on a punishing tour schedule; in Europe and Scandinavia they became huge stars. *Off The Record* (1977) continued with the punchier direction while *Level Headed* (1978) delivered their last hit in the form of the Top 10 "Love Is Like Oxygen". And then Connolly declared that he was leaving to go solo in 1979, which meant the band continued as a trio with Scott singing for a while before they added **Gary Moberley** (keyboards).

Three albums – *Cut Above The Rest* (1979), *Water's Edge* (1980) and *Identity Crisis* (1982)

Sweet have been at the dressing-up box again.

RON HOWARD/REDFERNS

– were trundled out and though the tours were successful enough, one quarter of their former magic was off pursuing a slightly less heavy path. Eventually the band called it a day but their legacy lived on in the new generation of 80s glamsters. The enduring influence of the band was given a further boost when "Ballroom Blitz" featured heavily in the hit comedy movie *Wayne's World* in the early 90s. Various versions of the band had already re-formed and toured as far back as the mid-80s, but the renewed interest meant that two versions of the band – one fronted by Connolly, the other by Scott – could go on tour well into the 90s; in the

OFF THE RECORD

SWEET

case of Scott's line-up well into the new millennium. Sadly, in 1997 Connolly died as a result of liver failure, his health already seriously ravaged by the excesses of hard living from the 70s. Tucker also succumbed to illness when he died of leukaemia in early 2002.

⊙ Give Us A Wink
1976; RCA

There's no Chinn and Chapman here, just a whole lot of The Sweet. These are diamond-edged songs, bristling with tough riffs and bedecked with fine harmonies and hooks, plus a nice line in smutty lyrics.

⊙ Ballroom Hitz – The Very Best Of The Sweet 1996; Polygram

This is a fascinating trip through time, including all the early hits, from "Funny Funny" right through to "Love Is Like Oxygen". One minute they're a lightweight bubblegum band, the next they're smacking you over the head with some mean-sounding guitar grind. Sweet indeed.

SYSTEM OF A DOWN

Formed Los Angeles, US, 1995

Of all the bands to emerge from the mid-90s nu-metal morass, **System Of A Down** are surely the most original and thought-provoking of the lot.

Way back in the early 90s, somewhere in the seedy netherworld of the Los Angeles music scene, two bands found themselves sharing a studio. **Daron Malakian** (guitar/vocals) was a member of one outfit and **Serj Tankian** (vocals/keyboards) was a member of the other. A mutual appreciation society formed and soon the two of them were joining forces in a band known as **Soil** with **Shavo Odadjian** (bass) managing them. A few line-up changes later and Odadjian was their official bass player with drummer **John Dolmayan** the final part of the equation, creating a unique metal band with an overt Armenian heritage. And the name? Look no further than a Malakian-penned poem called "Victims Of A Down". System was thought to be a stronger word for a band moniker, and so they set about turning the post-grunge world of rock upside down with a stunningly tight combination of disparate sounds, provocative political posturing and a stage show famed for its gymnastic intensity. Producer **Rick Rubin** witnessed one of their live meltdowns at the Viper Room in Hollywood and the band signed to American Recordings in September 1997.

The first recorded result of Rubin's collaboration with the band, *System Of A Down* (1998), left the metal scene reeling with its audacious synthesis of grinding metal, jazzy weirdness, thrash, rap, Middle Eastern and Armenian influences. Chief in creating this paradigm-busting noise was Tankian's bizarre vocal performance, captured on tape at Rubin's house, which veered between demon-possessed shriek and bowel-rupturing roar, sweetly turned melody and Middle Eastern-inflected stylings. The songs covered the personal and the political. "Soil" dealt with the suicide of a friend; "D-Devil" merged four of Tankian's poems and covered subjects as diverse as cloning and plagiarism; "Cubert" was about limited and clichéd people; "P.L.U.C.K" (Politically Lying, Unholy, Cowardly Killers) dealt with the Armenian genocide. Shot through with anger and an unfettered sense of artistic integrity the debut consolidated the hype that already surrounded the band. The same year found the band on the road with heavyweights Slayer and then taking part in the Ozzfest. System had truly arrived in style.

By the time of *Toxicity* (2001) the band's musical growth was evident as a result of some serious touring commitments. The album, once again, mashed together a plethora of different styles and featured the usual quirky and awesomely tight time changes. In terms of lyrics, the subject matter veered from the expected to the characteristically wacky – from acerbic political satire ("Prison Song"), to notorious killer Charles Manson's views on the environment ("Atwa").

The band's next album, however, seemed to come about more by accident than design. The emergence of *Steal This Album* (2002) was a result of various unreleased songs from the *Toxicity* sessions appearing on the Internet. System were forced to bring forward their plans for a trawl through the vaults to stem the flow of poor-quality bootlegged material. The resulting album was properly mixed and mastered but packaged to look exactly like a homemade bootleg compilation and included material from all stages of the band's career.

What made the album particularly noteworthy was the inclusion of "Boom!", an antiwar song for which the band chose renowned film-maker **Michael Moore** to direct the video. Moore had previously directed Rage Against The Machine's "Sleep Now In The Fire" video and his political perspective marked him as a natural choice for System's polemics.

With the decks cleared of material the band were free to pursue other artistic endeavours. Odadjian began to develop his video directing skills by working on Taproot's promo clip for "Mine" before moving on to hip-hop videos; Tankian and Malakian started producing other bands – the latter actually helped out volatile punk metallers Amen issue their *Death Before Musick* album on his own EatUrMusic imprint. Incredibly, while all this activity continued, the band found time to begin work on their next album, taking time out to play the moving Souls concert at the Greek Theater in Los Angeles on 24 April 2004 – remembrance day for the Armenian genocide. The aim was to raise awareness and money for charity and, naturally, the song "P.L.U.C.K." took on a special resonance.

It was a year before the band gigged again in the US. The Souls 2005 benefit show was a perfect opportunity to unveil songs on their massive two-part album: *Mezmerize* was released in May 2005 with its follow-up *Hypnotize* arriving in the autumn.

System Of A Down
1998; American

Raw and brutal, the band's Armenian heritage shines through in the vocal stylings while the metal provides a powerful and coruscating counterpoint. Includes the radio hit "Sugar".

Toxicity
2001; American

A major leap in creativity. The band's previous tendency to bludgeon a musical idea half to death during a song has been replaced with a more polished songwriting ability. There is much greater melody within the madness.

TAPROOT

Formed Ann Arbor, Michigan, US, 1997

The unassumingly pretty town of Ann Arbor might seem like the last place from which one of the best exponents of nu-metal might hail, but in an age in which the cunning use of cutting-edge technology can make all the difference, Taproot's rise is a fine example of the DIY ethic producing amazing results.

In the mid-1990s **Jarrod Montague** (drums) and **Mike DeWolf** (guitar) were both students at the University of Michigan, in love with music and keen to get a band going. Via a housemate, the two hooked up with **Stephen Richards** (vocals/programming) and **Phil Lipscomb** (bass), the result being plenty of loud and raucous jam sessions working on cover versions and some original material. Local gigging gradually built up their reputation, and the fledgling group burned copies of CDs for friends. Through their own website they let people know about upcoming gigs and started to promote their recordings, most notably their self-produced and financed debut album *Something More Than Nothing* (1998).

Taproot were looking likely to make it big, with interest from major labels, when their Internet activities garnered the attention of **Limp Bizkit** vocalist and industry mover and shaker **Fred Durst**. Durst could hear the potential in Taproot's nascent nu-metal noodlings and promised them a tasty deal. Unfortunately, the deal wasn't quite tasty enough for Taproot and they eventually went with Atlantic Records, resulting in a now notorious expletive-packed phone message left by the aggrieved Durst. Such toxic outpourings were not, however, as scorching as those on the band's major-label debut *Gift* (2000). It was casebook emotional turmoil set to bowel-quaking downtuned riffery, an angsty cocktail loaded with plenty of anger and bile. **Ozzy Osbourne**'s son **Jack** landed them an all-important spot at 2000's Ozzfest. Their trajectory was set when they made a repeat Ozzfest appearance the following year, the period in between punctuated with support slots for the cream of alternative metal. Sharing stages with the likes of Papa Roach, Linkin Park, Incubus and the Deftones exposed them to a perfect cross-section of the nu-metal-loving public.

In 2001, with pre-production under way for the follow-up album, producer **Toby**

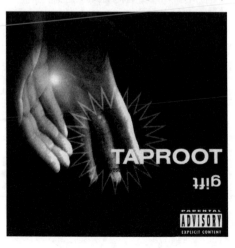

Ten Top Live Albums

It's possible to unleash a great band on stage and end up, at best, with a very mediocre result on tape. So what makes for a great live album? It all needs to be in place, that critical fusion of atmosphere, an extraordinary performance and a certain unquantifiable energy. What's more, if the conditions are right, the captured live experience can define a band's identity, becoming far more than just a stopgap or a way to fulfil contractual obligations to the record company.

The Who *Live At Leeds* (1970; MCA Reissued 2001)
Townshend supervised the remixing process for this album when the entire concert was finally made available. Aside from storming versions of their early songs it contains a near flawless performance of their rock opera *Tommy*; the energy level is quite incredible.

Deep Purple *Made In Japan* (1973; EMI Reissued 1998)
It's worth picking up this awesome live showcase in expanded form for the extra encore tracks. All together this is great fun – especially when Gillan cracks up during "Strange Kind Of Woman" – and the 20-minute version of "Space Truckin'" is hard to beat.

AC/DC *If You Want Blood – You've Got It* (1978; Atlantic Reissued 1998)
The last word in live hard-rock albums. If the amplifier hum and opening notes of "Riff Raff" don't hook you, then you must be dead. This album takes the studio tracks and transforms them into timeless classics, complete with extended solos and a crowd presence that is simply electric. Definitive and indispensable.

Aerosmith *Live Bootleg* (1978; CBS)
Packaged in a mock bootleg form, this amazing double album features some stupendously warts'n'all performances that are nothing short of terrific. "Sweet Emotion", "Toys In The Attic", "Sick As A Dog" and a nice'n'sleazy "Mama Kin" show just how swaggering and near-the-knuckle this lot could be in the pre-MTV era.

Cheap Trick *At The Budokan* (1978; Columbia Reissued 1998)
Live albums were ubiquitous when this little beauty first arrived. Though it had originally been intended as a Japan-only release it gave the band their first US top-ten single in "I Want You To Want Me". It was stunning on vinyl all those years ago and the twentieth anniversary CD reissue reinstates the songs originally cut due to lack of space.

Thin Lizzy *Live And Dangerous* (1978; Vertigo)
In the studio the band sometimes struggled to define their sound but this raw set – helped along by the odd overdub – captured Lizzy at their finest. The standout cuts are many, but the epic "Still In Love With You" makes for a superb mid-point peak.

Motörhead *No Sleep 'Til Hammersmith* (1981; Castle Communications Reissued 2001)
Setting the standard for rock live albums in the 80s, this contains proven crowd-pleasers throughout. Lemmy and the boys have rarely sounded this dirty and incisive on record. As with other early album rereleases, this version contains a number of excellent bonus tracks. A lesson in how to make something great even better.

Iron Maiden *Live After Death* (1985; EMI)
Singer Bruce Dickinson's cry of "Scream for me Long Beach!" has gone down in metal history as a catch-all quote, underlining the importance of this pounding double album. From the stunning sleeve, featuring mascot Eddie bursting free of the grave, to the acutely paced set recorded during the marathon World Slavery tour, this is the business, the well-oiled Maiden machine a titanic metal marvel crisscrossing the globe delivering a spectacular show night after night.

Nirvana *Unplugged* (1994; Geffen)
Cobain clearly shows his influences by leading the band through a set studded with covers from artists as diverse as David Bowie and Leadbelly. Stripped of their electric bludgeon the original songs are delivered with a clarity and force of emotion rarely heard, making this one brilliantly depressing set; "Pennyroyal Tea" has never sounded so ethereal and cleansing.

Led Zeppelin *How The West Was Won* (2003; Atlantic)
Ignoring the flawed *The Song Remains The Same*, it's amazing to think that for a band that excelled live, Zeppelin never had a proper gig document to their name. Guitarist Jimmy Page stumbled across the tapes for this set while trawling through the archives and the result is incredible; "Dazed And Confused" clocks in at over 25 minutes and "Whole Lotta Love" at just over 23, the band throwing in a selection of blues classics along the way.

Wright suggested that the band ought to loosen up its approach to songwriting. The result was the surprisingly mature *Welcome* (2002) which, far from treading the expected path of yet more post-adolescent raging, took a distinctly melodic direction reminiscent of Alice In Chains – not surprising really, considering Wright had worked with the latter band. Richards' cathartic lyrical leanings were still present and correct, as were the occasional lapses into nu-metal bawling, but for the most part the album charmed with its poised and measured melodic tack, even if the overall effect was rather maudlin and melodramatic. With the second album in the bag, the band hit the road once more with a seriously heavy bout of touring, before settling into the studio to create *Blue-Sky Research* (2005), with producer Michael Beinham.

 Gift
2000; Atlantic

Staccato riffs and relentless rhythms bounce around with fearsome abandon. Production is handled by the marvellously monikered **Ulrich Wild** – a man who, having worked with the likes of Pantera and Powerman 5000, knows a thing or two about heavy sounds.

TERRORVISION

Formed Bradford, UK, 1987; disbanded 2001; re-formed 2005

"We've been listening to heavy metal on eleven – and it's prompted us to record a country and western album!"
Leigh Marklew

Cheekier than a nudist camp on a hot day, lovably daft and shamelessly poppy, **Terrorvision** were from the Slade school of songwriting: make it loud and make it tuneful. The 1990s were the ideal playground for their distinctly English and idiosyncratic brand of hard rock, allowing them to rack up a decent run of hits, all the while having one hell of a good time.

The band consisted of **Tony Wright** (vocals), **Mark Yates** (guitar), **Leigh Marklew** (bass) and **Shutty** (drums), who originally came together as the **Spoilt Bratz** – a cartoonish name that somehow seems mightily appropriate given the Terrorvision sound.

Nevertheless they became Terrorvision and signed to EMI under their own imprint of Total Vegas, their first release being the *Thrive* EP in early 1992. The enjoyably loopy "My House" followed but on its first try it didn't trouble the singles chart, which was heaving under the onslaught of bands such as Nirvana. Their debut album was the fun *Formaldehyde* (1992), showcasing the band's ability to pen odd but catchy songs such as "American TV" and "New Policy One", both of which teased the lower reaches of the charts with their instantly appealing melodies – the latter taking liberties with the riff from the Police's "Every Breath You Take".

Good old-fashioned hard work made *How To Make Friends And Influence People* (1994) their breakthrough album. It went into the UK Top 20 and suddenly Terrorvision became synonymous with great sing-along rock'n'roll. Both "Middleman" and "Oblivion", the latter with its genius "doo wop" refrain, introduced them to *Top Of The Pops*; the only time they got remotely close to sounding serious was with the string-laden "Some People Say" and the slightly darker "Alice, What's The Matter?" – and even they featured the odd incongruous line guaranteed to raise a smile.

This combination of polished hooks and heaviness hit a critical highpoint with the top-ten *Regular Urban Survivors* (1996) album, preceded by the annoyingly memorable top-five single "Perseverance". This time round, the band presented themselves as widescreen heroes, the album sleeve being a cool pastiche of James Bond-style action-movie posters. The songs inside were equally adventurous, pushing their quirky edge to the max with tunes such as "Dog Chewed The Handle" and the masterfully mad "Hide The Dead Girl". The hits kept coming, and there was no reason to believe that they wouldn't match the standard on their next effort.

Sadly, *Shaving Peaches* (1998) suffered from a case of two many cooks: four producers were involved because Terrorvision couldn't find a suitable one who was free for long enough to do the entire album. The songs struggled through the uneven energy levels, and though they scored a #2 hit with a remixed version of "Tequila" – a tribute to a spirited binge that resulted in Wright breaking his legs while on tour – they weren't shifting enough units and EMI dropped them.

They bounced back with *Good To Go* (2001) on Papillon Records but things didn't look rosy with the new album sitting next to *Whales And Dolphins* (2001), EMI's 'best of' compilation. Sadly, when the new album stiffed it was thank you and goodnight from the boys from Bradford, though they did play a rapid one-off For One Week Only tour in early 2005.

ⓞ **Regular Urban Survivors**
1996; Total Vegas

This album is simply brimming over with great songs such as "Celebrity Hit List", "Bad Actress" and "Easy". It should have sold loads and turned them into superstars.

TESLA

Formed Sacramento, California, US, 1985; disbanded 1995; re-formed 2000

Named after the belatedly acknowledged inventor of radio, Nikola Tesla, this five-piece are surely one of the least pretentious bands to have made it big in the 1980s. A glance at the sleeve of their debut album *Mechanical Resonance* (1986) reveals a combo with a penchant for fluffy hair, but any overtly glamorous touches were left at the door. Tesla were about melodic hard rock of the 70s old school – more Montrose and early Aerosmith than the dopey posing of the majority of 80s rockers. So it was jeans and T-shirts, plenty of shape-throwing and a tireless blue-collar work ethic for this lot. "No machines!" proclaimed the sleeve proudly, and it wasn't lying: what you heard live was

exactly what you got on record – only a thousand times louder of course.

They originally came together under the name **City Kidd** with the stable line-up of **Jeff Keith** (vocals), **Frank Hannon** (guitar), **Tommy Skeoch** (guitar), **Brian Wheat** (bass) and **Troy Luccketta** (drums). Managed by **Cliff Burnstein** and **Peter Mensch** (who had worked with Metallica, Def Leppard, the Scorpions and AC/DC), they signed

to Geffen and appeared with sound almost fully formed on *Mechanical Resonance*. This was a record of tight and hooky hard-rock tunes displaying a maturity and finesse in the songwriting department it takes some bands half-a-dozen albums to achieve.

The album to truly get them noticed, however, was *The Great Radio Controversy* (1989). They had toured with Def Leppard, Alice Cooper and David Lee Roth and were now in a position where great things were expected from them. The second album delivered greater, grittier songs featuring some terrific dirt-under-the-fingernails solos from Hannon and Skeoch, but it was the largely acoustic, Free and Led Zep-flavoured "Love Song" that landed them with a US top-ten hit. If they'd listened to their record label it would never have been included on the album.

Ironically, it was the sensitive acoustic side of the band that sold the most records. *Five Man Acoustical Jam* (1990) narrowly missed out on the US Top 10. They inadvertently spawned the idea of unplugged live albums – which MTV would exploit so successfully – with a set that included a smattering of cover versions among a clutch of their own tunes stripped back to basics. Their cover of

"Signs", originally by Canadian hippies the Five Man Electrical Band (geddit?) did even better than "Love Song".

Their next effort *Psychotic Supper* (1992) featured the epic "Song And Emotion", dedicated to the memory of Def Leppard guitarist Steve Clark. The sound was a touch rawer, but *Psychotic Supper* would turn out to be the band's last supper as well. Grunge was just starting to take over the airwaves of the US and Tesla found that *Bust A Nut* (1994) – despite its heavier vibe and execution – just didn't whip up the kind of public fervour they were used to. They eventually split and the *Time's Makin' Changes* (1995) 'best-of' was their swansong.

The following years saw the various members playing in a variety of bands but when they finally played a one-off reunion in their hometown in 2000 they realized the chemistry was still there. They decided to tour and issued *Replugged Live* (2001), a double album featuring some of their best-loved songs belted out in front of thousands of screaming fans. A proper studio album was next and the forward-looking *Into The Now* (2004) saw the band return to the fray – almost as though they had never been away.

⊙ Psychotic Supper
1992; Geffen

The band reckon this is their finest set of songs and they're probably right. They were thriving on the intensely live feel of the recordings and hammering the songs home with the minimum of fuss. A gem, and no mistake.

TESTAMENT

Formed San Francisco, California, US, 1983

Testament surfed in on the so-called second wave of thrash in the mid-1980s, a time when many of their Bay Area brethren were already making waves. **Exodus** vocalist **Steve Souza** was in the line-up when they were known as **Legacy**, but the band personnel finally stabilized when the imposing figure of **Chuck Billy** (vocals) stepped in to complement **Eric Peterson** (guitar), **Alex Skolnick** (lead guitar), **Greg Christian** (bass) and **Louie Clemente** (drums). Billy provided a growl as formidable as his stage-commanding frame, which combined superbly with Skolnick's technical but fiery guitar style.

Their debut album, *The Legacy* (1987), was titled with a nod to their formative years and was released on Megaforce Records. It was hailed as an instant thrash classic: all scorching riffs and churning rhythms. The band had a lot of catching up to do, and they set about their task with great gusto over the next few years. The *Live At Eindhoven* (1987) mini-LP showcased the band in front of a rabid crowd in Holland – but their next studio effort truly made their name. *The New Order* (1988) featured a soon-to-be live favourite in "Disciples Of The Watch", but the real progress was in the writing and production, which sounded more focused and mature. Meanwhile, Skolnick was developing something of a well-earned reputation as a guitar wizard.

Practice What You Preach (1989) continued the trend with ever more inventive arrangements and a tight control on dynamics, their rising profile giving them their first UK top-forty album. But the desire to make a real breakthrough, coupled with bad timing, forced a compromise with their next album. The band were due to play on the major Clash Of The Titans tour alongside Slayer, Megadeth and Suicidal Tendencies and they needed an album ready in time. Many fans blame this for the drop in standards on *Souls Of Black* (1990); though the touring boosted the album into the Top 40 again the production lacked the necessary clout to do the songs justice. And then the next offering, *The Ritual* (1992), was an experiment too far for some. While still aggressive, the tempos were more mid-paced and the riffing never quite erupted into the full-tilt speed fans craved.

The changes may well have been down to Skolnick's desire to move away from metal and pursue his jazz leanings. He eventually left, marking a period during which only Billy and Peterson would remain unchanging elements in the band. **James Murphy** (guitar, ex-**Obituary**, ex-**Death**) stuck around for the bellicose *Low* (1994) and *Live At The Fillmore* (1995), while **John Tempesta** and **Jon Dette** respectively sat behind the drum kit. By now, Atlantic had presumably had enough of the band because their next effort arrived on Music For Nations. And, with nu-metal on the rise, Testament took on the challenge by becoming even heavier, calling their new album *Demonic* (1997) and getting **Gene Hoglan** (ex-**Dark Angel**, ex-Death) in on drums. For *The Gathering* (1999) Testament pulled

Testament: souls in black.

together an extraordinary line-up including Sadus bassist **Steve DiGiorgio** and **Slayer** drummer **Dave Lombardo**. The album raged with a white-hot intensity rarely matched in thrash circles.

The triumph, however, was muted by the news that Billy was suffering from a rare form of cancer and would have to spend some time receiving treatment. This did not stop the singer from instigating *First Strike Still Deadly* (2001), a fine collection of re-recorded songs from the band's formative days, with Skolnick and Souza as guests.

In the meantime Peterson unveiled his **Dragonlord** side-project, with *Rapture* (2001), a fusion of black metal stylings and pile-driving thrash of the old school. With Billy well on the road to recovery it was Peterson's turn to be put out of action: he fell down a flight of stairs before a European gig appearance and shattered his leg in three places. Nevertheless, as soon as he was able to drive to Testament's studio he began work on *The Gathering*'s true follow-up.

 **The Gathering**
1999; Spitfire

It may not be the sound of old Testament but the material on offer here is brutal and intense in the extreme. The band's command of dynamics is nothing short of breathtaking and Lombardo drives these songs along with a relentless and awesomely focused fury.

THIN LIZZY

Formed Dublin, Ireland, 1969

Way up there with the likes of Motörhead and AC/DC, **Thin Lizzy** were a band who lived it just like they played it. True advocates of the rock'n'roll lifestyle, they were just as at home in the middle of a boozed-up bar brawl as they were on stage. They were the epitome of 70s and 80s heavy rock values, with a renowned and charismatic songwriting genius leading them. Bass-playing, leather-trouser-sporting front man **Phil Lynott** – the son of Brazilian and Irish parents, sent to live in Dublin with his granny from an early age – was a genuine star, no question. He was capable of penning killer hit singles as well as smouldering, lighters-in-the-air ballads that would make women go weak at the knees, though his own personal demons (not to mention the booze and the drugs) would ultimately prevent him and the band from truly realizing their potential.

In fact, Thin Lizzy came damn near to never fulfilling any kind of promise at all in their early career. The band first came together when school friends Lynott and **Brian Downey** (drums), both of **Orphanage**, joined up with **Eric Bell** (guitar; ex-**Dreams**) and **Eric Wrixon** (keyboards). Wrixson lasted for only one single in 1970, the forgettable but collectable "The Farmer". Signed to Decca this line-up managed three rather lacklustre albums – *Thin Lizzy* (1971), *Shades Of A Blue Orphanage* (1972) and *Vagabonds Of The Western World* (1973), and one surprise classic hit single in "Whisky In The Jar", a reworking of an old Irish folk tune which went to #6 in the charts. Hit single or no, things just didn't seem to be moving as far as Bell was concerned – so he got out, leaving the band without a guitarist until ace six-stringer **Gary Moore**, who used to play with **Skid Row** (not to be confused with the Skid Row fronted by Sebastian Bach), stepped in. Moore, however, only stayed for four months, after which he was replaced by **Andy Gee** and **John Cann** (ex-**Atomic Rooster**) to complete touring commitments.

Lynott already had an idea that two guitars would be needed in the future so he recruited **Scott Gorham** and **Brian Robertson**; thus was born the famed Thin Lizzy twin-guitar attack. This line-up was powerful and extremely talented, leading to both great gigs and one of the band's most successful periods. *Nightlife* (1974) failed to give them any major hits but Lynott was honing his craft at last and the smoky, sultry ballad "Still In Love With You" was an album highlight and would go on to become a concert favourite.

However, progress was slow as the band chemistry had yet to develop, a situation hampered by Lynott's growing narcotic dependence. When it came, *Fighting* (1975) – with a cover featuring the band looking like a bunch of street thugs ready to punch someone's lights out – was a much better Lynott-produced set, kicking off with a rousing rendition of Bob Seger's classic "Rosalie" before

launching into "For Those Who Love To Live", a spirited celebration of the career of Irish footballer George Best.

Slowly, they were inching towards their ideal sound, and finally they struck gold with the Top 10 *Jailbreak* (1976), featuring the ideal concert-opening title track and a consistent set of quality tunes. The record was helped massively by hit single "The Boys Are Back In Town", a universally appreciated good-time party song that has been covered hundreds of times. On a roll they followed it up with *Johnny The Fox* (1976), another cocksure set of tough, street-level heavy rock driven by Lynott's Irish charm and craftsmanlike approach to great tunes; check out the cracking romantic irony of hit single "Don't Believe A Word".

It was a winning formula that faltered only when the drinking and brawling got the better of them; Robertson suffered a slashed hand defending a friend in a pub fight on the eve of a US tour, so Moore returned for the second of his turns with Lizzy, joining the band for a triumphant trek across America with Queen on the Queen Lizzy tour. When Robertson returned to the fold, *Bad Reputation* (1977) was another convincing slice of bad-boy boogie and was a British top-five hit.

The album that would finally ensure Lizzy's place in the rock firmament, however, was just around the corner. *Live And Dangerous* (1978) went to #2 in the album chart (held off the top spot by the soundtrack to *Grease*) and was hailed as a bona fide, 24-carat classic, the mutt's nuts of concert documents. Over time it has become regarded as the standard against which all other live rock albums are measured, which is somewhat ironic consid-

Phil Lynott on stage.

ering it was originally intended to be a stopgap effort to keep the fans going while they prepared for their next studio outing. The strength of *Live...* lay in its magical encapsulation of Lizzy in full flight, something which had eluded them somewhat in the studio. Plus, producer **Tony Visconti** masterminded a few sneaky overdubs here and there to buff what was already good into something terrific. From the ripping kick-off of "Jailbreak" through to the ballsy gallop of "The Rocker" it brought Lizzy leaping from the speakers and Lynott right into your front room.

Despite the triumph, though, Robertson wanted out of the band and went on to form **Wild Horses**, leaving the way open, once again, for Moore to step in and record *Black Rose (A Rock Legend)* (1979). It went to #2 again and proved to be their last consistently exciting album for a while, yielding a trio of decent hits: "Sarah", "Waiting For An Alibi" and "Do Anything You Want To", though the highlight was the Irish-folklore-inspired title-track.

Moore's days with the band were numbered, however, and he was sacked during the subsequent US tour. Bizarrely his replacement was ex-Slik/ex-Rich Kids guitarist **Midge Ure**, who was musically superb (though he never really got the hang of bullet belts and leather).

After the Japanese leg of the tour Ure went off to join Ultravox and **Snowy White** (formerly of Pink Floyd's touring band) replaced him for two solid, though not thrilling, albums: *Chinatown* (1980) and *Renegade* (1981), the latter featuring keyboard player Darren Wharton. Before *Chinatown*'s release, Lynott issued his first solo effort *Solo In Soho* (1980), though it was the hit single "Killer On The Loose" from the former that caused something of a stir. Many deemed it to be lyrically too provocative considering the UK was still reeling from the Yorkshire Ripper murders – but this didn't stop the song from going Top 10.

Following *Renegade*'s modest success White was replaced by ex-Tygers Of Pan Tang guitarist **John Sykes**. A far more visually arresting and flamboyant player Sykes was just what was needed to boost Lizzy once more, though Lynott was too embroiled in his own solo meanderings – *The Phil Lynott Album* (1982) – to capitalize on this from the outset. When he did, however, it was a newly revitalized Lizzy that released the astonishing fury of *Thunder And Lightning* (1983). It was heavier, gutsier and far more accomplished than anyone could have hoped for, the blistering and concise top-thirty hit "Cold Sweat" helping it to #4 in the album chart. The sleeve of a bass guitar serving as a lightning rod, and a studded

THRASH METAL

"Bang that head that doesn't bang" proclaims the sleeves of Metallica's debut album from 1983, *Kill 'Em All*. With those simple words the listener was introduced to an album that would launch this Bay Area band to the top of the thrash metal heap – at least for the duration of the 1980s. When thrash first came along many older metal fans just couldn't see the point; it seemed to sacrifice tunefulness for aggression and musicianship for primal bludgeon and speed for speed's sake. But what had spawned this mutant bastard of heavy metal?

It's impossible to pinpoint with accuracy, but a look at what was going on in metaldom at the time gives an idea. In the late 70s and early 80s the UK was enjoying the New Wave Of British Heavy Metal, with bands upping both the tempo and outright brutality of the music; **Venom** were trying to be as evil as possible, **Motörhead** had already penned some lightning-fast tracks, most notably "Ace Of Spades" and "Overkill", bands such as **Raven** and **Atomkraft** among many others were incorporating plenty of speed and violence into their sound. And then there was the influence of punk bleeding over. After all, where could metal go? Always reaching for the new extreme, for the next taboo to smash, punk-thrash metal, as it was sometimes called in the early days was the way to go.

In the US **Metallica** were definitely influenced by the NWOBHM – drummer **Lars Ulrich** was a big fan of UK bands such as **Diamond Head** – and the San Francisco Bay Area and LA scenes were developing into hotbeds of increasingly extreme metal. Alongside Metallica, **Exodus**, **Slayer** and **Megadeth** were among the US thrash vanguard with new bands arriving all the time. Over in New York groups such as **Anthrax** were upping the ante too. In Europe **Kreator**, **Destruction** and **Sodom** were also tapping into the latest underground sounds. And, of course, with the advent of thrash, early death and black -metal gradually evolved.

The influence of the early speed merchants can also be heard in most of the bands lumped in under new contemporary acronyms: the New Wave Of Swedish Heavy Metal and the New Wave Of American Heavy Metal.

fist punching through the earth in salute indicated what punters could expect inside: a rollickingly powerful metal album stuffed with terrific songs.

All of which was paradoxical, because Lynott and co had already decided to call it a day. Lynott felt it was all getting a bit stale and besides, the booze and the drugs were really taking their toll, not to mention the fact that Lizzy's finances were in a mess. The rest of 1983 was taken up with touring, including dates at the Reading Festival and Nuremberg as part of the European Monsters of Rock tour, culminating in four sold-out nights at the Hammersmith Odeon; this included the awesome spectacle of all of the band's previous lead guitarists on stage at the climax of the show. And just in case any fans had missed out, the following year's *Live/Life* album captured it all for posterity.

Following the demise of Lizzy, Lynott had little luck with his next vehicle **Grand Slam**, but he fleetingly struck pay dirt in 1985 when he and Moore scored a #5 hit single with the anti-war song "Out In The Fields". Sadly, ill-health brought on through years of alcohol and drug use would bring things to a rather tragic end: on January 4, 1986 Lynott died in hospital of major organ failure, having already been in a coma for eight days following a drug overdose – the end of a legend.

And so it would have stayed had it not and **Marco Mendoza** (bass) resurrecting the

band for a tour of Japan in 1994, as a result of the never-ending interest in Lynott and Thin Lizzy. The tenth anniversary of Lynott's death was marked by the band's biggest show since 1983. Dublin's The Point was soldout and the massive crowd outside unable to get tickets choked the streets to a standstill. Hence the touring and albums continue to this day, though many would argue that without the original outlaw-with-a-voice-of-gold leading from the front it's all a bit of a hollow exercise.

Jailbreak
1976; Vertigo

This is the place to start if you want songs up to the standard of "The Boys Are Back In Town". Lynott's charming swagger is evident throughout and the band gel into a tough and powerful, hard-rocking unit. Indispensable.

Live And Dangerous
1978; Vertigo

The history of this recording is rather more tricky than the sleevenotes suggest, but what really matters is the performance, which is faultless. A legendary live album featuring some all-time classics.

Thunder And Lightning
1983; Vertigo

Heavier and more mean-sounding than before, they sound so wound up it's incredible they decided to call it day. Worth it for the fantastic riffing of "Cold Sweat" alone.

3 INCHES OF BLOOD

Formed Victoria, British Columbia, Canada 2000

Few bands dish out classic heavy metal with quite the same fervour as these six individuals who emerged from the Victoria punk and hardcore scene. And therein lies the appeal. To look at, **Cam Pipes** (vocals), **Sunny Dhak** (guitar), **Jamie Hooper** (vocals), **Bobby Froese** (guitar) and brothers **Rich** (bass) and **Geoff Trawick** (drums) definitely do not fit the stereotypical image of a metal band. No long hair, leather or studs – just jeans and T-shirts.

Lurking beneath this unassuming exterior, however, beats the titanium heart of a relentless, blood-spattered, orc-slaying war machine. And the name? Simple: the result of a chaotic onstage headbanging frenzy. Vocalist Hooper was making like a one-man dandruff machine when his skull came into violent contact with Froese's guitar and one shocked punter was heard to scream that there were three inches of blood all over the floor.

In 2000 the first glimmerings of **3 Inches Of Blood**'s stainless steel potential were unveiled in their eponymous five-track EP. The blood-freezing scream of vocalist **Cam Pipes**, the last member to join the band, gave TIOB the razor-sharp edge to slash straight to the heart of their local music scene: the EP flew out of local record shops and the band garnered a fearsome reputation for pure, adrenaline-fuelled shows. It was a move to Vancouver in early 2001, however, that set the band on their sweeping course to success, via a series of triumphant gigs and winning first prize at the local university's talent competition.

Then came the band's first full-length assault on the senses: the unashamed tribute to all things metal that was *Battle Cry Under A Winter Sun* (2002). Gone entirely were any vestigial hardcore punk pretensions. It was a battle plan so brash and bold it could have been drawn up by Manowar themselves after a particularly hard night in Valhalla drinking Thor under the table. All the traditional elements were present and correct – the irrepressibly wired Iron Maiden gallop, the paint-stripping scream of King

Diamond, the incorrigible riff fury of Motörhead – but they were all supercharged with the irrepressible self-belief of youth. Not bad going for what was essentially a $1200 demo recording.

Here were stories of death and glory, of blood and fire, of steel crunching through bone from a band who enthused openly about 80s power metal. How could you go wrong with titles such as "Destroy The Orcs", "Headwaters Of The River Of Blood", "Skeletal Onslaught" and "Balls Of Ice", all rammed home with utter conviction, fearsome solos and drop-forged riffery?

It was gloriously over the top, and delivered with a wry smile and knowing nod to their influences. But TIOB were no joke novelty band. They took the hoary old clichés of metal and presented them to a new generation of heavy music fans without the bloated theatrics that tarnished the reputations of many bands from the 1980s. They looked hungry and utterly deranged on stage, not in any way like millionaires who had arrived at the venue in separate limousines and had their hair teased prior to strapping on their guitars. Their raw talent was recognized instantly, the debut single "Ride, Darkhorse Ride" being championed by influential DJ John Peel and awarded single of the week in *Kerrang!* magazine.

In early 2004 the band signed to Roadrunner Records – home to acts such as Slipknot and Type O Negative – and set about creating a worthy follow-up with veteran metalmen **Neil Kernon** and **Colin Richardson** producing and mixing respectively. The fact that Kernon had worked with Judas Priest, among many other legends, pointed the way forward and *Advance And Vanquish* (2004) was an astonishing consolidation, featuring new members **Brian Redman** (bass) and **Matt Wood** (drums).

While the debut had been relatively rough-and-ready, the new album benefited from a much clearer sound, accentuating the duelling guitars and rampant riffing. A trio of top tunes subtitled "Upon The Boiling Sea" made up a swashbuckling pirate saga; "Deadly Sinners" was a warning addressed to nonbelieving enemies of metal; and deadly robot wars epic "Wykydtron" provided a rousing sing-along chorus. The armour-plated icing on the cake was the cover art painted by **Ed Repka**, a man whose previous work had graced Death and

Megadeth albums, among many others. A triumph of both style and content, TIOB had created a perfect album for the post-grunge generation of metal fans.

⊙ Battlecry Under a Winter Sun
2002; Death O'Clock/Must Destroy

From the opening thunder of hooves and clash of steel this album is a lean, mean tribute to the finest influences in metaldom. The pace never flags as the band pay homage to some of the finest moments from Iron Maiden's *Killers* and Manowar's *Battle Hymns*.

⊙ Advance and Vanquish
2004; Roadrunner

Peddlers of false metal beware! TIOB are sharpening their axes and coming for you! This is headbanging nirvana, plain and simple, as tales of derring-do and heroic action are delivered with true panache. A superb second album.

THUNDER

Formed London, UK, 1989; disbanded 1999; re-formed 2002

In the tradition of great British bluesy hard rock, **Thunder** have made a name for themselves as a no-messing, good-time-guaranteed live act. But it wasn't always so. The band actually began as **Terraplane** back in the early 80s and were signed to Epic, who hadn't a clue what to do with them. Publicity shots of the band from around the time of their debut, *Black And White* (1985), show a band in costume hell – all mad mullets and multicoloured stripy jumpsuits, which was a pop image quite at odds with the hard rock they were aiming for. They had made a good impression at the Reading Rock Festival in 1982 but somehow allowed themselves to be transformed into a fashion disaster zone. Fortunately, by the time of *Moving Target* (1987) they had found a different tailor.

The sartorial improvement wasn't enough for them to keep the band together, however, and the team of **Danny Bowes** (vocals) and **Luke Morley** (guitar) kept hold of drummer **Gary "Harry" James** to form Thunder. With the line-up completed by **Ben** Matthews (guitar) and **Mark "Snake" Luckhurst** (bass) they wasted little time in securing a deal with EMI and blazing a trail in the tradition of bands such as Free and Bad Company. Their first album *Backstreet Symphony* (1990) was an unpretentious affair packed with catchy, well-honed rockers. The standard of writing was so high that over half of the album was issued as singles – standouts being "She's So Fine", "Dirty Love" and the ace title track. They became regulars in the UK singles charts, touring the UK and eventually playing the Donington Monsters Of Rock festival in the summer of 1990. They built their reputation as a peerless live unit, racking up sell-out shows including three nights at the Hammersmith Odeon. Europe loved them, and so did Japan. The readers of *Kerrang!*, *RAW* and *Metal Hammer* voted them best new band. For some reason, however, America seemed a tad resistant.

Their popularity in the UK was such that, upon its release, *Laughing On Judgement Day* (1992) debuted in the chart at #2 (held off the top slot by Kylie Minogue), and another great year for touring saw them play their second Donington festival and notch up yet more sold-out live shows. Amid all this frantic activity Snake was replaced by **Mikael Höglund** (bass), but the basic formula of finely crafted hard rock remained unchanged for *Behind Closed Doors* (1995), yet another top-five album.

Top Guitar Solos And Where To Find Them

Some axe heroes can't help themselves and just pile on the notes for a pyrotechnic display of virtuosity, while others wring every ounce of emotion possible from a very economical performance. But whether it's a neck-snapping, finger shredder or a three-note wonder, a great solo lifts a good song to the next level. As with riffs, it's simply impossible to pick out every single top solo, but the following 40 were created with some serious shape-throwing in mind.

"All Along The Watchtower" – **Jimi Hendrix, The Jimi Hendrix Experience** *Electric Ladyland* (1968)

"21st Century Schizoid Man" – **Robert Fripp, King Crimson** *In The Court Of The Crimson King* (1969)

"War Pigs" – **Toni Iommi, Black Sabbath** *Paranoid* (1970)

"Child In Time" – **Ritchie Blackmore, Deep Purple** *In Rock* (1970)

"Stairway To Heaven" – **Jimmy Page, Led Zeppelin** *IV* (1971)

"Won't Get Fooled Again" – **Pete Townshend, The Who** *Who's Next* (1971)

"Free Bird" – **Allen Collins, Lynyrd Skynyrd** *Pronounced Leh-Nerd Skin-Nerd* (1973)

"La Grange" – **Billy Gibbons, ZZ Top** *Tres Hombres* (1973)

"Dominance And Submission" – **Buck Dharma/Eric Bloom, Blue Öyster Cult** *Secret Treaties* (1974)

"I Got The Fire" – **Ronnie Montrose, Montrose** *Paper Money* (1974)

"Killer Queen" – **Brian May, Queen** *Sheer Heart Attack* (1974)

"Rock Bottom" – **Michael Schenker, UFO** *Phenomenon* (1974)

"Stranglehold" – **Ted Nugent, Ted Nugent** (1975)

"California Man" – **Rick Nielsen, Cheap Trick** *Heaven Tonight* (1978)

"Parisienne Walkways" – **Gary Moore,** *Back On The Streets* (1978)

"The Butcher And Fast Eddy" – **Pete Wells/Michael Cocks, Rose Tattoo** *Rose Tattoo* (1978)

"La Villa Strangiato" – **Alex Lifeson, Rush** *Hemispheres* (1978)

"Comfortably Numb" – **David Gilmour, Pink Floyd** *The Wall* (1979)

"For Those About To Rock (We Salute You)" – **Angus Young, AC/DC** *For Those About To Rock* (1981)

"Over The Mountain" – **Randy Rhoads, Ozzy Osbourne** *Diary Of A Madman* (1981)

"Mean Street" – **Eddie Van Halen, Van Halen** *Fair Warning* (1981)

"Bark At The Moon" – **Jake E. Lee, Ozzy Osbourne** *Bark At The Moon* (1983)

"Cold Sweat" – **John Sykes, Thin Lizzy** *Thunder And Lightning* (1983)

"2 Minutes To Midnight" – **David Murray/Adrian Smith, Iron Maiden** *Powerslave* (1984)

"Eat Me Alive" – **Glenn Tipton/K. K. Downing, Judas Priest** *Defenders Of The Faith* (1984)

"Fade To Black" – **Kirk Hammett, Metallica** *Ride The Lightning* (1984)

"Far Beyond The Sun" – **Yngwie Malmsteen, Yngwie J. Malmsteen's Rising Force**, *Rising Force* (1985)

"Ladies' Nite In Buffalo?" – **Steve Vai, David Lee Roth** *Eat 'Em And Smile* (1986)

"Dude (Looks Like A Lady)" – **Joe Perry, Aerosmith** *Permanent Vacation* (1987)

"Love Removal Machine" – **Billy Duffy, The Cult** *Electric* (1987)

"Sweet Child O' Mine" – **Slash, Guns N' Roses** *Appetite For Destruction* (1987)

"Ocean Size" – **Dave Navarro, Jane's Addiction** *Nothing's Shocking* (1988)

"Cult Of Personality" – **Vernon Reid, Living Colour** *Vivid* (1988)

"Fire In The Sky" – **Zakk Wylde, Ozzy Osbourne** *No Rest For The Wicked* (1988)

"Hanger 18" – **Marty Friedman/Dave Mustaine, Megadeth** *Rust In Peace* (1990)

"Jet City Woman" – **Chris Degarmo, Queensrÿche** *Empire* (1990)

"Alive" – **Mike McCready, Pearl Jam** *Ten* (1991)

"Killing In The Name" – **Tom Morello, Rage Against The Machine** *Rage Against The Machine* (1992)

"Black Hole Sun" – **Kim Thayil, Soundgarden** *Superunknown* (1994)

"Dead Eyes See No Future" – **Michael Amott/Christopher Amott, Arch Enemy** *Anthems Of Rebellion* (2003)

Surprisingly, *The Thrill Of It All* (1996) saw the band on a new label, Raw Power, and EMI began a prolific programme of Thunder compilations, kicking off with the 1995 *Their Finest Hour (And A Bit)* "best of". (EMI's cashing in was to continue with *The Rare, The Raw And the Rest* (1999), *Gimme Some …* (2000), *Rock Champions* (2001) and *Ballads* (2003), not to mention the many and various live albums and compilations issued through other imprints, several of them exclusively for the Japanese market.) The band replaced Höglund with **Chris Childs** for *Giving The Game Away* (1999). Their live shows were all about having a good time, with Bowes ever the genial host and typically resplendent in his Rupert-the-Bear trousers (maybe he found them at the back of his old Terraplane wardrobe).

Around the time of *Giving The Game Away* – in the wake of grunge and with nu-metal on the rise – it was becoming clear that Thunder had experienced a tailing off of interest. Blaming "outside business forces", they decided to fold and pursue other projects. Morley released *El Gringo Retro* (2001) and, with Bowes, worked on *Moving Swiftly Along* (2002). For a while it looked as if one of the UK's most entertaining bands was destined to become just another memory – and then came the offer of the Monsters Of Rock tour 2002 on a bill featuring Alice Cooper, The Quireboys and Dogs D'Amour. It was an opportunity too good to miss and just a few months after the arena-filling shows *Shooting At The Sun* (2003) appeared on the band's own STC label as did their *Plug It Out* (2004) DVD and yet another Bowes & Morley album, *Mo's Barbeque* (2004).

⊙ Backstreet Symphony
1990; EMI

Six singles were plucked from this little beauty, though that's not surprising considering the uplifting nature of the songs. They dish out the emotion on tunes such as "Love Walked In" and display an acerbic sense of humour on "An Englishman On Holiday". Wonderful stuff.

⊙ Live
1998; Eagle

Thunder are consummate showmen and this double album captures them in full flight, pulling out all the stops and playing their hearts out.

TOOL

Formed Los Angeles, California, US, 1991

 Standard practitioners of the metallic arts may content themselves with singing about dungeons and dragons. But there will always be room for bands who write about the demons of the mind, who want to make the listener excruciatingly uncomfortable with tortured visions of pain and dissolution, explorations of maniacal desire and tales of deep, crippling loss. Variously labelled art rock, hatecore and psycho-metal, **Tool** are a soul-skinning therapy session in the form of bravura guitar dissonance, bruising elliptical rhythms and skin-crawling vocals provided by a front man with a penchant for dresses and wigs.

Maynard James Keenan (vocals) was something of a Kiss fan in his youth – which might account for some of his inspired theatricality – but any pretensions of rock stardom were definitely on the backburner when he enrolled in the army. The desire to pursue a more arty career eventually got the better of him, and a change of direction led eventually to the genesis of Tool. Keenan met **Adam Jones** (guitar) who had been making his way as a sculptor and special-effects artist, a background that would prove invaluable for designing the sleeves for all the Tool albums, **Danny Carey** (drums) had been a member of **Pygmy Love Circus** and **Green Jello**, and **Paul D'Amour** (bass) came to join the band through a mutual friend of Jones.

Right from the beginning, it was clear that Tool were unique in both sound and vision and they were signed to Zoo Records within seven months of forming. Their first step was to release their *Opiate* EP in 1992, a six-track affair that showcased the band both in the studio and live. It was as claustrophobic as it was heavy, as raw as it was progressive. Tool were not about commerciality but melody harnessed to psychosis, with Keenan in turns crooning, wailing and roaring over a twisting and tumultuous array of riffs and rhythms, weird time signatures and peculiar phrasing that challenged preconceived notions of what heavy rock and metal could achieve.

Whether it was the dark content or the undiluted manner of its delivery, *Opiate* proved to be rather impenetrable to the average punter. Nevertheless, a tour pairing with the suitably heavyweight music of The Rollins Band gradually battered their name home and their own headlining slots were extraordinarily assured.

Undertow (1993) would prove to be something of an alternative metal watershed, however. Henry Rollins was impressed enough with them to provide vocal assistance on "Bottom" while the music was powerful, moving, and deliberately provocative. Calling a song "Prison Sex" – their comment on child abuse – might generate interest but it definitely won't get the tune on the radio. Like other arty luminaries such as Jane's Addiction, Tool were clearly working to their own creative agenda and they simply didn't care if songs were long and drawn out. Closing track "Disgustipated" – a wacky parable about the life of a carrot, and a satirical comment on religion and PC values gone

Top Riffs And Where To Find Them

The riff is the very backbone of rock and metal. It is impossible to write a great song without a good, crunchy riff. Anyone can string some fancy chords together but it takes genius to really come up with the goods because the tone and attitude are as important as the notes themselves. It's got to be raunchy, it's got to be hooky and memorable, and above all it's got to make the hairs stand up on the nape of your neck. It's impossible to list every classic riff, but the following 40 are guaranteed to give satisfaction:

"Whole Lotta Love" – **Led Zeppelin** *Led Zeppelin II* (1969)
"Kick Out The Jams" **MC5** *Kick Out The Jams* (1969)
"All Right Now" – **Free** *Fire And Water* (1970)
"Sweet Leaf" – **Black Sabbath** *Master Of Reality* (1971)
"Smoke On The Water" – **Deep Purple** *Machine Head* (1972)
"Breadfan" – **Budgie** *Never Turn Your Back On A Friend* (1973)
"Walk This Way" – **Aerosmith** *Toys In The Attic* (1975)
"Tush" – **ZZ Top** *Fandango* (1975)
"Detroit Rock City" – **Kiss** *Destroyer* (1976)
"Whole Lotta Rosie" – **AC/DC** *Let There Be Rock* (1977)
"Running With The Devil" – **Van Halen** *Van Halen* (1978)
"Another Piece Of Meat" – **Scorpions** *Lovedrive* (1979)
"Breaking The Law" – **Judas Priest** *British Steel* (1980)
"Ace Of Spades" – **Motörhead** *Ace Of Spades* (1980)
"Suicide Solution" – **Ozzy Osbourne** *Blizzard Of Ozz* (1980)
"Strong Arm Of The Law" – **Saxon** *Strong Arm Of The Law* (1980)
"Am I Evil?" – **Diamond Head** *Lightning To The Nations* (1981)
"Number Of The Beast" – **Iron Maiden** *Number Of The Beast* (1982)
"Fast As A Shark" – **Accept** *Restless And Wild* (1983)
"Holy Diver" – **Dio** *Holy Diver* (1983)
"Paradise City" – **Guns N' Roses** *Appetite For Destruction* (1987)
"Wild Side" – **Mötley Crüe** *Girls Girls Girls* (1987)
"Still Of The Night" – **Whitesnake** *1987* (1987)
"Twist Of Cain" – **Danzig** *Danzig* (1988)
"South Of Heaven" – **Slayer** *South Of Heaven* (1988)
"Vision Thing" – **Sisters Of Mercy** *Vision Thing* (1990)
"Trippin' On Ecstasy" – **Warrior Soul** *Last Decade Dead Century* (1990)
"Enter Sandman" – **Metallica** *Metallica* (1991)
"Smells Like Teen Spirit" – **Nirvana** *Nevermind* (1991)
"Slave To The Grind" – **Skid Row** *Slave To The Grind* (1991)
"Symphony Of Destruction" – **Megadeth** *Countdown To Extinction* (1992)
"Walk" – **Pantera** *Vulgar Display Of Power* (1992)
"Old" – **Machine Head** *Burn My Eyes* (1994)
"Negasonic Teenage Warhead" – **Monster Magnet** *Dopes To Infinity* (1995)
"Bullet With Butterfly Wings" – **Smashing Pumpkins** *Mellon Collie And The Infinite Sadness* (1995)
"Monkey Wrench" – **Foo Fighters** *The Colour And The Shape* (1997)
"Locked And Loaded" – **Halford** *Resurrection* (2000)
"Feuer Frei!" – **Rammstein** *Mutter* (2001)
"Cochise" – **Audioslave** *Audioslave* (2002)
"Life To Lifeless" – **Killswitch Engage** *Alive Or Just Breathing* (2002)

mad – was an arduous, ambient and baffling 15 minutes, 47 seconds long (much of it near-silent). The preceding "Flood" clocked in at a more modest 7 minutes, 45 seconds. To complement the weirdness, they played two sold-out shows at The Church of Scientology's Celebrity Centre in Los Angeles, and in 1994 Keenan recorded "Calling Doctor Love" on the *Kiss My Ass* Kiss tribute album, under the name **Shandi's Addiction**, alongside **Tom Morello** and **Brad Wilk** (of **Rage Against The Machine**), and **Billy Gould** (ex-**Faith No More**).

Tool became ideal candidates for the touring Lollapalooza festival due to their crossover appeal: they were brazen and heavy enough to appeal to the metal kids but distinct and alternative enough to appeal to the grungers. And Tool didn't disappoint. So intense were their performances that they were promoted from the second to the first stage. Keenly aware of the power of MTV, Tool put together a video for "Sober", featuring stop-motion animation provided by Jones – a technique they would revisit with future efforts – which went on to nab two *Billboard* awards. They were playing the game but to their own rules, subverting heavy rock to their own ends.

Over the next couple of years, serious bouts of touring with bands such as Rage Against The Machine (Keenan had guested on "Know Your Enemy" on RATM's debut album) brought them to the attention of an ever-widening audience who had been intrigued by press reports of this cerebrally challenging metal outfit. Their credibility was underlined by *Undertow* going platinum

and the video for "Prison Sex" being nominated in the Special Effects category at the MTV Awards, while *Spin* magazine voted them its number one artists of 1995.

Before their third album *Ænima* (1996) was recorded, D'Amour was replaced by **Justin Chancellor**. Not that this made any difference to the quality of the music, which continued to push the envelope for grime and misery-fuelled fury. The record featured a sample of comedian Bill Hicks, taken from one of his comedy albums (the band were great admirers of the iconoclast) and just as

Hicks courted controversy, Tool also caused a bit of a rumpus over opening track and single "Stinkfist". The connotations of the title were just too much for some radio stations and on video it was referred to as "Track No 1". What's more, Keenan's eccentric sense of humour landed him in trouble with Courtney Love (of Hole) when he produced joke T-shirts featuring the slogan "Free Frances Bean", the child Love had had by Kurt Cobain.

At this point the Tool story splits into two. While 1997 proved to be a very successful year for them, the band found themselves embroiled in a legal battle with their label that would halt the flow of any Tool product for another four years. (The *Salival* CD/ video package, featuring their acclaimed promo films, live and rare studio tracks was not to be released until 2001). In the interim, the various band members stretched themselves beyond the bounds of Tool. Keenan worked with Tori Amos and helped the **Deftones** out with vocals on their *White Pony* album, while Jones dabbled with The Melvins.

A key divergence from the plot was Keenan's **A Perfect Circle** project, which would go on to become a multi-platinum-selling behemoth in its own right. In the end, Keenan wound up contributing recording ideas to his Toolmates in the studio while on the road with A Perfect Circle. With their legal battle behind them they were finally free to concentrate on *Lateralus* (2001), which followed a few months after *Salival*. When the new record hit the stores the reaction was astonishing. It was a masterpiece, and various magazines and pundits dubbed it the most important heavy rock release of the year. Packaged in an inconspicuous black plastic sleeve, the full visual impact of the artwork was deliberately obscured. When unveiled the rainbow pyrotechnics of the "lyric booklet" were revealed – only there were no lyrics, just transparent page upon page of concentric designs which, when viewed as a whole, took on an arcane and mystical aura.

As a visual corollary to the contents, it could not have been more appropriate. *Lateralus* was sprawling, ambitious, and sense-swamping in its detail and emotional impact. For months the sense of anticipation had been almost palpable, and the fear of music piracy had led the band to set false media trails and release fake song titles on the Internet, both preserving their own mystique and keeping alive the voracious hunger for new material. When it was finally released, the album went straight to the top of the Billboard chart and into the Top 20 in the UK. The tour accompanying the record was one of the most eagerly attended of the entire year. In the US the band proved themselves to be in touch with their roots by embarking on a set of dates with prog-meisters King Crimson in tow.

They followed with even more triumphant live sets, including two sold-out dates at Madison Square Garden featuring performance artists Osseus Labrint from the video for "Schism". The end-of-year polls had Tool nominated and winning in most categories. It was a pattern repeated the following year, when "Schism" won a Grammy nomination for Best Hard Rock performance.

It's all been quiet on the Tool front over the last few years, what with their tendency to take forever to do anything and A Perfect Circle taking centre stage in 2003. However, a new album is rumoured to be due sometime in 2005.

⊙ Ænima
1996; Music For Nations

If *Undertow* saw Tool finally hitting their stride then this follow-up is their coming of age. Varied, harrowing, painful but ultimately highly rewarding, the songs within placed the band head and shoulders above their alternative metal contemporaries.

⊙ Lateralus
2001; Music For Nations

The incredible sleeve art is only half the story: the music within is sprawling and gloriously ambitious in scope and execution. A must-have release.

DEVIN TOWNSEND

Born New Westminster, British Columbia, Canada, May 5, 1972

If ever the word genius could be applied to a modern metal musician then Canadian-born singer and guitarist **Devin Townsend**

would be a prime contender. He has contributed to umpteen albums by a variety of bands and musicians and is a sought-after recording engineer and producer. He is also a hugely prolific writer of some of the most intensely heavy – both melodically and production-wise – music ever to be committed to CD. Whatever he turns his hand to, however, is characterized by a meticulous attention to detail and a dry sense of humour.

Townsend's first major break came when he sang on guitar wizard **Stevie Vai**'s *Sex And Religion* album at the tender age of nineteen (although it was probably guitar playing that got him noticed in the first place). Vai could tell he was dealing with a virtuoso and Townsend's contribution on vocals was a major highlight of this rather weird set of tunes. With such a high-profile gig under his belt stints playing guitar with a variety of other bands – **The Wildhearts** and **Frontline Assembly** among them – plus a number of tribute albums led eventually to the creation of **Strapping Young Lad**. This outfit created *Heavy As A Really Heavy Thing* (1995), largely featuring Townsend's own work in the studio as songwriter, singer, player and producer, while the second, *City* (1997), harnessed the professional power of veteran thrash drummer **Gene Hoglan** (**Dark Angel**, **Death**), **Jed Simon** (guitar) and **Byron Stroud** (bass). In the intervening years Townsend chucked out a joyous little punk piss-take album under the name **Punky Brüster** called *Cooked On Phonics*, making deadly fun of the growing number of soundalike pop-punk bands. The SYL material was also peppered with an ironic sense of humour, but delivered with the crushing force of full-on industrial metal, a gargantuan wall of sound that on repeated listens revealed intricate levels of detail and immensely gifted playing – so singular was the music that fans quickly dubbed his style Devy Metal.

This beautifully wrought brutal noise toured around the world, a flavour of which was captured on *No Sleep 'Till Bedtime: Live In Australia* (1997). Townsend's mercurial creative spirit demanded that he change tack somewhat and the slightly more laid-back **Ocean Machine** project, with **John Harder** (bass) and **Marty Chapman** (drums), was next, producing the album *Biomech* (1998). It was the darker, more ambient side of Townsend's muse: the epic, heavy wash of guitars and majestic

Devin Townsend: the evil genius of death-prog-jazz metal.

cyber-sweep of the music being an anti-dote to SYL's throat-ripping fury. It was the kind of proggy album Pink Floyd might record if they ever decided to crank things up to eleven. Around this time, frustrated by the limitations of being signed to someone else's record label, he set up his own: HevyDevy Records. His ultimate goal was to create the album he had always wanted to make, but the long writing and production process began to take its toll

and around this time he was diagnosed as suffering from bipolar syndrome.

When *Infinity* (1998) arrived (apparently inspired by Broadway musicals!) its vast array of sounds and moods expressed perfectly Townsend's state of mind and his unwavering control over creative chaos. Various musos turned up on the recording – including the Wildhearts' **Ginger** who co-wrote "Christeen" – while the sleeve notes informed the listener that the record had been "very hard to make" and described in detail the "blue" and "red" mixing sessions involved. Musically it was possibly the most diverse and electrifying heavy album to hit the stores that year – almost Zappa-esque in its off-the-wall invention. The degree of dedication that went into making this personal musical statement meant that only *Official Bootleg* and *Ass-Sordid Demos* (both 1999) kept fans happy before the albums *Physicist* (2000) and *Terria* (2001) followed in quick succession. By now Townsend's signature sound was well established. While the former brought an edgy melodic rush to the frenetic stampeding speed-metal thrash, the latter revisited some of the relatively calmer soundscapes of Ocean Machine, with a slightly more straight-ahead approach.

A torrent of creativity led to the release of two albums in 2003. *Accelerated Evolution*, described by Townsend as "no bullshit futuristic pop metal!", appeared under the name of **The Devin Townsend Band** and a self-titled SYL effort written with the tragedy of 9/11 in mind – and described as "war music" – focused the same rapid-fire artillery barrage as previous efforts. Two years later he was back under the SYL moniker with the slightly more accessible and melodic, though no less face-meltingly heavy, *Alien* (2005).

The restless, driven talents of Townsend make the output of most other musicians appear rather pathetic in comparison. For every album released by a "normal" band Townsend seems to issue two or three. Alongside his own recording and touring career, his brilliant studio techniques have also made him a sought-after producer and engineer. The last three or so years have seen him produce bands such as **December, Soilwork, Lamb Of God** and **Stuck Mojo**. Whether as a studio knob-twiddler or as a full-on prog-death-industrial metalhead, Townsend always brings to his work vast amounts of originality and inspiration, plus an ear for sonic perfection.

PUNKY BRÜSTER

Cooked On Phonics
Hevy Devy Records; 1996

This album was written and recorded in next to no time yet sounds ten times better than many expensively produced efforts. The concept storyline is an excuse for Devin to make ruthless fun of the 90s pop punk explosion. Unsurprisingly this is a lot more accomplished than most pop punk albums. An obscure gem.

STRAPPING YOUNG LAD

No Sleep 'Till Bedtime: Live In Australia
Century Media; 1998

It's quite amazing that SYL can reproduce this kind of white-hot intensity live and be funny too. "Far Beyond Metal" is hilarious – apparently Devin makes the words up as he goes along, which is astonishing considering the speed at which it's all delivered.

Alien
Century Media; 2005

This is a pounding yet relatively accessible effort from one of Devin's most uncompromising outfits. The scale of sound is cathartic and simply huge; hooky melodies surge and clash violently with martial, industrial rhythms and a veritable blizzard of berserk riffing. The effect is astonishing, akin to orchestrated pandemonium.

TWISTED SISTER

Formed New York, US, 1976; disbanded 1987; re-formed 2001

"It was the only Twisted Sister song I could bear to sing! Which doesn't say much for their lyrical content."
Lemmy on covering TS's "Shoot 'Em Down"

The success of such bands as Kiss and Mötley Crüe and the glam tendencies of 1980s metal should have made it easy for **Twisted Sister** to conquer the world but, for some reason, record labels remained stubbornly resistant to the band. Perhaps it was fear: they looked like transvestite scarecrows rather than pouting pretty boys, and in singer **Dee Snider** they had one hell of a motormouth frontman. He wasn't just a vocalist – with his shock of long peroxide-blond corkscrew curls he looked more like a freakish, nightmare cheerleader, preaching rock'n'roll rebellion in his own inimitable, foul-mouthed style. This wasn't so much hair metal as downright scare metal from a band of self-proclaimed "sick muthafuckers".

The band's origins dated right back to the very early 70s. **Jay Jay French** (guitar) was the only founding member to make it through various line-ups to be joined by **Eddie "Fingers" Ojeda** (guitar) and **Dee Snider** (vocals) in the mid-70s, and finally

Mark "The Animal" Mendoza (bass) and A.J. Pero (drums) as the 80s loomed. The classic line-up now in place they could focus on all they had learned through the years of playing in clubs around New York. Unable to secure a deal in the US, they eventually got their debut *Under The Blade* out in 1982 on the London punk label Secret Records. They were aiming for a sound as brash and loud as their outrageous image, and UFO's Pete Way on production did his best to capture the technicolour glam rampage the band were peddling. An appearance on Channel 4's groundbreaking music programme *The Tube* clinched it. Atlantic Records were only too ready to cough up the readies, and British metal fans took the band to their hearts, though it took America a little longer to realize what they were missing.

You Can't Stop Rock'n'Roll (1983) became a top-twenty hit in the UK and the band played the Donington Monsters of Rock festival as well as dates in Europe. The stomping anthems reached their peak of rabble-rousing perfection with *Stay Hungry* (1984), Snider ready to chomp down on a raw-and-ragged beef bone on the sleeve. The record became their first significant seller in America and their dates in Europe with Metallica went down a storm.

The in-yer-face image, lewd-and-crude lyrics and outspoken antics of their front man made the band a prime target for the censorship-promoting PMRC (Parents Music Resource Center) in the mid-80s. At one point Snider actually spoke at Senate hearings defending freedom of speech and expression in music. The singer revealed some years later

that he was certain he had been placed under security surveillance as an undesirable agitator of the nation's youth. Whatever the truth it didn't alter the fact that *Come Out And Play* (1985) was lacking in quality even if it did feature a duet with Alice Cooper on "Be Chrool To Your Scuel". It seemed as if the band were trying too hard to court mass appeal when their charm lay in their irredeemable ugliness.

Rumours began to circulate about dissent in the ranks. Pero bailed out and Joey Franco stepped in. *Love Is For Suckers* (1987), however, did nothing to halt the slide – the album was reputedly completed using various hired musos – and the band were by now seriously toning down their wardrobe and panto dame make-up. It came as no surprise when they finally pulled the plug. A "best of" entitled *Big Hits And Nasty Cuts* arrived some years down the line in 1992.

Snider formed Desperado – with Bernie Tormé (guitar), Marc Russell (bass) and Clive Burr (drums, ex-Iron Maiden) – which evolved into Widowmaker. Neither band made much impact, so the opinionated singer became a radio broadcaster while dabbling in music with Dee Snider's Sick Mutha Fuckers. Snider's outfit delivered *Live Twisted Forever* (1997), a live album and the vocalist also released the solo effort, *Never Let The Bastards Wear You Down* (2000).

Fans of Twisted Sister craved a reunion but for a while they made do with *Live At Hammersmith* (1994), a double album that had been recorded a decade earlier, plus a duo of rarities compilations *Club Daze Volume 1: The Studio Sessions* (1999) and *Volume 2: Live In The Bars* (2001). The classic line-up reunited in 2001 to play a benefit gig following the terrorist attacks on New York. The feeling was that the band had bowed out too suddenly in the 80s and they decided to extend their re-emergence into a full farewell tour which included dates at various European rock festivals in 2003. Rather than record a new album to go with the dates they rerecorded *Stay Hungry* as *Still Hungry*, going for a beefier, heavier sound. The DVD *Still Hungry: Live At Wacken Open Air* followed in 2005.

⊙ You Can't Stop Rock'n'Roll
1983; Atlantic

This is Snider and the boys in full-on us-against-the-world mode. It's about as subtle as a breeze block to the back of the skull but then you wouldn't want it any other way. Nasty and brilliant.

TYPE O NEGATIVE

Formed New York, US, 1989

"These songs are like my children and every parent thinks that their child is the most adorable in the entire world. I, however, am just the opposite and can frankly say that these are probably the worst songs that I ever heard."
Pete Steele

Death, pain, emotional torture – **Type O Negative**'s basic recipe for their maudlin dirge metal is straightforward, as man-mountain front man, bassist and chief songwriter **Pete Steele** will confirm. To those building blocks, add a misanthropic streak a mile wide, a sense of irony and a sick sense of humour, all of which make Type O one of the most fascinating bands ever to dabble with the basic goth template laid down by such bands as Sisters Of Mercy and Bauhaus.

It wasn't always quite so multifaceted. Steele began his musical career in New York punk metal band **Carnivore**. Far more aggressive and provocatively nasty, Carnivore's remit was to outrage as many people as possible. When the band fell apart in 1987 it took a couple of years for Steele to get his act together but with **Kenny Hickey** (guitar), **Josh Silver** (keyboard) and **Sal Abruscato** (drums) on board the Type O hate manifesto at last had full expression. Well, almost. Their first effort, basically a few reworked Carnivore ideas, was the catchily titled *Slow, Deep And Hard* (1991) on Roadrunner Records.

Key to their sound was Steele's impossibly deep and blood-chilling vampire vocal style, while the guitars were so distorted the result was almost comical. Maybe that was the point, because the lyrical contents and titles displayed a dark, intelligent sense of humour at work, as well as an unapologetically anti-PC slant. Steele's relationships with women were put through the shredder on "Unsuccessfully Coping With The Natural Beauty Of Infidelity" and "Prelude To Agony". Meanwhile, people on social security were given a pasting on the hateful "Der Untermensch". The whole album was choking on bile, not to mention a peculiarly sentimental sense of suicidal despair, and the apparent misogyny and misanthropy duly led to the band, and Steele in particular, being given a resounding kicking by the critics. They were labelled as women-hating racists, not that Steele cared one bit.

Things didn't improve much with *The Origin Of The Feces* (1992), a kind of fake live album, the cover of which featured a picture of Pete Steele's anus in loving close-up. Needless to say, the sleeve was changed on subsequent reissues. By the time of *Bloody Kisses* (1993), however, the quality of the music had improved hugely. Silver and Steele were the producers and the set was far more cohesive than before, not that they had abandoned their love of taunting political liberals. As ever, almost every track seemed calculated to offend someone. "Christian Woman" was about a young female who finds Christ upon the cross sexually arousing. "Black No 1 (Little Miss Scare-All)" skewered image-conscious goths. "Kill All The White People" was a

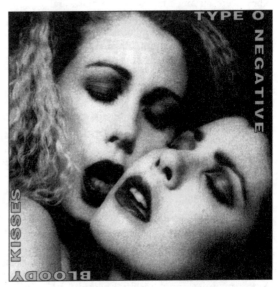

mock black power anthem. "We Hate Everyone" was their riposte to those who had labelled the band as homicidally rascist misogynists. Much of the rest of the album wallowed in morbid visions of deathly romance and lost love. It was epic, grandiose and absurdly theatrical, the Beatlesy melodies and video for "Black No 1" bringing them a whole new audience.

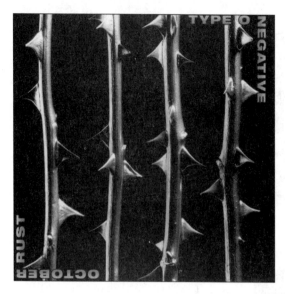

The next three years saw the band touring and allowed the label to capitalize on reissuing their previous efforts in order to raise their profile. One particularly astute attempt to garner publicity involved exploiting Steele's obvious photogenic qualities and trim physique by having him appear nude in *Playgirl* magazine in 1995. This was one of the key events that fans – particularly female ones – would remember as a prelude to what would prove to be their finest album, *October Rust* (1996). It was the first to feature new drummer **Johnny Kelly**, Abruscato having left to join Life of Agony.

Where *Bloody Kisses* had contained a relatively disparate collection of songs, some of which flaunted Steele's shamelessly self-indulgent dwelling on doomed romance, *October Rust* went for the full-on gothic experience with a lyric booklet of autumnal photos, the bleak, mist-shrouded trees reflecting the pagan overtones of the music. It was lush, layered and had an almost symphonic tone to the production. Only "My Girlfriend's Girlfriend" harked back to their infamous feminist-baiting ways. And to complement the theme of the album a stage set was created to resemble a forest glade.

Less sonically satisfactory was *World Coming Down* (1999), which lacked the atmosphere of its predecessor, the gloom and doom coming over as plain angry and no doubt fuelled by Steele's frame of mind, which was affected by the loss of various family members. "Everyone I Love Is Dead" and "Everything Dies", the latter accompanied by a particularly depressing video, set the tone for a collection that Steele was unsatisfied with. "There was just too much input from the record company, from management … and everyone was listened to, and as they say too many cooks spoil the broth" he boomed to the press.

Least Worst Of (2000) was a stopgap effort pulling together a few rarities, but with *Life Is Killing Me* (2003) some of the old Type O manic sparkle was back. When asked what the new album would sound like Steele was far more upbeat: "I would say it sounds somewhere between *World Coming Down* and *October Rust*. Where *October Rust* was full of wolves and women, and the woods and fire and ghosts, this next album is more about revenge, drugs and depression and death – all the good things in life."

Steele's obsession with impending loss, death and decay was satisfied by tunes such as "Todd's Ship Gods (Above All Things)" and "Nettie", about his father and mother respectively. Meanwhile, shadows of their hardcore thrash past appeared in far speedier numbers, such as "I Like Goils", an un-PC punk-metal song which could have slotted in quite nicely on *Bloody Kisses*. All in all, the album effectively took the slower, more mournful aspects of *October Rust* and added greater variety to the style and pacing, making it one of their strongest offerings to date.

October Rust
1996; Roadrunner

The smell and sense of seasons dying is almost tangible here. "Love You To Death", "Be My Druidess", "Die With Me" and "In Praise Of Bacchus" celebrate the destruction and decay of love. Meanwhile "Red Water (Christmas Mourning)" has Steele seeing ghosts and wallowing wantonly in the ecstasy of death, though the less said about their cover of Neil Young's "Cinnamon Girl" the better.

UFO

Formed London, UK, 1969; disbanded 1983;
re-formed 1985; disbanded 1988; re-formed 1990

I t's always gratifying when a mediocre group suddenly transform themselves to become one of the best. So it was with **UFO**, who started off in the late 60s with some awful space-rock albums.

The line-up of **Phil Mogg** (vocals), **Pete Way** (bass), **Mick Bolton** (guitar) and **Andy Parker** (drums) made something of a name for themselves on the Continent and Japan with *UFO1* (1970) and *UFO2 – Flying* (1971) and *Live in Japan* (1972). During this period they seemed to be rather clueless as to where to go next until a chance meeting in Germany. There they were supported by the Scorpions, who happened to have **Michael Schenker**, a very talented guitarist, in their ranks. They borrowed him when their six-stringer **Bernie Marsden** failed to show up for one of the gigs and he was so good they pinched him from the fledgling Teutonic rockers and kick-started a succession of ever-improving albums – thus ensuring their place in the heavy rock pantheon of notoriety.

First came *Phenomenon* (1974), which gave a taste of what they were capable of in the timeless "Doctor, Doctor" and storming "Rock Bottom", which saw Schenker putting his trademark Gibson Flying V

through the wringer with some stunning solo work. *Force It* (1975) went one step further by throwing keyboards into the mix, resulting in their first really accomplished collection with a raw and direct sound. The dabbling with keyboards worked well enough for them to bring in first **Danny Peyronel** for *No Heavy Petting* (1976) and then **Paul Raymond** for the essential *Lights Out* (1977). Heading into *Obsession* (1978), they were a force to be reckoned with, dealing in taut, muscular and

melodic rock, exactly the kind of thing to take them to the top in both the UK and the US.

The only stumbling block was themselves. Their growing success was allowing them to indulge in some seriously bad behaviour.

The rock excesses were leading to major ructions within the band, not least between Mogg and their fiery guitar genius. Schenker stayed long enough to participate in the landmark live effort *Strangers In The Night* (1979), which became their first top-ten album in the UK. Schenker then went off to begin a solo career and thus set up one of the longest-running soap opera plots in rock. He was so integral to the lead guitar-heavy UFO sound that fans seemed to count off the days until his return.

Paul Chapman (ex-**Lone Star**) was Schenker's replacement and, with his forceful style part of their hard-rock armoury, they fired off their first defiant volley with *No Place To Run* (1980). It was a potent return from the edge of what many fans thought was oblivion, but it turned out to be a temporary reprieve before the slide a couple of years later. The pressure-cooker internal dynamics of the band eventually led to Raymond quitting – he joined the **Michael Schenker Group** – to be replaced by **Neil Carter** for *The Wild, The Willing And The Innocent* (1981). So far, the band still seemed charmed as they produced yet another strong set, but with *Mechanix* (1982) and the lamentable *Making Contact* (1983) they were living on borrowed time. By the time of the latter, Way had decided that enough was enough. *Mechanix* had been a top-ten album but even that couldn't induce him to hang around any longer and he left while *Making Contact* was being recorded.

They staggered on but eventually fell apart, with the very strange and very rubbish *Headstone* (1983) – basically a compilation of live material and tracks culled from Scorpions and Michael Schenker Group albums – being their parting shot. Some thought it had got gruesome enough already, what with the booze and drugs and general poor performances, but Mogg gathered some hired hands and proceeded to drag UFO's name through the mud with *Misdemeanour* (1985) and the dreadful *Ain't Misbehavin'* (1988), a mini-album of demos.

The first glimmerings of a reunion appeared when Way – who had enjoyed some success with **Waysted** – hooked up again with Mogg in 1990. **Laurence Archer** (guitar; ex-**Grand Slam**) and **Clive Edwards** (drums; ex-**Wild Horses**) were roped in and UFO took off again (well, sort of) with *High Stakes And Dangerous*

Men (1992). It was a damn sight better than the last couple of albums but there was still an air of volatility and tension because of constant boozing.

The only way to make progress was to get the old line-up back together and that meant having Schenker on board. In 1993, they finally got themselves together to play some dates in Germany and America and in 1995 released *Walk On Water*. UFO were back, and fans were ecstatic – until it all went hideously wrong. Before a gig in Japan, Schenker attacked Raymond with a chair and during one of three sold-out gigs the guitarist stalked off stage. Keen to salvage something from their reunion Mogg and Way worked on *Edge Of The World* (1997) and *Chocolate Box* (1999), while Schenker went back to his solo career. Eventually they had another go with *Covenant* (2000), an album of decent quality featuring Mogg, Schenker, Way and drummer **Aynsley Dunbar**. The tour seemed to be progressing well until a drunken Schenker tried to get Mogg to play a solo mid-song during a gig in Manchester. It was clear that there was nothing else to do but cancel the tour as relations within the band fell apart. They recorded *Sharks* (2002) but didn't even bother to tour because it was felt that the whole house of precariously arranged cards could fall about their ears once more.

They said it couldn't be done but in 2004 the band returned with one of their strongest albums in several years, *You Are Here*. Raymond was back in the line-up and they had added guitarist **Vinnie Moore** and drummer **Jason Bonham**.

Obsession
1978; Chrysalis

The band were at the height of their powers here and they know it. Legend has it that "Pack It Up (And Go)" is a cheeky broadside aimed at Led Zeppelin. Elsewhere there is no letting up with highlights coming thick and fast. Just try out "Cherry" or "Hot'n'Ready".

You Are Here
2004; SPV

Moore is a guitarist of no small talent and his sterling lead work fits in perfectly with UFO's style, making this one hell of a miraculous return to form. Maybe there is life after Michael.

URIAH HEEP

Formed London, UK, 1970

In some ways, **Uriah Heep** find themselves in a similar situation to such bands as Nazareth. In the UK, where tastes in popular music shift unpredictably, their profile is relatively 'umble. Across Europe and Scandinavia, however, the Heep still tour regularly, occasionally popping over to the States to play the odd vintage festival shindig.

While it is true that these archetypal heavy rockers will forever be stars in Germany, there are few that would dispute that their heyday was during the early to mid-70s, when their albums regularly hit the charts. Right from the off, the band, formerly known as **Spice**, got into their stride with the sturdy *Very 'Eavy, Very 'Umble* (1970) on Vertigo. The famous sleeve art featured singer **David Byron** shrouded in fake cobwebs blasted over him by guitarist **Mick Box**. The remainder of the band comprised **Ken Hensley** (keyboards), **Paul Newton** (bass), **Ollie Olsson** (drums). "Gypsy", the opening track, was a bona fide classic that many a stoner band would find inspirational over the coming decades, but the most surprising aspect of the band's launch, given the high esteem afforded to their early work now, was the venom with which critics laid into them. The chief accusation was that they were essentially a poor man's Deep Purple – an understandable view given their driving Hammond sound and Byron's occasional primal yelp – but in reality the similarity was at best superficial. The follow-up, *Salisbury* (1971), featuring new drummer **Keith Baker**, gave them yet more future live faves in the shape of "Bird Of Prey" and "Lady In Black"; the songs were steadily improving as Hensley threw himself into the writing process.

With their live profile growing both in Europe and the US thanks to some arduous touring, the band brought in yet another drummer, **Ian Clarke**, and released their finest album yet, *Look At Yourself* (1971), on Bronze, which just broke into the UK Top 40. The best was yet to come, however, as the band settled into what many would regard as their definitive line-up featuring **Lee Kerslake** (drums) and **Gary Thain** (bass). *Demons And Wizards* (1972) came wrapped in a stunning Roger Dean sleeve and contained yet more classics in "The Wizard" and "Easy Livin'". At last they had a real chart success in both the UK (Top 20) and the US (Top 30), and the quality was maintained on *The Magician's Birthday* (1972) and the storming *Uriah Heep Live* (1973). By

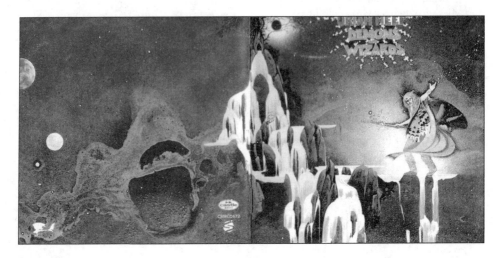

had to give as they tried to establish an acceptable new identity, and for *Conquest* Kerslake was replaced by **Chris Slade**, and Lawton by **John Sloman**. The next member to go was Hensley, whose characteristic keyboard style and compositional skills had been at the heart of the band: the fact that his songs dominated the albums had for a long time been a bone of contention. **Greg Dechert** stepped in, but not for long, because the band suddenly seemed to crumble away, leaving just Box to consider his position.

It took the guitarist a while, but once he had regained Kerslake and added bassist **Bob Daisley**, both of whom had been helping Ozzy Osbourne launch himself after leaving Black Sabbath, Heep once again were a going concern. **John Sinclair** was brought in on keyboards and **Peter Goalby** (ex-**Trapeze**) was their new vocalist for *Abominog* (1982), an album that again made them a top-forty name in the UK and spawned the "That's The Way That It Is" single and video, which found favour on MTV. They even played the Donington Monsters of Rock festival in 1982. *Headfirst* (1983) was in the same modern rock mould as its predecessor, but *Equator* (1985) suffered from lack of support from their new record label, Portrait (Bronze had eventually fallen apart with massive debts). It had been recorded with Bolder back in the band instead of Daisley, and line-up changes continued to dog their progress as Goalby and Sinclair bowed out, to be replaced by **Bernie Shaw** and **Phil Lanzon** respectively.

Into the late 80s and early 90s the band continued to tour extensively, punctuating their studio releases – *Raging Silence* (1989), *Different World* (1991) and *Sea Of Light* (1995) – with live albums. The most significant of these was *Live In Moscow* (1988), which celebrated the fact that Heep were the first heavy rock act to play the USSR. They

now even the critics were warming to the band – well some of them anyway – as they doggedly blasted away at their progressive blues agenda.

Sweet Freedom (1973) and *Wonderworld* (1974) kept them on a roll and the only major change came when Thain was replaced by **John Wetton** for *Return To Fantasy* (1975). Thain had become unreliable due to rock'n'roll excess and he died of a drugs overdose in 1976. The latter album gave them a #7 hit in the UK, but it also marked the last really decent record from the band for quite a while as they began to struggle with line-up changes and the snotty spectre of punk.

High And Mighty (1976) wasn't quite up to scratch, being somewhat lighter in sound, but *Firefly* (1977) required fans not just to tune into a new bassist in **Trevor Bolder** but welcome a new singer in **John Lawton**. Byron had been fired because of his growing alcohol reliance – which would eventually cause his death in 1985.

The records *Innocent Victim* (1977), *Fallen Angel* (1978) and *Conquest* (1980) led the band towards the uncertainty of the 80s. They had experimented with variations in sound – *Fallen Angel* featured what can best be described as a move towards poppy melodic rock – and had created some albums atypical of the usual Heep output. Something

US Hardcore
(The Influence On Thrash And Grunge)

Despite the rich vein of punk activity in the UK, 80s hardcore – a faster more aggressive form of punk – was very much a US urban phenomenon and led to a huge number of scenes centred on large cities spread across the country. Fans make distinctions between the Washington DC, New York, Boston, and Los Angeles sounds. Inevitably the scenes fractured into their own subgroups and movements such as **straight edge** – espousing the notion of personal responsibility and an almost puritanically clean lifestyle. Key bands of this era included the **Dead Kennedys** (San Francisco), **Black Flag** (Los Angeles), and **Minor Threat** (Washington DC). For many, however, the fountainhead of speedy hardcore were Washington DC's **Bad Brains**, without doubt one of the fastest bands of the time, whose *Rock For Light* (1983) album (bizarrely enough produced by Ric Ocasek of the Cars) is an all-time classic.

The result was a cross-fertilization between the hardcore scene and the growing thrash metal movement, which is quite neatly illustrated by New York's mid-80s hardcore supergroup **Stormtroopers Of Death**, featuring **Charlie Benante** (drums) and **Scott Ian** (guitar) of **Anthrax**, **Dan Lilker** (bass) of **Nuclear Assault** and **Billy Milano** (vocals) of hardcore outfit **MOD**.

In much the same vein as **Guns N' Roses**' *The Spaghetti Incident?* punk covers album, **Slayer**'s *Undisputed Attitude* (1996) shows where they got their taste for blistering speed with a manic fistful of hardcore covers. While guitarist **Jeff Hanneman** was the chief fan and instigator of such hyperfast riffing, the influence is undeniable in the music of **Megadeth** as well. Guitarist **Dave Mustaine** went on to record *The Craving* (1996) as a side-project under the name **MD45** with **Fear** singer **Lee Ving**. Likewise, during the 80s it seemed **Metallica** guitarist **James Hetfield** would only wear a T-shirt if it sported the name of a punk or hardcore outfit. The band famously went on to record covers of tunes originally written by the likes of **Discharge**, the **Misfits** and post-punkers **Killing Joke**.

The birth of grunge also owes much to punk and hardcore – scratch the surface and the discord and anger bleeds through readily. **Mudhoney**'s fuzzy, garage approach to rock can be traced back to a love for Black Flag, **Dicks**, **Fang**, **Void** and **Angry Samoans**. Meanwhile Kurt Cobain's favourite bands included **TSOL**, Void, **MDC** and **The Slits**, the punk influence showing clearly right from **Nirvana**'s debut, *Bleach* (1989). Even the more classic-rock-sounding of the grungers, such as **Soundgarden** and **Pearl Jam**, had punky influences, with bands such as **The Dead Boys** and **Fear** figuring among the originators of tunes they covered.

were treated like heroes there, in stark contrast to the UK where their profile was steadily waning.

Sonic Origami arrived in 1998, the live albums kept coming, and in 2001 they embarked on The Legend Continues Tour with Nazareth and Stray. They continue to plug away at the global live circuit in defiance of anyone daft enough to suggest that they have had their day.

Demons And Wizards
1972; Bronze

For some this will always be the key Heep album, recorded at a time when the template for rock and metal had yet to be cast with any permanency. The band were able to experiment and throw in progressive and psychedelic touches to produce one of their strongest early albums.

Abominog
1982; Bronze

This was a comeback album of sorts after the band seemed to disintegrate in the early 80s. They bounced back with fresh energy and vigour, much to the relief of the fans. The sleeve art is good too.

VAN HALEN

Formed Pasadena, California, US, 1973

Van Halen have been, without doubt, one of the most successful American hard-rock acts of the past 25 years. Their attraction can be squarely accredited to having an innovative sonic wizard on lead guitar and a kaleidoscopic whirlwind of a front man who could hold an audience of thousands mesmerized with an engagingly arrogant display of self-love.

Turning the clock back to Pasadena, California, in 1973, guitarist **Eddie Van Halen** and his brother **Alex Van Halen** (drums) – both classically trained musicians – asked a certain **David Lee Roth** (vocals) of local outfit **Red Ball Jets** (named after a brand of sneakers) to hook up with them; Roth's band had split and he had a rather useful amp setup that they had been hiring. The classic line-up was complete when former Snake bassist **Michael Anthony** joined the following year. Playing initially as **Mammoth**, they toyed with the suicidal name of **Rat Salad** (after the Black Sabbath track) before eventually settling on Van Halen at Roth's suggestion.

Peddling a raw mixture of 60s and 70s cover versions and original tunes, they became known as the loudest and heaviest band in the Los Angeles area, mainly through their opening slots at the Gazzari on the Sunset Strip. As a guitarist, Eddie was not only loud but also possessed of a technical virtuosity that left most people slack-jawed

in amazement. Roth, on the other hand, was developing the notion of rock'n'roll as vaudeville entertainment. Diagnosed as hyperactive as a child, he focused his energy into becoming one of the most flamboyant, self-regarding performers on the scene. His high-kicking star jumps from the drum riser have become one of his show-stopping trademarks. Their first break came when Kiss bassist **Gene Simmons** witnessed one of their characteristically over-the-top performances and offered to produce a demo tape for them, which was summarily ignored by the major labels. It was not until producer **Ted Templeman** saw them at the Starwood club that he persuaded Warner Brothers to sign the group.

With Templeman on board as producer *Van Halen* (1978) was created and is generally acknowledged as a landmark release in rock, comparable in stature to, say, AC/DC's *If You Want Blood…* or Led Zeppelin's *Four Symbols*. As a classic metal album, it sounds as fresh and dynamic today as it did when Roth had a full head of hair. The guitar blizzard that is "Eruption" is a brilliantly structured exercise in gratuitous finger-flinging solos and led to the establishment of a style of guitar heroics that has been much copied since but rarely bettered. Coupled with the dynamic six-string posturing, the power of the rhythm section was undeniable, Anthony's fluid bass style riding atop Alex Van Halen's unrelentingly muscular drums. Templeman's precise production also captured Roth's extrovert personality perfectly. With sales of over two million, the way had been paved for a string of platinum albums that would each outsell their predecessor. In addition, each release clocked in at just over half an hour, which in the days of vinyl helped maximize the quality of the recordings (a shorter record enables a fatter, volume-boosting, richer-sounding groove). *Van Halen II* (1979), *Women And Children First* (1980) and *Fair Warning* (1981) all displayed brilliant original songs, a penchant for dabbling with strange musical interludes and a diverse collection of hit cover tunes – exactly the blend that had got them noticed in the first place.

By the late 70s the band were truly enjoying the trappings and ludicrous excesses of stardom. Their legendary backstage rider stipulated that their provision of M&Ms should include no brown ones and they hired Francis Ford Coppola's soundstage at LA's Zoetrope studios to experiment with their new PA system.

Their fifth studio album, *Diver Down* (1982), was their weakest, but nevertheless made #3 in the US. The record contained more cover versions and instrumental noodling than was healthy but the band's reputation seemed untouchable and Eddie even provided some much-acclaimed guitar work on Michael Jackson's "Beat It".

With *1984* (1984) they signalled a return to form. The album featured effervescent synth work, along with blistering guitars and a sublime pop sensibility; tracks such as "Jump", "Panama" and "Hot For Teacher" made this a release no self-respecting rock fan could ignore. Tensions, however, were growing within the band and Roth became disenchanted with the way the other members did business. Shortly after the album's release, he did the unthinkable and left to pursue a solo career, which for a while paralleled Van Halen's early glories.

At first the band were advised to find an alternative name: after all, the idea of Van Halen without the brash presence of Roth seemed an appalling prospect. Who wanted to see an act where the only attraction was a deadly guitarist? Recruiting former Montrose vocalist **Sammy Hagar**, however, marked the rebirth of the band as a completely different entity (cheekily dubbed Van Hagar by their detractors). Hagar was an artist in his own right with a solid solo career, so it was a reinvention fraught with creative and commercial risks but the possibility of even greater success. In the end the latter proved to be true because their next album, *5150* (1986) – New York police code for criminally insane – spawned the anthemic mega-hit "Why Can't This Be Love". The formula with Hagar was repeated with *OU812* (1988), *For Unlawful Carnal Knowledge* (1991) and *Balance* (1995); all successful records but all lacking

Van Halen take time out for more intellectual pursuits.

that wonderfully tacky presence of a shamelessly self-publicizing, cartoon egomaniac on vocals. Meanwhile the band's first full live document *Live: Right Here, Right Now* (1993) merely proved that they could re-create their hits with unerring precision.

The run of continuing success had to end sometime, however, and sure enough Hagar left the band in the late 90s to continue his solo efforts. Van Halen had seemingly stumbled upon the right formula after **Diamond Dave**'s departure, but could they pull off such a feat again? Of course the rumour mill suggested that the way was clear for Roth to cut his losses in his flagging solo career and rejoin the band, but while he contributed to a couple of new tunes on *Best Of Vol 1* (1996), the possibility of a reunion was crushed when former **Extreme** singer **Garry Cherone** was selected as the new voice of Van Halen. It was a bizarre choice and one that failed. Although the resulting album *Van Halen III* (1998) was competent enough, it lacked that crucial spark of excitement. Coupled with this, Alex Van Halen injured his hand when falling plasterwork landed on him during a pre-gig warm-up in Hamburg, which delayed the band's plans for months. Cherone was eventually dismissed just one year later – and to make matters worse Eddie was diagnosed with cancer. Though he recovered, nothing could save the faltering relationship with their record company Warners, leaving one of the biggest bands in the world with plenty of unreleasable material and no singer. To add to this strange state of affairs Roth and Hagar toured the States in

2002, which prompts the question of whether Eddie and the boys have got what it takes to turn their fortunes around again. Or should they just retire and quit flogging a dying horse? In the last couple of years their only output has been a compilation double CD called *The Best Of Both Worlds* (2004) featuring three new songs.

 Van Halen
1978; Warners

A benchmark recording brimming with hard-rocking brilliance and re-creating their live blend of covers and originals. Producer Templeman extracts every last drop of energy from Eddie's guitar work and Roth's exuberant style makes it an essential party album.

 Fair Warning
1981; Warners

Once again packed with excellent songs and featuring their first experimentation with synths, which would grow with each subsequent release.

1984
1984; Warners

Nine original tunes which come damn near to matching the excellence of their outstanding debut. The synth work is more prevalent ("Jump", "I'll Wait") but it is their pop sensibilities that make this essential.

VENOM

Formed Newcastle, UK, 1980

I f you had to choose just one band as the main driving force behind the black metal scene then this fantastically over-the-top trio would have to figure pretty high on the charge sheet. For many aficionados of extreme satanic metal this lot were one of the main fountainheads of all that's unholy in guitar noise. What they lacked in commercial success they reaped in cult popularity; bands may come and go and deliver the latest fads but few can claim such enduring loyalty from their fans or, indeed, such a level of infamy. Though the **Venom** legend is peppered with personality clashes and discord it is also one that has endured.

Claiming to be in league with the horned one himself, **Conrad Lant** aka **Cronos** (bass/vox), **Jeff Dunn** aka **Mantas** (guitar) and **Tony Bray** aka **Abaddon** (drums) erupted onto the metal scene with *Welcome To Hell* (1981), a poorly produced but brutal thrash album. Having originally formed as a five-piece called **Oberon** in the late 70s, these pioneering and overtly theatrical minions of hell would go on to spawn a thousand imitators and become one of the most influential thrash groups of the early 80s, marking them as one of the key bands of the burgeoning New Wave Of British Heavy Metal.

Everything about this bunch was exaggerated, from the leather, studs and bullet belts, to the overt satanic imagery. It was cartoon time, and Venom had their very own prime-time show; the image cast by the trio in early

publicity snaps would be so influential that Scandinavian black metal bands would be copying such poses over a decade later. No one had ever experienced anything quite so depraved. They claimed not just to dabble in the black arts but to be regular (blood-)drinking buddies with the man downstairs. So cocky and confident were Venom of their success they displayed a mocking disdain for the usual routes to stardom. Not only was their debut recorded in a mere three days – it was a set of speedily recorded demos that formed the basis of the album – they allegedly refused to support any other bands and so had not actually played any live dates to speak of.

Their live debut – on a brief tour cunningly dubbed the 'The Seven Dates Of Hell' – was at the (then) Hammersmith Odeon in June 1984. Very few bands achieve such a remarkable cross-section in an audience, but Venom joined the ranks of acts such as Motörhead – one of their favourite bands – in attracting a vastly diverse crowd including metallers, bikers, punks and skin-

heads. Pumped up on the hype, everybody wanted to see whether these boys were as vicious live as their recorded material promised. Precedents were set that night for what would become Venom live-show staples: pyrotechnics of nuclear proportions threatened to toast those unfortunate enough to have seats in the stalls, the PA was one of the most powerful the band could obtain, and by the end of the gig every single piece of stage equipment was reduced to piles of smoking splinters.

This level of intensity can be experienced in their three follow-up albums, *Black Metal* (1982) – apparently recorded in six days this time – *At War With Satan* (1984) and *Possessed* (1985), which showed a band gradually learning how to play their instruments and write half-decent rock songs. But while *Black Metal* was a match for the infernal ferocity of their debut, *At War With Satan* seemed to lack good ideas in the writing department and *Possessed* suffered from yet another awful production job. Tensions were rising within the band – the trio were, by now, renowned for their volatile tendencies – and with the new wave of thrash and death metal bands from the US and the Continent gradually catching up with them (the upcoming Metallica had supported Venom just a year or two earlier) they just couldn't decide which path to take.

Inevitably, with the band's growing professionalism came a honing of their trademark lunacy and aggression. Although previously they had deliberately cultivated stories about attacking people who got in their way and drinking the blood of virgins, among many other cuddly and colourful rock antics, it didn't help their reputation that they eventually admitted to knowing very little about the occult.

The live album *Eine Kleine Nachtmusik* (1986) turned out to be the last outing for the classic trio line-up. The pressure within the band had grown unbearable and Mantas left, citing his bandmates' unwillingness to evolve as the main reason; just to prove the point he issued a melodic rock album called *Winds Of Change* (1988). When *Calm Before The Storm* (1987) arrived, the line-up had expanded to include two new guitarists: **Mike Hickey** and **Jimmy Clare**. It was a period of peculiar internal machinations for the band, not to mention a change in direction. Every now and then actual tunes could be discerned; so much for the band that had stamped the corrupted anti-piracy message "Home taping is killing music – so are Venom" on their early albums. The chief reason for this was the departure of Cronos. He broke ranks, as Mantas returned, to form an eponymous melodic rock outfit and start a fitness-training business, a move that endeared Venom even less to the diehard fans. A new vocalist, **Tony Dolan** aka **Demolition Man** (ex-**Atomkraft**), was brought in but no one really cared any more and stories of extreme disharmony began to spread. *Prime Evil* (1989), *Temples Of Ice* (1991) and *The Waste Lands* (1992) – recorded with various line-up changes – were of varying quality and showed a competent band still trying to make headway with the Venom name, if not the original sound.

It appeared as though one of the black metal vanguard had really gone straight to hell as the void left by Venom was filled with a huge number of compilation albums. *Black Reign*, *Kissing The Beast*, *Skeletons In The Closet*, *The Book Of Armageddon* and *Old, New, Borrowed And Blue* were sets of varying quality and it looked unlikely that the band would pull themselves together for long enough to do anything worthwhile. However, in 1996 there was *The Second Coming*, a live video and CD box set – recorded at their appearance at the Dutch Dynamo festival that May – showing that the old line-up could still muster some of their former g(l)ory on stage.

Unbelievably, a studio album, *Cast In Stone* (1997), soon followed, proving that the promise of cash can patch up all manner of differences. While it proved that Venom could still harness some of that ol' black magic when they put their minds to it, *Resurrection* (2000) – featuring new drummer **Antton** – was precisely the kind of thing the band's ever-faithful hellspawn were craving.

While the compilation albums have continued to pop up with alarming regularity, most recently the band's original brace of albums recorded for Neat Records have been

Venom set the table for Sunday lunch.

reissued with brand new sleeve notes, loads of vintage snaps and, best of all, a veritable horror feast of bonus cuts. With the current resurgence in all things metallic and the continued interest in the band's mythical status, Venom have taken the opportunity to plunge back into the fray. With a new guitarist in the ranks, **Mykvs**, the trio have been busy in the studio preparing a new album due in 2005. Mantas, meanwhile, has been busy with his **Mantas666** project.

Welcome To Hell
1981; Neat Records

An album so fast and heavy it's almost hilarious. This is the one to seek out if you fancy a spot of hell-raising.

Black Metal
1982; Neat Records

The definitive thrash blueprint followed by imitators the world over. Fast, brutal, ugly. But oddly amusing, too.

Cast In Stone
1997; SPV

Nasty stuff, but played with greater skill and precision. The satanic theatrics are still in place and a bonus second disc features ten rerecorded classics from the good old days.

THE VINES

Formed Sydney, Australia, 1995

T he turn-of-the-millennium rock scene was nothing if not volatile, with nu-metal seemingly a spent force and the arbiters of cool looking for the next big sensation. Step up **The Vines**, a young band who happened to be in the right place at the right time to capitalize on the resurgence in garage rock ignited by the success of bands from the Detroit scene – not least The White Stripes and pretty much anyone else who enjoyed kicking out the jams while sporting the obligatory thrift-store uniform of tatty jeans, T-shirt and battered Converse sneakers.

Despite the seeming overnight success, The Vines can be traced back to 1995 when **Craig Nicholls** (guitarist/vocalist), **Patrick Matthews** (bass player/backing vocalist) and drummer **David Olliffe** met at high school and shared the same kinds of dead-end casual jobs – flipping burgers and working in factories. Nicholls' dad just happened to have

been guitarist/vocalist in an obscure Australian band from the 60s called The Vynes, so a letter change later they had themselves a moniker with just the right vintage rock'n'roll resonance.

Instead of launching themselves into the fleapits of their hometown and learning their art through good honest gigging they chose to concentrate on writing some half-decent tunes first and so toiled in relative obscurity until 2001; it was then that their limited edition *Factory* EP was released to almost immediate acclaim from a press that was hungry for the spiritual healing power of trashy rock. In the UK in particular the *NME* latched onto the band with a fervour bordering on the fanatical, making *Factory* Single Of The Week and The Vines top of their 35-bands-to-watch feature in 2002. Meanwhile, things were taking off in the US: having signed a worldwide deal with Capitol Records, MTV2 latched onto the band even though they had no video product with which to promote themselves.

At this point Olliffe left the band to be replaced by **Hamish Rosser**, and a second guitarist, Nicholls' childhood best friend **Ryan Griffiths**, completed the line-up. The pieces were in place for the group's first headline live appearance in February 2002 at the Vic on the Park, a small pub in Sydney. Despite the tiny size of the gig, the press, especially *NME*, hailed it as some sort of second coming. Somewhat bizarrely the press and the record label were keen to push the band as a kind of Nirvana Mark II, no doubt because Nicholls' skinny frame and ability to wig out on the guitar revived decade-old memories of Kurt Cobain.

The album *Highly Evolved* (2002) was very good, but it was light years from *Nevermind,* the former being a synthesis of coruscating garage rock imbued with a sense of Beatles-esque psychedelia and an acute pop sensibility. It was a potent and stylish enough brew to land the band various prestigious TV slots, not least *Later With Jools Holland* in the UK, a programme that has become a showcase for what is deemed cool. Despite, or perhaps because of, these swift successes the band found themselves under extreme pressure while gigging towards the end of 2002 and came to blows on stage, prompting rumours of early burn-out.

While the first album had suffered something of a problematic genesis – various session players had apparently been drafted in to help out – the second was a chance for the four members to get their act together and prove they could exceed the expectations of the first. But the result, *Winning Days* (2004), was rather uneven. Fans embraced it for its unpredictable charms while the critics suggested the unevenness was down to the lads being unable (or just unwilling) to combine their desire for melody with neck-snapping rage in a convincing manner.

◉ Highly Evolved
2002; Heavenly/Capitol

A bristling, snarling album shot through with attitude. The balance between trippiness and balls-out rock is keenly felt and the best track has to be the 93-second rolling mayhem of the title tune – short, sharp and straight to the point.

◉ Winning Days
2004; Heavenly/Capitol

An odd one. "Ride", "Animal Machine" and "Fuck The World" sound as gloriously demented as their titles suggest. But when the stroppiness ends the outright melodic moments fail to elicit anything approaching a decent level of excitement. Thank goodness for the skip button.

VOIVOD

Formed Jonquiere, Quebec, Canada, 1983

You wouldn't think Canadian thrash could be a starting point for groundbreaking metal, but this imaginative and highly adventurous band epitomize just that.

It all started out innocently enough, with **Denis Belanger** aka **Snake** (vocals), **Denis D'Amour** aka **Piggy** (guitar), **Jean-Yves Theriault** aka **Blacky** (bass) and **Michel Langevin** aka **Away** (drums) jamming on classic metal tunes from the likes of Judas Priest and Motörhead, and, in much the same way as Metallica and many other bands, landing a spot on a Metal Massacre compilation album released by Metal Blade. Their "Condemned To The Gallows" track was thrashy enough to compete with much of the other material on offer but the band had plans above and beyond straightforward speed and aggression.

At the heart of **Voivod**'s campaign was Away's idea of creating a complete artistic image to their work, so he provided sleeve art as well as a central theme to the songs. The Voivod, an imaginary warrior creature from the land of Morgoth, would, over successive albums, provide the conceptual backbone to their writing. The first outing for this belligerent sci-fi creation and his nuclear conflict-scarred land was *War And Pain* (1984), which was one of the first extreme metal albums to emerge from Canada in the 80s. The band took their stylistic cues from Venom – all leather and spikes with Snake spicing things up by hanging the odd hand grenade from his bullet belt. It was energetic but basic stuff because the band were far from technically proficient at this point. Much better was *Rrröööaaarrr!* (1986), which allowed them to tour with the likes of avant-garde thrashers Celtic Frost.

The first inkling that things were changing came with *Killing Technology* (1987) and its longer songs, though the real breakthrough occurred with *Dimension Hatröss* (1988). The song structures were more sophisticated and Snake was singing more rather than relying on the thrasher's shriek he had employed on their early albums. By the time of the stunning *Nothingface* (1989) they had reached a creative peak. Piggy's riffing had taken on a jazzy flavour, while the rhythms were hammered home in weird time signatures, creating a menacing, churning welter of off-the-wall dissonance. Comparisons were drawn with King Crimson and Rush, though the influence of Pink Floyd was now rather obvious in the form of a cover version of the Syd Barrett-era "Astronomy Domine". The video for the latter became something of a cult favourite on MTV, and the band toured with Soundgarden and Faith No More.

They moved to MCA Records and *Angel Rat* (1991) should have broken them to a mass market, but things failed to take off when

grunge kicked in – the alternative metal stance of the band seemed to cut no ice with a public that was turned off by anything with an 80s connection. Blacky decided to leave and the band continued as a trio on *The Outer Limits* (1993) – featuring the 17-minute epic "Jack Luminous" – but they were really just treading water before the inevitable decline. Next to jump ship was Snake, marking the start of a period in the metal wilderness, even though bassist/vocalist **Eric Forrest** stepped in. The inevitable stylistic changes meant that *Negatron* (1995) and *Phobos* (1997) were pale shadows of their predecessors. In a near-terminal twist to the tale, the band were involved in a tour bus crash in the late 90s that put Forrest out of action, though he recovered sufficiently to keep playing. Meanwhile *Kronik* (1998) reflected the obsession of the times with remixes and threw in a handful of live tracks and rarities. *Voivod Lives* (2000) was the last album to feature Forrest.

The rebirth of Voivod came when ex-Metallica bassist **Jason Newsted** aka **Jasonic** entered the picture. He had been a long-time fan of the band's music and had jammed with them during the 90s under the band name of **Tarrat**. It was inevitable that Newsted would become involved on a more permanent basis, and with Snake back in the band Voivod were very much equipped to wreak jazz prog-metal havoc once more. *Voivod* (2003) took them back to the sound of their early-90s heyday and was a resounding critical hit. What's more the band ended up playing Ozzfest during the summer and Newsted was also asked to play bass in Ozzy Osbourne's band.

 Nothingface
1989; Mechanic/MCA

A peculiar hybrid of cerebral prog-rock and mesmerizing metal; sci-fi concepts just don't come more satisfying than this. Mutant melodies weave and twist through this brain-addling and complex journey while the band hammers it all home with furious conviction.

THE VON BONDIES

Formed Detroit, Michigan, US, 2000

There's no purer rush than that provided by primal rock'n'roll, and so it stands to reason that a band like **The Von Bondies** are one of the most exciting new bands

playing the devil's own music today. Everything that goes around comes around, as the saying goes, and while much of the mid- to late 90s was obsessed with nu-metal, rapcore, rap-metal or whatever else you want to call it, it was inevitable that the rock pendulum would swing back to the kind of hellish racket created by teenagers playing guitar till their fingers bleed in seedy garages the world over. And garages come no seedier than those in legendary Detroit. Within its urban sprawl can be found the raw material – the million and one tales of love and survival – that spawn great bluesy rock'n'roll. Think of the artists shaped by the city: The Stooges, MC5, Alice Cooper, Ted Nugent And The Amboy Dukes. The Von Bondies have a strong heritage to live up to – even if their leader, **Jason Stollsteimer**, claims not to own any classic Detroit rock albums.

At the turn of the millennium the Detroit rock scene was positively dripping with bands trading on the city's former glories: The White Stripes, the Electric 6, the Dirtbombs, the Detroit Cobras were all making waves. The Von Bondies were originally known as the **Baby Killers** but wisely opted for a name change, even if the music stayed the same. Jason Stollsteimer (guitar/vocals), **Marcie Bolen** (guitar), **Carrie Smith** (bass) and **Don Blum** (drums) took the energy of punk and the soul of Motown and channelled it into the classic template of overdriven guitar.

"It Came From Japan" (a tribute to rock'n'roll) and "Nite Train" (a tale about Stollsteimer getting loaded for the first time) were the first recordings to emerge in 2000. However, *Lack Of Communication* (2001) was what garnered major attention, being produced by The White Stripes' **Jack White**. The White Stripes also gave them the support slot on their European tour, providing the kind of exposure most young bands would kill for. Not surprisingly, within six months the Bondies were headlining their own shows and soon making prestigious appearances on various TV shows, such as *Later With Jools Holland*, and playing at the Leeds and Reading festivals.

The sudden upswing in their popularity of course meant plenty of new fans ravenous for every note and squall of feedback the band had produced. With supplies of the early singles disappearing fast *Raw And Rare* (2003) dished up some spontaneous and energetic

BBC sessions and a few choice live cuts to keep things rocking while the band worked feverishly at their major-label debut for Reprise. In a surprising turn of events the apparently cosy little world of Detroit's sunlight-fearing garage dwellers was rocked in a different way all together. Jack White was charged with assaulting Stollsteimer at the Magic Stick nightclub. White was eventually charged with assault and battery and pleaded guilty; Stollsteimer meanwhile had to recover from a black eye and a slightly bruised ego.

Rock'n'roll fisticuffs aside, the excellent rabble-rousing "C'mon C'mon" gave a tantalizing and mildly glammy taste of what to expect from *Pawn Shoppe Heart* (2004). The new album showcased a band that had largely transcended their roots to become a free-wheeling rock entity in their own right. It displayed all the brashness and swagger of the early material but a greater confidence and a knowing ear for melody and passion.

Where the rock will take them next is anyone's guess, but if you're willing to take a chance you could be in for one hell of a ride.

Lack Of Communication
2001; Sweet Nothing

Aggressive, impassioned and raw, this record takes the fury of punk and uses it to supercharge classic bluesy garage rock. No wonder Jack White wanted to be their producer.

Raw And Rare
2003; Dim Mak

Missed some of those early chunks of vinyl? Then grab this and make yourself happy. These Peel show radio sessions and live tracks snap and snarl with plenty of feral attitude.

Pawn Shoppe Heart
2004; Reprise

The first one sounded great but this one sounds even sexier, boasting a keen ear for hooks and a desire to shake you to your soul with the cleansing fire of rock'n'roll.

Formed New York, US, 1988;
disbanded 1995; re-formed 1999; disbanded 2000

Another of those bands that should have been world-beaters, **Warrior Soul** were an antidote to the brainlessness of hair metal and should have done well in the alternative 90s with their uncompromising and political agit-rock. But this band fell victim to the vagaries of a record label that didn't know how to deal with them – and, of course, their own vices.

Chief sloganeer, lyric-architect and polemicist **Kory Clarke** (vocals) had worked as a club video-DJ and poetry performance-artist, and was seeking a new vehicle to get his views on contemporary America across to as wide an audience as possible. Clarke was an iconoclast, an outspoken rock'n'roll revolutionary willing to take punk idealism and fuse it to a crushing metallic blast. With a band assembled at the tail-end of the 80s and signed to Geffen – after only five gigs – he immediately ran into problems when the label wanted to remodel the line-up.

Finally, with **Pete McClanahan** (bass), **John Ricco** (guitar) and **Paul Ferguson** (drums) on board, they released the quite magnificent *Last Decade Dead Century* (1990). Dubbed psyche-rock – presumably because it was psychedelic and psychotic – the critics loved it. *Kerrang!* declared it to be as unique as the first Metallica, Queensrÿche or King's X album, and the band were hailed as visionary artists. The record label didn't understand it

at all – especially Clarke's desire to read poetry live – and didn't know how to market them. Their management, the all-powerful **Q Prime** (Def Leppard and Metallica), tried to persuade the earnest frontman to tone it all down a bit – but failed. In the resulting publicity vacuum Clarke decided to make some of his own by picking verbal fights with various big-name bands – except Metallica, with whom they toured Europe.

The clash between Warrior Soul's stubborn – some would say naive – attempts to maintain some integrity and the demands of the industry resulted in a steady deterioration in relationships both inside the band and with the label. This wasn't immediately obvious with the punchy follow-ups, *Drugs, God And The New Republic* (1991), where they went for a more straight-ahead rock sound, and *Salutations From The Ghetto Nation* (1992). But with a label unwilling to promote the band, there was only one possible outcome.

By the time of *Chill Pill* (1993), with new drummer **Mark Evans**, it really looked as if the band had nowhere to go. Fans and critics still hailed them as unique but without the breakthrough to take them to the next level, the pressure was growing. Within the line-up the self-destruct button had been pressed, and the drugs kicked in with a vengeance – both Evans and McClanahan were on a narcotics-induced downward spiral – and after a major fist-fight between Ricco and Clarke things almost fell apart. With **Scott Dubois** (drums) and **Alex Arundel** aka **X-Factor** (guitar), they staggered on to the *Space Age Playboys* (1994) album, released on

Music For Nations, and they played their final UK gig at the Donington Monsters of Rock in 1995. The delightful *Fucker* (aka *Odds And Ends*) (1996) was a rarities collection snapped up by the fans. But by now the band were history.

The unstoppable Clarke then created the **Space Age Playboys**, a band designed to be the antithesis of Warrior Soul, an all-out trashy punk'n'roll party band, who managed *New Rock Underground* (1998) and *Live in London* (1999). The desire to re-form his former band proved to be too strong, however, and the old line-up came together for a reunion gig at London's LA2; the *Classics* (2001) album appeared, which rerecorded a spiky fistful of vintage Warrior Soul tracks with a much more immediate and in-your-face production. Sadly, the old tensions in the band prevented the reunion from being anything other than a short-lived distraction. Clarke was last spotted pursuing a solo career.

⊙ Last Decade Dead Century
1990; Geffen

Stark and poetically brutal, tracks such as "Trippin' On Ecstasy" and "Charlie's Out Of Prison" – the latter about Clarke's former drug-running employer – document the front man's brushes with narcotic culture; meanwhile tunes such as "Blown Away" and "Superpower Dreamland" bite deep into America's capacity for corruption and self-delusion.

WASP

Formed Los Angeles, US, 1982

White Anglo Saxon Protestants? Or the infinitely more entertaining We Are Sexual Perverts? Whatever really inspired their name, when ex-New York Doll **Blackie Lawless** (vocals/bass) decided to put the band together he created one of the most celebrated, reviled and downright enjoyably daft bands of the 80s. **WASP** were up there with the likes of Mötley Crüe and Twisted Sister as bands that struck fear into the hearts of moral guardians everywhere with their excessive shock-rocking ways, outrageous stage shows and gratuitously salacious lyrics. Of course, the kids loved them. Who wouldn't be impressed by Lawless's freakish dress sense and penchant for codpieces incorporating buzz-saw blades

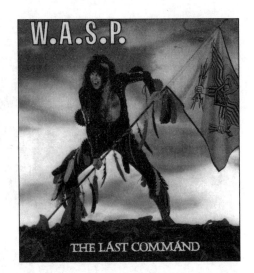

and flame throwers? And then there were the songs: Lawless's husky scream fronting lascivious slabs of anthemic metal detailing sexual conquests and promoting the rock'n'roll lifestyle up to and beyond the hilt.

It was an epic recipe virtually guaranteeing trouble from Tipper Gore and the Parents Music Resource Center, the right-wing pressure group formed with a view to censoring the fun out of rock'n'roll. Such was the violent reaction Lawless and his equally degenerate crew – the infamous **Chris Holmes** (guitar), **Randy Piper** (guitar) and **Tony Richards** (drums) – would regularly incite that the man might as well have painted a target on his forehead, because the threats of litigation, death and otherwise, came thick and fast once he had proclaimed his teen rebellion agenda. And that proclamation came loud and clear when, having signed to Capitol Records, they decided that "Animal (Fuck Like A Beast)" ought to be their first single.

In the end Music For Nations released the offending article in early 1984, WASP's infamy assured in one masterful stroke. No one would play the song on air, but after all the public outrage every self-respecting metalhead wanted it. Even now it is the song that springs to mind when anyone mentions Lawless and co. When their eponymous debut tore into the open air later the same year it became immediately clear where they were coming from, Lawless's astute commercial sensibilities bringing instantly hummable hooks to tunes like "I Wanna Be Somebody", "LOVE Machine" and "On Your Knees".

GLENN A. BAKER ARCHIVES/REDFERNS

WASP's Blackie (2nd from left) prepares a little surprise for Tipper.

Musically and theatrically WASP owed more than a debt of gratitude to Kiss and Alice Cooper, the lewd lyrics inspiring a stage show that was tacky, offensive and absurdly amusing. There were half-naked women tied to racks, nuns tortured and pigs ritually "slaughtered" – and the amount of raw meat thrown into the crowd regularly made the stage resemble an abattoir.

The band's off-stage antics drew plenty of attention too with Holmes rapidly developing a reputation for being an alcohol sponge. The man's boozing capacity soon became the stuff of legend and was eventually immortalized in Penelope Spheeris's 1988 documentary *The Decline Of Western Civilization Part II: The Metal Years*, where the drunk and incapable Holmes can be seen sloshing around in his mother's swimming pool, downing bottles of vodka and attempting to speak about his rock-star lifestyle.

WASP's debut follow-up, *The Last Command* (1985), was yet more of the same only with **Steven Riley** on drums. Appropriately enough for Holmes, one of the stand-out cuts was "Blind In Texas", an enjoyable little hymn to the virtues of firewater, while glammy, trashy tunes like "Ballcrusher" and "Sex Drive" ensured yet more attention from Tipper and her cronies.

It was so successful they decided to do the same thing all over again for *Inside The Electric Circus* (1986), this time with new bassist **Johnny Rod** and Lawless shifting his attention to guitar. One year later they scored a hit with "Scream Until You Like It", included on the soundtrack to tongue-in-cheek horror flick *Ghoulies II*, while *Live In The Raw* captured the full-blown, raunch'n'roll of the stage show. And then it all went a touch weird with *The Headless Children* (1989), which featured ex-**Quiet Riot** drummer **Frankie Banali** and ex-**Uriah Heep** keyboard wizard **Ken Hensley**, though the band was effectively a trio now. The music was as brazen as ever, but Lawless's attempts at vaguely socially aware lyrics sat awkwardly alongside tunes celebrating the crash-and-burn lifestyle. All of which marked the end of an era for the band. They had scored their biggest chart hit with their last album and scored in the singles chart with a cover of The Who's "The Real Me" and "Mean Man", but the band was falling apart.

Lawless decided that Holmes and his alcoholic ways had to go. With one of the band's key players gone, things rapidly hit the skids. Lawless continued under the WASP name for the next record, *The Crimson Idol* (1992), though it was in effect almost a solo effort. It was also a surprisingly successful concept album, a fact that astonished many critics who had thought the band and their main-man to be washed up, making his tale of a rock star in torment somewhat appropriate.

True, Lawless handled a large portion of the playing but he was greatly helped by ultra-slick lead guitarist **Bruce Kulick** (ex-**Kiss**, ex-**Meat Loaf**).

Kulick stuck around to help out with *Still Not Black Enough* (1995), which was even more of a solo Lawless effort. But with 1997's *Kill, Fuck, Die* things really went downhill, despite the fact that Holmes was back in the band. Lawless sounded mightily angry – and well he might have been, seeing how first grunge and now nu-metal had given him and his music a commercial pounding. As an effort to go head to head with the likes of Marilyn Manson, the album was less than satisfying, the industrial trimmings being somewhat at odds with the traditional WASP sound. Its follow-up, *Helldorado* (1999) – punctuated on either side by concert albums *Double Live Assassins* and *The Sting* – was back to the basic WASP blueprint, however, with Lawless seemingly trying to out-Spinal Tap himself with ludicrously idiotic tunes such as "Dirty Balls" and "Don't Cry (Just Suck)". It was far from pretty and hard to dispel the feeling that they were all trying far too desperately to reclaim some of the old glory.

With the next two albums – *Unholy Terror* (2001) and *Dying For The World* (2002) – the man was turning on the seriousness again. Holmes was only around for the former, a collection of songs partly inspired by Lawless's musings on religion and politics, while the latter album was written in the shadow of 9/11 with Lawless directing righteous anger at those who kill with heaven in mind. The next album, *The Neon God Part One: The Rise*, was far more in tune with the *Crimson Idol*-era WASP, yet another concept album about the rise of a dark messiah, the storyline of which was resolved in *Part 2–The Demise* (2004).

Quite where Lawless plans to take WASP in the future can only be guessed. The past decade has seen him trying to offset his rauchy, hellraising tendencies with more mature, and experimental outings. It hasn't always been successful but, for better or for worse, it has always definitely been WASP.

 WASP
1984; Capitol

Lawless's love of anthemic Kiss-style metal is evident throughout even if the band go way beyond the pale with their gratuitously sleazy lyrics. Definitely not for those of a sensitive disposition.

 The Last Command
1985; Capitol

Yet more OTT metal designed to offend parents and please teens. A mad splurge of blood and bodily fluids from the man with a taste for raw meat and a flame-thrower attached to his groin.

The Crimson Idol
1992; Capitol

Who would have thought that Lawless was capable of a half-decent concept album? The story might be a bit of a cliché but the metal is as mean as before.

WHITESNAKE

Formed London UK, 1978;
disbanded 1990; re-formed 1997 and 2002

There couldn't be any clearer indication of what you're going to get from **Whitesnake** than the cover of their *Lovehunter* (1979) album: a naked young lady astride a giant writhing snake. It really doesn't take a genius to work it out. The gentleman out hunting for lurve is, of course, **David Coverdale**, a vocalist with the kind of husky-blues bellow to make rock maidens weep and go weak at the knees.

Coverdale's career as the Lothario of bluesy hard rock began with **Deep Purple** and the albums *Burn*, *Stormbringer* and *Come Taste The Band*. When the Purple fell apart in 1976 Coverdale sought to get a solo career underway, which he did in fits and starts, with *David Coverdale's Whitesnake* and *Northwinds* (both 1977). Weird contractual problems and the prevalence of punk and disco prevented him from getting things going more quickly.

The albums were decent enough, with the accent on the blues, and featured **Micky Moody** (guitar) and **Roger Glover** (keyboards/bass). But Whitesnake first appeared as an entity with the *Snakebite* EP in 1978 featuring "Ain't No Love In The Heart Of The City", a cover of a Bobby Bland song that would become a live staple for the band. Coverdale had a line-up that included Moody, **Bernie Marsden** (guitar), **David Dowle** (drums) and **Neil Murray** (bass), the band's veteran standing providing a firm base upon which to build a following. *Trouble* (1978) was their first effort, which also brought in Deep Purple keyboardist **Jon Lord**.

Things didn't really pick up, however, until the infamously lewd cover of *Lovehunter* – the artist Chris Achilleas was renowned for his erotic fantasy work – hit the (top?) shelves and went Top 30 in the UK. The following year, however, the Snake were primed for success, Deep Purple drummer **Ian Paice** replacing Dowle. "Fool For Your Loving", the powerful opening track to *Ready An' Willing* (1980), went to #13 in the singles chart with the album hitting #6. The only downer – and it was a superficial one – was the incredibly drab monochrome band photo used for the sleeve. After the storm created

by *Lovehunter* they completely wimped out. Still, the songs did more than make up for it.

The surge in popularity sparked a release of *Live … In The Heart Of The City* (1980), a recording of a 1980 Hammersmith Odeon gig, plus the tracks that originally had been available only in Japan as *Live At Hammersmith*, recorded back in 1978. It was a superb concert set that displayed the raw power of the band and sealed their reputation as one of the UK's best live acts. They seemed unstoppable when *Come An' Get It* (1981) bounded up to #2 in the chart and sealed their place at the Donington Monsters of Rock festival.

Despite the headway made, internal pressures resulted in a bout of line-up shifts bringing in **Cozy Powell** (drums), **Colin Hodgkinson** (bass) and **Mel Galley** (guitar), replacing Marsden; there had been alterations in personnel before but from now the band changed with alarming regularity. Nevertheless *Saints And Sinners* (1982) – despite its patchy genesis – was embraced by heavy rock fans and contained "Crying In The Rain" and "Here I Go Again" which would reappear in revved up form on *1987*. A headlining slot at Donington beckoned in 1983 before *Slide It In* (1984) – a title that did them no favours among critics who still derided Coverdale for being sexist – delivered yet another macho fistful of pumping hard rock. The creation of their latest batch of trouser-trembling tunes had been marred by problems. Coverdale had sacked original producer **Eddie Kramer** and brought in old hand **Martin Birch** who had produced their other work. In the end the album was tweaked and in some places rerecorded with the help of the returning Murray and guitarist **John Sykes** (ex-**Thin Lizzy**, ex-**Tygers Of Pan Tang**) for the American market. On top of this the singer was suffering from throat problems, which seriously delayed putting together the next album.

It took three years to get *1987* into shape with the additional help of **Aynsley Dunbar** (drums), **Bill Cuomo** (keyboards), **Don Airey** (keyboards) and **Adrian Vandenberg** (guitar). The Coverdale- and Sykes-penned songs took the band into a completely different realm. The punchy blues numbers were largely replaced by polished, streamlined heavy rock with a distinct MTV sheen creating a huge-sounding album of massive commercial potential. They took full advantage, starting with the shuddering Led Zeppelin-inspired

JØRGEN ANGEL/REDFERNS

David Coverdale gets his microphone out for the ladies.

metal of "Still Of The Night". It was the start of a powerful video campaign that would feature the future Mrs David Coverdale, model Tawny Kitaen. The album was simply dripping with hit singles and "Is This Love" went to #2 in the US while "Here I Go Again" topped the chart. And if the music sounded impeccable then Coverdale recast the band for the ultimate live cock-rock line-up. Publicity shots featuring Coverdale, Vandenberg, **Vivian Campbell** (guitar), **Rudy Sarzo** (bass) and **Tommy Aldridge** (drums) show the band to be immaculately coiffed, taking the art of hair metal to new Olympic heights matched only by their stratospheric record sales.

Even this elite version of Whitesnake didn't last. Campbell was soon out and replaced by **Steve Vai** (ex-**David Lee Roth**, ex-**Frank Zappa**) with his even more technically proficient sound. *Slip Of The Tongue* (1989) – Coverdale yet again displaying his knack with titles – was every bit as majestic as its predecessor, but for many the addition of Vai took the band's sound away from its original blues roots, though they did recycle "Fool For Your Loving" for a modest hit single.

When they headlined the Donington Monsters of Rock festival in 1990 it looked as if this would be the last of Whitesnake. Coverdale then went off to work with **Led Zeppelin** guitarist **Jimmy Page** for *Coverdale/Page* (1993), which came as something of a relief after the more histrionic output from Whitesnake. Anyone who needed reminding of what they sounded like had the opportunity to pick up *Greatest Hits* (1994), which did exactly what it said on the

sleeve and wasn't a 'best of' by any stretch of the imagination. Under the name David Coverdale & Whitesnake the singer brought back Vandenberg and reformed the band for *Restless Heart* (1997), sensibly shedding the arena-pleasing sound of the 80s for a much bluesier feel. He also took Vandenberg off to Japan to record *Starkers in Tokyo* (1997), a successful little acoustic jaunt. Another three years passed before another solo album, *Into The Light*.

In 2002 Whitesnake re-formed to tour. They played the 2003 Monsters of Rock tour supported by Y&T and Gary Moore and headed off on some European dates in 2004 with the line-up of **Doug Aldrich** (guitar, ex-**Dio**), **Reb Beach** (guitar, ex-Dokken), **Timothy Drury** (keyboards, ex-Eagles), **Marco Mendoza** (bass, ex-**Ted Nugent**) and Whitesnake veteran Tommy Aldridge (drums). Meanwhile EMI set about plundering the archives for various compilations.

⊙ 1987
1987; EMI

It's a bit cheeky rehashing old tunes, but this entire album is so assuredly ROCK that you can forgive them. The songs are fantastic and absolutely synonymous with 80s metal. Indispensable.

⊙ The Early Years
2004; EMI

If you don't know which early album to go for (*Ready An' Willing* is ace) then this very fine compilation covers a lot of bases, assembling tracks from Mr Coverdale's career prior to the excesses of the MTV era.

THE WHO

Formed London, UK, 1964;
disbanded 1983; re-formed at various times since

"The last time I got my rocks off to something was when I saw Pete Townshend ... I looked and thought this fucker's dangerous! I was frightened but excited..." Angus Young

The booze, the drugs, the breakdowns, the cars in swimming pools, the wrecked hotel rooms, the trashed equipment, and, of course, those stupendous windmill power chords – **The Who** are way up there

THE WHO SELL OUT

Replacing the stale smell of excess with
the sweet smell of success,
Peter Townshend, who, like nine out of ten stars,
needs it. Face the music with Odorono,
the all-day deodorant that
turns perspiration into inspiration.

THE WHO SELL OUT

This way to a cowboy's breakfast.
Daltrey rides again. Thinks: "Thanks to Heinz
Baked Beans every day is a super day".
Those who know how many beans make five
get Heinz beans inside and outside at
every opportunity. Get saucy.

which is undoubtedly the classic rebellious ode to alienated youth "My Generation", one of the most oft-covered tunes in popular music. It was one of the standout cuts on *My Generation* (1965) and was inducted into the Grammy Hall Of Fame in 1999.

The following year *A Quick One* earned the distinction of being the first Who album to feature a mini-opera in "A Quick One, While He's Away". On the deluxe remastered version of the awesome *Live At Leeds* (1970) Townshend introduces the mini-epic as the parent to The Who's ambitious *Tommy* (1969). Before their first fabled excursion into full-blown rock opera territory they eased themselves into concept album mode with *The Who Sell Out* (1967). Taking a light dip in psychedelic waters, though the album had no storyline, the songs were linked together with fake adverts with the intention of creating the ambience of a pirate radio broadcast. It gave them one of their strongest live tunes in the hit single "I Can See For Miles", which provided them with their first truly major break in the US chart. Another (incomplete) rock operatic fragment appeared at the end of the album in the form of the "Rael" tracks.

The story of the famously deaf, dumb and blind kid was to be one of their most celebrated pieces of work. Complex, both musically and symbolically, and commanding an enduring fascination, *Tommy* and its success would lead to a symphonic version in 1972, the 1975 cult film directed by Ken Russell, and a Townshend-aided 1993 Broadway musical adaptation.

Townshend's desire to push The Who even further towards concept works led to the mythical *Lifehouse* project, which was to have been a synthesis of film script, performance art and Who music with a view to revolutionizing the face of modern rock. The project, however, failed to find a focus. Recording sessions in New York didn't go

in rock'n'roll lore as one of the most influential bands in history.

Back in the early 60s the band were known as **The High Numbers** and had a distinctly more mod than rocker outlook, but as they progressed they expanded their horizons to include psychedelic pop and eventually heavy rock via concept albums and rock operas.

Chief composer was **Pete Townshend**, whose full-on scything guitar drove the songs forward. But each of the band members contributed their own style to the sound. **Roger Daltrey's** vocals exuded primal sexual aggression; **Keith Moon** was a charismatic madman behind the kit, playing the drums as a lead instrument; and **John Entwistle's** fluid and complex bass lines more than underpinned the rhythm. Together they took a basic r'n'b sound and blasted it into energized fragments, much like their equipment, which regularly got smashed, to the delight of audiences who would come along to their early gigs purely to witness the band freaking out.

Their first single, issued as The High Numbers, was "I'm The Face" but as The Who they scored the first of many high-charting hits with "I Can't Explain". It went to #8 in the UK and began an impressive run of single successes, the most famous of according to plan and this, plus their deteriorating relationship with their manager **Kit Lambert**, almost pushed the guitarist over the edge. The copious boozing and drugs didn't help either. Ultimately, what was salvaged by producer **Glyn Johns** in the band's London recording sessions became *Who's Next* (1971), one of the greatest rock albums ever recorded, a chart-topper in the UK and a top-five hit in America.

Amid the release of various solo efforts from everyone bar Moon, Townshend's preoccupation with mod culture and the lonely desperation of youth came through in the band's last rock opera, *Quadrophenia* (1973). The title referred to the four personality traits displayed by the lead character, a mod named Jimmy. Like *Tommy*, the story worked its way into the UK's pop-culture consciousness and was turned into a celebrated film in the late 70s.

The *Odds And Sods* (1974) collection came next, while Moon finally got his act together for the poor *Two Sides Of The Moon* (1975), his only solo album. By this point the various members were embroiled in a variety of extracurricular activities – Daltrey, in particular, had launched an acting career – but came together for *The Who By Numbers* (1975), a move towards a more discrete song format. The change was consolidated with *Who Are You?* (1978), but shortly after the record was released, after years of leading a seemingly charmed life, Moon died of a drugs overdose following a party; ironically, the drug in question was medication prescribed to control alcoholism.

With one-quarter of the band's inimitable chemistry gone, it looked like The Who might fold but they recruited ex-Faces drummer **Kenney Jones** and came back with *Face Dances* (1981) and a hit single, "You Better You Bet". *It's Hard* (1982), however, was their last studio album, and the band split in 1983.

Since then The Who have re-formed on various occasions to play live, their first being an appearance at Live Aid in 1985. In 1989, they got together for a 25th-anniversary tour of America with **Simon Phillips** taking Jones's place. More reunion appearances took place in the mid-90s, and in October 2001 they played the Concert For NYC benefit for families of the victims of the 9/11 terrorist attacks. In June 2002, with a US tour about to get under way, Entwistle died from a cocaine-induced heart attack. His

replacement was renowned sessioneer **Pino Palladino**, who had played on some of Townshend's solo efforts.

Alongside the reunion gigs there has been a steady flow of Who compilations, including *Thirty Years Of Maximum R&B* (1994), a huge 80-track box set of favourites and rarities; *My Generation: The Very Best Of The Who* (1996); and *The Ultimate Collection* (2002).

⊙ Live At Leeds
1970; MCA

Townshend supervised the remixing process for this album when the entire concert was finally made available. It contains a performance of *Tommy* and the energy level is quite incredible. A live classic.

⊙ Who's Next
1971; Track

Heavier than *Tommy*, the fragments of a vague concept idea still float around these magnificent songs. "Baba O'Riley" and "Behind Blue Eyes" are stupendous, and if "Won't Get Fooled Again" doesn't have you windmilling with Pete then you are a lost cause. The remixed and remastered reissue contains a whole host of bonus goodies.

⊙ The Ultimate Collection
2002; Polydor

This album is very boldly titled but thankfully delivers in spades. The double-CD set takes in the band's mod beginnings and leads the listener all the way through to their later studio output. Of course the classic hits stand out and though a compilation could never hope to do justice to the likes of *Tommy* or *Quadrophenia* the track selection plucks out some very worthy highlights.

THE WILDHEARTS

Formed London, UK, 1989;
disbanded 1997; re-formed 2001

"The whole point of the band was to sound as good as my fave bands, the Replacements and Hüsker Dü, to be as violent as Big Black and as tuneful as Cheap Trick." Ginger

When it comes to writing witty and effortlessly hooky heavy-rock tunes, **Wildhearts** main man **Ginger** is nothing short of a master. Not only that – he produces new songs at an unbelievable rate. Singles always come with non-album tracks, albums turn up with bonus discs of new material, side projects feature loads of original fresh cuts. He is a challenge for fans and completists alike. Coupled with this prolific work rate comes a personality that thrives on mayhem. In The Wildhearts' relatively short but turbulent career they have developed a reputation for chaos and unpredictability. Despite the day-to-day roller coaster ride, the band have a rabidly loyal following based upon their ability to write eminently chart-ready tunes and to positively slay in concert. They are endearingly manic, utterly compelling and one of the best heavy bands the UK has ever produced.

Born in South Shields, **Ginger** (guitars/vocals) went through the usual teenage motions of mis-spending his formative years playing in a variety of rock bands, before moving to London and ending up in honky-tonk boogie merchants **Quireboys**. The role of hired gun on extra guitar duties proved to be far too restrictive and he ended up sacked for being his usual lairy self. As a passionate songwriter, he was keen to find a suitable outlet for his creative energies and after being cut loose and wallowing in the gutter for a while he set about creating the bastard-monster that is The Wildhearts.

Going through countless personnel changes over the years, the first vaguely stable line-up consisted of Ginger along with **Chris Jadghar** aka **CJ** (guitars, ex-**Tattooed Love Boys**), **Danny McCormack** (bass) and **Bam** (drums, ex-**Dogs D'Amour**). After a series of demo sessions, the band were eventually snapped up by EastWest.

Their first release, the brilliantly titled *Mondo-Akimbo-A-Go-Go* EP (1992), showed signs of a rushed genesis – the production woefully lacked anything remotely like balls – and was whipped out to coincide with a special guest slot supporting the Manic Street Preachers. Working through his bitter feelings about record companies, Ginger's lyrics on "Turning American" and "Nothing Ever Changes But The Shoes" were spiteful and venomous. The record as a whole, though, lacked the razor-sharp attack of subsequent releases. The whole thing was soon re-recorded in Seattle with producer **Terry Date** (**Pantera**, **Soundgarden**).

Showing a distinct love for perverse titles, the rerecordings were released, with four new cuts of prime frothy punk metal, as mini-LP *Don't Be Happy ... Just Worry* (1992). Among the new tracks the outstanding "Splattermania" detailed a love of gory horror movies, while a maturer side was evident in "Weekend (Five Days Long)", a song for those who know what it's like to be dead-end bored and aimless.

Despite the brevity of their career so far the band were already developing a militantly uncompromising attitude as an antidote to what they saw as the daily bullshit they had to deal with, an attitude which extended beyond the music and into their cover art. So far this had included a bloody ox's heart pierced with a toy arrow, and their trade-mark demon smiley face surrounded by dis-embowelled cartoon smiley faces. This attitude became even more apparent on the subsequent tour slots with Love/Hate and Izzy Stradlin when each night they blitzed through a scuzzy 35-minute set at ear-bleeding volume. They lasted a single night on the Stradlin tour (Nottingham Rock City) before they were ditched for bad behaviour. Typically, they responded by publicly slagging Stradlin off in the press. More touring with Pantera and Wolfsbane followed and they finally found a permanent drummer in the shape of **Ritch Battersby**.

Their first full album – recorded with earlier sticksman **Andrew 'Stidi' Stidolph** – *Earth Vs The Wildhearts* (1993), received rave reviews from almost every quarter for its mix of speed and ragged melody. Ginger's lyrics detailed everything from life in London ("Greetings From Shitsville") through to a sensitive take on relationships ("My Baby Is A Headfuck"). Never content to cruise along in neutral the band busily set about upsetting their record company again with the artwork to their first single release, "Greetings... "; it featured their producer, **Simon Efemy**, defecating into a pitta bread pouch. The original photos were never used but the single was, of course, limited to a brown vinyl seven-inch release.

Coinciding with the release of their first top-forty single, "Caffeine Bomb", in March 1994, the album was rereleased with the new song included. The Wildhearts' equivalent to Motörhead's "Ace of Spades", it skidded into the charts helped along by a hilarious appearance on *Top Of The Pops*. The band took the stage looking like an explosion at a jumble sale: multicoloured shiny spandex, fluorescent brothel-creepers, glam face-paint, and sun goggles. The Full Roar tour followed and was topped off with the headlining slot on the *Metal Hammer* stage at Donington.

Meanwhile, behind the scenes, things were falling apart. Danny appeared to lose his marbles after a debauched bout of chemical recreation, and Ginger and CJ were constantly fighting. In the end, the management sacked CJ who went off to form **Honeycrack** with **Willie Dowling** (their unofficial keyboard player). This was to prove the beginning of their troubles with guitarists. **Devin Townsend** (guitars), then of Stevie Vai fame, was drafted in as a short-term replacement for the group's Reading Festival slot. The show was a stormer, with the usually effervescent Danny dislocating his knee during set-opener "Caffeine Bomb". He finished the set sat at the edge of the stage, and to add insult to injury the band were nearly fined for playing just over the legal noise limit.

The winter brought the release of the fanclub-only record *Fishing For Luckies* (1994) at a special bargain price, an opportunity for people to hear a more esoteric side to the band. It was an excuse to take their songwriting to new levels of weirdness with the majority of the six tracks clocking in at over seven minutes. One moment they came on like The Pogues with "Geordie In Wonderland", the next they hammered through an 11-minute prog-metaller, "Sky Babies", apparently inspired by Ginger's UFO fixation.

By January 1995 the band had obviously decided that they had gone far too long without any major trouble. Following an erroneous report in rock magazine *Kerrang!* that Danny was about to be booted out of the band, they marched into the magazine's offices and set about trashing the offending

journalist's computer. The resulting publicity simply added to the growing myth of The Wildhearts' volatility.

Fishing for Luckies

In a season of mixed fortunes, they found themselves searching for another guitarist after Townsend's tenure ended. The replacement came in the shape of **Mark Keds** (ex-**Senseless Things**) just as they made another appearance on *Top Of The Pops* in support of "Geordie In Wonderland". It was agreed that Keds would be a permanent member after he had fulfilled contractual obligations in Japan.

The next studio release, *P.H.U.Q.* (1995), was hailed as a masterpiece across the board. Featuring hints of punk, the focus was more on a fat, heavy, textured rock sound, an approach best appreciated on the cracking "Jonesing For Jones" and "Caprice". At last they were developing beyond the cartoony image into a band of true substance. The critical acclaim, however, was not matched by record sales, and the band's relationship with EastWest, which Ginger had described as "hate-hate", began to deteriorate further. Meanwhile the summer brought the infamous Phoenix Festival debacle. Keds failed to return after his stint in Japan was over and the band had to pull out of their booked slot. In typical diplomatic fashion they threatened to "kick his head in" if they got their hands on him. Unknown quantity **Jeff Streatfield** (guitars) was his replacement.

Late summer brought more drama in the shape of a threatened split after the planned tour. They had grown to hate EastWest so much that they simply refused to play ball. When the record company decided to release

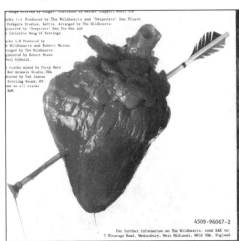

Fishing... plus three unreleased tracks through normal retail outlets at full album price, it looked like the last straw. Sickened by the crass cynicism of the marketing ploy, Ginger urged fans not to buy it.

The offending plans were eventually put on ice and after a protracted period out of the limelight the band re-emerged without East-West and a whole fistful of new tunes. Distributed through Warners, "Sick Of Drugs", on the band's own Round Records label, slipped easily into the charts on a wave of excitement and expectation and peaked at #14 in the UK. To accompany the new single the band decided to rerelease *Fishing For Luckies* (1996) as a resequenced and full-length album containing no less than eight fresh tracks. As everyone had expected, The Wildhearts had too much left to say and do to let themselves go under as the result of a feud.

The remainder of the year brought yet more rumours of an imminent split and a blatant EastWest cash-in release, *The Best Of The Wildhearts* (1996), seemed to underline the possibility. The rumours seemed to have been spawned by the band's early return from supporting on the US leg of AC/DC's world tour. On their first proper outing to the States the band had run out of money and tensions had grown to critical point. Anyone familiar with The Wildhearts' ability to thrive on near disaster will find nothing unusual about their recovery. Having cleared the air, they managed to hold on to the same line-up, sign to the hip and trendy Mushroom Records label and set about recording a new album without the usual interference from company executives. Apart from a

thoroughly shredded version of Elvis Costello's "Pump It Up", one of the first songs to emerge from the sessions was "Anthem" penned by McCormack, his first successful foray into writing.

The band finally emerged from the studio having forged a new sound on *Endless Nameless* (1997). The usual melodic trademarks were present but buried under a deliberately harsh industrial-style production job, making it frustratingly inaccessible at best and at worst completely unlistenable. It was as though they had set out with the express purpose of annoying as many people as possible. Sounding like an explosion in an anvil factory, it was a clattering, metallic mess, the kind of thing only a band on the verge of folding might release as a final "fuck you" to everyone, especially the music industry. It proved to be the last thing they would release for a time, as the band split, though they did re-form a short while later for a tour of Japan.

It looked as though one of the UK's best bands were through. In the vacuum, *Anarchic Airwaves* (1998) and *Landmines And Pantomimes* (1998), both releases disowned by the band, gave the fans plenty of rarities, B-sides and radio session tracks to work through. Meanwhile, The Wildhearts' popularity in Japan resulted in the huge *Moodswings And Roundabouts* (1998) box set and *Tokyo Suits Me* (1999) live album.

The various members didn't stop working in the time that the band were out of action, however. Everyone seemed to have a pet project to keep them busy. The two most prominent members were Danny McCormack, who went off to form the **Yo-Yos**, and, of course, Ginger whose incredible work rate seemed to double as he became the most ubiquitous man in rock. He wrote with mad guitar genius Devin Townsend (the tune "Christeen" turned up on *Infinity*); he worked with **Backyard Babies** and the garagey supergroup **Super$hit 666** (with members of Backyard Babies and **The Hellacopters**) – they recorded an eponymous album in 1998 which was finally released in 2000; he played his first acoustic show, which eventually became the hilarious *Grievous Acoustic Behaviour* (2001), with CJ, Danny McCormack and Ritch Battersby making guest appearances among the tiny, drunken crowd crammed into London's 12-Bar Club; he also set up a singles club. And then there was the **Clam Abuse** project with **Alex Kane** (Anti-Product) which produced the *Stop Thinking* album in 1999. The major thing that kept Ginger going, however, was the creation of supergroup **Silver Ginger 5** – featuring "Random" Jon Poole (bass, the Cardiacs), Conny Bloom (guitar, ex-Electric Boys) and Tom Broman (drums) – which resulted in *Black Leather Mojo* (2000) being released first in Japan before hitting the shelves elsewhere. For those suffering major Wildhearts withdrawal symptoms it was the next best thing, a bombastic and majestically excessive exercise in epic, hook-laden heavy rock.

It wasn't until 2001 that The Wildhearts reconvened to bring chaos to venues around the UK. The reunion tour would have been a peerless triumph had it not been for Danny McCormack's very public battle with heroin, which rendered him unable to play all the dates. Fortunately they borrowed support band Anti-Product's bassist **Toshi** to complete the tour – as luck would have it, Toshi had played in a Japanese Wildhearts tribute band so knew the songs backwards.

Sadly, Danny's problems meant that his input into subsequent recordings was minimal. A brace of superb singles followed, including "Vanilla Radio" and "Stormy In The North, Karma In The South", which found their way onto overseas mini-LP *Riff After Riff After Motherfucking Riff* (2002), before the first full-on technicolour blitz the band had indulged in since *Endless Nameless*. *The Wildhearts Must Be Destroyed* (2003) was a tough, melodic, sublime return to form, the true successor to *P.H.U.Q.* with Ginger handling both guitar and bass duties alongside CJ and Stidi – for the live shows Jon Poole was on

hand to provide bass. From the chunky chanted chorus of opener "Nexus Icon" to the closing blast of "Top Of The World" it was a succinct 32-minute rampage, a "fat-free whippet of an album" according to Ginger himself.

Naturally, with Ginger's rock'n'roll muse working overtime, a vast number of songs didn't fit the mood of the album and turned up as bonus tracks on the singles, so many that *Coupled With* (2004) featured another twenty tracks of prime Wildhearts, plus a video clip.

Honest, volatile, foul-mouthed and gloriously heavy, The Wildhearts will doubtless continue to grace the world of metal with their irrepressible energy for a long while yet – provided they can keep their act together.

Don't be Happy … Just Worry
1992; EastWest

Hard to find as the original double CD, this was re-released in 1994 as a single disc. Vastly improved after the tracks were rerecorded with Terry Date, it is still merely a hint of what the group were capable of; cartoon metal of the highest quality.

Earth Vs The Wildhearts
1993; EastWest

At last the band began to fulfil their early promise. The arrangements sometimes drift off into no-man's-land but the witty lyrics and harmony-laden hooks make this essential. Again it was re-released in 1994 with the single "Caffeine Bomb" included. A party classic and no mistake.

P.H.U.Q.
1995; EastWest

Including the Top 20 "I Wanna Go Where the People Go", this album is packed with classics. Ginger's lyrics are humorous and bitter while the overall sound is heavier and more textured than previous releases.

Fishing For Luckies
1996; Round Records/Warners

By the time this originally emerged the band truly hated their record label. This subsequent version, put out after parting with EastWest, virtually doubles the original number of tracks and is certainly worth investing in just to check out the deliberate weirdness the band were capable of as an antidote to writing three-minute classics.

The Best of The Wildhearts
1996; EastWest

Cynical cash-in or not, this is the kind of collection that will have fans arguing over the relative merits of what is included and lamenting over the exclusion of particular favourites. A mere taste of what the band can do, but pretty good all the same.

Landmines And Pantomimes
1998; Kuro Neko

A neat little package of B-sides, out-takes and previously unreleased top tunes which yet again prove that, had the band been able to keep their self-destructive tendencies in check, commercial success could have been attainable.

The Wildhearts Must Be Destroyed
2003; Gut Records

For such a prolific band only eleven tracks make it to this superb album. But every song has been lovingly crafted for maximum effect. The result is that rare beast, an album with no duff moments whatsoever, just honest-to-goodness rock guaranteed to plaster a ten-mile smile on your face.

ZAKK WYLDE

Born Jackson, New Jersey, US, January 14, 1967

"It's gotta sound pissed and it's gotta be hungry." Zakk Wylde

Legendary booze-hound guitarist **Zakk Wylde** has earned himself something of a reputation for honesty in a business that simply oozes bullshit and rewards a surreptitiously slipped knife between the vertebrae. In interview he is always ready to provide his profanity-strewn unalloyed point of view –

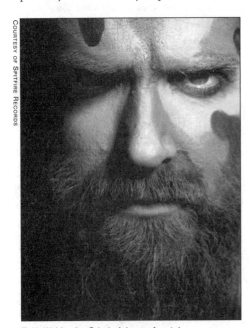

Zakk Wylde: the Grizzly Adams of metal.

whether or not that means banging heads and upsetting his paymasters – and in his music he gives one hundred percent, both in the studio and live, where his charismatic shape-throwing style and bullseye-painted Gibson Les Paul have become well-known trademarks.

The battle-ravaged, self-assured beer monster of today is a stark contrast to the fresh-faced youth of nineteen who was plucked from obscurity in a New Jersey bar to join **Ozzy Osbourne**'s band in 1987. When it seemed like a potential sports career might not take off, Wylde decided that music was for him and duly absorbed as many classic rock influences as possible, as well as incorporating classical styles into his technique, making him the perfect choice for Ozzy's *No Rest For The Wicked* (1988) album. He idolized Ozzy and had both the musical chops and the blond locks required to remind fans of Ozzy's first guitarist, Randy Rhoads (deceased in a freak plane accident).

From the late 80s and well into the new millennium, Wylde maintained his role as Ozzy's chief guitar sidekick, but also developed a highly credible solo career running in parallel. His first foray into running his own unit came about in the early 90s when the Ozzmeister decided that he needed to withdraw from the limelight leaving Wylde free to set up **Pride And Glory**, a power trio that issued one southern rock-inflected, eponymously titled album in 1994 through a deal with Geffen. It showcased Wylde's powerful and bluesy vocal style, and allowed him to indulge in the kind of rootsy blue-collar rock'n'roll made famous by the likes of The Allman Brothers and Lynyrd Skynyrd. Naturally there was a healthy dose of Black Sabbath in there too, but it was definitely the sound of a guitarist stretching himself creatively beyond the bounds of his day job. Sadly, industry wheeling and dealing put paid to a promising little outfit.

The mid-90s brought a brief dalliance with **Guns N' Roses**, which again came to nothing. Consequently, under his own name, Wylde issued the largely acoustic *Book Of Shadows* (1996), which again featured songs of genuinely heartfelt grace and beauty; an atmosphere of loss and longing pervaded the entire album which was a million miles from the metallic bluster of the songs he had worked on for Ozzy's 1995 album, *Ozzmosis*.

By 1998, however, with Wylde now a grizzled, hirsute rock veteran – a look somewhat at odds with his earlier smooth-cheeked poster-boy image – it was time to turn on the juice with the **Black Label Society**, an outfit fuelled on alcohol and hi-octane Sabbath riffery, making unholy swamp metal best suited to Hell's Angels' hangouts and dingy, smoke-filled gin-joints of ill repute. The *Sonic Brew* (1999) sleeve featured a cunning pastiche of a Johnny Walker Black Label whisky bottle and the legend within claimed that the music used only "hand-selected beats, full-bodied guitar riffs, savory bass, and quenching melodies". It was an alcoholic sledgehammer to the cranium of anyone expecting more sensitive material in the vein of *Book Of Shadows*.

Stronger Than Death (2000) was more of the same volatile and punch-drunk metal, with Wylde's gritty vocals even rougher and more world-weary than before. The full-on BLS warhorse experience was then captured on *Alcohol Fueled Brewtality* (2001), an incredibly sludgy and crushingly raucous live set. The sound went way beyond straightforward Sabbath fuzz and into the realms of Pantera at their raging heaviest.

Some material that had originally been intended for Ozzy's *Down To Earth* album turned up on the next studio set, *1919 Eternal*

(2002), the title inspired by Wylde's father (his birth year) and his never-say-die philosophy on life. "You gotta make records you like making. You have to be true to who you are. The whole thing is I don't make boy band music, I don't write stuff to sell 23 million records. I do my own music, know what I'm saying? You know, what am I supposed to start doing? Rapping and wearing fucking shorts and Vans and trying to be something I'm not? Maybe if I did fucking rap I'd sell some more fucking records! But I can't!" boomed Wylde in typically shy and retiring style when asked if this would be the album to take BLS stratospheric. The world had gone nu-metal mad but Wylde gave everyone exactly the kind of sonic pummelling in which he always specialized.

By this point Wylde was in a position to split his time at Ozzfests between BLS opening the bill and then taking up lead guitar for Ozzy's headlining set, meaning that greater numbers of fans were hearing the BLS creed. As a result *The Blessed Hellride* (2003) debuted at #50 in the *Billboard* chart, but with *Hangover Music Vol VI* (2004) a slightly mellower feel brought greater depth to the usual aural thrashing, which was resumed with gusto on the subsequent *Mafia* (2005).

Book Of Shadows
1996; Spitfire

This is a surprisingly laid-back piece of work dripping with southern influences and an aching sense of loss. There are songs of great power and beauty to be found here. Who'd have thought it possible?

Sonic Brew
1999; Spitfire

A dirty, scuzzy metal record fuelled on cheap whisky and beer – just how we like it. Wylde's playing is punishingly heavy and economical.

The Blessed Hellride
2003; Spitfire

Yet more emotionally dark tales set to a ferociously heavy backdrop of guitars and jackhammer rhythms. Can Wylde get any heavier?

Y&T

Formed San Francisco, California, US, 1974; disbanded 1991; re-formed at various times since

This highly talented four-piece never really took off the way they should have, considering their consummate songwriting skills and the formidable delivery of lead guitarist and vocalist **Dave Meniketti**. Nevertheless, during the 80s they thrived on their reputation for hard-rocking shows and were always a reliable addition to any festival bill.

Joining Meniketti were **Joey Alves** (guitar), **Phil Kennemore** (bass) and **Leonard Haze** (drums), going under the name of **Yesterday And Today**. Legend has it that Haze pulled the name out of nowhere while on the phone to a gig promoter; as they hadn't settled on a suitable moniker he used the title of a Beatles album.

The band first issued a couple of albums on London in the States – their eponymous debut in 1976 and *Struck Down* (1978) – but it wasn't until a deal with A&M and *Earthshaker* (1981) that they really hit their stride. The album was tight, focused and covered all those important bases: women, rock'n'roll and riffs aplenty. "Dirty Girl" was a nice'n'sleazy highlight, as was the crunching riffery of "Hurricane". To mark their arrival as a band reborn they became the more urgent-sounding **Y&T**.

What followed was Y&T's peak period with albums such as *Black Tiger* (1982), *Meanstreak* (1983), and *In Rock We Trust* (1984), landing them support slots with the likes of AC/DC, Ozzy Osbourne and Kiss. They even made it onto the bill at the Donington Monsters of Rock festival in 1984. Everyone agreed that live, the band were a killer unit. Inexplicably, however, they never managed to harness the same kind of vitality in the studio.

By the time of *Down For The Count* (1985) – which featured the would-be hit single "Summertime Girls" – they were struggling to take that all-important step up to the big league. Sadly that never really happened, even though *Open Fire: Live* (1985) at least showed what they were capable of in front of a crowd.

By the time of *Contagious* (1987) and *Ten* (1990) the band had gone through a couple of line-up shifts – drummer **Jimmy DeGrasso** and guitarist **Stef Burns** had joined – but ultimately the band were

floundering somewhat. They eventually split with *Yesterday & Today: Live* (1991) being their swansong – at least for a while. The band re-formed for *Musically Incorrect* (1995) and *Endangered Species* (1997), which proved to be a popular move in Japan, where the band have a major following, though inevitably they felt squeezed by grunge and nu-metal.

Since then Y&T have been something of an on-and-off project while Meniketti has built up his own solo career. They have undertaken various tours including a slot supporting Whitesnake on the latter's 2003 Monsters of Rock tour.

⊙ Earthshaker
1981; A&M

Something of an underrated hard-rock gem, this album features all the hallmarks of classic Y&T – great melodic riffs and Meniketti's ace chest-beating vocals – and marked them down for great things … which failed to materialize.

⊙ Open Fire: Live
1985; A&M

Only ten tracks but at least it showed the band in full flight, which is more than can be said for the lacklustre studio efforts.

ROB ZOMBIE/ WHITE ZOMBIE

Born Haverhill, Massachusetts, US,
January 12, 1966,

"We don't see much of him. He's in make-up all day. Swear to god, he must spend six hours a day in make-up…"
Dave Wyndorf on touring with Rob Zombie

If there is one definite thing that can be said of **Rob Zombie**, it's that he hasn't been an instant sensation. Some artists come and go overnight without leaving a mark on the rock scene. Rob Zombie, however, has been working assiduously at achieving his goals since the mid-80s. An avid comic book collector and a major fan of horror movies, Zombie has directed all his energies to create art inspired by and appealing to his own twisted cult tastes, first through the trashy horror metal groove of **White Zombie** and then a whole host of associated projects, culminating in a successful solo music career and a burgeoning offshoot directing movies.

The original line-up of White Zombie was Rob (vox), **Tom Guay** (guitars), **Sean Yseult** (bass) and **Ivan de Prume** (drums), drawn together by a mutual love of Black-Sabbath-style metal and schlocky horror B-movies. As with many freshly formed bands, they developed an unshakeable do-it-yourself ethic when it came to their music and image.

Their early years of living in squats and half-starving in order to save money eventually bore fruit (and pretty rancid fruit at that) in the shape of the *Psycho Head Blowout* EP and then their full-length debut *Soul Crusher* (1988), both released on the Silent Explosion indie label. Distinctly extreme in style, their funky death-metal credentials were firmly established with wickedly titled tracks such as "Ratmouth", "Die Zombie Die" and "Shack of Hate".

Their next outing on Caroline Records, *Make Them Die Slowly* (1989) – this time with **John Ricci** on guitar – was produced by rock veteran **Bill Laswell** and, though more polished, it cemented their cult underground status. The group clearly had a vision of where they were going but the lack of funds meant that they were still doing things for themselves and living on next to nothing. On their first European tour, as the stories have it, their record label gave them a mere $3 a day to live off.

It took another three years – and the introduction of another guitarist in **Jay Yuenger** – before a major label finally tapped into their full potential. A move to Geffen and the production work of **Andy Wallace** eventually allowed the band to entertain and horrify to maximum effect. *La Sexorcisto: Devil Music Volume 1* eclipsed their previous efforts on the songwriting and image front with ease, the explosive solid grind of the guitars and Zombie's twisted lyrics giving the world of rock exactly what it wanted – tracks like "Welcome To Planet Motherfucker/ Psychoholic Slag" and the Grammy-nominated "Thunderkiss 65". White Zombie had truly arrived as the horror cartoon merchants from hell; a stereophonic technicolour tornado of outrageous bad taste.

After *La Sexorcisto* the band toured for over two years and played a staggering 350 shows worldwide; the album went platinum in America and earned them a Grammy nomination. But the true indication that they had come of age was that they became firm favourites with MTV losers, Beavis and Butthead! Despite the snowballing commercial success however, de Prume left early in the touring schedule to be replaced temporarily by **Phil Buerstatte**. It wasn't until the end of the marathon tour that they picked up a permanent sticksman in **John Tempesta** (ex-**Testament**).

Their next effort *Astrocreep 2000: Songs Of Love, Destruction, And Other Synthetic Delusions Of The Electric Head* (1995) proved that they hadn't lost their touch when it came to freakish titles or their deft handling of horror comedy. The White Zombie sound was rapidly becoming an all-encompassing experience rather than just a collection of songs. The album featured extensive sampling, whilst Rob Zombie growled menacingly over the mesmerizing metal groove of such enticingly titled classics as "El Phantasmo And The Chicken-Run Blast-O-Rama" and "Supercharger Heaven". Another album of conceptualized dementia, this one featured fractured sampling, along with more of the Zombie growl and groove. But excess, not to mention dementia, was the whole point with White Zombie, whether in Rob's cover art and video direction, their live pyrotechnics or the crunching guitar lines.

The next White Zombie album, *Supersexy Swingin' Sounds* (1996), was basically a selection of remixes, allowing various artists to perform sonic Frankenstein experiments on tunes from *Astrocreep 2000.*

To any astute observers of the band it was pretty clear that the Zombie existed mainly as a vehicle for Rob and his own creative agenda. He got into making movies and even found time to launch his own Zombie A-Go-Go record label specializing in supercharged surf-rock. With so much Rob-centred activity grabbing the fans' attention a solo project was inevitable and when *Hellbilly Deluxe* (1998) proved to be a huge commercial hit, White Zombie were truly dead and buried. The solo album made a respectable dent in the UK charts but went to #5 in the US. Looking at the titles on offer there was

very little difference between the deathly groove and grind of his previous band and the "13 Tales Of Cadaverous Cavorting Inside The Spookshow International", as the album was subtitled.

Sticking to a tried-and-tested formula *American Made Music To Strip By* (1999) was a remix of his solo effort featuring the talents of **Limp Bizkit**'s DJ Lethal, **Nine Inch Nails'** **Charlie Clouser** and **Rammstein** among several others; he then concentrated on a widely eclectic series of projects, ranging from soundtrack work to producing his own horror movie, catchily titled *House Of 1000 Corpses*. Changing his musical approach not a jot, the B-movie-meets-metal formula of *The Sinister Urge* (2001) was a cornucopia of sonic delights featuring contributions from the likes of **Ozzy Osbourne**, **Slayer**'s **Kerry King**, Limp Bizkit's DJ Lethal and legendary drummer **Tommy Lee**.

That done Zombie threw himself back into working on the sequel to his first movie and preparing for the launch of his very own horror comic before indulging in yet more contributions to various soundtracks. All of this was just a prelude to *Greatest Hits: Past, Present And Future* (2003), the bonus DVD of which contained ten videos directed by Zombie himself. The album contained everything from White Zombie tunes to soundtrack selections and a couple of new efforts.

● La Sexorcisto: Devil Music Volume 1
1992; Geffen

Brutal riffs combined with a cool and calculated stab at the heart of trash movie and rock culture. A dazzling fusion of weird lyrics and cartoon satanism; guaranteed to upset those of a sensitive nature.

● Astrocreep 2000: Songs of Love, Destruction, And Other Synthetic Delusions Of The Electric Head
1995; Geffen

Another swingeing attack on good taste. An admirably sustained science-fiction horror experience. Packed with fractured and frenetic sampling, it overloads your ears and brain with its crazed patchwork of riffs and pulsing rhythms. Awesome.

● Hellbilly Deluxe
1998; Geffen

Crunchier than a mouthful of roaches and equally creepy, Zombie goes for the jugular with this thumpingly dark slab of grinding spookshow metal. This contains such mutant marvels as "Superbeast" and "Dragula".

ZZ TOP

Formed Houston, Texas, US, 1969

When these gloriously hirsute hombres first got it on in the beer halls of Texas more than thirty years ago, little did they know that they would be presented with a diamond award for selling ten million copies of one of their albums – *Eliminator*, of course – or inducted into the Rock'N'Roll Hall Of Fame in 2004. For three guys playing unpretentious hard-rocking blues'n'boogie, they pack a kick meaner than an ornery mule on mescaline.

The mysteriously named band – they apparently got the idea by amalgamating the names of different brands of cigarette paper – originally came together from a collision of two psychedelic bands. **Billy Gibbons** (guitar/vocals) had been playing in the **Moving Sidewalks**, during which time he picked up a few six-string tricks and licks from none other than James Marshall Hendrix while on tour. Legend has it that when appearing on the Johnny Carson talk show Hendrix said Gibbons was one of the most promising guitar players in the US. Meanwhile, the **American Blues** – their stage gimmick was that they had dyed their hair blue, geddit? – featured **Dusty Hill** (bass/vocals) and **Frank Beard** (drums).

The trio took the basic blues template as practised by the likes of Lightin' Hopkins, BB King and John Lee Hooker and gave it a little ZZ magic to create the kind of smoking hard-rock groove that would make them into superstars. The fourth part of the band's magic was supplied by promo-man turned band manager and producer **Bill Ham**. In the early days it wasn't unusual to see Ham's name included in the songwriting credits.

The first ZZ Top effort was a single, "Salt Lick", that would give collectors a hard time to track down in years to come, though it did eventually surface again as part of the *Chrome, Smoke And BBQ* (2003) box set alongside a few other rarities. Appropriately enough, the trio's debut on London Records was called *ZZ Top's First Album* (1970) and featured some fine cuts, such as the superb "Brown Sugar", but while displaying the band's knack for humorous lyrics the set suffered from a rather thin sound. *Rio Grande Mud* (1972) was more assured and featured

their first minor hit, "Francine", though the album's real masterpiece was the near eight-minute epic "Sure Got Cold After The Rain Fell". Neither record troubled the upper reaches of the charts but the band were by now renowned in the southern states as a seriously talented, dynamite live band.

The breakthrough came with the classic *Tres Hombres* (1973). Their signature single "La Grange", based upon the tale of *The Best Little Whorehouse In Texas*, became a hit and the album breached the US Top 10. The true watershed, however, was in the sound they achieved. Gibbons had been searching for the perfect guitar tone and here it was, brittle, crunchy, thicker than a bucket of molasses and twice as sweet. The dirty groove they hit as a result was spine-tingling, making every song vibrant and alive. Their popularity was burgeoning under Ham's astute managerial direction to the point that 80,000 people turned out for their First Annual Texas Size Rompin' Stompin' Barndance Bar-B-Q in Austin, Texas.

By this point ZZ were beginning to topple concert records set by the likes of Elvis Presley and Led Zeppelin. The live triumphs and new recording expertise were combined on the half live, half studio *Fandango* (1975). Among the songs revelling in the new Gibbons guitar grit was the stupendous US top-twenty hit "Tush", the funky tribute to pirate radio stations "Heard It On The X" and the rollicking party track "Balinese". The next album *Tejas* (1976) was the one to take the band in all their spangly cowboy-outfitted glory to the world. ZZ Top's Worldwide Texas Tour was an attempt to take Texas to the people in a stage show that, according to news reports, exceeded even the Rolling Stones' efforts of the time. The stage was shaped to look like the Lone Star state and was backed by screens to simulate the wide open spaces of the wilderness, complete with sunrise and sunset. The rig took forty men two days and two nights to erect. There were cacti, a longhorn steer, a two-ton buffalo, buzzards and rattlesnakes – and the experts to look after them. Not bad going for the self-proclaimed "little ol' band from Texas". It was the kind of spectacle that's hard to top. So they didn't try. They went on holiday instead – for two years. *The Best of ZZ Top* (1977) was the last album to appear on London.

ZZ Top: beards, blues and boogie ... Southern style.

Though the band were well known outside the US, it was during the 80s that they became global superstars through their cunning colonization of MTV with a brace of videos featuring a certain customised car and some comely young ladies. During their long break they began to cultivate their extraordinary fuzzy face furniture, except for Beard, who would tickle newcomers to the band by being the one who didn't. They eased themselves into world domination mode via the excellent *Degüello* (1979) on Warners, a bluesy rocker with a tight modern production, and *El Loco* (1981), which was maybe just a tad too wacky for its own good.

With *Eliminator* (1983), the band embraced synths and studio technology with a vengeance. Nasty rumours abounded that Beard never even picked up a drumstick while the album was being recorded, that it was all done on machine, but that meant little to the millions that sent it into the Top 5 in the UK and Top 10 in the US. Not only did it chart high but also it stayed in the charts for years. The singles "Legs", "Sharp Dressed Man", "TV Dinners" and "Gimme All Your Lovin'" commanded the airwaves and that bright-red hot-rod car became the band's calling card. It was even flown by helicopter over the festival ground prior to the band's headlining appearance at the 1985 Donington

Monsters of Rock show. *Afterburner* (1985) stuck the car on the sleeve in space shuttle mode – perhaps unsurprisingly, a couple of years later the band booked themselves onto the first future passenger flight to the moon.

While *Afterburner* took the robo-blues rock sound to its logical conclusion *The Six Pack* (1987) was a silicon chip too far. The box set contained their early albums in remixed and remastered form, destroying the warm analogue charm of their old work. They had already alienated some of the blues purists along the way and this seemed like a pointless exercise in sonic manipulation.

The arduous tour to support *Afterburner* took 22 months and after that the band took another Texas-sized holiday. *Recycler* didn't turn up until 1990, with "Doubleback", one of its standout cuts, appearing on the soundtrack to *Back To The Future III*; the band also made a cameo appearance in the film. It signalled a return to a more organic sound but also began a period of reduced output as the band's superstar status and mammoth touring schedules kept them busy outside the studio. *Greatest Hits* preceded the disappointing *Antenna* (1994) – out on RCA – by two years, and while the sound of the new songs was akin to ZZ of old their constant tinkering with production values masked some of the basic rock'n'roll punch that had made them so appealing back in the 70s and early 80s. *Rhythmeen* (1996) got closer still to the spirit of their earlier work while still incorporating electronic frills, but with grunge and nu-metal both vying for the attention of younger rock and metal fans, ZZ were constantly in search of the sound of the moment upon which to fuse their smouldering blues-rock. The result was the misfiring *XXX* (1999), featuring a handful of live tracks in the tradition of *Fandango*, which didn't even get an official release in the UK.

By now they had well and truly transcended their origins and become a celebrated Texan phenomenon, taking part in charity events and celebrity functions, even playing at President George W Bush's 2001 inauguration shindig. With such activities eating into their time it was four years before *Mescalero* (2003) gate-crashed the party with yet more grinding blues and modern production twists. Just to underline ZZ's influential status Gibbons dropped by the **Queens Of The Stone Age** studio to help record a version of their classic "Precious And Grace" (from *Tres Hombres*) for the next Queens album.

Tres Hombres
1973; London

What a guitar sound – it doesn't get any better than this. With riffs and solos flowing from his soul, Gibbons leads the trio on their best early album. Every single song is a classic with honourable mentions going to "Master Of Sparks" and "Sheik".

Degüello
1979; Warners

This album is in the spirit of *Tres Hombres*, only with a more adventurous sound. ZZ's alter egos The Lone Wolf Horns turn up to provide some seriously saxxy accompaniment on some of the tracks. Highpoints include "Fool For Your Stockings" and "Cheap Sunglasses".

Eliminator
1983; Warners

The blues in collision with computer-aided rhythms doesn't look too promising on paper, but it's a testament to the band that this works so well. The groove is tight and insistent and the outright silicon-enhanced rockers are balanced with some slow and primal blues.

Inoex Of Banos Ano Artists

Page numbers in **bold** type refer to the main entry of a band/artist.

A

B

C

D

Z